HISTORY
OF THE
CHICAGO POLICE

PATTERSON SMITH SERIES IN
CRIMINOLOGY, LAW ENFORCEMENT & SOCIAL PROBLEMS
A listing of publications in the SERIES *will be found at rear of volume*

PUBLICATION No. 164: PATTERSON SMITH SERIES IN CRIMINOLOGY, LAW ENFORCEMENT & SOCIAL PROBLEMS

HISTORY
OF THE
CHICAGO POLICE

BY

JOHN J. FLINN

REPRINTED WITH A NEW INTRODUCTION BY
MARK H. HALLER
AND A NEW INDEX

Illustrated

MONTCLAIR, NEW JERSEY
PATTERSON SMITH
1973

First published 1887
under the auspices of the Chicago Police Book Fund

Reprinted 1973 by Patterson Smith Publishing Corporation
Montclair, New Jersey 07042

New material copyright © 1973 by
Patterson Smith Publishing Corporation

Library of Congress Cataloging in Publication Data

Flinn, John Joseph, 1851–1929.
    History of the Chicago police.

    (Patterson Smith series in criminology, law enforcement
& social problems. Publication no. 164)
    Reprint of the 1887 ed. with a new introduction and a
new index.
    1. Chicago – Police – History. I. Title.

HV8148.C4F7 1973b   363.2'09773'11   75-172577
            ISBN 0-87585-164-9

This book is printed on
permanent/durable paper

INTRODUCTION TO THE
REPRINT EDITION.

In the 1840s and 1850s, America's major cities abolished the night watch and the police functions of constables and replaced them with unified police departments. By the era following the Civil War, police departments in the various cities were not only remarkably similar to each other but had taken on an organizational structure that, with adaptations because of technological changes, would persist to the present. John J. Flinn's *History of the Chicago Police,* covering the period from the founding of the city in the 1830s to the Haymarket Riot of 1886, is in effect the story of the creation of a modern urban police force.

The police, from the beginning, have been a subject of continuing controversy. Elite groups attacked them for their obvious corruption and inefficiency, their failure to enforce laws regulating saloons, and their cooperation with criminal groups. Yet the elite often rallied to support the police when they put down riots or broke up gangs of robbers or burglars. Labor leaders were often bitterly critical of police behavior during strikes, although they often shared with the police the same blue-collar and ethnic background. Flinn's history is not a critical study, however; it is a general defense of the city's police and a specific defense of their role in the controversial Haymarket Riot. Flinn, however, has gone beyond a simple defense to provide an interesting and useful portrait of the police role in a growing, brawling, nineteenth-century city.

John J. Flinn was born in Ireland of an Irish father

and Scottish mother on December 5, 1851. Because his father
was a carriage-maker who also had a contract with the British
government to carry the Irish mails, the family was reasonably
well-to-do and able to provide young Flinn with a good
private-school education. When he was fourteen, his mother
brought him, his two brothers, and his two sisters to Boston,
Massachusetts, where Flinn had two more years of schooling
before the family moved to Missouri. In the early 1870s he
worked as a reporter for various Missouri papers and in 1875
moved to Chicago, where he held a variety of newspaper
jobs, including that of associate editor of the fledgling Chicago
Daily News. He also wrote literary sketches and occasional
poems. A Republican with a strong interest in politics, he
served as United States consul to Saxony during the presi-
dency of Chester A. Arthur. In 1889 he started his own publishing company and brought out a series of histories and
guidebooks relating to Chicago. His *History of the Chicago
Police* (1887) was the first, followed quickly by a *History of
Chicago* (1889), *The Standard Guide to Chicago* (1891),
various guides to Chicago's World Columbian Exposition
(1892–1893), and a *Hand-Book of Chicago Biography* (1893).
In a way, then, he made himself an unofficial booster and
historian of the city.[1]

Flinn's Chicago was a marvel of urban growth even for
that period of rapid urbanization. A mud town of some 50
persons in 1830, it boasted a population of 30,000 in 1850, and
of 300,000 by 1871 when the famous fire leveled its buildings.
With hardly a pause, the city grew to more than one million
by 1890, more than two million by 1910, and more than three
million by 1930. (The city's land area grew from half a square
mile to more than 200 square miles.) Chicago, like all great
metropolises, was a city of contrasts. As a port city and then
a rail center, it attracted a large floating population—and
the facilities that service it: skid rows, saloons, bordellos, and

---

[1] John J. Flinn, ed., *The Hand-Book of Chicago Biography* (Chicago,
1893), p. 153.

cheap lodging houses. Rapidly, too, the city developed working-class family neighborhoods, as well as elite neighborhoods of mansions for the financiers, manufacturers, merchants, and professionals who guided Chicago's economic growth and grew wealthy as the city grew larger. In 1890 nearly 80 percent of the city's population was foreign-born or the children of foreign-born parents. The diversity of languages, religions, and ethnic groups lent an exotic and exciting texture to the life of the city. The police had to respond to the many needs of this changing and heterogeneous population.

POLICING THE CITY

Flinn's *History* is valuable in several ways as a study of the police and of urban life. One major strength of the book is the portrayal of the degree to which Chicago, like other nineteenth-century cities, was periodically torn by rioting and group violence. Indeed, the high points of Flinn's story are the principal riots: the Lager Beer Riot of 1855, the railroad riots of 1877, the streetcar strike riots of 1885, and the famous Haymarket Riot of 1886. Between them came a series of less serious disturbances: the election riot of 1857, the bread riot of 1873, the riot of Bohemian Lumber Shovers in 1876, the McCormick strike rioting in 1885, plus numerous others not included in Flinn's *History*. His serious treatment of group violence illustrates two important aspects of urban life during the period. The first is the degree to which many citizens perceived the city to be threatened by these uprisings —they felt besieged in their own city. The second is the depth of the cultural and class tensions, continually festering, which periodically erupted into violence. The fear of rioting was a major factor leading to the creation of a police department; and the continuing reality of group violence shaped much of the activity of the police as well as public attitudes toward them.

Although Flinn's general attitude toward rioting was that the police were "as heroic as any soldiers that ever faced an

enemy'' (p. xiii) and that the leaders of the rioters were
wrong to resort to violence, he is nevertheless sympathetic
in depicting the conflicts that resulted in that violence. He is,
for instance, bitterly critical of the nativist agitation that pro-
voked the Germans to riot in 1855: the election of a nativist
mayor, his creation of a police department with only native
Americans as members, his raising of the saloon license fee
from $50 to $300, and his decision to enforce the long-
neglected Sunday closing laws, thus depriving the Germans
of their traditional day of relaxation at a local beer hall. The
issue of saloon control was far from trivial. In city after
city elections turned on this issue, as many persons, led
by those of German and Irish background, fought to protect
their ''personal liberty'' to drink, while others, led by native
Americans of New England heritage, campaigned to control
or eliminate the evils of the saloon.

Flinn is almost equally balanced as he describes the issues
that resulted in violence between police and workers during
strikes. Even in the events leading up to the climactic Haymarket Riot of 1886, he stresses the essential justice of the
workers' goals. Only the anarchists, who he believed misled
the workers and turned legitimate grievances into illegitimate
violence, are treated with bitter contempt. The riots, as Flinn
makes clear, were rooted in conflicts that deeply divided the
city's citizens.

A second strength of the book is the portrayal of the day-
to-day activities of the police. By the period after the Civil
War, the two functional divisions of the police had been set:
the patrolmen who walked the beats, and the detectives who
were responsible for preventing or solving specific crimes.
Their basic methods of operation have remained largely unchanged to this day, except to the extent that improvements
in transportation, communication, and technology have altered
the context in which patrolmen and detectives work.

Patrolmen, of course, had the basic responsibility of preventing crime by walking a beat in a particular section of the

city. During the late nineteenth century they worked twelve hours a day and seven days a week. While crime prevention was their official object, Flinn makes clear that a variety of functions devolved upon them in the neighborhoods they patrolled. They took injured persons to their homes or to hospitals, mediated family quarrels, returned lost children to their parents, directed traffic on the downtown streets and at bridges across the river, controlled crowds at fires, helped remove dead horses from the streets, investigated violations of licenses by saloons and other small businesses, reported broken gas lamps, and performed the other innumerable social services that have always constituted most police patrol work.

Flinn also describes the beginnings of the technological advances that would gradually change patrol work. Especially important was the introduction of call boxes and horse-drawn patrol wagons in the early 1880s. Before then the patrolman walked his beat largely cut off from communication with the station house. In the absence of telephones, citizens could not report crimes to the station except by actually visiting it, nor could the station communicate directly with the patrolman. Patrolmen, if in trouble, could sound their "creakers." But if they wanted to make an arrest, they had to walk the prisoner to the station, commandeer a passing wagon, or even, on occasion, push a drunk to the station in a wheelbarrow. With the introduction of call boxes and patrol wagons, patrolmen—or citizens—could call the station and summon assistance. By requiring patrolmen to call the station hourly, the department could also hope to monitor the patrolman's performance of his duty. The strong resistance to the introduction of call boxes, as Flinn hints, stemmed from the fact that many patrolmen spent their time socializing in saloons or sleeping in a favorite hiding-place. But because the men at the station house soon learned to cover for those patrolmen who failed to make their hourly reports, the call boxes did not seriously interfere with such habits of patrol.

During the nineteenth century, the police station served

as a neighborhood complaint and welfare center, with personal contact made necessary by the lack of modern communication. Here persons brought family quarrels, complained about unruly adolescents or noisy neighbors, or reported crimes—often petty but sometimes serious. In the early decades of the twentieth century the increasing use of the telephone gradually meant that citizens no longer went personally to the station to make complaints. By World War I, some policemen had begun to patrol on motorcycles; in the 1920s the department began purchasing police cars, and in 1930 radios were installed in them. A citizen could now report a crime by telephone, the station could dispatch a patrolman by radio, and patrolmen, using radios, could keep in continual contact with the station. At the time of Flinn's writing, of course, this modern patrol system, with its greater speed of response but reduced personal contact, lay in the future.

Through Allan Pinkerton's stories and other fictionalized accounts, detectives were portrayed to the public as men who solved crimes through remarkable deductive abilities based upon a few obscure clues and shrewd insight into human nature. To some extent, Flinn describes detective work in accordance with this highly romanticized and inaccurate tradition, but he also presents enough information to provide a realistic corrective. He makes clear, for instance, that the detective's chief stock-in-trade was his knowledge of the underworld (p. 372):

Some had wide acquaintance among the colored denizens of "Cheyenne"; others had confidential relations with members of the sporting fraternity, who might be relied upon for valuable information; others, by long years of service in all branches of the department, were familiar with all the more noted criminals who had "worked" Chicago in earlier years . . . ; others, trained in the districts from which the criminal population of Chicago is most largely recruited, were thoroughly familiar with the younger generation of thieves and pickpockets.

The cultivation of informers and the maintenance of extensive informal relations within the underworld meant that detectives often granted freedom from arrest in return for information. Even honest detectives were so involved with the underworld that it was not always clear whether they were partners of criminals or guardians against crime. Detectives felt, however, that only through contacts in the underworld could they hope to solve highly publicized crimes or repress general underworld activity when newspapers played up a crime wave.[2]

There were other aspects to standard detective work. One was the development of techniques of interrogation, which included not only the use of the third degree but also the "sweat box"—subjecting a man to prolonged questioning until he broke down. So common was this practice that Flinn describes without comment how a detective solved a case by placing a suspect in the sweat box for two days (p. 386). Another task of the detective division was to keep track of those types of businesses most likely to serve as fences in the disposal of stolen goods. A pawnshop detail, for instance, toured the city's many pawnshops looking for goods that were known to have been stolen. By the 1880s, too, the major police departments, including Chicago's, had begun to photograph arrested felons, to record important identifying marks, and to assemble a rogues' gallery. The photographs were often exchanged with other cities and made possible the arrest of criminals who fled the state. The use of fingerprints for identification did not come into use until the early twentieth century, and few police departments had crime laboratories until the 1930s. But these later developments have not superseded the basic tools of the detective: the use of informers and of interrogation.

For Flinn, the high points of his history are the descriptions of police strategy and heroism during riots. The heart of

---

[2] For an interesting description of detective work in another major city, see Roger Lane, *Policing the City: Boston 1822–1885* (Cambridge, Mass., 1967), chap. 8.

his book, however, lies in his descriptions of patrolmen and detectives going about their daily work.

THE POLICE AND THE LAW

There are several aspects of police activity that Flinn does not emphasize—some because coverage would undermine the generally favorable portrayal of the police that was his goal, and others because they were so commonplace that he would not recognize the need to explain them for future generations.

One important characteristic of nineteenth-century policing in America was the degree to which patrolmen, as well as detectives, carried on their crime-control activities outside of formal legal controls. As Flinn points out, newly-appointed policemen received an exhortatory lecture by a police inspector, along with the cloth for making their own uniforms, and were immediately sent out to begin patrol duty. They received no formal instruction in criminal law or the legal rights of suspects. Not only were policemen untrained in law but they operated within a criminal justice system that placed little emphasis upon legal procedure. Those arrested by the police were generally tried before elected police justices who seldom had legal backgrounds. Defendants rarely had attorneys, and the few attorneys who did practice in the justice courts were more likely to peddle their political influence with the justice than their skills as lawyers. Persons charged with petty crimes—the overwhelming majority—were processed rapidly before justices, and the decisions in their cases frequently depended upon their dress and demeanor rather than upon any legal case against them. A policeman's superiors in the department and the courts reinforced the informal and nonlegal nature of patrol work.

Policemen on patrol, particularly in high-crime areas, were often expected to be able to dominate their beats physically, and to handle suspicious persons or minor crimes without resort to arrest. Herman F. Schuettler, Deputy Superintendent of Police in 1906, reminisced about his days as a patrolman in the 1880s: "It was not customary for a policeman to arrest anyone for a small matter, then. The hickory had to be used pretty freely."[3] In addition to making free use of the "hickory," policemen ordered teenage "corner loungers" to disperse, warned known criminals and strangers to leave the neighborhood, and threatened saloons with revocation of their licenses if they operated in a disorderly manner. The necessity of walking prisoners all the way to the station—often a dangerous as well as arduous undertaking—provided a further reason for the police to punish rowdies and wrongdoers on their own authority in the street rather than bother with the technicalities of arrest.

As the railroad crossroads of the midwest, Chicago was a major center for transients, and much of the normal work of the patrolman involved the control of wandering tramps and unemployed men who lived along the skid rows near the central business district. From this population came the beggars whose activities, particularly in the business district, the police were expected to suppress; from this group came many of the petty thieves and disorderly drunks, as well as the ill and disabled who often turned to the police for assistance. Although Flinn's *History* suggests that the police were chiefly concerned with serious crime, the arrest statistics show otherwise. Of the 5,000 persons arrested during the first three months of 1874, for instance, only a little more than 5 percent were indicted for felonies. By contrast, some 1,600 were arrested for disorderly conduct, another 1,068 for drunkenness, and some 600 for vagrancy. Most of those arrested were young, unmarried men without work: over one-fourth were between the ages of 10 and 20 and another one-third between 21 and 30. Nearly 40 percent were unemployed and an additional 18 percent were day laborers. When brought before a justice, most were dismissed and a few were fined.[4] A good part of

---

[3] Chicago *American,* June 17, 1906.
[4] *Report of the Board of Police . . . for the Year Ending March 31, 1874* (Chicago, 1874), *passim*.

normal police work, then, consisted of the arrest, processing, and eventual release of teenage boys and young unemployed men. The police also provided lodging without arrest—indeed until the construction of a municipal lodging house in the early twentieth century, the unemployed could sleep in the police stations. During the winter and in periods of unemployment thousands of homeless and transient men did so.

The police, of course, recognized their function in the control of this part of the population of the city. Flinn, for instance, quotes Superintendent Michael C. Hickey as stating in 1876 (p. 157):

> Our city is centrally located, rapidly increasing in population, and the hundreds of railroad trains that daily arrive here very naturally bring among their passengers a share of that dangerous class of vagrants called ''tramps'' who now infest the principal cities of the country. Our patrolmen stationed at the railroad depots are watchful, and render good service in noting . . . these arrivals, and whenever practicable compel them to leave the city on the very next train. The number of men who have no home in the city, and who have been provided with lodgings in our station houses during the last year, is 7,467. Some of them are vagrants who travel from place to place, not caring to have a home, and preferring always to beg or steal rather than work. . . . There are also among them many who would gladly make an honest living, but are out of employment by reason of the general depression in business which now affects all sections of the country. These are entitled to more humane treatment, and should be rendered facilities for bettering their condition and preventing them from becoming criminals.

By default, then, it fell to the police to manage a population created by the massive immigration and rapid urbanization of the nation.

Detectives, unlike patrolmen, were responsible for investigating serious crimes and preparing cases for trial before the legally trained judges of the county criminal court: they therefore often needed to master the rudiments of criminal law and procedure. Yet even here the appearance of legal procedure was greater than the reality. As already mentioned, many of the interrogation techniques were of doubtful legality. Although felony cases were usually prosecuted by the State's Attorney and defendants often had defense attorneys, many cases were disposed of through dismissal or through pleas of guilty after bargaining between the defendant and the prosecutor. Again, there was only minimal legal oversight of police practices.

Normal detective activities, then, displayed little concern with due process: the main expertise of a detective was his familiarity with the underworld. One way to reduce crime was to harass known thieves into leaving town. The chief method, as Flinn suggests (p. 371) was to "vag" the criminal —to arrest him for vagrancy (having no visible means of support) and take him before a justice to be fined. Langdon W. Moore, a New York counterfeiter and bank-robber allied with several Chicago thieves, who used the city as a base of operations for robbing small-town banks, described how the system worked:

> I was not known to the Chicago officers at this time, and could go and come when I pleased. It was not so with the men I had been working with. They were residents of the city, and were well known to the detectives. Before we had been there a week, one of the party was arrested, charged with being a vagrant without visible means of support. At the same time he had on his person several hundred dollars in cash. He was taken to court and put under bonds . . . of five hundred dollars to appear for trial. Before the case was fixed, another of the party was arrested. . . . In this way one was picked up after another, until the three were arrested, and put under five hundred dollars bail each.[5]

Faced with such harassment, a thief might well decide to leave the city.

When a particularly well-publicized crime occurred or when newspapers complained of a crime wave, the police reacted by making mass arrests. The following is a newspaper description of such an operation in the early 1890s, when the police were attempting to reduce crime in the South Side entertainment district:

> All Thursday afternoon and evening the Harrison Street wagon was kept busy rattling over the pavements bringing in colored and white men and women of evil reputation. Some were arrested in the streets and alleys, and others were taken from the most notorious brothels on Plym-

---

[5] Langdon W. Moore, *His Own Story of His Eventful Life* (Boston, 1893), p. 466.

outh and Custom House places. About 200 men and women of vile character were captured.

Last night the raiding was kept up with unabated vigor and at least 200 more prisoners were landed at the station.

After a notorious crime, those arrested in dragnet raids were searched and interrogated to determine if they were connected with the crime. Although the harassments may occasionally have influenced underworld figures to name the perpetrator in order to call off the police pressure, the raids served to give the appearance of vigorous police activity but seldom resulted in discovery of the culprit. Yet this standard—and illegal— police technique was so firmly entrenched that in 1906 the police chief explained: ''We can't do away with [the dragnet]. The detectives and patrolmen get their orders to bring them all in. . . . And the chances are that nine times out of ten the persons picked up are not guilty of the crime. But if the tenth time we should get the guilty man we are well repaid, as is society.'' [6]

Thus the police—a *law*-enforcement institution—developed in Chicago (and other American cities) with little formal concern for law. The standard techniques of patrolmen and detectives—the use of summary punishment by police, the system of harassing arrests, the employment of extralegal interrogation, the trading of information for freedom from arrest—were widely approved by society and became deeply ingrained in the police subculture of the nineteenth century. These attitudes and techniques, although modified, have remained essentially unchanged within the police subculture of the twentieth century.

CORRUPTION AND POLITICAL CONTROL

A final characteristic of policing during Flinn's period was the extent to which it was marked by widespread corruption and political control. Although Flinn does not entirely

---

[6] First quotation from Hagop Costikyan, ''Criminal Law and Criminals (1892),'' term paper (March 1928), Ernest W. Burgess papers, II-A, University of Chicago Library; second quotation from Chicago *Tribune*, February 18, 1906.

ignore such matters, he usually passes over them lightly. For instance, he lists Jacob Rehm, former city marshall and three times superintendent of police, as one of the founders of the People's Party in 1872. This party, formed in the wake of Mayor Joseph Medill's decision to enforce the saloon-closing laws, had as its major goal the nonenforcement of saloon laws. With the sweeping victory of the party in 1872, Rehm was rewarded with the superintendency of the police. While Flinn records Rehm's resignation three years later, he fails to explain that Rehm resigned when a federal raid showed him to be cashier for a whiskey ring that was defrauding the government of the excise tax. Rehm's successor, Michael C. Hickey, also resigned shortly afterwards, "pending an investigation of charges of corruption brought against him" (p. 190). Flinn omits the information that Hickey was charged with leasing property for use as a house of prostitution. As a final example, Flinn mentions (p. 382) that detective James H. Bonfield was reduced in rank for failure to give political support to William H. McGarigle in his 1882 race for county Sheriff. He mentions that McGarigle, after losing the race for Sheriff, was appointed warden of the county hospital, became involved in a scandal, and soon was "a fugitive from justice" (p. 212). What this leaves out is that McGarigle was a major contact within the police department for Mike McDonald, a leading gambler-politician as well as a fixer for thieves. Since McGarigle served both as chief of detectives (after 1875) and Superintendent of Police (beginning in 1880), his political activities and his ties to the underworld are important in understanding the police department of his time.[7]

Manipulation of the police departments was crucial for competing political parties and factions in the burgeoning cities of the nineteenth century. The largest of the city de-

---

[7] For facts about Bonfield and Rehm, see David R. Johnson, "Law Enforcement in Chicago, 1875–1885," unpublished research paper (spring 1968), pp. 14–15. There is a discussion of McGarigle's career in the Chicago *Tribune*, October 29, 1882, pp. 4 and 10.

partments, they were a major area for patronage jobs. (Chicago's police department did not come under civil service regulations until 1895.) Policemen often had to make payments to political leaders to secure their jobs and to receive promotions; and, like other city employees, they were faced with periodic assessments during election campaigns. When, as frequently happened, political factions used violence to control polling places on election day, it was necessary that the police either assist or, at least, look the other way. Finally, the police were important in aiding the dominant political factions to collect regular contributions from a wide range of businesses, legitimate and illegitimate. Gambling dens and houses of prostitution, as well as saloons, retail stores, street vendors, and other businessmen made payments to political organizations in return for favors or to avoid harassing arrests. From the point of view of ward politicians, a major role of the police was to assist in the maintenance of the political machine.

Despite the lack of civil service protection, policing became a relatively secure and attractive occupation in the period after the Civil War. The salary received by patrolmen was higher than that for almost any other blue-collar job in the city, and, of course, employment was not subject to periodic layoffs arising from economic conditions. Although policemen were sometimes removed to create jobs for the supporters of rival political factions, this apparently became relatively uncommon. Instead, politicians influenced the police by control over assignments and promotions. Favorable assignments and a successful career in the department depended upon a policeman's receptivity to the demands of dominant political groups. Even after the passage of civil service regulations in 1894, in fact, politicians continued to control the department through influence over assignments and promotions. Partisan manipulation of the police, then, was a legacy of the nineteenth century that continued well into the twentieth.

While political manipulation created police cynicism, it

did not always seriously conflict with the police view of their proper functions. Many policemen were horse-racing fans and saw nothing wrong with placing bets on a nag, nor did they share the views of elite reformers that saloons should conform to Sunday-closing regulations. Thus they had little inclination to enforce gambling or saloon laws. Policemen, moreover, like many other Chicagoans, believed that prostitution was inevitable in a large city, but they favored its restriction to certain districts. As one newspaper explained: "The disreputable women, the pickpockets and petty thieves are better 'bunched' in one section of the city than scattered all over it. The police know where to find them. Respectable people know how to avoid them." [8]

As a result of such attitudes, many policemen used their positions to make money on the side. Beyond what was expected of them as servants of politicians, they shook down prostitutes and gambling houses, accepted free drinks and meals from saloons, and sometimes made arrests to shake down defendants or their families. In the local precincts, police magistrates, bail bondsmen, defense attorneys, and police officers often cooperated in using arrests to make money from hapless defendants rather than as a means to enforce the law. Detectives, as well as patrolmen, entered into partnerships with con men, pickpockets, and other thieves, providing protection from arrest in return for a share of the profits. The interrelations of the police and the underworld were many and complex.

Flinn's *History* is of more than merely antiquarian interest. Patrolmen today ride in cars with radios, and detectives have access to crime laboratories and fingerprint files; but behind these technological changes lie many of the attitudes and operating methods that developed in our police forces in the middle decades of the nineteenth century.

MARK H. HALLER

Temple University, January, 1973

---

[8] Chicago *Chronicle*, July 3, 1899.

JOHN A. ROCHE,
Mayor of Chicago.

HISTORY

OF

THE CHICAGO POLICE

FROM THE SETTLEMENT OF THE COMMUNITY
TO THE PRESENT TIME,

UNDER AUTHORITY OF

THE MAYOR AND SUPERINTENDENT OF THE FORCE

BY JOHN J. FLINN,

ASSISTED BY JOHN E. WILKIE.

To Benefit the Policemen's Benevolent Association.

ILLUSTRATED.

CHICAGO:
UNDER THE AUSPICES OF THE POLICE BOOK FUND.
1887.

[facsimile of the original title page]

To

The Officers and Men

of

The Chicago Police Force

who, in the past,

Served the Garden City so Faithfully

and

Defended Her so Heroically--

Who, in the Present,

Watch Over Her with Jealous Care--

This History is Dedicated

by

The Writers.

INTRODUCTION.

Let me say at the outset that the preparation of this work was undertaken with a very evenly-balanced mixture of diffidence and confidence. Had the great fire of October, 1871, resulted only in the destruction of buildings, we would look, almost in vain, for traces of it to-day. The black and desolate track which marked the wake of that calamitous and awful conflagration is hidden beneath a New Chicago; the memory of our people is becoming dimmed and confused regarding its course and boundary, and the marvelous, almost miraculous recovery of the city from this terrible blow has reconciled our citizens to the event, dreadful as it was, and heart-rending as were the incidents which surrounded it. The buildings destroyed have been replaced by others more substantial, more beautiful. The fortunes lost have been recovered in so many cases that the exceptions are not remarked. The conglomerate mass of melted iron, shattered granite, pulverized brick, powdered glass and smouldering merchandise, which covered like a hideous pall the once beautiful district, on the memorable morning of Oct. 10, in the hands of Providence fertilized the soil, and prepared it for the golden harvests which were to follow. But the fire destroyed many things which can never be replaced, among them the official records of the city and county—an irreparable loss in many respects, a loss that will be felt more and more as the years roll by, and that will be regretted most, perhaps, by those who, like myself, undertake to write any portion of the history of this remarkable city. For with the loss of these records the very basis upon which history should properly stand—the written archives of the past—was swept away.

Knowledge of this fact made me diffident, inspired me with dread lest my ability and energy, such as they are, should prove unequal to the task of penetrating successfully through and beyond the smoke and confusion of those October days. Whatever facts could be obtained must be gathered from the remembrances of old citizens, from various early historical sketches, from documents and prints in possession of the Historical Society, from the ante-fire directories and newspaper files, from reminiscences contributed to the press since 1871, and from miscellaneous contributions to local history, in manuscript and print, widely scattered through the homes, book stalls and libraries of the city and State.

The confidence I felt was inspired by the hearty expression of good will, the kind assistance volunteered, the valuable information cheerfully given on all sides. It was my aim—how well carried out the reader must judge—to make this history of the Chicago police one that could be relied upon for all time to come as covering the period of which it treats, accurately and honestly. To carry out this intention I have spared no pains to obtain the most reliable and fullest information. I have exercised all the ingenuity of which I am possessed in an earnest endeavor to arrive at facts.

Although this volume is written with special reference to the part which the police have played in the history of Chicago during the past fifty years, it would be neither possible nor advisable to separate their work altogether from that performed by other departments of the city government, nor to isolate it from the material and social progress of the city, which they have to so large an extent contributed in strengthening. A history of our police must, if it be a true one, deal with every interest that is dependent for existence upon peace and good order—and what human interest isn't dependent upon those two conditions?

In the preparation of this volume I have had the assistance of Mr. John E. Wilkie, of the Chicago *Tribune*, whose contributions have added greatly to its worth. The detective and patrol services have been placed under his especial charge, as his ability to handle these branches of the subject was not only recognized by myself but by the heads of the police department.

Every means of obtaining reliable and official information, when necessary, have been placed in the hands of Mr. Wilkie and myself by the Superintendent of Police and his officers and men. The Historical Society has afforded much valuable information, through the courtesy of its secretary, Mr. Hager; Librarian Poole, of the Public Library, has kindly opened the way for the examination of such authorities as that institution possesses; the scrap books of private individuals; such written history as exists—everything within reach that could throw a light upon the history of the Chicago police force have been carefully collected and examined, and it is hoped that the compilation herewith presented to the public may be thought worthy of the subject with which the volume deals.

I have just laid down a weather-beaten, moth-eaten, curious old volume written by one Joseph Pembroke, "A Gentleman Traveller," and printed in London in 1778. It tells of the writer's experiences in London and the continental cities, and three or four of its chapters are devoted to what might be called an inquiry into the police organizations of the great centers of population in Europe—if such a thing as police organization, as we understand the term, then existed.

Macaulay and other English historians, De Quincy. Dickens and other English writers, have pictured London to us as it was during the last and previous centuries,

What Pembroke tells us is not only confirmatory of the stories already familiar to most of us, but gives us in addition a very clear and striking view of daily occurrences in the British capital, such as would find their way these days, under the head of police news, into the newspapers.

It is only at very rare intervals now that the crime of garroting is committed in any populous community. In London little more than a hundred years ago it was a crime of nightly occurrence. Highway robbery within the shadow of St. Paul's was no uncommon act of daring, even though the punishment was fixed at death, with or without some species of refined torture. Ladies and gentlemen returning from the theater, or a private gathering had their " chairs " or carriages stopped, pistols pointed at their heads, and were compelled to deliver their money to some city Dick Turpin. Members of the British parliament going home after a late sitting, were met by highwaymen and compelled to hand over their purses without delay. Members of the nobility, and even princes of the blood royal, were frequently accosted by armed robbers in their gardens or on the public roads, and subjected to the same painful and expensive humiliation.

It was all a man's life was worth to venture out after dark. In some sections of the city, and close to the very center of business activity, people were murdered for their money in broad daylight; after nightfall the cry of " Robbers!— help!" was heard on all sides, and received but little attention.

People of means were usually accompanied by an armed guard consisting of from one to half a dozen men. Frequently the robbers overpowered the guard, took the master as a hostage, and refused to give him up until his relatives or friends paid the price of his liberty.

House breaking became a regular branch of trade. It was the constant aim of people of wealth to hide all knowledge of their means from their neighbors, for should it become known that they possessed either money or valuables, a visit from burglars inevitably followed. And these house breakers were always ready to shed blood if their mission proved or threatened to prove disappointing. Like the highwayman their challenge " Your money or your life!" meant just exactly what it said.

Thousands of people did succeed, of course, in deceiving others regarding their means, and thousands of people avoided the garroter and the highway man by keeping out of their way, or by chance or good luck, but highway robbery and burglary were not the worst features of life in London under the condition of things then existing. Women and young girls were abducted on the streets, oftentimes by the debauched young aristocrats, who rode or walked rough shod over all the rights of the common people. Assaults of the most abominable, the most atrocious character, were of every day occurrence. Sometimes, when the family of the woman or girl, who had been thus shamefully and brutally treated, was one of more than ordinary consequence, public indignation would assume the form and substance of a mob, and the mob would change its character three or four times before the military had succeeded in scattering it. It had its origin in the claim of some respected citizens who felt that they had been outraged; it attracted the idlers and roughs of the city, it was swollen by underground criminals, pickpockets, garroters and highway men, it was finally, perhaps, augmented by political malcontents bent upon revolution—it usually ended, almost invariably ended, in doing a vast amount of injury to the persons and property of innocent persons, without obtaining any satisfaction from, or doing any harm to the guilty ones.

Riots were periodical. Disturbances were almost perpetual. Only when the military were in possession of a district could it be said that peace prevailed. But the military while suppressing the criminals, and the rioters were oftentimes a greater affliction than a blessing. Commanded by dissolute officers, and composed of soldiers who had contracted all the vices prevalent in their own and foreign lands —frequently hired mercenaries—they respected no private rights, and exacted from the unfortunate people, conditions no less revolting than those which they denied the criminals they had just succeeded in displacing.

In Amsterdam there was even less pretense on the part of the municipal government to protect the lives and property of the people. London had its "watchmen," often brave, generally faithful, but without discipline or number sufficient to cope with the criminal and lawless elements of a great city. In Amsterdam, for years one of the great commercial centers of Europe, a rival of London, Paris and Vienna, every man took care of himself, and to use an old saying, the devil took the hindmost.

There garroting, highway robbery, burglary, and every species of crime known or unknown in our days, were rampant. Murders, assassinations, assaults on the public streets and quays were every day affairs. The merchant on his way to the Bourse was armed with a sword or pistol. Over the desk of the banker was suspended a blunderbus, not for ornament, but for use at a moment's notice. People wore their money in belts fastened around their waists next to the skin, or buried it in their cellars. The aristocrats never appeared on the streets save accompanied by guards. The general pursuit of gain—the desire to acquire wealth— alone prevented society from falling to pieces. People mistrusted each other, and it was impossible to tell whether the gentleman who sat next to one in the theater, at the coffee house or in the church, made his living legitimately or by pointing the persuasive muzzle of a pistol at his fellow citizen after dark.

In Madrid, in Vienna, in Naples, at Rome, the same condition of things existed. It is hardly necessary to go into details with regard to life in Paris during the eighteenth century. This city was one of the first in Europe to attempt police regulation. She got no nearer to the desired end, however, than the establishment of a very crude, half military, half civic organization, under governmental care, known then as now as the gens d'armes. That it proved to be inadequate, insufficient, incapable, need not be said. No such sickening crimes, no such atrocious barbarities, no such inhuman cruelties as stained the history of France during the last century would have been possible had there existed in Paris a police organization such as we find in most of the large cities of the world to-day—an organization that would have throttled crime before it developed into anarchy.

In Paris for half a century before the revolution there was little regard for private rights. The city had grown to vast proportions. The people had gradually shaken off the dread their fathers felt for the noblesse. Feudalism was dying out, and with it all respect for authority. As in other populous centers, only to a greater degree in Paris, all the old forces that had held society together were weakening, losing their hold upon the masses, and none of the new forces, that came in to take their places later on, had made their appearance. Humanity had been held in the iron grip of tyranny and despotism—that grip was relaxing under the pressure of an ever-expanding intellectual growth, and when at last it was compelled to let go altogether, there was nothing to hold in check the passions or proclivities of a free people. Paris was the theatre upon the stage of which was enacted the greater part of the bloody tragedy that filled the civilized world with horror. In the hands of a soldiery as little inclined to submit to discipline as the people were to submit to law, the French capital during the revolutionary epoch, or from the meeting of the States General to the triumph of the Convention, was a community of lawless, desperate, uncontrollable people. There was no civil power capable of checking crime or preserving the peace, for it was not thought possible in those days, nor for many years afterward, that police were better qualified to deal with muni-

cipal disturbances than military organizations, whether
regulars or militiamen, regiments of the Grand Army or
battalions of the gens d'armes.

But time and experience have proved to be wonderful
instructors in this as in every other particular. Louis Napoleon discovered for France what Sir Robert Peel discovered
for England, that a good constabulary had come to be the
mainstay of peace and order in every community. To-day
Paris has one of the finest police organizations of any city
in the world, and the " Peeler " organization which Sir
Robert substituted for the incapables who existed under
Charles the First's organization of 1640, is the pride of every
Englishman. The German government, with all the regard
it holds for strictly military development, has planted in
every one of its large and populous cities, a police system
which is the admiration of visitors from other lands, so perfect is it in even the simplest details. Austria, too, from
Vienna to Buda Pesth, has her police officers, uniformed
and equipped so much like our own that it would be difficult
to distinguish a difference between them.

Every progressive government on earth has given close
attention to the organization and discipline of police within
the past twenty-five years. As home guards they have
proved to be far more effective and trustworthy than soldiers, feeling their responsibility to their fellow-citizens
more keenly, and being themselves interested deeply in the
peace and welfare of the communities to which they are attached.

It is not necessary to go over to Europe in order to
learn how deplorable were the conditions surrounding life
in large cities before the present admirable police organizations were brought into being. New York, Boston, Baltimore, and some of the younger cities of this country suffered under the "watchman" era from the depredations of
thieves, the villainies of highwaymen, and the riotous excesses of mobs proportionately as much as any cities in

Europe.   Even Chicago, before our present police system
went into effect, in the days when " constables " and town
" marshals " held full swing, had reason to feel that humanity needed at times a stronger curb.   There were times
when mobs met mobs, when peaceable citizens were compelled to take up arms to save their lives and defend their
property even here.   But those days are happily ended.
There is no longer any necessity for mob law in Chicago.
Recent occurrences have demonstrated that the vicious
classes cannot maintain themselves outside of their holes.
To exist here at all they must keep quiet.

For years it was held that as the policeman's duty did
not extend beyond the apprehension of law breakers and
criminals, and the preservation of the peace, he was a person
inferior in every respect to the soldier who shouldered a
musket and went to the war, or to the militiaman who
shouldered a musket without calculating that he would ever
have to make any other use of it.

In New York city, in the riots of 1863 and 1877; in Baltimore during the "plug ugly" disturbances; in St. Louis during the riot of 1859; in Pittsburg during the riot of 1877; in
Chicago during the riot of 1877, on the Black road and at
the Haymarket in 1886—in many cities, under many circumstances—the police of the United States have marched
with measured tread into the very jaws of death and proved
themselves not only to be peace preservers but warriors,
fearless as any soldiers on any field.

They have proved that no danger appalls them, no appearances frighten them.   Whether in a hand to hand
grapple in a dark alley, with the knife of the city thug glis-
tening ere it makes its deadly plunge, or face to face with a
mob bent on murder, or yet, shattered in limb by the flying
missiles from an exploded bomb—wherever they are, under
whatever circumstances we may find them—in whatever
peril we may see them—they are still as heroic as any soldiers that ever faced an enemy, and their heroism is all the

more ennobling for the reason that their greatest deeds of valor are not seen of men, are not accomplished under the inspiration of patriotic cheers, are not destined to bring down the light of glory on their heads—are done simply "in the discharge of their duty."

In the preparation of this work I have consulted, and I cheerfully acknowledge the assistance of the following: Judge Catons's *Address before the Chicago Historical Society;* Blanchard's *Conquest of the Northwest;* the Fergus Historical Publications; Brown's *History of Illinois;* Bross' *History of Chicago;* Colbert's *History of Chicago;* Colbert and Chamberlain's *Great Conflagration;* Sheahan and Upton's *Chicago—Its Past, Present and Future;* M. L. Ahern's *Political History of Chicago;* Paul Hull's *The Chicago Riot;* the files of the daily papers; pamphlets and other material in possession of the Chicago Historical Society, and I have endeavored to give credit wherever it belonged.

JOHN J. FLINN.

South Evanston, November, 1887.

CONTENTS.

Page.

LIST OF ILLUSTRATIONS.

HISTORY
OF THE
CHICAGO POLICE

CHAPTER I.

In the beginning, that is to say, centuries after the last vestige of Aztec civilization had disappeared, when even the homes of the Mound Builders were crumbling into fine dust, and before the sun of European enlightenment had dawned upon the "flat heath, pierced by a small tranquil stream"—the destined site of this great city—there was nothing. Unless one would call some miles of soggy, desolate downs, relieved here and there by a clump of trees—oak, maple or perhaps cottonwood—dotted with miniature islands covered with swamp-reeds, and rising high and pyramidal above the surrounding waste of decayed and living weeds, with a murky stream, to which there were no apparent banks, crawling through the tangle of useless vegetation, losing itself now and then in the marsh, and finally emptying its dirty waters into the lake—unless one would call this something, there was nothing.

Nothing certainly to charm the eye of one who might approach it from the West, nothing to captivate the pioneer, the traveler or the adventurer who viewed it from the South or North. Where there was not swamp there was sand; when a dense fog was not rising from the midst of the dreary waste, shutting out at times even the mid-day sun, clouds of finely pulverized sand from the lake shore blew across the marsh, descending again upon the weeds and grasses and making the picture more desolate and repelling than ever.

Perhaps it was providential, perhaps accidental, at any rate it was lucky that Marquette and Joliet, the original white discoverers of Chicago, fell in with a band of Illinois Indians who undertook to show them the Southern shores of the great lake, whose Northern waters they were already familiar with, for these Indians had told marvelous tales of the grandeur and beauty of the big water, and the lands that fringed its Southern banks. Otherwise the missionary explorers might have been tempted to turn back when they found themselves on the bosom of a stream, green with stagnation and along whose sides nature appeared to be in one of the last stages of decomposition. The indomitable will which characterized these early discoverers, the high sense of duty which inspired them, sustained the good men in the task they had undertaken. They came to spread the light of Christianity among the Illinois, and nothing could hinder their progress save death.

Up the Illinois then came Marquette, Joliet, their stout-hearted followers and dusky guides; into the Desplaines they plowed, finally through the Chicago river, out on the greenish waters of the lake.

It was a beautiful September day in the year 1673, when Marquette and Joliet turning their boats about, directed their visions toward the shore.

Rising above the graveled beach, upon which the wavelets splashed and murmured, were long lines of sand-hills, sparkling against a back-ground of autumnal foliage, through which the setting sun penetrated, giving a golden tint to the turning leaves on oak and maple. Their view embraced the horse-shoe bend which to-day assists in forming the natural harbor of Chicago. Before them was the stream from which they had just emerged, trailing like a serpent through a white sandbar that stretched far out into the lake. The river's mouth was hospitable enough to all appearance, and one on which the gaze of Marquette was riveted for some moments.

The Indians had already named the river, and the name they gave it was destined in all probability to outlive the memory of the great explorers. It has often been remarked by American historical writers, that there was a great deal of hard, practical common sense in the crude nomenclature of the aboriginies. When they desired to give anything a name, they generally gave it a name which fitted so closely that it was bound to stick. Much as they have been credited with poetic imagination, their minds were probably entirely innocent of the slightest tendency in that direction. Hence, when they named the stream to which the very settlement, let alone the glory and prosperity of this city is due, the Chicago river, they intended to convey an idea in the plainest and clearest possible language.

They had during the hunting season found it profitable to penetrate the marshes through which the river ran, in search of game, which abounded thereabouts to their hearts content. They had spent days and nights upon the stream or upon its banks. They were familiar with it. They were acquainted with its good points and with its little drawbacks. They weighed both in the scales of their Indian intelligence and decided to name it the Chicago river, the word "Chicago" in the language of the Illinois Indians meaning "Onion," in the language of the Pottawatomies, meaning "pole-cat."

A recent historian, says: "It is highly probable that it was thus named because wild onions grew in great profusion there. That it was a synonym of honor, is demonstrated from the fact that the Illinois tribes named one of their chiefs Chicago, and thus elevated above his peers, he was sent to France in 1725, and had the distinguished honor of being introduced to the Company of the Indies."

This explanation the reader will be quite willing to accept with some mental reservation. It is more than likely that the Chicago river, in the days before a city grew up along its banks, was tainted somewhat with the odor which has now made its name famous through the length and breadth of the land. That the Indians gave it an appropriate name, will not be questioned at this late day.

As "Chicago Portage," the point where the Chicago river emptied into Lake Illinois (as Lake Michigan was then called) became geographically known, when known at all. The bold spirits who penetrated into the wilderness and established trading posts on the rivers and lakes may have been familiar with it, but to the outside world, and even to the great majority of the pioneers, it was entirely unknown. It was not a point of importance at any time during the troublesome times that followed the Anglo-French Colonial war, in which George Washington under Braddock, first achieved military distinction. This war stripped France of all territory lying upon the great lakes and east of the Mississippi, and Chicago Portage passed under the English flag without knowing it. In all the subsequent events, the cession of Louisiana to Spain, the insurrection of the Indians under the great Pontiac, and spurred on by the French traders, the attempt of the Illinois Chief Chicago to drive back the English; the English attempt to prevent settlements beyond the Ohio river; the annexation of the Northwest to Canada; the preparation for a colonial revolt against King George—through all these events Chicago Portage slumbered obliviously in her desolate neck of the woods, as blissfully ignorant of the world as the world could possibly be of her.

The Southwest was settling up rapidly. The Mississippi had become dotted with thriving towns. The commerce in furs had assumed enormous proportions even along the banks of the Missouri. LaClede (in 1763) had established a trading post on the Father of Waters and named it St.

THE KINZIE HOUSE.

FIRST RESIDENCE EVER BUILT IN CHICAGO.

From Blanchard's "Conquest of the Northwest."

Louis; it had grown to the dimensions of a large town, and had established considerable of a reputation throughout the valley long before the place destined one day to rival and later to surpass it was dreamed of. Even during the Anglo-Spanish war, when St. Louis had 800 white and 150 colored inhabitants, and when it was considered such an important point that Gen. Clark with a detachment of 1,500 men marched against it—for it was a Spanish town—Chicago Portage was entirely unknown. If there were any settlers hereabouts they were of that unassuming and orderly class which even in war times attract no attention. It is the general belief, however, that there were no inhabitants located at Chicago Portage, save a few Indians and some stray hunters.

While negotiations for the purchase of Lousiana were still in progress, the project of building a fort—a sort of an outpost of civilization—at the Southern extremity of Lake Michigan, was being entertained by Congress. From the close of the revolution it had been remarked that British influence among the warriors who over-ran the West, and who could be counted in bands of thousands along the upper lakes, was gaining headway, and it became necessary with the acquisition of the new territory, that the United States government should make some demonstration of its strength in order to counteract the pernicious effects of England's tactics. The Indians could be made very troublesome to us by the artifices of a nation that was secretly, if not openly, still an enemy of the republic. Hence the proposition to build a fort.

The mouth of the St. Joseph river on the east bank of the lake, was first proposed as the proper site for the outpost, but the friendly Indians were hostile to the measure, withheld their consent to its construction, and the government commissioners, in the interest of peace, decided to select another location. This decision may be pronounced the beginning of the history of Chicago.

Across the lake from St. Joseph was the Chicago Portage, where a piece of territory six miles square had been ceded to the government by the Indians by the treaty of Greenville, in 1795. The mere fact that these six miles square had been ceded to the government, appears to have been the most potent influence brought to bear upon the commissioners. Beyond the fact that the government owned this little piece of land in the wilderness, there was no particular reason why the fort should be located there—except that the Chicago river emptied into the lake at this point, and from the Chicago communication could be had by water with the interior. So that thus early the river was our friend. The undertaking was considered at the time a bold one, as the post would be far removed from the borders of civilization, and the safety of its defenders would depend to a great measure upon the friendship of the Illinois and Pottawatomie Indians. No force which the government intended to place within the fort could, of course, be expected to cope with a general uprising, but it was the only available point, and an order for the construction of the works was issued by the war department in 1803.

There were no American outposts nearer than Detroit and Michilimacinac at this time. A company of United States soldiers was stationed at the latter place under command of Capt. John Whistler, an officer of the revolution, and to him was entrusted the work of establishing the new fort. Two young lieutenants, William Whistler, his eldest son, and James S. Swearington, from Chillicothe, Ohio, were under his command. To the latter he gave in charge the difficult and dangerous task of conducting the soldiers through the forests of Michigan to Chicago, while with his wife, his son and his son's wife—a young bride—he embarked on the United States schooner "Tracy" for the same destination.

It was on July 4, 1803, that the schooner anchored outside the sand bar. The mouth of the river was choked with sand, driftwood and weeds. On the sand bar the

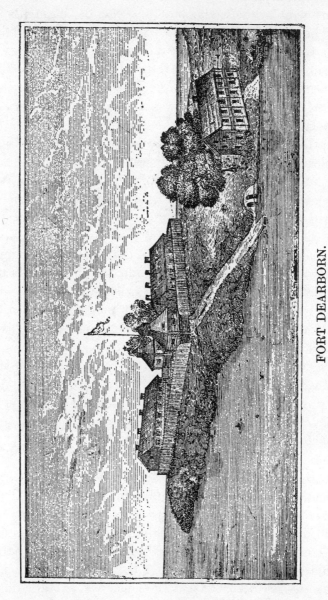

FORT DEARBORN.

BUILT 1803-4.—DESTROYED BY THE POTTAWATOMIES, 1812.

(From Blanchard's "Conquests of the Northwest.")

schooner discharged her freight of ammunition, arms and provisions into small boats, in which they were rowed into the river and landed on the spot where the fort was to be built. There were, at this point, three rude huts occupied by French fur-traders, with their Indian wives and broods of half-breeds. But the news of the projected work had been noised around the country, and nearly 2,000 Indians were present to witness the debarkation. In the presence of these natives, the United States flag was planted on a spot which the historian of the Northwest says, was "made venerable with the memories of 130 years of transient French occupation."

The Indians exhibited no signs of hostile intentions, indeed they exhibited no sign at all save those of childish wonder. They had never seen a vessel before and the schooner amazed them. Its size appeared to their sight perfectly immeasurable. They had never conceived of anything that could float upon water larger than a birch-bark canoe. After looking at the schooner for several hours they finally named it, in their own language, the " big canoe with wings."

It is not likely that if the Indians understood the full meaning of the debarkation—if they realized that the powder and shot, the arms and equipments of the fort, which were scattered on its proposed site, were intended to bring about the destruction of their power and their final extermination from the hunting grounds along the river and by the great lake— if they could appreciate how grasping, unyielding, relentless and deadly was the enemy represented by this first installment from the schooner—they would not have stood quietly by and permitted the invasion with good humored stolidity.

Capt. Whistler must have had a great deal of confidence in the Indians. Otherwise he would not have permitted Capt. Tracy to sail away with his schooner almost immediately, leaving the little party practically at the mercy of the natives.

The soldiers arriving overland, the first thing to be done was to erect a block house. " This," says Rufus

Blanchard in his "Discovery and Conquests of the North-west," "was an easy task but for the hauling of the logs to the ground selected for its site. They had neither oxen nor horses with which to do this, but the soldiers geared themselves with ropes and performed the onerous toil." The summer and autumn of 1803 had passed away before the Fort was completed, but before cold weather set in the garrison had provided themselves with tolerably comfortable quarters. The defenses, as described by the same historian, consisted of two block houses, one at the southeast and the other on the northwest corner of the grounds enclosed. These were large enough for a parade ground and were surrounded by a substantial palisade. A sally port connected the enclosure with the river by means of a subterranean passage. Immediately north of the fort, the main branch of the Chicago river rolled its quiet waters to the lake, and on the west, half a mile of wet prairie or swamp intervened between the fort and the south branch. On the east were the shifting sand drifts, through which the river found its way to the lake by a detour southwardly along the shore, half a mile south of its present outlet. Three pieces of light artillery and small arms constituted the armament. Attached to the fort was a two-story log building, sided with clapboards riven from logs like barrel staves. This was called the United States factory which meant a place to store goods belonging to the government, designed for gratuitous distribution among the Indians. It stood outside of the palisade to the west, and was under the charge of an agent who was sutler to the fort and was subject to the orders of the commander. The garrison of the fort consisted of one captain; one second lieutenant; one ensign; four sergeants; one surgeon and fifty-four privates.

In Eastman's History of Chicago, it is said: "This fort then occupied one of the most beautiful sites on the lake shore. It was as high as any other point, overlooking the surface of the lake; commanding as well as any other view on this flat surface could, the prairie extending south to the belt of timber along the south branch and on the north side, and the white sand hills, both to the north and south, which had for ages past been the sport of the lake winds."

Around the fortification little by little began to gather the wild and restless adventurers, who blazed the road of civilization across the trackless forests. Now and then hunters dropped in, liked the place, and stayed. Little by little the three log huts which the schooner "Tracy" had found there, became part of a little village of similar huts, but the occupants instead of being French fur-traders with squaw wives, were more closely allied by race and disposition to the soldiers within the palisades. Indians there were and continued to be in great numbers. Though not naturally hostile, still there was always more or less danger that a personal quarrel with one of the soldiers or settlers might precipitate trouble. The post continued to be entirely isolated from the rest of the Caucasian race on the continent, and save for an occasional visit from a supply schooner, its little garrison might well become impressed with the belief that all the world had forgotten them.

Everything connected with the little fort is of interest to one who studies the history of Chicago for the purpose of gleaning therefrom the material for a record of her guardians, whether they wore the uniform of government regulars or the blue blouses of the police. The little garrison which we find sheltered inside the block house or behind the palisades were Chicago's first police force, the Indians they had to contend with were her first anarchists, and a few years later, near this very spot, occurred the first riot and massacre.

And here let us listen to a story every word of which is true, and in it we will discover all the elements that go to make up a first-class Indian novel. A backwoodsman named McKenzie had been one of the pioneers of Virginia, in the days when Virginia's borders extended to the Ohio river.

During Denmores' war on the frontier, so the story is told, the Shawanese, then the great formidable power of the forest, now entirely annihilated, or lost among the surviving tribes, in one of their border forages came suddenly upon the home of the McKenzie's, killed the wife and carried two of the daughters, Margaret, aged ten, and Elizabeth, aged eight, into captivity. The Indians took them to old Chillicothe, the capital town of the Shawanese nation, where they were adopted into the family of a "high bred Indian Chief," and reared according to custom, under the tender care of his obedient squaw. Ten years later when the girls had ripened into blooming womahood, Margaret was allowed to accompany the chief whom she was taught to call her father, on one of his hunting excursions to the St. Mary's river, in the present State of Indiana, near Fort Wayne. During this journey the white maiden was chaperoned by a discreet and matronly squaw. Arriving at the hunting ground a young chief of the same tribe fell in love with Margaret, a love which she was far from reciprocating. She declined the offer of his heart and hand, and he determined to carry her off by force. On the night of the intended abduction, becoming aware of his plans, she escaped into the woods. Her dog followed, and the two hastened to the stockade, where the horses were kept, half a mile down the St. Mary's river. Her lover was at her heels before she reached the place. She turned and set her dog on him. The dog grappled with the dusky lover, and while the conflict was raging she reached the stockade, jumped upon a horse and fled through the wilderness, seventy-five miles to her Indian home at Chillicothe. Her horse never rested until he had brought her into safety. Next day he died. The fate of the dog remains a mystery to this day.

John Kinzie was born in Quebec, in 1763; when an infant he lost his father, and his mother took unto herself a second husband, a Mr. Forsyth. The family then removed to New York. John who was about ten years old, determined to go back to his native place, and accordingly he boarded a sloop bound for Albany. On board the vessel young Kinzie made the acquaintance of a Quebec gentleman who took a fancy to him, paid his fare, and landed him safely at the end of the journey. He never got any nearer to Quebec. At Albany he became an apprentice to a silversmith, and he is next heard of at Detroit, as a fur trader, during the English occupation of that town.

Margaret and Elizabeth McKinzie, shortly after the former's escape from her lover, were taken by their Indian foster-father to Detroit. Here young Kinzie met with them. He and Margaret fell in love with each other and soon afterward they were married. About the same time Elizabeth met a Scotchman named Clark, and they were soon married. The two young women and their husbands lived in Detroit for about five years afterward, and during this time Margaret became the mother of three children, William, James and Elizabeth; and Elizabeth had two children, John K., and Elizabeth.

The father of the two girls, about twenty-five years after their abduction from his home, received tidings of his children, and hastened to Detroit to see them. So happy were the girls to see their father again, and so loth was he to leave them, that they agreed to return with him to his old home. The husbands consented. No final separation was intended, says Mr. Kinzie's biographers, but time and distance divorced them forever.

Mr. Kinzie afterward married the widow of an English officer at St. Joseph. Margaret married Mr. Benjamin Hall, of Virginia, and Elizabeth married Mr. James Clybourn, also of Virginia. One might naturally suppose that this romance of real life might end here, but no. David, the eldest son of Benjamin Hall and Margaret, made a journey to Chicago in 1822, where he remained three years. On his return to Virginia, he gave such a flattering account of the place that a large number of persons were induced to emigrate hither. The first of them was Archibald Clybourn, the oldest son of Elizabeth, who became one of the leading citizens and a historical character. His mother, Elizabeth, the former captive, and her second husband, Mr. Clybourn, shortly afterward removed to Chicago. Mr. Benjamin Hall also came out here. From these sisters descended a long line of men and women who were distinguished in the early history of Chicago, and their blood mingles today with that of many of the leading people of the city.

John Kinzie shortly after his second marriage, determined to come to Chicago. His wife was the mother of a daughter by her first husband. By his second wife he was the father of a boy, John H. Kinzie, then about six months old.

In the spring of 1804, John Kinzie, his wife, daughter and the babe, with their effects packed in saddle bags, and lashed to the backs of the horses, took the Indian trail that led from Detroit through Ypsilanti, Niles and St. Joseph around the southern extremity of Lake Michigan to Chicago. Soon after his arrival, Mr. Kinzie purchased of a Frenchman named Le Mai, a small trading establishment, and here his little family were housed. He improved the hut from time to time, until at a later period, he built a comfortable home.

John Kinzie was practically the first genuine citizen of Chicago. He came here to live and grow up with the country. He came here to assist in developing the place, and he soon gathered around him others of the same steady and indefatigable type. He was also the first prominent business man, and the same restlessness that has characterized those who came after him, was developed to a large extent in the person of this pioneer.

We have now located at Chicago, firstly, a police department, in the nature of a garrison of United States regulars; secondly, a lawless mob in the nature of Illinois and Pottawattamie Indians; thirdly, the rabble in the nature of adventurers, hunters and shiftless half-breeds, and fourthly, the prominent citizen, represented in the person of Mr. John

Kinzie and a few small French fur traders. Now it may be said that Chicago is fairly started out in life. Here are the essentials for the formation of a community.

The baby that John Kinzie carried from Detroit, swung in a swaddling pocket from the horn of a saddle, is married and years afterward his accomplished wife writes a book on frontier life, a book full of thrilling interest and containing many graphic pictures. It is entitled, Wabun. In speaking of her father-in-law's first experience in Chicago, she says:

"By degrees more remote trading posts were established by him, all contributing to the parent one at Chicago. At Milwaukee with the Menominees; on the Illinois river and Kankakee with the Pottawatomies of the prairies; and with the Kickapoos, in what was then called Le Large —being the widely extended district afterward created into Sangamon county. Each trading post had its Superintendent and its Engages—its train of pack horses and its equipment of boats and canvass. From most of the stations the furs and peltries were brought to Chicago on pack horses, and the goods necessary for the trade were transported in return by the same method. The vessels which came in the spring and fall (seldom more than two or three annually) to bring the supplies and goods for the trade, took the furs that were already collected to Mackinaw, the depot of the Southwest and American fur companies. At other seasons of the year they were sent to the place in boats coasting around the lakes.

"Of the Canadian Voyageurs or Engages, a race that has now so nearly passed away, more notice may very properly here be given. They were unlike any other class of men. Like the poet, they seemed born to their vocation. Sturdy, enduring, ingenious and light-hearted, they possessed a spirit capable of adjusting itself to any emergency. No difficulties baffled, no hardships discouraged them, while their affectionate nature led them to form attachments of the warmest character to their 'bourgeois' or master, as well as to the native inhabitants, among whom their engagements carried them. Montreal, or, according to their own pronunciation, Maraialle, was their depot. It was at that place that the agents commissioned to make up the quota for the different companies and traders found material for their selections."

In Blanchard's history we learn that the terms of engagement of these Voyageurs were usually from four to six hundred livres (ancient Quebec currency) per annum as wages, with rations of one quart of lyed corn, and two ounces of tallow per diem, or its equivalent in whatever sort of food

was to be found in the Indian country. Instances are known
of their submitting cheerfully to fare from fresh fish and
maple sugar for a whole winter when cut off from supplies.
It was a common saying, "Keep an Engage to his corn and
tallow and he will serve you well, give him pork and bread
and he will soon get beyond your management."

The families that became neighborly with the Kinzies at
once, and were friendly for years afterwards, were the Le
Mais, the Ouilmettes and the Pettels. Of these the Ouilmettes were perhaps best known in after years, and the name
is perpetuated to this day by a little suburban village on the
lake shore north of Evanston. It is now spelled as pronounced,
Willmette. This village is located in a large reservation of
lands which was granted to the founder of the family as a
reward for his early achievements and his devotion to the
interests of the settlement.

The young bride of Capt. Whistler who accompanied her
husband in the first schooner to Chicago Portage, was alive
only a few years ago. Henry W. Hurlbut, a citizen of Chicago, visited her in 1875. In a pamphlet on "Chicago An-
tiquities," he describes his interview with her as follows:

"It was a coveted privilege which we sought, as any one might believe, for it was during the tremendous rainstorm of the evening of the
29th day of October, 1875, that we sallied out to call on Mrs. Col. W. A.
Whistler. When we entered the parlor the venerable woman was engaged
at the centre table in some game of amusement with her grand-children,
and great grand-children, seemingly as much interested as any of the
children. She claimed to enjoy good health, and was apparently an unusual specimen of well preserved faculties, both intellectual and physical.
She is of a tall form and her appearance still indicates the truth of the
common report that in her early years she was a person of surprising elegance. A marked trait of hers has been a spirit of unyielding energy and
determination, and which length of years has not yet subdued. Her ten-
acious memory ministers to a voluble tongue, and we may say briefly she
is an agreeable, intelligent and sprightly lady, numbering only a little
over eighty-eight years. "To-day," said she, "I received my first pension
on account of my husband's services."

"Mrs. Whistler lives in Newport, Kentucky. She has one son and
several grandsons in the army. Born in Salem, Mass., July 3, 1787, her
maiden name was Julia Ferson, and her parents' were John, and Mary

La Duke Ferson. In childhood she removed with her parents to Detroit, where she received most of her education. In the month of May, 1802, she was married to William Whistler (born in Hagerstown, Md., about 1784) a second lieutenant in the company of his father, John Whistler, U. S. A., then stationed at Detroit."

What wonderful changes this woman had seen! A bride of sixteen years she arrived at the mouth of the Chicago river in the Wilderness. There are but three log huts, and not a person of her age, sex or cultivation that she can associate with nearer to her than Detroit. She watches the building of old Fort Dearborn. She sees a little settlement grow up around it; she is there and has children born to her before the Kinzies arrive; she sees the slow but steady transformation of the country about, the marshes disappearing through numerous drains, the fields cultivated, and the savages becoming less numerous week by week; she lives to see the fields that surrounded the block-houses and palisades covered with handsome houses—sees streets cut through what was once a dense morass, survives to the beginning of this decade, and her faculties remain clear enough to behold Chicago the fourth city of the American continent!

CHAPTER II.

THE EVENTS LEADING UP TO AND CULMINATING IN THE MASSACRE OF FT. DEARBORN—ENGLAND'S TREATMENT OF THE YOUNG REPUBLIC —THE ANGLO-FRENCH WAR—EMBARGOS ON COMMERCE AND NON-INTERFERENCE—THE WAR OF 1812—TECUMSEH AND THE POTTA-WATOMIES—THE RAID OF THE WINNEBAGOS—EVACUATION OF THE FORT—THE MASSACRE—EARLY HEROISM.

When England in 1783 was compelled to acknowledge the defeat of her armies and the success of the American revolution, she did so grudgingly, and with a determination to make independence a costly and burdensome luxury for the late dependent colonies. She had it in her power to annoy the young republic, and she never missed an opportunity. No minister was sent to represent the court of St. James at the American seat of government, and this courteous recognition was withheld in spite of the fact that an American minister represented the republic in London. She excluded our commerce from her colonial ports, compelled American merchants to trade in English waters, under the monopolizing system that she had established by means of her armament on the high seas, directed by her laws of trade. Her war vessels sailed the American lakes and menaced our infant commerce at every point; they supplied her forts, still held on American soil, with arms and munitions, which were presented cheerfully to the Indians that they might plunder and murder American settlers, and thereby retard the progress of the country. By every means in her power, nearly always secretly, but now and then openly and brazenly, she continued a guerilla warfare upon the people who had just compelled her armies to surrender.

The war of independence had left the country in a crippled condition financially.   During the revolution production had almost ceased, the demands made by the patriots in the field exhausted the resources of the people. They had won their liberty, but it found them impoverished. England knew this, and knew also that the republic would not dare to undertake another war in her then enfeebled condition.   Western people cared little for the indignation and outrages heaped upon the Eastern mercantile classes by England's maritime policy, but they had reason to complain bitterly of the atrocities committed along the borders by Indians armed with English weapons, and supplied with English ammunition and provisions.

All this time it was by no means certain that a federal government would be established under a constitution that would insure the permanency of the republic.   American statesmen were quarrelling among themselves over the form of the central government which should be instituted to take the place of the continental congress; there were bitter and personal disputes between the delegates from the different colonies or states, and for a time it looked as if the war for independence would result only in shattering the federation which appeared to be so closely cemented while there was a common enemy in sight.

These internal disputes increased England's opportunities, and Washington at length became impressed with the necessity of taking vigorous measures for the protection of the results which his masterly genius had assisted in achieving.   As a first step he determined to establish our commercial relations on a firm and profitable basis. Prosperity, he reasoned, would speedily put an end to disputes at home; foreign powers, and especially England, must be taught to respect the American flag and the rights of those who sought its protection.

The result was Jay's treaty of 1794, which allowed America to trade direct with the West Indies.   England relinquished the Western ports wrongfully held by her since the signing of the peace, trade immediately sprang up, and prosperity continued until the mad war between England and France, during the progress of which the principals violated all treaty-rights and treated with disrespect the natural rights of neutrals.

In 1805 the French fleet was destroyed at Trafalgar by the great Nelson, and England became in fact mistress of the seas. Napoleon in 1806 had issued his famous edict closing all the ports subject to French authority, and the ports of all nations friendly to France, against English commerce. English merchandise wherever found was to be subjected to seizure. Millions of dollars' worth of English goods were seized, and much of them destroyed, in the ports of Holland, Belgium and Italy. England, to counteract the effect of this mandate, inspired by the almost insane hatred which Bonaparte felt toward everything English, issued in November, 1807, "plenary orders for the confiscation of ships and goods bound for the ports of France and her allies, from wherever they might come, and her ability to execute these orders made them effective, and ultimately recoiled with force against Napoleon, the prime mover in this attempt to fight natural destiny." Of course the United States, struggling to expand her commercial relations, suffered from both decrees. The English decree was specific in its language pointing toward the restriction of American trade. The following paragraph will illustrate the general tenor of the situation:

"All trade directly from America to every port and country in Europe at war with Great Britain, is totally prohibited. All articles, whether of domestic or colonial produce, exported by America to Europe, must be landed in England, from whence it is intended to permit their re-exportation under such regulations as hereafter may be demanded."

Here was a dilemma for a young government to grapple with. Our farmers, traders, exporters, had been reaping the benefit of European misfortunes. The people had turned in and tilled the lands until the country was able to supply the European armies and the hostile European nations with breadstuffs and raw products of every description. The embargo acts of France and England stopped all this. An American vessel bound for a French port was subject to seizure and confiscation by English men of war. An American vessel bound for an English port was subject to seizure and confiscation by French men of war. The United States Congress, thinking that if our supplies were cut off altogether the war would have to be brought to a close, passed the embargo act of 1807, and the non-intercourse act of 1809. The French resented these acts, and seized American vessels in French ports as lawful prizes. England did not object seriously, "but continued her right of search and the consequent impressment of American seamen into her service, a very questionable prerogative that she had never abandoned since our colonial vassalage, if her necessities required its practice. The colossal proportions which the war between England and France now assumed, by which they were daily weakening each other, may have extended the limit of American forbearance to declare war; instead of doing which she made an offer to England to rescind her embargo. This offer England rejected, on the ground that she would not accept a favor from America which might benefit France."

In 1810 France repealed her obnoxious decrees against the commerce of the United States, upon the contingency that our government, after reopening commercial relations with France, should continue its restriction against England. The treaty or understanding went into effect without any official notice of the fact being sent to England. By a blunder some American merchantmen were soon afterwards seized by France, and England took advantage of this event to insist that all the original embargo decrees were still in force. While negotiations were in progress between this country and France several appeals were made by the representatives of this government and influential citizens to England, praying that the embargo which the latter nation had placed upon our commerce be removed.   England would not agree to do this, but in reply called the attention of the American Government to the fact that it had been engaged in secret and insidious negotiations with France to the detriment of Great Britain.   Finally the British Government, in 1812, in its ultimate reply, attempted to justify its previous acts, and said: "If at any time hereafter the Berlin and Milan decrees (Napoleon's embargo edicts) shall, by some authentic act of the French Government, publicly promulgated, be expressly and unconditionally revoked, then the order in council of the 7th of January, 1807, (the British embargo decree) shall be revoked."

As the result of this unsatisfactory reply, and as our relations with France had again become friendly, the United States Government, on June 18, 1812, declared war upon England.

This history would have little to do with the important events which it has glanced over so hastily, were not Fort Dearborn, on the outskirts of American civilization, very closely interested in the conflict which was about to ensue. Little did the garrison and the inhabitants of this post dream at the time that circumstances were combining which, within a few short weeks, would bring terror and the horrors of a massacre to the little outpost.

President Madison, two months before the declaration of war, had ordered Gov. Meigs, of Ohio, to raise 1,000 men for Western service.   He promptly raised this number and 300 more, which force he turned over to Gen. Hull at Dayton.   The commanding officer marched to Detroit. Malden, the most important British post on the upper lakes, was situated on the Canadian side of the main channel of the Detroit river, and commanded the direct passage of that stream.   A schooner, which carried some invalids, hospital stores, and a trunk containing his official papers, had been sent ahead by Gen. Hull in company with a boat.   The

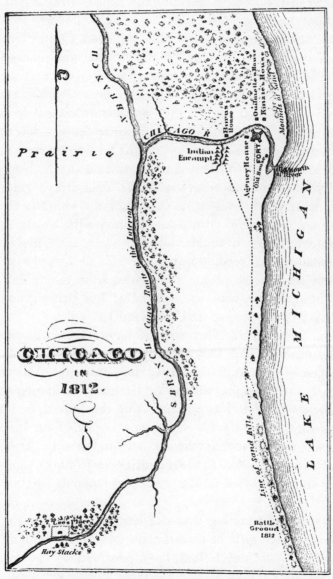

CHICAGO IN 1812.
(From Blanchard's "Conquests of the Northwest.")

schooner during the night ran ahead of the boat and was captured in the Detroit river by the British brig "Hunter." The boat fortunately escaped capture. The day after the capture of the schooner Gen. Hull received a letter from the War Department, by way of Cleveland, announcing the declaration of war with England. This was the first intimation he had received of the Government's action. He was ordered to proceed to his post at Detroit with all possible speed, and to make such arrangements for the defense of the country as in his judgment might be necessary.

He reached Detroit on July 7, and on the 12th crossed over to the Canadian shore with his little army. Here he issued a spirited address to his soldiers and the French Canadians, who were naturally at enmity with England, and the watchword "On to Malden," became an inspiring cry on all sides. A reconnaisance of 280 men were sent forward to the British post. Five miles from that point they came into collision with an outpost of the British, and the first blood of the war of 1812 was spilled.

Gen. Isaac Brock, Governor of Upper Canada, was alive to the situation, and had already marked out his plan of campaign. Fort Michilimacinac was the first place to be attacked, and, skipping all the preliminary incidents, suffice it to say that it fell into the hands of the British and their Indian allies on July 16. "It was regarded as the most important post in the Northwest, except Detroit. It had an annual export trade of furs amounting to $240,000, and the custom house duties on imports were about $50,000 per annum."

The Indians, finding that the British were successful in the opening struggle of the war, flocked to the standard of our enemy. Tecumseh had been elevated to the rank of brigadier-general, and was already rendering excellent service to Gen. Brock.

The officers who were originally in command of Fort Dearborn had been replaced the year previously by Capt.

THE NEW FORT DEARBORN.

AS IT APPEARED IN JUNE, 1853.

(From Blanchard's "Conquests of the Northwest.")

Heald, Lieut. Helm (who had married John Kinzie's step-daughter), Ensign George Ronan, and Surgeon Dr. Van Voorhees. A reinforcement of twelve militiamen had increased the garrison force to sixty-six soldiers. John Kinzie, Jr., born in Canada, opposite Detroit, just before his father emigrated to Chicago, was a lad of eight years. Ouilmette, a French laborer in Mr. Kinzie's employ, had married an Indian wife, and was blessed with several children. He lived near the Kinzie residence. On the same side of the river and about eighty rods to the west lived Mr. Burns, his wife and children. Four miles up the south branch lived Mr. White on a farm known as Lee's place. He had three French laborers in his employ. The spot which this little farm covered is now in the heart of the saw and planing-mill district. Besides the farms mentioned there were a number of half-breeds, who lived in huts or camps, according to their circumstances. Inside the palisades of the fort dwelt the families of Capt. Heald, Lieut. Helm and Sergt. Holt, "whose wives were destined to become heroines of history, and to their number may be added Mrs. Bisson, sister of Ouilmette's wife, and Mrs. Corbin, wife of a soldier."

According to a paper read before the Chicago Historical Society by Judge Caton, in 1870, and published by Fergus in 1876, the data for which was received from one of the oldest Pottawatomie chiefs, the hunting grounds of these Indians were limited on the south by Peoria Lake, and on the west by Rock River. "Since the days of the great Pontiac, their alliance with his tribe, the Ottawas, had been cemented into a chain of friendship strong and enduring; both had ever been active allies of the French since 1673, as appears from the contemporary history, and both were unrelenting foes to the English during the long and bloody French and Indian war, and Pontiac's war which followed, a period extending from 1755 to 1764; and when their beloved chief Pontiac was basely murdered by an Illinois, both of these tribes took summary vengeance on the whole Illinois tribe, and at Starved Rock slaughtered the last remnant of them, except eleven warriors, who fled under cover of darkness to St. Louis. And this was the victory which gave the Pottawattomies so much ascendancy in northern Illinois.

But the French had in a great measure been driven out of Illinois by the English, and the English had worked their way steadily into the confidence and affections of the Indians. They had been taught by English agents and emissaries that the Americans were attempting to rob them of their hunting grounds, and led to believe that if they would join their futures with the British, the Americans would be driven out of the country, and be forever prevented from trespassing upon their lands. The Shawanees had been thoroughly blinded by the English, and had given themselves over bodily to the enemy, with Tecumseh at their head. This great chieftain was as eloquent as he was brave. He talked to the Pottawattomie chiefs, worked upon their credulity and gained their adhesion to the English cause. Several of them had fought by his side at Tippecanoe the year before, and Brown's History of. Illinois informs us that even then Tecumseh contemplated the destruction of Fort Dearborn, and would have carried his plans into execution were it not for the defeat he suffered in that memorable engagement.

He was an energetic men, and he wandered through the wilderness constantly in search of new allies to assist him in driving the white settlers east of the Ohio river. He succeeded in forming an alliance of this character with the Winnebagoes of Rock River.

Tecumseh's influence was great, and he succeeded in winning over to his side the great body of the Indians of all tribes east of the Mississippi. A short time before trouble actually began, some Indians who had come to Fort Dearborn on business, seeing Mrs. Heald and Mrs. Helm playing at some outdoor game, one of them said to the interpreter: "The white chiefs' wives are amusing themselves very much; it will not be long before they are hoeing in our corn fields." A few weeks later the Winnebagoes raided the settlement, and the circumstances point directly to the conclusion that the massacre of all persons found outside of the palisades was contemplated in the design. This is known to history as "The attack on Lees' Place."

It was late in the afternoon of April 7, 1812, when a party of twelve Indians entered the log house of Lees and seated themselves with the utter disregard for manners which characterized the Indian race generally. In ordinary times this would not have aroused suspicion, but the actions of the Indians now alarmed the inmates, who were anticipating trouble. Two of the men, under pretense of a desire to feed the cattle, left the house, and immediately fled toward the fort, alarming the Burns household on the way. Here Mrs. Kinzie sat by the side of Mrs. Burns, who was lying on a couch with a new-born babe. On hearing the alarm sounded by the fugitives across the river, she lost all consciousness of the sick woman and thought only of her own children, to whom she fled like a wild woman, shouting: "The Indians! The Indians! Killing and scalping!" Mr. Kinzie was engaged in the chaste amusement of playing a violin, to the music of which the children were dancing. On hearing his wife's announcement, the family was hurried into two boats and rowed rapidly to the fort. The Burns family was rescued by Ensign Ronan and six soldiers, who carried the poor mother on a mattress into the fort. The Indians had murdered Mr. White and one of his French laborers, and killed a dog belonging to the latter. All the white residents, half-breeds and friendly Indians, were now gathered under the protection of the fort, the families taking up their quarters in the agency house, which was placed under additional protection, the verandas being planked up, with port holes cut in the sides, to be used in case of an emergency.

The fort was amply provisioned for a long siege, and police organization at once went into operation. Patrolmen were appointed to look out day and night for signs of trouble. An order was issued to prohibit any citizen or soldier from leaving the enclosure without a guard. A few nights after the attack Indians were seen prowling around the fort. They were fired upon by the patrolmen, and one of them was killed. Numerous visitations were made after this, sheep found outside the fort were killed, and other cowardly depredations were committed, but soon these annoyances ceased, and after a few weeks the inhabitants began to move abroad with their old time confidence. The Pottawatomies all this time wore the guise of friendship, disclaimed all knowledge of a complicity in the recent outrages, and pretended to entertain the best of sentiments toward the soldiers and settlers.

Everybody familiar with American history will recall readily the disastrous defeats and humiliations which befell our armies in the Northwest during the early months of the war of 1812. It is not necessary to the purposes of this volume that these events should be detailed, except where they bear directly upon the little settlement surrounding Fort Dearborn. Owing to the almost criminal tardiness and inefficiency of the government then administering the affairs of the nation, Gen. Hull was left without sufficient reinforcements, with inadequate supplies, and almost entirely at the mercy of the British, who were pressing him from all directions and carrying on a vigorous and admirable campaign. Fort Michilimacinac had fallen. Finally the garrison of Detroit, together with the town and the entire territory of Michigan, were surrendered to the enemy. This was a dreadful blow to the pride of the nation and a menace to its very existence. Gen. Hull was tried by court martial and sentenced to be hanged, a sentence never exe-

cuted, and time has done him the justice to acquit him of
the responsibility which a weak and vacillating government
placed upon his shoulders, in order to hide its own defects
and conceal its own disgrace.

Some days before surrendering he had the manli-
ness and the foresight to acquaint Capt. Heald, the commander of Fort Dearborn, of the situation, to warn him of
the impending danger, and to urge upon him and the little
garrison the expediency of evacuating the fort and retreating to Fort Wayne, if they believed themselves unable to
hold out against an attack until succor should reach them.
The message was sent in ample season, and was entrusted to
Winnemac, the Pottawatomie chief, who happened to be at
Detroit at the time.   He left on his mission July 28, 1812,
and arrived safely at his destination on Aug. 9.   This was
the first intimation Fort Dearborn had received of the declaration of war, and the unfortunate disasters which had befallen the Americans at Michilimacinac and Detroit.   The
news created confusion and consternation, bordering upon
panic.   To add to the horrors of the situation there was
anything but harmony existing between Capt. Heald and
his subordinates.   On the receipt of Gen. Hull's communication, Heald determined upon evacuation, without consulting with his officers, in spite of the opposition of Kinzie
and against the opinion of Winnemac, who had proved his
friendship and might have exerted his influence to prevent
the sad results which followed.   Gen. Hull had ordered
that the supplies contained in the fort be distributed among
the surrounding Indians.   At length when it was found that
Heald was fully determined to evacuate, Kinzie begged him
to do so at once, before the American defeats and the peril
and weakness of their position became noised among the
savages.   Heald, who was bent upon obstinacy, insisted upon
postponing the move till he could summon all the Indians,
in order to divide among them the supplies.   Winnemac
saw clearly the danger of this policy, and advised that the

fort be abandoned without delay, with everything left as it was, so that while the Indians were ransacking the place for spoils, and gorging themselves with the provisions, the garrison might safely escape. Heald would not listen to this suggestion, though backed by Kinzie, who knew the Indian nature thoroughly, and next morning at roll call the original plan of the commander was read. The subordinate officers that afternoon united in a further appeal to Capt. Heald, laying before him all the dangers which they saw in his plans. They told him that the Indians on learning of the recent disasters to the government could not be restrained; that their friendship, even when encouraged by a distribution of supplies, would be but a frail reed to rest upon, and that not even the popularity of Kinzie among them would be sufficient to stay their desire for pillage and bloodshed when once aroused. They also raised the point that their retreat, encumbered as it must be by women and baggage, would be slow, and that it were better to hold the position and wait for succor, or to fall into the hands of the British, than to run the risk of being massacred on the road by the pursuing Indians. But all to no avail. The subordinate officers thenceforth remained silent. Daily the number of Indians increased around the fort; they became insolent, stared impertinently at the ladies, used their fire-arms freely, going so far as to discharge a gun in one of the ladies' parlors, and behaved themselves generally with disrespect, as if bent on mischief. On August 12, a council of Pottawatomies was assembled and called to order by Capt. Heald in the presence of Mr. Kinzie, who accompanied him to the place of meeting outside the palisades. The subordinate officers refused to attend, on the ground that they had reason to suspect that the Indians would turn the council into a massacre. It passed off peaceably and friendly enough, however, Capt. Heald promising to evacuate the fort and distribute the supplies, and all surplus ammunition and arms within the garrison. The Indians were also to receive a liberal re-

ward in money before starting, and an additional reward on
arriving at Fort Wayne, upon their promise to escort the garrison and settlers to that point in safety. Capt. Heald appeared to be well satisfied with these arrangements, but his
satisfaction was not shared by the others. The news of the
American defeats had been withheld from the Indians by
Capt. Heald, but it was conveyed to them quickly by Tecumseh, who pronounced this a glorious opportunity to anni-
hilate the whites and drive them forever out of the hunting
grounds of the red men.

The effect of this intelligence upon the Indians was at
once manifest. They became more offensive than ever. At
length Heald saw his mistake, and at the instance of Kinzie
he decided to destroy all the ammunition and arms which were
not needed by his men. The next day the supplies, consisting of clothing, ornaments and provisions, were distributed;
but the Indians plainly exhibited their displeasure and dis-
appointment that the arms, ammunition and liquor were
withheld. That night prowling Indians found fragments
of muskets, firelocks, flints and broken powder casks thrown
in a well, and at the river bank a number of headless whiskey casks, the contents of which had been emptied into the
stream. Reporting these discoveries to the multitude of red
skins now assembled, their indignation knew no bounds.
The Indians justly looked upon this act of Capt. Heald as
a piece of treachery, depriving them of the gifts which they
prized most highly, and as Blanchard says, "It compromised all the good fellowship that existed between the
Indians and the garrison, on which alone Capt. Heald had
based a frail hope of security."

The garrison had made friends among the chiefs.
Black Partridge was one of them. Next day he called on
Capt. Heald and said, "Father, I come to deliver up to you
the medal I wear. It was given me by the Americans, and
I have long worn it in token of our mutual friendship, but
our young men are resolved to imbrue their hands in the

blood of the whites. I cannot restrain them, and I will not wear a token of peace while I am compelled to act as an enemy." Brave words well spoken. They came when the provisions of the fort had been given away, and when there were but twenty-five rounds of amunition to a man! The contest would not be a battle; it would be a massacre.

Rumors of the threatened danger at Fort Dearborn had reached Fort Wayne. Capt. Wells, stationed there, was a brother of Mrs. Heald. When a lad he had been taken captive by the Indians, and was reared by Little Turtle, a celebrated warrior. As a young man he fought side by side with the Indians at St. Clair. Growing older, he bade his adopted father good bye, and joined Gen. Wayne in 1794. When the Revolution closed he went back to Little Turtle, and converted the chief to belief in the Americans. When the war of 1812 broke out he reported for duty at Fort Wayne. Hearing of the danger which threatened his sister and the garrison of Fort Dearborn, he speedily departed with fifteen Miamis to the rescue, arriving at the latter place on the 14th, and finding the garrison without hope of deliverance from its frightful position. Evacuation at any cost had been determined on, as starvation was the only alternative.

It was agreed that on the next morning at 9 o'clock the fort should be evacuated, and the march begun to Fort Wayne. Mr. Kinzie entrusted his family to the care of some friendly Indians, and had volunteered to accompany the troops, his influence on the Indians being considered a better protection than the muskets of the soldiers. That morning he received a message from To-pe-nee-bee, a chief of the St. Joseph's band, warning him that the Pottawatomies who had engaged to escort the garrison, were bent upon treachery, urging him not to accompany the troops, and promising that a boat containing himself and family should be allowed to pass over to St. Joseph in safety. Kinzie felt his responibility and was prepared to assume it; he knew that his presence with the retreating party would to some extent, at least, prove a safeguard, so he declined to take advantage of the kindly offer, but accepted it for his wife and children. The latter were crowded into a boat and rowed to the mouth of the river, where a messenger from To-pe-nee-bee detained them. Kinzie bade his family good bye, and hastened to join the garrison party.

The evacuation was one of the saddest spectacles that one could imagine. As the inmates left the palisades, they were preceded by the post band which played the Dead March. Not a man or a woman among them expected to reach Fort Wayne. They felt, one and all, that their doom was sealed. Capt. Wells led the little band of Miamas, which formed the van. He had blackened his face in token it is said, of his impending fate.

The evacuating party consisted of the garrison, about sixty-five men, officers included, the Miamis and leader, sixteen men, the wives and children of the officers, soldiers and settlers, some half-breeds and a few friendly Indians— about one hundred and twenty-five persons, all told. They took their route along the southern shore of the lake. Extending from the water's edge to the center of the block between the present Michigan and Wabash avenues, was the beach. This was skirted by a range of sand hills. To the west of these hills, or from, say State street inward, was the prairie, or swamp lands, dry in the month of August, 1812. The little band of whites and their Indian friends marched on the beach, the line of which had been used as the common highway heretofore. Much to their alarm, the Pottawatomies took the prairie on the west side of the sand ridge. This looked suspicious to begin with.

They must have reached a point on the shore at the present Eighteenth street, when Capt. Wells, who had been riding in advance, came galloping back to the main body with the announcement: "They are about to attack us;

(meaning the Pottawatomie escort) form instantly and charge upon them!"

These words were echoed by a volley from the openings between the sand-hills. The massacre had begun.

Great credence is placed upon the story of the massacre told by Mrs. Helm, wife of the Lieutenant, and step-daughter of John Kinzie. She was an eye witness of the attack, and had an opportunity of observing, as well as a bewildered and frightened woman could, the terrible beginning of the assault. But owing to the ill-feeling prevailing among the garrison officers it is very fair to presume that she dealt rather severely with the conduct of several of the principals on the white side, in her narrative. She tells for instance of the cowardly conduct of the Surgeon, Dr. Van Voorhees, who was almost immediately tomahawked, and casts reflection upon the behavior of Capt. Heald, while she lauds the behavior of Ensign Ronan, her husband and her father. It is very likely that all conducted themselves as well as men generally do when placed in such a terrible position. Mrs. Helm was carried off the field to a place of safety at the lake shore, and hidden almost under the water by no other than the faithful chief, Black Partridge, who saved other lives that day.

At the very first discharge of the enemies' muskets, Capt. Wells' band of Miamis precipitately fled across the prairie, and left the others to their fate. The Miami chief, after accusing the Pottawatomie chief of treachery, and uttering a threat of future vengeance, followed his flying braves.

The whites fought with all the courage and energy of desperation. One after another, the charges of the Pottawatomies were repulsed with great losses on both sides. Ensign Ronan, mortally wounded, and kneeling in the sand, loaded and fired with deadly precision until he fell exhausted. Kinzie and Capt. Wells were fighting like madmen to protect the women and children. Presently, while the whites were charging on a squad of Indians hidden in a ravine, a young

Indian brute climbed into a baggage wagon in which were the children of white families, twelve in number, and slaughtered every one of them. The number of whites had been reduced to twenty-eight after hard fighting near the ravine. The little band, according to Mrs. Helm, succeeded in breaking through the enemy and gaining a rising ground not far from Oakwoods. The contest now seemed hopeless, and Lieutenant Helm sent Peresh Leclerc, a half-breed boy in the service of Mr. Kinzie, who had accompanied the detachment and fought manfully on their side, to propose terms of capitulation. It was stipulated that the lives of all the survivors should be spared and a ransom permitted as soon as possible.

It was then that tidings came of the massacre of the children. "Is this their game?" cried Capt. Wells, "butchering the women and children? Then I will kill, too!"

So saying, he started for the Indian camp where the Indians had left their squaws and children, pursued closely by Pottawatomies. "He laid himself flat on the neck of his horse, loading and firing in that position, as he would occasionally turn on his pursuers. At length their balls took effect, killing his horse and seriously wounding himself. At this moment he was met by Winnemac and Wau-ban-see who endeavored to save him from the savages who had now overtaken him. As they supported him along, after having disengaged him from his horse, he received his death blow from another Indian, Pee-so-tum, who stabbed him in the back." His heart according to a historian of Illinois (Brown) was afterward taken out, cut to pieces and distributed among the tribes. Mrs. Corbin, wife of a soldier, surrounded by savages, fought like a tigress and refused to surrender, although safety and kind treatment was promised her, and was finally cut to pieces. Sergeant Holt finding himself mortally wounded by a ball in the neck, gave his sword to his wife who was on horseback, telling her to defend herself. She too was surrounded by Indians who endeavored to capture her alive. She fought with mad desperation, and finally broke away from the annihilating party and fled to the prairie. The Indians admired her bravery, and the cry followed her pursuers to save her life. She was at length seized from behind. She was afterward turned over to a trader on the Illinois river, and later restored to her friends. Mrs. Heald, who was wounded, was on the point of being scalped, when near the boat occupied by the Kinzies, to which spot she had been conducted by her captor, when a friendly Indian under the instructions of Mrs. Kinzie, saved the lady's life by making the savage a present of a mule, and a promise of ten gallons of whiskey. Mr. Kinzie, later in the day, extracted a ball that had penetrated her arm. The Kinzie family were protected during the massacre, and afterward removed to their home near the fort.

The battle was over by this time. The whites had surrendered after the loss of about two-thirds of their number. Notwithstanding the terms of the armistice, that the lives of all the survivors should be spared and protected until ransomed, the Indians slaughtered a large number of the wounded.

At the fort during the massacre, the Indians left behind had begun the work of destruction. "The cattle were shot down as they ran at large, and lay dead and dying around, but it was not until next morning that the torch was applied, which now left nothing but blackened debris to mark the spot where the fort had stood."

Kinzie's family was threatened with destruction later, and there was more or less atrocious barbarity and bloodshed afterward, several prisoners being murdered in cold blood on the day following the fight, but the worst was over. Black Partridge, Winnemac and other friendly chiefs did their utmost to insure the safety of the few survivors, and to them is due the fact that a solitary white face or half-breed was permitted to escape. Once when the massacre of

Kinzie's family and all the other survivors had been determined on in spite of the protests of the friendly chiefs, Billy Caldwell, a chief of the Pottawatomie nation, whose father was a British officer, and mother a Wyandotte woman, saved their lives by his sudden appearance and an admirable piece of diplomacy, through which he made the Indians feel ashamed of their cowardly proceedings and treachery.

Three days after the massacre, John Kinzie and family were conducted to St. Joseph, the wife and children being permitted later to leave for Detroit, where he joined them in the following January. Capt. Heald and his wife, both wounded, were also sent across the lake to St. Joseph. Lieut. Helm, also wounded, was conveyed by more friendly Indians to their village at Au Sable. Later he and his wife, arriving at Detroit, were arrested by the British and subjected to various indignities and brutalities. Mrs. Burns with her infant became the prisoners of a chief who carried them to his village, and afterwards were liberated. Mr. Lee, his son and all the other members of the household at "Lee's Place" on the river, except Mrs. Lee and her infant, fell victims on the 15th of August. Black Partridge saved the mother and child from the infuriated savages during the massacre. The noble chief later proposed marriage to this woman, but was induced to give her up for a liberal ransom. The man who paid the ransom, a trader, Mr. Du Pois, afterward married her himself.

Chicago toward the close of 1812 and until the 4th day July 1816, just thirteen years after the arrival of Capt. Whistler, was as desolate a spot as it had been one hundred and fifty years before. At the close of the war of 1812, that is to say in 1814, the project of constructing a new fort to replace the one destroyed, was broached in Congress, and President Madison in the same year called the attention of that body to the necessity of a canal that would connect Lake Michigan with the Illinois and the Mississippi rivers. It was also suggested about this time, that a line of forts be constructed along the water highway from Chicago to St. Louis. President Madison's suggestion is said to be the first expression ever given to the idea which afterward was carried out in the construction of the Illinois and Michigan canal. The construction of the new Fort Dearborn was placed in the hands of Capt. Hezekiah Bradley, who arrived with his detachment on July 4, 1816.

"The bones of the victims of 1812," says Blanchard, "still lay scattered over the sand drifts, amongst the sparse growth of bunch grass and stunted shrubbery that grew there, and thus remained till 1822, when they were carefully gathered and buried with the measured respect of military etiquette, and they are now a part of the dust beneath the feet of a countless throng of busy citizens."

The new fort occupied the exact site of the one destroyed, and resembled it somewhat in structure, there being block houses, store houses, etc., surrounded by palisades. The government at this time also ordered a survey of the water-course between Chicago and the Illinois river, which was conducted by Maj. Long. Mr. John Kinzie and family returned to Chicago during the summer and occupied the old residence which the Indians had respected; a treaty was concluded during the same year, with the Ottawas, Chippewas and Pottawatomies, which practically resulted in freeing Northern Illinois of the presence of the savages. Communication had been opened with towns and settlements in Southern Illinois. The tide of emigration had begun to flow toward the West. The waste places were taken up rapidly under the homestead act. Illinois was admitted into the Union in 1818. Chicago began to assume the appearance of a thrifty village, and from that time on, though interrupted now and then by dreadful calamities, her course has been upward and onward.

CHAPTER III.

FROM 1829 TO 1837—THE LAST ATTEMPT OF THE INDIANS TO DRIVE THE
WHITE INVADERS BACK—CHICAGO SURVEYED AND PLATTED AS A VIL-
LAGE—THE VILLAGE GOVERNMENT—TOWN ORGANIZATION UNDER A
BOARD OF TRUSTEES—TOWN AND POLICE CONSTABLES—ONE OF THE
FIRST RECORDED POLICE CASES—PRIMITIVE METHOD OF DEALING
WITH A THIEF—INCORPORATION OF THE CITY—THE FIRST HIGH CON-
STABLE.

Indian disturbances from time to time menaced the peace
of Chicago after the rebuilding of Fort Dearborn, the most
notable event of the kind, culminating in the "Winnebago
troubles," in 1827, but nothing of a serious nature transpired within the limits of the village, and the slow but
steady progress of the settlement was practically uninter-
rupted. The name "Chicago" first appeared in a school
atlas about this time. The fur trade had grown to very
considerable proportions. Wool was cultivated to some extent, but commanded very low prices. In 1829, Chicago
was surveyed and platted into village lots. The legislature,
sitting at Vandalia, had taken preliminary steps looking to
the construction of the Illinois and Michigan canal, but circumstances arose which prevented the completion of the
work for many years afterward. In 1830, there were thirty
votes cast in the village, Reynolds, the Jackson candidate
for governor, receiving twenty-two of them, and three-
fourths of all the voters were French or half-breeds. The
judges at the election were Russell E. Heacock, Chicago's
first lawyer, Gen. John Baptiste Beaubien and James Kinzie. The clerks were Medard B. Beaubien and Jesse Walker.
Cook county was organized in March, 1831. Col. R. J.

Hamilton, according to William Bross' history, became in the course of a single year, probate judge, recorder, county clerk, treasurer and commissioner of schools, some of which duties he fulfilled without gratuity. "The county of Cook, in 1831, embraced all the territory now included in the counties of Lake, McHenry, DuPage, Will and Iroquois," says Mr. Bross. No mention is made of a police force in those days, but, judging from the number of taverns in the place, we might suppose that a few constables could have been kept moderately well occupied. There were two companies of infantry in the fort, commanded by Major Fowle, and the prominent citizens were Elijah Wentworth, James Kinzie, William Lee, Robert A. Kinzie, Samuel Miller, John Miller, Mark Beaubien, J. B. Beaubien, Dr. E. Harmon, James Harrington, Dr. Walcott, and the blacksmith, a Mr. McKee. All of the above were active men, some of them keeping taverns, others grocery stores, others dry goods stores, and others trading with the Indians, or combining professional with commercial pursuits. The settlement nearest to Chicago was Naperville, called after the first settler. Galena was at this time quite a prosperous mining town. "Chicago was yet essentially an Indian town," says Blanchard. "Peltries and furs, guns, blankets, kettles, knives, hatchets, vermilion and whisky were its stock in trade, and Indians were its suppliers and consumers. Quiet·reigned then because no one had occasion to offend the Indians, and when they became intoxicated the squaws took care to keep sober in order to restrain them." "The Pottawatomies paid one-half the expense of building the first bridge from the South to the West Side," says *Western Annals*.

It was in 1831 that the Black Hawk war broke out. Interesting as the story would be, it is not necessary here to follow the details of that memorable conflict—the last effort of the Indian tribes in the Mississippi valley to check the progress of the white settlers. It was the desperate attempt of a doomed race to assert itself against the growing power

of a grasping invader—the last united struggle of a hunted
people, driven from point to point across half a continent,
to make a stand against the Anglo-Saxon host that robbed
them of their inheritance and threatened them sooner or later
with annihilation.   The Black Hawk contest was a terrible
one for the whites, a fatal one for the Indians.   It plunged
the young state of Illinois into all the horrors of a barbarous insurrection, and made her prairies and wooded river-
banks the scenes of most atrocious outrages and diabolical
massacres.   It brought consternation and panic into every
border settlement and made Chicago the refuge of the
frightened whites, who flocked for protection under the guns
of Fort Dearborn.   Inside the palisades of the fort, in a
very few days, Gen. Scott's command, which had been ordered to the West to assist in suppressing the Indian uprising, suffered a loss of 90 men from that most frightful of all
diseases, the Asiatic cholera, and the whitened bones of these
unfortunate men were exposed by the erosion of the lake,
ten years afterward (about 1840,) in their burying ground
on the lake front, foot of Madison street.   Thirty of their
comrades had perished on the steamer which brought Gen.
Scott's troops to Chicago.   The Black Hawk war was the
school in which many American heroes received their training.   One in particular the memory of readers will recall—
Abraham Lincoln—but many of the officers and men who
served in this contest, proved themselves to be skilled and
courageous soldiers in the war with Mexico, while some of
them who, as boys, had joined in the pursuit of Black Hawk's
warriors, fought with distinguished brilliancy in the rebellion.

The Indians were scattered, driven, killed, until but a
remnant remained, to be removed beyond the possibility of
causing further annoyance to the white invader.   "The conquest of the northwest was now completed.   The spasmodic
throe of a lingering native power that had been quickened

into a fleeting activity by the courage of Black Hawk, had vanished."

It was on August 10th, 1833, that Chicago became organized as a town under the general laws of the state, and at the election held that day only twenty-eight votes were cast. A board of trustees was elected, consisting of P. J. V. Owen, George W. Dale, Medard Beaubien, John Miller and E. S. Kimberly. One of the first measures of public utility was the construction of a log house to answer the purpose of a jail, in the public square where the City Hall and Court House now stand. Another public building was shortly afterward added. It was an estray pen, or pound, and the total cost of the same was twelve dollars. Under the preceding Board of Trustees one of the greatest public improvements demanded was the building of ditches on either side of Clark street, then the leading street of the town, so as to make the thoroughfare passable. The treasury was empty and the president of the Board was driven to the necessity of negotiating a loan for sixty dollars in order to carry out the work. This amount was expended faithfully and the debt was paid on maturity. It is mentioned here because it was perhaps the first financial transaction ever entered into by Chicago as an organized community.

In 1833 the *Chicago Democrat* was established by John Calhoun, whose daughter married Col. J. K. C. Forest, at present the oldest active journalist of this city. The publication of the first copy of this paper marked an epoch in local history. The fact that it was fairly prosperous from the beginning proves that intelligence and enterprise were even then prominent characteristics of Chicago people. On the 11th of June, 1834, the following significant "item" appeared in this paper :

Hardly a vessel arrives that is not crowded with emigrants, and the stage that now runs twice a week from the East is thronged with travelers The steamboat Pioneer, which now performs her regular trips to St Joseph, is also a great accommodation to the traveling community Loaded teams and covered wagons, laden with families and goods, are daily arriving and settling upon the country back.

The tide which has continued to flow up to the present day, was setting in. "During the summer of 1833," says Colbert's history, "not less than 160 frame houses were erected and the number of stores increased from five or six to 25." From the same source we learn that the year 1834 "witnessed the establishment of closer relations with other points east and west." On the 30th of the same month (April), the corporation announced that emigration had fairly set in, as more than 100 persons had arrived by boat and otherwise during the preceding ten days. On Saturday, July 11th, the schooner Illinois, the first large vessel that ever entered the river, sailed into the harbor amid great acclamations, the sand having been washed away by the freshet of the spring previous. In its issue of Sept. 3d, the *Democrat* stated that 150 vessels had discharged their cargoes at the port of Chicago, since the 20th of April preceding. "The total number of votes polled in the whole county of Cook, this year, was 528. The poll list of Chicago had increased to 111 out of a population of 400, besides 200 soldiers in the fort. It is noteworthy that not less that 13 of the 111 were candidates for office at the October election."

We learn from Colbert's work, also, that in the spring of 1834 stage communication was opened up between Chicago and the country westward, by means of J. T. Temple's line for St. Louis, the line for Ottawa being piloted out by John D. Caton, who had previously been over the unmarked miles on horse-back. A large black bear was seen on the morning of October 6th, in a strip of timber on the corner of Market and Jackson streets. He was shot, and the people afterward "got up a game wolf hunt in the same neighborhood and killed not less than forty of those animals before nightfall. It was just at this point, thirty-seven years after, almost to a day, that the flames leaped across the river from the west division and swept northward to the limits of the city." In this year a drawbridge was built across the river at Dearborn street: active measures were taken to prevent the spread of cholera, and a committee was authorized to build a cholera hospital, if the disease should make its appearance in the town; the first Sunday liquor law was passed; the sum of forty dollars was paid for repairing bridges, and the town was divided into four wards "by an ordinance intended to prevent fires." " Prior to this year," says the same authority, "all the stores were located on South Water street—indeed, Lake street and all the streets southward of it, only existed on paper." In the autumn of 1834, Thomas Church erected a store on Lake street which was soon the busiest in the whole town. The packing statistics of the year show that Mr. Clybourn packed 600 cattle and more than 3,000 hogs, in a packing house of his own, recently built on the south branch. The same year Gurdon S. Hubbard packed 5,000 hogs on the corner of Lake and LaSalle streets. The first waterworks of the future city was established about this time, the sum of $95.50 being paid for the digging, stoning, and stone of a well in Kinzie's addition on the North Side.

In 1835, numerous hotels were added to those already in existence under the name of taverns. Among these was the Tremont House, which had been erected, however, the year previous on the spot where its magnificent successor stands to-day. The Green Tree, the Saganash, the Graves and the Tremont were the leading hostelries in those days. About this time the town ventured upon another financial transaction. The treasurer was authorized to borrow $2,000, at not more than 10 per cent. interest, payable in twelve months. Rather than face the responsibility he resigned, and his resignation was followed by that of the street commissioner. Another notable event of this year (1834) was the establishment of the *Democrat's* rival, the *Chicago American*. In 1835, two additional buildings were erected in Court House square—a brick structure for the use of the county officers, and an engine house, costing $220. The first fire engine was bought in December of the same year for $896.38, and a second ordered, and the first fire company was organized two days afterward.

It was some time afterward that the legislature passed an act (approved February 11, 1853), including all the land east of State street from Twelfth street to Chicago avenue, within the corporate limits, except the Fort Dearborn reservation, lying between Madison street and the river, which should not belong to the town until vacated by the United States. This was the original 600 acres, the ownership of which induced the government to establish a military post here in the first place. South Water street property, with wharfing privileges, sold toward the close of the year at $25 per front foot.

In 1836, the schooner Clarissa was built on the river front, and a large assemblage visited the first launching in the town. This year, also, ground was broken for the Illinois and Michigan canal. The dream of the earliest settlers was about to be realized. In order to exhibit the remarkable growth of Chicago as a commercial point, between '33 and '36, the following will serve as an illustration:

	NUMBER OF VESSELS ARRIVED.	TONNAGE.
1833.	4	700
1834.	176	5,000
1835.	250	22,000
1836.	450	60,000

The town was indeed making remarkable progress in every direction, and soon it became evident that her first corporate garments were becoming too small for her. She was resolved upon being a " city," and her career as a town ended on the 3d of March, 1837. On the 4th, by an act of the legislature, she was incorporated as a city, and William B. Ogden, the democratic candidate, was elected mayor over John H. Kinzie, who ran on the whig ticket. The former received 469 votes, the latter 237. The South division cast 408 votes, the North 204, and the West 97 at this election.

We have now followed the early history of Chicago down to a point where minor events must henceforth sink into insignificance, and we pass into a period which gives attention only to enterprises of great moment. It is neither possible nor expedient to follow, within the scope of this work, the manifold interests which have contributed since 1837 toward making Chicago one of the most remarkable, most prosperous and most populous cities on the globe. That is a work already well performed by others. Our mission now is to tell how the peace has been preserved in Chicago all these years; how order has been maintained among a populace embracing representatives from every civilized, semi-civilized and uncivilized land on the face of the earth; how the passions and the vices of avaricious and turbulent seekers after wealth have been held in check; how crime, the inevitable companion of such phenomenal growth in population and wealth, has been restrained, and how the property and persons of the people who have flocked in hundreds of thousands to this city from every point of the compass have been protected.

Not all of those who poured into Chicago in the early days were people bent upon making an honest fight for life, for fortune or for happiness. While the thriving city that grew up around the Fort Dearborn reservation drew very largely upon the honest and hardy yeomanry of the East, and attracted, at first by hundreds and afterward by thousands, the brightest and most energetic citizens of older towns and cities, and while as a rule the people who turned their eyes and their footsteps toward Chicago, and made it their abiding place, proved themselves deserving of all the blessings of freedom and self-government—yet the spirit of adventure, the thirst for easily-acquired gain, the easily-acquired gain itself, the opportunities for the dishonestly-inclined, the looseness of a half-organized society, the swelling tide of unregulated European immigration, the temptations of a city where women were greatly in the minority, where Homes were scarce, the very prosperity of the place, and the advantages which it held out to all, from the black-

leg to the banker, from the thief to the mechanic, contributed toward the collection of elements which required the
unremitting vigilance of good citizens to hold in check.

As far back as 1850, Chicago had an unenviable reputation
throughout the country, and she became known as the wick-
edest city in America before she had attained her majority.
It is not necessary here to attempt any defense of the city's
morality, nor to endeavor to disprove the charges made against
her from time to time.   We remember very well that the
great fire was spoken of in a thousand pulpits throughout
the land as the visitation of an angry Providence, and that
the destruction of the greater part of this city was pointed
out to intelligent audiences by learned men as the fall of the
second Sodom.   That Chicago deserved much of the odium
which was cast upon her there is no denying, but that she
could not have been anything other than she was is unques-
tionable.   She had in her wonderful growth received as sus-
tenance and nourishment the very cream of the world's
population; that she was compelled to swallow much of the
scum of civilization was the penalty her sudden rise from
obscurity into greatness imposed upon her.

The first constable of whom we have any record was Archibald Clybourn, and he was appointed before the organization of Cook county.   "He was made constable of the First
Precinct of Peoria county, comprising all that part of the
country east of the mouth of the DuPage river, where it
empties its waters into Aux Plains river.   This was rather a
hard beat for a constable even in those times, but the probabilities are that beyond serving civil processes, he paid
little attention to the duties commonly falling to the lot of
constables in new settlements.   This Archibald Clybourn
was the oldest son of the Elizabeth McKenzie, the captive
maiden mentioned in a preceding chapter.   He became one
of the most prominent of the earlier settlers.

Long before Chicago was incorporated as a town there
were regularly elected constables to act as village guardians.

John Kinzie was the first justice of the peace, elected July 28, 1825, and he was followed by Alexander Walcott and John B. Beaubien. There were certainly constables attached to these courts, but no record of them remains. At the special election for justice of the peace and constables, held at the home of John Kinzie, July 24, 1830, thirty-three votes elected John S. C. Hogan to the first named office, while Horatus G. Smith was elected constable, receiving one vote less. At a special election held at the same place, Nov. 25, 1830, Stephen Forbes was elected justice of the peace, but the name of the fortunate constable cannot be ascertained. Presumably, however, Mr. Smith continued in office. This same Stephen Forbes was elected first sheriff of Cook county in August, 1832. He received 106 votes against two cast for James Kinzie, who was the last sheriff under the old county organization and the predecessor of Forbes. The new county took its name from Daniel P. Cook, a member of congress, from Southern Illinois. Contemporaneous with Forbes were Samuel Miller, Gholsen Kercheval and James Walker, who were sworn in as our first county commissioners, March 8, 1831, before Justice Hogan. Archibald Clybourn was the first county treasurer and Jediah Wooley the first county surveyor.

In the spring of 1833, before the village board of trustees ceased to exist, John D. Caton, who afterward became one of the most distinguished jurists of the west, occupied a room with Giles Spring, another adventuresome young attorney. Both were very poor, as clients were scarce and but little money was paid out in law-suits. Each managed in some way to pay $5 per week for board, or to escape paying it, as the case may be. The first criminal trial we have been able to find any mention of, occurred about this time. A man named Hatch had been robbed by a fellow boarder of $34 in Bellows Falls money, (this was in the "wild cat" period) at Old Geese's tavern. Heacock, Chicago's first lawyer, was the justice and he issued a warrant which was served by Constable Reed, who was a carpenter. The prisoner was captured and conveyed to the carpenter's shop, which was used as a "sweat-box." Here the culprit, surrounded by a crowd of interested spectators, was subjected to a systematic search. Caton had been retained by the prosecution, and he compelled the prisoner to shed his clothing. The attorney, notwithstanding the protests and objections of Spring, for the defense, compelled the prisoner, finally, to strip himself of drawers and stockings, and in one of the latter the stolen money was found. The court sat upon the carpenter bench, and in the presence of this evidence ordered that the prisoner be committed for trial next day. There was no jail and the constable had to sit up with him all night. Next day, at Old Geese's tavern, the trial took place, Caton and Spring distinguishing themselves before a dining-room full of country-gawkes, half-breeds and Indians, and the prisoner was convicted. He gave straw bail, however, pending a motion for a new trial, and escaped. It was generally believed at the time that Spring helped the prisoner to escape, so determined was he to beat his room-mate, Caton.

There was a black town-crier employed by the village, named George White. Shortly after the occurrence above mentioned he called the inhabitants together to attend the sale of a man named Harper under the vagrant law. Harper had once been a man of some respectability and education, but border life and border whisky had so demoralized him that the community determined upon taking this extreme measure. There was a large attendance at the sale, Constable Reed acting as auctioneer. Negroes had been sold in this way, but the sentiment of the people revolted against the sale of a white man. Finally the negro town-crier bought Harper for a quarter, but some of the villagers helped the unfortunate vagrant to escape to the woods that night. He never was seen in these parts again.

The constables under the village organization were seldom called upon to perform any important service. In cases where the peace was seriously menaced, the garrison at the fort was ready to act, and citizens generally turned out to preserve order in case of any extraordinary fracas. After the organization of the county the sheriff assumed the responsibility of arresting the greater criminals, and the town constables were seldom called upon to act singly in any dangerous police enterprise.

The early inhabitants, as a rule, settled their own differences in their own way. There were no ordinances worth mentioning, and, consequently, no violations of them to be attended to. The constable was a man who, like Reed, followed some trade and who considered his official position simply a sinecure to which but little profit was attached.

Under the village organization the fines inflicted upon law-breakers were shared in by the informers. Half the fines usually went to the person giving information. This system was also in practice after the town became organized and public notices were posted in conspicuous places, which represented that for certain violations of local laws fines would be imposed, one-half of which would be given to the person whose testimony would lead to the conviction of the offender.

On August 10th, 1833, the first town election was held under general statute law, with the result heretofore stated. As only 28 votes were cast at the election it will be seen that the necessity for a police force was not great. No constable is mentioned in connection with the election, but that one was appointed or otherwise provided for is certain, for even under the village organization there were constables. In 1834, when Eli B. Williams was elected President of the Council Board of Trustees, the name of a constable fails to occur likewise. But in 1835, at the August election, O. Morrison is chosen constable and town collector.

This year, also, the Board of Trustees adopted several important ordinances bearing upon police regulations. The sale of liquor was prohibited on Sundays, gambling houses were ordered closed, street nuisances were defined, and the

use of fire-arms on the streets was positively prohibited,
penalties being provided in each instance. Constable Morrison was re-elected in 1836. The year had been a most
prosperous one for Chicago, and the town was expanding in
all directions. The population had grown from about 200 in
1833 to very nearly 4,000. The work on the canal and harbor improvements had attracted large numbers of persons,
while speculation in lands, the rapid increase in valuation,
and the opportunities offered to settlers in the vicinity, contributed toward swelling the population. It became plain to
the more watchful and enterprising citizens that the growth
of the place was going to be rapid, and that the existing
municipal organization was incapable of meeting the emergencies likely to arise. The President of the Board of Trustees,
therefore, on October 26, 1836, called a meeting of delegates
from each of the three geographical divisions of the town,
the South, West and North Sides, to meet the Board in conference as to the advisability of applying to the legislature
for a city charter. This meeting was held on November
25th, and the result was the appointment, by President Eli
B. Williams, of five delegates to draw up a charter for presentation. The men who composed this committee were
Ebenezer Peck, J. D. Caton, T. W. Smith, William B. Ogden and Nathan H. Bolles. The committee presented the
charter to the Board of Trustees on December 9th; after being slightly amended it was adopted, and on March 4th,
1837, the legislature passed the bill approving it. The first
charter election was held on May 2d, 1837, William B. Ogden, being the democratic, and John H. Kinzie the whig
candidate for mayor. The former was elected, receiving
467 votes against 237 cast for Mr. Kinzie. The total vote
of the South division was 408, of the North 204, of the
West 97, and of the whole city 709. At this election John
Wentworth cast his first vote, being challenged on account
of his youthful appearance, and sworn as to his legal age,
before his ballot was counted. At this election, also, John
Shrigley was chosen high constable.

CHAPTER IV.

FROM 1837 TO 1854—THE NEW CHARTER AND ITS PROVISIONS FOR A POLICE
SERVICE—RATHER A WEAK FORCE—A SATIRE ON THE CONSTABU-
LARY—SAMUEL J. LOWE AND M. HUNTOON—THE DAYS OF OSCAR SMITH,
PHILLIP DEAN, AMBROSE BURNHAM, LUTHER NICHOLS AND DARIUS
KNIGHTS—CRIME IN THE YOUNG CITY—THE MOBBING OF STEPHEN A.
DOUGLAS.

The city charter required that some very radical change
should be made in local governmental affairs, and proper
provision was made for the police branch of the service, although it was not expected that the powers of the young
municipality in this direction would be called into play for
some time to come. Chicago was growing too rapidly to feel
comfortable in her old garments, but she had not developed
sufficiently to wear the new ones with grace. So she adopted
the simplest methods possible under the charter, and waited
patiently until she could take advantage of the larger possibilities for which it gave ample scope.

The new charter created a municipal court which had
jurisdiction concurrent with the county court, over all municipal matters. The high constable was an officer of this
court, bearing about the same relation to it that the sheriff
did to the county tribunal. The common council was em-
powered to appoint one constable for each of the six wards
into which the city was districted, and these, acting under
the high constable, were to constitute the first city police
force. But there appears not to have been any necessity for
a police establishment of seven men. How many men John
Shrigley had under him is not known, but, judging from in-

formation respecting subsequent years, he was probably limited to two or three.

He held the chief's position under Buckner S. Morris, Chicago's second mayor, and in 1839, when Benjamin W. Raymond succeeded to the head of the city government, Samuel J. Lowe was elected high constable, and his assistants were Daniel B. Heartt, D. C. Allen and M. Huntoon. Whether from motives of economy, or because there was no real necessity for a force of four men, is not known, but certain it is that shortly after Mayor Raymond's accession the police force was reduced to two men—Messrs. Lowe and Huntoon.   S. Lisle Smith was then the city attorney and the common council met on Clark street, in the old City Hotel building.   It may not be out of place to mention here, that in the early days of Chicago "Clark," in Clark street, was invariably spelled with a final "e."   When "Clarke" finally gave way to "Clark" is uncertain, but it must have been some time during the fifties.   The city attorney's office was located "over Clark's druggist store," and the river was crossed on "Clarke" street, by ferry.   The *Daily American*, of April 11, 1839, says:

Our office is now at the head of navigation and the ferry is constantly in motion with the life of the city. We would caution men of business against being too intent in conversation with those on the boat who are bound for the other shore, as the boat—like " time and tide "—waits for no one, and they may find themselves going the wrong way.

There was a rival ferry at State street, and this competition was loudly commended by the paper just quoted.   In the same paper of Tuesday evening, April 25, 1839, we find the following:

☞ The scoundrel who set fire the other night to the old postoffice building is *suspected*. He and all other suspicious loafers about the city had better, as soon as possible, make themselves scarce, or *the city watch will be at their heels*.

The "city watch," of course, consisted of Lowe and Huntoon, but whether they ever got at the heels of the suspicious loafers is a matter that must forever remain in doubt.   There were many of these loafers in the young city, however, desperate characters, too, but, judging from the following in the *American* of May 20, same year, life and property were faithfully guarded by the city watch:

The grand jury after a session of four days has adjourned after finding six indictments, four for larceny, and two for perjury. When we consider the number of indictments found at previous times, the public must be satisfied that crime is fast diminishing.

In the common council about this time S. J. Lowe is allowed "$30 for services as police constable during the riots and disturbances of August last, and other services." These riots and disturbances, it appears, consisted of a row between some residents and soldiers of the garrison, who were all more or less excited by the immoderate use of alcoholic stimulants. Horse stealing was the bane of the early agricultural settlers here, as it has been elsewhere ever since, and the *American* calls attention to the organization at Naperville of a society for the detection and punishment of horse thieves, and suggests that a similar society be organized in Chicago. On June 19, 1839, the common council requests "City Marshal Lowe"—this is the first time he is mentioned as city marshal—"to make monthly reports of all his doings, and suggests such measures for the better order and government of the city as he should deem expedient." Sam Lowe had at least four titles during his management of police affairs. He was "High Constable" at first, then "Head Constable," later on we find him mentioned as "Chief of the City Watch" and still later as "City Marshal." The watch house was for a time located on the lake front, and afterward in the rear of the first court house, and in front of the jail, facing Randolph street, nearly opposite the west wall of the present Sherman House. It was built of upright oak boards and its dimensions were about 15x20.

The "tippling houses" and "groceries" furnished the watchmen of '39 with the greater part of their work. The soldiers in the fort were in the habit of resorting to these places, particularly on pay days, and collisions with the residents were not infrequent. Another source of constant employment, especially in the summer season, was the hunting down and butchering of worthless dogs. Where they came from, nobody could tell, but, judging from the frequent references to them, they were as numerous in proportion to the population as they are now.

A newspaper published at Jackson, Mich., evidently not over-friendly to Chicago, printed the following in the summer of '39:

The population of Chicago is said to be principally composed of dogs and loafers.

To which the *American* replies, directing its remark to the editor of the Jackson paper:

You had better emigrate. We will *classify* you.

For some time the press had been making complaints about the police force. Attention was called frequently to the number of brawls in the rum shops, street fights, etc. Besides complaint was made that " small pigs and fowls" were "running at large in the 6th ward," and finally the *American* charged the "watch" with dereliction of duty on the 4th of July, when a serious row had taken place in a whisky shop. It is presumed that the high constable, accompanied by the head constable, the city marshal and the chief of the watch, called upon the editor to make an explanation, for on July 12, the *American* contained the following piece of satire and defense of the constables:

OUR CITY POLICE.—The constabulary patronage of our city is alarming. The liberties of the people are positively in danger from the number of police. We learn that there is kept up from one end of the year to the other, without increase or diminution, the enormous number of *two* police marshals. This is indeed a small standing army of " office-holders " and unless the number be diminished at least two-thirds, we apprehend the worst consequences. Seriously speaking, we regard it as a great evil that the number of our police is so contemptibly small. Perhaps Messrs. Lowe and Huntoon who are indefatigable in the performance of their duty, may be able to preserve the order of the city in "these piping times of peace," but on extraordinary occasions, such as the 4th of July and election day, a greater force should be provided. We unintentionally did these two worthy officers an injustice when speaking a few days since of a row at Burg's grocery. We were not aware that the 4th of July muster roll was the same as the " peace establishment." It is certainly unreasonable to expect *two* men to be keeping order in six wards at the same time.

A destructive fire broke out on Sunday morning, October 27, of this year, in which eighteen buildings were reduced to ashes—the first great calamity of the kind recorded in the young city. At the time it was looked upon as a crushing blow, but the place rapidly recovered from it, and from many another destructive conflagration involving terrible losses in life and property. All of these fires were so overshadowed by the blaze of October, 1871, that they appear to have been entirely lost sight of now.

Lowe and Huntoon continued on the police force, and additional assistance was given them "on extraordinary occasions, such as the 4th of July and election day," but in 1842, when Orson Smith was elected city marshal and street commissioner combined, he had but three assistants—Henry Rhines, Hugh K. Henry, and William Wesencraft. The population of the city then was 7,580, and it must have been a hard task for this little force to preserve anything like order, inasmuch as every second shop was a grocery, and the groggeries were the favorite resorts of two-thirds of the population. Orson Smith was the first regularly elected city marshal and he held the office during the administration of Mayors Augustus Garrett and Alanson S. Sherman till 1844. The only police constable mentioned in the latter year is William Wesencraft, but there must have been others, as the population had now reached 10,864. Of this number, "972 were Irish, 1,056 German, 531 Norwegian, and 683 other foreigners," making the total foreign population 3,242. There were 43 lawyers and 28 physicians in the town, and the total expenditures of the city administration were $21,-488.20. At the election held on March 4, of this year, 2,133 votes were cast in the six wards.

In 1845, Augustus Garrett again becoming mayor, Phillip Dean was elected marshal and street commissioner, and William Wesencraft held on as police constable, but constables were elected additionally in each of the six wards. Dean served as marshal until 1847, when the number of wards in

the city was increased to nine, and nine constables elected.
In 1848 Ambrose Burnham was elected city marshal, and the
police force consisted of the following constables, one from
each ward, in the order named: Carding Jackson, A. H. Pahl-
man, A. J. Chappel, Daniel T. Wood, Henry Misner, J. E.
Willick, Bartley Ford, Erni Pattriolett and William Boomer.
These men served during the dreadful cholera epidemic, and
are mentioned as having performed their duties faithfully
and in many instances heroically. Mr. Burnham held over
till the accession of Mayor Curtis in 1850, when he was succeeded by James Howe, who was city marshal during the succeeding four years. In 1850 the force consisted of nine men,
there being some changes, as follows: C. T. Bogue, W. H.
Wells, Michael O'Brien, A. S. Fay, H. Misner, J. N. Norton, B. Ford, Michael Maguire, John McHale. These policemen each had charge of the ward they represented, from first
to ninth, and the population of the different wards was then:
1st, 2,829; 2d, 3,398; 3d, 3,250; 4th, 3,200; 5th, 3,400;
6th, 2,380; 7th, 3,560; 8th, 3,224; 9th, 2,384—whole, 28,-
620; increase in ten months, 5,573.

Robberies and burglaries were of frequent occurrence
then, and the *Gem of the Prairie* was unspairing in its
abuse of the police for not attending to their duties. In its
issue of May 3, 1850, after describing a burglary in Hubbard's building, in which the safe of Winslow J. Ball was
broken open, it said:

The city watch knew nothing of it, of course. They were probably
regaling themselves in pleasant quarters at the time.

Sam. Lowe, the ex-high constable, had now become
a justice of the peace, and he appears to have been
kept busy attending to city criminal matters About this
time there was a bloody fracas at the "Farmer's Home," a
tavern that stood upon the corner of LaSalle and South
Water streets. Soldiers from the fort had been drinking
there, and the usual disturbance followed. Constable Hines
interfered in the interest of good order and was knocked

down with a club, "which cut his head open frightfully."
Another constable was served in like manner, and then both
were forced out of the room. At this stage, three additional
city watchmen appeared and demanded admission. On
being refused they broke down the door with huge clubs.
"Once inside, they assaulted the soldiers, knocked them
down with their clubs and dragged them bleeding to the
calaboose." Notwithstanding this gallant conduct on the
part of the "watch," a Tax-payer writes to the *Gem of the
Prairie*, under date of August 17, 1850, protesting against
the method of selecting watchmen, alleging that although
the power was in the council, it was delegated to one man—
meaning the mayor—bad material was selected, and the
force was composed of strangers instead of respectable citizens. The writer further says that he heard "a man" remark
that "the city was best protected when the watch was
asleep." Complaint is made by other citizens that Erie and
Champlain sailors, of unknown character, were preferred to
well-known residents for positions on the force.

J. N. Barker was the assistant marshal at this time, and
he gives notice to the public that he will collect the census returns for 1850. Duties foreign to regular police service were
enforced upon the officers generally, and toward the close of
the year the *Gem of the Prairie* confesses that the police
cannot be justly blamed for the numerous robberies reported,
as the force is entirely too small. The paper demands a
large and an immediate increase in the number of men.

The salaries paid at this time were very small, the marshal
receiving only $800, and the cost of supporting the entire
night watch was but $6,344 per annum. The city attorney
received $500 per annum for his services.

It was customary in those days to compel prisoners convicted of offenses against the city ordinances, and who were
unable to pay their fines, to work them out in the "ball and
chain gang" upon the public streets, doing scavenger work
and repairing. Every prisoner had a chain fastened around

his ankle, at the end of which was a heavy ball of iron, to prevent his escape should he take a notion to attempt to elude the vigilance of the watchman placed over the gang. This was looked upon by many citizens as a barbarous custom, disgusting to the sight of all, and demoralizing to the unfortunate fellows who were forced to submit to it. The anti-slavery movement was growing at the time, too, and everything that had a tendency to degrade mankind was becoming obnoxious. The *Tribune* of September 6, 1851, contained a strong editorial protesting against the use of the ball and chain, and condemning the custom as inhuman and a disgrace to the age. Soon afterward the bridewell was completed, and the " chain gang " disappeared forever. The bridewell was opened in 1851. This city prison was located on the corner of Wells (Fifth avenue) and Polk streets. It was built of three-inch oak planks, set upright and roofed with the same material. It was 100 feet in length, 24 in width, and one story high. There were cells for 200 persons. Employment was found for culprits in handling and piling the lumber used in street planking. Later, when the plank road system was abolished, they were forced to labor in a stone yard, provided for them near by. Walsh was superintendent of the bridewell till 1857.

The same year, in September, the corner stone of the new Court House and City Hall was laid in the public square with imposing ceremonies. The procession was half a mile long, says the report, and it was composed of the masonic fraternity, which had charge of the ceremonies, military companies and the volunteer fire brigade. Every able-bodied man in town belonged to an engine or hose company. He might belong to other organizations, but he was not considered a citizen in first-class standing unless he "ran with the machine."

In 1852 Walter S. Gurnee was mayor and James L. Howe was marshal. The police constables were A. B. Wheeler, S. H. McDearman, John N. Norton, J. Y. Cutler, Richard

Carthew, R. V. Wightman, James Daly, Michael Grant and William Cannon. Added to these were special constables Luther Nichols, George Rommeiss, Charles O'Malley, Owen Dougherty and William Harrison. Of all these, Charles O'Malley, will be most pleasantly remembered by the past and present generation. As a police justice he attained a national reputation in later years for the originality of his decisions and his utter disregard of common and statutory law. He is dead. Owen Dougherty was a well-known character also for many years. But perhaps Luther Nichols is deserving of more recognition as a historical personage than any of the others.

He was a native of Gilbertsville, Ostego county, New York; born in 1805, and enlisted as a regular soldier in 1828, arriving in Chicago with his wife and one child as a soldier of the 2d United States Infantry, under the immediate charge of Major Whistler. When he reached Chicago it was during the Black Hawk war, and Fort Dearborn was crowded with refugees from the surrounding country. It was a few days after the arrival of the company of 50 men, to which Nichols was attached, that Gen. Scott arrived with his cholera-stricken command. Upon Scott's arrival Major Whistler built a barrack for his men at the foot of Madison street. During the cholera Nichols, with six other soldiers, was detailed to inter the remains of cholera victims, which were thrown overboard from the troop vessel during the trip down the lake, and which the winds had washed ashore along the south beach. He was present at Rock Island when the treaty was signed with the Indians, and was discharged from the service in 1833. He became a citizen of Chicago and served in many responsible positions.

In 1852 the Chicago *Tribune* was printed at 53 Clarke street. It was a whig newspaper and its editors were William Duane Wilson and Henry Fowler. It then claimed the modest circulation of 2,000 daily and 2,000 weekly. The *Journal*, published at 107 Lake street, was also politically a whig, and its editors were R. L. and C. L. Wilson; circulation, daily, 1,000; weekly, 2,000. The *Illinois Staats Zeitung* was published at 190 Randolph street; its editor being George Schneider, and its daily circulation 500. The *Daily Times and Citizen* was published at 50 Clarke street, a Free Democrat in politics, and its editor was Z. Eastman; circulation, 800. The *Democratic Press* was published at 45 Clarke street; politically, democratic, and its editors were J. L. Scripps and William Bross; circulation, 800. There were in all seven daily papers published here. The population on June 1st, 1852, was stated at 38,733; American, 19,314, and foreign, 19,419.

In 1853 Charles M. Gray was mayor and James L. Howe continued as city marshal. Daniel T. Wood replaced John N. Norton, Thomas Hennessy succeeded R. V. Wightman; and Charles O'Malley, Thomas Melvin and James Quinn were substituted for James Daly, Michael Grant and William Cannon on the constabulary. The City Hall was then temporarily located over the South Market Hall, on State street, but the mayor's office was room No. 1, "Court House, Court Square." The county jail was in the basement of the Court House. The Recorder's Court, with the same jurisdiction as our present Criminal Court, was established in 1853. Previous to its establishment criminal business was transacted in the Circuit Court. Hon. Robert S. Wilson was the first judge of the new tribunal, Phil A. Hoyne was the first clerk, and he was succeeded by Col. J. K. C. Forest. Daniel McElroy was state's attorney from 1853 to 1856.

In 1854 Isaac L. Milliken succeeded to the mayorial chair and Darius Knights became marshal. Luther Nichols was appointed Captain of the Watch or assistant marshal, and held the position for one year. The police justices were his honor, the mayor, Calvin DeWolf and P. Lamb, and the police constables were Charles T. Bogue, A. B. Wheeler, John Beech, Michael Hickey, Richard Carthew, T. Hennessy, James Keefe, Michael Grant, and William Duffy. The population at this time was said by one statistician to be 58.538, but another estimate placed the figures at 65,872; these figures, however, included some 4,000 "marines," in port at the time the count was made.

It is of some importance to understand that of this population 35,857 were reported to be of foreign birth, for people of foreign birth in those days were facing an issue that had more than once culminated in bloodshed, and threatened to produce a state of feeling which might at any moment cause an internal rupture, more lamentable and frightful in its effects, and far less satisfactory in its ending or results, than the civil war, that convulsed the nation a few years later.

Know-nothingism was in its bloom in 1854. The cry, "Put none but natives on guard!" echoed from one end of the country to the other. Dastardly outrages had been and were being committed upon foreign-born citizens in the East, for no other reason than that they were foreign-born, and "Down with the Irish!" "Down with the Dutch!" "to h— with the Pope!" were the political rallying cries of the fanatics who, for the time being, seemed to forget that their fathers, grandfathers, or great-grandfathers had been perhaps but poor, poverty-stricken emigrants themselves.

These cries were raised in Chicago, and there were not wanting newspapers ready and willing to nurse the bigotry and intolerance that gave them voice. From the very first Chicago has been indebted to foreign-born citizens for the greater part of her prosperity and glory. Her first white discoverers were French missionaries; her first traders were Frenchmen; her first genuine resident-merchant and citizen—John Kinzie—was born on foreign soil; her leading business men during the first quarter of a century of her existence as a settlement were largely German, Irish and Norwegian emigrants; fifty, and even sixty per cent of her population in the earlier days of her existence as a city were foreign-born, and in 1854, when know-nothingism was in its bloom, as we have said, 35,857 of her 65,872 residents claimed foreign nativity. And ever since then population statistics from year to year have shown that a minority only of the citizens of Chicago have been native-born.

The know-nothing hue and cry went up in every hamlet, town and city from the coast to the Mississippi, and it found many strong adherents and devoted followers in Chicago, but the masses of our people were strongly opposed to the narrow doctrines advocated by its noisy promoters, and some of its most bitter antagonists were men who could look back over a long line of American ancestor

Adding to the disturbed condition of the public mind was the free soil question, then at its whitest heat. By some unfortunate and unfathomable misapprehension on the part of a large class, and undoubtedly through the cunning maneuvering of the fanatical element, the know-nothing cause became entangled in the free soil movement, to such an extent that it was difficult for a person to be a know-nothing and not be a free soiler, or to be a free soiler and not be a know-nothing. Foreign-born citizens throughout the North were strongly opposed to permitting the encroachments of slavery upon free territory, or to the spread of the institution upon any pretext, but they were prevented from forming an alliance with the free soilers because the know-nothings controlled or at least influenced their movement. They had their choice, therefore, between the democratic party, which was willing to add Kansas and Nebraska to the list of slave states, or the free soil party which, while it was strongly in favor of advancing the interests of the Ethiopian, was openly at enmity with the citizens who chanced to have been born in other lands. The Kansas troubles added their heat to the general conflagration of public feeling. Politics were mixed; parties were demoralized. Men who were whigs on one question were strongly democratic on another. The lines of policy were hanging loosely on both sides, and neither creed could define its position to the satisfaction of its followers. In the midst of this turmoil whigism was soon to writhe in the throes of labor and bring forth at the cost of its own life a child—the republican party—which could and would define its policy; the democracy was to undergo a similar ordeal, but the result was destined to be one of its usual miscarriages, with sinking spells which were to occur frequently for years afterward.

Stephen A. Douglas, senator from Illinois, was on the wrong side of both questions, when looked at from the native Northern standpoint. He was unfortunately on the wrong side of one question when looked at from the foreign-born Northern standpoint; but the latter were willing to wink at his "Squatter Sovereignty" doctrines, so broadly, so liberally, so manfully did he advocate his own opinions, and so tolerant was he of the opinions of others.

"On the know-nothing question Douglas took a noble and even advanced ground," said Mr. Fred Cook in an article which appeared in the Chicago *Times* in 1877. "In fact he was the first to make war upon the proscriptive spirit of the native party, and it was he who marshaled the democratic party against the hosts of intolerance and political as well as religious fanaticism—for this party, like another, until 'christian statesmanship' put it to the blush, claimed all the cardinal virtues and followed meekly in the wake of the pulpit."

Chicago, before the know-nothing and free soil questions were raised, was a democratic stronghold. An "old settler" is credited with the following statement regarding the political bias of the young city: "If the town pump," he said, "had been nominated for mayor in those days on the democratic ticket, it would have been elected. A nomination was always equivalent to an election, and I remember once when Dr. Kimberly got the nomination for clerk of some court, in the democratic convention that was held in the little old Court House, that stood on the northeast corner of the square, he fainted dead away, he was so overpowered by it. You see the nomination gave him a nice thing, and the nomination and election coming that way in one fell swoop is calculated to knock off the strongest, as I happen to know, for I have run for office once or twice myself." But in 1854, as we have already pointed out, the party lines were ragged, and "Fusion" this way or that way was the fashion in politics. The democratic party was afraid to take up arms against the know-nothing doctrine, and its leaders begged the question until Stephen A. Douglas, in a Fourth of July address at Philadelphia, had the nerve to combat it. Had he stopped after giving the know-nothings the most scathing overhauling they ever received it would perhaps have been better for him, but his position on the Nebraska question "so offended the free soil element in his party that a general stampede followed, and this free soil element, together with the know-nothings in Chicago, determined to give him a warm reception when he reached home." The *Democratic Press*, a free soil organ, edited by John L. Scripps and Hon. William Bross, and published here at the time, heaped the most bitter denunciation upon the shoulders of the "Little Giant," and so great was the opposition to him, by the know-nothing element on the one side and the free soil element on the other, that a writer says, "not more than a corporal's guard of true souls could be found to give the little senator a brave backing."

Douglas arrived in Chicago on the 25th of August, 1854, Congress having adjourned on the 1st of the same month. He found the town up in arms against him. From the bitterness and noise of the opposition it seemed as though he had not a solitary friend left. Notice was given him publicly and privately that he would not be permitted to express the views he had aired in Washington and Philadelphia, before a Chicago audience. Threatening letters were sent to him and he was even warned that his life was in danger. Nevertheless he announced his determination to address the public on the evening of Sept 1, in the old North Market Hall, Michigan street near Clark. "All sorts of wild rumors

were afloat," says a report of the meeting, "one being to the
effect that Douglas had selected a body guard of five hundred Irishmen, who, with arms in their hands, were to be
present and compel the people to silence while he spoke."
Of course there was no foundation for such a reckless statement.

The gathering did not take place inside, but immediately
in front of the Market House.   Mayor Milliken, who had consented to preside at the meeting, being a democrat and a
strong personal friend of Douglas, took every precaution to
preserve the peace.   Marshal Darius Knights and Luther
Nichols, captain of the watch, with almost the entire regular constabulary, and a large number of specials sworn in
for the occasion, were on hand, but their presence was next
to useless, for the constables were careful not to offend their
fellow citizens, nor to interfere with them in the interest of
peace when the question at issue happened to be a political
one, and besides, each and every one of them had his own
personal and political sentiments to indulge and his own
prejudices to nurse.   But a majority of the constables were
Irishmen, and their sympathies were naturally with the senator.   However, during all the disgraceful and riotous proceedings of the night, it is certain that Mayor Milliken's
police shirked their duty, or were overawed by the howling,
angry mob with which they had to deal.

The senator had scarcely begun his address before it became evident that trouble was brewing.   Mr. Bross, who was
at the time acting as a reporter for his paper, *The Democratic
Press*, is credited with opening the opposition ball by calling certain of the senator's remarks to question.

Mr. Bross, under the excitement of the moment, threw
a fire-brand into the midst of the combustibles, without thinking, perhaps, what the consequences would be.
It proved to be the signal which the mob was waiting
for, nevertheless. Pandemonium ensued. "Douglas was
instantly assailed by all manner of epithets," says Cook,

"every name that vile tongues could invent were hurled at him. In a moment he was surrounded by a howling, raging mob, hungry to do him personal injury. But all undaunted he fearlessly faced the enemy, at the same time keeping down a little company of friends on the platform, who were all eagerness to resent the insults and affronts so brutally heaped upon their idol. He boldly denounced the violence exhibited as a preconcerted thing, and in defiance of yells, groans, cat calls and every insulting menace and threat, he read aloud, so that it was heard above the infernal din, a letter informing him that if he dared speak he would be maltreated." It was reported at the time that he had been pelted with rotten eggs, but this has been denied, and rotten apples, it is said, were the most offensive missiles used.

The late Mr. James Sheahan, for many years one of the ablest of Chicago journalists, in his "Life of Stephen A. Douglas," thus refers to this episode:

We never saw such a scene before and hope never to see the like again. * * * Until ten o'clock he stood firm and unyielding, bidding the mob defiance and occasionally getting in a word or two on the general subject. It was the penalty for his speech in Philadelphia. It was the penalty for having made the first assault upon know-nothingism. It was the penalty for having dared to assail an order including within its members a vast majority of the allied opposition of the Western states. We have conversed since with men who were present at that mob; with men who went there as members of the order, pledged to stand by and protect each other; with men who were armed to the teeth in anticipation of a scene of bloody violence, and they have assured us that nothing prevented bloodshed that night, but the bold and defiant manner in which Douglas maintained his ground.

The little body guard which stood by Douglas throughout this ordeal, and finally forming a line around him, placed him in a carriage and escorted him to the Tremont house, are now nearly all gone. The most notable of them were: Hon. Frank C. Sherman, General Hart L. Stewart, Cornelius and William Price, Tom Mackin, Elihu Granger, Dan McElroy, Dan O'Hara, Col. Dick Hamilton, Elisha Tracy and Ike Cook.

It was Chicago's first experience with a mob, and when the angry passions which had been excited so readily by political differences had cooled down, citizens began to ask themselves what would have been the result that night if a single shot had been fired? What was there to check a riot? Upon what protection could peaceable citizens depend? The police force was unworthy of consideration. The example set by this mob might be followed by other and more desperate ones. Better protection was demanded on all sides. The more the subject was discussed the more dangerous the situation appeared. It only required a few months to prove that this alarm was not groundless.

CHAPTER V.

FROM 1854 TO 1858—THE POLICE SERVICE GROWS IN IMPORTANCE—
DECLINE AND FALL OF KNOW-NOTHINGISM—THE CELEBRATED "LAGER
BEER" RIOT—RACE AND RELIGIOUS PREJUDICE—DESTRUCTION OF "THE
SANDS"—AN ANTI-SLAVERY MOB—HARD TIMES IN THE YOUNG CITY—
SUFFERINGS OF THE POOR AND FRIGHTFUL INCREASE OF CRIME—THE
ADMINISTRATIONS OF MAYORS BOONE, DYER AND WENTWORTH RE-
VIEWED.

We have reached a most remarkable period in the history of this city. The events of 1855 were extraordinary enough to have impressed themselves upon the memory of every old citizen indelibly, and such would have been the case were it not that the war of the rebellion and the great fire of '71 built barriers mountain-high between the Chicago of the Past and the Chicago of the Present. And is it not possible, nay, probable, high in our estimation as the events of the Present may be, and fraught, as we think them, with such vital importance to the city, that some overshadowing calamity, some mighty revolution in our affairs, may occur, which will make them appear insignificant to those who come after us?

The anti-Popery riots of the last century in London would have shrunken into obscurity had not Dickens woven from the career of the hair-brained fanatic, Lord George Gordon, the story of Barnaby Rudge. Historians pass over the episode, deeming it too trivial to merit the attention of their erudite minds; but the touch of the novelist has brought it out in relief as one of the most interesting and entrancing chapters in the history of the English people. When the coming American novelist, if he be a Chicagoan, is searching for facts upon which to frame his romances, he will in all likelihood gloat exultingly over the musty, ragged, incomplete records which will be then in existence, to tell the story of intolerance, bigotry, race prejudice and religious fanaticism which culminated in the lager beer riot in 1855. Throughout the entire country bitterness had taken the place of good fellowship. "It was," says a writer in later years, "one of the hottest and most unreasoning political periods in the history of the country. Passion ran high on all sides. The temperance question was alive; the Catholic question almost precipitated a religious war, and know-nothingism hung on the outer wall a banner inscribed, "Put none but Americans on guard! Each one of these questions was well calculated to rouse the very worst passions, and under this stimulus sprang up a generation of 'b'hoys' that, until the war of the rebellion, were the terror of all large American cities."

Dr. Levi D. Boone, the candidate of the American or know-nothing party, was elected mayor of Chicago in March, 1855, after one of the most bitter political contests that has ever occurred in this city. Indeed, the entire city government was in the hands of the "Native American party," and no better illustration of the length to which race prejudice was permitted to extend can be found, than in the fact that every applicant for employment under the city administration was compelled to prove that he had been born on American soil. The mobbing of Douglas, together with the probability that trouble would result from the enforcement of a stringent temperance law, which the legislature of the preceding winter had ordered to be submitted to the people, for ratification or rejection—and which it was believed would certainly be ratified—convinced all good citizens that the constabulary should be increased. The new council passed ordinances immediately, providing for the creation of a police department and a force of eighty or ninety men. Every man appointed on this force was a native American. It should be remembered that this discrimination was enforced in the face of the fact that one-half the population was foreign-born. "What a change less than a quarter of a century has brought!" said Mr. Cook, in the Chicago *Times* in 1877. "A prescriptive spirit of that sort could not now maintain itself for a moment even in the most intolerant community in the country, and least of all in Chicago. Now the Chicago police force is divided among all nationalities. And this is well, not so much because every nationality has an individual right to be represented in the force—it has nothing of the sort—but because business can be best expedited in that way, and the ends of justice and the interests of humanity are so best subserved. Now the German districts are largely patrolled by German policemen, the Scandinavian by Scandinavian, and so on through the whole list. By this means each policeman is his own interpreter, and many serious blunders and mistakes are avoided."

The temperance crusade at this time, the impartial reviewer of these events is constrained to say, was not instituted from any very exalted motives on the part of public functionaries, nor to conserve the ends of public morality; but purely and simply to strike at the habits and customs of one class of foreigners—the Germans. The assault which was made upon the social life of these foreign-born people was entirely unprovoked and outrageously wanton. The men who attempted to deprive them of the privilege of drinking beer were, with few exceptions, notorious for their own convivial habits. While claiming apostolic purity in their warfare upon intemperance, their aim was to drive out the beer sellers by imposing heavy and intolerable burdens upon them in the way of taxation. The mayor who drank grog himself was not above resorting to the sheerest trickery in order to deprive his fellow-citizens of German birth or extraction from indulging their taste for beer, but he lived to see his mistake, and to feel ashamed of the narrow-minded views which were his in '55.

He had scarcely taken his oath of office before he recommended to the council that the liquor license fee be raised from fifty to three hundred dollars per annum, and that no license be issued for a longer period than three months. In later years he claimed that he made this recommendation thinking it would be a wise precaution, since it would "drive out all the lower class of dives and leave the business in the hands of the better class of saloon keepers, who, when the temperance law should go into force, could be rationally dealt with." Even were this his motive, his reasoning was most illogical, for the smaller liquor dealers were by no means the worst, nor were the larger dealers by any means the best. What he intended was to drive out the small beer dealers who were scattered particularly throughout the North Side, where the Germans were in the ascendency, knowing that as they depended for existence upon the custom of an economical and law-abiding people, and, as their profits were but small, in comparison with those of the down town whisky-dealers, they could not meet the demanded increase in the license fee, and would be compelled to close up. The ordinance was passed, of course, and the beer dealers banded together to defeat its execution.

It was the last straw and it broke the camel's back. As long as the know-nothings confined themselves to mere abuse, ridicule and misrepresentation, the German-born citizen paid little attention to the agitation, wisely calculating that the mad prejudice would soon wear itself out. But soon as an attempt was made to deprive them of rights which they had enjoyed under a despotic government, of rights guaranteed them by the constitution of the United States, they felt that if they did not now assert themselves as men in behalf of their liberties, "there would soon be instituted for the white alien a slavery as abject as the negroes' servitude on the Southern plantation."

The excitement throughout the city ran high, but the *Nord Seite* was in a perfect ferment. Meetings were held, speeches were made, resolutions were adopted, and pledges were registered that the Germans of Chicago would die, if need be, rather than submit to this outrage upon their rights.   Loud-mouthed, shallow-brained and mischief-loving agitators stepped to the front, and the result was a frenzied state of public feeling, for and against the ordinance.   The Irish and Scandinavian citizens who drank alcoholic liquors, or didn't drink liquor at all, were naturally in sympathy with the Germans, who had a weakness for malt, and made common cause against the fanatical party.   The line for once was clearly drawn.   All native Americans were not know-nothings, but all know-nothings were native Americans, and they had arrayed themselves against foreign-born citizens of every nationality.

As if to blow the flames into a whiter heat, the mayor attempted in the midst of this excitement to enforce the almost forgotten Sunday law, which had been adopted when the place was a mere village, and had been a dead letter for years.   The back and side doors of the whisky shops were open to the natives on the Sabbath, but the German beer gardens and saloons were ordered to be closed tight.   Naturally the Germans resisted, and the result was that over two hundred of them were arrested for violation of the license and the Sunday ordinances.   Some of them were committed to the city prison and others were liberated under bonds.   The saloon keepers decided to unite for defense and resistance, contributed toward a common fund and engaged counsel to represent all.   It was decided between counsel for the defense and the city attorney that a test case should be tried, the agreement being that the decision should settle the dispute.   The case was set for the 21st of April, and was to be heard before Squire Henry L. Rucker, whose office was in the public square, between the Court House and the watch house.   The case was called, but before proceedings were well under way an uproar was heard outside.   The liberated saloon keepers had collected their friends on the North Side, and, preceded by a fife and drum, the mob, about

500 strong, had marched in solid phalanx upon the justice
shop, as many as could entering the sacred precincts. After
making themselves understood that the decision of the court
must be in their favor, if the town didn't want a taste of
war, they retired and formed at the intersection of Clark
and Randolph streets, and held possession of these thoroughfares to the exclusion of all traffic. Crowds gathered from
all sections of the city, friends and enemies, and the uproar
around the Sherman House was deafening. The situation
was a threatening one, but Mayor Boone, narrow-minded as
he was, had the courage of his convictions, and a high and
clear sense of his duties as the city's chief magistrate, and
he prepared to grapple with it with admirable energy.

Under the new organization of the police force, Marshal
Darius Knights remained, but its real head was Cyrus P.
Bradley. He was Chicago's first Chief of Police, and it
was he who reorganized the service in 1855. Bradley was
born at Concord, N. H., Nov. 14, 1819, and located in Chicago when about 18 years of age, when he entered into the
employment of H. H. Norton, Walters & Co., near Fort
Dearborn. He married in 1843 the daughter of John
Hodgson, and in 1849 was appointed collector of taxes for
South Chicago. His heroic conduct during the floods in
detaching vessels from the ice-gorge and breaking up the
jam, brought him more prominently into notice. He had been
identified for some time with Pioneer Fire Engine Co. No. 1
and was one of its first foremen. In 1860 he succeeded Ashley
Gilbert as fire marshal, serving for two terms, and he was
one of the organizers of the Firemen's Benevolent Association, acting as its secretary till 1885, when, after serving
two terms as sheriff in the meantime, he was appointed
Chief of Police by Mayor Boone, and from the spring of
1856 to the spring of 1860 he, with B. C. Yates, J. H. Williams and Chris. Noyes, conducted a private detective agency,
and afterward conducted a similar institution alone. His
detective ability ranked high. Before the war he was a mem-

ber of the Light Artillery, which became known as batteries "A" and "B," but he did not go into actual service. When the war broke out he was superintendent of police, and did valuable service as provost marshal, "by placing an iron-bound embargo," says his biographer, "upon fugitives from the draft. Policemen were placed at all the depots and on vessels in the harbor, and all persons subject to the draft were compelled to show they were not leaving to avoid service." He resigned the superintendency in 1862, was afterward elected secretary of the Police Board, continuing in that capacity till 1864, and from that date to his death was connected with the government secret service, doing splendid work in the detection of counterfeiters. He died March 6, 1865.

Previous to Bradley's time there had been no regular day patrol, but now the force was put on constant duty. Luther Nichols was captain. Knights, Bradley and Nichols were men of great force of character and wide experience, and they seconded the efforts of the mayor to restore due respect for the law.

After the mob had completely blockaded Clark and Randolph streets, Captain Nichols waited upon Mayor Boone and demanded orders. "What shall I do?" he asked. "Clear the streets and disperse the mob," was the answer. This Captain Nichols proceeded to do, at the head of a squad of policemen, and, notwithstanding the apparently determined stand it had taken, the mob was quickly scattered. A number of men who offered resistance were arrested and quietly locked up.

This was entirely satisfactory so far, and the mayor, taking a look over the ground, congratulated himself that the disagreeable business was over. But it wasn't. This was in the morning. The South Side was quiet, but the North Side was preparing for another demonstration. It was decided to form into line in the afternoon, cross over the river and rescue the prisoners. The rioters armed themselves with shot guns, rifles, pistols, clubs, knives, and every species of weapon within reach. Wild rumors of their intended raid began to reach the South Side, and these rumors were quickly confirmed to the satisfaction of the mayor. He at once swore in one hundred and fifty special policemen, and had, therefore, at his command nearly two hundred and fifty men in all.

Speeches were being made to the mob over on the North Side. The excited people were told that unless they succeeded now in checking the outrages that were being heaped upon them, they might just as well prepare to leave the country, for the know-nothings would never stop until they had burnt down their homes and murdered their families. The cry was for war, and the response was manifest in the large numbers of young and old men, ordinarily peaceful, and even women, armed to the teeth, who flocked toward the avenging army.

It was about 3 o'clock when the mob began to move, making its way down Clark street to the bridge. Here it met with a disaster that it had not calculated upon. The mob moved in two detachments, there being quite an interval between the first and second. The first passed safely over the river, and then the bridge-tender, acting upon the mayor's orders, swung the draw and prevented the second detachment from following. As soon as the rioters, comprising the latter, realized how neatly they had been tricked, a howl went up that was heard in the Court House square. They demanded that the bridge-tender close the draw at once. They threatened him with death. They coaxed him with honied words. They offered bribes. Some talked of shooting him. The bridge-tender shouted across the yawning space that he was acting under orders from the mayor, and that much as he would like to accommodate the gentlemen in waiting on the north abutment, he could not conveniently disobey the orders of his superior. The parley went on for some time, till at length the mayor, having per-

fected his arrangements, ordered the bridge opened, and the
rioters swarmed across, only to be met by a solid body of
policemen thrown across Clark, between Lake and Randolph streets. A collision was expected, and it came. Cries
of "Shoot the police," "Pick out the stars," rose from the
mob, accompanied by the cracking of guns and pistols.
The police replied without waiting for orders, and for several minutes there was a hot engagement in the vicinity of
the Sherman House. A German, whose name is lost, lev-
elled a double-barrelled shot gun at Officer Hunt and blew
off his left arm. Sheriff Andrews, who had joined the police, with a posse, saw this, and ordered a young man named
Frazer, standing by his side, to return the fire. He did so,
shooting the German dead. A large number were wounded
on both sides, and several mysterious funerals occurred on
the North Side within the next few days, which convinced
the authorities that a number of the rioters had been fatally
wounded. There is positive knowledge, however, of only
one death, the man killed by Frazer. Officer Hunt is still
in the police force, and for many years has been detailed
for special duty in the comptroller's office. The city council, at the suggestion of Mayor Boone, voted him $3,000 in
consideration of the loss of his arm, and for over twenty
years afterward he had this amount out at interest, with Dr.
Boone for his financial agent.

Instead of releasing the prisoners the riot added sixty
more to their number.

The excitement was so great throughout the city that the
Montgomery guards, an Irish military company commanded
by R. R. Swift, at that time a prominent financier, and the
Chicago Light Guards, an American company, were called
out. Swift, it is said, was ordered by Mayor Boone to protect the Court House with his artillery. He had two guns,
and claimed that at most he could only protect two sides of
the structure at a time. The mayor then drew up a diagram for him, to demonstrate that by placing one gun at

LaSalle and Washington streets, and the other at Randolph and Clark, he would be able to command all the approaches to the square. This settled the matter for Swift. As soon as he saw that it could be done, the terrible responsibility of his position flashed across his great financial mind, and he withdrew from his command, appointing a lieutenant to act in his place—a man who, it is confidently held, would not have hesitated to mow down the mob had it made its appearance in the square.

But the riot was over. The mob was defeated. Not, however, the cause for which the North Siders fought. Nearly all the cases against the imprisoned rioters were dismissed, no disposition was manifested to carry the bitterness much further; there was a very loud demand from fair-minded people of American birth that the disreputable tactics of the know-nothings be stopped; the reaction had begun to set in; the minds of the people were expanding under the teachings of the founders of the republican party, and little by little the "Native American" idea faded until it finally vanished out of sight forever.

The native American party had run things with a high hand during 1855, and with anything but satisfaction to the citizens. Levi D. Boone was succeeded by Thomas Dyer as mayor; James M. Donnelly succeeded Darius Knights as marshal; J. W. Connett succeeded Luther Nichols as captain, and Cyrus B. Bradley was retired. The office of chief of police was abolished. Under the new organization the city was divided into three police districts, and a station established in each division. Police station No. 1 was located up stairs in the north end of South Market Hall, on State, between Lake and Randolph streets, and was in charge of 1st Lieutenant H. Shockley and 2d Lieutenant Charles Chilson. Police station No. 2 was located up stairs in the east end of West Market Hall, on West Randolph, near Desplaines street, and was in charge of 1st Lieutenant M. Finocan and 2d Lieutenant Frederick Gund. Police station No. 3 was located up stairs in the south end of North Market Hall, on Michigan, near Clark street, and was in charge of 1st Lieutenant John Gorman.

There were three police justices: Calvin De Wolf, South Division; Nathan Allan, West Division, and T. J. Prendergast, North Division. Benjamin R. Knapp was clerk. Marshal Donnelly's office was in the Court House, South Side, as was also Captain Connett's. The receipts of the police department, fines, etc., for the year ending February 1, 1856, were $21,260.26, and the expenditures $87,248.29, which sum covered the cost of suppressing the lager beer riot, in addition to the regular expenses of the department. The population was less than 100,000; there were 156 street lamps on the South Side, costing $8,687.00, 31 on the West Side, costing $984.00 and 94 on the North Side, costing $2,760, for the year. The strength of the police force remained about the same—between eighty and ninety men.

During Mayor Dyer's administration hard times had begun to strike the country, and they were nowhere felt more keenly than in Chicago. Toward the latter part of 1856 and early in 1857, the streets were thronged with idle men and crime increased alarmingly. Burglaries were of almost nightly occurrence, daring robberies were committed on the streets, and the police were everywhere denounced for their alleged inefficiency. Financial panics and mercantile disasters succeeded each other with startling regularity and rapidity; failures were reported from all sections and some of the oldest houses in the land went under. Discontent was general, and Chicago was overrun by desperate characters.

The municipal election was an exciting one, there being considerable bad blood engendered by a vigorous and bitter campaign. In the 7th ward, then known as "the bloody ground," Charles Seifert was beaten to death at the polls, and there was serious rioting and many heads broken in the 10th ward. John Wentworth took his seat in March, 1857, and found the city in a pretty low condition morally and financially. James M. Donnelly remained as city marshal, but Bartholomew C. Yates succeeded James W. Connett as captain. Station No. 1 was in charge of 1st Lieutenant Luther Nichols and 2d Lieutenant D. E. Ambrose, and Geo. W. Hunt was sergeant. Station No. 2 was in charge of 1st Lieutenant John M. Kennedy and Sergeant William Wiggins, the 2d lieutenancy being vacant. Station No. 3 was in charge of 2d Lieutenant Henry A. Kauffman and Sergeant L. Prindle, the 1st lieutenancy being vacant. The police justices were: John Lyle King, Jr., M. Grants and John C. Miller; F. S. Hooke being clerk. In addition to the regular force a "fire policeman" was appointed for each ward. This year C. F. Chilson was fire policeman for the 1st ward, Ira Colman for the 2d, Delos N. Chappell for the 3d, Robert Cunningham for the 4th, William K. Norwood for the 5th, Joseph Mitchell for the 6th, Jacob Myers for the 7th, C. K. Nichols for the 8th, Jacob Knaus for the 9th and Robert Scuden for the 10th. Then there were the "bell ringers"— M. Joyce and C. Boltz for the Court House, Nicholas Lacey for Twelfth street, J. M. Mattey and Martin Schuffer, West Harrison and Jefferson streets, and Philip Petrie for Fourth, near Milwaukee avenue. The superintendent of the reform school was D. B. Nichols.

Four new wards were added to the city and the following were the boundaries of the ten:

1st Ward.—All that part of the South Division east of State street.

2d Ward.—All that part of the South Division between State and Clark streets.

3d Ward.—All that part of the South Division between Clark and Wells streets (now Fifth avenue) extending south to city limits.

4th Ward.—All that part of the South Division lying west of Wells street extended.

5th Ward.—All that part of West Division between West Randolph and West Harrison streets.

6th Ward.—All that part of West Division lying north of West Randolph street.

7th Ward.—All that part of North Division lying west of North La-Salle street.

8th Ward.—All that part of North Division between Wolcott and North LaSalle street.

9th Ward.—All that part of North Division lying east of Wolcott street.

10th. Ward.—All that part of West Division lying south of Harrison street.

Mayor Wentworth, shortly after taking office, appointed E. S. Hansen to be 2d lieutenant South Division; Charles M. Taylor to be 2d lieutenant West Division, and John Noyes 2d lieutenant North Division, to fill vacancies existing in them, caused by promotion.

Various legends are afloat to this day regarding the raid made in Mayor Wentworth's time upon the "Sands." There are as many versions of the story as there are persons who tell it. It would be impossible to extract from the variety of accounts one that would stand the test of investigation, and it is deemed best to give here the plain unvarnished tale as it appeared in the Chicago *Tribune* on April 21, 1857, the day after the raid:

THE DENS IN THE SANDS BROKEN UP—NINE BUILDINGS TORN DOWN AND SIX BURNED.—Decidedly the vilest and most dangerous place in Chicago is, or rather was, the locality in the North Division near the lake shore, known as the Sands. For some years past it has been the resort or hiding place of all sorts of criminals, while the most wretched and degraded women and their miserable pimps congregated there in large numbers. A large number of persons, mostly strangers in the city, have been enticed into the dens there and robbed, and there is but little doubt that a number of murders have been committed by the desperate characters who have made these dens their homes. The most beastly sensuality and darkest crimes had their homes in the Sands, so famous in Chicago's police annals.

Previous to yesterday several unsuccessful attempts had been made to break up the "Sand Houses," but the land upon which they stood was in litigation in the United States courts, and the litigants, in view of the uncertainty of the law, were disinclined to take any violent measures to eject the occupants.

A short time since Hon. W. B. Ogden purchased the interest of one of the litigants, and a few days since Mr. Ogden's agents notified all the occupants to vacate the premises forthwith, or their buildings would be torn down, and at the same time, to avoid as much difficulty as possible, purchased the buildings of such of the owners as would sell them for a reasonable price.

Finding that the occupants were determined to retain possession as long as possible, yesterday morning the agent, accompanied by a deputy sheriff, arrived with writs of ejectment, and assisted by a large posse and some thirty policemen, headed by the mayor, had five disreputable houses and four shanties torn down. The inmates were allowed a sufficient time to move their furniture into the streets; hooks and chains were then fastened to the buildings, one after another, and down they came. This was in the morning, and the proceeding attracted a crowd of several thousand persons.

One or two of the houses were not destroyed, the occupants promising to vacate them to-day.

Yesterday afternoon, about 4:30 o'clock, six of the remaining buildings, all houses of the worst character, were burned to the ground. As the fire broke out in three of the buildings simultaneously, it is probable that they were set on fire by the inmates, out of spite to the owner of the property who had just purchased them. They were wooden buildings and of little value.

Thus this congregation of the vilest haunts of the most depraved and degraded creatures in our city has been literally "wiped out," and the miserable beings who swarmed there driven away. Hereafter, we hope the "Sands" will be the abode of the honest and the industrious, and that efficient measures will be taken to prevent any other portion of the city from becoming the abode of another such gathering of vile and vicious persons.

The story is told on good authority that Mayor Wentworth had advertised a dog fight for large stakes, which was to occur outside the city, in order to entice away the male inhabitants of the "Sands," on the day of the contemplated raid; and that device succeeded. There is, however, no record of this piece of diplomacy on the part of Mr. Wentworth, but he has never denied that the story was well founded. Judging from the frequency of the raids which the police made on brothels during the following six months, it appears plain that the immediate effect of the raid was to scatter the former denizens of the sandy lake shore throughout the city, and the newspapers commented upon the result at the time in anything but complimentary terms. The *Tribune*, which had been friendly to his highness, as it persisted in calling Mr. Wentworth, became his bitter enemy before his term expired. Every issue of the paper contained accounts of the most daring robberies, burglaries and assaults. Letters from leading citizens were printed complaining of the terrible increase of all manner of crime. The people became almost panic-stricken, and honest citizens returning to their homes or visiting friends after dark, ran the risk of being mistaken for criminals and shot. Nineteen years later, or in 1876, a very similar condition of affairs existed in this city, which was due to precisely the same cause—hard times. In 1857, as in 1876, laborers and mechanics were driven from sheer want and by the sufferings of their families, to try their fortunes as garroters, highwaymen, burglars and thieves.

John Wentworth stoutly maintained during these trying times that the police were performing their whole duty; that the circumstances were such as to defy at times the most vigilant watchfulness on the part of the officers and men, and that, while admitting the increase of crime, the *Tribune* had greatly exaggerated the offenses committed and purposely misrepresented the true condition of affairs. In the paper mentioned, on the morning of July 9, 1857, attention is called to the fact that the mayor had caused the different lieutenants of police to make an official report to him of the burglaries committed during the month of June; that Lieutenant Hansen of the 1st district (South Side), reported 33 robberies; that the lieutenants of the 2d district (West Side) did not report at all, but admitted a large number, and that the lieutenants of the 3d district (North Side), reported 3. The *Tribune* charges that these reports were intended rather to disguise than to expose the real state of affairs; that unfit men were appointed to the police force, and that the public was at the mercy of the criminal classes. Mr. Medill and Dr. Ray were the editors of the *Tribune*, and John Wentworth was proprietor and practically the editor of the *Democrat*. The one bitterly criticising and denouncing the mayor, the other, of course, warmly defending and applauding him, made the controversy during Wentworth's term an exceedingly interesting one. Neither paper spared abusive language nor epithets of questionable decency, and sometimes, during the most violent stages of the warfare, careful fathers and husbands hesitated before introducing the sheets into their families.

Gambling hells had prospered for a number of years previous to Wentworth's administration and numerous attempts were made to suppress the evil. On Thursday evening, July 17, 1857, one of the largest gaming houses in the city, on Randolph between Clark and Dearborn streets, was raided, and 18 arrests were made. The raid was managed by Capt. Yates, who received just praise, but the gamblers were one and all discharged afterward, and the police became discouraged, as they have often been discouraged since over the final result of descents of a like nature. Officers Grant and Brown caught a burglar a few nights afterward, and the *Tribune* congratulated the people over the fact that there were at least two men on Wentworth's force who realized that they had other duties to perform besides drawing their salaries.

It was in connection with the gambling cases that John Wentworth committed " assault and battery " upon Charles Cameron, many years later a well-known local politician, and at one time city attorney. Mr. Cameron swore out a warrant against the mayor and the case came up before Justice Beattie. The marshal was ordered to bring " Long John " into court, but his honor refused to appear, denying the jurisdiction of the tribunal. Mr. Cameron testified that he was sent for by two men confined in the watch house on a charge of gambling. While conversing with them about their case a policeman came up and ordered him away. He informed the officer that he had been retained as attorney by the prisoners, and that he had a right to converse with them. The policeman then went away, and a moment thereafter Mayor Wentworth came up, and roughly shoved him toward two police officers, and ordered him locked up. Cameron further testified that he gave his name and business to the officers, in the watch house, and was informed that the charge against him was that of " resisting an officer." He denied that he did so, when the mayor

again "took hold of him and pushed him into a cell." Other
witnesses corroborated the testimony of complainant. The
mayor was fined $25, and a judgment for $200, forfeited
bail, was likewise entered against him. The matter was afterward adjusted amicably, and Cameron and Wentworth in
later years became fast friends.

The city narrowly escaped a serious riot on Sunday, August 30th. The country was wild over the "fugitive slave
law" and the "Dred Scott case," and in Chicago the sentiment was almost as pronounced in favor of abolition as it
was in Boston. Any negro who was fortunate enough to
escape from bondage could rest assured of a hospitable reception and full protection here. A Kentuckian named
Thompson, accompanied by a negro boy, arrived in the city
on the day named. Some evil-disposed person started the
rumor that the negro was an escaped slave, and that Thompson was carrying him back to his mastsr. The rumor
spread rapidly, and the story told attained a sensational
character early in the afternoon. Soon crowds began to
gather around the hotel where Thompson was stopping, and
threats of summary justice were freely made and applauded
by the crowd. Many of the leading citizens were in the
mob, as wild and lawless in their talk as the "lower" classes.
By evening the mob had swollen to alarming proportions,
and now it was not Thompson that was threatened, but the
landlord of the hotel which harbored him. Many in the
crowd threatened to burn down the building, liberate the
negro and hang Thompson and the hotel proprietor. All
this time the latter and his guest attempted to make explan-
ations from an upper window, but the mob would not listen.
At length Allan Pinkerton, Alderman DeWolf, Mayor
Wentworth, Capt. Yates and some other responsible citizens
held a meeting and decided to investigate the case. They
visited the hotel and learned to their satisfaction that Thompson was simply conveying the negro from Kentucky to some
relatives in Monmouth, Ill.; that there was no attempt at
kidnapping, and that the negro himself was only worried

lest harm should befall his white companion. The committee reported these facts to the mob; there were many who
doubted the truth of the report, but affidavits made by the
members of the committee were read to the excited multi
tude, and the excitement soon afterward faded away.

In a report submitted to the common council on Sept. 7,
the estimated expenditures of the police department for the
year were put down at $127,000, and the estimated receipts
from fines, etc., at $42,103.

One of those terrible conflagrations which periodically
occurred in Chicago previous to 1871, but which have been
blotted out from the memory of old citizens by the great
fire, broke out at 4 o'clock on Monday morning, Oct. 19, of
this year, in the stores 109 and 111 South Water street. It
destroyed property on South Water and Lake streets to the
value of $500,000, and 18 charred and unrecognizable bod-
ies were taken from the ruins. At this fire the police did
gallant service in assisting the firemen, and in the prevention of robberies. The city was full of idlers and thieves,
and it required the utmost energy on the part of Capt. Yates
and his men to prevent robberies during the panic which the
fire created.

The winter of 1857 was one of the hardest the people of
Chicago ever passed through. There was nothing doing.
Bad financiering, a currency of uncertain or of no value,
wild cat banking, speculation and reckless extravagance for
several preceding years had borne bitter fruit. The result
was hardship, poverty, discontent and crime, throughout the
land, and in Chicago the outlook was little less than hopeless.
Life and property were in constant danger from mobs and
criminals, and John Wentworth's administration went out
amidst a general clamor from all classes for a change that
would at least check the declining tendency of trade and industry. Even the newspapers reduced their size, and the
Tribune of those days bears evidence of a terrible struggle
to keep alive.

CHAPTER VI.

FROM 1858 TO 1866—THE DAYS OF LEATHER BADGES—MAYOR HAINES
INTRODUCES UNIFORMS—JACOB REHM, IVER LAWSON—SALARIES OF
POLICE OFFICERS—A FULL ROSTER OF THE FORCE IN 1859—WENT-
WORTH'S SECOND TERM AND ITS ECCENTRICITIES—ESTABLISHMENT
OF THE BOARD OF POLICE—THE ENTIRE FORCE DISCHARGED—
BRADLEY AND NELSON—FAMILIAR NAMES APPEARING—THE WAR
EPOCH REVIEWED.

During the administration of John Wentworth, he practically acted as chief of police. He made all appointments
and no officer could be removed without his consent. He
directed the work of the force, and on many of its raids commanded the men personally. The patrolmen wore leather
badges, of his invention, a few of which are still in existence, and preserved as priceless curiosities. The men carried heavy canes by day and batons by night. Instead of
patrol boxes and electric signals they were provided with
"creakers," such as had been used by the watchmen of
London for three centuries before, devices with which to
call assistance in case of distress. It would be difficult to
find such a thing as a "creaker" in Chicago now, but they
are still in use in some European and Canadian towns by the
police, while the farmers of Great Britain and Ireland, and
of some portions of the Continent, utilize them to scare crows
from the grain fields. In later days the police whistle superseded the "creaker."

Under John C. Haines, who succeeded Mr. Wentworth
as mayor in 1858, the policemen of Chicago took upon themselves a brighter hue. The uniform was then a short blue
frock coat, blue navy cap with gold band, and a plain brass
star. When Wentworth was once more elected mayor, two years

later, he stripped them of their gaudy plumage, and again replaced the stars with leather badges worn on the hat bands of the men. Jacob Rehm became city marshal in 1858, this, however, was by no means his first connection with the police force of the city. John M. Kennedy was appointed captain of the police, a position which he held for two years. The bridewell was still located at Wells and Polk streets. D. B. Nichols managed the reform school, and the 1st district station during the year was removed from the South Market Hall to the armory building on Franklin street. The following were the officers of the police force, and the salaries they drew in 1858 and 1859:

OFFICERS.	INCUMBENTS.	SALARIES.
Police Justice	Andrew Akin	$1,200
" "	J. L. Milliken	1,200
Pros. Atty.	C. R. Jones	1,200
Police Clerk	Neils Larsen	1,200
City Marshal	Jacob Rehm	1,500
Capt. of Police	J. M. Kennedy	1,500
1st Lieut. S. D.	Wells Sherman	624
2d " "	Richard Bellinger	624
Sergeant, "	M. M. Gillespie	448
1st Lieut. N. D.	F. Gund	624
2d " "	J. C. Davis	624
Sergeant, "	W. H. Prince	468
1st Lieut. W. D.	W. R. Greene	624
2d " "	John S. Palmer	624
Sergeant "	Thos. Bronnell	448
Lieut. Hosp. Station.	Michael Grant	624
Fire Police, (S. D.)	Ira Colman	468
" " (N. D.)	Charles Warner	468
" " (W. D.)	D. H. Howard	468

By a most fortunate discovery we are enabled to throw a bright light upon the police establishment of Chicago, as it existed in 1859. John C. Haines was still mayor, Akin and Milliken were the police justices, C. R. Jones was the prosecuting attorney, Neils Larsen was the police court clerk. Here we find the mayor was provided with a "staff," consisting of Geo. W. Hunt, (the hero of the lager beer riot), E H. Chapman and John Oliver. This "staff" was detailed for duty around the mayor's and other city offices. Then there were two "police constables" who served writs in relation to violations of city ordinances. These were B. F. Cravens and Asa Gaines. And there was a "hack inspector" named A. Smith. The day "lock-up turnkey" was R. G. Cook, and the night "lock-up turnkey" was C. M. Beach.

The marshal's office had a force of its own, and for the first time the police department appears to be managed from headquarters, and not from the mayor's office. Jacob Rehm was marshal and his clerk was Charles Hodgson, who became first secretary of the board of police commissioners later on, and died of the cholera in 1868. The detective force consisted of Asa Williams, J. H. Williams, W. M. Douglas, John Macauley, H. A. Kaufman, N. S. Tenbroeck and Tobias Almendinger. But, more interesting and important than all, we are enabled to give the name of nearly every man connected with the regular police force in 1859 and 1860. Important and interesting, because the latter year closes a period in the history of Chicago, because the war of the rebellion scattered these men broadcast, because it is the only complete roster of the force, as it existed before the firing on Sumpter. Some of the men mentioned below are still living in Chicago, many live in other parts of the country, but the greater part of them are dead. Here is the roster:

WEST DIVISION.

First Lieutenant _____N. R. Green.
Second   "   _____John S. Palmer.
Fire Police_____D. H. Howard.
   "   "   _____P. Karlhofer.

PATROLMEN.	BADGE.	PATROLMEN.	BADGE.
James Hogan	No. 1	H. Simsalt	No. 14
A. Hare	" 2	F. C. Boone	" 15
R. Shippey	" 3	Thos. Biese	" 16
O. T. Belkland	" 4	R. Moore	" 18
H. Bale	" 5	H. Fink	" 19
F. Elmers	" 6	J. A. Hutchins	" 20
P. Milling	" 7	Geo. Eisenbeis	" 21
John Stening	". 8	M. Koff	" 22

PATROLMEN.	BADGE.	PATROLMEN.	BADGE.
George McAuley	No. 9	M. Coffey	No. 23
C. P. Throop	" 10	John McCarthy	" 24
P. Delany	" 11	Wm. Sawyer	" 25
H. Perry	" 12	J. E. Palen	" 26
J. J. Foote, Sergt.	" 13		

NORTH DIVISION.

First Lieutenant ....Frederick Gund.
Second   " ....J. C. Davis.
Sergeant ....W. H. Prince.
Fire Police ....C. Warner.

PATROLMEN.	BADGE.	PATROLMEN.	BADGE.
E. Langdon	No. 27	J. G. Halleck	No. 41
C. McAuliff	" 28	S. Fleis	" 42
T. Dehli	" 29	T. D. Fox, (bridge)	" 43
P. O. Patterson	" 30	C. Miller	" 44
P. Phillips	" 31	M. Bishop	" 45
A. H. Robertson	" 32	J. A. Gund	" 46
J. H. Grimner	" 33	S. Marx	" 47
F. Reichenbacker	" 34	M. Keble	" 48
J. Bass	" 35	G. Leander, (depot)	" 49
A. Vallender	" 36	P. Kuhn	" 50
John Schmidt	" 37	J. F. Stewart	" 51
N. Reeis	" 38	T. Johnson	" 52
P. Portman	" 39	M. Petrie	" 53
C. Jackson	" 40		

SOUTH DIVISION.

First Lieutenant ....Wells Sherman.
Second   " ....Richard Bellinger.
Sergeant ....M. M. Gillespie.
Fire Police.....................................Ira Colman.

PATROLMEN.	BADGE.	PATROLMEN.	BADGE.
J. Nelson	No. 54	D. McCarthy	No. 68
N. McAuley	" 55	P. Dorin	" 69
C. Kolb	" 56	J. Knight	" 70
H. Wood, (depot)	" 57	P. Schneider	" 71
P. McIntyre	" 58	C. Quinn	" 72
L. Colman	" 59	H. H. Harris	" 73
O. S. West	" 60	E. Denman, (post office)	" 74
F. Clayton	" 61	A. Wagner	" 75
T. Barrett	" 62	G. Cooker	" 76
P. Welch	" 63	D. Clayton	" 77
H. Pilgrim	" 64	H. P. Barnes, (depot)	" 78
William Mein	" 65	D. Sipple	" 79
J. Hall	" 66	G. Ward	" 80
J. Merrifield	" 67	J. B. Gray	" 81

J. J. Grant in charge of armory.

HOSPITAL STATION.

Lieutenant_____M. Grant.

PATROLMEN.	BADGE.	PATROLMEN.	BADGE.
Adolph Mueller	No. 82	James Quinn	No. 85
John Gillespie	" 83	William Wallace	" 86
J. B. Butts	" 84	James Fritz	" 87

BRIDEWELL POLICE.

Thomas Cunning, —— Schilling, Philip McGrath, —— Bloom, S. Y. Prince, G. C. Cunningham and —— Brazee.

John Wentworth was again elected to the mayoralty in 1861, and a revolutionary movement was immediately inaugurated in the management and composition of the force. Iver Lawson became marshal in March of this year and held the position till March, 1861. John Lyle King was prosecuting attorney, Andrew Akin remained as police justice, but L. H. Davis superseded Justice Milliken. Neils Larsen was still clerk of the court. Mr. Lawson was harbor master as well as marshal. The bridewell keeper was William Justice. Salaries remained about the same, the following being the pay-roll for leading members and attaches of the police department:

OFFICES.	INCUMBENTS.	SALARIES.
Police Justice	Andrew Akin	$1,200
Police Justice	L. H. Davis	1,200
Police Clerk	Neils Larsen	1,200
City Marshal	Iver Lawson	1,500
First Lieut. (S. D.)	Wells Sherman	624
Second Lieut. (S. D.)	Richard Bellinger	624
First Lieut. (W. D.)	J. H. Williams	624
Second Lieut. (W. D.)	M. Grant	624
First Lieut. (N. D.)	F. Gund	624
Second Lieut. (N. D.)	John McAuley	624
Lieut. Hosp. Stat.	A. Mueller	624

A "board of complaint;" consisting of the city marshal and the commanders (lieutenants) of the three precincts, was created by Mayor Wentworth. This board met in the basement of the Court House, "where all who had complaints to make were heard and answered." The police force was reduced in each of the three divisions to about one-half its strength in 1859, the heads of some of the oldest officers were chopped off, and many important changes were made in the rules and regulations governing the force. The eccentricities of the mayor, his method of dealing with police officers, his interference in the most trivial details of police affairs, created very general discontent among the people. While reducing the numerical strength of the force from what he claimed to be economical motives, he left large districts of the rapidly-growing city at the mercy of the criminals who infested Chicago in shoals during the three or four years preceding the civil war. The force under Wentworth toward the close of his administration had been reduced to a captain, six lieutenants and about 50 patrolmen, and it proved to be entirely inadequate to meet the demands made upon it. Loud complaints were made on all sides against the mayor's so-called economical policy, and the result was the passage by the legislature on February 15th, 1861, toward the closing days of Wentworth's administration, of "An Act to establish a board of police in and for the city of Chicago, and to prescribe their powers and duties." This act provided that after its passage "there shall be organized in the city of Chicago an executive department of the municipal government, to be known as the board of police of the city of Chicago, which board shall consist of three commissioners, to be chosen, one from the South, one from the West and one from the North Division of said city, who shall constitute said board. That until election and qualification, in the manner and at the time herein provided, the governor shall nominate, and by and with the advice and consent of the senate, appoint the first commissioners of said board of police, who shall be and they are hereby declared the first commissioners of said board of police, and who shall respectively hold their offices for two, four and six years, from and after the next general municipal election in said city, and until their successors are duly elected and qualified. * * * The said commissioners, when appointed, shall, within ten days after their appointment, or as soon thereafter as may be, proceed to organize said board and decide by lot their respective terms of office. * * * One of said commissioners shall go out of office at the end of each and every two years from and after the next general municipal election."

The officers of the board provided for were a president and treasurer, the clerk of the police court being named as *ex-officio* secretary. The duty of the board was defined as follows:

It shall be the duty of the board of police hereby constituted, at all times of the day and night, within the boundaries of the said city of Chicago, to preserve the public peace, to prevent crime and arrest offenders, to protect rights of persons and property, to guard the public health, to preserve order, to remove nuisances existing in public streets, roads, places and highways, to provide a proper police force at every fire in order that thereby the firemen and property may be protected; to protect strangers and travelers at steamboat and ship landings, and railway stations, and to obey and enforce all ordinances of the common council within the said city of Chicago, which are applicable to police or health. Whenever any crime shall be committed in said city of Chicago or within the county of Cook, or the person or persons accused or suspected of being guilty shall flee from justice, the said board of police may, in their discretion, authorize any person or persons to pursue and arrest such accused or suspected person or persons, and return them to the proper criminal court having jurisdiction of the offense, for trial.

The new law prescribed that the force should consist of a general superintendent, one deputy superintendent, three captains, six sergeants and sixty police patrolmen, "and as many more police patrolmen as may be authorized by the common council of the city of Chicago." The act went into minute details as to the jurisdiction of the board, the duties of officers and men, questions of discipline, etc. It practically stripped the mayor of all authority or control over the police department, and placed them solely in the hands of the three commissioners. The law received the signatures of Shelby M. Cullom, who was then speaker of the house of representatives, of Francis A. Hoffman, "speaker" of the senate, and of Richard Yates, governor, who gave it his approval on February 21st, 1861. The governor appointed as the board of police Alexander C. Coventry, from the

North Division, William Wayman, from the West, and Frederick Tuttle, from the South. Upon its organization, Mr. Coventry was elected president of the board, and Mr. Wayman treasurer. The former had drawn "by lot" the six year and the latter the four year term, leaving Mr. Tuttle to serve only for two years.

Just before the end of his term of office, John Wentworth once more attracted general attention and created universal indignation by indulging in one of those freaks, bordering upon lunacy, which characterized the greater part of his official career. The legislature which passed the act providing for a board of police, the governor who approved of it, and the men who constituted the board itself, were all politically antagonistic to Wentworth and his methods. He was aware that the board intended to revolutionize the police system; that many of his most faithful henchmen would be discharged, and that the organization he had formed, such as it was, would be smashed to pieces. His authority over the police had been snatched away from him abruptly and completely. He had no more power to order a policeman to do this or that than the most ordinary of private citizens. He felt humiliated and offended, and determined upon a very foolish method of obtaining revenge.

On the night of March 21, 1861, he summoned the entire police force to his office in the City Hall. The board of police was holding its first meeting at the same time, in the northeast corner of the Court House basement. The police, officers and men, hung around the mayor's office until the night was far advanced. Finally, when the board had adjourned, and Wentworth had satisfied himself as to the course it intended to pursue, he had the men drawn up in line before him. He made a speech, in which he lauded the expiring administration, claiming it to be not only one of the most efficient but economical the city had ever known. He praised the men who stood before him, and pronounced them the finest police officers in America. Then he informed them that the new executive power had superseded him in all authority over the police affairs of the city; that the board was bent upon discharging every one of his men, and that rather than suffer them to undergo this humiliation he had decided to discharge them himself. Thereupon he dismissed the entire police force at 2 o'clock in the morning, and left Chicago at the mercy of the criminal classes.

Until 10 o'clock next morning the city was without a police force, but the board, at first stunned by Wentworth's insane *coup d'etat*, soon recovered itself, and within a few hours had sworn in many of the officers dismissed by Wentworth, besides a considerable number of new men, for active service. Public opinion was decidedly against Wentworth, whose conduct was pronounced at once reckless, disgraceful and disloyal.

This act led to the immediate reorganization of the police under the new law. At the first regular business meeting of the board, held March 27, Jacob Réhm was appointed deputy superintendent of police, and until the 6th of April, he had full charge of the police force of the city. On the 6th of April, the board, by resolution, requested Cyrus P. Bradley to assist Mr. Rehm in organizing the police force, and on the 23d of the same month, by unanimous vote of the board, Mr. Bradley was made general superintendent. A recent contribution to the *Herald* of this city, in alluding to Bradley's assumption of this office, contains some facts in relation to the police of his time, worthy of being recorded here. It said of Bradley, his first move was to select Captain John Nelson as his assistant, and as the city at that time had a population of 109,000, and special officers were necessary, he also, by authority of the board, appointed the first regular central detail of detectives, composed of the following named officers: Samuel A. Ellis, who had been on the force since 1856, attached to the North Market station, and now employed as clerk at the detective headquarters; James Morgan, who is yet on the force, and widely known as the horse-thief detector; Horace Elliott, a cousin of Superintendent Bradley, and who has weathered all the storms of changing administrations, and yet remains to be known as one of the most competent thief-takers in the country; Isaac Williams, now living in Omaha; Wm. Douglass, who became insane, and afterward committed suicide; John Wall, who is now in the coal trade at Covington, Ky.; John Macauley, now a wealthy property owner on the North Side, who made a world-famous reputation as the man whose evidence convicted a score or more of Molly Maguires in Pennsylvania; Chris Streble, who afterward died in Germany; William Ten Broeck, now justice of the peace in Lake View; Henry Kaufmann, formerly police magistrate on the North Side, and Joseph Dixon, afterward deputy superintendent.

On the night of June 18, Wentworth gathered his policemen around him, and gave orders that every over-hanging sign, awning, and all posts or other obstructions to the view or the free passage of citizens along the principal downtown streets be immediately removed. He had already employed all the express and draymen in the city to co-operate with the force. In many respects Chicago was still a mere country town. The merchants were in the habit of erecting permanent awnings in front of their stores, after the fashion still in vogue in the smaller towns of the South. These were useful for the display of advertisements, and protected the goods which were exhibited underneath, but they were anything but ornamental. Besides, all sort of swinging signs were hung out over the sidewalks and streets, a constant menace to life or limb in case of a wind storm. Then again, the dry goods men placed boxes on the sidewalk's edge, upon which they piled cotton, calico and other stuff, to attract the attention of passers-by. The thing became at length an intolerable nuisance, and Wentworth determined to wipe it out. On the night named every swinging sign, awning, post or box found protruding two feet beyond the front of buildings were deposited in a pile at the north end of the South Market Hall, on State street In the morning when the town woke up it was hardly recognized by the people, so complete was the change. There was much complaining on the part of the merchants for a while, but in this "eccentricity," at least, public opinion was with "Long John."

Julian S. Rumsey succeeded John Wentworth as mayor, in 1861, and during his administration the police board made numerous changes and several improvements in the organization of the force. Under Bradley the men were disciplined thoroughly, sometimes severely, and the Chicago force proved to be of the greatest value to the state and national governments in the matter of assisting in the detention of conscripts, the arresting of deserters, the suppression of bounty-jumping, the detection of counterfeiters, etc., and in generally preventing or punishing the peculiar crimes and criminals created or developed by the outbreak of the rebellion. Charles Hodgson was elected clerk of the police board in 1861. R. J. Paulsen was captain of the North Division.

An amendment to the city charter extended the term of our mayors from one to two years at this time, and Francis C. Sherman was the first mayor elected under the new order of things, serving from the spring of '62 to the spring of '64, or through the most perilous and exciting times of the war epoch. In '62, the police justices were C. D. Fitzz and Charles J. Mueller, and the police clerk was John Atwater. Justice Fitzz was superseded by Charles McDonald later on, and Martin Palser was given Atwater's place. Ira Colman had charge of the bridewell. There was no change in the composition of the board of police in '62, and the patrolmen numbered 60. In '63, we find that Francis Adams is city attorney, the same able lawyer who, in later years, acted as corporation counsel under Mayor Harrison. Thomas Barrett, a well-known member of the force, occupied the position of police constable, and important changes took place in the make-up of the board of police and the management of the department.

On the 20th of February, 1863, Jacob Rehm was promoted to the superintendency, C. P. Bradley having resigned. On the 14th of the following month Supt. Rehm tendered his resignation. but the board refused to accept it. On the 1st of April C. P. Bradley was elected secretary of the board of police, and on the 6th of May John S. Newhouse presented his credentials as commissioner from the South Division, *vice* Frederick Tuttle whose term had expired. The board organized by electing Mr. Newhouse president, and William Wayman treasurer, C. P. Bradley secretary, and Charles Hodgson clerk. By a change in the law the mayor became an *ex-officio* member of the board.

Supt. Rehm's office was at this time in the Central station (called so for the first time), on LaSalle, southwest corner of Washington street. The city is now divided into "precincts." The 1st precinct station is situated in the Armory building, corner of Franklin and Adams. Here John Nelson is captain. M. C. Hickey, afterward superintendent, is 1st sergeant, and Thomas Clayton, in later years a distinguished officer, is 2d sergeant. There are 36 patrolmen attached to this station.

A sub-station of the 1st precinct is established at 26th and State streets, which is placed in charge of Acting Sergeant O. S. Abbott.

The 2d precinct station is still located in the west end of West Market Hall, on Randolph opposite Desplaines street. William Turtle, in later years the head of Turtle's Detective Agency, is captain here, William W. Kennedy, still among the living, is 1st sergeant, and Geo. W. Miller, who afterward took to the law, is 2d sergeant. The force consists of 20 patrolmen.

The 3d precinct station remains at the north end of North Market Hall, on Michigan, east of Clark street, and

Frederick Gund is the captain in charge. John N. Norton is 1st and Charles H. Jennings is 2d sergeant. There are 18 patrolmen here.

About this time the number of wards in the city were increased to 16. In addition to the police justices there were three police magistrates—Robert Malcomb, North Division, John Summerfield, South Division and Jarvis Stanford, West Division. Ever† Van Buren was judge of the Recorder's Court; Daniel O'Hara was its clerk, and the state's attorney's office was held by Joseph Knox. The city directory for 1863 claimed a population for Chicago of 150,-000. The claim was generally considered to be well founded. The directory itself was greatly enlarged, having some 700 pages, several of which were given over to an alphabetical list of new streets. The publisher calls attention to the fact that great trouble had been experienced by the canvassers. The people feared that they were enrolling officers under the conscription law, and in consequence hundreds of names were withheld. Yet the directory for the year contained 4,000 more names than its predecessor. The publisher also calls attention to the fact, that when in 1844 he claimed that Chicago would one day have a population of 100,000 people, he was ridiculed on all sides. The volume was published by Messrs. Halpin & Bailey.

In 1864, we find the name of Mark Sheridan, who was destined to become prominently identified with the force, for the first time connected with police matters. He is on the police committee of the city council, representing the 5th ward. Associated with him is George Van Hollen, afterward a defaulter and refugee, who represented the 11th ward with L. L. Bond. Iver Lawson is also a member of the council.

Returning to '63, we find that on July 3d of that year, the resignation of Jacob Rehm is accepted, and on the same day, at the regular meeting of the board, Commissioner Wayman nominated William Turtle for the superintendency.

Commissioner Newhouse nominated Charles Walsh, of Camp Douglas fame, and Commissioner Coventry nominated Capt. John Nelson. Each member of the board thus having his favorite, says Colbert, and none of them being willing to withdraw his friend's name, no appointment was made, and Secretary Bradley exercised the powers of superintendent. On the 2d of September Commissioner Newhouse again nominated Charles Walsh and was seconded by Mayor Sherman, who was an *ex-officio* member of the board, but Coventry and Wayman voting in the negative the motion was lost. On the 23d of April, 1864, on motion of Commissioner Wayman, seconded by Commissioner Newhouse, William Turtle was appointed general superintendent. C. P. Bradley, on motion of Commissioner Wayman, was honorably discharged and removed from the office of secretary of the board, and William Abbott was appointed to that position. Early in '64, the police board consisted of Alexander C. Coventry, president, John S. Newhouse, Thomas B. Brown and Francis C. Sherman (*ex-officio*). In May of the same year, on the resignation of Mr. Newhouse, Hon. John Wentworth was appointed to fill the vacancy, and he held the office until Nov. 7, 1865. W. W. Kennedy succeeded to the captaincy of the 2d precinct on the promotion of Turtle, but no other changes of note occurred in the body of the force. James B. Bradwell is a justice of the peace. The city directory contains 39,414 names.

In 1865, John B. Rice becomes mayor. The police committee of the city council consists of Messrs. Lawson, Russell and Shackford. George Knerr is keeper of the bridewell. The police justices are A. D. Sturtevant and Isaac L. Milliken. William Vocke is clerk of the police court. George E. Cooper is police constable. The board of police consists of Alexander C. Coventry, John Wentworth, Thomas B. Brown and the mayor. Its secretary is Roswell Scott.

At the Central station Adam Morganthaler is 1st sergeant. The 1st precinct is commanded by Capt. Nelson, M. C.

Hickey is 1st and Thomas Clayton is 2d sergeant, and the detail is increased to 50 men. The 2d precinct station is removed to No. 14 Union street, Capt. Kennedy still in charge, but Nathan A. Briscoe becomes 1st and Charles Burdell 2d sergeant. The detail is increased to 40 men. The 3d precinct station is still in charge of Capt. Gund; Charles H. Jennings is 1st and Thomas D. Fox is acting 2d sergeant.

It might be mentioned here that in May, 1864, the fire alarm telegraph system was inaugurated with 165 boxes. It was considered a great event in the history of the city, and the first trial gave general satisfaction. The population was then estimated to be 195,000. Great public improvements have been undertaken and carried out during 1864–65. In addition to the fire alarm telegraph, the papers congratulate the people over the success of the lake tunnel, the leveling of the Illinois canal, so as to purify the river, (which in those days is spoken of as a nuisance), the laying of the seventeen miles of water pipe, etc. The letter delivery system also goes into effect, and the people are informed that "No citizen living at a distance from the postoffice is necessarily now obliged to visit the postoffice, but can, if he chooses, have his correspondence brought to his own door."

Before closing what may be termed " the war epoch " in the history of the Chicago police, some mention should be made of the condition of the city, from a moral aspect, during the troublous and exciting years from 1861 to 1865. The following from the pen of one of the brightest journalists in Chicago will give a clearer insight into the police events of those years than anything that could be substituted for it. There are some inaccurate statements contained in it, in regard to dates, but they are trivial, and are corrected elsewhere:

At the old Armory station, corner of Adams and Franklin streets, opposite the gas house and in the midst of "Connelly's Patch," are centered the most interesting reminiscences of early police days. Here Jack Nelson held command until his promotion, when he was succeeded by Michael C. Hickey, who in turn became chief in later years. The sergeants were Tom Barrett, possibly, with the exception of Sam Ellis, the oldest man on the force in point of service, who now swings the keys as night lock-up keeper at Harrison street, and Adam Mergenthaler, who died some years ago. The present genial Captain William Buckley was station-keeper at the old Armory. Charles S. Perry was lock-up keeper, and is now attached to the Desplaines street station. Uncle Solomon Moloney, then at the Armory, is still on duty as keeper at Harrison street. These names include those living who were identified with the old stone structure about which cluster so many pleasant as well as unpleasant memories.

Of the patrolmen of that day Simon O'Donnell was the "dandy copper" of the Lake street squad. To be a member of that squad in those days carried with it honor and pride, and no crossing policeman ever appreciated the truth of this fact more than did the magnificent Simon, who rose from the ranks to be chief of police, and is now captain of the West Twelfth street district. Lake street was then the retail thoroughfare of the city, and Simon's crossing the busiest one in town. He was the pink of politeness, and long before he left those corners was called the "ladies' favorite." His partner was Officer Shippy, who afterward became lieutenant at Cottage Grove avenue station.

One of the most exciting periods in the history of the force was during the year 1862, when the city was infested with "bad" men from all over the West, the special attraction being the possible chances for bounty-jumping and the presence of people ready to be fleeced. There was also a coterie of sluggers here, who were constantly creating disturbances and making trouble for the officers. Among the South Side patrolmen was Officer James Powers, who had, upon more than one occasion, established his prowess in hand to hand contests with local law breakers. He was a fearless

man, and never hesitated to perform what he knew to be his
duty. In the winter of 1862, "Big Denny" O'Brien, a
tough from Davenport, Iowa, spent several weeks in Chicago.
He was drunk from the time he struck the town until driven
away. Being a professional pugilist and a quarrelsome fellow, he was in trouble night and day. He was one day driving up and down Clark street, exceeding the speed prescribed by the ordinance, when Officer Powers ordered him
to stop. Some words passed, when suddenly O'Brien sprang
upon Powers, and there ensued one of the most bloody and
desperate fights in the annals of the Chicago police. Powers
defended himself against the attack of the burly ruffian, but
was finally struck down and terribly beaten with his own
club. O'Brien escaped, and for several weeks his victim was
not expected to live. He finally recovered, and a short time
thereafter was badly injured while endeavoring to arrest a
burglar on Wabash avenue. In the struggle Powers was
thrown against the curb stone, receiving serious internal injuries. He was granted a furlough, went to Ireland, and on
the return journey fell dead in the depot at Cleveland. One
of the characters of the time was a certain "Captain" Hyman, a professional blackleg and gambler, who was wont
while in liquor to go about town intimidating people by
whipping out a revolver and threatening death to anybody
who crossed him in any way. One evening during an exciting political contest in 1862, "Captain" Hyman took possession of the Tremont House office, and, revolver in hand,
defied anybody to arrest him. The guests fled and the
house police, as well as the officer on that beat, were afraid
to go near him. He walked to and fro at the top of the high
flight of steps leading up from the Dearborn street entrance,
and refused to allow anyone to leave or enter the house.
Word was sent to Captain Jack Nelson at the detective headquarters, corner of Washington and La Salle streets. The
captain jumped into old "Shang" Noyes' hack and drove
rapidly to the hotel. He was told the situation, and with-

out the slightest hesitancy stepped into the stairway in full view of the desperado. Hyman did not recognize him, and was about to shoot when Nelson said, "Put up that gun and come down here!" Hyman recognized the voice and cried out, "Don't shoot, Jack; I ll come down," and imitating Captain Scott's squirrel, he descended and was driven to the station. The siege of the hotel had continued for upwards of an hour, and Hyman afterward said that he would never have been taken by anyone but Nelson. Said he: "Jack is a brave man, knows no fear, and can shoot too quick for me."

Nelson had to contend with many of the roughest characters that have ever been known in Chicago. There were Hyman and O'Brien, of whom mention has been made; Jerry Monroe, then a husky fellow, constantly looking for trouble, while Black Jack Yattaw, the present bumboat pirate, used to come down from Racine quite often and endeavor to run the city. The resorts where gentlemen of this ilk mostly did congregate, were Roger Plant's "Under the Willow," which stood on the southeast corner of Wells and Monroe streets; Ben Sabin, a Buffalo tough, kept a saloon on Wells street, while the saloons of Tim Reagan and Andy Routzong, on Clark, near Van Buren street, were constantly under the strictest police surveillance, because of the desperate character of both proprietors and their patrons. All along the east side of Market street, from Van Buren to Madison streets, were located dozens of low-down dens and sailors' boarding houses, where broils and murders were of frequent occurrence. River street, from South Water to the bridge, and North Water street, from Wolf's Point to Clark street, were also headquarters for as desperate a class of men as ever disgraced the city.

From these dens came the seemingly endless crowd of bounty-jumpers and desperadoes, who at one time became so bold in their operations that respectable citizens proposed to organize a vigilance committee for the purpose of clearing the city of these pestiferous and dangerous classes. Captain Nelson had but a small force, but under the watchful and intelligent leadership of Chief Bradley, and through his own individual effort, he succeeded in preserving order, and made for himself a record second to no man who has ever occupied an executive position on the police force of Chicago. He died of consumption during the spring of 1868, universally regretted by all good citizens.

To be a policemen in those days was no sinecure. Patrol wagons were unknown, and the police were accustomed to impress into the service any description of vehicle which might be at hand to transport drunken and unruly men to the lock-up. Lieutenant Beadell, of the Cottage Grove sub-station, who at that time traveled a beat in the Bridgeport district, tells a story of how, for the want of some better · conveyance, he loaded drunken Jimmy Kilfoil, a notorious Archer avenue bum, into a wheelbarrow and pushed him from the vicinity of the old steam quarry to the Archer avenue station, a distance of two miles.

It was during Chief Bradley's time that General Burnside suppressed the publication of the Chicago *Times*, and both Bradley and Nelson took an active part in preserving the peace on that eventful day, when it seemed as though every able-bodied man in the city was crowded into the streets adjacent to the *Times* office on Randolph street. It was during this memorable day that a lawyer named Doolittle, known as a red-hot rebel sympathizer, harangued the crowd from a dry goods box in front of the Matteson House, at the corner of Dearborn and Randolph streets. He was very bitter in his denunciation of the government, and came within an ace of losing his life in consequence. Told repeatedly to cease his abusive references to President Lincoln, he paid no attention to the demands, and was finally pulled from his perch by an angry mob, who proceeded to carry out their threat to lynch him. Somebody found rope enough, made a noose, put it about his neck and started for the nearest lamp-post. Officers George Cooper, now employed by the Chicago City Railway Company, and Asa Williams, made an effort to rescue Doolittle, and assisted by "Horse" Eddy and several other level-headed persons in the crowd, cut the rope and fought their way to the House of David, carrying the now frightened lawyer with them. Doolittle was rushed into the saloon, and after a time was taken through the alley to State street and told to make himself scarce. He did so without a second invitation.

The famous Garrity brothers were then in their prime, and a constant source of annoyance and trouble to the authorities. One of Mike Garrity's earliest and most desperate exploits occurred about this time. Detective Bellinger arrested Garrity as he was coming out of the north door of the Court House, on a warrant charging him with complicity in a burglary committed in Iowa. Garrity resisted the officer and a desperate and bloody encounter took place. Bellinger was disarmed and terribly beaten by the crook, who escaped, but was afterward recaptured, taken to the scene of his crime and sentenced to the penitentiary for a term of years.

In those days the police raided the gamblers occasionally, but the knights of the green cloth seemed to thrive nevertheless. Frank Connelly was proprietor of a den over the "Senate," at the corner of Dearborn and Randolph streets. It was known as a high-toned game, and no "shoestring gamblers" were encouraged to play there. The first raid upon Connelly's place resulted in the capture of several well-known business men, who, when arrested, were transported to the Armory in carriages at Frank's expense. He afterward paid the fines of the entire party, and immediately opened his house as though nothing had occurred to disturb the serenity of the situation. Connelly was the Hankins of that day, and it was in his place that George Holt, the gentleman par excellence of all Chicago professional gamesters, first became known. It will be remembered that Holt was killed several years ago in Calhoun place by a falling bucket of coal, which struck him full upon the head, breaking his neck.

The old-time police officers, in referring to the gambling fraternity of those days, still laugh over a most ludicrous scene which occurred in a "coon" gambling house run by a colored man named Steve Stampo. It was located in the second story of an old frame building on Monroe street opposite North's theatre. A raid was ordered on the place, the officers surrounded the house, and Officer Henry Pilgrim got on to the roof from an adjoining building. Directly over the table where about a dozen darkies were playing cards there was a glass transom or skylight. It had been snowing and Pilgrim, while endeavoring to find the skylight, walked through it and descended right in the midst of the crowd of players. He struck the table and the "coons" struck out for liberty. Several of the players jumped through the windows, carrying sash, glass and everything else with them, but they were all captured as they struck terra firma.

Chicago now has nearly thirteen hundred police officers, and this magnificent force has no superior on the continent. Since its first organization methods have changed. Many modern appliances in the way of telegraphic service have been adopted by which the work of the department has been simplified. The patrol wagon, originated by a Chicago man, has become a necessary adjunct to every well equipped department in the land. But the fact remains undisputed that to Cyrus P. Bradley is due no small measure of credit for the excellent discipline which originated with him and has since his day been rigorously enforced and maintained by his successors. He was a man of exceptionally fine executive ability, possessed all the attributes of a successful police officer, and, dying at the early age of forty-four years, left behind him the impress of his ability.

Charles Hodgson, the first secretary of the police department, died of the cholera in 1868. He was universally

respected by the entire force.   Ben Cleaves, afterward cor
oner, and the successor to Gustave Fischer, the absconding
sheriff, was at one time a member of the early police force.
Simeon Y. Prince and "Major" Yelveston the old Armory
janitors; ex-Captain Luther Nichols, who became too old
for active service, and was detailed for years to enjoy himself about the Board of Trade Building, Charley Beach,
William A. Carman, or "Billy" as he is familiarly called,
and who has served under every superintendent since the or
ganization, first as patrolman, stationkeeper, clerk and custodian, and now the efficient assistant to Secretary Shepard,
are other members of the old guard, as is also Detective
Denny Simmons, of the Central detail, Officer Nathan A.
Briscoe, now on duty at Madison street; William B. McCauley, now at Webster avenue station, and George W. Hunt,
who lost an arm in the lager beer riot of 1855.

CHAPTER VII.

FROM 1866 TO THE CLOSE OF 1871—THE GROWTH OF THE SERVICE UNDER
THE BOARDS OF POLICE—DIVIDED DUTIES AND THEIR RESULTS—WIL-
LIAM TURTLE, JACOB REHM AND W. W. KENNEDY AS SUPERINTEND-
ENTS OF THE FORCE—NEW SUB-STATIONS ESTABLISHED—WICKED CHI-
CAGO BEFORE THE FIRE—THE POLICE DURING THE GREAT CONFLA-
GRATION—HEROIC AND UNSELFISH CONDUCT—LIEUT.-GENERAL PHIL
SHERIDAN IN CHARGE—CITIZEN PATROL PARTIES—END OF THE MILI-
TARY OCCUPATION AND ELECTION OF JOSEPH MEDILL.

Changes in and amendments to the law establishing a
board of police for the city of Chicago were frequent, and
not always judicious. Starting out with authority simply
over the police, we find the board in 1866 in control of the
fire and health departments as well. "The police, fire
and health departments," says a "Guide to Chicago," published this year, "are considered eminently effective. The
heads of the departments or board of fire and police commissioners elected by the people of Cook county is composed
of Thomas B. Brown, A. D. Titsworth and Frederick Gund.
The same board is also *ex-officio* a board of health, so that
three of the most important functions of the city government are vested in its members, namely, control and direction of the fire, police and sanitary affairs of the city."
The truth is that too much was imposed upon or assumed
by the board, and its incapacity soon became manifest.
The extraordinary growth of the city during the war had
amazed the most enthusiastic and sanguine of its people.
The increase in population had exceeded the wildest predictions of ante-bellum residents. Buildings were erected

with astonishing rapidity, and with an utter disregard of the probability of fire. To have properly supervised the construction of dwellings and storehouses would have demanded the entire attention of the board. As it was, while the greatest attention was paid to the extinguishment of fires, and the very latest and best apparatus was employed for that purpose, no attention was paid to their prevention, or none worthy of mention. Buildings were thrown together in hap-hazard style, pine being the principal material, and whole sections of the city were covered with what a few years later proved to be tinder boxes. There were sanitary regulations enough, but to enforce them was another thing. The board had taken the responsibility off the shoulders of the common council, without being able to fulfill the obligations it imposed, and the result was, as might have been expected, a most deplorable and disgusting condition of sanitary affairs. Then, again, the police department was neglected, because of the divided attention of the board. As the population grew, crime increased. There was the usual percentage of criminals in every day's arrivals. The local columns of the newspapers published here in '66 are overflowing with criminal news, and there is a loud and unremitting cry for better police protection. The greenback epoch was entering upon its decline. The disbandment of the armies glutted the labor market. The depreciation of values checked production. Great enterprises projected in the days of unlimited inflation were suspended. The period of reaction, which was to culminate in the panic of '73, had set in. The extravagance, the prodigality of war times had left their impressions upon the public mind, and it was hard to erase them. The drop of wages from $10 to $5, from $5 to $2 per day was stunning. It came hard for people who had worn broadcloth to come down to cassimeres or cotton jeans. It was trying to be compelled to eat plain home-made bread after having lived so long on costly pastry; or to eat pork when porterhouse had almost become a necessity. The great masses of the people bore the change philosophically and nobly, but it plunged many thousands into vice, degradation and crime.

Chicago was the one city in the nation that appeared to be unaffected by the reaction. The place continued to grow in the face of all obstacles. The eyes of the country were turned toward the wonderful young metropolis on the shore of Lake Michigan. Adventurers, gamblers and thieves, as well as capitalists, mechanics and honest laborers, were attracted toward it. It outgrew all the provisions which had been made for the welfare of its inhabitants. It was, in truth, a great city with a village government.

William Turtle did not remain long at the head of the police force. On Nov. 29th, 1865, he tendered his resignation, which was immediately accepted, and Jacob Rehm, on January 13, 1866, was appointed general superintendent. John B. Rice was still mayor; Daniel D. Driscoll was city attorney. The police justices, were Isaac L. Milliken and Austin D. Sturtevant, and William Vocke was clerk. The board of police now consisted of Thomas B. Brown from the West Division, A. D. Titsworth from the South and Frederick Gund from the North. Mr. Brown was president, John Nelson continued to act as deputy superintendent, and Charles Hodgson as secretary, and W. H. C arman was clerk of the board. The clerk of the detective office was Charles T. Hale.

Now we find that M. C. Hickey has been promoted to the rank of captain of the first precinct. Thomas Clayton is advanced to the 1st and Thomas Barrett to the 2d sergeantcy. The detail at the first precinct station is increased to 55 men. A sub-station of this precinct is established at the corner of Archer road and 22d street. It is placed in charge of Sergeant Adam Morganthaler, who has 6 men under his command.

The second precinct is commanded by Capt. W. W. Kennedy, and the station at 14 Union street has for sergeants

Chas. Berdell and N. A. Briscoe. The detail numbers 40 men. A sub-station is established at the corner of Lake and Paulina streets in charge of James Garrity, sergeant, who commands 6 men.

Thomas D. Fox is captain of the third precinct, the head station still being located in the North Market Hall. C. H. Jennings is 1st sergeant, and the second place is vacant. There are 38 men here. This precinct also indulges in the luxury of a sub-station, located at North avenue and Larrabee streets, and W. B. Macauley has it in charge. He commands 6 men. So that the entire force, exclusive of officers, in the year 1866, consists of 151 men.

In 1867, John B. Rice still filling the mayor's chair, things are in rather a topsy-turvy condition. The Court House and City Hall are being rebuilt, and the headquarters of the police department are removed temporarily to 140–142 Madison street. The board of police also meets here. It consists now of Thomas B. Brown, A. D. Titsworth, Frederick Gund and W. James. The latter had been added as a representative of the fire department. Mr. Brown stills acts as president, Jacob Rehm is superintendent, John Nelson is deputy, E. P. Ward is secretary and W. H. Carman chief clerk of the board. Adam Morganthaler becomes 1st sergeant under Captain Hickey at the Armory, and Thomas Barrett takes Morganthaler's place at the substation. Now there are 57 men at the Armory. James Garrity becomes 2d sergeant at the Union street station, and W. M. Douglas takes his place at the sub-station, Lake and Paulina. A new sub-station is added, located at the corner of 12th and Johnson streets, and in charge of Sergeant Briscoe, who commands 16 men. The West Division force consists altogether of 58 patrolmen.

The only change in the 3d precinct is the transfer of Macauley to the head station, where he becomes 2d sergeant, A. Gund taking his place at Larrabee street. There are 43 patrolmen in this precinct.

We have a copy of the official report of the work performed by the force in 1867, as follows:

Number of arrests	23,315
Males	19,276
Females	3,937
Married	7,809
Single	15,391
Fines	$143,821
Stolen property reported	$268,432
Stolen property recovered	$206,003

This speaks well for the efficiency of the force. The principle charges made during the year on arraignment before the police courts were: Arson, 100; adultery, 50; assault with intent to kill, 104; assault with a deadly weapon, 83; assault with intent to rob, 17; assault with intent to commit bodily injury, 54; burglary, 127; forgery, 64; inmates of disorderly houses, 1,670; keeping disorderly houses, 542; larceny, 1, 765; murder, 3; riot, 340; rape, 3; robbery, 66.

This year the legislature amended the police law once more. It was required that the commissioners should devote their whole time to the public service, and each was to receive an annual salary not exceeding $2,500, the exact amount to be fixed by the city council. The salaries of police officers were regulated as follows: General superintendent, not less than $3,000; deputy superintendent, $2,500; captain's, $1,500; sergeant's, $1,200; patrolmen, not less than $800 nor more than $1,000. An act passed two years later (March, 1869), fixed the salary of each commissioner at $3,000, captain's at $2,000 and sergeant at $1,500. During 1867 the number of patrolmen was increased to 173.

In Zell's *Guide to Chicago*, published in 1868, we read that: "The police are under the control of three commissioners elected by the people, and a superintendent and deputy superintendent appointed by said commissioners. The headquarters or Central station is located at 140 Madison street. 250 men compose the entire force. The following are the stations:

"City Armory, corner of Franklin and Adams streets.

"Sub-station, Archer avenue and 22d street.

"2d precinct station, 14 N. Union street.

"Sub-station, W. Lake and Paulina streets.

"Sub-station, W. 12th and Johnson streets.

"3d precinct station, Michigan street, near Dearborn avenue.

"Sub-station, North avenue and Larrabee street."

Mayor Rice entered upon his official duties April 18, 1865, four days after the assassination of President Lincoln. He was elected on the republican ticket. As already noted, the mayoralty term had been extended to two years under a previous enactment, and the legislature of 1869 changed the time of holding city elections from April to November. With a second election in 1867, and holding over under the new law, he remained in office four and a half years. He is still mayor, then, in 1868. Hasbrouck Davis is city attorney, and the police board remains unchanged. John Nelson having died in April of this year, Wells Sherman is appointed deputy superintendent in his place. Thomas A. Moore is appointed to fill a newly created office, that of "sergeant of detectives." F. Gerbing becomes sergeant of the 3d precinct sub-station, and beyond a very considerable increase in the number of men, there are no notable changes. The detective force in 1868 consisted of 12 men, and Colbert, in alluding to this branch of the service, says the detectives "will compare favorably with that of any city in the world in point of efficiency though not in numbers. No mystery is too intricate to be unravelled, and no crimes too dark to be brought to light by their efforts. In shrewdness, perseverance and efficiency the force is unequalled by few and surpassed by none. Thomas Moore is sergeant of the detective force. The Lake street squad, 29 in number, are generally considered as belonging to the Central station."

Prof. Colbert, now a leading writer on the Chicago *Tribune*, wrote the above in 1868. He also gave us the following outline history of the three precincts then in existence. While we have gone over the ground in detail, there are many dates of importance and points of interest in Prof. Colbert's review, which ought not to be omitted from this history:

The 1st precinct station, better known as the Armory, he says, is located on the corner of Franklin and Adams streets. In 1856, during the administration of Mayor Dyer, the South Chicago police force consisted of 20 patrolmen, under command of H. Shockley, as 1st lieutenant, Charles F. Chillson as 2d lieutenant, and G. D. Hunt as sergeant. The station was then in the basement of the Court House. The next year, 1857, the old market house on State street, between Lake and Randolph, was fitted up as a station. The force this year was increased to 23 patrolmen, and on the 4th of March, upon John Wentworth's accession to the mayoralty, Luther Nichols was appointed 1st lieutenant and E. S. Hansen 2d lieutenant, and the force increased to 26 men. In the latter part of this year D. E. Ambrose was promoted to the position of 2d lieutenant to fill the vacancy caused by Hansen's resignation. In 1858 the station was removed to its present location (old Armory). B. L. Cleves was appointed during the early part of John C. Haines' administration in this year, sergeant, and Michael Grant 2d lieutenant. And, again, during the year, M. M. Gillespie was appointed sergeant. In 1859, during John C. Haines' second term, Wells Sherman was appointed 1st lieutenant, and Richard Ballinger 2d lieutenant. The force consisted of 26 patrolmen. John Wentworth, during his second term, (1860), retained Sherman and Ballinger, but removed Gillespie from the sergeantcy from economical motives, and reduced the force to 21 men. In 1861 the same commanders continued in office and the force was reduced again to 20 patrolmen. On the 17th of March, 1861, after the adoption of the metropolitan system. John Nelson was appointed captain and C. M. Beach sergeant, and on April 1st George A.

Simmons was appointed 2d sergeant. The force at that time consisted of 18 men. On the 1st of March, 1863, Thomas L. Clayton, who joined the force as patrolman in 1859, was promoted to the position of 1st sergeant, and John A. Norton was made 2d sergeant. The force was increased to 26 men. On the 1st of June, same year, M. C. Hickey was made 2d sergeant, vice Norton resigned, and the patrol force was increased to 34 men. In 1864, the same officers and same number of men were retained. During 1865 the force of the 1st precinct was increased to 52 men. In May, Adam Morganthaler was promoted to the position of 3d sergeant. On Jan. 13, 1866, M. C. Hickey was appointed captain, vice Nelson promoted, and Thomas Barrett was made sergeant. May 27, 1868, Richard Shippey was made sergeant. The force (South Side force) now (1868) consists of 82 men with 5 sergeants, there being two sub-stations.

The second precinct is located at 14 North Union street, and it is at present (1868) in charge of Capt. W. W. Kennedy. This station was first established in the east end of the old West Market Hall, on the 16th of June, 1855, under Mayor Boone. Michael Grant was first lieutenant, William Tenbroeck 2d, Charles Warner sergeant. At that time the force consisted of 14 patrolmen. In 1856, under Mayor Dyer, John Gorman was 1st lieutenant, Chas. Deuchy 2d, and Francis Humelshine sergeant. There were 20 men, 4 American, 1 German and 15 Irish. In 1857, under John Wentworth, John M. Kennedy was made 1st lieutenant, Chas. M. Taylor 2d, D. E. Ambrose sergeant ; 35 men. In 1858, under John C. Haines, G. H. Sitts was made 1st lieutenant, and William Wiggins sergeant, with 40 men. In 1859, Haines' second term, W. R. Green was 1st lieutenant, John S. Palmer 2d, Thos. Brummell sergeant; 35 men. In 1860, under Wentworth, J. H. Williams was 1st, Michael Grant 2d lieutenant, and Jacob Schoenwald sergeant; the force was reduced to 16 men. In 1861, the metropolitan system was inaugurated, and Turtle made captain, W. W. Kennedy 1st sergeant, and George M. Miller 2d sergeant ; 18 men. In 1862–63, the same officers and same number of men were retained. In 1864, Capt. W. Turtle was appointed to the superintendency of the force, W. W. Kennedy was made captain, and Geo. M. Miller 1st sergeant; 22 men. In July, 1864, Miller resigned and went on the superintendent's staff. In April, same year, the station was removed from the old West Market building, to its present quarters, (Union street) which was purchased and fitted up as a police station at an expense of $8,500.

In June, 1865, N. A. Briscoe was appointed 1st sergeant, and the force was increased to 50 men. In Nov., 1865, James Garrity was appointed sergeant and assigned to the charge of the sub-station on the corner of Lake and Paulina streets, with a force of 8 patrolmen. November 3d, 1866, Wm. M. Douglas was appointed sergeant; May 15, 1867, James B. Crane was made sergeant. The force (West Side force) now consists (1868) of 87 men, with five sergeants, there being three sub-stations. A new four-story brick is about to be erected on the corner of Madison and Union streets, at a cost of $20,000, to be used as the second precinct station.

The third precinct station was originally located on the north end of the North Market Hall, on Michigan street, and was established June 16, 1855. S. P. Putnam was 1st lieutenant, John Noyes 2d, and George Leander sergeant. At that time the force consisted of 20 men. In 1856, under Mayor Dyer, Michael Finnigan was 1st lieutenant, Fred. Gund second. The force then consisted of 21 men—2 American, 5 German and 14 Irish. In 1857, (under Wentworth) Jacob Rehm was 1st lieutenant for a while, succeeded by H. A. Kauffman, John Noyes 2d, and Phillip Petrie sergeant; 33 men. In 1858, under Haines, Wells Sherman was 1st, and Richard Bellinger 2d lieutenant; 35 men. In 1859, Fred. Gund was 1st, and James C. Davis

2d lieutenant; 40 men. In 1860, under Wentworth, John Macauley was 2d lieutenant and the force was reduced to 16 men. In 1861, when the metropolitan system was inaugurated, William Paulsen was made captain, and Samuel S. Houston and John N. Norton sergeants. The force was reduced to 14 men. In 1863, Fred. Gund was made captain, and M. C. Hickey and Chas. H. Jennings sergeants; 21 men. In 1864, Sergeant Hickey was transferred to the 1st precinct, and Jacob Sauter appointed to fill his place. The force was again reduced to 14 men. In 1865, Sergeant Sauter died and Thos. P. Fox was appointed in his stead, William Macauley being made 3rd sergeant, to take command of a sub-station. November 18, 1865, Sergeant Geo. M. Miller was made captain, Mr. Gund having been made police commissioner. April 30, 1866, Wells Sherman succeeded as captain, vice Miller resigned, and May 2d, James A. Gund was made sergeant, vice Macauley changed to Lake street squad. Frank E. Gerbing was made sergeant June 5, 1867; May 13, 1868, Sergeant Fox was appointed captain, vice Sherman promoted, and Sam. Ellis was made sergeant. Jan'y 14, 1868, John Baus was made sergeant, vice Gund deceased. The force (North Side force) now consists (1868) of 60 men, with three sergeants, there being one sub-station.

In 1869, the board of police remained unchanged, but W. W. Kennedy is promoted to the general superintendency of the force. There was no change in the city officers, and but few in the department of police, beyond the change in its head. The first precinct station had 57 men. A new sub-station on Cottage Grove avenue, between 25th and 26th streets, in charge of Sergeant Richard Shippey, was provided with a force of 22 men.

The headquarters of the second precinct were changed to the new station house on the cornor of Union and Madison streets, where it remained for many years afterward, or until the present Desplaines street station was ready for oc-

cupancy. It was always known by the old name of the
" Union street station." Here George Miller was captain,
James Garrity was 1st, and N. A. Briscoe 2d sergeant. It
had a detail of 45 men. The Lake street sub-station had
21 men; Twelfth street (James B. Crane , sergeant), 26
men; Chicago avenue, near Milwaukee avenue, (Chas. Berdell, sergeant), 20 men. The third precinct headquarters
were removed to Huron, between Clark and Dearborn streets.
Captain Fox continued in command of the precinct. F. E.
Gerbing was 1st, and A. W. Hathaway 2d sergeant of the
Huron street station. The detail numbered 48 men. The
sub-station, corner of North Larrabee street and North avenue, was in charge of Sergeant John Baus, who commanded
30 men.

In 1870, Hon. R. B. Mason became mayor. The city attorney was I. N. Stiles, and William J. Onahan was city
collector, a position which he held after a lapse of a decade
under Mayor Harrison, and which he now holds under
Mayor Roche. The police justices were A. A. Banyan and
John Summerfield, and court for the South Side was held at
the old Armory. On the West Side the police court was
located in the Union street station, and on the North Side in
the Huron street station. Canute R. Matson, present sheriff
of Cook county, was clerk of the police court, and his deputy
for the West Side was Adam L. Amberg, and for the North Side
Martin Scully. We find that the office of the board of police
and the headquarters of the department are again located in
the basement of the west wing of the Court House, where they
were to remain until driven out by the fire of the following
year. There is no change in the leading official positions.
John P. Paine is mentioned as a clerk in the detective office.
Louis J. Lull is 2d sergeant at the Armory station. At the sub-
station, 22d and Archer road, Thomas Clayton and Edward
Woods are 1st and 2d sergeants, with 26 men, and Thomas
Barrett becomes sergeant of the Cottage Grove avenue station, with 22 men. Jonas W. Johnson becomes 1st ser-

geant at the Union street station, under Captain Miller. Sergeant Briscoe remains. The force here consists of 48 men. The sub-station at Twelfth and Johnson streets has 26 men, and for the first time we meet the now familiar name of Simon O'Donnell, who has been promoted out of the ranks to the position of 2d sergeant, James Garrity occupying the 1st place. The West Lake street station is in charge of Sergeant Douglas, who has 21 men. The West Chicago avenue station is in charge of Sergeant Chas. Berdell, who commands 20 men. There are no changes in the third precinct, except that a new sergeant, M. Bishoff, is appointed to serve with John Baus at the Larrabee station, which has 30 men.

The year 1871 opens up with no changes of importance in the personnel of the city government, and with but few in the department of police. Hon. R. B. Mason is mayor, in the second year of his term, and the staff he selected upon assuming the duties of his office remains with him. The affairs of the city appear to be in a more prosperous condition than ever before. Great fortunes have been made during the decade just past. Merchants are broadening and lengthening their facilities for trade. Old-fashioned frame storehouses are rapidly disappearing, and on the principal thoroughfares, granite, iron and glass have entered largely into building enterprises. A monster hotel is under way; great blocks of substantial and beautiful business houses are going up on all sides. Some of the streets already compare favorably from an architectural point of view with any in the world. Handsome churches and costly public edifices are scattered plentifully throughout the city. The money famine, which is beginning to pinch other sections of the country, has not yet been felt here. There is no end to the schemes which men of capital and energy have planned or projected. The population increases rapidly, and careful investers are looking with greedy eyes upon Chicago real estate. Matters political are quiet. The establishment of sub-stations in the more turbulent districts have done much toward preventing and repressing the vulgar crimes. Supt. Kennedy is looked upon as a most efficient officer, and there is great confidence in the force. True, the city in some respects is very wicked. It has a larger number of saloons, grogeries, dives, concert halls, dance houses, and places of like or lower character than a truly moral community could very well afford to boast of. It is known as a "fast" city throughout the length and breadth of the land.   People of respectability do things, and tolerate things here, which are perfectly shocking to the moral sense of respectable people elsewhere. Men, reckless of public opinion, and women, regardless of feminine delicacy, are continually creating social sensations, which shake whole neighborhoods of gentility, not to say respectability, from center to circumference. The beauties of the stage find much to attract them to Chicago, and receive much attention of a peculiar kind while filling their engagements here. The painted woman drives an elegant equipage, paid for, perhaps, by some prominent citizen; whole thoroughfares are given over, abandoned, to bagnios and brothels. Now and then a frightful tragedy, in which some young man, favorably known in commercial circles, is a principal or a victim, or some woman of hitherto unquestioned good character is involved, demands a moment's reflection from the busy people, but as a rule the inhabitants of Chicago in 1871 are not spending much time in seriously contemplating the moral situation, nor worrying their minds over questions of social purity.   The aim of the average Chicagoan, in the days of which we speak, is first of all to make money, next to spend it—how, when and where is nobody's business. The *Tribune* in 1871 is endeavoring in a conservative way to bring about a change in the moral atmosphere, the *Evening Journal* likewise demands that a higher price be put upon integrity and virtue than they now command. The *Times* calls " a spade a spade," and by exposing depravity in all its hideous forms, hopes to check it. The *Republican,* in a more guarded way, aims at the same result with the same weapons. The *Evening Post* is inclined to reflect the light and airy sentiments of the day, without taking them into serious consideration, and the young *Evening Mail* throws a sunset halo over the scene, painting Chicago in the rosiest of hues. The *Daily News* has not yet made its appearance, a fact which may possibly account for the deplorable moral turpitude of the times. But the ablest, highest or most conscientious Chicago journalist in 1871, whether it was the philosophic Medill, the caustic Storey, the skeptical Matteson, the poetical Benjamin F. Taylor, the brilliant McCullagh, the satirical Wilkie, the sedate Wilson, the statistical Forest, the philanthropical Bross, the amiable Shuman, the astronomical Colbert, the historical Chamberlain, or the genial, generous and scholarly Sheahan, could have done but little toward correcting the evils which everywhere abounded. Water or fire, a deluge or a conflagration, was necessary, in order that the careless, reckless, godless inhabitants of the young Western metropolis should be brought to their senses.

Before the awful calamity of October came upon the city, the police force consisted of about 310 men, all told. Three additional sub-stations were added during the year, known then as the "South Branch," "North Branch" and "Webster avenue" stations. W. W. Kennedy was superintendent. Wells Sherman was deputy superintendent. The board of police consisted of Thomas B. Brown, who represented the West Division, Mark Sheridan, South Division, Fred. Gund, North Division, and W. James, the fire department. Mr. Brown was president, and E. P. Ward was secretary. The 1st precinct was commanded by Capt. Michael C. Hickey; William Buckley and Louis J. Lull being the sergeants at the Armory, to which 70 patrolmen were attached. The 22d street sub-station was in charge of Sergeants Morganthaler and Clayton, with 24 men. The Cottage Grove avenue sub-station was in charge of Sergeant Barrett, with 23 men.

The South Branch sub-station was in charge of Sergeant Ed. W. Wood, with 16 patrolmen. The second precinct was commanded by Captain George Miller, with Sergeants Jonas W. Johnson and Chas. H. French in charge of the Union street station, to which 56 patrolmen were attached. The West Lake street sub-station was in charge of Sergeant Douglas, with 21 patrolmen; the West 12th street sub-station was in charge of Sergeants N. A. Briscoe and Simon O'Donnell, with 26 men; the West Chicago avenue station was in charge of Sergeant Charles Berdell, with 20 men. The North Branch sub-station was in charge of Sergeant Joseph Garrity, with 10 men. The third precinct was commanded by Captain Thomas D. Fox; the Huron street station being in charge of Sergeants Charles Rehm and A. W. Hathaway, with 48 men. The North avenue sub-station was in charge of Sergeants John Baus and M. Bishoff, with 30 men. The Webster avenue sub-station was in charge of Sergeant Macauley, with 19 men.

It is not the province of this volume to enter upon the details of the great fire. It would be out of the question to treat that subject as it ought to be treated, and at the same time do justice to the department with which our work is concerned. A History of the Chicago Fire Department is yet to be written, and when it is written the great fire must receive the earnest attention of the writer. For the present we must view the subject strictly from a police standpoint.

The police force immediately preceding the fire is said by some authorities (notably by James W. Sheahan and George P. Upton, in their book, "Chicago, Its Past, Present and Future"), to have numbered 400 men; but as the force only numbered 425 in March, 1872, according to Supt. Kennedy's report, we are led to believe that it was much smaller in October, 1871. All data concerning the principal stations in the 1st and 3d precincts was swept away by the fire, and nothing of an official character was left to tell the story of the quarter of the year ending with Sept. 30th. And for many days succeeding the fire, the policemen of these stations had nowhere to report, except at headquarters, and confusion reigned supreme throughout the burnt district. One hundred and fifty of the police force were left homeless and almost penniless by the fire. Most of these were on duty during the nights of October 8th, 9th and 10th, doing what little they could to assist the firemen, to help the distracted and fleeing people, to protect property and to keep the peace, while their own houses were being swept away, and their own families were being driven before the flames, to the lake side or the prairie. Testimony is not wanting to prove that many of the officers and men performed heroic service during these dreadful nights, and during many nights afterward, when the city was but a desolate and ghastly waste of ashes. "I desire to bear testimony to the cordial co-operation and efficiency of all branches of the service," said Supt. Kennedy, in his report to the council, "especially during the trying times succeeding the disastrous conflagration of last October, when about 150 of our men were burned out, and while their families were houseless and homeless they rallied with but few exceptions to their posts of duty immediately after the fire, and did their utmost, along with the balance of the force, in the restoration and maintenance of order. To them and to the entire force, as the executive head of the department, I desire to bear testimony for their faithfulness and coolness in their duties, when so many of our citizens were apparently panic-stricken."

The fire had done its worst when it consumed everything in its path, but a new and even a more dreadful terror than that just passed seized the public mind when it became rumored that incendiaries and robbers were attempting to complete the disaster which had already befallen the community. Not only the 75,000 homeless people who had fled before the advancing columns of flames, but the thousands who still had roofs to cover their heads, in the sections that had escaped the calamity, were panic-stricken by this newly threatened calamity. There was no water, and a fresh outbreak of fire on the West Side, or on the South Side, below the black line of debris, would probably result in the complete annihilation of the city. No wonder, then, that horror seized the people when the rumor spread that incendiaries, with an eye to plunder, were at their devilish work. The citizens at once formed themselves into patrol parties, to protect what little there remained in the burnt district, and to prevent, if possible, the designs of the incendiaries and thieves upon those sections which had escaped the fire. These patrol parties in the main did excellent service, but they did not always act with discretion, and it was popularly believed that many innocent persons met death at their hands. Undisciplined, inexperienced, panicky and inclined to look with suspicion upon every stranger who came along, they served to increase rather than to diminish the alarm of honest people in many quarters.

While the flames were leap_ng from house to house and from block to block on the South Side, and driving thousands of frightened people before them over the bridges and through the tunnel, there were gathered together in a little West Side church a few of the city officials. There, on the night of October 9th, on a coarse piece of paper, was drawn up with a lead pencil the famous proclamation of Chicago to the civilized world. It is preserved in the rooms of the Historical Society, plainly framed, and may now be easily read, for it is as legible as ever. It ought to be encased in a cabinet of solid gold, and placed beyond the possibility of loss or destruction. With many other treasures, above price, it is at the mercy of the first neighborhood fire, in the miserable quarters which are provided for the use of the Historical Society—quarters which, by the way, are a sad commentary on the vaunted public spirit, home pride and culture of our citizens. The proclamation touches upon police matters, but if it did not, it deserves a prominent place in any work which aims to follow the history of this city, no matter how lightly. It runs as follows:

WHEREAS, in the providence of God, to whose will we humbly submit, a terrible calamity has befallen our city, which demands of us our best efforts for the preservation of order and the relief of the suffering.

Be it known that the faith and credit of the city of Chicago is hereby pledged for the necessary expenses for the relief of the suffering. Public order will be preserved. The police and special police now being appointed will be responsible for the maintenance of peace and the protection of property. All officers and men of the fire department and health department will act as special policemen without further notice. The mayor and comptroller will give vouchers for all supplies furnished by the different relief committees. The headquarters of the city government will be at the Congregational Church, corner of West Washington and Ann streets. All persons are warned against any acts tending to endanger property. All persons caught in any depredations will be immediately arrested.

With the help of God order and peace and private property shall be preserved. The city government and committees of citizens pledge themselves to the community to protect them and prepare the way for a restoration of public and private welfare.

It is believed the fire has spent its force and all will soon be well.

R. B. MASON, *Mayor.*
GEORGE TAYLOR, *Comptroller.*
CHARLES C. P. HOLDEN, *President Common Council.*
T. B. BROWN, *President Board of Police.*

CHICAGO, OCTOBER 9th, 1871.

The telegraph brought the words: "*Be it known that the faith and credit of the city of Chicago is hereby pledged for the necessary expenses for the relief of the suffering,*" to every part of the globe, and they unlocked the hearts and opened the purses of mankind to Chicago. The men who were dictating and the man who was writing this proclamation, were being beggared in that very hour, but they dictated and wrote as if inspired, and their words filled the world with confidence in the future of Chicago.

The mayor, by proclamation, requested all good citizens who were willing to serve, to report at the city headquarters and be sworn in as special policemen. Hundreds immediately responded. Citizens were requested to organize a police force for each block in the city and to send reports of such organizations to police headquarters, which had been removed to the Union street station.   Gen. Sheridan saw the situation at a glance and immediately appealed to the secretary of war, Gen. Belknap, for assistance.   The government, through the secretary, immediately responded, throwing open its supply depots to Gen. Sheridan, and ordering at once seven companies of regulars to report here for duty. A regiment of old soldiers, sworn in for twenty days' duty by Gen. Sheridan, was immediately organized.   The preservation of the peace and good order of the city was entrusted by the mayor to the gallant Sheridan, and from the moment he assumed control the confidence of the people began to return and to grow.   On the 12th he reported to Mayor Mason: "No authenticated attempt at incendiarism has reached me, and the people of the city are calm, quiet and well-disposed.   The force at my disposal is ample to maintain order should it be necessary, and protect the district devastated by fire.   Still I would suggest to citizens not to relax their watchfulness until the smouldering fires of the burnt buildings are entirely extinguished."

Lieut.-Gen. P. H. Sheridan was practically the superintendent of police of Chicago from the 11th to the 23rd of October.   On the latter date he wrote to the adjutant-general of the army, Washington, D. C., as follows:

SIR:—The disorganized condition of affairs in this city, produced by and immediately following the late fire, induced the city authorities to ask for assistance from the military forces, as shown by the mayor's proclamation of Oct. 11, 1871.   To protect the public interests intrusted to me by the mayor's proclamation, I called to this city Companies A and K of the Ninth Infantry, from Omaha, Companies A, H and K of the Fifth Infantry, from Leavenworth, Company I, Sixth Infantry, from Fort Scott, and accepted the kind offer of Major General Halleck to send me Companies F, N and K of the Fourth, and Company E of the Sixteenth Infantry, from Kentucky.   I also, with the approbation of the mayor, called into service of the city of Chicago a regiment of volunteers for twenty days.   These troops, both regulars and volunteers, were actively engaged during their service here in protecting the treasure in the burnt district, guarding the unburnt district from disorders and danger by further fires, and in protecting the storehouses, depots and sub-depots of supplies, especially for the relief of sufferers from the fire.   These duties were terminated on the 23d inst., the regulars started to their respective stations, and the volunteers were discharged. It is proper to mention that these volunteers were not taken into the service of the United States, and no orders, agreements or promises were made giving them any claims against the United States for services rendered.

I am, very respectfully, your obedient servant,

P. H. SHERIDAN,
Lieut.-General Commanding.

The volunteer regiment spoken of was partly composed of companies of the state militia, ordered by Lieutenant-General Sheridan or some of his subordinates to report to him or them, and of recruits enlisted under their authority. The regiment was constituted as follows:

Col. Frank T. Sherman, Chicago Volunteers, commanding.

Major C. H. Dyer, Adjutant.

Major Charles T. Scammon, Aid-de-camp.

Lieutenant-Colonel H. Osterman, First Regiment National Guards, Illinois State Militia.

Major G. A. Bender, First Regiment National Guards, Illinois State Militia.

Captain Fisher's company (A); Captain Pasch's company (D); Captain Como's company (G) ; Captain Paul's company (H) ; Captain Kelter's company (I), all of First Regiment National Guards, Illinois State Militia.

Captain Rogers' company (B); Captain Merrill's company (C); Captain Baker's company (K), all of First Chicago Volunteers.

Captain Colson's company, University Cadets.

Captain Crowley's company, Montgomery Light Guards.

Captain McCarthy's company, Mulligan Zouaves.

Captain Ryan's company, Sheridan Guards.

Captain Salter's company, Chicago Cadets.

Captain Williams' company, Hannibal Zouaves.

Also four companies of the Norwegian Battalion of National Guards, commanded by Major Alstrup.

Exaggerated reports of disorder, tumult, riot, loss of life, lynchings, etc., were sent out by excited or unscrupulous newspaper correspondents for a week after the fire. The truth is, the people, while panic-stricken at first, very soon regained their composure and went about making the best of it, attending to their own business, and looking neither to the right nor to the left, but to the future, which looked bleak enough before the ashes cooled. Whatever the intentions of the criminal classes may have been, the fact that Sheridan was in command, and that he had a small army of regulars behind him, compelled them to be very careful in all their enterprises. That a number of persons met death at the hands of excited citizen-policemen is most probably true, but that the number exceeded, or even reached, half a dozen, all told, is very improbable.

In Colbert and Chamberlain's work, "Chicago and the Great Conflagration," we find the following version of the causes which led to the rather sudden surrender of authority on the part of Lieut.-General Sheridan:

The period of military rule came to an end on the 23d of October. It was doubtless hastened by a melancholy occurrence which serve.l to elicit some serious animadversions on the policy of employing military usages to the extent which characterized this period. Thomas Grosvener, Esq., prosecuting attorney for the city in the police courts, was fatally shot on the morning of the 21st, by a young man named Treat, belonging to Col. Sherman's "home guard," and acting as sentinel near the Douglas University, of which he is a student. Mr. Grosvener, going home after midnight, was challenged by the sentinel and refused to halt. Treat told him he should fire upon him if he did not obey. The reply was, "Fire and be d——d." The sentinel, true to his word, drew up and fired, shooting Grosvener through the lungs. He was soon afterward arrested and held for the action of the grand jury. The popular voice generally sustained the boy, and blamed the victim for his rashness; but a gloom was spread over the community by the event, not only because the deceased was a popular man, but because the situation had really become such as not to require military aid any longer. Accordingly, on the 23d, Mayor Mason, after some sharp correspondence with the board of police commissioners, who had been piqued from the first at the temporary diminution of their consequence, relieved Gen. Sheridan of the duty which he had asked him to accept twelve days before. And thus ended the period of death, of panic and of military law.

The losses sustained by the police department in the great fire are summarized as follows: Buildings, $53,500; office and station furniture and supplies, $10,000; boat-house, two boats, grappling irons and fixtures, $500; muskets to the number of 620, $8,680; total, $72,680. Besides these losses, six brass cannon, carriages, cassions, harness and equipments, value not estimated, were destroyed; also a large amount of property in the hands of the custodian, which had been lost, stolen, unclaimed or detained as evidence in criminal cases, amounting in value to about $20,-000.

For the relief of the members of the department who suffered by the fire, the following amounts were received from the sources named:

Boston police dept.,		$1,384.00
St. Louis " "		1,000.00
Worcester " "		165.00
Baltimore " "		925.00
Cleveland " "		2,000.00
Buffalo, " "		500.00
Milwauk'e " "		200.00
Memphis " "		189.00

Sullivan & Blanchard,		
Detroit,	$	25.00
Louisville police dept.		300.00
Quebec " "		40.25
Brooklyn " "		3,047.71
Mass. constabulary,		212.00
New Orleans police dept.		56.76
Total		$10,044.66

Local politics began to claim public attention before the burnt district had entirely cooled off. A vigorous fight was made by the better class of citizens of both the democratic and republican parties to throw the "bummer" politicians overboard, and nominate only citizens of known integrity and ability for city and county offices. The result was the combination of citizens, which ended in the triumphant election of the "fire-proof" candidate, with Hon. Joseph Medill at their head. Police and Fire Commissioner Fred. Gund sought re-election, but was overwhelmingly defeated, the people seeming to be determined to root out all those who could be considered in any way responsible for the calamity that had befallen the city. Mayor Mason retired from office, and Mayor Medill was sworn in at the council meeting held on the 4th of December, 1871.

CHAPTER VIII.

FROM 1871 TO 1877—THE RISE OF CHICAGO FROM HER ASHES—JOSEPH
MEDILL'S PROPHECY—HIS ADMINISTRATION—WHERE HE MADE A
MISTAKE—THE FANATICAL PARTY EXPOSES ITS HEAD AGAIN AND
IT IS AGAIN CRUSHED—TROUBLE IN THE POLICE BOARD—WASH-
BURN'S UNFITNESS FOR THE SUPERINTENDENCY—COLVIN'S ELEC-
TION—JACOB REHM—M. C. HICKEY—A BLACK HORIZON.

The police department was the first to recover from the
demoralization caused by the fire in 1871, and aside from
the comparatively small losses which it sustained in buildings,
equipment, records, etc., it soon ceased to feel the effect of
that calamity. The headquarters of the department remained at the Union street station, West Side, until the
temporary City Hall, which attained celebrity as the "Rookery" was thrown together, at the corner of Adams and La
Salle streets. This building was erected and ready for occupancy within a few months after the fire. The old Armory station was undergoing repairs when the fire occurred,
and the 1st precinct headquarters were located for the time
being in the old bridewell building, on Wells street, (Fifth
avenue). When the ground had cooled sufficiently to allow
it, the headquarters were moved into the frame school house
on the corner of Wabash avenue and Harrison street, and a
few days later to the frame school house which was situated
on the corner of Harrison street and Pacific avenue. Additions were made to this structure and it served all purposes
passably well until the new Armory was erected at a cost
of $40,000. The precinct station of the North Division was
located for a time after the fire at No. 180 Dearborn avenue,
and was removed to its present quarters, East Chicago avenue in 1873, in a building erected at a cost of $24,303.63. In

his inaugural address Mayor Medill noted the fact that the members of the police and fire departments were paid nearly $900,000 for their services on the Saturday preceding the fire, so that the city was not indebted to them in any large amount, when the great calamity occurred.

Although but a few weeks had elapsed between the time of the dreadful visitation and the assumption by Mr. Medill of the mayorial chair, the spirit and confidence of the people had already been restored, and this is seen nowhere more plainly than in the inaugural address delivered by that gentleman. "I point with pride and admiration," he said, in concluding his remarks, "to the gigantic efforts our whole people are putting forth to rise from the ruins and rebuild Chicago. The money value of their losses can hardly be calculated. But who can compute the aggregate of anguish, distress and suffering they have endured and must endure? Their wounds are still sore and agonizing, though they have been greatly alleviated by the prompt, generous and world-wide charities that have been poured out for their succor and relief; and I claim in their behalf that they are showing themselves worthy the benefactions received. They have faced their calamity with noble fortitude and unflinching courage. Repining or lamentation is unheard in our midst, but hope and cheerfulness are everywhere exhibited and expressed. All are inspired with an ambition to prove to the world that they are worthy of its sympathy, confidence and assistance, and to show how bravely they can encounter disaster, how quickly repair losses and restore Chicago to her high rank among the great cities of the world. Happily there is that left which fire cannot consume—habits of industry and self-reliance, personal integrity, business aptitude, mechanical skill and unconquerable will. These created what the flames devoured, and these can speedily re-create more than was swept away. Under free institutions, good government and the blessings of Providence, all losses will soon be repaired, all misery caused by the fire assuaged, *and a prosperity greater than ever dreamed of will be achieved in a period so brief that the rise will astonish mankind even more than the fall of Chicago."*

We have italicized the concluding lines of Mr. Medill's inspiring, and, it would seem, inspired peroration, for, in the light of subsequent events, they stand out boldly and unassailable, as a prophecy fulfilled. But few men in Chicago had more confidence in the future than had Mr. Medill, although at the time these words were uttered the South and North Divisions of the city were still covered with the black and hideous ruins of the great conflagration, and it may be said that he but voiced the general sentiment of the people who had just elected him, with loud acclamation, as the man who could bring order out of chaos, and guide the stricken city through the most perilous epoch in her history.

In 1872, as has been stated, the headquarters of the police department were located in the temporary City Hall. The board of police consisted of Mark Sheridan, Jacob Rehm, L. H. Davis, and Mancel Talcott, and in the board James E. Chadwick represented the fire department. W. W. Kennedy retained the position of general superintendent during the early part of the year. The police committee of the city council was composed of J. C. Knickerbocker, P. H. Hickey, Louis Schaffner, George P. Powell and Monroe Heath.

The first precinct station, Harrison street and Pacific avenue, was commanded by Capt. Michael C. Hickey, and William Buckley and Edward Hood were sergeants. The force of the station numbered 64 men. The sub-station, on 22d street, was in charge of Sergeants Clayton and Morganthaler, with 21 men; the Cottage Grove avenue sub-station was in charge of Sergeant Thomas Barrett, who commanded 20 men; the South Branch sub-station, Archer avenue and Deering streets (now known as the Deering street station) was in charge of Sergeant J. L. Lull, who commanded 17 men.

The second precinct station was commanded by Capt. C. H. French, and Jonas D. Johnson and James Garrity were sergeants at the precinct station, the force consisting of 60 men; the sub-station, 609 West Lake street, was in charge of Sergeants W. N. Douglas and Thomas Moore, and had a force of 19 men; the sub-station, 12th and Johnson streets, was in charge of Sergeants N. A. Briscoe and Simon O'Donnell, and had a detail of 36 men; the sub-station on West Chicago avenue was in charge of Sergeant Charles Berdell, and had a force of 15 men; the North Branch (rolling mills) station was in charge of Sergeant William B. Macauley, and had a detail of 12 men.

The third precinct was commanded by Frederick Gund, that gentleman having resumed his captaincy after retiring from the board; Charles Rehm and Amos W. Hathaway were the sergeants attached to the precinct station, 180 Dearborn avenue, and the detail was 40 men; the Larrabee sub-station was in charge of Sergeants John Baus and M. Bishoff, and had a force of 18 men; the Webster avenue sub-station was in charge of Sergeant Thomas D. Fox, and mustered 15 men.

The conduct of police affairs under Mayor Medill exhibited no signs of weakness or vacillation during the early months of his administration, and doubtless his term would have been a most successful one, from every point of view, had not that ever-disturbing element, which is supposed in a vague sort of way to be composed of the "better class of citizens," insisted upon taking part in the management of public affairs. The police department was well managed in the spring of 1872. Some of the best men that were ever attached to the force held prominent commanding positions; strict discipline prevailed; there was that *esprit* among the men of every grade—too often missing since that time—which contributed largely toward bringing the force up to a high standard. Mr. Medill had seen many imperfections in the police establishment when he entered upon his duties as mayor, and with the assistance of friendly members of the board of police commissioners had striven hard to correct them, and in many instances had succeeded.   The force was very small, considering the condition of the city at the time.   The work of rebuilding was under way, and thousands of strangers were flocking into Chicago from every point of the compass.   All classes of tradesmen found ready employment, and the demand created by the stupendous undertaking involved in the rebuilding of the city, drained the labor market in other sections of the country.   It was estimated that for some time during the spring and summer of '72, mechanics and laborers arrived here from outside points at an average rate of 5,000 per week.   Good wages and plenty of work made money easy in Chicago during those days, and, as a natural result, every train-load of strangers contained a large percentage of disreputable characters, who had turned their footsteps toward Chicago with an idea in view of preying upon the honest people of the community.   Gamblers, bunko-steerers, confidence men, sharpers and criminals of every description arrived in shoals; besides, the fire had demoralized a large number of residents, who had up to October 9, 1871, ranked among respectable people.   Reckless dissipation on the part of those who had lost part or all their possessions in the conflagration was not uncommon.   Some took to stimulants; others to gambling; the decade after the fire is strewn with the whitened bones of human wrecks, caused by that great calamity.   Saloons, concert halls, dives, brothels and gambling hells flourished.   The temptations were great and the means of yielding to them plentiful.   Nobody who could or would work need suffer for want of money.

The police suffered from numerous disadvantages.   The city was undergoing a complete metamorphosis; locations were obliterated, old landmarks destroyed; the neighborhoods that had been respectable had become disreputable, the slums of anti-fire days had become purified; the streets were almost impassable for months after the fire; shelter and hiding places for criminals abounded in the ruins or in the rising buildings; new faces were in the majority among the criminals, and the most experienced officers had to learn their trade over again, just as if they had been assigned to duty in a new city. Notwithstanding all these drawbacks they did splendid work in preventing and punishing crime. They had more serious matters to deal with than the enforcement of unimportant city ordinances, and while they were struggling to hold the burglar, the footpad, the murderous thug in check, they had to give free rein to the grog shop keepers, the bunko-steerers, the confidence men and the minor class of criminals generally.

Then the reformer came to the front, and, as usual, he was not satisfied with reforming by degrees, but insisted, as he often had before, as he often has since, and as he often will again, that everything should be reformed at once; that nothing should remain unreformed. There was room for reformation; everybody realized that, and the reformer was given full rein. Meetings were held at which he made speeches damning the administration in general and the conduct of police affairs in particular. Jacob Rehm had retired from the police board, and E. F. C. Klokke took his place. The board, in the spring of 1872, was constituted as follows: Mancel Talcott, president, Mark Sheridan, E. F. C. Klokke and L. H. Davis, the latter representing the fire department.

There had been organized a "Committee of Seventy," composed of leading citizens and a large number of clergymen, who were bent upon the immediate and unconditional purification of the city. Some of them were men of large, some of fair to middling calibre, but most of them had narrow views and were impelled onward by motives which, when probed to the bottom, proved to be of a very low order. The first and second named classes very soon withdrew from the contest, leaving the last named in full possession of the field. They appointed a sub-committee of fifteen to call upon the mayor, and demand the enforcement of the reform measures

which they had agreed among themselves were absolutely
necessary to the salvation of the city. The Sunday law
must be enforced first of all. There must be no selling or
buying of liquors in Chicago on the Sabbath; temperance
must be enforced everywhere, and the morality of the city
must be speedily elevated. The mayor received the committee courteously, but informed the gentlemen that, while
he agreed with them fully as to the desirability of bringing
about the reforms they demanded, yet it would require some
time to change the habits of the people, and that any attempt
to deprive them of what they conscientiously believed to be
their rights, no matter how forcibly they might be argued
or dealt with, would inevitably result in dismal failure.
But he was endeavoring, and would endeavor still further,
to bring about a satisfactory change in the moral condition
of the city, but, he assured them, it must be a slow process,
as Chicago was to all intents and purposes beginning life
anew, and it would require some time before the people became settled in their ways. When the present strain upon
the public mind had relaxed, he believed the disreputable
classes would be eliminated rapidly, but it would be bad
policy now to force an issue which was obnoxious to many
thousands of the most industrious of citizens. The Germans, for instance, could not be reconciled to the belief that
beer drinking on Sundays was an offense against morality.

And yet Mr. Medill, undoubtedly against his better
judgment, yielded little by little to the pressure which the
committee of seventy brought to bear upon him. His first
mistake was the dismissal of Superintendent of Police Kennedy, on July 29, and his second was the appointment of
Elmer Washburn to fill the vacancy. Washburn had distinguished himself at the head of the government secret
service during the war, and was, at the time of his appointment, warden of the Illinois penitentiary. He had not the
slightest experience as a policeman, and was entirely unfa-
miliar with the duties of a police superintendency. In a

word, he lacked every requisite supposed to be necessary to the successful management of a police force. He entered upon his duties with the assumption that everything up to date had been mismanaged; that everything then existing was wrong; that the speediest and best method of correcting the existing evils was to demolish the entire police establishment first, and then reconstruct it after his own methods. And then he undertook, in response to the "sentiments of the better classes," to regulate the habits, to revolutionize the customs of more than two-thirds of the people. During his brief career as superintendent of police, the force was pretty badly shaken up. There was no longer any interchange of opinion between the chief and his captains. He would listen to no suggestions, simply waving his subordinates off, and telling them that they would hear from him officially. He employed a corps of clerks, who were kept busily engaged in preparing orders. Written orders were a weakness with him. A question that might have been answered by a nod of the head, was replied to with ponderous verbosity and a bombardment of officialisms over the length and breadth of a sheet of legal cap.

On his assumption of the duties of superintendent there were no changes in the force from those heretofore reported, except that a sub-station had been established at 22nd street and Wentworth avenue, which was placed in charge of Sergeants Frederick Ebersold and Dennis Fitzpatrick, and given a detail of 21 men. The reformers continued to hold meetings, as did also the anti-reformers, and various subcommittees waited upon the mayor. The committee of seventy insisted that the prevalent epidemic of lawlessness and crime was caused mainly by drunkenness, and advocated as a partial remedy, the enforcement of the Sunday closing law. Still Mr. Medill held out, claiming that "the movement was impracticable, for the reason that both sellers and purchasers would deem it an arbitrary and inconsistent interference with their prerogative on one certain day out of the seven in the week; that the law was directed against the keepers alone, and not against the drinkers as well, therefore being discriminative; and, further, because it would require one policeman for each drinking place, to see that the law was enforced, or, say three thousand altogether, whereas the tax-fighters made it hard to support a force of four hundred and fifty policemen." As the committee of seventy was composed very largely of tax fighters and tax evaders, this thrust of Mr. Medill made a painful wound. The committee came out in print with a reply in which they claimed that although the liquor interest was active and united, and exerted a controlling influence in politics, the facts went to show that whenever an honest effort had been made to enforce the Sunday liquor law, it had been successful. Mayor Medill was accused of pandering to the whisky element and of moral cowardice.

Mancel Talcott, a member of the board of police, was an outspoken advocate of the blue law proposition, and some other members of the board committed themselves to it to such an extent that Mayor Medill finally felt called upon to submit to the demands of the reformers, and he therefore ordered the enforcement of section 4, chapter 25, of the city ordinances. Then disintegration set in. It was a crushing blow not only to the republican party, but to genuine reform, for the masses of the people were opposed to the measure and determined to resist it. Not since Mayor Boone's time had the fanatical element attempted to raise its head. The same prejudices were beginning to make themselves felt now. Little by little it leaked out that the temperance movement in Chicago was only another name for know-nothingism. It was to be not so much a war upon intemperance as a crusade against foreigners. The decanter might be passed around in the haunts of the natives, but the beer glass must not leave its peg in the beer hall, or circulate under the umbrageous silver-leaf poplars of the beer garden. The "Dutch" beer saloons, the Irish tippling houses, the Scandinavian whisky shops must go—particularly if they were small places in humble neighborhoods—but the back and side doors of the fashionable sample rooms, and the bar-rooms in the club houses would be accessible to those fortunate beings who had taken their first mouthful of air in this blessed land of freedom. This is the way the "foreigners" then residing in Chicago looked at it, and they made common cause against the invasion of what they were pleased to call their rights.

A committee of Germans waited upon Mayor Medill and, it appears, went away satisfied that he did not sympathize with the movement, although he had been forced into it Henry Greenebaum belonged to a citizen's committee of twenty-five, also bent upon strengthening the moral fabric, but when he learned that the committee favored the enforcement of the Sunday law, he resigned the chairmanship and withdrew his membership indignantly. Mancel Talcott, who had been one of the leading advocates of the blue law, resigned from the board, because his seat was becoming uncomfortable, and his place was filled by the appointment of C. A. Reno, who was made president. The other members now were Sheridan and Klokke. The police, officers and men, were discontented with Washburn's method, and the latter came into conflict with the commissioners. Charges of neglect of duty were preferred against him by the secretary of the board. The mayor was true to his friend Washburn, sustained him and removed Reno and Klokke from the board, removals which the board refused to recognize, on the ground that its members were appointed under commissions from the governor, and instructed Secretary Ward to recognize no other authority in the management of police affairs than that of the board. The mayor appointed to fill the places of Reno and Klokke, which he had declared vacant, Messrs. Carlisle Mason and L. P. Wright, and the council confirmed them. Thereupon Mark Sheridan announced that his duty to the public would compel him

to act with the new appointees. Commissioner Sheridan
made an explanation of his change of front. The mayor
and comptroller, he said, having refused to adjust claims of
persons who had furnished supplies to the department, there
was no doubt in his mind that they would recognize Messrs.
Mason and Wright, and while he felt that the claims of
Reno and Klokke were legal, he was constrained to act with
their successors—under protest, however—in order to advance the interests of the city and maintain the interests
of the police and fire departments. He was satisfied that
the power claimed by the mayor under and by virtue of
the act known as the "Mayor's Bill," was contrary to the
spirit of our republican institutions, and that, even if the
power did exist, the arbitrary exercise of it would not be
justified or sustained by the courts. The board as newly
constituted on February 26, 1873, dismissed the charges
against Superintendent Washburn, and on April 7 the
board sustained the mayor in the dismissal from the force
of Sergeants Rehm, Bishoff, Douglass and Macauley, they
having obeyed the orders of the board and Acting Superintendent Dr. Ward.

The pathway being made comparatively clear of obstacles
now, Superintendent Washburn, on April 28, issued an order
that the Sunday closing ordinance be enforced. Mark Sheridan antagonized this order with all his vigor, and entered
a protest against it in the records of the board, in which
he quoted from the Constitution the provision : "The right
of the people to be secure in their persons, homes, papers
and effects against unreasonable searches and seizures,
shall not be violated." Commissioners Wright and Mason
entered a resolution on the records denouncing Sheridan's
protest as incendiary in character and as "tending to incite the police force to disobey the orders of the board."
From this time on there was a constant friction in the
board ; protests and counter-protests, conflicts of authority, strong language, personal altercations and almost vio-

lence. Sheridan and Washburn, at one stage of the proceedings, were within an inch of coming to blows. On July 12, Captain M. C. Hickey resigned ; on July 29, Commissioner Mason resigned, and Reuben Cleveland was appointed in his stead. During the remaining months of the Medill administration the bitterness continued inside and outside of the board room; meetings were held almost nightly, which denounced the policy pursued by the mayor and his superintendent ; the foreign-born population was thoroughly aroused and united, the democracy catered to its wishes and demands ; demagogues rose up and took the lead, and then came that most remarkable of all the political combinations that Chicago has ever given birth to—the People's party.

The times had changed, money was becoming scarcer and scarcer every day; people of usually strong resources were becoming pinched; capitalists were growing timid; improvements were either suspended or inclined to languish; mechanics and laborers were thrown out of work; the poor were already beginning to feel the want of necessities, hundreds were driven to crime by poverty alone—the reaction had come at last; the golden shower that followed the devouring flames had ceased—the great financial panic was on the threshold, ready to step in at a moment's notice and crush the life out of enterprise and industry.

But the great majority of Chicago people were shutting their eyes to the impending evil. Politics absorbed all their thoughts. The People's party, on the one side, clamoring for more freedom, the Law and Order party on the other side shouting for less license, drowned for the time being the premonitory rumblings of the financial earthquake that was soon to make the earth tremble beneath their feet.

The Germans had gone over to the democracy; the Irish were united with the Germans; all foreign-born citizens were bound together by a common tie—that of mutual protection. The democracy encouraged the strange alliances formed, and did everything possible to widen the breach between the "better classes" and the "foreigners." Meetings—great, suffocating, mass meetings—were held in every ward, every precinct, and the Medill administration was everywhere—by the People's party—denounced, lampooned, ridiculed, excoriated. True, Mr. Medill had been led, as before remarked, into the fanatical noose against his better judgment, and he had never in reality endorsed the Sunday closing movement as a wise piece of policy. He knew that it was a piece of folly, and that it would be succeeded by greater follies still by the opposition. The city had passed through a similar episode once before, and it suffered the worst consequences. No reasonable person could doubt but that to insist upon the enforcement of a law which was bitterly opposed by every foreign-born citizen, and an enforcement which would inevitably result in the unification of the foreign vote, was simply idiotic. But the editor-mayor had taken sides in the contest and he couldn't stultify himself. He did the next best thing—turned the conduct of affairs over to an acting mayor, and took a trip to Europe, thoroughly disgusted with his experience as a local politician.

One of the largest and most demonstrative of the German indignation meetings, held during the municipal campaign, laid down as planks in the platform on which they proposed to stand, the principles that the temperance and Sunday laws were obnoxious to a large and respectable portion of the people; that the civil service of the general, state and local governments had become a mere instrument of partisan tyranny and personal ambition; that the arrest of any person, whose offense was only punishable by a fine, instead of procedure by mere process or summons, was an outrage; that the police power of the state, county or city should not be wielded in the interest of factions of society; that intemperance in all things should be discouraged; that inspectors should be appointed to detect impurities in beverages sold; that the granting of liquor licenses to persons of bad repute be prohibited; that a person should be held responsible only for his own wrong-doing, and for this reason, not landlords but saloon-keepers be held accountable for liquor sold on premises; and not saloon-keepers but drunkards responsible for the habits of drunkenness. Among those who took a prominent part in the advocacy of these principles, and indeed who took a prominent part in all that concerned the interests of the People's party, were the following German and Irish-American citizens: Conrad Niehoff, Richard Michaelis, A. C. Hesing, Carl Bluhm, Peter Hand, L. Schwuchow, Francis A. Hoffman, Jr., Frank Schweinfurth, William Floto, C. Tegtmeyer, Dr. Malther, Max Eberhardt, Emil Muhlke. R. Thieme, J. Schiellinger, G. R. Korn, William Schwartz, B. Eisendrath, Carl Dahinten, Phillip Stein, H. Schanellin, W. Schaeffer, R. Frieberg R. Christensen, J. C. Meyer, A. Erle, F. Sengl, J. H. Mc-Avoy, Barney G. Caulfield, W. J. Onahan, George Von Hollan, Jacob Rehm, Michael Evans, P. M. Cleary, John Corcoran, Thomas Brennan, Michael Keeley, Justice Boyden, Herman Leib, Peter Hunt, Edward O'Neill, Arno Voss, R. Kenny, John Bonfield, Edward Phillips and Adolph Schoeninger.

The convention of the People's party made the following nominations, and they were endorsed by the "Liberal and Democratic Central and Executive Committee of Cook County:" For mayor, H. D. Colvin; for city treasurer, Dan. O'Hara; for city collector, George Von Hollan; for city assessor, Charles Dennehy; for judge of the Superior Court, S. M. Moore; for judge of the County Court, M. R. M. Wallace; for county clerk, Hermann Lieb; for clerk of the Criminal Court, Austin J. Doyle; for county treasurer, H. B. Miller; for county superintendent of schools, George D. Plant; for county commissioners, Christian Busse, John Herting, William P. Burdick, Thomas Lonergan, A. B. Johnson, and for police commissioner, C. A. Reno; city attorney, Egbert Jamieson; clerk of police court. Martin Scully.

The Law and Order party nominated the following: For mayor, L. L. Bond; for city treasurer, David A. Gage; for city collector, A. L. Morrison; for city assessor, W. B. H. Gray; for city attorney, I. N. Stiles; for police court clerk, K. R. Matson; for judge of the Superior Court, Joseph P. Clarkson; for judge of the County Court, M. R. M. Wallace; for county clerk, J. W. Brockway; for clerk of the Criminal Court, W. K. Sullivan; for county treasurer, Phillip Wadsworth; for county superintendent of schools, A. G. Lane; for county commissioners, A. J. Galloway, S. Olin, William M. Laughlin, W. B. Bateham, S. W. Kingsley; for police commissioner, Reuben Cleveland. This ticket received the endorsement of the "Committee of Seventy." Of the nominees, David A. Gage on the Law and Order ticket, and George Von Hollan on the People's ticket, turned out subsequently to be defaulters. Every candidate on the People's ticket was elected, the majorities ranging from 10,000 to 13,000. The vote for mayor stood: Colvin, 28,791, Bond, 18,540. The general impression prevailed that the "Committee of Seventy" had by its endorsement ruined whatever small chances of success the "Law and Order" ticket had at the start. "The committee of seventy," said the *Tribune* after the fight, "some three months since, smelt the battle afar off, and came out of its winter quarters. It proceeded to organize the recent campaign, in which it met with a crushing reverse. Hereafter it will be remembered in the history of local politics for good intentions, for miserable inefficiency as a political organization, and for its failure to execute the designs for which it was organized."—Severe language coming from a paper that had given a warm support to the defeated ticket. Several attempts, rather weak-kneed, were afterward made to restore the Sunday law movement to life but the city council granted the right of traffic in liquor on Sunday, and Mayor Colvin endorsed this action.

In his inaugural address to the city council, Mayor Colvin made the following remarks in relation to the police force:

Our police system should be conducted upon the principle of the prevention rather than the punishment of crime. Nor should the city seek to obtain revenue by any of the prevalent forms of vice. When it does, it becomes *particeps criminis* in the iniquity it professes to punish or suppress. My nature revolts against this barbarous and brutal practice, not pursued for the purpose of extirpating vice, but with the object of adding a few paltry dollars to the public revenue. It shall never receive my sanction. All that can usefully be accomplished in this direction is the mitigation of the more glaring or demoralizing effects of that which in all ages and among all races has existed as an evil that may be mitigated or perhaps regulated, but which has never yet been exterminated. Police officers should be made to understand and feel that laws are enacted as much to protect the unfortunate as to punish the wicked. In no case should a person be inhumanly treated, simply because he has been arrested for some petty offense or misdemeanor. I am decidedly opposed to the practice of police officers receiving money in the shape of rewards for services rendered from any corporation or individual. Let them look to the city alone for remuneration.

Of course Mr. Washburn could not remain under an administration which had been elected partly as a rebuke to the methods which he had pursued, and Jacob Rehm was appointed superintendent almost as soon as Mayor Colvin was sworn in. E. F. C. Klokke was appointed to the police board. M. C. Hickey had re-entered the force in the meantime, and was again promoted to a captaincy, vice Louis J. Lull.

In the winter of 1872, the poverty of the people made itself felt in a miniature riot on La Salle street, near the rooms of the Relief and Aid Society. The charge was made that the society had gobbled up a great part of the many contributions for the relief of the fire sufferers, and was distributing it among its members. The riot broke out suddenly, and soon the streets surrounding were blocked. Joseph Dixon, who happened to be at headquarters at the time, was detailed to lead a company of policemen against the rioters, which he did with a skill that won him great praise and later on promotion. He charged upon the mob, drove a large number of the rioters through the tunnel, scattered others east and west on Randolph and Lake streets, and kept the great body of them at bay until Captain M. C. Hickey arrived with reinforcements from the Armory, when quiet was soon restored. This uprising was not of long duration, but it is remembered by old residents as the " bread riot."

The expenses of conducting the department of police for the year ending March 31, 1874, were $653,258.65, and the amount asked for the following year was $718,468.29. This increase in the estimate was said to be due to the fact that an increase in the force had become absolutely necessary. The board of police submitted the following figures in support of their demand:

Number of men on duty, at one time....................... 244
Average number of acres to each beat................... 93½
Average number of miles to each beat................... 14½

In his report for the three months ending March 31, 1874, Superintendent Rehm said:

Before entering into or giving the details of the working force for the said year, I beg permission to state that since my assuming the position of general superintendent of police in December last, the members of the department have, with very rare exceptions exhibited an evident determination to faithfully perform their respective duties, the result of which is that we can to-day point with pride to the fact that less crime has been committed, less arrests effected for violation of city ordinances, and a much better showing of stolen property recovered during the last three months than for any other three months of the year, and this notwithstanding the fact that many of our citizens,on the approach of winter, were apprehensive of a season of crime and depredations on account of the unusual number of people out of employment.

It had been one of the hardest winters in the history of Chicago—the winter after the panic—and the streets were constantly thronged with idlers. But the hard times had not yet seriously affected the morals of the people, and although poor and suffering the workingmen of the city abstained from crime. It required nearly two years of pinching poverty to drive some of them to the road, where they degenerated into common tramps, some to criminal practices in the city, and others still to the excesses which culminated in the riots of 1876 and 1877.

The police force in March, 1874, consisted of a general superintendent, 3 captains, 17 sergeants and 525 patrolmen, divided up as follows: Harrison street station, 111; Twenty-second street station, 48; Cottage Grove avenue station, 30; South Branch station, 27; Union street station, 86; West Twelfth street station, 56; West Lake street station, 30; West Chicago avenue station, 29; East Chicago avenue station, 51; North Branch station, 12; Webster avenue station, 14; Larrabee street station, 19. The superintendent recommended that several of the stations be enlarged; that the number of sergeants be increased to 20, and that 85 patrolmen be added.

For the year ending March 31, 1875, the board of police commissioners reported that the expenditures for the year had been $722,876.92, and asked for $823,180.00, to meet the expenses of the next twelve months. This increase in the amount asked for was due to the fact that the board proposed to add 150 new men to the force. In some respects the year had proved to be an exceptionally quiet one for the police, the value of goods stolen being only $182,590.00, as against $347,598.00 during the previous year; a little more than one-half. But in other respects the policemen appear to have suffered some hardships, as the following table will show. During the year the policemen

Shot by burglars, numbered	3
Shot by thieves, "	2
Dangerously beaten while making arrests	4
Cut with a hatchet by prisoner	1
Stabbed by prisoner	1
Foot broken at fire	1

The report says, "There were many others who received injuries of a less dangerous character, and from the effects of which the policemen were laid up for several days," and these significant words are added, "We think it worthy of note that while the aggregate number of arrests is more than three thousand less than for the year immediately preceding, the arrests for grave crimes, as burglary, larceny, etc., largely exceeds the number for that year."

The city council only provided for forty of the eighty-five policemen asked for by the superintendent during the year, and he joins with the board now in asking that an increase of 150 be made. In concluding his report he asks that the salaries of the twelve patrolmen, detailed as roundsmen, be fixed at $1,200 per annum. This is the last report we have from Superintendent Rehm. Shortly after writing it he was superseded by M. C. Hickey, who assumed command of the force as general superintendent. The board of police commissioners was legislated out of existence at the same time, but its functions were in a great measure preserved and exercised in the person of the city marshal, that office having been revived for some unfathomable reason. The duties of the city marshal were to most people a mystery at the time, and even now, looking over the records left us by R. E. Goodell, it is almost impossible to determine what the object was in establishing such an office. He received a salary of $4,000 per annum, and he had a secretary who received $2,500, and three clerks who received $1,200 each. He was not a police officer, neither were his secretary and clerks, and yet all combined they exercised a little more authority than the heads of the police department. The truth is, the police establishment was gradually approaching the system which we have settled down to now, but it made very awkward strides toward it in 1875, and sometimes it looked as though it was going backward. In the year 1887 the inspector of police practically performs all the duties that in other days fell to the lot of police boards, marshals and deputy superintendents, except that he does not wield the executive power. The superintendent of police under the boards was a mere instrument to be used by the majority of the commissioners, without personal independence. The office was necessarily a political one, and it could never be lifted out of politics as long as it was an office within the gift of partisan commissioners. The boards of police commissioners left us as a relic the city marshal, and when the city marshal passed away the police force began that period of real and useful development in which it is becoming more perfect year after year.

During the first nine months of Superintendent Hickey's management of the police department, there were but few changes worthy of note. The Colvin administration had become the target for a pretty generous expenditure of abuse, and the occupant of the mayor's chair was receiving in solid chunks some very fair samples of the public opinion which had been hurled at his predecessor. But the city was quiet; the times were hard, dull, uneventful. There was more or less crime of a desperate nature recorded daily; garrotings, highway robberies, sand-baggings were becoming a little too frequent to be novel or interesting, but still the policemen held the vicious pretty well in check, and the turbulent element had not yet dared to measure its strength with the constituted authorities.

There were now four police precincts, the West Chicago avenue station having been constituted one. Captain William Buckley had command of the first precinct; Captain Samuel A. Ellis, the second; Captain Jonas M. Johnson, the third, and Captain Fred. Gund, the fourth. Joseph H. Dixon was deputy superintendent. The force numbered, exclusive of four captains and twenty sergeants, 565 men, and Superintendent Hickey, like his predecessor, demanded a considerable increase, but instead of granting this request the city council, on July 26, 1876, passed an ordinance demanding a reduction of 25 per cent. of the expenses of the department, a reduction that made it necessary for the superintendent to dispense with 75 patrolmen, from an already insufficient force. The force toward the end of 1876 included a general superintendent, one deputy-superintendent, four captains, nineteen sergeants and five hundred and ninety-two patrolmen.

Serious troubles occurred among the Bohemian lumber shovers during the summer, but the police finally smothered what for a few days promised to become a dangerous riot.

The country swarmed with tramps ; the lumber yards, vacant buildings, sheds, railroad depots, and all public places were thronged with idlers; the disputed result of the national election contributed toward prolonging the hard times; crime of all kinds was on the increase; it was dangerous to venture out after dark; people were sandbagged, garrotted or "held up" on some of the leading streets, a terrible winter for the poor had set in, a gloomy spring had followed; and when the first faint murmurs of the mob-uprising along the line of the Baltimore & Ohio railroad were heard, a responsive chord was struck here, and the Chicago mob was only too eager to repeat the performance that had enveloped Pittsburg in flames, and caused ruin and bloodshed across half the continent.   The riot of '77 was on.

CHAPTER IX.

THE YEAR 1877—OUTBREAK OF THE GREAT RAILROAD STRIKE IN THE EAST—THE CONDITION OF AFFAIRS IN CHICAGO AT THE TIME— HARD TIMES FOR MECHANICS AND LABORERS—WAS THE FIRE A BLESSING OR A CURSE?—THE DECLINE OF WAGES AND DEGEN- ERACY OF THE WORKING CLASSES—WHY THE CITY WAS RIPE FOR A RIOT—THE OUTBREAK IN CHICAGO—MISTAKES OF THE AU- THORITIES—BREAKING UP MASS MEETINGS—THE RANDOLPH STREET AFFAIR—TROUBLE AT McCORMICK'S—LIEUT. CALLAHAN'S GALLANT CONDUCT AT THE ROUND HOUSE.

Early in the month of July, 1877, telegrams were printed in the Chicago papers announcing that small bodies of employes, here and there, along the line of the Balti- more & Ohio railroad were quitting work. These dispatches were quite brief, and simply announced that there was a difference between the men and the company as to the question of wages, and for the most part were hidden away under single headlines, at the bottom of inside columns. There was something, however, about these telegrams which struck the telegraph editors of the different papers as being peculiar, to say the least. From a three or four line announcement at the start, they gained in length daily, until at the end of a week twenty lines were con- sumed. But the most peculiar feature about them was that they came over the wires with as great a degree of regular- ity as the Wall street stock report. Evidently the associated press correspondent was a persistent fellow, for, although he didn't have very much to say, he said something every day, and generally something just a trifle fresher than he said the day before. The burden of these dispatches was that the employes of the company were discontented with their lot, that many were throwing up their jobs and that the trouble was inclined to spread rather than to subside as the days slipped by.

But little attention was paid to the news here. If it was read at all, it was looked upon simply as a trivial matter, unworthy of more consideration than is usually given to the vast number of unimportant telegrams which are printed daily in the newspapers. But the "B. & O. trouble," as it came to be called, would persist in parading itself before the public. The three-line telegram expanded into a twenty-five line dispatch, grew until it occupied a quarter of a column, and then until it attained the dignity of a displayed head. More than that, it was accompanied now by telegrams from different points, and shortly by telegrams from all points in the Baltimore & Ohio system. Then came the more startling information that the "B. & O. trouble" had spread to the Pennsylvania and other lines, and now the public began to take a livelier interest in the situation. Almost as quick as a flash this news was followed by the information (on Thursday, July 19, 1877), that a gigantic railroad strike, involving the employes of all the great trans-continental and tributary companies, was on, and that serious riots had occurred already at many points in Pennsylvania and West Virginia. On Saturday information of a still more alarming nature came over the wires. There was a general uprising of the working classes in the Keystone state. On Sunday morning the people of Chicago were horrified by the news that Pittsburg was in the hands of a mob; that the property of the railroad companies was in flames; that blood had been spilled freely on the streets; that a reign of terror prevailed in all the large cities of Pennsylvania, West Virginia and Ohio, and that the spirit of riot, like some spectral courier of a dreadful epidemic, was advancing westwardly, and conquering as it came.

That Sunday morning, noon and night, will always be

remembered by the people who then resided in Chicago as the most remarkable, perhaps, in the history of the city.

The morning papers had presented the news from Pittsburg up to 5 a. m., when rioting was still in progress at Pittsburg. By 8 a. m. the streets presented a week-day appearance; by 9 a. m. they were crowded; by noon they were thronged, and with one accord the people flocked toward the newspaper offices where bulletins began to make their appearance.

Let us stop right here and take a hasty glance at the condition of Chicago. In the preceding chapter an effort has been made to exhibit clearly the tendency of the times in this very direction. From the close of the war there had been a slow but steady decline in the market price of labor; a slow but steady decline in the ability of the working classes to make both ends meet; a slow but steady decline in all values; a constantly diminishing confidence in the future. Hard times were setting in here when the great fire occurred. The financial panic which occurred in 1873 might have—in all probability would have—occurred in 1872, had not the extraordinary demands created by the rebuilding of Chicago, and the vast amount of money put into circulation in consequence, averted it—staved it off. The blow was all the heavier, for being postponed, when it came. The great fire, even though it resulted in giving employment for a time to thousands of men, who would otherwise have been deprived of work, was not an industrial gain, but an industrial loss. Every dollar lost in the fire was just as much lost after Chicago was rebuilt as before. The calamity to our city, in a word, simply aggravated the industrial prostration then prevailing. It was pure nonsense when unthinking individuals pronounced the Chicago fire a blessing in disguise. Nothing that is lost can by any method of reasoning be figured out as a gain, and the fruits of thirty years of untiring industry was blasted by the fire of October, 1871. It would have been difficult to convince the stonemasons, bricklayers, carpenters, etc., who were drawing from $7.50 to $10.00 per diem, during the six months following the fire, that within a year they would be glad to get $4.00 or $5.00 for the same amount of labor, or, that within three years it would be offered without a purchaser, at from $2.00 to $2.50! It is difficult for anybody to realize what a dreary, drizzling, rainy day really is when the sun is shining brightly, the air is dry and exhilerating and the burnished arch of the blue canopy above is cloudless. That mechanics were drawing $10.00 and common laborers $5.00 per diem was all sufficient to convince the unthinking individual, above referred to, that the Chicago fire was a blessing in disguise. How many days of enforced idleness did the destruction of property by the fire, did the cost of replacing it, did the inflated prices demanded for material and labor, cost the workingmen of Chicago—the workingmen of the country? It is impossible to answer that question correctly, yet here are some facts:

In the fall of 1872, before the work of reconstruction was half completed, police reports inform us that the city swarms with idle men. Many hundreds who came here, worked and made good wages, remained when the demand for labor was exceeded by the supply, and, so police statistics show, were compelled to walk out of town penniless. Under Superintendent Washburn the police justices are kept busy in "bagging" mechanics who have degenerated into vagrants, and the justices are giving them "time" to leave town. Under Superintendent Rehm the idlers increase and many laborers and mechanics, who have heretofore led honest lives, have descended to criminal practices in order to keep body and soul together. There are in all 24,899 arrests made in 1874, and the majority of them are laborers and tradesmen. In the building trades alone we have the following exhibit; only the most important being noticed:

TRADES.	ARRESTED 1884.
Architects	4
Blacksmiths	95

TRADES.	ARRESTED 1884.
Brass finishers	31
Brick makers	5
Boiler makers	18
Carpenters	433
Coppersmiths	10
Cabinet makers	24
Contractors	26
Glaziers	24
Gilders	5
Gas fitters	99
Laborers	4,542
Masons	307
Machinists	116
Marble cutters	15
Painters	181
Plumbers	78
Plasterers	168
Stone cutters	53

This year there are 8,483 persons arrested who refuse to give their occupations, and it is a significant fact that most of them were persons of good address and generally well educated. During the same year 573 gamblers were hauled in, showing that it must have been some years later when gambling was "entirely suppressed" in this city. Passing on to 1876, we find Superintendent Hickey talking as follows to the city council in his annual report:

Our city is centrally located, rapidly increasing in population, and the hundreds of railroad trains that daily arrive here very naturally bring among their passengers a share of that dangerous class of vagrants called "tramps," who now infest the principal cities of the country. Our patrolmen stationed at the railroad depots are watchful, and render good service in noting and checking these arrivals, and whenever practicable compel them to leave the city on the very next train. The number of men who have no home in the city, and who have been provided with lodgings in our station houses during the last year, is 7,467. Some of them are vagrants who travel from place to place, not caring to have a home, and preferring always to beg or steal rather than work. Some of them, too, are of the class who place but little value on human life. There are also among them many who would gladly make an honest living, but are out of employment by reason of the general depression in business which now affects all sections of the country. These are entitled to more humane treatment, and should be rendered facilities for bettering their condition and preventing them from becoming criminals.

This year there were 3,192 persons arrested for vagrancy, and the total number of arrests figured up 27,291, the great majority of them being charged with minor criminal offenses. Again the trades cut an important figure in the police reports, and the number of mechanics and laborers arrested is greatly in excess of those reported for any previous year.

Reference has been made to the lumber-shovers' strike elsewhere. Investigation into the cause of the trouble revealed the fact that thousands of men employed in the lumber district were receiving from seventy-five cents to one dollar per day for their labor, and that they were threatened with a still further reduction. Nearly all had families. They lived in one-room huts, built of clapboards hastily thrown together. Their families were on the verge of starvation, and the men were driven to desperation. Laboring men in other branches of trade were scarcely better paid. Indeed, they were glad to get anything, no matter how small, for their services, and employers were not generous enough, as a rule, to pay more than the bottom prices for any kind of service. Mechanics, too, were working for what they could get. A number of strikes had occurred during the past three years, but they proved failures one and all, and in most instances the men returned to work at less than they were getting when they struck. There were ten pairs of hands ready and willing to take the place of every single pair that quit work.

The unsettled state of national affairs, caused by the Hayes-Tilden dispute, only served to make matters worse. People had looked forward to the election of 1876 with a great deal of hope, expecting that it would prove to be the turning-point from depression to prosperity. But they were disappointed. Discontent was general among the wage classes. Socialism had been planted here, and it grew luxuriantly in the soil so well prepared for it. There were socialistic societies by the hundred, which held regular meetings throughout the city, and great mass meetings occasion-

ally on Market street, the Haymarket, or the lake shore.
The grievances of the wage-workers were palpable and
great. Things could not very well look more hopeless for
them. The demagogue was in his glory, and he demanded
war upon capital, vengeance upon the "privileged classes."
A great unemployed labor demonstration had paraded the
streets. Thousands of poorly clad, hungry looking men
were in line. A banner with the startling device, "Bread or
Blood," was boldly carried through the down-town streets.
All this before the news came from Pittsburg. The news
from Pittsburg was all that was necessary to precipitate
trouble here. Everybody knew that. The business man
knew it, the "Prominent Citizen" knew it, the mayor knew
it. The superintendent of police knew it. A few hours more
and the outrages committed in Pittsburg would be repeated
here. This everybody felt instinctively; yet nothing was
done to prepare for the impending, the inevitable, uprising.

On the forenoon of Sunday, July 22, the *Daily News* issued an "extra," containing the latest news from Pittsburg,
and this was followed by others at intervals varying from a
half hour to an hour throughout the day and late into the
night. About 3 o'clock in the afternoon extra editions
were issued from the *Times* and *Tribune* offices, and these
papers likewise continued to send out special editions with
every arrival of fresh intelligence. Pittsburg was in the
hands of a mob; the railroad shops were burning; the total
destruction of one whole section of the city was threatened;
the state militia and the mob had come into collision, and
the militia had been compelled to seek safety in flight, leaving their dead, dying and wounded on the streets; Philadelphia was threatened with a similar experience; there was
rioting at Allegheny City, at Wilkesbarre, at Harrisburg, at
Wheeling; trouble was brewing at Cincinnati; the excitement in St. Louis was at fever heat; the riot fever was
spreading in all directions, and it looked as though the
country was about to be convulsed by an uprising bordering

closely upon an insurrection. The "extras" contained editorial comments upon the news, taking a very gloomy view of the situation for the most part, and counselling the people of Chicago to keep cool, while exciting them to a feverish pitch by printing the news under warlike headlines. Certain of the papers that denounced the rioters in their early editions defended them toward evening, as the strength of the uprising became more strikingly manifest. The papers sold by the hundreds of thousands. The down-town streets were jammed with excited people. As a rule the bulletins were read in silence, and the news contained in the special editions was received in the same manner. The silence was oppressive. Men looked alarmed, but gave no vent to their feelings. There was a portentious seriousness depicted upon the faces of all. It was not a matter to joke about, to laugh over, to sneer at. It made men think. Certainly the future looked anything but bright.

That night the communists and socialists held high carnival. Numerous meetings were held, at all of which resolutions sympathizing with the Pittsburg rioters were passed. Couriers were sent out from communist headquarters with messages to the different meetings, and next morning it was announced that a monster mass meeting of wage workers would be held on Market, between Madison and Washington streets.

Then it was time to act. The morning papers brought later intelligence from the East, and this only served to fan the excitement into a warmer glow. Deputations of citizens called upon the mayor and asked him to take immediate measures to prevent destruction of property and loss of life here. He promised to do so. Some prominent citizens, headed by Mr. Levi Z. Leiter, called upon the editor of the *Daily News*, and begged him to suspend the publication of his paper for the time being, as the news he was furnishing to the public only served to excite the populace. He promised not to suspend it. Deputations waited upon the superintendent of police and asked him to take instant precautions against the possibility of a riot. He had already taken them. Deputations called upon the sheriff, telegraphed the governor, and interviewed Lieut.-Gen. Sheridan. Thus were deputations running here and running there, now and then, by accident, doing a sensible thing, but generally helping to precipitate the trouble which they were struggling, in an idiotic sort of a way, to avoid.

The men who kept cool and viewed the situation like reasonable beings advised, first of all, that the meeting announced to take place on Market street be suppressed, or, rather, be prevented from gathering. Mayor Heath remembered that there was something in the constitution which guaranteed the right of the people to peaceably assemble and relieve their minds, and he thought it best not to interfere. That settled it. The communists, socialists, vagrants, loafers, thugs, thieves and criminals in general were only waiting for the slightest exhibition of weakness on the part of the authorities; Mayor Heath furnished it, and the city was at their mercy.

There were newspapers which backed the mayor in his decision, which talked loudly of the rights of workingmen to meet and discuss the situation, and which held, in very elegantly constructed editorial leaders, that the right of free speech should never be abridged; there were newspapers which did that on Monday, and that talked in a different strain altogether on Wednesday, when they saw that a great blunder had been committed. Neither the mayor nor the superintendent of police appeared to realize—they certainly did not recognize—the magnitude of the issue presented then, nor for some time afterward.

The mass meeting on Monday night was a monster affair, the participants filling every inch of space between the tunnel and the south side of Madison street. Cars were unable to pass on the latter thoroughfare during the three hours that were consumed by the speakers. The communist leaders were there early and stayed late. Upon the different stands, or rather wagons, used by the speakers, and scattered through the vast assemblage were missionaries of the communist societies propagating doctrines of riot, incendiarism, revolution. Some of them who took part in that meeting had reason at a later date to regret their utterances that night; others had reason to feel ashamed of them. The wildest harangues of the communist leaders were cheered to the echo; their most treasonable sentiments applauded; their most incendiary demands received with manifest approbation. The crowd was ready for anything. Just as occurred nine years later, near the Haymarket, the sneers, the ridicule, the contemptuous remarks of the speakers were turned in great part toward "the cowardly police." Would the police, the well-fed, idling, lazy police, dare interfere with the rights of honest workingmen? No! Would they dare attempt to prevent such gatherings as this? No! If they did attempt to interfere with men who were exercising the right of free speech, what then? Why, my fellow citizens, they would be swept away like chaff before the wind. [Loud and continued cheering].

And so went the meeting to the close. There were officers present in plain clothes. There were here and there on the outskirts of the crowd a few policemen in uniform. But not the slightest attempt was made to interfere with this gathering of free American citizens who were aching to overturn the institutions of the country, to crush out all semblance of law and order, and to trample society in the dust. Superintendent Hickey's report of this meeting was undoubtedly based upon unreliable information. "A mass meeting of workingmen," he says, "was held on Monday evening on the corner of Market and Madison streets, and about five thousand persons were present. The meeting was addressed by several speakers who rather counseled prudence and moderation than violence, and although some speeches were made by noted communists, and a few at times became somewhat boisterous, the meeting adjourned in a quiet and orderly manner, about 10 p. m., the crowds dispersing off the streets, and all went peaceably to their homes." The facts are as stated nevertheless. A few speakers—probably three or four —had attempted to quiet the mob by using moderate language and advising peaceable proceedings.and lawful conduct, but they were hissed and howled down. It became necessary, of course, for the administration and the superintendent of police to attach as little importance as possible to the meeting, but the truth is, and it was so recognized at the time, that if a bold stand had been taken, such a stand, for instance, as the police took in New York about the same time, when Murray scattered the mob in Tompkins' square, there would have been no such scenes of lawlessness as followed during the remainder of the week.

Orders had been issued on Monday to the different captains of police, "to hold their commands in readiness at their respective precinct stations until further orders, and to hold themselves in readiness to move at the shortest possible notice."

Early on Tuesday morning the trouble began. The old automatic telegraph instruments were kept busy at headquarters recording the movements of a dozen different mobs, that were marching in as many different quarters of the city and gaining in volume as they moved. These mobs were marching from place to place, compelling workingmen in every branch of trade to quit work and help to swell their numbers. There was no resisting the demands of the rioters, and the most peaceably inclined and contented of mechanics and laborers were forced to drop their tools, don their coats and join the rabble brigades. The communists were in their second heaven, the *canaille* was at the very summit of its glory. Chicago was apparently as completely in the hands of the revolutionary element as Paris ever had been.

A mob which had been small when it started, but which

Scene below viaduc

was every minute attaining the most formidable proportions, was marching north on South Canal street, following the tactics already indicated. It compelled all workingmen along its route to abandon their labors. Whenever it came to a warehouse or factory where non-union men or "scabs" were employed, it assaulted the men, drove them from the buildings and proceeded to wreak destruction upon the property of their employers. The employers, in many instances, hearing of the advancing column, ordered their men to quit work, closed up their places, and trusted to Providence for the rest.

The mayor saw the necessity for speedy and vigorous action, but somehow or other, he was not prepared to take it. When orders were sent to Captain Seavey at the Union street station, to intercept the mob on Canal street, and compel them to disperse, the mayor stipulated that none of the rioters should be injured, if it could possibly be avoided. Lieutenants Blettner and Simmons, with twenty-five men each were detailed to meet and handle this mob, and if they and the men under them had had their way about it, the riot would have been stifled then and there, but they were under orders to be kind to the lawless ruffians, and no discretionary power whatever was left in their hands. No further proof of the ease with which the riot could have been squelched, if taken in time and handled with vigor, is necessary than the fact that the mob, upon the mere appearance of this little detachment of police, scattered in all directions. A few arrests were made; not even a club was used; the police did not seem to be in earnest; the mob felt, even though scattered, that if they had taken a determined stand the police would not have molested them. This first move on the part of the police filled the rioters with encouragement rather than alarm. The strongest possible evidence that this was the case began to accumulate before the day was over. At about 3 o'clock that afternoon, a mob had surrounded a gun store on State street. Orders were sent to

Captain O'Donnell to see that this mob was dispersed. He dispatched a squad under command of Lieut. Bell, and the street was cleared without difficulty. This demonstration and the fact that the Pittburg rioters had raided gun stores and pawn-brokers' offices, in order to obtain fire arms, led to the issue of the following :

TO ALL PAWNBROKERS.

As a measure of precaution as well as protection to yourselves, in the event of a riot, I would respectfully request that you remove all re-volvers, or other firearms, from your windows, to some safe place where they cannot be taken from you, and let them so remain until such time as all danger is past.   M. C. HICKEY,

Gen'l Supt. of Police.

Not only the pawnbokers, but dealers in firearms gener-ally, complied with this request on the part of the superin-tendent, and many of them volunteered to turn over their sup-plies of firearms and ammunition to the "custody of the city authorities for safe-keeping, on condition that all such prop-erty not returned to them when the excitement subsided should be paid for by the city." There was some patriotism in this offer, but it had the drawback of being too strongly diluted with selfish business interests to be entertained by the superintendent.

All through the afternoon reports of mob-gatherings were received from every part of the city. Strikes were in progress from the lake to Western avenue; from the North Side rolling mills to the town of Lake. The disposition or propensity to strike became a mania. Workingmen who had no earthly cause to complain, who could not call to mind a grievance, threw down their tools, tore off their "overalls," snatched up their coats and hats, shook their clenched fists at their employers, and—joined the nearest mob. The rail-road employes, the lumber shovers, the saw and planing mill men, the iron-workers, the brass finishers, the carpenters, the brickmakers, the bricklayers, the stonemasons, the furniture makers, the polishers, the shoemakers, the tailors, the painters, glaziers, butchers, bakers, candlestick makers—

all went out without motive or reason, and helped to swell the crazy mobs that paraded aimlessly through the streets.

As is usual in such cases the less dangerous of the characters followed—the most desperate, reckless and unprincipled led. Hundreds of those who shouted for higher wages and better treatment were vagabonds who had not done an honest day's work for years; hundreds were confirmed criminals, hundreds were professional thieves. But the most dangerous element of all were the foreigners who belonged to the communistic societies and who were endeavoring to bring about a period of the blackest anarchy. These people, especially their leaders, were willing to unite with the thugs and thieves of the city to secure the accomplishment of their designs. They were active and indefatigable in their work, and wherever a mob appeared they stood in the front ranks, urging the rabble and the misguided workingmen forward to the commission of acts of lawlessness, violence and brutality.

The police force at this time consisted of a general superintendent, a deputy superintendent, four captains, eighteen lieutenants, eleven sergeants and four hundred and eighty-one men. The force available for active duty "in the field," however, scarcely numbered 250 men. It was simply out of the question, of course, that such an insignificant force could successfully cope with a score of mobs, scattered broadcast throughout the city. The patrol wagon had not been dreampt of at the time, and the men rode in street cars, or traveled on foot from one point to another, being utterly unable to promptly respond to the calls sent in. All day Tuesday they were kept on the march, from post to pillar, from pillar to post, sometimes to meet and disperse a mob which would immediately re-form; sometimes on a wild goose chase, but always going, never resting, until worn out with hunger and fatigue they were almost ready to sink exhausted on the streets. Many of them had not taken a mouthful of food for twenty-four hours; many had bleeding feet, and

Deputy Superintendent Dixon states that he saw officers that night, and on the nights following, take off their boots in order to empty them of the blood which had been accumulating in them for hours. Officers who went through those days of tribulation, still on the force, will say that this is no exaggerated picture. The oppressive heat added to their sufferings, and it became evident all too soon—dreadful discovery as it was!—that the police were unable to meet the emergency.

The emergency never would have arisen had this riot been snuffed out when it first made its appearance. The Monday night mass meeting was the first mistake; the order to deal gently with the mobs Tuesday morning was the second mistake, the failure to make an example of some of the rioters during the afternoon was the greatest mistake of all. The opportunity for suppressing the troubles had slipped from the hands of the mayor and the superintendent. The police alone could no longer be depended upon to restore peace, or to maintain it!

Captains Seavey, O'Donnell, Gund and Johnson, and Lieutenants Blettner, Simmons, Callahan, Bell, Hathaway, Gerbing and Baus had been in active command of details sent out to disperse the rioters, and had done the very best they could, but without success, to crush out the riot. Their hands were tied. They had the privilege only of making a display of force, not of using it. The mobs found this out, and treated the policemen accordingly. They insulted, ridiculed and stoned the men with perfect impunity. "No blood must be spilled," said the kind-hearted mayor, and it came to the point where the only blood being spilled, or likely to be spilled, was that which flowed through the veins of the policemen.

The streets were flooded with circulars on Tuesday afternoon announcing that another great mass meeting of workingmen would be held on Market street, between Madison and Washington, that evening. The business people and

the law abiding citizens generally demanded of the mayor
that this meeting should be prohibited, and Superintendent
Hickey finally received instructions to prevent the gathering.
By 8 o'clock that evening another tremendous crowd had
assembled and the inflammatory speeches had begun. The
greatest alarm prevailed throughout the city, for it was
feared that this meeting would lead to more terrible results
than any that had yet been experienced. Lieutenant Gerbing in command of 50 men, and Lieutenant Baus with 25 men,
were honored with the execution of the chief's orders to
break up this meeting. Those on the outskirts of the crowd
observed the advancing column of blue-coats some time before their appearance became known to the vast multitude
which was packed tightly between Madison street and the
tunnel entrance. Without any preliminary flourish, Lieutenant Gerbing advanced front on the crowd and opened a
fusilade of blank cartridges, followed immediately and rapidly by three or four others. The panic-stricken crowd
stampeded immediately, tramping each other down, yelling
for mercy, swearing, howling, but ever scrambling or running toward the tunnel, through which several thousand
rushed over to the West Side. The police advanced in
splendid order, forming a line almost completely across the
wide street at this point, now and then sending a parting
salute of harmless gunpowder after the flying mob. Some
resistance was shown here and there, but the clubs were
brought into play, and in less than ten minutes the square
was as quiet as a country graveyard.

The firing had been heard throughout the South Side,
for half a mile, and over on the West Side, and all sorts of
wild rumors were set afloat immediately. The police had
mowed down the mob! Three hundred were killed and
twice that number wounded! Market street was covered
with the dead, the dying and the injured! The police had
likewise suffered dreadful losses! Etc., etc., etc.

After the mob had been dispersed quiet reigned su-

preme; the streets were deserted and an oppressive calm
pervaded the entire community. The worst had not come,
and everybody seemed to feel it. The rioters, learning that
blank cartridges only had been used in the Market street
charge, were disgusted with themselves for running away,
and the communistic leaders took advantage of this fact to
inspire the rabble with the belief that if they would only
stand firmly together, the police might easily be overpowered.
The demagogues, too, were loud in their denunciations of the
mayor and police for daring to interfere with "a meeting of
peaceable citizens," and for trampling upon "the right of
free speech," and workingmen were told that if they submitted quietly to this outrage they must expect henceforth
to be treated as slaves by their masters and the hireling
police.

Mayor Heath began to realize the danger at last, and now
in response to the indignant demands of the people, expressed through the press, he determined to crush out the
riot at any cost. His first move was to call upon the law-
abiding citizens of every ward in the city to form themselves into armed organizations for the preservation of the
peace and the protection of life and property; he appealed
to the governor, and the first and second regiments were
called out. All other military organizations were asked to
come forward and assist the municipal authorities, and all
responded; over three hundred special policemen were
sworn in, armed and assigned to regular patrol duty in
place of the regulars who were now on active duty far from
their beats; arms and ammunition were contributed by citizens in immense quantities, and stored at the City Hall.
Deputy Superintendent Dixon took command of the forces
on the outside. Lieut. Frederick Ebersold was made quartermaster, military regulations and discipline were introduced;
the street car, teaming companies, wholesale houses, and
private individuals gave the use of their horses to the city,
and cavalry companies were organized—the whole town was

aroused, either for defensive or offensive purposes, and Chicago presented the appearance of a city in a state of seige. Superintendent Hickey estimates that on Wednesday there were not less than 20,000 men under arms. Gen. Joseph T. Torrence, commanding the military operations, established his headquarters in the office of the superintendent of police.

On Wednesday morning the rioters were more aggressive than ever before. They committed several dastardly assaults upon workingmen who declined to join their ranks; they destroyed a vast amount of property in outlying manufactories; they attempted to set fire to one or two planing mills; they succeeded in burning down one building; they flourished revolvers, shotguns and rifles; they expressed their determination to take possession of the city and wipe out all authority.

In the lumber district they assembled in great numbers and from there moved toward McCormick's factory, a place that has ever attracted the attention and experienced the enmity of mobs. These agricultural implement works were surrounded by about 900 men. Lieut. Vesey, with a squad of policemen, was ordered to disperse them. He was reinforced by Lieut. Callahan, who commanded 36 men. The mob used stones and other missiles freely and fought the policemen desperately; but Vesey and Callahan held their men under restraint until the proper moment arrived, when they swooped down upon the mob, demoralizing it completely. Two patrolmen were seriously injured and a number of the strikers were wounded. The first blood had been spilled by the police. Vesey and Callahan proved themselves to be brave, cool, and competent commanders during this little engagement; the law-abiding people began to look toward them with confidence, and they were from this time on entrusted with the most difficult and important undertakings.

Volunteer cavalry and infantry companies were immediately dispatched to the "Black Road" region, with instructions to patrol the surrounding district and prevent the mob from reassembling. A mob had collected also at the corner of Sherman and Taylor streets—a hard locality at that time—and after organizing itself in a semi-military fashion, marched north on the river bank to Van Buren street bridge, crossing over to the West Side, going north on Beach street to Polk, and driving workingmen from their benches along the route. At the west end of Polk street bridge, Lieut. Ebersold, with 35 men who had been sent in pursuit, intercepted and dispersed them, without loss on either side. In the meantime a mob had collected at the Illinois Central elevator, near the lake shore. Lieut. Bell, with 50 men, and Sergeant Brennan, with a squad from the Central station, were ordered to this point, but found it no easy matter to disperse the crowd. Another mob, at Fifteenth and Dearborn streets, were stopping the street cars; the North Side tailors were out on a strike and closing up the merchant tailoring establishments, and Lieutenants Bell and Baus were sent respectively to each of these points, where they succeeded in quelling all disturbances. There were probably fifty different mobs moving at this time, and it was out of the question for the police to follow them up. The rioters paid no attention whatever to the "specials" or volunteers. Superintendent Hickey, in speaking on this point, says: "Special policemen are comparatively worthless for quelling disturbances or dispersing crowds, for however good their intentions or efforts, the truth is that twenty policemen in uniform are better and more effective for the purpose than fifty specials in plain dress. This was clearly proven when a mob had congregated on the North Side. Most of the regular force at that time being on duty elsewhere, a squad of twenty specials were sent to disperse the crowd, but the rioters defiantly turned upon them and they were forced to retire to the station. Lieutenant Hathaway, in command of fifteen men from the regular force, dispersed them without serious trouble, although the crowd and the excitement had greatly increased in the meantime." The windows of the shot tower, Crane Brothers Mfg. Co., Carlyle Mason's work shop, and other places were broken in by the mob, as were also three of the North Side tanneries. The rioters dodged the police around corners, scattered and reformed again and by their maneuvering simply tired the force out. It was impossible to get them concentrated. This the police endeavored to accomplish, and Captains Seavey and Johnson detailed squads of patrolmen at different points with the view of hedging in and consolidating the mobs, so that they could be attacked as a whole; but this idea had to be abandoned. All the saloons were now ordered closed, and the situation every moment becoming more serious, the mayor requested the proprietors of all the manufactories to resume business, promising them protection, and ordering all idlers off the streets, under penalty of suffering in case of a conflict with the rioters. Messrs. J. V. Farwell & Co., Field, Leiter & Co., Gen. Stockton, C. B. Holmes (South Division street car company), James K. Lake (West Division street car company) and many others, loaned their teams and wagons to the city for the transportation of the policemen from point to point. Handbills were again distributed calling upon all workingmen to assemble on Market street that (Wednesday) evening, and a request was made by "The Workingmen's Party of the United States," that the meeting be allowed and given police protection. This request was denied and the meeting proclaimed. Precautions were taken this time to prevent the assembling of the crowd. A force of 150 men was assembled at headquarters, and Lieut. Gerbing, with 50 men, was ordered to proceed to the place of the proposed meeting and prevent the gathering of a crowd. This was about 8 p. m., and already about 2,000 persons were assembled; stands for the speakers had been erected and the square was illuminated with calcium lights. Lieut. Gerbing's company formed as on the previous night and drove the mob before them. This time, however, the clubs in the hands of the policemen were freely used and many a head was broken; one of the loudest-mouthed of the speakers had his skull cracked; the stands were torn down and thrown into the river, and the streets were again cleared completely. Market street was now occupied by Lieutenants Hood, Blettner, Baus and Gerbing, who commanded a force of about 200 men. It was expected that the West and North Side contingents of rioters would soon be along to participate in the meeting. This expectation was partly fulfilled, but before the West Side mob could cross over the Randolph street bridge they were confronted by a line of police drawn up at Market and Randolph streets, attacked and driven back. "A desperate hand to hand fight occurred here," says the official report, "the police hammering them [the rioters] mercilessly with their clubs, and the rioters throwing stones and pieces of coal which they got from a yard close by. It may to some appear strange why the police had not fired indiscriminately into them by this time, but when it is remembered that right in front of the mob and close to the drums and banners, which were in advance of them, there was a crowd probably of one hundred and fifty small boys and children, and that a volley fired into them at that time would unavoidably have killed innocent children and not the rioters, I think it will be conceded that the police acted with prudence and excellent judgment in the emergency. As it was, and after the rioters had been repeatedly repulsed and returned, Lieut. Gerbing finally ordered his command to shoot over their heads. A volley was instantly fired in the direction of the mob, and although not with fatal results, it had a good effect, for they at once disbanded and were forced in opposite directions, some being driven across the bridge and others toward the lake."

A mob of about four hundred men had assembled in the meantime at the round house of the Chicago, Burlington & Quincy railroad, on West Sixteenth street, and proceeded to smash the windows and wreck the rolling stock of the company. Several cars and locomotives were ditched, and the rioters, it seems, had planned to set fire to the building and destroy its contents. Capt. Seavey was notified at once, and ordered Lieut. Callahan with a squad of policemen to the scene. The men were crowded into omnibusses and driven rapidly toward the round house. Arriving there the mob opened fire on the 'busses, using revolvers and stones, and the driver was thrown off his seat, breaking his arm in the fall. In a moment more the most desperate attack thus far had begun. As the policemen left the omnibusses they were met with a perfect shower of bullets and a hailstorm of stones. Lieut. Callahan took in the situation at a glance. The mob was swelling every moment until it now numbered some three thousand rioters. Many of these had taken part in the trouble at McCormick's the day before; they knew Callahan and bore him a grudge. He drew his men up in line and parried the bullets and stones as best he could, and endeavored in every way to gain time. He had sent in for reinforcements, as he dreaded to attack such an immense crowd, composed mainly of the most desperate ruffians, with such a small force of men. Sergeant Ryan with twenty men had been patroling the district near the round house, and, hearing of Callahan's position, hastened to his assistance. The stones and bullets from the mob began to fly thicker and thicker around the heads of the policemen, and finding that the rioters were determined upon ugly work, Lieut. Callahan ordered an attack.

The policemen acted like old soldiers and went into the fight eagerly. A volley from their ranks, which laid a number of the rioters low, was followed by a charge, the officers keeping up a pretty steady fire. The mob responded with their revolvers, missiles and yells, holding their ground pugnaciously. Callahan's command, however, kept up the fire, and gave every evidence of being prepared for a long engagement. Several of the brave fellows had fallen, some seriously injured, and this served to infuriate their companions. With one wild shout the policemen finally precipitated themselves upon the rioters, using their revolvers in one hand and their batons in the other, doing terrible execution everywhere, until the solid body of rioters in front of them broke and scattered, the great majority of them retreating toward the Halsted street viaduct.

The fight lasted about half an hour, and Lieut. Callahan, finding that his men were out of ammunition, and that many of them were injured, returned to the Twelfth street station. They presented a sorry sight as they marched back. But two or three of them escaped injury of some kind. Nearly all were badly bruised by flying stones, and the following officers of Callahan's command were more or less seriously injured by bullets, stones or other missiles:

Patrolman Patrick O'Hara, died since by drowning.

Patrolman A. Samolsky, at present a constable.

Patrolman Patrick Shanly, at present on the force.

Patrolman Thomas Dooley, at present on the force.

Patrolman Thomas N. Dane, whereabouts unknown.

Patrolman Matthew Twohy, died subsequently.

Patrolman William Flynn (who shot Fitzgerald at the polls), still on the force.

Patrolman George Demar, at present on the day squad.

Patrolman James B. Carroll, whereabouts unknown.

Patrolman S. S. McCormick, whereabouts unknown.

Patrolman Thomas McCann, whereabouts unknown.

Patrolman Michael Conneroy, at present on the force.

Patrolman Edward Laughlin, now lieutenant on the force.

Patrolman James Lacy, died subsequently.

Patrolman Henry Gant, whereabouts unknown.

In the battle at the round house James Flashuck, shot with a pistol ball, died next morning; Wensen Movoskosky, shot with a pistol ball, died in half an hour; five others, whose names and residences it was impossible to discover, were shot and died from the effects of their wounds, and about twenty-five were seriously wounded. Lieut. Callahan so distinguished himself in this and other struggles with the rioters, that his name became one of the most prominent on the force. Citizens vied with each other in doing honor to his pluck and ability. After the excitement had cooled down, the citizens of the West Twelfth street district presented him with an elegant and costly gold watch and chain. The watch bore the inscription: "To Lieutenant M. Callahan, from the citizens of Chicago, Sept. 11, 1877, for efficiency, honesty and fidelity." Justice Scully, in presenting this testimonial, made an address most flattering to the gallant lieutenant, and the latter replied in a neat speech. Later on his name was mentioned conspicuously for the superintendency, but at his request his claims to this advancement were not pressed. He had made many bitter enemies, as well as substantial and enthusiastic friends, by his conduct during the riots, but the former were more active than the latter, and they never rested until, upon a change of administration, they succeeded in having him reduced to a sergeantcy, a position which he holds at present, at the West Madison street station. He is a man of excellent education, good address and fine physique. He bore his reduction with the same good grace that he bore his laurels in the riot of '77.

CHAPTER X.

THE YEAR 1877—PROGRESS AND FINISH OF THE RIOT—THE NUM-
EROUS CONFLICTS ON THE HALSTED STREET VIADUCT—A WARLIKE
DISPLAY—THE MILITARY, VOLUNTEERS AND POLICE—BLOODY WORK
BETWEEN TWELFTH STREET AND ARCHER AVENUE—DIXON AT
THE FRONT—A HEROIC BOY—THE TURNER HALL EPISODE—A
SPEEDY RESTORATION OF PEACE—THE MILITARY REGIME IN THE
DEPARTMENT.

The rioters who had assembled and suffered a repulse
from Lieut. Callahan's heroic little command in the vicinity
of the Chicago, Burlington & Quincy round house, proved
later to be a wing of the grand mob, which, by this time,
was consolidating on Halsted street, between the viaduct
and Archer avenue. At length it seemed probable that the
two or three hundred scattered detachments would become
centralized, and that a crushing blow might be dealt the uprising as a whole. A force of 200 policemen, under command of Lieuts. Blettner, Macauley and Bell, had been dispatched to the ground, with instructions to show the mob
no mercy. The authorities had come to the conclusion that
mercy to the mob meant danger to all peaceable citizens,
and now they were determined to make amends for the mistakes committed at the start. Previous to the arrival of the
police, however, the mob had been carrying things at their
will. The first street car that attempted to cross the viaduct was pelted with a shower of stones, the conductor and
driver both driven from their positions, the horses lashed
into madness until they ran away, and finally the car was
overturned at the junction of Halsted and Evans streets,
where it was "pulled to pieces by a pack of howling young

devils," says the *Tribune's* account, "contained within boys not older than 14 years." The other cars that arrived at the viaduct were stopped, the conductors rifled of the contents of their pockets, and the passengers compelled to leave their seats and walk. M. J. Pribyl, a dealer in firearms at 522 Halsted street, had paid no attention to the request of the superintendent in relation to hiding dangerous weapons from view. He had a fine display of revolvers, guns, etc., in his window. The store was pillaged by the mob, which carried off thirty-five guns, as many revolvers, and as many more pistols. Most of those who assisted in gutting Pribyl's place were thugs and thieves. The workingmen had nothing to do with it. South of the viaduct the mob assumed serious aspects at several points. The crowd of howling young devils, who were pulling the open street car to pieces, extinguished the street lights (for it was now quite dark), which the mob only allowed the lamplighters to light, after much discussion, in the first place. It became rumored then that pillaging was about to commence, and immediately every shopkeeper along the street locked his doors, barred his windows, and prepared to defend his property. A crowd of young men and boys marched upon the hardware store of E. R. Lott, No. 785 Halsted street. The iron bars were wrenched from the windows, the shutters forced off, the windows broken, and some one, hoisted through an aperture thus made, succeeded in opening the door. The rabble, principally composed of young thieves, rushed in and commenced the work of plunder. The gas was lit, and the older persons in the mob seized the most valuable goods on the shelves and in the show cases. A large amount of cutlery and small hardware was carried off in a buggy, and the thieves only desisted when the articles left were too heavy to be taken away by hand.

The mob appeared to be thinning out at the viaduct, and an attempt was made to run the street cars, but the crowd would not permit it. The police arrived about this time, coming from the south, and the mob quickly scattered. As the blue-coats passed the point where the cars were wrecked, several shots were fired out of one of the buildings, but no harm was done. The police marched along, clearing the sidewalks as they advanced across the Halsted street viaduct, but encountered no more opposition until they came to the corner of Halsted and Fifteenth streets, where a large crowd of laborers had assembled. The police formed in line here, charged the crowd with their clubs, and scattered them in all directions. Several, who stubbornly held their ground or resisted, were pretty badly beaten. The mob gathered again about a block away and marched west, hooting and yelling as they went. In a few minutes Lieut. Hood, commanding about 100 men, came down Halsted to Twenty-second street, clearing everything before him. The first three companies remained in the vicinity of Thirteenth street, which was considered the most dangerous point, while guards were placed at all the street crossings, to prevent the rioters from again gathering on Halsted. Besides the casualties already mentioned as having occurred at the round house, a large number of persons were severely, some fatally, injured, during the various attacks of the evening on Halsted street.

During Wednesday, mobs had disturbed the peace and created a great deal of alarm on the South and North Sides, but no considerable damage was done. It was evident to all that the worst had not come, but it was more evident still that the city was only naif-way prepared to meet the real danger ahead. A mass meeting was held in the Moody and Sankey tabernacle, which had been erected on the site of the old gas works, fronting on Monroe, between Franklin and Market streets, on the afternoon of Thursday. The immense hall was packed with the leading business men of the city, and law-abiding people generally. It was called to order by the Rev. Robert Collyer, who nominated Hon. C. B. Farwell for chairman. Mr. Farwell, on taking the chair, suggested that the wisest thing to do was to appoint a strong committee of three men from each division of the city, and let them attend to such matters in organization as may be deemed necessary, after consulting with the mayor. Gen. Drew said he had a proposition to offer, which had already been approved by the mayor and Deputy Superintendent Dixon, to the effect, that the mayor call for 5,000 volunteers, or more as they may offer, to report forthwith at headquarters, there to be organized into companies of 100 each, to be placed in charge of competent officers—men who had served in the rebellion; let them be armed with heavy canes or clubs, or, if they have revolvers, let them bring them along; organize them as fast as they report, and let them be turned over to the superintendent of police as special policemen.

While Gen. Drew was speaking, the following proclamation from the mayor arrived, and it was read to the meeting:

MAYOR'S OFFICE, CHICAGO, JULY 25, 1872—3:30 o'clock.—In my proclamation of yesterday I requested all good citizens to organize in their respective districts and blocks and do patrol duty in their immediate neighborhood. Though this request has to a large extent been complied with, I must again remind the people that such organization must be made thorough and effective. I also request 5,000 good and experienced citizens, composed as largely as possible of ex-soldiers, to report at headquarters, to do such general duties as may be assigned them.

I again warn all idlers and curious people, especially women and children, to keep off the public highways, as the authorities in case of necessity will not be responsible for consequences.

The public and citizens are ordered to arrest all disorderly persons and to take them to the police stations in the vicinity. The aldermen of the city are requested to take charge of such organizations and provide rendezvous for the same.   M. HEATH, Mayor.

This proclamation was greeted with cheers, and Gen. Drew, continuing, said that it covered the ground precisely. The necessity for organization was making itself felt more strongly every moment. "With the discipline most necessary in cases of this kind," said Gen. Drew, "the assistant (deputy) superintendent of police assured me he could put down every demonstration inside of 24 hours, and I have no hesitation in asserting that it can be done. I would also, in addition to that, have the military held in reserve, in case of any disturbance beyond the control of these men, so that they could be brought to their rescue, and I undertake to say that there is no question that this whole demonstration can be put down and law and order and peace be preserved here, and everybody go about his business." [Applause].

Hon. Carter H. Harrison, then a member of congress, seconded the suggestions of Gen. Drew, and urged that every manufacturer in Chicago be requested to resume business next morning. "Idleness, it is said, is hell's workshop," cried Mr. Harrison, "and when men are idle the devil's hammer—whisky—is employed. After that no man can be held responsible for the consequences. [Cheers]. The people of Chicago are industrious, the laborers are workingmen of the truest stamp, and to-day there is the remarkable phenomenon exhibited of a city of 500,000 men, women and children—a city composed of industrious workingmen—controlled by a mob of 200 or 300 idlers and ragamuffins. [Cheers]. It is not laboring men who are making the strike. A few laboring men commenced it; but it is the idlers, thieves and ruffians who are carrying it on. * * * We have stopped the railroads, and what can Chicago do without the railroads? We cannot get bread without them."

The fear of a failure in the supply of breadstuffs had begun to make itself felt; people were already talking of an impending famine inside the city, as not a train of cars had been moved for three days, and there was little prospect of the blockade being raised. It should be remembered that the railroad strike extended to all the towns and cities within a radius of 700 miles of Chicago, and that other towns and cities were, like Chicago, partly or wholly in the hands of mobs.

"I have noticed," said Mr. Harrison, in closing his remarks, "that when the police have arrested a rioter or a striker, not one single word was said against it. When the policeman lays his hands on a man's shoulder and says, 'You are my prisoner,' the feeling of law-abiding reverence for those who are the officers of the law will make the man go to prison. Keep your military back. If necessary let them stay to protect banks or waterworks, but don't let the soldiers shoot down defenseless women. The blue-coated man of the police, and you who are going to enroll as his assistants, when a man attempts to stop another from working, can go and arrest him for doing violence to the law, and by to-morrow night we will have peace in this great city of the West." [Applause].

Robert Collyer said that he had lived in Chicago for 20 years and he considered this the most serious time he had ever seen. "What our friend has just said is true—we are cowed by an insignificant mob. The great wheels of commerce and trade are stopped. I think our mayor has done well in his large forbearance. There are some fearful evils that might have been sprung on us before we were ready, but we must be ready this afternoon to meet any crisis that may come. I cannot expect to live long," said the great preacher, solemnly. "I thought I might live twenty years, I would like to. Do you know, fellow-citizens, as God lives and as my soul lives, I would rather die in twenty minutes in defense of order and of our homes against these men than live twenty years as happy a life as I have lived all these fifty years! [Applause]. I wish our mayor in his wisdom and courage had suggested larger measures. My thought was this: That we should have this committee that has been mentioned to consult and act with the mayor as a committee of defense, and have sub-committees in the different districts and wards of the city. We should then organize a force of 30,000 special constables and we should subscribe $1,000,000 as a fund to draw on to take care of those men who cannot take care of themselves. I am poor, but I am ready to give $200 to begin with." [Applause].

The reverend gentleman moved that a committee of nine,

to consist of three from each district of the city, be chosen to act with the mayor in the public defense, and the motion was adopted.

Hon. Leonard Swett, in the course of a brief speech, made a suggestion which was acted upon later and bore good fruit. He said: "Now, I am told by persons familiar with the army officers here that if the mayor of this city were in a proper manner to request them, the government of the United States would within twenty-four hours place substantially a regiment of soldiers in this city. * * * * I throw out this suggestion for what it is worth. I understand that the government itself cannot take the initiative. I understand it will not send troops here unless requested to do so. But I am told that if the citizens want the protection of the government, that it is ready and will be immediately extended. I suppose the mayor, perhaps, would not like to act without *an expression of opinion*. The object of this meeting is to express opinions. Therefore it would seem to me proper that this meeting should ask the mayor, who knows all the measures that have been inaugurated, to call upon the government to send troops here immediately, so that we may have no outrage, so that we may not undertake to restore the business, as they are now undertaking in Pittsburg, after the damage is done."

Henry Greenebaum suggested vigorous measures, and Col. Roberts offered the following, which was adopted:

Resolved, That this meeting is in full sympathy with the proclamation of the mayor, calling for 5,000 men, and that we will at once report at police headquarters for duty.

Ex-Mayor Boone, who had suppressed the lager beer riot, was in the audience, and in response to demands for a speech said that if the police were armed they could dispose of the rioters within twenty-four hours.

The city council that night held a special meeting, and passed resolutions calling upon all good citizens to aid the mayor and police in the work of maintaining peace; to enroll themselves as special policemen, and to obey carefully the orders of the mayor. Ald. Lawler at the same meeting offered the following:

WHEREAS, It is a well-known fact that thousands of workingmen are idle in the city of Chicago at the present time, whose families are suffering for the necessaries of life, all for the need of employment for their labor, and who believe that the city authorities should provide labor for them by immediately commencing work upon the city improvements for which the appropriations have been made; therefore, be it

Resolved, That the mayor and comptroller be and they are hereby directed and instructed by the city council of the city of Chicago to borrow the sum of .$500,000, the same to be applied toward commencing the erection of the city's portion of the new Court House, and also for completing the sewers for which an order was passed May, 1877.

The matter was referred to the finance committee, and favorable action was taken upon it soon afterward. A committee of five aldermen, consisting of Gilbert, Cullerton, Rawleigh, Baumgarten and Kirk was appointed to co-operate with the mayor.

The communists continued to hold meetings, and their headquarters were continually surrounded and crowded by a most vicious and dangerous class of ruffians. During Thursday the following circular was issued:

WORKINGMEN OF CHICAGO.

The success of our honest effort to increase wages depends entirely upon your good conduct and peaceable though firm behavior. We hereby declare that any riotous action in our meetings will be immediately put down by us.

The grand principles of Humanity and Popular Sovereignty need no violence to sustain them. For the sake of the cause which we hold most dear, let every honest workingman help us to preserve order. Let us show the world that, with all our grievances and misery, we can still act like men and good citizens.

THE COMMITTEE,
Workingmen's Party of the United States.

Greatly to the surprise of citizens in general and to the satisfaction of all law-abiding citizens in particular, two companies of United States regulars—" E " and " F " of the Twenty-second Infantry—arrived at the Chicago, Milwaukee & St. Paul depot, West Side, during the afternoon. They were fresh from the Indian campaign on the plains, and were rushed through at full speed, stopping only an hour or so in St. Paul, whence they came direct to this city. They were tanned and grizzled, with unwashed faces and unkempt hair, their clothing covered with dust an inch thick. Capt. Dickie, under whose command they were, was in no better condition upon arrival than his men. The accommodations on the trains were very poor, and they had no opportunity of cleaning up from the time they commenced their forced ride to Chicago. They were met by Lieut.-Col. Frederick D. Grant, who brought orders from Gen. Sheridan, and the companies were formed into marching line, and led over the bridge and down Madison street. Here a great crowd, composed to some extent of portions of the Canal street mob, which had become disintegrated, lined the streets, but no disturbance occurred. On the way down cheer after cheer went up from the business blocks on both sides of the street, and the soldiers received many a "God bless you." From the tops of the highest buildings, where shoemakers and other tradesmen who had not struck were at work, came the loudest cheers. The sight of armed men, enclosed in an armor of cartridges, cleared the way in front, but behind them came a mass of men, women and children that completely blocked the whole street. So small an affair as the arrival of two companies of United States troops was sufficient to attract thousands. Finding that the troops were going directly to the Exposition building, the vast crowd soon dispersed quietly. The regulars were well supplied with ammunition. Supplies had been quietly arriving during the previous twenty-four hours. Gen. Sheridan had made all preparations for meeting any request which the mayor might make, or any emergency; in fact, he had anticipated the wishes of the people. The "boys in blue" were stationed for a while at the Armory building during the afternoon, but they were not called upon to act. Four additional companies, under command of Capt. Clark, arrived from Omaha next day. The first and second regiments were under arms all this time, but as the feeling was still strongly in favor of allowing police methods free scope, they did little more than guard duty. The first regiment was ordered to be ready for active duty at 3 a. m. Thursday, and the second regiment boys were also informed that there would be hot work for them on the following day.

All through the early part of Wednesday night the city was alive with rumors of dreadful work on Halsted street. These rumors reached police headquarters, and squads of regulars and specials were sent out to reinforce the jaded men on duty along that thoroughfare. Whenever the rioters made their appearance they were clubbed or driven into their holes, but no great or serious disturbance occurred. All the bridges leading to the West Side were swung, the tunnels were guarded, and armed men patrolled the down-town streets. At every corner two or three or half a dozen "specials" could be met, but the South Side remained through the night as quiet as a graveyard. There were no cars running, the hackmen had long since declined to drive for love or money, pedestrians were few and far between, and the only busy centers in the city were the newspaper and telegraph offices.

" The policemen of this city." said the *Tribune* next morning, " are doing their duty faithfully, intelligently and manfully in this trying emergency. In every instance where they encountered violent mobs yesterday, they dispersed them by their sudden and resolute charges. The result is an eloquent testimonial to their drill, discipline and *esprit de corps*."

All this time Deputy Superintendent Joseph Dixon was chafing under the inactivity at headquarters. Policemen were constantly reporting with torn clothing, battered faces and bruised bodies. The rioters insulted the officers everywhere and heaped outrages upon them. It was perfectly safe to hurl a stone at a passing squad of policemen, for the men were instructed not to fire, and it was out of the question for them to break ranks. The rioters began to perceive that they had the policemen at a disadvantage, and they lost no time in making the best of their opportunity. In a square fight, when the mob was drawn up in line against the police, the latter routed them every time, but it was the firing from ambush, the guerilla warfare carried on by the ruffians who had joined the strikers, that the men dreaded. Dixon was in favor of making an example out of the first solid body of rioters the police might come in collision with. There had been too much child's play, and it became a question now whether the mob or the police force should go down.

Dixon was a police officer of iron nerve, brave and as perfectly inflexible in the discharge of his duty as John Bonfield. He was born in Scotland, in 1835, his mother being a native of that country and his father an Englishman. The family came to America, and to Chicago in 1836. Young Dixon attended school here, his first teacher being a man named Murphy; afterward he received instruction from Prof. Tyler, and later at the hands of A. G. Wilder, attending the public school in the old St. James Episcopal church on Cass street. As he approached manhood he learned the carpenter trade, (there are more representatives of this trade on the police force to-day than of any other, many of the leading officers having worked at the bench). He was known as a pretty wild young fellow, his weakness taking the form of running away from home. He shipped on the lakes, worked on the Mississippi, and had seen Memphis, Boston, Philadelphia and New York, on his own account, before he was 17 years of age. In 1858, under Jacob Rehm, he was appointed complaint clerk in the city marshal's office, held the place one week and was detailed for detective duty. He remained under Rehm, doing good service until the reorganization of the force, and was appointed a regular detective by the board of police commissioners. When Turtle took

charge he dropped out, and remained off the force until
Rehm again assumed command, when he was reappointed.
He was made assistant or deputy superintendent in 1874, under Hickey, and remained in that capacity during the Colvin,
Heath and seven months of the Harrison administrations, a
part of the time, toward the close, as acting superintendent,
Superintendent Seavey being too ill to perform his duties.
Upon demanding his resignation, Mr. Harrison intimated
that there were grave charges of irregularity against Dixon,
but upon being called upon to make them public, he refused
to do so and declined to give the retiring officer any satisfaction on this score. It was generally understood that the
removal was the result entirely of political causes. After
leaving the police force Mr. Dixon was made warden of the
county hospital. While acting in this capacity, he was approached with the proposition afterward made to and unfortunately accepted by McGarigle, to become a go-between for
the county commissioners and contractors. Declining to
have anything to do with the crooked transactions of the
board, a conspiracy was hatched to get rid of him. Fred.
Bipper, who afterward had a hand in the McGarigle case, it is
said, was one of the leaders in this movement to ruin Dixon,
and a fellow named Stevens, who had sworn to frauds
alleged to have been perpetrated by the warden, was afterward sentenced to the penitentiary for perjury, admitting his
guilt, and proving to the satisfaction of Judge Sidney
Smith and State's Attorney Mills that Dixon was the victim
of a most villainous plot.

Joseph Dixon did much toward unravelling the celebrated
La Grange murder mystery, and fastened the crime to the
satisfaction of all but the jury upon Joseph St. Peters.
Dixon searched until he traced the pistol which St. Peters
had used to a West Side pawn-shop, and from this weapon he
produced perfect *fac similes* of the ball which had entered the
heart of Alvina Clark. There was no question but that the
unfaithful wife of the latter and St. Peters had planned and

executed the murder. The murderer was able to prove an alibi, by jumping on a freight train, and arriving in the city only a short time after the murder had been committed. Dixon was connected with the hunting down of the Walworth (Wis.) bank robbers, arresting Joe Brown for the crime, after a desperate struggle. "Buck" Holbrook was Brown's pal, and was afterward killed at Hennepin, Ill.; he assisted in the breaking up of the notorious Stillwell gang, at Annawan, Ill.; he hunted down the murderer Zeigenmeyer, and cleared up the mystery of William Gumbleton's death, necessitating a trip to Germany and the display of consummate detective and diplomatic ability, all the surroundings and circumstances of which go to make the Zeigenmeyer case one of the most remarkable on record; he assisted materially in suppressing the "bread riot" in 1872; he was engaged in the celebrated Julius Wilche case ; with Sam Ellis exposed the guilt of the murderer John Biddle, following him to Milwaukee; brought the diamond robbers who plundered Giles Brothers to justice; helped to capture the great "pepper robber;" worked up the Sherry and Connolly case; had a hand in the Race murder case, and has probably sent more ruffians to the penitentiary than any single man ever connected with the Chicago police department. Dixon and Ellis, when they worked together, were the terror of thieves and burglars, forgers, confidence operators and murderers; they were recognized as the ablest detectives in the West, and they seldom failed in any of their undertakings.

Superintendent Hickey was an Irishman by birth, fairly well educated, intelligent and quick-witted. He entered the force in 1854, and displayed such ability that he soon achieved promotion. Retiring from the force shortly afterward, he became a police justice, which position he filled with credit, and he re-entered the force in 1861. He rose to a sergeantcy and then to a captaincy, and was recognized as one of the best executive officers in the department. On

October 4, 1875, he was appointed superintendent of police by Mayor Colvin, vice Jacob Rehm resigned, and the same day Joseph Dixon was appointed deputy superintendent. Several attempts had been made to smirch the reputation of Hickey, the most bitter was during Washburn's superintendency, when he resigned, pending an investigation of charges of corruption brought against him. The board of police found him innocent, and ordered his reinstatement. Later on, similar charges were brought against him by the McMullen Brothers, proprietors of an evening newspaper, the *Post and Mail*, but he was again vindicated, and held his position until removed by Mayor Harrison, when Capt. Seavey was appointed in his stead.

Dixon and Hickey had always pulled together harmoniously, and each expressed the greatest respect for the other. But Dixon saw that Hickey was being influenced by the mayor, and was making a mistake in the management of affairs during the riot of '77. As soon as the news of the Pittsburg riot reached Chicago, Dixon called upon Captain Tobey quietly, and induced him to organize a battery, which he did, with one gun, using an express wagon for a caisson. Learning that there were one hundred stands of arms stored in McCormick's hall belonging to the government, he sent Major Heinzeman (of the police force) and Lieut. Gerbing to get them. They reported back with one hundred and twenty-five stands. He pushed all his arrangements in the same quiet manner, and had his plans laid so that the riot could have been nipped in the bud, had not orders been issued that no arms should be displayed or used. The trouble went on increasing until Thursday, and then the deputy superintendent informed his chief and the mayor that it was suicidal to play with the mob any longer. Mounting a horse—the first one he could find—and taking with him a mixed company of specials and regulars, he made for the South Halsted street viaduct.

Superintendent Hickey's report tells us that at 6 o'clock

on Thursday morning all necessary details were arranged, and Captain Seavey was ordered to detail a force of 75 men to patrol the lumber district and southwest portion of the city. About 8 o'clock it was ascertained that a large body of rioters were gathering at the Sixteenth street viaduct, on Halsted street. Sergeant Ryan and Officer Ward, in command of 25 men each, were patroling this vicinity and went to disperse them, which was easily done, and the police marched in the direction of the lumber district and the Eighteenth street bridge. Shortly after this the mob again commenced to assemble at the viaduct, and a squad of police was sent to disperse them. Upon the appearance of the police the mob yelled, commenced throwing stones, etc. It soon became warm in the vicinity, for the police returned the fire. The mob made a movement as if to overwhelm the police, but the blue-coats made a bold stand and several rioters were punctured with cold lead. The firing on both sides was continuous for some time, and the police, having exhausted their supply of cartridges, retired slowly and in good order. Reinforcements arrived from the Twelfth street station, about 25 men, but soon after the information came that this force, all told, was insufficient to cope with the mob, which was gaining in strength every moment. Captain Seavey was ordered to the front with all his available force, and instructions were sent him to show the rioters no mercy, but to hold his ground, and that reinforcements to any extent were coming to his assistance. Captain O'Donnell was also ordered to send all his available force to report to him (Seavey), and 50 men from the fourth precinct, in command of Lieut Bishoff, and 50 from the Central station, in command of Sergeant Brennan, were also sent to the scene of disturbance.

When the combined force advanced on the mob again, every policeman in the ranks seemed determined to make the rioters feel that matters had become serious. They moved in a solid column, taking in the entire width of the street, and sweeping everything before them. The rioters jumped over fences, sneaked away through back yards and alleys, and in less than five minutes the field was in possession of the lawful authorities.

It was evident from the opening that the territory between Canalport avenue and the viaduct was to be the scene of nearly all the rioting of the day, as there was a very vicious gang of boys and young men in that neighborhood, and as there were rumors that a crowd from the stock yards intended coming down to their assistance, it became necessary to consolidate a large force of police and military in the vicinity. Deputy Superintendent Dixon was on the ground giving instructions to the captains, lieutenants and men, and personally supervising every movement. He impressed upon the officers the necessity of keeping cool, and of shooting to hit every time. "There must be no firing over the heads of the mob to-day," he cried, "we've got to crush out the riot to-day, or the riot will crush us out to-morrow. Are you ready? March!"

Two cavalry companies were the first to arrive as a support for the police, and these were followed by the second regiment, at the time composed almost entirely of young Irish-Americans. The regiment turned out about 300 strong and was under command of Col. Quirk. It was understood that the military were simply to look on and see the policemen do the work, the intention being not to interfere unless the regular peace preservers were driven to the wall. The mayor had also given the state soldiery to understand that should they open fire, they must direct their aim above the heads of the rioters. Col. Quirk's position was at once delicate, dangerous and awkward. His command in reality was under the protection of the police, and when the latter were off on a charge, or compelled to retreat up or down a side street, his men were pelted with stones and fired at from pistols in the hands of the mob. Two ten-pound guns manned by firemen and citizens were placed be-

tween two companies of the regiment, the intention being to
fire grape and canister into the mob if everything else
failed.

The entire military reserve halted at Twelfth and Halsted streets for a rest. In the meantime two squads of police and the cavalry patrolled Halsted street as far as the
viaduct. There was a large gathering of people just north
of the railroad track on Jefferson and Union streets, but
they offered no violence to any property, although many of
them were strikers. The police started in that direction, but
came back and marched across the viaduct, followed by the
cavalry, going out to the bridge over the South Branch, to
meet a mob from the stock yards and Bridgeport. Then
the officers and soldiers marched back to the viaduct where
the crowd would persist in taking possession of the south
approach. The structure was cleared once more, and the
police kept on up the street, being assaulted with stones now
and then, to which little or no attention was paid. Between
nearly all the houses on South Halsted street there were narrow openings or private passages, and in these boys, young
men and sometimes middle-aged men, concealed themselves
and threw stones at the policemen as they passed, immediately disappearing through the back yards.

The skirmishes on the viaduct and on the bridge only
brought from the South and upper portion of the West Side
crowds who flocked through mere idle curiosity to the viaduct. The viaduct was the center of interest, because it
spanned the tracks of the Chicago, Burlington & Quincy
railroad, the Chicago & Alton railroad and other lines, and
below were hundreds of cars, dozens of locomotives and the
army of railroad strikers. From this point a general survey
of the railroad tracks could be taken, and as every attempt of
the companies to move a car was frustrated by the strikers,
the mob on the viaduct cheered. From this point, also, passenger trains, which now and then succeeded in running the
gauntlet, were stoned and the windows smashed. Many pas-

Clearing out West Twelfth St

ner Hall in Riot of 1877 (p. 197).

sengers, mostly suburban residents, were injured by being struck with stones or splintered glass while passing the viaduct.

Superintendent Hickey arrived on the ground early, and apparently throwing off all restraint, went into the fight with the same determination that inspired Dixon and the other officers. The superintendent was an eye witness of the exciting scenes which took place on Halsted street that day, and he has given us a vivid picture of the struggle for supremacy between the police and the rioters. When the superintendent arrived on the scene he had at his command, and practically subject to his orders, the first regiment, under Col. W. T. Sherer, the second regiment, under Col. James Quirk, both under the immediate command of Gen. Joseph T. Torrence; two six-pound guns, ready for action, in command of Col. Bolton and Capt. Tobey; two companies of cavalry, and 350 policemen, regulars and specials. Upon the arrival of the military reinforcements the police were well nigh exhausted, and although they were in possession of the viaduct, the disorderly crowd was by no means dispersed, for Halsted street from Twelfth street to Archer avenue was densely packed. The curiosity-seekers swelled the crowd to immense proportions, and made the task of preserving order doubly difficult for the police. Many innocent persons, as usual, were clubbed severely, and some were shot, but the general opinion was that they deserved all the punishment they received.

After the collision on the viaduct the police advanced south on Halsted street, dispersing the crowd as they went. A mob had started from the packing houses at the stock yards at an early hour, intending to cause a strike at the rolling mills and march to the assistance of the mob at the viaduct, as before stated, but the laborers at the rolling mills refused to go out. From this point the mob started northeast on Archer avenue, evidently intending to join the crowd on Halsted street, but when they reached the bridge the police met them, and here occurred another desperate struggle. An attack was made upon the police and military and citizen cavalry by the rioters, who used stones and revolvers pretty freely. Three platoons of policemen, in charge of Lieuts. Hood, Carberry and Bishoff, were ordered to cross the bridge for the purpose of cutting off the stock yards crowd. As soon as the police arrived they immediately became lost to sight in the dense concourse of rioters. At this moment some villain had swung the bridge to prevent additional forces from crossing, and this separated the policemen who had already crossed from their comrades. At this juncture, while the fight was raging on both sides of the river, and amidst a shower of bullets and stones, a little hero named James O'Neill, not over eleven years of age, came to the rescue in a manner that at once astonished the spectators and elicited the cheers of the policemen and many of their enemies. He had been left on the bridge when it was swung open, and the levers being in place when abandoned by the miscreant who had turned the draw, the little fellow, putting forth almost the strength of a full-grown man, swung the bridge into position, and thereby allowed the reinforcements to pass over. The men who had been waiting with impatience on the north abutment charged across impetuously, using their revolvers with deadly effect and rescuing their isolated companions from their perilous position. So warm was the execution here that the mob became panic-stricken, soon scattered, and fled pell-mell before the blue-coats, who fired a perfect hailstorm of bullets into the retreating rabble, and hammered the heads and shoulders of the lagging ones with their batons and revolver stocks.

Deputy Superintendent Dixon had taken command in the southwest portion of the city by this time. Upon his arrival at Twelfth street station he found the wildest excitement prevailing in the vicinity. The cells were filled with prisoners of war, just brought in; the corpse of one rioter was lying rigid upon the floor, and another was breathing his last close by. The station was surrounded by an immense crowd of men, women and children. Rumors had been circulated to the effect that several hundred rioters had been killed, and the wives of many of the men engaged in the riot were already bewailing the supposed deaths of their husbands. Dixon telegraphed for assistance for the protection of the station and the removal of the prisoners. Lieut. McGarigle soon arrived with a squad of men and omnibuses for the purpose named, and soon the captured rioters were locked up in safer quarters.

The deputy superintendent then proceeded to the front, and finding the police almost out of ammunition made arrangements for supplying them, then continued south on Twenty-second street, to where the police and second regiment were stationed. Nothing of importance occurred until they arrived at the corner of Archer avenue and Halsted street, where there was a large crowd of rioters. Dixon ordered that these be dispersed, and his order was speedily executed. After resting a few minutes the police and military marched south, the latter being defended, front and rear, by blue-coats. The police in the rear of this column was again attacked by the mob, when Dixon ordered Lieutenant Bishoff from front to rear, in order to support Lieutenant Carberry, whose command was suffering from the attack. There was a desperate conflict for a few minutes, when the rioters broke and fled. By this time Gen. Torrence had taken personal command of the military, but he was able to announce almost immediately after his arrival that the back-bone of the riot was broken.

There were skirmishes, running fights, charges, retreats, engagements without number throughout the day, and the policemen were almost exhausted. A little more of the incessant labor which had been imposed upon them and they would have been compelled to abandon the fight to the military. Luckily, however, this was not necessary, and although the militia were ready for any emergency, and conducted themselves more like veterans than volunteers, no emergency which called for harsher methods than those practiced by the police arose that day or afterward.

Early in the day and while the trouble was progressing at the viaduct, a meeting of communists was held in Vorwaert's Turner Hall, on West Twelfth street. A mob soon began to gather in this vicinity, crowding the sidewalks, filling the streets, and creating the greatest disturbance and alarm in the neighborhood. Poles and Bohemians were there in large numbers, and the wildest threats were made. The hall was packed and demagogues were endeavoring to excite the mob to the fighting pitch. The vilest epithets were hurled at the police and city authorities, and the direst vengeance was promised before the troubles ceased. Just about 10 a. m. a detachment of regular and special policemen, who had been detailed at Harrison street station for duty in the neighborhood of Halsted and Sixteenth streets, marched across the Twelfth street bridge on their way to the West Twelfth street station. The force numbered about 25 men. As they neared the crowd, the howling and hooting were renewed and the mob drawing itself up into a dense body on the sidewalk in front of the hall, opened on the squad a shower of stones and other missiles. The police stood the attack for a few minutes, but the stones fell thicker and faster, until the forbearance of the policemen was stretched to its utmost limits. A charge was ordered and the policemen turned upon the mob with their clubs, striking right and left, and breaking a large number of heads and limbs in a very few minutes. Outside the station, about a block and a half from the scene of conflict, were about a score of police in wagons. They were awaiting orders from headquarters. Seeing the trouble at Turner Hall they immediately came to the assistance of the fighting squad, and taking the crowd of rioters in the rear soon forced their way through until they formed connections with the Harrison street detail. Officer Ryan was in command of the attacking party, and Sergeant Brennan commanded the reinforcements. The mob inside the hall now commenced to discharge pistols and to throw stoves, chairs and other articles of furniture through the windows. Special Policemen Ladacher and Shimly were badly injured, the former by a pistol ball, the latter by a falling chair. Brennan and Ryan, uniting their forces, entered the hall, and caused one of the most exciting stampedes ever witnessed. The occupants fairly walked over, or rather rolled over each other into the street. Many were badly injured, a number fatally, it was supposed, and the crowd was taught a lesson that kept them quiet for the remainder of the day.

As was generally believed on Thursday night the mob was cowed. There were but few disturbances Friday. The stations were overflowing with prisoners. The hospitals were filled with the wounded. The undertakers were kept very busy in the socialistic headquarters for a month afterward. The strike was over. Business was speedily resumed, and by Saturday the city was quieter than it had been for years. There were no strikes and no talk of strikes. There were no socialistic or communistic meetings. The great railroad strike was really the turning point from bad to good times. Business began to improve and a period of prosperity, which healed up old sores and veiled the past from view, set in. The capitalists and merchants of Chicago saw for the first time the danger which threatened them from great uprisings of this kind. The regiments were better treated. Armories were built. Deputy Superintendent Dixon raised money which was used in supplying every station in the city with muskets. A military spirit pervaded the people. The police was re-organized on a military basis. The superintendent became a colonel, and wore shoulder straps. The deputy superintendent became a lieutenant-colonel, and also wore shoulder straps. The captains and lieutenants wore shoulder straps. Every man on the force hoped that some day in the future he would wear a shoulder strap. The shoulder straps were ridiculed, but the result of all this so-called military affectation was soon manifest. The discipline of the force became almost perfect; the men were drilled regularly; they were taught to handle guns, to form in hollow squares, to go through the street-fight maneuvers, and to bear themselves like soldiers. But the newspapers would not tolerate the military idea. They continued to ridicule it. The public was not pleased with it. Finally, when Colonel Hickey went out, the title went out with him; Captain Seavey became plain general superintendent and Joseph Dixon did his lieutenant-colonelcy up in a brown paper parcel, with his shoulder straps, and became once more a common deputy superintendent.

The number killed in the riot has been variously stated at from twenty to thirty-five. That many died of their injuries is certain. The number injured, more or less seriously, was about two hundred. The police escaped remarkably well, considering the close quarters in which they were frequently placed, and the brutal assaults made upon them. Aside from those mentioned in connection with the round house fight, the following were wounded: Patrolman Fitch A. Taylor, second precinct, wounded by a bullet; Patrolman Michael Keeley, second precinct, wounded by a bullet; Lieutenant Carberry, first precinct, cut in the forehead by a stone. The policemen suffered more or less from bruises inflicted by stones and other missiles, but they suffered more from fatigue than from any other cause. Many of them had been without sleep for thirty-six hours; others were marched around without food until they became completely exhausted; several of them never recovered from the hardships of the campaign on South Halsted street.

There were about 300 of the rioters arrested during the disturbances; a number of them were placed under bonds for appearance before the Criminal Court, but the disposition to keep the matter before the public languished, and little by little all proceedings were dropped.

It was in describing the fight on the South Halsted street viaduct that the late Stanley Huntley, at that time a reporter on the *Tribune*, and now widely remembered as the author of the side-splitting "Spoopendyke Papers," used the expression, "And the pale air was streaked with blood." The connection in which it was used is as follows: Huntley had been captured by the mob and re-captured by Gen. Torrence's command. Mounted upon a street-car horse, kindly furnished him for the occasion, he takes in the situation. This description is, of course, exaggerated, partly imaginative, and satirical:

From the viaduct south the avenue was crowded with roughs. They poured in from the side streets, their hands full of stones. The police met them, head on. The sickening crash of clubs followed, and the pale air was streaked with blood. Huge, bloated women at the windows yelled encouragement and defiance. Pistol balls shrieked as they flew. The clash of sabers and the shouts of maddened men made the hot air hideous. Horses were spurred into the mob and swords rose and fell with cruel significance. Alleys were gutted of molten masses of enraged humanity. Great massive blows fell on their passion-stained faces and tore the rage out of them. Shrinking figures darted behind boxes and fired upon the cavalry. The prisoners shrieked for rescue and sank groaning in the wagons under the cut of clubs. Stones rattled on the streets and tracks, and from the windows came showers of missiles. It was clear that the trouble was .at hand. A volcanic mob pressed the troops from behind. A sea of human lava blocked its way in front. The cavalry was divided, one company charging in the rear and another hurrying forward to assist the overworn police. Down the side streets they charged, the flash of pistols in their faces, and the air they breathed dusty with stones. * * * The reporter desires to say a kind word for his horse. It was a car horse. Whenever a bell or a clock struck the rider waited patiently for another bell or clock, and then the horse started on again. Whenever a rioter raised his fist or stick, the horse went to the opposite side of the street and pulled up. The reporter remonstrated once, but the horse turned around and bit the rider's leg. He was a good horse, but he was inexperienced in mobs.

The Chicago *Daily News* was, in the summer of 1877, a quarter-sheet, five-column paper, little larger than a hand-bill. It had been struggling for about 18 months to maintain itself against its older, wealthier and more pretentious rivals in the evening field of journalism, but with only partial success. It was the pioneer here of that species of newspaper which since then has prospered in every part of the country. But there was no long felt want for it in Chicago; the style of journalism which it introduced had never been craved for here. It summarized, epitomized and crystallized the news of the day, generally giving a line where its contemporaries would give ten. Up to the outbreak of the riot it had no opportunity of making itself felt. On the Sunday of the Pittsburg riot it issued hourly "extras." It continued to issue "extras" at all hours of the day and night during the week. From a circulation of about six thousand it advanced in a single day to over 90,000. Before the troubles blew over they had blown the *Daily News* into popularity and prosperity. The penny paper had distanced its evening rivals in the art of news gathering, and its position for all time was secure. The sudden rise of the *Daily News* from obscurity to prosperity, may be referred to as one of the incidents of the riot of '77.

CHAPTER XI.

EFFECT OF THE RIOT OF '77 ON POPULAR OPINION REGARDING THE
POLICE FORCE—TRYING TO GET AN INCREASE—SUPERINTENDENT
SEAVEY'S BRIEF CAREER AND UNTIMELY DEATH—SIMON O'DONNELL
AS CHIEF—WHAT HE IS CREDITED WITH—McGARIGLE TAKES HOLD—
HIS MANAGEMENT AND UNFORTUNATE MISTAKE—AUSTIN J. DOYLE'S
ADMINISTRATION—THE PATROL SERVICE—INCREASE OF THE FORCE—
FREDERICK EBERSOLD AND JOHN BONFIELD STEP UP HIGHER.

Some good results followed the riot of '77. As already
stated, the military organizations of the city received more
attention than ever before, and more liberal contributions.
But of more interest to us is the fact that the Chicago policeman ceased to be looked upon as a mere uniformed idler
from that time on. The policeman did not stand high in
popular esteem previous to this time. There were individuals on the force at all times who were respected and admired for the faithfulness and efficiency with which they discharged certain duties, but this did not hinder the public
from looking upon the average blue-coat as barnacle and a
nuisance. He was only tolerated because there still remained a doubt as to the wisdom of trying to get on without
him. Nothing could be more indicative of this sentiment
than the frequency with which propositions to lower the salaries of police officers came up in the city council, and the
language used by aldermen in reference to the force when
these propositions were debated. Looking over the printed
reports of these meetings now, we find some rather bitter
criticisms that came from the mouths of city fathers who
have since patted the police force on the head, so to speak,
and pronounced it the finest in the world. The truth is, that
after the fire there was so much crime, there were so many
outrages committed in this city in spite of the police service, that all confidence in them, if any had existed before,

was dying out. But no such force as Chicago had for several years after the fire was competent to protect the lives
and property of the people. The police did the very best
they could, but there was a limit to the territory which one
man could patrol, and a limit to his endurance. In a word,
there were not men enough to cover one-third of the area
mapped out for police inspection and protection.

The manner in which the force conducted itself during
the riot won for it the highest public commendation, and
this is reflected very strongly in the press. "The police,
both regular and special," said one evening paper on July
28, 1877, "proved themselves brave, resolute, earnest and
strong for the cause of good order, both officers and men.
The next man who tries to cut down the number or pay of
the force will be laughed at by the council."

The experiences of the week had taught all good citizens
likewise that mobs should not be played with for a single
instant. The *Tribune*, which was a warm and devoted friend
of Mayor Heath, was constrained to print the following on
Saturday of riot week:

The mob riots were suppressed on Thursday. They ought to have
been extinguished on Tuesday and they would have been if the mayor
had permitted the police to attack them and had promptly called out the
two city regiments to aid them. But he did neither, but gave up the
town to roving vagabonds during the entire day and night, not even
guarding the water-works or gas-works. Tuesday the police fired blank
cartridges, and little or no headway was made against the increasing em-
boldened mobs. Wednesday the police fired high and very few cut-throats
were hurt. Thursday the police concluded to end the foolishness about
blank cartridges and high firing and began to do a little low firing. It
had a most admirable effect on the mobs and convinced them that the
police were at last in earnest and meant business. Thereupon the mobs
dispersed. Had the police been ordered out promptly on Tuesday with
orders to commence work with low firing, fewer would have been hurt
than were, and the city would have been saved the disgrace of three days'
rule of the commune.

The United States regulars were not called upon to act,
but their presence in the city had a most quieting effect
upon the mobs, while from the moment of their arrival

public confidence began to rise.   There was no question in anybody's mind but that these regulars would have mowed down the communistic mobs in short order.   Fortunately, however, the "low firing" of the police made their presence in the struggle unnecessary.

In his annual report for 1877, Superintendent Hickey had the following:

I trust it will be considered pardonable for me also to say a word in behalf of the police for their bravery, endurance, good judgment and strict attention to duty in this emergency.   All will bear witness to the fact that not one of them flinched or showed any indication of shirking duty at any time, but fought twenty times their numbers, although almost exhausted from incessant work, and marching from place to place throughout the city for four days and nights, and having little or no rest during that time.

Captains O'Donnell, Seavey and Johnson, Lieutenants Callahan, Vesey, Carberry, Bishoff, Bell, Ebersold, Blettner, Simmons, Hood, Baus, Gerbing and Hathaway, and Sergeants Ward and Brennan, won personal distinction during these troubles.   The North Side police, under Capt. Gund, had very little opportunity of displaying their valor.

Superintendent Hickey, at the close of the year, appealed to the city council for a considerable increase in the force. At this time there were connected with the service one general superintendent, one deputy superintendent, four captains, eighteen lieutenants, eleven sergeants and four hundred and eighty-one patrolmen, distributed as follows: At headquarters, two lieutenants, one sergeant and fifty-three men; at Harrison street, one captain, two lieutenants and sixty-four men; at Twenty-second street, one lieutenant, one sergeant and forty-one men; at Cottage Grove, one lieutenant, one sergeant and twenty-nine men; at Deering street, one lieutenant, one sergeant and eighteen men; at Union street, one captain, two lieutenants and seventy-four men; at West Twelfth street, one lieutenant, one sergeant and forty-four men; at Hinman street, one lieutenant, one sergeant, and twenty-three men; at West Chicago avenue, one captain, one lieutenant and twenty-two men; at West Lake street, one lieutenant, one sergeant and thirty men; at Rawson street, one lieutenant, one sergeant and thirteen men; at Chicago avenue (East), one captain, two lieutenants and forty-two men; at Webster avenue, one lieutenant, one sergeant and eleven men; at Larrabee street, one lieutenant, one sergeant and seventeen men.

Capt. V. A. Seavey succeeded to the general superintendency in 1878, vice M. C. Hickey, removed. Deputy Superintendent Dixon remained, however. The new superintendent had distinguished himself in the riots, and was generally popular. The appointment, coming shortly after the accession of Carter H. Harrison to the mayoralty, took him somewhat by surprise, and he displayed commendable modesty in assuming his new position. For the superstitious there is something of interest connected with poor Seavey's entrance upon the duties of superintendent. With the idea of avoiding all appearance of display, he drove over from the West Side in a buggy, and, tying his horse in the alley known as Quincy street, in the rear of the old Rookery, he entered police headquarters through an open window, which extended from the ground almost to the ceiling. "My God, Seavey!" said a local politician who was present, as the new chief entered in this unceremonious fashion, "why did you come in that way? Don't you know it will bring you bad luck? It means death!" Seavey only laughed, sat down at his desk, and took up the business of the department, as though he had been superintendent all his life. In May, 1879, he was attacked by a complication of physical diseases, all resulting, as it afterward proved, from Bright's disease of the kidneys; he left the city on a furlough on June 3rd, Deputy Superintendent Dixon having been appointed to act in his place, but returned unimproved in health, and gradually sank until he passed away on September 7th. He had been connected with the force for over ten years, and the honors which attended his obsequies proved that he had won the esteem and admiration of his fellow citizens in every rank of life. During the time he was able to devote his energies to the general superintendency he proved himself to be an able executive officer in every respect. On his promotion Lieut. Hood succeeded to the captaincy of the Union street station. During the year the number of patrolmen had been reduced by cutting off 76 from the roll. Of the 409, 88 were detailed for station, bridge, tunnel and other outside duties, leaving the number available for regular patrol service 321. "As there are 38 square miles of territory, with 600 miles of streets," said Superintendent Seavey in his annual report, "to be patrolled by this number, averaging three and one-fourth miles of street for each patrolman on duty at night, and four and one-half miles for each of those on day duty, it should not be surprising if the cry of 'Where are the police?' is occasionally heard. It will be seen that we have less than one policeman for every 1,200 inhabitants; New York has one policeman for every 428 inhabitants; Philadelphia, one to every 650; Boston, one to every 530; New Orleans, one to every 380; Baltimore, one to every 520; San Francisco, one to every 600; St. Louis, one to every 1,000; Brooklyn, one to every 770; and so on through the entire list of cities; none can be found with so small a police force as our own." He held that the force was entirely insufficient, and said: "The police force, including officers, numbered 600 men when the population of the city was 125,000 less than it is at present, but within the last three years it has been reduced two lieutenants, two sergeants, and 160 patrolmen, although it was at the time and is now freely admitted that the number employed has never yet been sufficiently large for the requirements of the city, and to properly protect the interests of the people. It will, no doubt, be claimed that the annual report of the superintendent of police is always made the occasion for recommending an increase of the police force. This, it appears, has been so, but it also appears to have been the rule of late to largely reduce the force whenever an increase was asked for. There is scarcely any difference of opinion as to our necessities in this respect at the present time. Therefore I respectfully recommend that the present force be increased by the appointment of 100 additional patrolmen."

With the advent of the Heath administration a determined and systematic policy of retrenchment in every department of the city government was inaugurated and pursued. The police force was not the only sufferer. Expenses were cut down to the minimum. Mayor Heath's financial policy in a very short time restored the credit of Chicago abroad, but it impaired the usefulness of the police to a great extent. Mayor Harrison, upon entering office, took up Mayor Heath's policy, and followed it closely. For a time the force of the police and fire departments proved to be entirely inadequate; but it became an absolute necessity to place the financial credit of the city on a solid basis, and everything for a time was sacrificed to that object. Hence the reduction in the force. If the fact that the force was inadequate was constantly borne in mind by its critics, there would have been little ground for complaint; but while the population was steadily increasing, and the inhabited portion of the territory within the corporate limits steadily broadening, the force was being reduced rather than increased, that fact was not taken into consideration. Salaries were paid in "city scrip," too, and this was subject to a fluctuating rate of discount. Besides, the salaries paid were not such as to command the services of good and trustworthy men at all times. Prosperity was returning, and many men left the service, for the reason that they could do better in other walks of life. No increase was granted, and at the end of the year the force consisted of five captains, seventeen lieutenants, twelve sergeants, three clerks, one custodian, ten detectives, twenty-eight station keepers, and (including pound keepers, lock-up keepers, police court bailiffs, day squad men and special details of all kinds) 376 patrolmen.

Superintendent Seavey suggested that the Morse system of telegraphy be extended by the employment of five operators. "The dial instruments for many years in the department," he said, "are incapable of giving the service required, as they are too slow and unreliable for use in cases where the rapid transmission of messages to and from the different stations becomes necessary."

There was in possession of the department this year a quantity of arms, purchased by the Citizens' Association, consisting of four twelve-pound and two six-pound guns, with caissons, harness and limbers complete; one ten-barrel Gatling gun, with gun carriage and equipments complete; 296 Springfield breech-loading rifles, and 60,000 rounds of ammunition. These arms, equipments and ammunition were held by the department with the understanding that they were to be returned to the association at the demand of the executive committee. The department had also at this time 102 Springfield rifles of its own, which had been purchased by citizens and presented to the police.

It was part of the discipline of the police under Hickey and Seavey, and afterward under some of their successors, that the members of the force be compelled to attend drill duty in their respective precincts, and receive instruction in company movements, once each week during the summer months. The force, under this regime, attained a high degree of efficiency in the handling of firearms, in marching, etc. Detective Leander Bauder acted as drill master.

In 1878, four officers died, one of whom was the victim of a most foul and cowardly murder. The first three were Officer Dominick S. Barbaro, who died of consumption; Officer Bartholomew Hoffman, who fell a victim to the same disease, and Officer James Kern, who died from injuries received in accidentally falling into an excavation in the rear of 176 Clark street, while on duty. The murdered officer was Albert Race, who was shot and instantly killed on the evening of October 4, 1878, while in the performance of his duty, in front of Lesser Friedburg's "fence," or pawnshop, No. 494 State street. He had been a member of the force for about 5 years, and was generally esteemed as a faithful and efficient officer. In connection with the names of men who figured in this case afterward, references are made to the crime. Here it will be only necessary to relate the bare facts. Officer Race was patrolling his post in the vicinity of the pawnbroker's shop, a place that bore a most unenviable reputation. About 9:45 o'clock p. m. he observed a horse and wagon standing in front of the place, and noticed that the wagon contained a large quantity of dry goods. Suspecting at once that the goods had been stolen, he stood aside until a man emerged from the pawnshop and took possession of the vehicle. Another quickly followed, and while the two sat in the wagon, Officer Race proceeded to question them as to its contents, and was about to prevent them from moving, when one of the two drew a pistol and, pointing it at the policeman's head, killed him instantly. The theory was that Friedburg would not pay as much for the stuff as the thieves demanded, and they were about to take it elsewhere. The assassin jumped from the wagon, but the other drove a short distance, and then abandoned it. The wagon was recovered at once and driven to the Harrison street station. Here it was quickly discovered that the goods had been stolen that same evening from the Chicago branch of E. S. Jaffrey & Co., New York, which was located in the present Herald building, corner of the alley, between Madison and Washington streets, on the west side of Fifth avenue. Johnny Lamb and "Sheeney" George were arrested for the crime, and the latter sentenced to be hanged, but owing to the character of the witness against him ("Sheeney" George, who turned state's evidence), he finally escaped punishment.

For some months previous to the death of Superintendent Seavey, Deputy Superintendent Dixon acted as general superintendent of police. His resignation being demanded under circumstances mentioned elsewhere, Mayor Harrison appointed Simon O'Donnell deputy superintendent, and until the death of Superintendent Seavey he acted in the capacity of general superintendent. When death finally created a vacancy in the position, O'Donnell was appointed chief, a promotion which he strenuously endeavored to avoid. During his incumbency the responsibilities of the place weighed heavily upon his shoulders and the gallant commander of the third precinct never felt lighter-hearted than the day he stepped out of the high office to the humbler captaincy in the uniform of which he felt comfortable and entirely at home.

Although it is a point which has been disputed, some of the oldest members in the force give Simon O'Donnell's administration credit for the conception of the patrol service idea. Austin J. Doyle was unquestionably the author of the scheme; but it is contended it was O'Donnell and not McGarigle who gave the secretary of the department the encouragement he needed at the outset, in order to put his plans into practical shape. It was Simon O'Donnell who first called attention to the incapacity of the existing Criminal Court, which was presided over by one judge, and in which it was utterly out of the question to prosecute the number of causes brought before it by the police department. Soon afterward an additional or auxilliary court was created. Simon O'Donnell, too, while departing from the usual custom of appealing to the city council for an increase of the force—which under his superintendency reached the lowest numerical point in ten years—informed that body frankly and flatly that at least 800 men were necessary to render ample police protection to all interests and parts of the city. While no public tumults, aside from an occasional serious strike, marked the period of his administration, the force under him exhibited a marked degree of discipline and fidelity in all its undertakings, and personal loyalty to the chief often counted for more than any official orders in bringing to the minds of subalterns a high sense of their responsibilities and duties.

E. P. Ward, who had filled the position of secretary of police from the abolition of the marshalship, was succeeded, after the first election of Mayor Harrison, by Austin J. Doyle, who acted in that capacity during the superintendency of O'Donnell and McGarigle. The position at first was merely a clerical one, but it grew to be second in point of importance only to the superintendency. During Secretary Doyle's occupancy of the place, he took an active interest in everything which concerned the material welfare of the force. It is not necessary here to go over the ground already covered in the chapters which give the history and describes the workings of the patrol service, in the organization of which Mr. Doyle took a most important and prominent part. He was born in Chicago, Sept. 18, 1849, received a first-class common school education, and during his early manhood was connected with some of the leading mercantile houses, in various capacities. Under Daniel O'Hara, he became a clerk in the Recorder's Court, in 1865; was appointed first deputy of the court in 1868, and in 1873, on the People's ticket, was elected clerk of the Criminal Court, studied law while filling this office, and was admitted to the bar later on. On the resignation of Superintendent McGarigle, he was promoted from the secretaryship to the superintendency of police, which position he held until he retired to become superintendent of a horse railway company.

William J. McGarigle, who succeeded Simon O'Donnell as general superintendent, was born in Milwaukee, Wis. He received a collegiate education. As a young man he became attached, in a responsible position, to the United States Express Company, and handled, it is said, vast amounts of money while in that service. Afterward he became connected with the Chicago, Milwaukee & St. Paul Railroad Co.

In November, 1870, he married Anna Bodmer, of Milwaukee, a woman who in later years exhibited the most exalted wifely devotion for him. He entered the Chicago police force in 1872, as a patrolman, being assigned to the Webster avenue station. Shortly afterward he became one of Superintendent Washburn's numerous secretaries, and later, a clerk of detectives, and in 1875, he was appointed lieutenant and made chief of detectives, afterward being placed in command of the third precinct, from which position he was promoted to the superintendency. His connection with the patrol service, and other events in his official career, are mentioned in their proper places. He resigned the superintendency in 1882, to make the race for sheriff; was defeated; became connected with a mercantile house; was appointed warden of the county hospital, and, while holding that office, became involved in transactions which have thrown a dark shadow over his career. He is at present a fugitive from justice.

The police force in 1880 consisted of one general superintendent, one secretary, five captains, seventeen lieutenants, sixteen sergeants, three clerks, one custodian, eleven detectives, twenty-eight station keepers, and (including pound-keepers, lock-up keepers, police court bailiffs, day squad men or special details of all kinds), three hundred and ninety patrolmen. The force at headquarters, all told, was 27; the day squad consisted of one lieutenant, one sergeant and 36 men. Including officers of every grade, the following were the details at each station at the close of 1880: Harrison street, 54; Twenty-second street, 37; Cottage Grove avenue, 27; West Twelfth street, 47; Hinman street, 23; Deering street, 18; West Madison street, (Union street) 69; West Lake street, 25; West Chicago avenue, 24; Chicago avenue, 41; Larrabee street, 17; Webster avenue, 13; Rawson street, 13.

The most important event of the year was the introduction of the signal patrol service.

During the year Michael Murphy, patrolman, Rawson street station, died of a complication of diseases, and William F. Mackay, patrolman, Twenty-second street station, was killed by a railway train on the Chicago, Burlington & Quincy railroad.

The total number of men on the force at the close of 1881 was five hundred and six. A captain was placed in command of the day squad, and the detail was increased to 49 patrolmen, four of whom were detailed for duty on the "police telegraph wagon," as the vehicle was called. The West Madison street sub-station was organized and added to the third precinct.

The mortality among the policemen this year was remarkably high. George Gubbins, lock-up keeper at the Harrison street station, died of cancer. Patrolman Timothy Mahoney, of the Deering street station, was shot dead by two burglars, on the night of June 12. The burglars were masked and had entered the house of Mr. Richard Jones, No. 3815 Emerald avenue, when the family was awakened and gave an alarm. The burglars, hearing the alarm, pointed a revolver at Mr. Jones and threatened to shoot him if he did not remain quiet. They left the house, Jones following them. Coming across Officer Mahoney at the corner of Halsted and 38th streets, he informed the officer of what had happened. Officer Mahoney ran after the burglars, telling Jones to follow. The policeman overtook the burglars at the next corner, and Jones, who was half a block distant, testified that he could see a struggle going on, in the glare of the lightning, for it was a stormy night. Three shots were fired in quick succession and Officer Mahoney fell to the ground fatally wounded. He was unable to give an account of the trouble before death seized him. The bullet which caused his death had entered just above his heart. He was 40 years of age. A public subscription of $5,000 was raised for his afflicted family.

During this year, on June 20, one of the ablest detectives that was ever connected with the American police, expired at St. Joseph's hospital. This was Lieut. Edward J. Keating. He was born in Kane Co., Ill., and at the time of his death was 35 years of age. As a patrolman in the secret service, and as its chief, he made a record which stands out prominently now, though many changes have occurred since his time. For several years the names of Keating and Kipley, the two who worked hand in hand and shoulder to shoulder in the unravelling of so many mysteries, and the apprehension of so many miscreants, were famous in the police annals of Chicago. In giving the records of his old associates in this volume, the name of Edward J. Keating occurs frequently and always prominently.

Patrolman Patrick O'Brien died at the West Twelfth street station, on the afternoon of August 3d, from a pistol shot wound in the left breast, inflicted by one Thomas Cahill, residing at 50 Rebecca street. [See biography of Patrolman James Ray, inspector's office].

Patrolman Daniel Crowley died at his residence, 94 Miller street, on the night of August 3, from the effects of a pistol shot wound inflicted by Edward Kelly, at the corner of Quincy and Desplaines streets, while on his way to the station with a female prisoner. The murder was a cold-blooded one. Passing the corner mentioned, two men stood on the sidewalk, one of whom asserted that Officer Crowley's prisoner stepped on his foot, accompanying the statement by the use of foul language. The policeman ordered the fellows to be quiet and move on about their business, when one of them (Kelly) drew a revolver and shot the policeman. The ball took effect in the thigh, and blood poisoning ensued. Officer Crowley was but 34 years of age, and had entered the force in 1877. He was at the time attached to the third precinct.

Patrolman Mortimer Hogan, of the Hinman street station, died of meningitis August 12. He contracted the disease at the funeral of the murdered officer, Patrick O'Brien, a few days previous.

Detective and ex-Captain Thomas F. Simmons, of the first precinct, died at his residence, 671 Fulton street, on September 20, of consumption. He had been connected with the force for twelve years, and was at one time a very prominent officer.

Patrolman Michael Mitchell, of the Deering street station, died of consumption Sept. 23d, at his residence, 3727 Emerald avenue.

During the year, the Policemen's Benevolent Association paid to widows and orphans of deceased officers, $5,565; paid to sick and injured members, $834; paid for funeral expenses, $1,125. The superintendent speaks very highly of the association in his annual report, and advises all members of the force to become attached to such a useful organization.

During the year, Captains Buckley and O'Donnell remained in command of the Harrison and West Twelfth street stations respectively, but John Bonfield is captain of the third, and Amos W. Hathaway is captain of the fourth precinct, and the day squad is commanded by Capt. Frederick Ebersold. Austin J. Doyle succeeds W. J. McGarigle as chief, and the office of inspector is created and incorporated with that of secretary of the department, under the official title of secretary and inspector.

The first incumbent of this position was Dominick Welter, who was born at Echternach, Grand Duchy of Luxemburg, (a province that has given many distinguished officers to our police department), Nov. 9, 1839. His family arrived in this country in 1850, locating at Tiffin, Ohio. Young Welter attended the public schools and assisted his father in the bakery business, learning also the tobacconist trade. At the age of 17, he enlisted in the 7th United States infantry, which was assigned to duty in the far northwestern territories. Returning to his old home in

Ohio in 1861, he enlisted as a private in the "Tremont Guards," known as the 4th Ohio cavalry, and attached to the Army of the Cumberland. He was promoted to a lieutenancy in 1862, and to a first lieutenancy in January, 1863. Taken prisoner at Chickamauga, on Sept. 20, 1863, he was confined for eighteen months in the Libby prison, Richmond, Va.; at Macon, Ga.; Charleston and Columbia, S. C., and Salisbury, N. C., where he suffered all the tortures that have made the names of these horrible prisons infamous. While a prisoner in 1864, he was promoted to a captaincy, and at the close of the war he was a major. While he had visited Chicago as early as 1852, he did not locate here permanently until 1870, when he opened a tobacco house and did a prosperous business, which he turned over to his son when he became inspector of police in 1882. He distinguished himself in connection with the military organization here in 1877, when he became connected with the only cavalry company here, just previous to the riots of that year. From this, the First Cavalry, I. N. G., was organized, and Major Welter became its commanding officer, March, 1881. In December, 1884, when three hundred men were added to the police force, it is thought that Major Welter over-exerted himself in drilling the recruits, and that this led to his untimely death. He died at his old home, Tiffin, Ohio, where he had gone in the hope of restoring his health. A detachment of Chicago police escorted the body to Chicago; the stations were all draped in mourning, and he was buried at St. Boniface cemetery with military honors. The cortege consisted of Chief Marshal Stockton and staff, second regiment band, one hundred and fifty members of the fire department, drum corps of Battery "D," Chief of Police Doyle and staff, 400 men from the police department, members of the detective force, Trocher & Winters' band, 1,000 men from the Independent Order of Foresters, Major Nevans' band, 100 representatives from the Luxemburg Unterstuetzungs Verein, 50 men from the Catholic Benevolent Legion, 50 national veterans, drum corps of the first regiment, 250 men of the 1st infantry, 20 men of the colored battalion, cavalry band and first regiment cavalry, the caisson bearing the casket, the pall bearers, wagons bearing floral tributes, friends, and city and county officials. Major Welter was a member of the Catholic Benevolent Legion, the Policemen's Benevolent Association, the State Police and Fire Association, and one of the directors of the High Court of the Independent Order of Foresters.

While secretary and inspector he performed his duties with very general satisfaction. Always a popular favorite, he succeeded in winning the affection and respect of his associates in the police department, and in retaining them to the end. Though not a policeman in the strict sense of the word, his military education was of great value to the department, and he succeeded in bringing the discipline of the force up to a high standard.

This was another year in which the great reaper, Death, mowed down many members of the force. Two deaths were the result of violence.

Patrolman John Huebner died at his residence, 565 North Paulina street, on the 4th of February, from the effects of a gunshot wound received twenty-four hours previously, while attempting to arrest two burglars, near the corner of Holt and Bradley streets. They had entered the house of John Henning, 5 Bauman street, and made a noise which attracted the attention of Mrs. Henning, who immediately alarmed the family. Several shots were exchanged between Henning and the burglars, and Officers Foley and Kearns, on duty in the neighborhood, hearing the reports, hastened to the spot. At Ashland avenue they sighted the burglars and attempted their capture, but the criminals dodged through an alley, and ran northward, the officers keeping up a running fire in the pursuit. Officer Huebner was on Bradley street, and ran to head off the burglars. As he reached Holt street he caught one of them.   The other fired several shots at the officer, all of which took effect, and the burglars escaped.   He was forty-two years of age, and his wife and eight children were provided for by the Policemen's Benevolent Association.   The murderer was afterward caught, convicted and hanged.

Patrolman Valentine Bittel, of the day squad, died of dropsy at his residence, 719 Holt avenue, February 24.

Patrolman William Lobbeke, of the fourth precinct, died at his residence, No. 181 Dayton street, on May 9, after two months' illness.

Patrolman Patrick O'Leary, of the second precinct, died at his residence, 615 South Union street, May 11.

Patrolman Edmund Welch, of the first precinct, died at his residence, 24 Charles place, of inflammation of the bowels, May 24, aged thirty-five years.

Patrolman Matthew Twohey, of the second precinct, died at his residence, 238 West Taylor street, of consumption, June 23, aged thirty-six years.

Desk Sergeant Patrick H. Hussey, of the fourth precinct, died at his residence, 761 Dudley street, June 2, of consumption.

Patrolman Henry O'Neil, of the day squad, died at his residence, 201 De Koven street, October 1, after ten days' illness, aged thirty-five years.

Patrolman Patrick McGrath, of the third precinct, died at his residence, 3 Owasco street, October 21, after six weeks' illness, aged forty years.

Clarence E. Wright, patrolman, met with a sudden and cruel death at the hands of William Allen, *alias* Joe Dehlmer, at 37 West Washington street, November 29. [See "Bill Allen Case," Patrol Service].

There was no change in the precinct commands during 1883, but the force shows a slight increase, the total number of men connected with the department being 637.   The patrol service was greatly extended and improved, and the work done was excellent. In his report for the year, Superintendent Doyle says: "No additional men will be needed for the service, except where new stations hereafter may be built. No citizen need call upon this branch of the department without a ready response; thirty per cent of last year's arrests were made by this branch of the service." He asked, to meet the expenses of running the department during the succeeding year, an appropriation of $992,273.50, as against $703,579.66 for the year just closed, and backed this up with some statements of general interest. "In regard to the detective force," he said, "I will simply offer this suggestion that there are at present 850 regular passenger and freight trains coming into and departing from the city daily on the twenty regular lines of railroad owning their own tracks; two more roads have been admitted recently, and it is safe to predict that before the end of 1884 the number of such trains will be 1,000 daily. There are numerous prisons within a radius of 100 miles of the city, each of which is discharging convicts daily, and from all of which the railroads lead directly to Chicago. A competent and efficient detective force is needed to locate and watch the movements of these professional criminals—the facilities for reaching and leaving the city (by land and water) surpassing those of any in the world. I trust, therefore, that you will agree to the proposition that the amounts estimated for detective and secret service are very moderate, when the exigencies of the service are taken into consideration. Permit me to call attention to a few facts showing deficiency in the regular day and night patrol service, which can only be remedied by increasing the number of patrolmen. The 300 men employed as regular patrolmen cannot work night and day without rest or sleep; they are, therefore, divided into two details, three-fourths (or 225) being detailed for night duty, and one-fourth (or 75) for traveling during the day. In order to distribute the night work fairly, each man travels three months at night and one month in daytime, giving him only three months of day duty during the year. The area of territory embraced in the city limits is about the same as that of New York City, where the police force numbers 2,560 men. The inhabited territory of Chicago, which needs to be traversed by patrolmen, is about 18,000 acres; divide this number by 225, and you have one night patrolman for each 80 acres; divide by 75, and you have one day patrolman for every 240 acres. There are 80,000 buildings in this city; divide this number by 225, and you have one night patrolman for each 350 buildings; again by 75, and you have one day patrolman for each 1,050 buildings. The population of this city may reasonably be estimated at 675,-000; divide by 225, and each 3,000 people are guarded at night by one patrolman; each 9,000 by one patrolman in the daytime. This in the 'Convention City' of the United States. An immense transient population is daily domiciled within its limits; this population must be protected to a great extent by the day squad and detective department. When you consider that the average beat for a night patrolman measures one-half by one-quarter of a mile, and comprises a territory such as, for instance, is bounded by Halsted street, Center avenue, Madison and Jackson streets, a fair idea may be conceived of the responsibilities of one night patrolman. Multiply the territory by the figure 3, and you have the area to be covered by the day patrolman."

The estimated advance in the salary list aggregated 5 per cent. increase over the amounts paid the preceding year, but the superintendent thought this would be more than made up by grading the force into three classes; the force previous to the last year's appointments, constituting the first grade, at $1,000 per year salary; those appointed the last year, constituting the second grade, at $900 per annum, and new men, to constitute the third grade, to be paid $62.50 per month, for the first eight months. Superintendent Doyle advocated the grading of patrolmen warmly, and insisted that it was only reasonable and logical that the experienced men were worth more than the partially experienced or inexperienced.

The force was largely increased during 1884, the total number of men connected with the service at the close of the year being 924. The "Day Squad" changed its name to the "Central Detail," and had one lieutenant, one sergeant and 99 patrolmen; the Harrison street station had 63 men, all told; the Twenty-second street station, 48; the Cottage Grove avenue station, 46; the Thirty-fifth street station, 34; the West Twelfth street station, 79; the Hinman street station, 49; the Deering street station, 35; the Desplaines street station, 73; the West Madison street station, 31; the West Lake street station, 42; the West Chicago avenue station, 61; the West North avenue station, 27; the Rawson street station, 28; the Chicago avenue station, 64; the Larrabee street station, 48; the Webster avenue station, 42.

New stations were added, as will be seen, and the precinct commands were changed as follows: First precinct, including Harrison street, Twenty-second street, Cottage Grove avenue and Thirty-fifth street districts, commanded by Captain Frederick Ebersold; second precinct, including West Twelfth street, Hinman street and Deering street districts, commanded by Captain Simon O'Donnell; third precinct, including Desplaines street, West Madison street and West Lake street districts, commanded by Captain John Bonfield; fourth precinct, including West Chicago avenue, West North avenue and Rawson street districts, commanded by Captain Amos W. Hathaway; fifth precinct, including the Chicago avenue, Larrabee street and Webster avenue districts, commanded by Captain William Buckley.

In the summer and fall of 1885, some important changes occurred in the department. Captain Ebersold became inspector of police in August, vice Major Welter, deceased, and two months later was appointed general superintendent, vice Austin J. Doyle, resigned; Captain Bonfield succeeded to the inspectorship; Captain Buckley was transferred back to the first precinct; Captain Ward was placed in charge of the third precinct; Lieut Schaak became captain of the fifth precinct, and George W. Hubbard became captain of the Central detail. The force, at the close of 1885, numbered 926 men, all told. A period of great disturbance had already set in, and for two years the police department of Chicago attracted the attention of all Christendom.

CHAPTER XII.

THE YEAR 1885—COMMUNISM, SOCIALISM AND ANARCHY—THE BOARD OF
TRADE DEMONSTRATION—SEDITIOUS SPEECHES AND A DISGRACE-
FUL PROCESSION—AN OUTRAGE ON THE STREET—SPREAD OF COM-
MUNISTIC DOCTRINES — THE GREAT WEST DIVISION STREET-CAR
RIOTS — BONFIELD'S FAMOUS MARCH — THE EXCITING SCENES AND
INCIDENTS ON MADISON STREET—SOCIALISTIC PICNICS AND PROCES-
SIONS—THE MOTTOES OF THE " REDS"—APPROACHING THE DREADFUL
CULMINATION.

The first three months of 1885 were uneventful, from a
police standpoint. The winter had been the most severe experienced in this region for years, and there was no small
amount of suffering among the poor. Trade of all kind
had been slack, and Chicago had for months failed to present to the visitor that animation and spirit for which
she has become celebrated. On Tuesday, April 7, Carter H.
Harrison was again, for the fourth time, elected mayor, de-
feating Judge Sydney Smith, but by such a small majority
that contest proceedings were commenced. The campaign
had been an unusually bitter one, and partizan feeling ran
high. In time this bitterness wore itself out and the contest was abandoned, owing to the unwillingness of the republican leader to make a fight. Mr. Harrison's re-election,
therefore, prevented any important changes from occurring
in the department. During the spring another of the periodical McCormick strikes broke out and assumed serious
proportions and characteristics. There was the usual amount
of rioting, the women taking part as well as the men in the
various demonstrations along the "Black Road"—a name
given to the stretch of road that connected Blue Island avenue with the reaper works, for the reason that it was filled
in with cinders from the mills and factories in the vicinity—

and an unfortunate collision had occurred between the men and Pinkerton's detectives, resulting in loss of life among the strikers. After a prolonged struggle, a settlement was brought about on Saturday, April 11, and Monday morning the hands returned to work, with the conviction that the managers of the McCormick factory had determined upon a more liberal policy. An advance of 15 per cent. was given on piece work and other concessions were made.

The palatial new Board of Trade building, foot of La-Salle street, was to be inaugurated with elaborate and gorgeous ceremonies on the night of Tuesday, April 28. There were to be a grand reception of invited guests and a magnificent banquet. The Board of Trade had long been the target of Parsons, Spies, Fielden and the other leading socialists and anarchists, and the fact that the new structure was to be opened with such a lavish display of elegance, created the greatest indignation in proletariat circles. A mass meeting of members of "The International Working People's Party" was called to assemble on Market street on this same Tuesday evening, and the circular announcing the meeting wound up as follows:

After the ceremonies and sermons, the participants will move in a body to the Grand Temple of Usury, Gambling and Cut-Throatism, where they will serenade the priests and officers of King Mammon and pay honor and respect to the benevolent institute. All friends of the bourse are invited.

There were about 500 men and a few women assembled on Market street, near Randolph, at 8 o'clock that evening, and a band of music performed the Marseillaise and other airs calculated to awaken revolutionary feeling. A delay was occasioned by the neglect of the North Side anarchist societies to report on time. While waiting for them, a number of men with muskets wheeled around the corner and thinking that they were a detachment of the "Armed Group' of socialists, a large crowd left the meeting and advanced to welcome them. It turned out, however, that they were members of Company "G," second regiment, out on drill. Upon making this discovery the cheers of welcome were changed to yells of scorn and defiance. Insulting epithets were hurled upon the militiamen, but they paid no attention to the rabble and marched quietly on.

About one thousand persons were assembled when Albert R. Parsons called the meeting to order. He said they had assembled to take into consideration their position in society, and announced that after some speeches had been made a procession would be formed which should march around the "Board of Thieves," singing the Marseillaise, that the members of the board might hear the notes which had inspired the hearts of lovers of liberty in every land. He was interrupted with cries of "*Vive la Commune*" and cheers. Samuel Fielden then took the stand, amid cheers and cries of "*Vive la Commune*," and opened by saying that Boards of Trade were a curse and a menace to the welfare and comfort of the people. At this point the North Side contingent of "Reds" made their appearance, carrying red and black flags. The speaker, pointing to these flags, said that the red one represented the common blood of humanity—equal rights of blood, whether it coursed through the veins of falsely-named aristocrats or through the veins of tramps or beggars. The other was the black flag of starvation, and it was fitting that it should be unfurled when a Board of Trade is being opened, for a Board of Trade meant starvation for the masses—privileges for a few—disqualifications, insult, robbery—everything that was mean and contemptible. The new Board of Trade building, it was said, cost nearly $2,-000,000. Before it had been in operation many years it would have cost the people of Chicago and of the Northwest $1,000,000,000. [Cheers and a voice "Blow it up with dynamite!"] Men had paid $5,000 for memberships, who had never in their lives earned one single meal. While the masses were being gradually impoverished, while 2,500,000 persons were out of work, these men were building $2,000,-

000 Boards of Trade. This Board of Trade was an establishment where thieves were at work, and the commercial colleges of the city were the establishments which trained these thieves to prey upon the people. [Applause]. His hearers who had to work all their lives, who would be glad to huddle their families into any kind of a squalid shanty, to wear the meanest clothes, to sit down to the meanest victuals, to take a 25-cent seat in a cheap theatre, had come out to express their opinion and say that this thing of building $2,000,000 houses in which to rob the people must be stopped. [Cheers]. Last summer one of these thieves went on the Board of Trade and came off in twenty-four hours with $1,000,000 more to his credit in bank than he had before. Where did he get it? [A voice, "Stole it from us"]. "He stole it from you and I," said the speaker. He hoped his hearers would forgive him for quoting what Jesus Christ said of the lily. [Laughter]. The profit-mongers of the United States toiled not, neither did they spin, yet they had the best of everything. The men who had put up the money were not invited to the grand banquet. [Voices, "We are going anyway," "We will invite ourselves," and laughter]. If they went they would not be welcome, but they were going anyway. [Cheers and cries of "You are right," and "That's business"]. How long were they going to stand this? How long were they going to sit down to a 15-cent meal, with a piece of pie thrown in, when those fellows sat down to $20 dishes? Ought not these fellows to be glad to come and ask them if they could have a piece of pie? But they allowed themselves to be robbed by them without protest. There must be a change, and they had to make it. [Applause]. If they had the spirit of manhood in them they would resolve to band themselves together "to destroy from the face of the earth every unproductive member of society." [Cheers].

A. R. Parsons then stepped upon the barrel which was used as a platform, and said, a temple was being dedicated to

the God of Mammon, and it was to be devoted exclusively
to the robbery, the plunder and the destruction of the people. When the corner-stone of the Board of Trade was laid,
Bishop Cheney was there to baptize it. [Derisive laugh-
ter]. What a truthful follower that man must be of the
tramp Nazarene, Jesus, who scourged the thieves from the
Board of Trade of Jerusalem. [Cheers]. And another pious
man was to take part in the present ceremonies—the Rev.
Dr. Locke. [Cries of "Shoot him," "Lock him up," and
laughter]. "Let us not be foolish," said Parsons; "let us
not be deceived by these matters any longer. Have we got
the right to live? [Voices "Yes" and "No"]. Do we want
our natural rights? ["Yes"]. Then, if you do, let every man
lay up a part of his wages, buy a Colt's navy revolver,
[Cheers, and a voice "That is what we want"], a Winchester
rifle [Several hisses and voices "And ten pounds of dynamite;" "We will make that ourselves"], and learn how to
make and to use dynamite. Then raise the red flag of rebellion [Cries of " Bravo!"], and strike down to the earth every
tyrant that lives upon this globe. [Cheers and cries of
Vive la Commune]. Until this is done you will continue to
suffer, to be plundered, to be robbed, to be at the mercy of
the privileged few. Organize for the purpose of rebellion,
and you may be free." [Cheers].

As soon as Parsons had concluded, the order was given
to form into line, and from the reports made at the time a
description of the night's proceedings will be interesting, viewed in the light of subsequent events. The main
body of the crowd stretched itself along the middle of the
street until it had a line about a block in length with five or
six abreast. These were the socialists, anarchists and communists. They were headed by the brass band. Just in
front of the band red and black flags were borne on lofty
poles. The flags were carried by women, four of whom
walked together and took turns with the staffs. About the
middle of the line there was another pair of flags, black and

red, also borne by women. A large crowd of spectators gathered on the sidewalks. The column marched south on Market street to Madison, where it turned east and continued in that direction until Clark street was reached. The echo which redoubled in the narrow streets seemed to awaken some excitement, and the noise increased with the length of the walk. The crowd, however, was continually being augmented by the spectators, who not only clogged the sidewalks, but who fell into line, as a matter of convenience, hoping thereby to be in better position to see the fun, should any occur. The mob got a good view of the new Board of Trade building in passing La Salle street, which caused many alternate expressions of admiration and disgust. The excitement increased as the column neared the illuminated structure, and many in the crowd were becoming gleeful over the prospect of a riot, in which, possibly, some policemen would get hurt. The programme was to march to the very door of the building, and there to sing the "Marseillaise" to brass band accompaniment, so that the "eaters of $20 pie" could not fail to hear their voices and understand their object. Not a policeman was in sight, and the 2,000 which composed the mob were, perhaps, congratulating themselves upon the fulfillment of a long-cherished desire to interfere in some way with the pleasures of somebody supposed to represent capital, when the head of the column turned from Clark street around the corner of Adams and marched west to La Salle street.

Superintendent Doyle had been requested early in the morning to protect the building, and those who would visit it, from the threatened serenade. Every policeman in the city was ordered to hold himself in readiness, and two hundred men from the different stations were required to report to Captain Ebersold at the Harrison street station. Two hundred more were kept in reserve in the stations, and the other two hundred, of the six hundred men comprising the night force, were within easy reach. Twenty minutes after call, six hundred men could have been concentrated in front of the Board of Trade building, and a second call would have increased that number to 1,000.   At 9:05 o'clock the 200 men detailed for active services were divided up into five detachments and were marched to every intersection of streets leading to the building. Capt. Ebersold gave the detachments their positions and ordered them to allow no procession to pass them in the direction of the Board of Trade. They were then marched out in command of Inspector Welter. The divisions were in command of Lieut. Ward at Adams and La Salle streets, Lieut. Sheppard at Jackson street and Fifth avenue, Lieut. Duffy at Sherman and Van Buren streets, Lieut. Laughlin at Clark and Jackson streets, and Lieut. Beadell at Pacific avenue and Van Buren street; Lieut. Hubbard commanded the men detailed for service within the building.   Beside the squads, a large number of policemen in plain clothing, together with the detectives, were scattered through the mob, and along the streets, so that the department was kept acquainted with everything that was going on.

The band struck up the "Marseillaise" as the procession turned west on Adams street, and the mob sang the revolutionary song in French, German and English.   The head of the column had just entered La Salle, when it was brought to a sudden stop.   "Halt," cried Lieut. Ward, and the music ceased.   August Spies was in the lead as usual, and walking out in front of the band he asked in an indignant tone for the captain in command.

"I am in command," said Inspector Welter.

"Why do you stop us?" asked Spies.

"Because this street is too crowded with carriages and pedestrians for the passage of a procession."

"Break through!" yelled men in the mob, and spectators on the sidewalks, who sympathized with the anarchists.   "Go in and enjoy the cut-throats' music," cried others.

"March your men away," commanded Inspector Welter,

addressing Spies. "There are plenty of other streets open to you. Go there. Don't stop here and obstruct the streets."

The band struck up again and the procession moved across La Salle to Fifth avenue. At Jackson street a weak attempt was made to break through the police cordon, but the idea was abandoned before a blow was struck. When the corner of Monroe and Clark streets was reached, in the circuitous return march around the Board of Trade center, a carriage, containing Mr. Kadish, an old and respected citizen, and his wife, came up with the procession; some fellow in the crowd yelled, "Turn over the Board of Trade carriage," and the next moment a cowardly miscreant threw a large cobble stone through the glass door of the carriage, which struck the lady in the face, cutting her severely and deluging her dress with blood. After this exhibition of deviltry, the procession made its way speedily to Fifth avenue, and took a position in front of the *Arbeiter Zeitung* office, and here A. R. Parsons, appearing at one of the windows, made a speech to a crowd numbering about 1,000. He was followed by Spies, who edited the *Arbeiter Zeitung*. These speeches afterward were raised in judgment against both. Not content with advising rebellion, anarchy, assassination, arson and plunder, Spies had the fool-hardiness to take a number of persons into his sanctum, where he exhibited for their edification numerous devices which he claimed "the people" would use in a short time to strike terror into the hearts of tyrants. He admitted a reporter into his confidence and showed him a quantity of dynamite, some bombs and a perfect armory of weapons. "If they'd attacked us," said one foreigner introduced to the reporter, "we'd have fixed them," and he pulled a large six-shooter out of his pocket. A dozen others drew similar weapons. "Every one of us has got one of them—we're armed to the teeth," said the confiding anarchist. "Come in here," said another, as he led the way to the printing office. "See here," he said:

"Every man in this parade had some of these," and he showed a long cartridge which, on close inspection, was found to be half filled with nitro-glycerine. "I guess that would have raised a little racket," he added. These cartridges were the same used by burglars in blowing safes open. "Here's some ear-splitters," he remarked jocularly, and he pointed to a big box filled with cartridges six inches long. "The office is full of such stuff as that." And so it proved to be, many months afterward.

Strange as it may appear now, there were no arrests made, at least none of the leaders were arrested, or molested, and although the papers exposed the anarchistic conspiracy fully, and called the attention of the mayor to the desperate character of the leaders, to the ignorant brutality of their followers, and to the treasonable doctrines which were being propagated, the *Arbeiter Zeitung* and its editors, stockholders, constituents and subscribers, were permitted to go ahead, fomenting discord among the peaceable-minded, breeding discontent among the laboring classes, and fermenting deviltry among the ignorant and the vicious. One of the most truthful as well as the strongest arguments brought forward at a later day as a reason why the leading conspirators against public order should be leniently dealt with, was based upon the fact that for years the city authorities had permitted them to express the most incendiary and treasonable utterances, without making the slightest attempt to restrain or punish them. At first socialism of the Utopian and poetical school was talked by the men who desired a social revolution, and the followers of the socialistic Dr. Schmidt numbered at one time 12,000 voters, and were represented in the city council and state legislature. Then came the propagation of communistic doctrines, not as they are understood by the teachers of social science, but as they were understood by the rabble who sought the communism of Paris only, and from this point the descent was natural and easy toward anarchistic teachings. Fielden had read much, and thought much, and was ambitious to become the Danton of the American revolution; Parsons was a raving enthusiast who wanted to be its Marat, and the ambition of Spies led him to dream that he might some day become a Robespierre, in a sea-green coat, dictating terms to the privileged classes from the City Hall, as his idol had dictated terms to the royalty and nobility of France from the Hotel d'Ville in Paris. The three had read and pondered over the history of the French revolution, as boys of weak intellect read and ponder over a cheap novel of adventure, until, like the boys of weak intellect, they became inspired with the Quixotic idea that they might go out into the world, paralyze society, and revolutionize the governments of Christendom, beginning, of course, with the government of the United States.

They had already an armed group; they had meeting places in all sections of the city; they had missionaries out among the workingmen; they printed thousands of pamphlets; they had a daily newspaper and they never missed an opportunity of pushing themselves to the front, or of demonstrating their strength at workingmen's meetings, or in political gatherings.

On the evening of April 30, about sixty prominent anarchists met at 54 Lake street, when the only woman in the room, a Mrs. Swank, (Sclavonic names predominate among the anarchists) was called upon to preside. At this meeting Parsons boldly advocated the use of dynamite as a means of overthrowing the "privileged classes"—*i. e.*, the classes who had accumulated private property. "Dynamite," he said, "is the gift of science to mankind struggling to be free; it is the true peacemaker. The dread of dynamite, that terrible destructive agent which every laborer could produce at his own hearthstone, would force the owners of private property—the privileged classes—to do justice and remove the cause of discontent.

At 3 p. m., on Sunday, May 3, the anarchists held a large

meeting on the lake front. A. R. Parsons here addressed what he called "The International Workingmen's Association." Parsons was a great inventor of names, and he used them lavishly in designating the different bodies which entered into the great sedition movement which he was endeavoring to build up. Sometimes he called his followers "The Workingmen's Party of the United States," sometimes "The International Brotherhood," again, "The International Workingmen's Association." At times he would address his hearers as "Fellow Slaves," and then, by a strange inconsistency, wind up by appealing to them as "Citizen Freemen." After a number of inflammatory addresses were made at the time mentioned, Parsons announced that meetings would be held every pleasant Sunday afternoon from that time forward. The newspapers with one accord appealed to the mayor to prevent the gathering of these meetings, as they were usually attended by the very worst element of the city's population, but the question of free speech arose in his honor's mind and nothing was done.

About this time the horrible Italian strangling case, which first became known as "The Trunk Mystery," attracted public attention, and occupied the time of the detective force. In the solution of this case, and the conviction of the barbarous assassins who had a hand in it, Detectives Bonfield and Coulson took a distinguished part. This case is referred to elsewhere.

Another meeting of anarchists was held at the lake front on May 10, and was addressed by Parsons, Fielden and Spies; their language, if anything, being a little more rabid than ever. "We are here," said Parsons, "to consider the causes of and remedies for public discontent. We are those who are called anarchists, socialists, dynamiters, loafers, bummers, rascals and thieves, or any worse name the representatives of the press can invent." He was not in good voice, he said, and would, therefore, introduce Mr. Owens. Mr. Owens proved to be a man after Parsons' own heart, and he talked anarchy until the crowd began to thin out. These meetings were held regularly, as announced.

Numerous strikes occurred in May. The Union ore shovellers on the docks, the Joliet Steel Works' employes, the stained glass workers, the employes of a large printing house, and even the hospital nurses went out, but quiet was soon restored. In June, there were great railroad strikes throughout the West, notably in St. Louis, and the switchmen's strike of this city caused a great deal of commotion and anxiety, keeping the police busy, but doing no mischief outside of the railroad yards. There was serious rioting at Lemont, too, and some of the rioters were shot by members of the state militia, an occurrence which gave the anarchists a fresh text, and helped to swell their meetings. Printed circulars, relating the circumstances, highly colored, of the Lemont episode, were distributed by the anarchists, but they failed utterly in their effort to create a disturbance here. It was not until June 30 that an opportunity, such as they had been long seeking for, exhibited itself. On that day all the street-car conductors and drivers employed by the West Division Railway Company went out on a strike. No cars were run, except during the morning on Milwaukee avenue and Van Buren street. Three weeks previous to this time, the conductors and drivers held a meeting, and petitioned the company to increase and equalize their wages, shorten the term of service of probationers, and dismiss an assistant superintendent, who had made himself offensive to the employes. The company complied with these demands with apparent cheerfulness, the pay was advanced, the term of probationers was shortened, and the offensive assistant superintendent received his walking papers. The men, at a meeting subsequently, expressed themselves as being perfectly satisfied with these concessions, and it seemed as though peace would continue to prevail for some time to come. On the day following the last mentioned meeting, however, some of the drivers and conductors who had been foremost in petitioning the company were dropped from the service, and between that time and June 30, fifteen in all had been discharged. It was evidently, so the men said and believed, the aim of the company to drop the men who had been instrumental in forcing the concessions. After these dismissals occurred, the carmen met to consider the situation, drew up resolutions, and sent an appeal to the company, asking for justice. A person connected with the company's business office received this appeal, and, the carmen claimed, tore it up contemptuously in the presence of the committee. This irritated the men greatly. Another meeting was called at which it was stated that many more of the conductors and drivers would be discharged, but that the company required their attendance as witnesses in damage suits then pending. The meeting, after considering the subject carefully, decided that it was best to bring the company to terms by ordering a strike.

Early on the morning of the 30th, the conductors and drivers of the Halsted street line were at the barn, but refused to take out their cars. Lieut. Byrne, of the Deering street station, was present with a small squad, but there was no trouble to call them into active service, and the best good humor prevailed. At the Western avenue stables the men were present in full force, but refused to work. Captain (now inspector) Bonfield was on the ground with a squad, and later, a number of deputy sheriffs reported for duty. A driver and conductor having been secured by the company, Deputy Sheriff McCartney took a position by the driver's side, and the car started toward Madison street, amid the jeering and hooting of the crowd. The car made the trip.

Superintendent Doyle had instructed Captain O'Donnell to look after the barns in the second precinct, Captain Bonfield in the third, and Captain Hathaway in the fourth. The sheriff detailed deputies to act independently of or in conjunction with the police force. During the first day of the strike the men behaved themselves in a praiseworthy man-

ner. The sympathy of the public was with them; West
Siders, male and female, young and old, walked to and from
their places of business cheerfully, and suffered all manner
of inconvenience, in the hope that the carmen would win.
On the second day, enterprising individuals began to take
advantage of the street-car lock-up, and the West Side
arteries soon swarmed with omnibuses, express wagons,
furniture trucks, rheumatic hacks, wheezy carriages, and
broken-down vehicles of every shape and condition, the
drivers of which were all engaged in soliciting and obtaining patronage at from 3 cents to 10 cents per passenger.
The people not only bore the ordeal with patience, but
rather enjoyed the novelty of the situation, and not a mur-
mur was raised against the strikers. That day the carmen
issued the following:

To THE PEOPLE OF CHICAGO:—The conductors and drivers of the
West Division Railway Company desire the public to explicitly understand that they do not desire to be judges of whom the company shall
employ or discharge, but on this occasion, considering the efficiency of
the discharged men, and their long terms of service in the employment,
it is, in our estimation, a spiteful and arbitrary act on the part of the
officials. If the company can produce and substantiate their charges
against those men, we are willing to abide by the decision of the public.

The public decided that the men were right and the strike
went on. On the forenoon of July 1 the company made an
effort to run its cars from the Western avenue barn. A plan
had been decided upon over night, and in accordance with
this three cars made their appearance almost simultaneously
on the street. The first was No. 504, and was in charge of
C. W. Howe as conductor and G. W. Nash as driver. Sup-
porting these were eight policemen. The second was 576,
in charge of J. V. Boswell, conductor, and Thomas Snow,
driver, and seven policemen. The third was No. 500, in
charge of H. Adams, conductor, F. A. Skinner, driver, and
fifteen deputy sheriffs. The conductors and drivers were
either new men or barn employes, and they looked anything
but comfortable as they passed through the street which,

from the barn to Madison street, was thronged by idlers and roughs who now began to take a prominent part in the proceedings, to the exclusion of the carmen. Policemen had been stationed at intervals, and in good-sized squads around the corner, and for a block or two down Madison street, and although the crowd hooted at and insulted the drivers, conductors, deputy sheriffs and officers, it was kept well out of the track, and the cars proceeded, closely together in a block, toward the east. Two patrol wagons acted as an advance guard and after passing through the densest part of the crowd wagons and cars traveled at a brisk speed. Laborers employed along the street, as well as pedestrians, hooted the procession, but it proceeded, unmindful of all remarks, toward the South Side. Randolph and State street was reached at 11:50, the down trip having been made in 30 minutes. It was noon when the cars reached Madison street bridge on their return trip, and at that time the employes of all the factories west of the river, for three or four blocks on either side of Madison street, were let out for their dinner hour. These naturally gravitated toward the main West Side artery, where it was but reasonable to expect that there would be excitement, in view of the carmen's strike. As the first patrol wagon was sighted yells went up from the crowds, and stones, dirt, and other missiles within reach, began to fly. From Desplaines to Halsted, and even beyond, the fusilade was kept up, but no more serious attack was made. The policemen in the wagons and cars, as well as the deputy sheriffs, behaved with admirable coolness, and bore the assault and the insults with good humored resignation in the main. At Halsted street a young tough aimed a stone at Captain Bonfield's head. That officer saw him, and quick as a flash pulled his revolver and fired, aiming low so as to merely disable the fellow. But the ball missed its mark, when he collared the miscreant and threw him bodily into the patrol wagon. Deputy Sheriff George F. Horton was struck by a stone which crashed through the glass window of the street-

car, and cut him severely in the face. At Halsted street
Mayor Harrison disarmed a man who, with a pickaxe, was
endeavoring to rip up the track, and turned him over to the
police.

As the cars passed Madison and Carpenter streets Officer
M. W. O'Brien arrested a young man named John Sullivan
for throwing stones. Sullivan, making a loud outcry, resisted the officer, and soon an immense crowd surrounded
the two. It became apparent at once that the sympathies of
the crowd were with Sullivan, and cries of "Rescue him,"
"Kill the copper," and "Hang him," came from the mob. Not
less than three thousand excited men were yelling at one
time. When the cry "Hang him" was heard a man jumped
off an express wagon, rope in hand, ready to assist in the cere-
mony. All this time Officer O'Brien kept a tight grip on his
prisoner, and with revolver drawn bravely faced the howling
mob. Little by little he backed toward the sidewalk, and
then to a store front, where he looked at the crowd with determination bordering on defiance. The mob was momentarily becoming more threatening, and just as it was closing in
upon the policeman a young hero named F. E. Sullivan
elbowed his way through, took a position at Officer O'Brien's
side, pulled a revolver and threatened to kill the first man
who should attempt a rescue. This encouraged some other
law-abiding people in the crowd, and Officer O'Brien soon had
a body-guard around him. The prisoner was quickly placed
in a hack, and before the mob realized it, was on his way to
the Desplaines street station.

Early in the morning there was trouble all along South
Halsted street—there is always trouble along South Halsted
street when there is trouble anywhere else. Deputy sheriffs
had attempted to move a car, but the mob unhitched the
horses and upset the car on the side of the street. Several
cars which had been started out, insufficiently guarded, were
treated in a like manner on Madison street. On Lake, the
excitement was so great, for a time, as to attract the crowd

from Madison street. Things looked quiet, and before the street-car people had heard from the first detachment sent out, they attempted to start some other cars, placed in charge of deputy sheriffs, who agreed to drive. Deputy Sheriff Finn was struck by a stone on the side of the head, as his car reached Leavitt street, and the trip had to be abandoned.

On the morning of July 2d, greatly to the surprise of the strikers, the mob and the public in general, the company made no effort to move its cars. A conference had been held between the street-car and the city officials, and it was decided that a determined and systematic effort would be made next day to break the back of the strike and establish street-car communication between the West and South Sides. During the evening Superintendent Doyle, Lieutenant Shea, of the detective force, Lieutenant Hubbard, of the Central detail, and other police officers, held a consultation to determine what course to pursue. It was a council of war, and at its conclusion Superintendent Doyle informed the representatives of the press that if the company decided to run its cars next day the police department, while it could not supply drivers or conductors from the force, would do all in its power to protect the company's employes and property, and to preserve the peace. Captain Bonfield said, upon being questioned, "If the railway company wants to run its cars it is entitled to protection and should have it. The cars shall be run if the company desire it, and people who do not wish to get hurt had better keep out of the way." The Central detail was ordered to report at 6:30 on the morning of the third—a half hour earlier than usual.

Mayor Harrison suggested arbitration all this time, but President Jones, of the railway company, said he did not see that there was anything to arbitrate. All the men asked for, he said, was their peremptory reinstatement, and if this demand were complied with it would carry with it the implication that the men and not the company should dictate who should be employed and who discharged.

A mass meeting of the striking carmen and their sympathizers was held at the Haymarket that night, and among the speakers was Congressman (then alderman) Frank Lawler, who said it was a shame that the street-car conductors and drivers should be driven to this means of enforcing a principle which all men admitted to be correct and laudable. The street-car company was making very poor returns for the franchises and benefits which had been heaped upon it, and added: "The company will learn that it must take back the old employes. It must realize that unless it carries out its agreement with the people [to run its cars regularly] the city council in session next Monday night will say 'We cancel and revoke your charter.'"

Popular opinion was so strongly on the side of the strikers that nearly all the men arrested were discharged without punishment, and in response to the request of a committee Mayor Harrison released the man whom he had himself arrested at Halsted street, for attempting to tear up the track. L. Z. Leiter, a stockholder in the company, called upon the mayor and protested that the city was threatened with anarchy, at the same time demanding that the lawful authorities should make themselves felt. The mayor replied that in mingling with the crowds he found that nine out of every ten citizens were in sympathy with the strikers, and that the wisest and speediest way of bringing about a settlement was by submitting the question in dispute to arbitration. Again the carmen addressed the public, submitting a long statement of their grievances, and complaining particularly of the treatment they had received at the hands of James K. Lake, the superintendent, whom they held responsible for the entire difficulty.

Between 5 and 6 o'clock on the morning of July 3d, four hundred policemen, detailed from the different districts, reported for duty at the Desplaines street station. Captain Bonfield, in whose district most of the trouble had occurred, and where the troubles of the day just opening were expected to occur, was placed in command of the entire force, the captains present from other precincts acting under his orders. Superintendent Doyle, however, was present, and when all had reported, and the men were ready to march, he addressed them from the steps of the station, as follows:

You have all been on review and dress parade in fine form. To-day you will probably have a different kind of duty, and I want this department to show itself. Whatever your private views or mine may be, property must be defended, the law must be upheld and you are its defenders. Each division has its commanders and they assume all responsibility. Pay strict attention to your commanders; they will tell you what to do. Wait for orders. I am sure you will do your duty. Move!

Seventeen patrol wagons, loaded down with blue-coats, speeded west on Washington boulevard. Between Ashland and Western avenues, on Madison street, these wagons were posted at intervals on the cross streets, close to the corners, the horses' heads facing north and south. Looking up or down Madison street they could not be seen, but they were so many hidden forts covering the thoroughfare, and ready at a moment's notice to sweep it clean. From the wagons patrolmen were sent east and west along the street, stationed so as to cover the sections between the avenues mentioned. It was the duty of these outposts to prevent the gathering of crowds, and to compel all persons to keep moving. But the crowds were dense, and the policemen were not inclined to be too severe. While they were not wanting in courage or in fidelity to the city, yet they could not but sympathize with the strike, like everybody else, and this made them too lenient with the other sympathizers. A detachment of 200 policemen started, as the wagons left, and marched west on Madison street, leaving strong details at Halsted street, Ogden avenue and other threatening points. The street was lined with people, as though a great procession was expected to pass.

An attempt was made here to start ten cars from the barn, but the third car had scarcely reached Madison street before Danielson, the driver, was pulled off the platform by the mob.   Captain Bonfield [see Chapter XVII] rescued him and placed him on his car.   It was at this point that Captain Bonfield arranged the cars into "blocks."   Taking nine cars he divided them into three divisions.   The first of each division was an open car, loaded with policemen, facing front; the second was a closed car, guarded by twenty policemen, inside and on the platforms, to be used as a prison van or ambulance; the third was an open car, loaded with blue-coats, facing back.   These three divisions having been arranged, Captain Bonfield took his position at the head of a double advance platoon, covering the entire width of the street, and his famous march began.

Just as the start was about to be made the mob attempted to close in on the police and storm the cars, when Capt. Bonfield called upon the crowd to fall back.   "You must not molest us," he shouted, loud enough to be heard by the entire crowd in the vicinity; "you have all been warned, and now I repeat that unless you disperse you will get hurt." There was no reason to assume that Capt. Bonfield did not mean what he said.   He was placed with his men in a desperate position.   He must carry out the orders he had himself given.   To hesitate now, in the face of any consequences, would bring the entire police establishment into disgrace, and law and order into ridicule and contempt. What had been undertaken must be carried out at all hazards.   It were madness to spare a few heads or a few limbs, or even a few lives, if they stood in the way here, for to spare them now would mean a wholesale massacre in case the police failed and the military were placed in control. He was dreadfully earnest as he spoke to the mob, his face almost white, and his voice trembling with suppressed emotion.   Scarcely had he finished before a stone was hurled at the police.   "Shoot the first man that throws a stone! March!" he commanded.

There have been more dreadful, bloodier marches than this, but certainly very few in which the commanding officers and their men were so completely at the mercy of their assailants. Capt. Bonfield knew, and every man in his command knew, that the police had taken the unpopular side of the fight. If they didn't know it at first, the yells, hootings, ˙jeers, sneers, insults, curses, missiles, which were piled upon them after leaving Western avenue, soon brought them to a realization of it. The mob had to fly before the advancing column of blue-coats, but the rioters hurled back defiance and stones as they fled.

Between Western avenue and Leavitt street the mob raised a barricade of lumber, gas pipe, curb stones, beer kegs, etc., across the street. Building was going on in the vicinity, and there was plenty of material for obstructing the progress of the police at hand. As fast as the police removed these obstructions others were raised, and this method of warfare began to assume an appearance so decidedly Parisian and communistic in character that Capt. Bonfield became ˙satisfied of the presence of anarchistic leaders in the mob. And he was right. They had not only mingled with the crowds for the past three days, but they had been the instigators of nearly all the violence that had been attempted. They hoped before Bonfield could reach Halsted street to have created a general uprising. But few of the conductors or drivers were in the mob. It was composed almost wholly now of roughs, socialists, thieves, and foolish respectable people, who meant no harm, but contributed toward doing a great deal of it. These foolish respectable people were pushed toward the front, and the thugs, thieves and anarchists threw stones and insults at the police over their heads. In the different charges made by Bonfield's men many of these "innocent people" were badly hurt, but it was as plain then as it is now, that had they been elsewhere, attending to their business, they would have escaped injury.

As the mob was routed from one stronghold after another, it consolidated in advance of the police. At Leavitt

street a brick building was in course of construction. From
the material piled on the street the mob pulled five twenty-
foot iron girders, and laid them across the tracks. On these
they piled timber, gas pipes, brick, and other material, until
they had a barricade five or six feet high. Entrenched behind this they taunted, insulted and pelted the police, while
other obstructions in front were being cleared away. The
policemen went to work patiently and with a will, and soon
opened the street for traffic. No shots were fired. At
Hoyne avenue a number of men, employed by the gas company in putting down a new main, had covered the track for
half a block with two feet of black clay, which had to be
cleared away before the cars could pass. Of course this
was done with malicious intent, and a number of the men
were arrested. At Honore street there was another barricade, and a charge was made on the mob. The street was
again opened, but the police met with obstructions at nearly
every corner, and the club had to be used freely. At Peoria,
Green, Halsted and Union streets, rough crowds had assembled, and the police had reason to fear a desperate
attack before the bridge was reached; but the demeanor of
Bonfield and his command kept the mob at bay, although
the vilest epithets were hurled from the crowd, and missiles
were thrown with unceasing regularity and admirable precision. The policemen used their clubs whenever necessary, and the taps which they gave were not gentle, by any
means. The mob saw that business was meant, and, seeing
this, it gradually but reluctantly withdrew. The trip from
Desplaines street to State was without incident, and the
return trip was a comparatively easy one, as the police stationed along West Madison street had prevented the reassembling of crowds, and saw that no obstructions were
placed on the track. Western avenue was reached at 9:20,
the trip back having consumed only an hour. Here the horses
were changed, and the nine cars, manned and led as before,
started upon their second journey. At Hoyne avenue the

mayor ordered the police to prevent the crowd from getting on the sides of the street, it being his idea that the thoroughfare should be swept clean. At Robey street the verandas of several houses were occupied by women, who were evidently in sympathy with the strike, and were not ashamed to proclaim it. They reviled the police as they passed. On the sidewalk in front of them was a large crowd of men, who appeared to be enjoying the remarks made by the women. The officers charged upon these fellows, when all save one broke and fled. This was a young man, and he held his ground boldly and defiantly. He was told to move, but refused to stir. Then he was clubbed, and pushed into a yard opening on the street, the women in the meantime berating the officers, and crying, "Don't touch Fred; don't you dare touch Fred," and shaking their fists at the blue-coats. But Fred was all unconscious of the subsequent proceedings, and when he awoke a radical change had taken place in his views respecting the rights of free-born citizens. At 3 p. m., when the cars arrived at State and Madison street, the crowd was great, but peaceable. For the first time now the cars began to receive passengers, and a procession of five cars started west from State street, made up as follows: The first was occupied exclusively by the police. This was an open car Then came a closed car, which received passengers, the third and fourth had more passengers, and the fifth was packed with policemen. At 5 p. m. the remainder of the cars left State street, carrying about eighty passengers, in the order named above. The first was an open car, managed by Captain (now superintendent) Ebersold, Lieutenant Shea, Lieutenant Laughlin, and fifty-two men. Next came cars guarded by policemen and well filled with passengers, and the last car was occupied by policemen, under command of Lieutenant Arch.

During the day, about twenty-five persons had been badly clubbed; and loud complaints were made by those who had been in the crowd, and the friends and relatives of the injured persons. Among the first to complain of the police management was President Billings, of the West Side Gas Company, who protested to Mayor Harrison against the arrest of the men who had thrown clay on the track. To him the mayor said: "You are a stockholder in the street-car company which has called upon me for protection. Your men violated the laws, and because we arrest them, you make a row about it. That is a pretty position you have placed yourself in." This incident occurred on West Madison street, and the crowd seeing through the situation, cheered the mayor. Complaints were made at headquarters, at the mayor's office, and in the newspapers, of the alleged brutality of the police. Most of these complaints were directed against Captain Bonfield. As a rule, the newspapers sustained and defended him. "The police," said Superintendent Doyle, "have in every instance ordered the people to move on. When they didn't comply with the order, they were moved by force. No one was clubbed for the fun of clubbing him. None of the officers went on to the cars for fun. Something had to be done to maintain law and order in the city. Citizens do not seem to understand that they have no right to congregate on the street corners or in the streets. An ordinance prohibits it. They must go along quietly about their business. If they stand around they violate the ordinance by refusing to move on when commanded. If citizens would obey the law there would be no trouble."

The mayor said. "Several gentlemen have called upon me and asked why I did not order the police to shoot into the crowd. I sent for Captain Bonfield, against whom complaints are made, and he said to me, ' Mr. Mayor, I am doing this in mercy to the people. A club to-day, to make them scatter, may save the use of a pistol to-morrow.'"

On the morning of July 4, the papers announced that several suits would be commenced against the city by the persons clubbed; that Captain Bonfield would be prosecuted, and that warrants would be sworn out against him. In reply to questions, Captain Bonfield said he had heard nothing of suits or warrants, and refused to say anything in defense of his own conduct, leaving that to the verdict of the public, when the popular mind had become cooler. A detective informed him that a plot had been discovered, which had for its object the taking of his life. He smiled and made no comment. The backbone of the riot was broken. Bonfield could afford to wait patiently for a change of public sentiment, and although the workingmen of the city were bitter against him at first, and the Knights of Labor denounced him, yet it became clearer, as the days rolled by, that he had simply performed his duty, nothing more, nothing less.

The following correspondence passed on the evening of the 3d:

MAYOR'S OFFICE, CHICAGO, July 3.

MR. J. R. JONES, *President West Division Railway Company.*

DEAR SIR:—I have use for all my force to-morrow, on account of the large number of fires, accidents and disturbances occurring every Fourth of July, making necessary the use of the entire police and fire departments, and leaving them wearied the following day; and in the excited state of public feeling, it is impossible to run your cars for the general transportation of passengers on your lines. I therefore hope you will not, under the circumstances, urge your call on me for protection in running your cars to-morrow and Sunday.   Respectfully,

CARTER H. HARRISON, *Mayor.*

To which the following reply was made:

OFFICE OF THE CHICAGO WEST DIVISION RAILWAY COMPANY, }
CHICAGO, JULY 3. }

THE HON. CARTER H. HARRISON, *Mayor.*

DEAR SIR:—I beg to acknowledge the receipt of your communication of this date, and to hasten to reply that I entirely agree with you in the opinion that it will be unwise to attempt to run our cars to-morrow and next day. We shall be ready to commence in earnest next Monday morning, and I beg to express the hope that you will then be in a position to continue to render us the same efficient aid which you are now rendering.   Your obedient servant,

J. R. JONES, *President.*

All was quiet and peaceable on Saturday the Fourth of July, and on Sunday, although the streets were constantly jammed with vehicles engaged in passenger traffic, and more or less hilarity was indulged in by the people. The mayor still urged arbitration, and suggested three of the Circuit judges as arbiters. The carmen took kindly to the suggestion and selected Judge Prendergast. The street-car people would not consent, President Jones replying that the company was acting within its rights, and lawfully, and protested that it should be placed upon a level with men who had openly violated the law. On Monday morning the following was issued:

WHERE s, The excitement growing out of the strike of the conductors and drivers of the West Division Street Railway Company, did during the last week cause acts of lawlessness to be committed when said company attempted to operate its cars; and

WHEREAS, Such lawless acts would have been to a great extent avoided if citizens had not congregated along the streets when the cars were being operated, or had dispersed when ordered so to do by the police, as they should have done under the law; and

WHEREAS, Said company has notified me that its cars will again be operated in accordance with chartered rights and duty, Monday, the 6th day of July instant; therefore, for the sake of peace and of the good name of Chicago, and for the preservation of life and property, notice is hereby given that the people must refrain from congregating on the streets when the cars of said company are being run, until all excitement shall have subsided, and that all persons must immediately move on when ordered so to do by the police; and

NOTICE is further given, that the police of Chicago must and will, at all hazards, protect the property of said company, while in performance of its chartered rights, and must and will protect the servants of said company while engaged in their lawful duties.

I do most earnestly appeal to all citizens to aid in protecting the good name of Chicago.

CARTER H. HARRISON, *Mayor*.

The socialists, at their regular Sunday meeting on the lake front, used Bonfield's march for a text, and Spies and Fielden, who made speeches, advised the street-car men and all other workingmen to buy guns and fight for their rights like men. Notice was given by Alderman Weber at a West Side mass meeting that he would move the revocation of the company's charter in the council Monday night. The best the company could do was to run thirty-three cars on Monday, being short of men, and there being few who were willing to take the places offered; the disposition of the public grew more hostile to the corporation, and at length President Jones was forced to agree that the matter complained of by the strikers would be speedily investigated and full justice done. This was satisfactory and ended the strike. On Tuesday the cars ran as usual. The superintendent of the road was shortly afterward removed, and since then the corporation and its employes have had no serious difficulty. The police came out of the affair with credit and with no casualties worthy of mention.

Many persons will remember the riot which occurred at Silver Leaf Grove during the progress of a socialistic picnic in 1876. It was a bloody affair, while it lasted, and forever afterward caused decent people to shun that spot as a summer resort. Ogdens' Grove thenceforth became the picnicking ground for labor societies, and particularly for socialists, communists and anarchists.

All the terrorists in the city turned out on Monday, July 12, following the street-car troubles, to attend a picnic at Ogdens' Grove. The West Side division of anarchists formed at Clinton and Lake streets in the morning, and Mrs. Parsons and four other women occupied conspicuous places in the pageant. Several decorated wagons filled with women were placed at intervals in the line. The banners that were carried bore such inscriptions as "We Mourn, but not so much for Gen. Grant as for a Little Child that Starved to Death Yesterday," [Gen. Grant had just died at Mount McGregor]; "Government is for Slaves, Freemen Govern Themselves;" "Millions Labor for the Benefit of the Few—We want to Labor for Ourselves;" "In the Absence of Law all Men are Free;" "The Fountain of Right is Might—Workingmen Arm !" "Every Government is a Conspiracy of the Rich Against the People;" "Our Civilization—The Bullet and Policeman's Club." German mottoes to the same effect were carried, some of which, being translated, read as follows: " Private Capital is the Product of Robbery;" "Down with All Laws;" "Hurrah for the Social Revolution—Liberty Without Equality is a Lie!" Patches of red cloth were worn on the hats of the men, some wore red sashes, there were red shoulder-knots on the "Blue Smock Brigade." The red flag was flaunted to the breeze boldly. Copies of an inflammatory paper were distributed among the crowds. The North Side contingent was partly composed of men armed with carbines and muskets. The display made was one calculated to create alarm. At the grounds Parsons, Fielden and Spies addressed about 2,000 people, denouncing the police in particular, appealing to their followers to arm themselves, to learn the use of dynamite, how to make bombs, and how to be prepared for the social revolution which was certainly near at hand.

On Sunday, September 5, the anarchists indulged in another demonstration, and all the policemen in the city were held in readiness for duty. This demonstration was gotten up for the purpose of throwing odium on the "Trade and Labor" display in which the workingmen of the city were to participate next day. Before the anarchist procession moved, Fielden made an incendiary speech from a platform on Market street near Randolph. "There is going to be a parade to-morrow," he said. "Those fellows" (meaning the workingmen who were not in sympathy with anarchy), "want to reconcile labor and capital. They want to reconcile you to your starvation and your shanties. They have invited the chief murderer, Harrison, and assistant murderer, Bonfield. Have they forgotten Bill Pinkerton and his bloody gang?"

The procession, headed by Parsons, who acted as grand marshal, moved on, many of the men and women singing the "Marseillaise." There were fifty young girls, above whom was held a banner bearing the inscription "American Corps," and a number of women occupied seats in decorated wagons. Dozens of red flags were carried, and the mottoes were as treasonable and inflammatory as those borne on the previous occasion. "Hail to the Social Revolution," "Our Civilization—Powder, Lead and the Club," "The Greatest Crime to-day is Poverty;" "Down with Government, God and Gold," "Subscribe for the Firebrand" (the name of an anarchist paper), were among the most striking.

Parsons, Fielden and the rest made speeches at the grove, where there were three or four thousand people assembled.

The anarchists were free to come and go as they pleased, to hold meetings, to parade the streets, to expose their sentiments, banners, to dispense their poisonous doctrines, to breed discontent, to excite the ignorant to the commission of crime, to propagate sedition and to advocate murder, arson and social revolution. Everything pointed to a dreadful culmination. It came soon enough.

CHAPTER XIII.

THE YEAR 1886—THE GREAT EIGHT-HOUR MOVEMENT—THE INFLUENCE OF
THE FOREIGN-BORN IN AMERICAN INDUSTRIAL AFFAIRS—ANTAGONISM
OF THE ANARCHISTS TO THE PROPOSED SHORT-HOUR SYSTEM — HOW
THEY FOUGHT THE MOVEMENT—PARSONS, SPIES, FIELDEN, SCHWAB—
BREEDING DISCONTENT — A GRAND OPPORTUNITY FOR THE REDS —
DISGRACEFUL SCENE ON FIFTH AVENUE—THE McCORMICK RIOT.

Toward the latter part of 1885, and during the spring of
1886. the attention of all observant people, and more especially of the employing and employed classes—those two
grand divisions of mankind in America, between whom and
other citizens there is a line, but so delicately drawn that
its definition seems at times almost impossible—was firmly
riveted upon a movement which promised to revolutionize
the industrial habits of the people, and threatened to up-
root and discard the practices which had been ingrafted
into the race by the slow and subtle process of time. People
still on the sunshiny side of life will remember when the
working day in the United States began with the rising of
the sun, and only ended—not always even then—with the
going down thereof. And those were days when the necessaries of life were dearer and the price of labor cheaper
than they have been at any time during the past ten years.
In Europe, to-day, the hours of labor range from twelve to
fourteen hours. French and German artisans, mechanics
and laborers are accustomed to begin the day's work at 5
a. m. in summer and at 6 a. m. in winter, ceasing half an
hour for breakfast at 9, an hour for dinner at noon, and
continuing at their labor until 7 o'clock p. m. in summer,
and 8 o'clock p. m. in winter, making the length of their
working days eleven and one-half hours. In England and

throughout the United Kingdom, the hours of labor are only a trifle shorter. These remarks have special reference to manufacturing cities, and the figures given are based upon an extended series of consular reports made to the state department at Washington. In return for this labor the compensation obtained by the workingmen for the same class, kind or quality of labor is, as a rule, one-half, and in many parts of Europe two-thirds, less than is received by American workingmen.

It may be claimed here that European customs have nothing whatever to do with the arrangement of affairs in this country; that we are not now, and never have been, guided by them, and that we never will permit European ideas to control, or even enter into, our method of doing things. This would be a protest at once dignified and worthy of American citizenship, could it maintain itself against the overwhelming evidence which rises up to crush it as a false statement, with no foundation of fact upon which it may be firmly established. The truth is, that European customs, brought over here by European immigrants, have had, and are having, a great deal to do with the arrangement of our affairs; that the employed classes of the United States are now, and have been, in great measure, guided by them, and to a most alarming extent, and that the American people have permitted certain ideas of European origin and growth, and of the most pernicious character, to enter into their method of doing things. Were the capitalists, the employers, of the United States to take as readily and as lovingly to the teachings of European capitalists and employers, as the workingmen of this country do to the teachings of newly arrived immigrants, fresh from their eleven and a half hours of daily labor and their fifty cents of daily hire, then, indeed, this would be a land of misery, within the borders of which every man of spirit might be justified before God in raising the cry of insurrection. And in the face of the innumerable and, for the most part, inexcusable strikes and riots planned or fomented by workingmen of European birth and education, which from time to time have hampered, obstructed, and now and then paralyzed the industries of this country, it seems strange that the European idea of dealing with the employed classes has not been adopted in this country by employers, even to a limited extent.

The hours of labor in the United States have gradually undergone a reduction during the past thirty years, until to-day the generally adopted period of doing labor is limited to ten hours. This was the case in 1878 when the eight-hour movement was fairly launched by the passage of an eight-hour law for government employes. The arguments advanced in favor of a reduction in the hours of labor from ten to eight hours were logical. First, it was a reform asked in the name of political economy, all political economists being agreed (as Samuel C. Hunt, of Boston, said in his letter of Nov. 10, 1879, to Hon. Hendrick B. Wright, chairman of the Congressional committee on the Depression of Labor) that the standard of wages is determined by the cost of subsistence rather than by the number of hours employed; that "the natural and necessary rate of wages," as Adam Smith says, "is such a rate as will supply not only the commodities that are indispensably necessary for the support of life, but whatever the custom of the country renders it indecent for creditable people, even of the lowest order, to be without." It was asked in the interest of civilization. " The battle for the reduction of the hours of labor is a struggle for a wider civilization," says Hunt. "Civilization demands a prosperous and contented people with increased wants, and means to supply them. To refuse aid to willing hands to cultivate our idle lands, to import a servile race [the Chinese] that thereby the cost of subsistence may be reduced to a far lower standard and a lower level for all be reached, and to insist on long hours of toil when thousands are standing idle, all are heavy blows aimed at the very foundation of our modern civilization. A decrease in the hours of labor means rest, and rest is invariably accompanied by increased wants. Release the poor drudge in the mine or the factory from his long hours of toil and give him daily hours of recreation and leisure, and you at once raise him in the social scale. Rest cultivates. We insist that every reduction of the hours of labor heretofore made has elevated the working people; that increased leisure has invariably produced new wants, has added to the necessaries of life, and consequently has raised the social condition of the people. The setting apart of one day in seven for rest, wherein no man shall labor, is a prime factor in the growth of civilization. We never hear the charge that wage-workers receive seven days' wages for six days' work, simply because conscientious conviction has been hardened into national custom." It was held that the whole history of the short-hour movement in England proved conclusively that every reduction in the hours of labor was followed by an increase in wages. It was asked because of the changed relation between production and consumption. The changed condition of our industrial system, arising from the rapid development of mechanical appliances whereby hard labor has been so largely superseded, called for remedial legislation looking to the establishment of shorter hours of labor. "Political economists," adds Hunt, "recognize the evil and propose to meet it by such measures as will preserve to the people what custom has heretofore rendered it indecent to be without. To do this, less hours of daily toil are essential. A reduction of hours means less idle hands, more persons profitably employed. By increasing the number of employed consumption will be stimulated, over-production checked and a more balanced relationship between the two established."

These arguments, as stated, were made in 1879, and all that could be, or were afterward, added to them were merely amplifications of the ideas here advanced. To go deeper into the subject would be merely to end in the discovery, after wading through an ocean of pamphlet and newspaper literature devoted to the question, that the arguments advanced by Hunt covered the case from beginning to end.

The most advanced, that is, the most intelligent, of American employers saw the wisdom and recognized the logic of this position. We are speaking for Chicago in this matter more particularly, and here, it may be said, the great majority of the leading employers were in sympathy with the eight-hour movement, hoped it might be carried out to a successful issue, but doubted whether the times were ripe for it. The great question to be solved was, how can the movement be made so general, that the increased cost which will follow its adoption in one, may not be taken advantage of by another locality, to the detriment of the industrial interests of the first? In other words, if Chicago adopts the system and New York does not, New York will have, at the same cost, a clear gain over Chicago manufacturers of two hours of labor daily from every employe,—representing about six hundred and eighteen working hours per annum—being enabled thereby to produce at less cost than Chicago manufacturers, to undersell them and perhaps ruin their business by this unequal competition. "Make the movement a national one," said the Chicago employers, "or so general that eight hours shall constitute a day's labor in every center that comes into direct competition with Chicago, and we will cheerfully agree to its principles."

It would be out of the question, perhaps, to prevent it, but very early in the agitation the socialistic element found its way into and exercised such an influence in the conduct of the movement that it suffered seriously in repute. In October, 1880, we find that Albert R. Parsons is a member of the National Eight-Hour Committee, and from year to year, until the anarchistic element was driven out bodily by the honest workingmen of the country, the poisonous doctrines advocated by Fielden, Parsons, Spies, and others in this community, were infused into the movement, weakening and almost killing it.

As a pure and simple proposition to reduce the hours of labor to eight, the anarchistic socialists had very little faith in its efficacy as a panacea for existing evils, real or imaginary. They wanted to use the movement as a tool, by the aid of which they might bring about the condition of the social chaos they so much desired. To admit that a reduction of two hours for a day's labor would be sufficient to make any workingman more contented with his lot, or that it would satisfy the demands of the downtrodden masses, was to admit something utterly senseless and absurd. The eight-hour movement, if desirable to the socialistic anarchists at all, was only desirable because there was a chance—a bare possibility—perhaps a probability, that it might lead to a bitter warfare between labor and capital, resulting finally in what?—strikes, riots, revolution, anarchy! In their hearts they hoped that the eight-hour movement would not succeed. Having been driven out of the councils of its friends, and having no longer any reason for hiding their hypocrisy, they openly antagonized it, denounced its advocates as frauds and hirelings of the capitalists, and urged the working classes to have nothing to do with what they called a mere sop—a bone thrown by the master to the dog to make him cease his whining appeals for food! The socialistic anarchists did not want the eight-hour question settled—it would in all likelihood be the means of making the great masses of the people so much more contented and happier than they were before, that the "social revolution" might be indefinitely postponed. Anything before that! Awakening at last to the discovery that the movement was on the high road to a triumphant victory, that the employers were falling into line, that public sentiment was overwhelmingly favoring it, and that the 1st day of May, 1886, would almost assuredly see the blessed dreams of its friends realized—seeing the danger of a long peace where they had hoped for an extended war—they determined upon using another and a more powerful argument against it—it must be shattered with dynamite.

A man no sooner becomes a criminal than he hates and fears the uniform of a police officer; no sooner becomes an anarchist than he hates anything and everything that is representative of law and order—be it a blue-frocked patrolman or a granite court house. The police and the courts stand between him and his proposed victim—society. To pull it down to his own level, and then trample it in the mire, he must first climb over the policeman's body and grope his way through the debris of the court house. The policeman must be felled before even the court house can be stormed, and it is to the policeman, therefore, that the anarchists first turned their attention in their organization of the damnable conspiracy which was to end in murder, robbery, arson and chaos.

The Eight-Hour Association of Chicago was very active, and the movement gained more and surer headway here than elsewhere. Of this committee there were at least two members—Schilling and Greenhut—who were pronounced socialists, but of a much more moderate character than Parsons, Spies or Fielden. Yet they held views antagonistic to public opinion, and their presence in the movement did not help to strengthen it. The first of May was set apart for the general inauguration, as far as possible, of the eight-hour system. The anarchists, whenever possible, made their presence felt at meetings, by demanding ten hours' pay for eight hours' work—something that had not been counted on by the true friends of the movement, for they believed that the wage question would settle itself very speedily, after the more important one, at least for the time being, was gotten safely out of the way. "Ten hours' pay for eight hours' work," was a cry taken up by the more ignorant of the mechanics and laborers; and then the employers, viewing this as a breach of faith, began to distrust the sincerity of the leaders in the agitation. If there was anything in the arguments, that rest was what the working classes needed, that rest would create new wants, and that new wants would create a condition of industrial affairs which would demand, as well as justify, increased wages— if there was anything but the merest twaddle and the flimsiest nonsense at the bottom of these arguments, why, in the name of sense, did the advocates of the eight-hour movement now demand ten hours' pay for eight hours' work, thereby discounting the innumerable blessings which were to result in the near future from the shortening of the working day? The Chicago committee saw quickly that the cry of "Ten hours' wages for eight hours' work" was a most dangerous one, and that it could only have emanated from unfriendly quarters. In its address to *"All the Trade and Labor Associations of Chicago and Vicinity,"* issued but a short time before the first of May, the following passage occurred:

> The workingmen of Chicago are ready to make sacrifices in wages, in order that more people may find employment, and for the general good of the whole community. Surely such a self-sacrificing spirit should meet with a cordial response from the employing classes.

And it did receive a cordial response. There was no opposition of character to the movement here among employers, other than that which grew out of honest differences of opinion regarding the probability that the movement, instead of becoming general at once, would be local to Chicago for some time to come, owing to the fact that the matter had not been properly agitated, nor the inauguration of the system arranged for in other parts of the country, and especially at points which were recognized competitors of this city in certain lines of manufactures.

Albert R. Parsons aired his own views, and voiced those of other leaders in the anarchistic-socialist party, when he said in his paper, *The Alarm*, as early as October 31, 1885:

> The private possession or ownership of the means of production and exchange places the propertyless class in the power and control of the

propertied class, since they can refuse bread, or the chance to earn it, to all the wage classes who refuse to obey their dictation.   Eight hours, or less hours, is, therefore, under existing conditions, *a lost battle*.   The private property system employs labor only to exploit (rob) it, and while that system is in vogue, the victims—those whom it disinherits—have only the choice of submission or starvation.

August Spies, writing in the same paper, in reply to a reader who had called it to task for its enmity to the eight-hour movement, said:

We do not antagonize the eight-hour movement, viewing it from the standpoint that it is a social struggle, we simply predict that it is a lost battle, and we prove that though even the eight-hour system should be established *at this late day*, the wage-workers would gain nothing. They would still remain the slaves of their masters.

Parsons pronounced the eight-hour movement a lost battle seven months before it was to be fought, and Spies follows him up with the statement that it is *too late* now to demand a concession of this kind—as the workingmen would still remain the slaves of their masters, whether the movement succeeded or not.   What was needed was a social revolution—no half-way measures—the complete annihilation of private ownership, the leveling of all to a common plane, the division of wealth and the rule of the commune.

A number of men had been discharged from the McCormick harvester factory.   The principal owner, the manager and the superintendent of these works claimed that the men were discharged because they were no longer needed.   The workingmen claimed that they were discharged because they had been prominent in the organization of unions, foremost in the demands which were from time to time made upon the McCormick company, and prominent in the work of drawing up petitions which were now and then presented to obtain redress for various grievances among the employes. The workmen in the factory had been perfecting their organization for a long time, or since the strike in which the Pinkerton men had taken so conspicuous a part, and all arrangements having been perfected for a long struggle, they demanded that a guarantee should be given that no man in the factory, or anyone serving on a committee, should be discharged for having acted as a representative of his comrades. This guarantee had been given at the termination of the strike of the April previous, but was not lived up to. Now it was absolutely refused. Of course it had been forcibly extorted, rather than peaceably achieved, in the first place, and the company, finding itself in a position to resist now— having a plentiful supply of finished work on hand—decided to throw off the yoke and resume its independence. While the question was still pending and the men were awaiting an answer, the works were "shut down" February 16, 1886, at 9:30 a. m. Although this was a move for which the workmen were hardly prepared, yet, as they read the notice that work had been suspended, they took the announcement complacently enough. The works were going to be shut down, anyway, by the proposed strike—and all expected to strike before the guarantee demanded could be secured—the company had simply been the first to act; that was all.

For a number of days all was quiet on the Black Road. The locked-out mechanics, artisans and laborers assembled in the vicinity of the works from time to time, and listened to the speeches of anarchist missionaries, but no violence was attempted. The police kept a close watch on the district, but had reason to fear no serious trouble. It was simply a question, which could lay idle the longest, the works or the men? and that was a conundrum that time alone could answer. The trade societies, and especially the leaders of the eight-hour movement, appealed to the locked-out men to be patient, entreated them to be guarded in their language, and begged them to abstain from all acts of violence. The anarchist leaders told them that the works had been shut down to starve them out of their holes; to drive them to submission, and to teach them such a lesson that would forever prevent them from demanding their rights again. Dramatic pictures of squalid hovels, with starving wives

and famishing babies, by empty tables and chilling hearthstones, were painted by the anarchist orators, and held up
for exhibition before the ignorant men who usually composed their audiences.   Little by little the men were
wrought up to a high pitch of excitement by these agitators,
until the feeling began to grow within them that they had
the right to march upon the works, throw them open, and
set the machinery in operation, in spite of the protests of
the owners, or raze the factory to the ground if resistance
was made.

After several acts of violence had been committed, and
matters around the McCormick works began to assume a
serious aspect, the company employed a large number of
Pinkerton detectives, and the police department placed five
hundred men on the ground to preserve the peace and maintain order.

In the meantime the anarchists were busy.   They had
organized two " armed groups," which drilled nightly; they
experimented with dynamite, issued instructions for the
making of bombs, practiced target shooting in the country,
and entered into the work of preparation for the great social
upheaval, which they predicted and hoped for, with more
vigor than they had ever exhibited before.   The police, in
searching for a murderer at this time, stumbled upon a lot
of dynamite and other material of a destructive nature, in
the sleeping room of one Chris Komens, 231 West Twentieth street.   Among the articles found were a breech-loading
Springfield rifle, twenty rounds of cartridges, lead pipe, and
a pot and ladle used in forming it into balls, a number of
hollow lead balls, intended to be used as bombs, one bomb
loaded and almost ready for the percussion cap, a wrought
iron pipe, which was transformed into an infernal machine,
other articles of like character, and a pamphlet in the
German language, by Johann Most, instructing the reader
how to make explosives.   The police discovered that Komens
was a member of one of the anarchistic-socialist groups,

known as No. 3, which formerly held its meetings at 519 Blue Island avenue. The rules of the "group" required every member to "purchase a navy revolver, a foot and a half long," says Mr. Paul Hull, in his book entitled "The Chicago Riot." This proceeding alarmed the gentle Teuton in whose place they met, and he notified the members that he preferred that they meet elsewhere. The members were armed with muskets, similar to that found in Komens' house. Each gun was numbered to correspond with that of the person who owned it or had it in possession. Komens' gun was No. 400. Instructions were given in the manufacture and use of explosives. The bombs were to be thrown into crowds, or the ranks of police or militia, from housetops or wherever convenient. The group numbered over one hundred active members. About 1885 the society divided into two sections, and began to meet elsewhere.

On March 2 a mass-meeting of the locked-out workmen assembled in the vicinity of Eighteenth street and Center avenue—a locality in which socialism and communism of the anarchistic stripe had flourished for years—and was addressed by A. R. Parsons and Michael Schwab. The meeting, as these orators stated it, was assembled not only for the purpose of making the grievances of the workingmen known, but to "protest against the armed force which had been enlisted against them. To beseech an employe not to take the place of another became an attack on the state, and these armed men, employed by the state, (the policemen) came forth at the behest of capital, struck down the peaceable citizen, clubbed and searched them, and cast them into the patrol wagons and hustled them off to prison. The banditti of 'law and order' maintained the legal right of capital to do what it pleased with labor, and the authorized 'pickpockets' searched every workman for weapons of defense." The McCormick company, after several threatening outbreaks, and upon the advice of the press and leading citizens, finally made a concession to the men as to the matter of wages—a matter that developed after the lock-out—but reserved the right to employ non-union men. The shops were thrown open, and although the great majority of the men returned to work, they harassed, annoyed, insulted and assaulted the non-unionists or "scabs" who worked by their side, and committed so many outrages, that the company had to protect itself and the men who were willing to work peaceably, still further, and the result was a fresh outbreak and a renewal of the strike. The Black Road now became the daily and nightly scene of villainous outrages perpetrated upon the non-union men. They were followed on their way to the works and beaten. Crowds awaited the closing down hour in the evening and waylaid the "scabs" as they returned home. The police were kept jumping, in their wagons, from one point to another in an almost vain effort to preserve the peace and protect the lives of the non-union men. There was a reign of terror in the neighborhood, and as the days passed the situation became more alarming. The anarchists were everywhere. Mr. Dyer D. Lum, their defender, tells us in his "Concise History of the Great Trial of the Chicago Anarchists in 1886," that "These stormy scenes but intensified the general feeling of resistance and determination to unite in making the strike of May 1 all embracive. Meetings [of anarchists] were held nightly in various portions of the city, and the prisoners [that is to say, the condemned seven] became prominent as orators or organizers. Their frequent speeches at meetings held on the lake front had made the names and faces of most of them familiar to workmen. The *Arbeiter Zeitung*, on which Spies and Schwab were editors, entered ardently in the work and was instrumental in bringing about a reduction in hours from fourteen and sixteen to ten for the bakers, brewers and other unions. [The credit for this work was afterward claimed by Oscar Neebe]. The speakers of the International were engaged nearly every evening in addressing or organizing unions, [i. e., groups]. On the Monday preceding the first of May the Central Labor union [composed exclusively of anarchistic socialists] held an immense eight-hour demonstration, at which there were estimated present 25,000 persons, and who were addressed by Spies, Parsons, Fielden and Schwab." As Spies, Parsons, Fielden and Schwab had already sang a requiem over the grave of the eight-hour movement, as they never lost an opportunity of ridiculing it, and as they did their level best to make it so odious that employers would be driven to oppose it, the manifest absurdity of this eight-hour demonstration will be apparent. The speeches of the quartette before the multitude of discontented workingmen—nearly all foreigners, and for the most part of Sclavonic origin, although there were more Germans in the assemblage than there should have been—were calculated rather to embitter the ignorant among them against the movement than to reconcile them to it. The anarchists dreaded the success of the movement more. than ever, as the date set for its inauguration approached.

Having done everything in their power to make the success of the movement impossible, the following from the pen of August Spies appeared in the *Arbeiter Zeitung* on May 1, when some 25,000 or 30,000 workingmen had already struck for eight hours, more than two-thirds of them demanding ten hours' pay, in spite of the promises and remonstrances of the eight-hour leaders:

The dies are cast! The first of May, whose historical significance will be understood and appreciated only in later years, is here. For twenty years the working people of the United States have whined and have begged their extortionists and legislators to introduce an eight-hour system. The latter knew how to put the modest beggar off, and thus year after year has passed by. At last, two years ago, a number of trade organizations took the matter up, and resolved that the eight-hour work day should be established on May 1, 1886.

That is a sensible demand, said the press, howled the professional importers, yelled the extortionists. The impudent socialists, who wanted everything, and would not content themselves with rational demands of this kind, were treated to the customary shower of epithets.

Thus things went on. The agitation progressed and everybody was in favor of the shortening of the work day. With the approach of the day, however, on which the plan was at last to be realized, a suspicious change in the tone of the extortionists and their priestcraft in the press, became more and more noticeable. What had formerly, in theory, been modest and rational, was now impudent and senseless. What had formerly been lauded as a praiseworthy demand, when compared with socialism and anarchism, changed now suddenly into criminal anarchism itself. The cloven feet of the hellish crew, panting for spoils, became visible. They had intonated the eight-hour hymn simply to lull their dupes, workingmen, to sleep, and thus keep them away from socialism.

That the workingmen would proceed in all earnestness to introduce the eight-hour system was never anticipated by these confidence men; that the workingmen would develop such stupendous power, this they never dreamed of. In short, to-day, when an attempt is made to realize a reform so long striven for, when the extortionists are reminded of their promises and pledges of the past, one has this and the other has that to give as an excuse. The workers should only be contented and confide in their well-meaning exploiters, and some time between now and doomsday everything would be satisfactorily arranged.

Workingmen, we caution you. You have been deluded time and time again. You must not be led astray this time.

Judging from present appearances, *events may not take a very smooth course.* Many of the extortionists, aye most of them, are resolved to starve those to "reason" who refuse to submit to their arbitrary dictates, i. e., to force them back into their yoke by hunger. The question now arises, will the workingmen allow themselves to be slowly starved into submission, or will they *inoculate some modern ideas into their would-be murderers' heads?*

The italicized words in this article were not as clear to outsiders on the first of May as they were a few days later. They were not, indeed, italicized at all in the *Arbeiter Zeitung.* Doubtless the members of the different anarchist groups knew well enough what Mr. Spies meant, to make emphasis of any kind unnecessary.

"As illustrative of the hatred earned by thus championing the cause of their fellow workers," says Mr. Lum, "attention is called to the following leader in the editorial columns of *The Chicago Mail* of the same day, May 1:"

There are two dangerous ruffians at large in this city; two sneaking cowards who are trying to create trouble. One of them is named Parsons; the other is named Spies. Should trouble come they would be the first to skulk away from the scene of danger, the first to attempt to shield their worthless carcasses from harm, the first to shirk responsibility.

These two fellows have been at work fomenting disorder for the past ten years. They should have been driven out of the city long ago. They would not be tolerated in any other community on earth.

Parsons and Spies have been engaged for the past six months in perfecting arrangements for the precipitation of a riot to-day. They have taken advantage of the excitement attending the eight-hour movement to bring about a series of strikes and to work injury to capital and honest labor in every possible way. They have no love for the eight-hour movement, and are doing all they can to hamper it and to prevent its success. These fellows do not want any reasonable concession. They are looking for riot and plunder. They haven't got one honest aim nor one honorable end in view.

Mark them to-day. Keep them in view. Hold them personally responsible for any trouble that occurs. *Make an example of them if trouble does occur.*

"Certainly a more personally vindictive article," says the socialistic historian Lum, "than any the prosecution have been able to produce from the pen of either Spies or Parsons. How these gentlemen have borne themselves when 'trouble' came is a matter upon which no question can be raised; how far the implied threat has influenced their conviction, is not, however, beyond question."

The same hand that wrote the *Mail's* leader quoted above, is tracing these lines to-day, and its owner, looking back over the past seventeen months, sees that the warning he then gave was fully warranted and justified by subsequent events, and that the predictions made were in every way fulfilled. Parsons and Spies were the most dangerous of all the ruffians concerned in the anarchist conspiracy, because they were endowed generously with brains, liberally with education and plentifully with the smooth and subtle faculty of attracting the ignorant and the brutish about them—a faculty which they used unstintingly and in the furtherance of every one of the innumerable devilish propensities of their natures. When "trouble" did come, Parsons was the only one of the anarchist leaders to turn tail and fly. He made his appearance afterward in court and gave himself up to the authorities, but this he did upon the positive assurance of his over-sanguine counsel that he would certainly escape punishment. After his conviction, his incarceration in the county jail was characterized by one continuous and unremitting whine. He shirked his responsibility as an anarchist leader from the moment the bomb was thrown. And how was it with Spies? He had no time to fly, but was putting his affairs in shape, so that he could make a sudden departure, when arrested. Making a disgusting display of bravado at the start, he soon ingratiated himself into the affections of a sympathetic but very foolish virgin, and through her sentimental tears cowardly appealed for mercy.

Editor George Schilling, of the *Eight-Hour Day*, a paper published in the interest of the movement for shorter working hours, published an editorial under the head of "The Situation," on Saturday morning, May 1. As it represents the views of the real friends of the proposed change, as opposed to those expressed by the anarchists, it is proper to quote from it fully:

The results of the coming week will be watched with intense interest by friends and foes alike. The atmosphere is filled with strikes and rumors of strikes. Some of the unions, we regret to say, have gone off half-cocked, and are compliciting this eight-hour question too much with that of wages, and herein lies the greatest danger to the movement in this city. Many of the manufacturers say they cannot pay the 20 per cent. increase in wages until the same demand is successfully made of their Eastern competitors. This looks reasonable, and the *Eight-Hour Day* deprecates the action of those unions who have thereby complicated the situation, and are likely to endanger the success of the movement.

Competition is a factor in the question, and the workingmen of Chicago have no right to exact short hours and high wages from their employers unless similar demands are made elsewhere.

This was the situation in a nut-shell, and an answer complete and convincing to the article written by Spies on the same subject. Mr. Schilling added:

The coming week is the most responsible in the history of the labor movement in Chicago. Strikes must be averted, if possible. Those under way should be settled through the art of diplomacy instead of continued hostilities. The various fragments of partially organized work-ingmen must be brought under one head, one eight-hour council, so that the entire movement may be conducted with the precision of clock-work. Men who have more passion than brains, and are full of braggadocio, must be put aside.

But Schilling, and men like him, who were aiming solely for the success of the eight-hour movement, were no longer in control of the situation. It had slipped noiselessly from their grip. Short hours with long pay, and short hours with increased pay, were now the rallying cries. The eight-hour question gradually fell back to the rear. The workingmen were no longer fighting for a grand principle. They openly confessed, in many instances, that what they wanted was not shorter hours, but more wages, while many threatened that, in case short hours were granted, they would still insist and strike for advances in wages. Before May 1 the furniture workers, foundrymen, the employes of several of the railroad companies, and the lumbermen, were out on a strike for ten hours' pay for eight hours' work. On May 1, the "Day of Emancipation," as it was called, some thirty thousand men struck work in every department of industry, from the men who handled freight in the railroad warehouses to the girls who sewed uppers in the shoe factories. The streets were thronged with idle men and women, the manu-factories were silent, and business in general was almost at a standstill. A large number of employers, before evening, yielded to or compromised with their hands—some granting ten hours' pay, others nine hours' pay, for eight hours' work. Some went even further, and promised their em-ployes Saturday afternoon holidays, but the great majority of the large employing concerns held out against the de-mands made. By far the most serious strike was that of the freight handlers, as it practically paralyzed the business of the railroad companies, and in turn prevented merchants from receiving or shipping goods. The Chicago, Milwaukee & St. Paul had begun to hire non-union men, promising them full protection and high wages, before the day closed.

Parsons left for Cincinnati that night. Spies, Schwab and Fielden were, however, active in their attendance at meetings, and the red flag made its appearance in different parts of the city. The day closed with an immense ball, under the auspices of the Trades and Labor Assembly, at Cavalry Battery, which passed off pleasantly. All this time the police were kept busy. The greatest activity prevailed at headquarters. Frederick Ebersold was now superintendent and John Bonfield inspector of police. A closer watch than they suspected was kept on the movements of the anarchists. The superintendent, from the telephone at headquarters, directed the movements of the police, ordering the patrol wagons here and there, and keeping, as it were, the entire city, and particularly that portion of it where trouble was likely to occur, under his watchful eye. Detectives were on the alert. Every man on the force was prepared for an emergency. Sunday, May 2, passed over very quietly—so quietly that many were led to believe that the excitement had cooled down, and that all trouble would be averted. The railroad managers, it was announced, were about to hold a joint meeting, and the impression prevailed that the demands of the strikers would be complied with. This action, if taken, would influence or compel those in other lines of trade to follow, and the eight-hour day would be a reality. Some of the great employing concerns had already given their men to understand that their demands would be complied with. Good feeling seemed to prevail in most quarters. The anarchists were driven to desperation. If the eight-hour fight should win, all was lost for them. But they were quiet this Sabbath day, too, and no red flags were flaunted from their headquarters on West Lake street. Said one of the daily papers of that morning: "The thinking men will now have an inning, and the red flag spirit will, doubtless, be somewhat crushed." Delusive dream! The red flag spirit was at that very moment preparing for its boldest stroke.

On Monday, May 3, the number of strikers had quad-rupled and the excitement in all quarters of the city increased in proportion. All classes and grades of workingmen had quit their shops. The mania was spreading and the dry goods clerks threatened to leave their places behind the counter. A number of processions moved through the streets, and on Fifth avenue occurred a scene, one of the most disgraceful in the history of Chicago, that caused the blood in many an honest and patriotic heart to boil with indignation. A procession of about 500 tailor-girls had been moving down that thoroughfare. It was composed wholly of the daughters or wives of foreigners, principally of Bohemian, Polish and Hungarian origin. Many of the young women, doubtless ignorant of their meaning, and in-spired with the excitement of the day, carried and waved red flags. In passing the office of the *Arbeiter Zeitung*, which was then located on the avenue named, a lot of frowsy-headed ruffians, among them Spies and Schwab, waved red banners and flags from the windows, and gesticulated like madmen in a frenzy of delight, over the appearance of the miserably-clad women, many of whom were undoubtedly dressed in ragged apparel for effect—as the poorest women in Chicago never look as shabby as most of those creatures did that day. The blood-red flag of the commune had never been flaunted as boldly before in the business part of the city, and a number of citizens were on the point of rushing into the *Arbeiter Zeitung*, gutting the place and stringing up the vagabonds responsible for the treasonable proceeding, when the flags were hauled in, followed by the frowsy heads, and better councils prevailed.

That afternoon ominous news came from the Black Road. The McCormick strikers had been mysteriously quiet for several days. Now the passions of the men broke out afresh and hostilities had begun in earnest. Some five or six thou-sand Sclavs, among whom were a few Germans of the lowest order, assembled on the commons or prairie, which lay on either side of Blue Island avenue at the terminus of Robey street, at about two o'clock. These men had been gathering from an early hour in the morning, and they dotted the Black Road and prairie very thickly when the 1,400 men employed in the McCormick factory crossed over to begin their day's work. About 75 per cent. of these were non-unionists, or "scabs," as the strikers were pleased to call them. A detachment of the strikers had been placed near the gate of the factory, and as the workmen approached they were either prevailed upon not to enter, compelled to stay out, or gained admission through force. During the forenoon crowds hung about the gate, or leaned against the high board fence which surrounded the works. A meeting was called for the afternoon, at which all the strikers and their friends were urged to be present, and hence the gathering of five or six thousand on the prairie. The striking lumber shovers had contributed toward swelling the crowd, and according to the statement of August Spies, who addressed the meeting, "fully 10,000 persons must have been present" when he arrived. A number of speeches were made in the Polish, Bohemian, Hungarian and German languages, and after the less celebrated orators had finished, Spies addressed the multitude. There were some detectives scattered among the crowd and around the factory, but very few policemen were present, as no immediate trouble was anticipated out that way, and the entire force was kept busy in the different districts of the city where strikes were in progress. The speeches made in Polish and Bohemian were of the most inflammatory nature, and Spies capped the climax by urging the already excited men to incendiarism and violence. Here was a chance to crush out the eight-hour movement, and the opportunity was not to be wasted. He advised the men to arm themselves with dynamite, rifles, shot-guns, pistols, clubs, sticks, stones— anything that they could use effectively—and make a bold stroke for freedom here and now. No time was to be lost. The work must be begun at once.

The detectives and policemen who were present became alarmed early in the speech-making. They saw that trouble was inevitable. Word was sent to headquarters, and soon patrol wagons, loaded with blue-coats, were on their way to the Black Road.

Many of the excited men had already left the meeting before Spies closed his speech, and he testifies:

During my speech I heard some voices in the rear, which I did not understand, and saw about 150 men leave the prairie, running up the Black Road, toward McCormick's reaper works (one-quarter mile south of where the meeting was). Five minutes later I heard pistol shooting in this direction, and upon inquiry was informed that the striking mold-ers of McCormick's works were trying to make the "scabs," who had taken their places, stop work. About this time—I was just closing my speech—[Spies should have said, "About this time, I thought it best to close my speech "]—a patrol wagon rattled up the street, filled with police-men ; a few minutes later about seventy-five policemen followed the patrol wagon on foot, who were again followed by three or four more patrol wagons. The shooting continued, only that, instead of single shots, regular volleys were now fired. I left the meeting, and hastened up to McCormick's.

Mr. Spies' statement is all correct, save as to the last sentence. He left the meeting—there is no question about that; but he didn't hasten up to McCormick's. On the con-trary, he hastened—that does not express it—fled to a Blue Island avenue street-car, and was soon on his way to the *Arbeiter Zeitung* office, where the work of preparing the " Revenge Circular " was undertaken a little later on. The detectives who turned in the police alarm were J. M. Hanes and J. J. Egan. How quickly it was responded to, the statement made by Spies seems to show. Locked within the telephone room at headquarters was Superintendent Ebersold from that moment until late in the evening, dis-patching patrol wagons from point to point, ordering de-tachments here and there, and covering the field of opera-tion as intelligently—more intelligently—than if he had been on the ground. Not a wagon or a company moved or acted without his special instructions. With the station nearest to the trouble always in direct communication with him, he heard reports, and acted upon them quickly, decisively and energetically. During that exciting afternoon, the mobs, moving in different directions, must have felt some surprise at being headed off and scattered at every turn. Chief Ebersold, through his able lieutenants, had information immediately regarding every movement made, and the patrol wagons, which dashed hither and thither without apparent object, and with such apparent recklessness, were all moving in response to the plans being executed at headquarters. The scene laid before Ebersold like a checker-board, and he moved his men as carefully as the most expert of players, until the surface was entirely in the hands of the blue-coats, and the Reds had been wiped out. Never had the patrol system been worked to greater perfection.

But while he was engaged in handling the force, bloody work was going on. Patrolmen West and Condon were the only policemen at the McCormick factory when the first outbreak and assault occurred. As the crowds came thick and fast across the prairie and on the Black Road toward the works, the factory bell rang out for the men employed within to quit work. Then the workmen began to pass out, dinner buckets in hand. It was about half-past 3 o'clock. The mob gathered around the gates. Three or four of the workmen were assaulted and brutally beaten. Others were driven back to the enclosure. Officers Condon and West fought like heroes to protect the workmen, and brandishing their clubs and revolvers kept the crowd at bay. Condon, at length, was struck on the side by a heavy stone, and hastened toward Western and Blue Island avenue to turn in an alarm. Here he found that he was so badly injured as to be unable to speak. Somebody standing near sent in the alarm for him. This hurried the reinforcements. Officer West was driven from his position at the gate, pursued down the switch track alongside the McCormick works, pelted with stones and badly beaten. Then the Hinman street patrol wagon, in command of Sergeant Enright, and manned by Officers Fugate, Rafferty, Falley, Quintan, Walsh, Peasnick, Zimmick, and McCarthy, came dashing toward the mob that surrounded the gate, cut an avenue through it, and entered the enclosure. Quick as a flash the men were out of the wagon and fighting back the infuriated rioters, while stones and bullets whizzed around their ears and missiles of every conceivable character were hurled against them in blinding showers. Not a pane of glass nor a window sash was left whole in the northern portion of the McCormick works. The mob wrecked the gateman's house, and it was driving the brave little body of policemen into close quarters when another wagon-load of men arrived, dismounted, and opened fire upon the mob, and then came Captain Simon O'Donnell, and after him another large reinforcement. Captain O'Donnell was well known to the mob, and thoroughly hated because of the vigorous manner in which he had dealt with the professional rioters in his district. He drove from the Twelfth street station in a buggy. As he was passing through Blue Island avenue, some thirty rioters surrounded his vehicle and ordered him to get out. He lashed his horse, cut the rioters' faces with his whip, and drove through them. Then they hurled stones and bricks at him, some of them striking him on the body. He dropped the curtains, wheeled the buggy around and faced his pursuers and assailants, revolver in hand, and the stones fell from the hands of the ruffians harmlessly. There was that in the captain's face which told them they had gone far enough. The captain then charged upon the mob and the cowardly miscreants fled, and Captain O'Donnell drove rapidly to McCormick's. One of the patrol wagons was attacked by a detached mob before reaching the factory. Every ruffian in the crowd appeared to be provided with stones. These were showered down upon the wagon-full of patrolmen, and the horses became frightened. Some of the rioters attempted to climb into the wagon. The driver gathered up his lines, lashed his horses, the policemen in the wagon bent low to escape the shower of stones, while revolvers kept the mad crowd at bay. The men were needed, and speedily, elsewhere. Were it not for this fact that mob would have suffered.

As the patrol wagons dashed up, one after another, the mob became less aggressive, wavered and scattered. Every one of the wagons was saluted with a volley of stones as it passed through the dense crowd. Officer Shepherd knocked a would-be assassin senseless with his club, as he was taking deliberate aim with a revolver at a wagon load of policemen. The entire district was covered with rioters, but the wagons dashed hither and thither, dispersing the crowds wherever they were inclined to gather in large numbers. This was kept up for an hour after the assault on the works, and the police at length had the entire district under subjection. A man named John Vogtik was shot through the left loin during the battle at the gate. Another was killed. Several others were shot less seriously. One man had his finger shot off, another had a gash cut across his scalp. Fifty or more were badly bruised and otherwise injured. Many of the rioters were clubbed and went home with swollen heads and sore shoulders. Assistant Superintendent Bensly, of McCormick's factory, was badly bruised. Officer Kaiser was badly wounded in the head by a stone thrown from the mob. All was quiet in the Black Road at 6 o'clock that evening. One of the most exciting events of the day remains to be described.

Officer Casey, of the third precinct station, with three other policemen, undertook to convey John Vogtik, the wounded man mentioned above, to his home, No. 422 West Seventeenth street. The patrol wagon in which the wounded man lay was followed by a savage mob, bent upon seeking vengeance for the shooting of their comrades. The crowd was composed almost wholly of Bohemians. As the wagon turned the corner of Center avenue the mob divided up into smaller bodies and did not follow, but each crowd appeared to be discussing the situation among themselves.

"The Policemen in the Wagon Bent Low to Escape the Shower of Stones, while Revolvers Kept the Mad Crowd at Bay."

ANARCHIST BANNERS CARRIED BY THE ANARCHISTS IN THEIR
NUMEROUS PROCESSIONS IN CHICAGO.

They stood quietly around while the policemen carried their wounded fellow-countryman into his house, and by the time that he was deposited on a bed, and the policemen had returned to the street, the entire neighborhood had turned out *en masse* and clogged the street on both sides of the wagon. Casey remained behind to get the report of Vogtik's condition, and was detained in the house about five minutes after the other officers had taken their seats in the wagon. Many of the neighbors had crowded into the house, and into the bedroom where Vogtik lay. On being asked who shot him, Vogtik, evidently misunderstanding the question, pointed to Casey. The crowd inside would not and did not wait for an explanation, but immediately communicated the news that Vogtik's murderer was in the house, to the mob outside. Instantly there was a demand for Casey's blood. He was seized and dragged out to the sidewalk. "Lynch him," "Hang him," "Kill him," were the cries heard on all sides. Casey, although a Hercules in strength, was powerless in the hands of this mob, which hemmed him in on all sides. But he made a desperate struggle, and in his efforts to escape his uniform was torn in shreds. A ruffian in the mob brought a rope, and one end of it was thrown over the arm of a lamp-post in front of Vogtik's house, the mob setting up a cheer and yelling with delight when they beheld this proceeding. As Casey's eyes fell upon the dangling rope, and as he realized the dreadful and humiliating end which this barbarous crowd had prepared for him, he made an almost superhuman effort, threw off his captors, freed himself of their clutches, and ran for his life, followed by the disappointed, howling, murderous *canaille*. Casey fired several shots as he ran, and succeeded in keeping safely in advance of the mob until he reached Center avenue, where the patrol wagon, containing his comrades, met him, they having turned back upon hearing the shots from his revolver. He was helped into the wagon in an almost exhausted condition. The mob seemed to be inclined to attack the wagon at first, but the policemen drew their revolvers, and the crowd fell back.

When the Black Road had been quieted, the police escorted the workingmen confined within the McCormick factory to their homes. The wives and daughters and mothers of the Bohemian and Polish rioters at intervals attacked the officers of the law with stones and sticks, but more frequently with vile abuse in Sclavonic and broken English. One woman struck an officer with a stone, and the police were finally compelled to make a harmless charge upon these females, in order to scatter them.

In taking home a wounded socialist, one of the patrol wagons, containing five men, was attacked by an immense mob. An effort was made to overturn the wagon, and the massacre of the police appeared to have been determined upon. One of the rioters had aimed a blow at Officer Kayzer, who in turn fired, and the socialist fell.

Lieutenant (now captain) Hubbard, with one hundred men, remained at the Central detail in reserve throughout the day. Nearly all the other stations, particularly those in the disturbed districts, were well provided with reserves. Every point, where trouble was likely to occur, was covered by the force. The disposition and discipline of the men were admirable. There were no hitches whatever, and from morning until night, the police machinery of the city acted like clock-work. " We have perfected arrangements for prompt and decisive action in all cases," said Inspector Bonfield that night. "I believe we are strong enough to suppress any uprising. I do not believe it will be necessary to call out the militia, because I do not anticipate any serious trouble. There will be more or less rioting, a few sanguinary conflicts, some blood spilling perhaps, but I do not anticipate anything like a repetition of the riot of 1877." Inspector Bonfield could not calculate upon the devilish secret designs of the anarchists; no man could. He supposed that the police department had human beings, not bloodthirsty demons, to deal with.

CHAPTER XIV.

THE FOURTH OF MAY, 1886—FROM MORNING UNTIL NIGHT—THE OUTRAGES
COMMITTED BY THE MOBS IN THE VICINITY OF EIGHTEENTH STREET
AND CENTER AVENUE - LIVELY WORK FOR THE POLICEMEN IN THE
ANARCHIST SECTION—THE "REVENGE CIRCULAR"—SCHWAB'S INCEN-
DIARY EDITORIAL, AND THE CALL FOR A MASS MEETING—SPIES'
SIDE OF THE QUESTION—THE HAYMARKET GATHERING—WHY THE
MEETING PLACE WAS CHANGED.

A fairer morning than that which smiled across the blue
waters of Lake Michigan on the 4th day of May, 1886,
never dawned upon the city of Chicago. The wounded,
crippled, bruised and bleeding anarchists who looked out
upon it must have been maddened by the perfect beauty
of the new day, the clearness of the sky, the fresh-
ness of the atmosphere, and the glorious awakening of
Nature from her long sleep, made manifest in every peeping
grass-blade and swelling bud.

The night, to all appearances, had passed over peaceably,
and, to those who sought the city's business center in• the
early morning, it seemed as though the excitement occasioned by the eight-hour strikes and the troubles at Mc-
Cormick's were about to subside at last. A feeling of tranquillity prevailed down town, and to such an extent that even
yesterday's events, fresh, impressive and alarming as they
were but a few hours since, were already fading from the
public mind, and gliding smoothly and swiftly into history,
as mere episodes along the road of Chicago's marvelous
progress. This sudden change from public alarm to popular tranquillity was one which, in a great measure, had become peculiar to Chicago. The panic occasioned by the
great fire was dreadful while it lasted, but it died completely
out in a single night, and some two hundred thousand souls,

who had gone to sleep in despair, arose next morning
buoyant with hope and confident of success. The riot
of '77 reached its climax one afternoon, and the city was
crazed with excitement; next day the riot was hardly an
interesting topic of conversation. So it was on other occasions, and so it promised to be now. The police had finally
grappled with the McCormick rioters in dead earnest, and
whenever they were aroused to that point, then peace was
brought around sure and sudden. What need to bother any
further with the disturbance? It was all over.

The friends of the eight-hour movement were really
chuckling over the defeat of the anarchist element on the
Black Road. Parsons, Spies and the rest had taken charge
of the campaign down that way, and had met with ignoble
failure. It was plain now that they would not dare to raise
their heads again. Spies had retreated on a street-car at
the sound of the first pistol shot, and, of course, he would
not have the impudence to say another word. Everything
looked very favorable for the movement. At the stock
yards and Pullman, the strike for short hours was general.
Many employers announced voluntarily a reduction of hours,
at the old pay. The packing houses were yielding—under
protest, of course, but yielding nevertheless. The lumbermen were inclined to look upon the movement favorably,
notwithstanding that threats of burning the yards had been
and were being freely made by the employes. The state of
business was such that manufacturers, as a rule, could not
afford to shut down. The demands of trade were pressing.
The times were good. It was just at the opening of a season
which gave every promise of being a most prosperous one.
One by one during the morning, and faster still by noon,
they fell into line, took their old hands back under the new
arrangement, and cheerfully set to work to make the best of
it. There may have been many—undoubtedly there were—
among these manufacturers who bent their heads to the inevitable, with the mental reservation that when trade slack-

ened they would throw these eight-hour strikers out of
doors, and bring them to better terms. But the great majority of Chicago employers, who made the concessions demanded, did so in good faith.

In his dirty little office on Fifth avenue, the bloody-
minded Spies had already put a finishing touch to the eight-
hour agitation. He was driven to the point where a desperate card had to be played—and he played it.

He claims to have left the meeting, which he was engaged in addressing when the shooting was heard at Mc-
Cormick's, in order to join the mob that was surging toward
the works. It has been established, as before stated, without any doubt, that he immediately took a street-car. After
seeing some indescribable butcheries performed by the hellish police at McCormick's gate, "I ran back," he says, "to
the meeting, which in the meantime had been adjourned.
The people were leaving it in small knots, going home, some
of them indifferent and unconcerned at the news from Mc-
Cormick's, others shaking their heads in indignation. I
was frantic, but my senses returned as I glanced over the
stolid faces of these people; there was no response there!
And, seeing that I could be of no possible assistance here,
I took a car, without uttering another word, and rode down
town to my office. Just in what frame of mind I was, I cannot describe. I sat down to address a circular to the workingmen—a short account of what had transpired, and a word
of advice: that they should not be so foolish as to try to resist
an armed, organized 'mob,' in the employ of the capitalists,
with empty hands,—but I was so excited that I could not
write. I dictated a short address, but tore it up again, after
I had read it, and then sat down—the compositors were
waiting for the copy, it being after the regular hours—and
wrote the now famous so-called 'Revenge Circular' in English and German. The word 'Revenge' was put on as a
headline by one of the compositors (without my knowledge),
who 'thought it made a good heading.' I ordered the circular

printed, and told the office assistant to have them taken to
the different meetings that were held in the evening.   There
were only a few hundred of them circulated.   After I had
given this order, I went home."

And so, after doing that which was intended to create
disturbance, incite crime and lead to murder, and that which
within a very few hours afterward was destined to bring sor-
row and misery to a hundred hearthstones and consternation
to the people of a city which had made the mistake of tolerat-
ing him and wretches like him too long, this devil-inspired,
anarchistic maniac, feeling easier in his mind, went home.
Here is the actrocious circular:

Revenge! Workingmen, to arms! Your masters sent out their bloodhounds, the police. They killed six of your brothers at McCormick's this
afternoon; they killed the poor wretches because they had the courage to
disobey the supreme will of your bosses; they killed them because they
dared to ask for the shortening of the hours of toil; they killed them to
show you, free American citizens, that you must be satisfied and contented with whatever your bosses condescend to allow you, or you will
get killed. You have for years suffered unmeasurable iniquities; you
have worked yourself to death; you have endured the pangs of want
and hunger; your children you have sacrificed to the factory lords—in
short, you have been miserable and obedient slaves all these years. Why?
To satisfy the insatiable greed, to fill the coffers of your lazy, thieving
masters. When you ask them now to lessen the burden they send their
bloodhounds out to shoot you—kill you. If you are men, if you are the
sons of your grandsires who have shed their blood to free you, then you
will rise in your might, Hercules, and destroy the hideous monster that
seeks to destroy you. To arms! We call you to arms!

YOUR BROTHERS.

What if some printer, into whose mind the poison of
the atmosphere which surrounded the hyenas who crawled
up and down the narrow staircase of the *Arbeiter Zeitung*
office had penetrated—what if some half-witted or drunken
employe, had put on as a head-line the word "Revenge!"
It does not add one jot nor tittle to the diabolical nature of
the circular, nor would its omission lessen the atrocity of the
composition.

In the trial of the scoundrels who planned, instigated

and precipitated the throwing of the bomb on the night of
May 4, the state held as its theory "that for a number of
years there existed in the county of Cook a conspiracy, embracing a large number of persons, having for its object the
destruction of the legal authorities of the state and county,
the overthrow of the law itself and a complete revolution of
the existing order of society, and the accomplishment of
this, not by agitation or through the ballot box, but by force
and terrorism, a conspiracy deliberately formed and thoroughly organized."

Lest there should still remain a doubt in the minds of
intelligent people regarding the existence of this conspiracy,
let us watch during the next twenty-four hours, as we try to
describe them; how events became dove-tailed; how apparently trivial circumstances became woven; how arrangements, seemingly disjointed and without relation, settled
down finally into one concerted design for the creation of a
disturbance which the conspirators hoped would end in the
social revolution they had so long dreamed of.

A man on horseback scattered a batch of the "Revenge
Circulars" at a socialistic gathering in front of 54 West
Lake street before the ink with which they were printed was
yet dry, and there is evidence going to show that in the
course of a few hours he had covered the districts inhabited
by the dangerous element which followed the leadership of
Spies, Parsons and Fielden.   While the courier of the conspiracy was scattering the seed of riot and sedition, Michael
Schwab—a person with whom forgetful people later on expressed some sympathy—was preparing the following for
the *Arbeiter Zeitung:*

Blood has flowed. It had to be, and it was not in vain, that Order
drilled and trained its bloodhounds. It was not for fun that the militia
was practiced in street fighting. The robbers who know best of all what
wretches they are; who pile up their money through the miseries of the
masses; who make a trade of the slow murder of the families of workingmen, are the last ones to stop short at the direct shooting down of the
workingmen. "Down with the Canaille," is their motto. Is it not his-

torically proven that private property grows out of all sorts of violence? Are these capitalistic robbers to be allowed by the canaille, by the working classes, to continue their bloody orgies with horrid murders? Never! The war of classes is at hand. Yesterday workingmen were shot down in front of McCormick's factory, whose blood cries out for revenge! Who will deny that the tigers who rule us are greedy for the blood of the workingman? Many sacrifices have been offered upon the altars of the golden calf amid the applauding cries of the capitalistic band of robbers. One need only think of Cleveland, New York, Brooklyn, East St. Louis, Fort Worth, Chicago, and many other places, to realize the tactics of these despoilers. It means, "Terrorize our working cattle." But the workingmen are not sheep, and will reply to the white terror with the red terror. Do you know what that means? You soon will know. Modesty is a crime on the part of workingmen, and can anything be more modest than this eight-hour demand? It was asked for peacefully a year ago, so as to give the spoilsmen a chance to reply to it. The answer is, drilling of the police and militia regulations of the workingmen seeking to introduce the eight-hour system, and, yesterday, blood flowed. This is the way in which these devils answer the modest prayer of their slaves.

Sooner death than life in misery, if workingmen are to be shot at. Let us answer in such a way that the robbers will not soon forget it.

The murderous capitalistic beasts have been made drunk by the smoking blood of workingmen; the tiger is crouching for a spring; its eyes glare murderously; it moves its tail impatiently, and all its muscles are tense. Absolute necessity forces the cry: "To Arms! To Arms!" If you do not defend yourselves you will be torn and mutilated by the fangs of the beast. The new yoke which awaits you in case of a cowardly retreat is harder and heavier than the bitter yoke of your present slavery. All the powers opposed to labor have united; they see their common interest in such days as these; all else must be subordinate to the one thought: How can the wealthy robbers and hired bands of murderers be made harmless?

The papers lie when they say that the workingmen who were near McCormick's yesterday shot first. [It will be seen by reference to the statement of Spies that he held this to be the information which he had received while addressing the meeting]. It is a bold and shameless lie of the newspaper gang. The police shot among the workingmen without a moment of warning, and, of course, the latter replied to the fire. [A deliberate misstatement of fact]. Why be so ceremonious with the "Canaille?" Had they been not men, but sheep or cattle, they must have reflected before shooting. But a workingman is quickly replaced. Yet these well-fed fellows [the police] boast of their costly meals in the company of their mistresses, of the splendid working of law and order.

Shabbily-dressed women and children in miserable huts weep for husbands and fathers. In palaces they still fill goblets with costly wine, and pledge the health of the bloody banditti of Order. Dry your tears, ye poor and suffering! Take heart, ye slaves! Rise in your might and level the existing robber rule in the dust.

In the same issue of the same paper, and evidently from the same harmless pen and innocent brain, appeared the following:

The heroes of the club yesterday pounded brutally with their cudgels a number of girls, many of whom were mere children. Whose blood does not course more swiftly through his veins when he hears of this outrage? *Whoever is a man must show it to-day. Men to the front!*

And then from the nest in which the above was hatched, came the following, a little later in the day, printed in English and German:

ATTENTION, WORKINGMEN!

Great mass meeting to-night, at 7:30 o'clock, at the Haymarket, Randolph street, between Desplaines and Halsted. Good speakers will be present to denounce the latest atrocious acts of the police—the shooting of our fellow-workmen yesterday.

THE EXECUTIVE COMMITTEE.

In the meantime a cowardly and dastardly mob was committing outrages in the southwestern portion of the city. All through the night Captain O'Donnell had a detail of 75 men engaged in patrolling the district adjacent to the Black Road, and this force was relieved by another of the same strength early in the morning of the 4th, although at the time the rioters appeared to have abandoned their intention of continuing the struggle, and Superintendent Ebersold had distributed about a score of detectives around the haunts of the desperate classes in the vicinity of Eighteenth street and Center avenue. The McCormick works were opened at 7 a. m., and the hospitable gates of the factory received and closed upon about 650 of the men whose lives were attempted the day before. The proprietor of the establishment expressed the determination to protect these men at any cost, and from the first he exhibited the most courageous devotion to the position he had assumed in relation to the anarchistic socialists.

At one of the corners of Eighteenth street and Center

Immediately following the bomb explosion, Crac

! went the pistols of the anarchists (p. 318).

avenue was the drug store of Samuel Rosenfeld. By 9 o'clock in the morning a mob of about 3,000 persons had assembled around the corner. It became apparent that the owner of the store was the object against whom the mob had an account which he would soon be called upon to settle. The rioters gathered more closely around the doorway. Then some of them entered the little shop. In a moment the noise of breaking glassware was heard, and then voices in the crowd outside were heard to yell—"Tear down the place!" "Kill Rosenfeld! He's a police spy!" It appears that Rosenfeld's telephone had been used by some of the police in sending messages to headquarters. This fact became known to the ignorant people in the vicinity, and Rosenfeld was branded as a spy. At the first outbreak the druggist took his family into the upper story of the building. Some thoughtful person telephoned the Hinman street station regarding the peril in which Rosenfeld and his family stood, and this was quickly responded to by the arrival of a patrol wagon full of officers, who rescued the Rosenfelds and conveyed them to the station for safety. A small guard was left behind, but the mob continued to grow, and it became necessary for Captain O'Donnell and Lieutenant Barcell, with a force of fifty men, to disperse the howling crowd.

It was thought that this dispersion would quiet matters, but no sooner had the police abandoned the spot than the crowd again collected. It was estimated that the mob numbered 10,000 when the real trouble finally began. There was a heap of chipped and broken brick close by, and this was the principal ammunition made use of by the mob. The attack was opened by somebody who threw a piece of brick through one of the windows. This was followed by a perfect shower. In a few seconds there was not a piece of glass the size of a silver dollar clinging to the sashes, up stairs or down, in the front of the building. A few moments more and the sashes were gone. Then the bottles and jars on the shelves were smashed, and volley followed volley into

the store until it occurred to the crowd that there were some
articles inside which might be captured whole with some degree of satisfaction. The jars labelled "Spiritus Fermenti"
were carried out in safety, and several other jars containing
other poisons, as a few mysterious deaths in the neighborhood shortly afterward went to prove. The drug store was
then completely wrecked. Everything within was destroyed,
including even the counters and shelving, and the unfortunate owner, whose only offense was that of accommodating
the officers of the law, was left penniless.

Rosenfeld's place offering no further attraction, the next
point of attack was Weiskopf's saloon. It was situated
under the hall where the anarchists held their meetings.
Weiskopf was accused of giving information to the police.
The mob was worked up to a frenzied pitch when the attack
was made here. Barrels of liquor were rolled out, the heads
broken in and the contents either emptied into the gutter or
gulped down by the mob. Bottles of whisky, wine and beer
were rapidly consumed, and then the work of demolishing
the fixtures began. Not a table or chair was left unbroken,
the ice box and bar counter being split as fine as kindling
wood. Lieutenant Shepherd, with a large force of men, were
quickly summoned, and the mob ran like frightened curs before them, skulking into cellars, back-yards and alleyways.
After driving them from the streets the police once more
retired.

The striking and riotous lumber-shovers, who, with the
old McCormick hands, were responsible for the lawlessness
of the previous day, had held a meeting in the morning, and
threats of burning the lumber yards and wrecking the Lumbermen's Exchange were heard. But they merely lounged
about on the sidewalks on Eighteenth street, between Brown
street and Center avenue, discussing the situation in a lazy,
surly manner. Toward noon their number had augmented
to such an extent that a force of police officers was sent to
watch them. The appearance of the blue-coats was hailed

with derisive shouts, says a report of the disturbance, and noisy demonstrations on every hand, but the mob kept at a respectable distance from the object of its hatred, until some half-dozen drunken fellows tried to force an entrance to the paint works of Cary, Ogden & Parker, on Eighteenth, near Brown street. There were half a dozen special officers on guard in front of the works. The fight was brief, but it attracted the attention of the crowds on the street, and in a short space of time hundreds of men were running toward the paint works. The specials fought gallantly against the odds, but they were forced back by the superior numbers of the strikers, and were finally compelled to take refuge in the building. One of them tripped and fell as he was stepping on the threshold of the works, and as the mob was close upon him, he drew his revolver to make a fight for life. He fired several shots point blank at the crowd and was fired at in return, but he escaped unharmed into the office. The firing attracted the attention of the police, who arrived on the spot with all possible haste.

On the Black Road the forenoon was gone and only here and there a few straggling groups had gathered around the McCormick works. It was drizzling, and the prospect for an unpleasant afternoon was good. This, and the apparent tranquillity of the district, led the police to think that hostilities would not be renewed, and information to the effect that the presence of such a large force on the scene was unnecessary, was about to be sent in to headquarters, when a yelping cur, to the tail of which a tin can had been tied by some mischievous youngster, came upon the scene and changed the entire current of the day's events. The dog yelped as only a dog can when in trouble of this peculiar nature, and soon the saloons and houses along the route of the distracted canine began to empty themselves of humanity. The yelping of the cur was hideous enough to have aroused any neighborhood, no matter how stolidly indifferent to vulgar exhibitions of this character it might generally be, but it served not only to arouse but to inflame the inhabitants of the district which lies around the intersection of Eighteenth street and Center avenue. If the yelping cur had been dispatched as a messenger, or touched off as a signal, the response could not have been more general. As if they had sprung from the ground, thousands of men were, within a few minutes, in view, and, acting as if by one accord, they turned their steps toward the intersection referred to. Here they were met by the scattering mob returning from the paint works, by the remnants of the Rosenfeld mob, and by other mobs coming from different directions, and it now became evident that the composition of the immense concourse was of too inflammable a nature to be overlooked. Intelligence of the gathering was at once sent to headquarters, and Superintendent Ebersold made speedy preparations to grapple with the anarchistic mob once more. By a mistake, or rather through the unauthorized use of Superintendent Ebersold's name, a company of the first regiment was called out by Col. Knox to assist in the suppression of the threatened riot, but the mayor and the superintendent assured that officer that the police department considered itself fully competent to deal with the case in hand quickly and satisfactorily. It was rumored down town that 7,000 rioters were marching upon McCormick's reaper works, and for a time it was feared that the events of 1877 were about to be repeated. But the rioters of 1877 had a different police organization to deal with.

The mob had become almost unmanageable before 3 o'clock, and the wildest advice given the crowd by the most desperate of the ruffians, who now and then rose above the surface and made a short speech, was received with cheers. A meeting was organized at the corner of Eighteenth street, while a drizzling rain was still falling. Here they were addressed by some of their own number, who openly advised warfare upon the McCormick factory, and the police in particular, and upon the law-abiding people of Chicago—known as the privileged classes—in general. While the speaking was still in progress, Detective Mike Granger, of the Central station, saw the handle of a pistol protruding from the pocket of one of the men, and stepped up to arrest him. This move was the signal for an anarchistic revolt, and the detective and five officers with him immediately found themselves surrounded by a howling, bloodthirsty mob. But the policemen lost no time. Forming into line, they charged upon the mob, and were "met by a volley of stones, bricks and bullets." Detective Granger fell senseless under a blow from a heavy missile, and Officer John Small, of the Hinman street station, received a pistol ball in the hand. The mob closed in on the four remaining men, and a massacre would have quickly resulted had not a reinforcement of ten men, from the Twelfth street station, made its appearance just in the nick of time. In a few minutes eight of the ringleaders in this outbreak were under arrest, and the mob was soon scattered.

Large reinforcements, however, continued to arrive, and the force of the Hinman street station was kept upon constant duty during the remainder of the day, traveling from point to point, suppressing disorders here or scattering mobs there, until they were jaded and well nigh exhausted at sunset, when relieved by the night men. The McCormick employes were all to leave the works without·a police escort, and the only set-back that peace and order appeared to receive was a fresh outbreak in the vicinity of Eighteenth street and Center avenue. This was at 7 o'clock in the evening. A meeting of lumber-shovers was being held in the hall referred to already. The crowd was so noisy that the patrol wagons of the Twelfth street, Thirteenth street and Hinman street stations were called. During the assault made upon the mob, with the object of scattering it, one of the men, Officer James Bulman, of the Twelfth street station, received a terrific blow from a brick on the back of the head.

John Vogtik, one of the wounded McCormick rioters, died during the day, and this served to keep alive the bad feeling in the vicinity of his house, 422 West Seventeenth street, but it was generally supposed that the worst was over, and the morning newspapers had wound up their reports of the day's proceedings with congratulatory paragraphs over the apparent final and satisfactory ending of the disturbances, when returns began to come in from the meeting at the Haymarket.

And for a long time there was nothing about these returns to excite the slightest interest, even among professional news collectors. True, a great deal of importance had been attached to the circular calling the gathering, early in the day, and certain it was that grave fears were felt in official and unofficial quarters regarding the outcome of an assembly called specifically for the purpose of exciting the passions of an ignorant and desperate class of men, and of inciting them, perhaps, to acts of brutal violence. The police were to be shown up in their true colors, as the paid tools of the capitalists; they were to be branded as the cold-blooded, cowardly murderers of the poor, and the mob which should gather in the Haymarket would be asked to wreak vengeance upon the lawful authorities who dared to enforce order at the muzzle of the revolver, as had been done at McCormick's.

There was a general feeling of insecurity and uneasiness around police headquarters all through the afternoon and evening. The Revenge Circular had been handed in, Schwab's bitter, treasonable and atrocious editorial had been translated for or read in the original by the commanding officers. Coming on top of these, the call for the Haymarket meeting looked very much like a part of a concerted scheme to carry out some design of the anarchist leaders, but what that scheme was nobody could even imagine; certainly nobody would venture to outline.

Superintendent Ebersold did not believe the worst was

over. A dozen times through the day he might have been seen hastily going to or coming from the office of the mayor, and nearly every time he carried a printed circular in his hand. He said little to anybody except the mayor and the staff officers. It was known that he had made repeated and futile attempts to convince Mr. Harrison that the proposed meeting should be prevented. If the mob was allowed to assemble, it might be a difficult and a dangerous proceeding to attempt to disperse it. Better take action in time and allow no gathering. The mayor was not certain but that the "people," as he called these pronounced enemies of society, government, law and order, had a right to assemble and discuss their "grievances" peaceably. He did not feel that he could molest them as long as they conducted themselves within the law, forgetting that the very call and advertised design of the gathering was to defy, denounce, ridicule and violate it. Arguments were of no avail, and the best the department was enabled to obtain from the mayor was an order that it "keep watch of the meeting, and if any of the speakers should advise their hearers to acts of violence," it would be the duty of the police, as conservators of the peace, to go to the place of meeting in sufficient force, and order them to peaceably disperse, the order to be as directed by law, viz.: Section 253, Chapter 38, Revised Statutes of Illinois. This was all right as far as it went, but Superintendent Ebersold felt that he had to deal with people who had no respect whatever for the statutes of the state of Illinois or the laws of the United States, and he proceeded to make arrangements which he deemed imperative, but was compelled to do so quietly, almost secretly, lest a veto might be put upon his actions by his superior officer.

There was another man at headquarters who dreaded the results of this gathering even more than the superintendent, although he, too, had but little to say concerning it, except to advise emphatically and unceasingly, in the presence of the chief and the mayor, that it be prevented at any cost.

He felt intuitively that something terrible would happen if the anarchists were permitted to assemble in response to the inflammatory call which had been issued from the *Arbeiter Zeitung* office. For some time the idea that a conspiracy was in existence, the object of which was to wreak vengeance on the police because of their activity in suppressing disorders, and to create a condition of affairs from which a social revolution would spring into life, had imbedded itself firmly in his mind. He had given the various proceedings of the anarchistic socialists, from the beginning of the eighthour agitation, the closest study; had weighed the apparently bombastic remarks of the leaders; had sifted the dark and mysterious hints thrown out by Spies, Parsons, Fielden and Schwab here and there; had remembered the statements made by inmates of the *Arbeiter Zeitung* office, that the *Internationale* was prepared for revolution; had watched carefully the meetings of the "armed groups," and had formed a very intelligent notion of the aims as well as the strength of the anarchistic organization. This man was John Bonfield, inspector of police, and with the reserve which is one of his characteristics, he kept his information and his views away from the public, deeming it necessary only to discuss the situation with the chief and some of his associate officers. That Superintendent Ebersold fully realized the importance of Inspector Bonfield's conclusion there is little doubt, but the gravity with which he looked upon the condition of affairs was not generally shared among the staff officers. Some of the captains doubted that an organized conspiracy existed, others that, even though it did exist, the miscreants at the head of it would dare to put their plans into execution, and others felt that nothing which the anarchists might do, even though they did their worst, would assume a degree of importance which would warrant any great alarm. Capt. Shaack had already succeeded in unearthing some important and startling information regarding the anarchistic plot, and he was engaged conscientiously in following up the clews which he had received, but it is doubtful if even he, on the afternoon of the 4th of May, felt that any immediate danger need be feared.

However, the superintendent and inspector, acting in harmony of opinion, made the necessary preparations to meet the trouble, if it should come. Capt. Ward, of the third precinct (near whose headquarters the meeting was announced to take place), was ordered to call all his available men to Desplaines street station. His command consisted of one hundred men, under Lieutenants Bowler, Stanton, Penzen and Beard. In addition to these, there were present at the Desplaines street station, early in the evening, twenty-six men, commanded by Lieutenant (now captain) G. W. Hubbard and Sergeant (now lieutenant) John E. Fitzpatrick. When Inspector Bonfield arrived at the station, the entire force present consisted of one captain, seven lieutenants, and one hundred and seventy-six men.

The force under Lieutenant Hubbard and Sergeant Fitzpatrick consisted of Patrolmen Cornelius W. Crowley, John P. Nelson, Patrick Lavihan, Jacob Ebinger, Solomon S. Steele, James Kerwin, J. O. D. Storen, William Lyonnais, Hiram A. Earl, John J. Kelley, James Mitchell, Lewis Golden, John W. Collins, James H. Wilson, Peter McHugh, Luke Colleran, Fred. A. Andrews, Michael O'Brien, John A. Weber, John F. Gibbons, James Cahill, John Riordon, John C. Morris, John Morweiser, Florence Donohue, and Daniel Hogan—all select men, the flower of the Central detail, pronounced by Mr. Paul Hull, who saw them march upon the meeting, "a company of giants."

Lieutenant Bowler's company consisted of Sergeant Richard J. Moore, Patrolmen George Miller, John J. Barrett, Michael Sheehan, John Reid, Lawrence J. Murphy, John E. Doyle, Arthur Conolly, Nicholas J. Shannon, Adam S. Barber, James Conway, Thomas McEnery, Patrick Hartford, Louis Johnson, Frank P. Tyrell, C. Keller, James Brady, John H. King, Peter Foley, John Wesler, Thomas

Meaney, Robert J. Walsh, Hugo Asping, Edward Griffin, and William L. Sanderson—a company that, within a few short hours, was destined to undergo a bloody ordeal.

Lieutenant Stanton's company consisted of Patrolmen Charles H. Coffey, Alexander Jameson, Timothy O'Sullivan, Thomas Halley, Jacob Hansen, Michael Horan, Peter Butterly, William Kelly, Joseph Norman, Thomas Hennessy, William Burns, Charles H. Fink, Matthias J. Degan, Bernard J. Murphy, Thomas Brophy, Charles J. Whitney, and Thomas Redden—another company that suffered dreadfully.

In Lieutenant Beard's company were, Sergeant John Post, and Patrolmen P. McMahon, Michael Keeley, George Kenan, Jacob J. Barcal, Richard Ellsworth, William I. Niff, Dennis T. Turney, Peter Cunningham, Joseph J. Fallon, Dennis Dunne, Daniel Pembroke, Michael Connelly, John Brown, Hugh McNeil, Nicholas H. Stahl, Patrick Prior, Charles E. Allen, Daniel Cramer, Martin Cullen, Frank Murphy, Timothy Daly, Peter J. Burns, and John Hartnett, Jr.

In Lieutenant Penzen's company were, Sergeant Edmund Roche, and Patrolmen P. H. Keefe, Andrew O'Day, Michael O'Donnell, John D. Hartford, Jeremiah Grogan, John J. Daly, Gustav A. Walters, Patrick Connors, John Plunkett, Thomas Kindlan, Matthew Wilson, Patrick Nash, Robert Bennett, Matthew Connolly, Patrick McLaughlin, Edward Gasquoine, Michael Walsh, Charles C. Fish, Edwin J. Cullen, George Lynch, William Sanderson, Henry F. Smith, and Daniel Daley.

Lieut. Steele, of the West Chicago avenue station, had under his command, Patrolmen C. W. Ganoio, Henry Weineke, Edward Ruel, Herman Krueger, Edward Barrett, Charles Dombrowski, and Patrick McNulty.

Orders were also dispatched providing for reserve details aggregating about 600 men, to be held at Harrison street. East and West Chicago avenue and Central stations, equipped for active service, and to be ready at a moment s notice for any emergency.   At each of these stations the precinct wagons were held in readiness.   The second precinct was not called upon for service, for the reason that during the two preceding days Captain O'Donnell's men had been kept in constant service, and there was still danger of an uprising in the vicinity of Eighteenth street and Center avenue.   A large squad of detectives in plain clothing was ordered to mingle with the crowd when it should assemble at the Haymarket, and to report to Inspector Bonfield, who was to assume personal command at the Desplaines street station, at the request of the mayor and with permission of the superintendent, at regular and frequent intervals, the state of feeling, the sentiments expressed by the speakers, and the probabilities or improbabilities of trouble, as the case might be.

Inspector Bonfield was specially desirous of assuming command of the force collected at the Desplaines street station, for he feared serious trouble, and he had reason to believe that the terrible possibilities of the gathering were neither fully understood nor appreciated by subordinate officers.   In the afternoon he said to the superintendent, "Chief, I think there is going to be bad work at the Haymarket this evening; one of us, you or I, ought to be present."   The superintendent had been at his post night and day since the preceding Friday.   The work which he had performed in directing the force at McCormick's, during the riot on the Black Road, was terribly wearing, and he felt almost exhausted.   "I will remain at headquarters," he said. "You had better be on the spot."   It was understood that the inspector should report to the superintendent frequently.

The meeting was announced to open at 8 o'clock, but, strange to say, at that hour none of the socialistic orators had put in an appearance, although it had ever been their custom to be on hand promptly.   Spies says that on the morning of the 4th he was informed by "A. Fischer, one of our compositors," that a general mass meeting would be held at the Haymarket that evening, and asked him (Spies) if he would come and make a speech on the "brutality of the police and the situation of the eight-hour strike." To this the author of the Revenge Circular replied that he hardly felt able to speak (but why, he fails to state, as on all previous occasions he felt more than able), but that if there was no one to take his place he would certainly be present. He adds that "delegates of a number of unions," Fischer informed him, "had called the meeting." "About 11 o'clock" (a. m.) he says, "a member of the Carpenter's union called on me, and asked that the hand-bill he showed me be printed in the *Arbeiter Zeitung* as an announcement. It was the circular calling the Haymarket meeting, and at the bottom it contained the words—'Workingmen, bring your arms along.'

"'This is ridiculous,' said I, to the man, and had Fischer called. I told him that I would not speak at the meeting if this was the circular by which it had been called. 'None of the circulars are as yet distributed; we can have these words taken out,' the man said. Fischer assented. I told them that if they did that it would be all right. I never for a moment anticipated that the police would wantonly attack an orderly meeting of citizens, and I never saw a disorderly meeting of workingmen. The only disorderly meetings I have ever witnessed were the republican and democratic pow-wows. I went home about 4 p. m., to take a little rest before going to the meeting. The reaction following the excitement of the previous day had set in. I was very tired and ill-humored. After supper my brother Henry called at our house. I asked him to come along to the meeting, which he did. We walked slowly down Milwaukee avenue. It was warm; I had changed my clothes; the revolver I was in the habit of carrying was too large for the pocket and inconvenienced me. Passing Frank Stauber's hardware store, I left it with him. It was about 8:15 o'clock when we arrived at Lake and Desplaines streets. I was under the impression that I was to speak in German, which generally follows the English. That is the reason why I was late."

That he was late is certain, as were Parsons and Fielden likewise. It is clear now why he was late, and why he left his revolver at Stauber's store. Spies knew what was going to happen that night as well as he could know anything, and he had been feeling nervous and "ill-humored" all the evening. He had worked the plot, with his brother anarchists, up to the boiling pitch, and now the "reaction had set in," as he says himself, and the frightful enormity of the crime which was about to be perpetrated stared him in the face and made him tremble. "When arrested, as I certainly will be," thought he, "if all our plans do not succeed, that is, if we are not masters of Chicago before morning, it is best that I shall not have a revolver in my possession. There is nothing like being on the safe side." Where, has been asked, were Parsons and Fielden? Why were they late, too? Was there a consultation going on somewhere? Why did the crowd of ten or fifteen hundred men hang around the Haymarket so patiently, awaiting the coming of Robespierre, Danton and Marat? The fact that they were late did not, as is usually the case, create impatience among the assemblage, and nobody undertook to interest the mob of sullen, low-browed ruffians who moved around carelessly, saying little or nothing, but now and then swarming into little groups, only to speedily break up again and continue their aimless wandering to and fro! The crowd began to grow larger toward half-past eight, but the new arrivals were mostly honest workingmen, drawn thither, perhaps, more through curiosity than because they had any sympathy with the meeting or the people under whose auspices it was to be held. "Small and large groups of men were standing around" when Spies arrived, "but there was no meeting. Not seeing anyone who might be entrusted with the management of the meeting, I jumped upon a wagon, enquired for Mr. Parsons (who I thought had been invited), and called the meeting to order. Parsons was not there." No, Parsons was not there. The gifted socialistic orator was still conspicuously absent. It had also occurred to him, most likely, that there would be some little trouble at this meeting, and he was in no hurry to reach it, hoping, perhaps, that the trouble would have occurred before he arrived. The idea of leaving his revolver, if he carried one, at the store of some brother socialist, had not dawned on him as a means of throwing off suspicion when difficulties should occur, but a happier idea than that was conceived in his fertile brain. "I will bring my wife and children to the meeting," he thought. "They need not be close enough to the spot where our friends are located to be in danger, but they will be at the meeting, and who will have the heart to say that I brought them there, knowing that a bomb was to be thrown in case the police interfered. Ah! that's a happy thought." Spies grew more nervous as Parsons and Fielden failed to put in an appearance, and jumped from the wagon with the intention of hunting them up. Then he learned for the first time, he says, that *Parsons, Fielden and others were holding a meeting at the Arbeiter Zeitung office.* A messenger was at once dispatched for the missing agitators.

It was almost nine o'clock when a strange movement of the crowd took place. As if by common consent the two thousand persons present moved off the Haymarket square to a point about half a block north on Desplaines street. Why the change was made nobody seemed to understand. All such meetings had heretofore been held on the Haymarket. This was the first time that Desplaines street was selected in preference. The section of Randolph street, popularly known as the Haymarket, begins at Desplaines street and runs west to Halsted. It is one hundred feet wide from curb to curb, or about one hundred and thirty feet between house fronts. On this square, in former times, stood the old West Market hall, frequently mentioned in this volume, and to the west of the building was the haymarket of the West

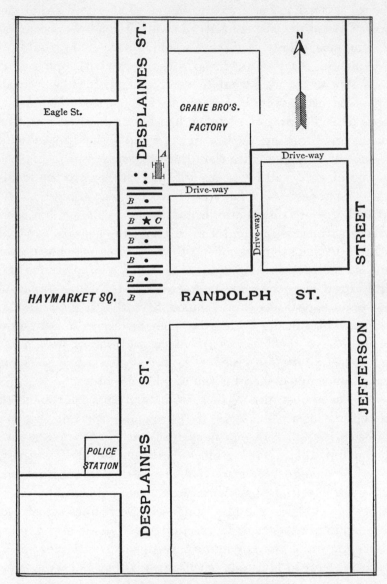

EXPLANATION OF DIAGRAM.

A—The Wagon.

₊—Inspector Bonfield, Captain Ward, Lieutenant Steele.

B B B B B B.—Six companies of policemen.

Division of the city. Hence the name. Because of the extreme width of the street at this point, the location had always been a popular one for large gatherings. Desplaines street, on the contrary, is only eighty feet wide. The crowd could stand in front of the speaker on the Haymarket and catch every word that was uttered. On Desplaines street it would have to spread out to the right and left, and the high buildings on either side would produce a disagreeable echo. But those who did not understand why the change was made could not be expected to diagnose the situation as clearly as this, on the spur of the moment, so all followed, and in a short time the Haymarket was deserted. Here, if anyone outside of the conspiracy had been suspicious, another strange thing might have attracted attention. A large truck wagon was already in position to receive the speakers, as though the arrangement had been made some time before the crowd began to move. Strange that the wagon should be in that spot, and stranger still, that those in the crowd, who were interested in the night's proceedings, should have known of it!

The average reader will perhaps be amazed when informed that no meeting was convened, no bomb exploded, and no massacre occurred at the Haymarket on the night of May 4, 1886. The "Haymarket massacre" is a misnomer, but by that name, and none other, will it go down into history, for common usage has fastened this title upon the terrible event of that awful night, and it is now too late to change it. The anarchist meeting was held, the bomb was exploded, and the massacre occurred on Desplaines street. It was intended by the fiendish conspirators who planned the meeting, that it should be held on Desplaines street and not on the Haymarket, and for the following very good reasons:

The Haymarket is a quadrilateral square, from any corner of which the entire length and breadth of the space between Desplaines and Halsted streets might be swept by a volley from the police, or, in case of such a revolutionary condition of affairs as the anarchists expected to inaugurate that evening, by grape and canister, should the military be called out. From this quadrilateral, when the bombs were exploded, as a number of them were to be thrown during the evening, there were no means of egress save through Desplaines street, which in all likelihood would be cut off by the police, through Halsted street, where Bonfield would certainly mass a large body of men, or through Union street, the only passage from the center of the Haymarket. Calculating that if the police entered the Haymarket, for the purpose of dispersing a meeting assembled there, they would probably march through the center of the square, it would be almost impossible for the bomb-throwers to do their fiendish work without being detected by law-abiding people in the crowd, while the width of the street at this point would give the police ample room for work, and under ordinary circumstances they could sweep it clean with their revolvers, the anarchists going down before them as well as the innocent and the ignorant in the crowd. All things considered, the Haymarket was not the place for the meeting. It developed in the trial of the anarchists that August Spies was the man who selected the Desplaines street wagon. His counsel in their brief and argument before the Supreme Court say:

It is proved alike by the witnesses of the state and for the defense that no move was made toward the calling to order of the meeting itself until August Spies, looking round for a suitable rostrum from which to address the crowd, selected the truck wagon which he found standing close to the edge of the sidewalk in Desplaines street, and directly in front of the steps leading up to the door entering into the Crane Brothers' manufacturing establishment. The wagon stood with the rear to the south, the tongue to the north, and the end of the wagon was some six or eight feet, or more, north of the north line of Crane Brothers' alley. [See diagram]. This is a short alley, as shown by the plat, which enters the block from Desplaines street toward the east, upon the south line of Crane Brothers' building, and extends about half-way through the block, then makes a junction with another short alley extending out from the point of junction southward to Randolph street. This alley is a perfect *cul de sac* as it then existed, and all egress from it could be stopped by a handful of men at the Randolph street exit.

This presentation of the case is plausible enough from the standpoint of the defendants. But let us see what Mr. Hull says in relation to this branch of the subject:

As remarked a moment ago, there was significance in the selection of this spot by the speakers, from whence to address the crowd. The building on the northeast corner of Desplaines and Randolph streets is seventy feet deep on Desplaines street. The next building north and on Desplaines street is a factory, and between the factory and the rear of the corner building, is a driveway or alley, ten feet wide, running east. It intersects another driveway running south to Randolph street and north to courts formed by the factory buildings. The north end of this driveway joins another which runs east to Jefferson street. Further north, and on Desplaines street, and on the east side of the street, is another alley running east. This alley cuts the block about two-thirds of the distance between Randolph and Lake streets. On the west side of the street an alley runs west, through the middle of the block, to Union street. Here were excellent avenues of escape, in case of danger, for those acquainted with the locality. The speakers' wagon stood just north of the driveway, on the east side of the street. Diagonally across the street was the opening of the alley running west to Union street. In case of necessity the socialistic brotherhood, being on the alert, could escape through the driveway on the east to Randolph street, and through the alley on the west to Union street, the police meantime being on Desplaines street. It had this advantage over the usual meeting place in the square—there the police could approach the crowd from Desplaines, Union or Halsted streets, as might chance, and the bomb-throwers would be in uncertainty as to where to station themselves. There would be no other means of escape, then, within range of the policemen's revolvers, up and down Randolph street. The street here is wide and the police could sweep it like a field with their shots. Their lines also would be spread out in order to cover the greater space. Their forces would not be concentrated as when on Desplaines street, and a bomb kills only at short range. With policemen marching in form to clear a street, a bomb would injure fewer of them in Haymarket square than on Desplaines street. It would require some seconds for a bomb-thrower to get out of the range of a revolver in Haymarket square. From the position taken in Desplaines street he could disappear in an instant. Did the anarchist leaders consider this when they selected this unusual position?

CHAPTER XV.

THE FOURTH OF MAY, 1886—HOW THE ANARCHISTS PLANNED TO ENTRAP
THE POLICE—THE NARROW STREET WITH ALLEY-WAY EXITS—THE
HAYMARKET MEETING—SPEECHES OF SPIES, PARSONS AND FIELDEN—
THE INFLAMMATORY REMARKS OF THE LATTER — "THROTTLE THE
LAW! KILL IT! STAB IT!"—WHY BONFIELD FINALLY MOVED—THE
BOMB—WHAT HAPPENED AFTERWARD.

It is a pretty well established belief now that the anarchist leaders did consider all these points before the selection was made.   Inspector Bonfield and the officers and men of the department are fully convinced that the object of the anarchists in changing the meeting place to Desplaines street was:

First.   To consolidate the police force in a narrow street, in order that bombs thrown into their ranks would produce a more effective slaughter.

Second.   To draw the police into this narrow space, so that when the bombs were thrown they would become confused, and, perhaps, shoot each other, and to afford the anarchists ample opportunity of firing from the ambush which the alley-ways afforded.

Third.   To give the leaders, and anarchists generally, avenues of escape, and to afford the bomb-throwers the protection of the alley-way opening into Desplaines street, close to the wagon.

There is a slight discrepancy among those who attended the meeting as to the exact time the speaking began, but it is generally put at a few minutes past 9 o'clock.

Fischer and Engel were present during the early part of the evening.   Later on, Schwab's gaunt form might be seen moving aimlessly through the crowd, as many witnesses have claimed, but he denied his presence there.   Parsons and Fielden arrived in due season, and, of course, Spies was there, and he was the first speaker. From the testimony of Paul C. Hull in the trial of the anarchists, the following summary of the remarks made by Spies is taken:

Mr. Spies told his version of the McCormick riots, which, as I remember, was, that he had been charged, he said, with being responsible for the riot and for the death of these men. He said—I believe he said—that Mr. McCormick charged him with it, or else somebody had said that Mr. McCormick had charged him with it. He said Mr. McCormick was a liar; that he (McCormick) was responsible for the death of our brothers, the six men, whom he claimed were killed at the riot; that he had addressed a meeting on the prairie—a meeting of his countrymen, I believe he characterized them—and when the bell of the factory rang, or at some point in the afternoon, a body of the meeting which he was addressing detached themselves and went toward the factory, and that there the riot occurred; that was in explanation of it. He then touched upon the dominating question of labor and capital and their relations, very briefly, and asked, what meant this array of Gatling guns, infantry ready to arm, patrol wagons, and policemen. And my recollection is that he drew the deduction from that, that it was the government, or the capitalists, preparing to crush them, should they try to right their wrongs.

The speaker, according to Mr. Hull, closed rather abruptly, and adds, in his account of the riot:

The briefness of Spies' speech can be accounted for on the supposition that he expected, every moment, to see a column of police coming down upon him. He had reason to believe that the moment the speaking was begun, the police would attempt to break up the meeting, and he felt that he would avoid responsibility in his utterances. Parsons spoke next. He began cautiously. He, too, was expecting the police. He dealt at length with labor statistics, and expounded that, whereas the laboring man produces one dollar, he receives but fifteen cents of it. In the early part of his speech he said: " I am a socialist from head to foot, and I declare it, although it may cost me my life before morning."

Mr. English, of the Chicago *Tribune*, in his testimony gave this abstract from Parsons' speech:

Don't you know that the military are under arms, and a Gatling gun is ready to mow you down? Was this Germany, or Russia, or Spain? [A voice, "It looks like it."] Whenever you make a demand for eight hours' pay, an increase of pay, the militia, and the deputy sheriffs, and the Pinkerton men are called out, and you are shot, and clubbed, and murdered in the streets. I am not here for the purpose of inciting anybody, but to speak out—to tell the facts as they exist, even though it shall cost me my life before morning.

It appears, therefore, from the testimony of two competent reporters, Mr. English, of the *Tribune*, and Mr. Hull, of the *Daily News*, that Parsons had some sort of an innate fear, some foreboding, some knowledge, regarding an event which would cause trouble—perhaps cost him his life—*before morning*. Parsons had never spoken in this vein before. His style was always defiant. He had never placed himself in the position of a prospective martyr. Like Spies he appeared to be ill at ease, and during the remarks which he made afterward, he spoke in a wandering, subdued manner, entirely out of keeping with his usual demeanor on the platform, while now and then he cast furtive glances in the direction of the Desplaines street station.

The crowd all this time was very quiet, uncommonly quiet. Not because the speech made was particularly interesting, or because any new points against the "privileged classes" were drawn out, but rather because a large number in the assemblage seemed to share the feeling exhibited by Spies and Parsons, that something might be expected to happen before morning.

Mayor Harrison was present while Spies and Parsons were speaking, and the meeting appeared to be so tame, in comparison with gatherings of this class which had been previously held in Chicago, that he came to the conclusion there would be no trouble during the evening, so informed Inspector Bonfield, and went home.

Mr. Hull adds in relation to Parsons:

He spoke at great length, as if killing time, but the police did not come. He grew bolder as he proceeded and warmed up to something like his old time heat. At one time he said: "We speak harshly of the scabs, but I tell you when a man has been out of work for six or twelve months, and has tramped about the country looking for a job, and been sent to the rock pile as a vagrant, he is going to take the first job that is offered him whether it is to fill a striker's place or not. There is not a man in this crowd but who would do the same. What is a scab? He is a flea or a dog. Now the trade unionists want to kill the scab or flea, while the socialist wants to kill the dog itself and prevent fleas." He closed by an appeal to arms by all men who loved their wives and children.

Fielden was the last speaker, and it was nearly 10 o'clock before he arose to address the crowd. His remarks were unusually mild at the beginning, but, like Parsons, he seemed to lose consciousness of the fear that was in him, and as he spoke he warmed up to the subject and soon his language began to flow in the old seditious and inflammatory channel. Mr. English, at the trial, testified to the following as some of his language:

There are premonitions of danger. All know. The press say the anarchists will sneak away; we are not going to. If we continue to be robbed, it will not be long before we will be murdered. There is no security for the working classes under the present social system. A few individuals control the means of living and holding the workingmen in a vise. Everybody does not know. Those who know it are tired of it, and know the others will get tired of it, too. *They are determined to end it and will end it.* There is no power in the land that will prevent them. Congressman Foran said, "The laborer can get nothing from legislation." He also said that the laborers can get some relief from their present condition when the rich man knew it was unsafe for him to live in a community where there were dissatisfied workingmen, for they *would solve the labor problem.* I don't know whether you are democrats or republicans, but whichever you are you worship at the shrine of rebels. John Brown, Jefferson, Washington, Patrick Henry and Hopkins said to the people: "The law is your enemy. We are rebels against it. The law is only framed for those who are your enslavers." [A voice: "That is true."] Men, in their blind rage, attacked McCormick's factory and were shot down by the law in cold blood, in the city of Chicago, in the protection of property. Those men were going to do some damage to a certain person's interest, who was a large property-owner, therefore the law came to his defense. And when McCormick undertook to do some injury to the interest of those who had no property, the law also came to his defense and not to the workingman's defense, when he, Mr. McCormick, attacked him and his living. [Cries of "No."] There is the difference. The law makes no distinction. A million men own all the property in this country. The law has no use for the other fifty-four million. [A voice, "Right enough."] You have nothing more to do with the law except to *lay hands on it and throttle it until it makes its last kick.* It turns your brothers out on the wayside, and has degraded them until they have lost the last vestige of humanity, and they are mere things and animals. *Keep your eye upon it. Throttle it. Kill it. Stab it.* Do everything you can to wound it—to impede its progress. Remember, before trusting them to do anything for yourself, prepare to do it for yourself. Don't turn over your business to anybody else. No man deserves anything unless he is man enough to make an effort to lift himself from oppression.

While Fielden was talking a sudden change had taken place in the atmosphere. The air which had been almost oppressive during the evening, now became chilly, and there were indications above of a sudden and severe storm. Rain had begun to fall, and many persons were moving from the crowd, and Mrs. Parsons suggested that the meeting adjourn to Zeff's hall, when Fielden in an irritable manner said no, the people were trying to get information and he would go on—he would say all he had to say there and then.

At the Desplaines street station Inspector Bonfield and his command were in constant receipt of information regarding the situation at the meeting. Detectives came in one after the other and reported what Fielden had said, how the crowd seemed to take his remarks, etc. The advice which he gave his hearers to throttle the law, to kill it and stab it, was reported, and some of the officers suggested that it was time to move. Inspector Bonfield, however, was not going to make a mistake, or act hastily. He sent the detectives back again, and while they were on their way others came in and corroborated the first statements. Still the inspector held the men back, and the officers around him in a joking way began to badger him, telling him he didn't have the nerve to break up the meeting, and that he was afraid to touch the anarchists. Inspector Bonfield replied to all this by saying that he wanted to act entirely within the law, and that when he did act, the others would soon discover whether he was afraid of the anarchist crowd or not. Now, reports began to come in that groups in the crowd which Fielden was addressing talked of proceeding to the St. Paul freight house, where "scabs" had been employed, and where they were housed for the night. The detectives, whom the inspector had dispatched to obtain more satisfactory information as to the threatening character of the meeting, returned, and the information which they brought convinced him that it was time to act. In relation to his action on that night, Inspector Bonfield says: "At different times, between 8:00 and 9:30 o'clock p. m., officers in plain clothes reported the progress of the meeting and stated that nothing of a very inflammatory nature was said until a man named Fielden took the stand. He advised his hearers, 'To throttle the law.' 'It would be as well for them to die fighting as to starve to death.' He further advised them, 'To exterminate the capitalists and to do it that night.' Wanting to be clearly within the law, and wishing to leave no room for doubt as to the propriety of our actions, I did not act on the first reports, but sent the officers back to make further observations. A few minutes after 10 o'clock p. m., the officers returned and reported that the crowd was getting excited and the speaker growing more incendiary in his language. I then felt to hesitate any longer would be criminal on my part, and then gave the orders to fall in, and our force formed on Waldo Place. The companies of Lieutenants Steele and Quinn formed the first division, Lieut. Steele on the right. The companies of Lieutenants Stanton and Bowler formed the second division, Lieut. Bowler on the right. The third division consisted of twenty-six men from the Central detail, under command of Lieut. Hubbard and Sergt. Fitzpatrick. Two companies commanded by Lieutenants Beard and Penzen brought up the rear. Their orders were to form right and left on Randolph street, and guard our rear from any attack from the Haymarket on Randolph street."

While the police were forming into line and marching toward the meeting, Fielden was talking. His language, according to the notes taken by Mr. English, ran as follows:

Is it not a fact that we have no choice as to our existence, for we can't dictate what our labor is worth. He that has to obey the will of any is a slave. Can we do anything except by the strong arm of resistance?

Socialists are not going to declare war, out I tell you war has been declared upon us, and *I ask you to get hold of anything* that will help to resist the onslaught of the enemy and the usurper. The skirmish lines have met. People have been shot. Men, women and children have not been spared by the capitalists and the minions of private capital. *It had no mercy, so ought you.* You are called upon to defend yourselves, your lives, your future. *What matter it whether you kill yourself with work to get a little relief, or die on the battlefield resisting the enemy?* What is the difference? An animal, however loathsome, will resist when stepped upon. Are men less than slaves or worms? I have some resistance in me. I know that you have, too. You have been robbed, and you will be starved into a worse condition.

At this moment the police appeared in view, and a tremor passed through the crowd, but Fielden continued to speak, although his remarks were not listened to, the attention of all being turned in the direction of the advancing column of blue-coats, which stretched across the entire width of Desplaines street, and swept it clean. Inspector Bonfield continues his story of the night's work: "In this order we marched north on Desplaines street (Captain Ward and myself in front of first division), until within a few feet of the truck upon which the speakers were standing, and around which a large crowd had congregated. The command 'halt' was given, and Captain Ward, stepping forward to within about three feet of the truck, said, 'I command you, in the name of the people of the state, to immediately and peaceably disperse,' and, turning to the crowd of persons on the right and left, said, 'I command you and you to assist.' Fielden turned and got off the truck, and as he reached the sidewalk, said, in rather a loud voice, 'We are peaceable.' Almost instantly I heard a hissing sound behind me, followed by a tremendous explosion. The explosion was immediately followed by a volley of pistol shots from the sidewalks and streets in front of us.

"The explosion was caused by a dynamite bomb, which was thrown into our ranks from the east sidewalk, and fell in the second division, and near the dividing line between the companies of Lieutenants Stanton and Bowler. For an insᴛant the entire command of tne above named officers, with many of the first and third divisions, were thrown to the ground, alas! many never to rise again. The men recovered instantly, and returned the fire of the mob. Lieutenants Steele and Quinn charged the mob on the street, while the company of Lieutenant Hubbard, with the few uninjured members of the second division, swept both sidewalks with a hot and telling fire, and in a few minutes the anarchists were flying in every direction. I then gave the order to cease firing, fearing that some of our men, in the darkness, might fire into each other. I then ordered the patrol wagons to be called, made details to take care of the dead and wounded, placed guards around the stations, and called for physicians to attend to our wounded men. It is surprising to many that our men stood, and did not get demoralized under such trying circumstances. It has been asserted that regular troops have become panic-stricken from less cause. I see no way to account for it except this: The soldier acts as part of a machine, rarely, if ever, when on duty is he allowed to act as an individual, or to use his personal judgment. A police officer's training teaches him to be self-reliant. Day after day, and night after night, he goes on duty alone, and when in conflict with the thief and burglar, he has to depend upon his own individual exertions. The soldiers, being a part of a machine, it follows, that when part of it gives out, the rest is useless until the injury is repaired. The policeman, being a machine in himself, rarely, if ever, gives up until he is laid upon the ground and unable to rise again. In conclusion, I beg leave to report that the conduct of the men and officers, with few exceptions, was admirable; as a military man said to me the next day, 'Worth the heroes of a hundred battles.' Of one officer I wish to make special mention. Immediately after the explosion, I looked behind me and saw the greater portion of the second division on the ground. I gave the order to the men to close up, and in an instant Sergeant John E. Fitzpatrick was at my side and repeated the order."

Captain Ward says, after telling of his recognition of Fielden on the wagon:

"I raised my baton, and in a loud voice ordered them to disperse as peaceable citizens. I also called upon three persons in the crowd to assist in dispersing the mob. Fielden got down from the wagon, saying at the time, 'We are peaceable.' As he uttered the last word I heard a terrible explosion behind where I was standing, followed almost instantly by an irregular volley of pistol shots in our front and from the sidewalk on the east side of the street, which was immediately followed by regular and well-directed volleys from the police, and which was kept up for several minutes."

Said Lieutenant Quinn in his report:

"The order 'forward' brought us to within about six feet of an improvised stand, a flat truck wagon, where several speak. ers were present, and a man then speaking to the assembly. The command, 'halt' was given, and at this moment, the speaker, pointing to our advancing force, remarked, 'There are the bloodhounds coming; do your duty and I will do mine.' Captain William Ward, of the third precinct, then stepped forward to the speakers' stand and, addressing the speakers, as also the entire assembly, said, 'I, as an officer of the law, in the name of the people of the state of Illinois, do hereby command you to disperse,' and at the same time calling upon law-abiding citizens to assist him in so doing. As Captain Ward had finished his last sentence a shell was thrown into our ranks; immediately afterward a volley of shots was fired into us from the crowd.. The command at once returned the fire, being assisted by the entire force on the scene, and were successful in dispersing the mob. After this, all available men of my command, as also a part of Lieutenant Steele's command, remained on the ground until 2 a. m. next day, by orders from Inspector Bonfield. I would further state that the conduct of the men in my command was excellent, without exception."

"After Captain Ward's order to the meeting, the speaker paused for a moment," says Lieutenant Bowler, "and the next instant a bomb-shell was thrown into our midst, wounding nineteen of my men out of a company of twenty-six. I was momentarily stunned, but soon recovered myself, and ordered what men I had left to charge on the crowd. We fired several shots each, and then used our clubs to good advantage. Both sides of the street were covered with wounded men, but most of the crowd was north on Desplaines street. After the shooting was over, Sergeant R. Moore, Officers Wessler, Foley, Meaney, Asping, R. Walsh and myself, went to assist the wounded. During the struggle I saw Inspector Bonfield, Captain Ward, Lieutenant Hubbard, Sergeants Moore and Fitzpatrick several times."

"The bomb fell directly in front and near the center of my company," said Lieutenant Stanton, "and about four feet to my left. I think it was thrown from the east side of the street. Shooting began immediately after the shell exploded, and continued from three to five minutes. I turned to look after my men, and found they were scattered and the most of them injured. I ordered them to fire, and proceeded to do so myself, and continued to do so until exhausted by the loss of blood from my wounds. I was then taken to the Desplaines street station, and soon afterward to the county hospital."

"Myself and Sergeant Fitzpatrick were side by side," said Lieutenant Hubbard, "the sergeant on my right, and both of us in front and center of our command. We proceeded north on Desplaines street to about 90 feet north of Randolph street, and when in the act of halting a bomb was thrown from the east side of Desplaines street, alighting in the center of the second division, about five feet from, and directly in front of, myself and Sergeant Fitzpatrick. The bomb exploded instantly, and mowed down about one-half of the second division, and six men of the left wing

of our command. The concussion made by the explosion
staggered and rendered me wholly deaf for a few minutes.
The remainder of the second division was forced back by
the havoc made by the explosion, together with our own injured, temporarily deranging our line.   Sergeant Fitzpatrick
reorganized the right wing of our command, and commenced
firing upon the crowd on the east sidewalk, I taking the
remainder of the left wing, and emptied our revolvers into
the crowd as they rushed south on the west side of Desplaines
street.   The firing continued until the order came from you,
[Inspector Bonfield] through Sergeant Fitzpatrick, to cease
firing, fearing that we might injure each other in the darkness.
We proceeded at once to reorganize the company, reload, and
ascertain how many of our command were missing, and found
nine short, seven of whom were injured and the other two
were assisting in caring for the wounded.   By your order
we proceeded to the southwest corner of Desplaines and
Randolph and stood guard until relieved and ordered to the
station.   A portion of our command was detailed to assist
in gathering up the wounded officers, as every few minutes
word would be received that an injured officer was at such a
number or place.

"Directly after the bomb exploded, it was followed by a
volley of pistol shots from both the east and west sidewalks.
Our men returned the fire as soon as possible.   I also saw
many persons lying on the walks, in doorways and alleys,
after the firing ceased, but when we had cared for our own
men, and began gathering up the dead and wounded of the
enemy, many had disappeared in some manner, and others
drawn into adjacent buildings.   The entire proceedings were
sudden, vicious and soon over; no one knows that better than
myself.   I would state in conclusion that the conduct of the
men was admirable, and that at the command, ceased firing
and fell in; the command immediately reorganized on the
very ground that they halted on at the beginning of the engagement."

No description of the scene which occurred after the explosion of the bomb could be more vivid than that which is given us by Mr. Hull, in his little work, "The Chicago Riot." Speaking of the dreadful night, he says:

It [the bomb] burst with a deep, sullen, prolonged roar, more deafening than summer thunder. No fire came from it and the cloud of smoke spread close to the earth. I saw the second and third companies of police, under Lieutenants Bowler and Stanton, fall to the ground as one man. An instant later all was confusion.

Then came the rattling reports of revolver shots from both sides of the street, and the smoke shut out my vision. These shots were fired from the crowd into the police. Then came the cry from some one, "Charge!" The police had rallied and shots came like the falling of corn on a tin pan, or the roll of a drum. The thought came to me that the police would fire high as they had so often done when dispersing crowds. I thought my position dangerous and foolishly rushed down to the street. I had much better remained where I was.

There was a furious and indescribable scramble for life around the corner, and at the instant I reached the bottom of the stairs, the police were directing their fire at this corner. I sprang into the crowd, thinking to gain a wide doorway just around the corner on Randolph street. At the first step a man in front of me was shot. I fell over him. At the same instant a man behind me was shot. He fell on my shoulders and head. For a moment I was unable to rise. The rushing crowd trampled on my legs and back. I was probably not down to exceed two or three seconds. I rose with an effort and sprang for the doorway. A policeman struck me with a club across the breast and staggered me back. The blow was not painful, but felt like the blow of a man's fist. Two men, who were in the doorway, were seized by officers and dragged to the pavement. The clubs smashed into their faces and on their heads for a moment. I stood still, my back to the wall, facing the police, holding my hat in my hand. The bullets buzzed like bees and the clubs cracked on human skulls.   *   *   *   *   *   *   *   I was acquainted with every officer, and I hoped they would know my face—white enough, probably, to show well in the darkness. I expected, every instant, to feel a bullet in my flesh; but I dared not run—I would have been beaten to death by my friends before they would have recognized me. Detective "Sandy" Hanley stood in the street, near me. I started toward him for protection. He caught a sidelong glance of me, drew his revolver on me, and fired. As the muzzle came down I threw up my hand and yelled, "Sandy!" He dropped his hand in time to fire the bullet into the cedar blocks at my feet. How many men, at a time like that, could have acted so quickly as this cool man?

Bailiff Kelley, of the Desplaines street court, has since told me how nearly he came to killing me. He said, "I stood a few paces to your

The police followed the retreating anarchists a

deadly volleys into their midst (p. 319).

right, and when I first saw you standing there I didn't know you. I drew aim on you, and was about to fire when I thought—'Why, d—— it, he stands there as if he had a right to,' and so I didn't shoot. I popped away at another man scooting across the square, and fetched him, too, and then I saw you again, and I thought I'd take a crack at you, anyway. I had just drawn on you, when an officer struck up my gun, saying 'that's a reporter.'"

The rapid shooting ceased within a minute after the explosion of the bomb. The officers had emptied their revolvers and were reloading. The mass of the crowd had disappeared, but the doorways, area-ways, and coal cellars in the vicinity, were full of men. As they rushed forth after the first sharp firing, to seek safety in flight, scores of them were clubbed to the ground and left lying there.

One man left a hiding place near me and started across the street. He ran past Officer Hanley, who had no club and had emptied his revolver. "Sandy" struck him a blow on the head with his fist. The man threw up his hand and plunged forward, almost against a policeman. That officer struck him a sounding whack on the side of the head with his club. The man gave another plunge toward another officer, who struck him a blow on the back of his neck, that dropped him on the ground like a bundle of rags. He did not rise. I moved toward the corner, to look at the scene of the explosion. I bent over a man who was shot in the body, and who moaned for help. I felt a strong hand seize me by the collar, and saw a club raised in the air. I wheeled and yelled "Reporter!" The officer recognized me. "Is it you, my boy?" he cried, "what the devil are you doing here?"—and he dashed after a man who had jumped from under the iron stairway. I will not attempt to tell to how many officers I introduced myself within the next two minutes, or describe the frantic and unsuccessful efforts I made to get my reporter's star from my suspender to the lappel of my coat.

In five minutes after the explosion of the bomb the riot was at an end. The first nihilist bomb ever thrown this side of the Atlantic had done its bloody work. The followers of the red flag had struck their first blow in Chicago, and it had torn down their emblem forever. * * *

The center of the street seemed full of writhing, groaning men, calling for help. Under the iron stairway, on the northwest corner of the street, two citizens lay, one insensible, the other moaning feebly and unable to rise. Down the basement stairway, under them, three men lay. Propped against the lamp-post on the corner was a wounded man, and, at his feet, in the gutter, another. Across the street, on the northeast corner, three men lay in the gutter. At the head of the basement stairway, one lay silently. Another sat up, holding a bleeding leg, and begging the officers not to kill him. Reclining on the stairs below them were two suffering men, and in the area-way below, three more. East and west on Randolph street wounded men lay in doorways. In the driveway ten men lay in a heap. In the alley, on the west side of the street, three men lay with wounded limbs or bodies. All the way to Lake street sufferers could be found. All of these were wounded in the legs or vitals, which accounted for their presence on the scene. Those wounded in the hand, or in such manner as to allow flight, had disappeared. Many were carried away by their friends. The police made no arrests, but quickly began the work of caring for their wounded brothers.

And this, then, was the grand culmination aimed at by Spies, Fielden and Parsons—the friends of humanity—the lovers of the people! This, then, was the triumphant climax achieved by the Robespierre, the Danton, and the Marat of the American social revolution! This, then—this bloody, sickening butchery—was to mark the birth of the newer and better order of things; this horrible massacre was to be the first object lesson in the new school of social science as taught by the anarchists. No wonder that it whitened the faces and sickened the hearts of the most desperate and reckless among the followers of the three arch-ruffians; that it put the ruffians themselves to flight, horrified over their own cowardly deviltry and stricken with panic!

From all that has been written and said concerning the terrible scene which followed the explosion of the bomb, it must have been a most appalling and horrifying spectacle. Inspector Bonfield tells how, his face being turned toward Fielden, he heard the hissing of the dreadful fuse as it was hurled from the mob at the mouth of the alley; how instinctively he realized in a second what the hissing noise meant; how all he had ever read of bombs, and the manner of their use, flashed through his mind during the brief interval which elapsed between the hiss and the explosion; how he thought of St. Petersburg, of Berlin, of London, while the dreadful thing was still in the air, and how, within this infinitesimal space of time, he had fully made up his mind to expect just what happened afterward. Lieutenant Bowler, Lieutenant Hubbard, Lieutenant Steele, Lieutenant Quinn, Sergeant Fitzpatrick, and their men, all heard the hissing or saw the fuse, and though it appeared like a lighted cigar that had been carelessly thrown into the air, all realized, as if by intuition, what it was and what it would do. And when the explosion came, it was like the dropping of a huge bowlder into a pool of water, so completely did everything on the surface sink around it. The dull report it made was followed by a frightful silence. Those surrounding the spot, when the explosive fell, were scattered, felled or stunned into unconsciousness. Strong men, who had been uninjured, stood transfixed, their heart-beats stopped, their breathing checked and muscles paralyzed. Immediately following the bomb explosion, crack! crack! went the pistols of the anarchists. It may have been but ten seconds, perhaps but five—probably but one—it seemed to those few who still retained their senses, and who stood around and gazing into the circle of prostrate, bleeding, dying policemen, their bodies piled one upon the other, bearing a resemblance to a sandbag entrenchment, that an hour must have elapsed between the explosion and the first pistol shot; when this was followed by a volley from the murderous miscreants, there was a sudden and a dreadful awakening. As if animated by one thought, every policeman who was able to use his arm had pulled his revolver and was firing—anywhere, everywhere—firing wildly, madly, taking no thought of aim, no thought of anything.

Bonfield was stunned, as all were, by the explosion, but he was one of the first to regain presence of mind. Hardly knowing what to do, but divining that something must be done and done quickly, his first thought was to restore order in the ranks of his men. In a loud voice he ordered the police to "form into line," or "close up," but the wild firing continued; panic had stricken the police, confusion followed panic, and then came Fitzpatrick's command in a clear ringing voice—a voice that sounded above the horrible rattle of the revolvers—ordering the men to "close up, form into line and charge!" It was a display of coolness seldom equaled on any field of battle, an exhibition of that element in the character of some men which makes them natural leaders. Bonfield heard the command, Fitzpatrick was at

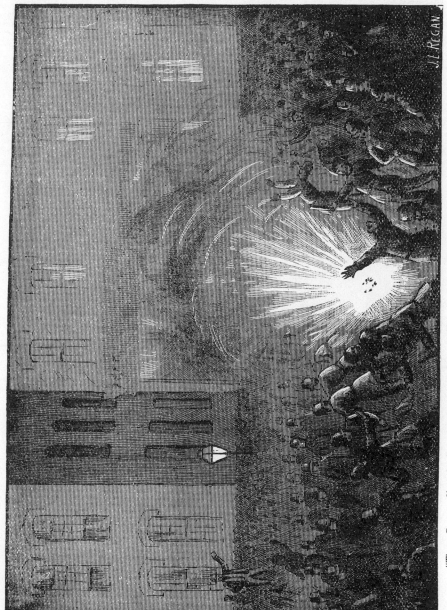

J.L. REGAN

"Those Surrounding the Spot Where the Explosive Fell were Scattered, Felled or Stunned Into Unconsciousness."

"Confusion Followed Panic, and Then Came Fitzpatrick's Command, in a Clear, Ringing Voice."

his side immediately; the entire force had felt the inspiration of the sergeant's coolness; Steele, Hubbard, Quinn,
Bowler and Ward were at their posts in a second, and rallying their men around them, they charged upon the mob.

As the police approached the wagon, before the explosion, the mob had fallen back in the center, until it formed
an inverted V, the points resting along the sidewalks, and
the apex reaching almost to Lake street. From the doorways, alleys and the inner line of this angular formation,
the pistols of the anarchists had been doing terrible work
for a few moments. The anarchists had undoubtedly expected that more than one bomb would be thrown, and had
not anticipated that the police would so speedily recover
from the shock. Now, as they beheld the blue-coats rushing toward them like madmen, the bloody-minded horde of
cowardly assassins became panic-stricken, wavered and fled,
and the police followed the retreating anarchists and sent
deadly volleys into their midst, as they plunged through
every avenue of escape. The shooting was kept up until
Inspector Bonfield, for the reason he has given elsewhere,
ordered that it cease.

When the mayor gave it as his opinion that there would
be no trouble during the evening, and when the weather
looked so threatening, as to almost convince Inspector Bonfield that all danger was past, that officer telephoned the
chief that he did not think it necessary to hold the reserve
details, at the Central and other stations, any longer. Superintendent Ebersold, feeling that the night would, after
all, be a quiet one, and being terribly fatigued, after giving
instructions to have the reserve dismissed for the night,
went to his home on the South Side. He could hardly keep
his eyes open, as he himself expressed it, and reaching his
bed-chamber, made hasty preparations for a good night's
sleep. To this moment he does not remember just how far
these preparations had advanced, when the telephone bell
rang sharply and ominously. Ominously, for he had left

everything in good order down town, and unless something extraordinary had occurred, he felt certain that he would not have been called up. Without delay he hastened to the telephone, and then he heard in a few words all that it was necessary for him to know in order to form a full conception of the terrible occurrence of the night. He was wide awake in a moment. As a soldier, he had been aroused in this manner often before. Throwing his clothing on somehow, he knew not how, harnessing his horse, and jumping into his vehicle, he was soon tearing along at a break-neck pace toward the Desplaines street station. When he arrived there, the building was illuminated from top to bottom, officers were carrying in wounded men on litters, surgeons and priests were working or praying, and the entire scene recalled to his mind the sad and sickening pictures he had often beheld after battles fought beneath Southern skies. The dead and dying were stretched upon the floor of the Desplaines street station, trained nurses, whom Warden McGarigle had dispatched from the county hospital, were quickly in attendance, and all attention that could possibly be given was freely extended to the sufferers. The alarm had been telephoned throughout the city, and from every station came plunging patrol wagons, loaded with officers, who were quickly at work upon the scene of the explosion, doing all they could for friend and foe alike.

When the cost of the explosion to the force was counted, the following casualties were reported by the officers named:

Of Lieutenant George W. Hubbard's command: Patrick Flavin, injured; Jacob Ebinger, injured; John J. Kelley, injured; James H. Wilson, injured; Fred. A. Andrews, injured; Michael O'Brien, injured; Daniel Hogan, injured.

Of Lieutenant James Bowler's command: John J. Barrett and Michael Sheehan, died from injuries received; John Reid, bullet wounds in both legs below knees; Lawrence J. Murphy, half of the left foot blown off by shell, two shell wounds in the right leg, one in the right hip, two

"The Dead and Dying were Stretched Upon the Floor of the Desplaines Street Station,"

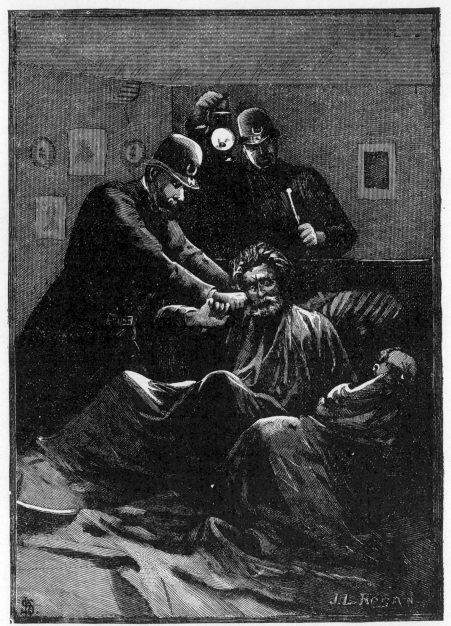

"Every Anarchist Hole was Entered and the Assassins in Some Instances were Dragged from Their Beds."

bullet wounds in the right leg, also one in the left side of neck; John E. Doyle, two bullet wounds in the right leg, below the knee, three shell wounds in the left leg, below the knee; Arthur Conolly, two shell wounds in the right leg, bullet wound in the right arm; Nicholas J. Shannon, bullet wound in the back, seventeen shell wounds in the lower part of both legs; Adam S. Barber, bullet wound in right heel, shell wounds in the lower and back part of both legs; James Conway, shell wounds through the lower part of the right leg; Thomas McEnery, ten shell wounds in both legs; Patrick Hartford, two shell wounds in the left leg, bullet wound through the right heel, three toes of the left foot shot off; Louis Johnson, shell wound in the lower part of the left leg; Frank P. Tyrell, two shell wounds in the fleshy part of the left thigh; August C. Keller, shell wound above the left hip, bullet wound in the left side; James Brady, four shell wounds in the lower part of both legs; John H. King, shell wound in the right jaw, and two bullet wounds in the right leg.

Of Lieutenant James P. Stanton's command: Lieutenant James P. Stanton, two wounds in calf of right leg, one in right thigh, one in right hip, one in right side, one in right forearm, wounded by pieces of shell, pistol wounds in right arm; Patrolmen—Alexander Jameson, severe pistol shot in left thigh, also in left wrist; Timothy O'Sullivan, severe pistol shot wound in right thigh; Thomas Halley, slightly injured by being trampled on; Jacob Hansen, right leg crushed by shell, amputated above the knee, two pistol shot wounds in left hip, left ankle fractured by shell; Michael Horan, dangerous pistol shot wound in right thigh, four inches above the knee, also severe pistol shot wound in right forearm; Peter Butterly, severe wound in each leg, below the knee, by shell, severe pistol shot wound in right forearm; Joseph Norman, severe shell wound in left hand, also in right heel; Thomas Hennessy, severe shell wound in left thigh, also several slight wounds in both legs, below the knees, caused by fragments of shell; William Burns, slight shell wound in right instep; Charles H. Fink, two dangerous pistol shot wounds in each thigh, and severe shell wound in left ankle; Mathias J. Degan, killed by shell wounds in abdomen and legs; Bernard J. Murphy, dangerous shell wound on right side of head, large wound through left thigh; Thomas Brophy, severe shell wound in left hand; Charles J. Whitney, dangerous shell wound in chest; Thomas Redden, left leg crushed by shell, also wounds in both arms and face.

Of Lieutenant Francis Penzen's command: Andrew O'Day, bruised in right knee; Patrick Nash, bruised in left breast; Patrick McLaughlin, bruised in right breast; Henry F. Smith, bullet wound in right shoulder.

Of Lieutenant J. P. Beard's command: Daniel Cramer, neck grazed by a bullet; Martin Cullen, collar-bone broken; Frank Murphy, three ribs broken and ankle badly bruised.

In addition to the above, Acting Lieutenant Edmund Roche, who was assigned to Lieutenant Stanton's place, the latter being injured, reported James Plunkett, of Lieutenant Beard's command, slightly injured, and Lieutenant Steele found it necessary to mention the fact that the only man who disgraced his uniform during the trying ordeal was Officer Charles Dombrowski, a new member of the force, who deserted his command and fled to a friend's house, on Halsted street.

Seven policemen were killed or died of their wounds as a result of the explosion. These were: Officer Mathias Degan. Although shockingly wounded, he attempted to walk to the Desplaines street station, but fell dead before he could reach it. The second officer to die was John J. Barrett. He was only 25 years of age and a stalwart young fellow; he died the second morning after the bomb-throwing. Officer George Miller was the third to die, after suffering dreadfully. On Friday of "Haymarket week," Timothy Flavin, the fourth victim died, after his leg had been amputated.   Officer Michael Sheehan died on the following Sunday.   Officer Thomas Redden, the sixth victim, died on May 17, and Officer Nels Hansen, the seventh victim, died after six weeks of excruciating torture.

How many of those in the mob were killed, wounded, or have since died of their injuries, it is almost impossible to tell.   That a large number paid a severe penalty for their attendance at this treasonable gathering, is certain, but the wounds of most of them were hidden, and the deaths of many of them were covered up.   Parsons fled at once; Fielden was slightly wounded; Spies and Fischer made rapid tracks for their homes, the *Arbeiter Zeitung* office, or the nearest anarchist headquarters.   The arrest of Fielden, Spies, Engel, Neebe, Schwab, Fischer; the sacking of the *Arbeiter Zeitung* office, and the discovery there of a vast supply of dynamite, arms, bombs, and infernal machines; the discovery of bombs in different parts of the city, under sidewalks and in lumber yards, some near the scene of the explosion, going to show that it had been intended to explode several that night; the brilliant work performed by Captain Schaack and his men, in the hunting down of the anarchists and the discovery of their dens, when every anarchist hole was entered and the assassins in some instances were dragged from their beds; the arrest of Lingg, one of the most dramatic events in the history of the police; the flight and sensational return of Parsons; the long trial; the speeches; the sentence; the appeal; the new sentence; the refusal of the Supreme Court of the United States to interfere; the efforts made to have the sentences commuted; the excitement and alarm preceding the 11th day of November; the shocking suicide of the "tiger anarchist;" the execution of Parsons, Spies, Engel and Fischer; the commutation of Fielden and Schwab—all these events, striking though they are, are too recent to be called history, and cannot be treated here at the length which their importance deserves.

CHAPTER XVI.

FREDERICK EBERSOLD—COMPARED WITH SUPT. MURRAY OF NEW YORK
—HIS EARLY STRUGGLES IN THE WEST—DETERMINED TO BE A SOL-
DIER—RECORD OF A BRAVE VOLUNTEER AND A GALLANT CAPTAIN
—AT SHILOH, KENESAW, VICKSBURG, AND WITH SHERMAN ON HIS
MARCH TO THE SEA—RETURN TO CHICAGO—FIRST YEARS IN THE
POLICE FORCE—STEADY PROMOTION—A SPLENDID RECORD.

There is a most remarkable similarity between the
careers of Superintendent Murray, of the New York, and
Superintendent Ebersold, of the Chicago police. The
former is a native of the American metropolis, was born in
1844, and first made his appearance on the scene as a Zouave
under the gallant Ellsworth. He received honorable wounds
at the battle of Bull Run. We next hear of him after the
war, in 1866, when he was appointed on the New York police force. In two weeks after he put on the blue uniform
he made several arrests, of such an important character,
that he attracted the attention of his superiors. He was at
once appointed roundsman, and at the end of a year made a
sergeant. During the six years of his sergeantcy he became conspicuous for his bravery in raiding several of the
most notorious dens in his district. He was next appointed
captain, and during the five months that he held this rank
he secured five hundred years of convictions for some of the
worst ruffians in his precinct. Then about eight years ago
he became inspector, and he is now chief of a force that ad-
mires and respects him. He has climbed from the bottom
to the top round unaided by outside influences. He has
been given nothing that he did not earn.

To bring the similarity closer (for in the recital of Superintendent Ebersold's career it will be seen that a striking

similarity exists even down to this point) it is necessary to recall the riots of 1877, which, originating on the Baltimore & Ohio Railroad, spread with an alarming rapidity, created a panic throughout the entire Union, and at one time assumed the characteristics of, and threatened to develop into a revolutionary movement.

The part which Chicago played in that great drama will be described elsewhere; for the present let us look at New York. The Astor Place riot in 1849, the draft riots in 1863, and the Orange riot in 1871, had taught the people of New York terrible lessons. In the first instance, the weakness of the authorities had permitted a tremendous disturbance to grow out of a most trivial affair—the rivalry between an American and an English actor. "The few constables could do nothing," says a writer, touching upon this subject, "so one of the ornamental city regiments was called out. There was an old white-headed, civic brigadier, all chapeau and epaulettes and gold braid, at its head. He was fatherly and benignant, and he read the riot act to the mob from his horse, and asked them in a beaming, persuasive way, to go home like good citizens. They replied with bricks (it was before the day of bombs). Then he regretfully fired blank cartridges at them, at which they pulled him off his horse and trampled a number of his men in the mud. Finally, being irritated to a proper sense of repartee, he came at last to bullets, and succeeded in killing several innocent people."

In the riot of 1863 the same course was pursued toward the mob, with the same results. When it finally became a question whether the city should be turned over to the rioters, the militia was called out, and hundreds of people were killed and wounded where, perhaps, a dozen would not have fallen, had there existed a well managed police organization in the first place. When the firing commenced, after hours had been wasted in vain attempts to argue with the leaders of the excited mob, the persons killed and wounded were nearly all innocent spectators. The real rioters and their leaders escaped almost to a man. And yet the measures taken were more prompt than in the Astor Place riot.

In the Orange riot experience taught the authorities that it wouldn't do to bandy words or waste time in dealing with it. The police force was not thought sufficient to cope with it. It had never been given a fair trial. The Eighty-fourth regiment was ordered out, was marched into Eighth avenue, and scarcely had it reached that thoroughfare before it commenced firing. The Sixth and Ninth regiments, which had just come up, followed suit. In a few minutes hundreds of victims were lying dead, dying and wounded on the street. It was a terrible blow, a cruel one, but there was no more rioting that day. The whole thing was over in a flash.

Six years afterward the riots of 1877 occurred. New York like many other American cities was ripe for a social conflagration. From 1873, when the panic struck Wall Street and all the money centers of the country, things had been going from bad to worse with the labor classes. There was nothing doing. The election of the year before, which promised to change things for the better, had only resulted in creating further distrust among capitalists. Foreign socialists, communists and revolutionists had been arriving steadily at Castle Garden. Workingmen who under ordinary circumstances would not have listened to their treasonable and incendiary utterances, gave them their attention now. They were told that nothing but a great popular uprising of the working classes, nothing but a terrific social revolution—something of a kind that would strike terror into the hearts of capitalists—could save their families from starvation, and themselves from absolute slavery. It was time to strike the blow! A revolution such as had convulsed France at the close of the last century must be started—a reign of terror must be inaugurated. There was to be a great meeting at Tompkins Square. It was to be the initial gathering of the revolution. The inflammable material was all prepared. The match would be applied at this meeting.

A very similar meeting occurred in Chicago, near another square, nine years later, with a very similar ending.

The Tompkins Square assemblage, like the Haymarket assemblage, was a wild one. It was ready for any thing. "The pulse of the city stood still," says a writer in describing it, "in the appalling presence of twenty thousand miserable desperadoes. Red-handed communists from the slums of Paris, and fiery-tongued Germans, smarting still from the imperial lash, poured their eloquence upon the rabble, and made them believe that in America they were still suffering the wrongs of their down-trodden fellows in Europe. That society was opposed to them. That wealth persecuted them! That law and order was made for their oppression!"

It was a terrible hour for New York. The peaceable people of the city trembled for their safety. If the Tompkins Square meeting should give the signal, murder, fire and desolation would sweep over the city before morning.

But Murray had his eye on that meeting, and watched it as carefully as did Ebersold and Bonfield the Haymarket meeting in Chicago nine years later, He bided his time. When the moment for action arrived he appeared in Tompkins Square at the head of five hundred policemen—mark it, there were no militiamen called out this time. He drove the twenty thousand before him into the back streets, into the alleys, into the slums, into the holes from which they came. In half an hour Tompkins Square was his. There were no communists or revolutionists to dispute its possession with him. The desperadoes from Europe and their sympathizers and followers had been scattered like chaff before the wind. There were many broken heads, broken arms, broken collar bones and broken noses in New York that night, but there was no conflagration, there were no murders. The peaceable citizens slept peacefully. The club had done its work effectively, quietly, satisfactorily.

How easy it is to recall some instances under Ebersold's

management of the Chicago police force, in which the club has accomplished results just as desirable!

It has been the steadfast faith of Frederick Ebersold, since he entered upon his duties as chief of the Chicago police force, never to bandy words or waste time in dealing with a mob. He believes it is cruel to parley with rioters, criminal to argue with them. First of all they must be scattered, struck down or handcuffed. Then they may be talked to with safety—with safety to themselves, and, which is more important, with safety to the community.

Chicago's experience with rioters previous to the disturbances of 1886 very closely resembled New York's in many particulars. "The Lager Beer Riot" of 1855 was a remarkable uprising of one of the strange elements that have entered into the composition of our peculiar population. A certain class of Germans were at the bottom of it, but before it got fairly under headway, all the toughs and thugs of the young city were engaged in it. There was no police organization worth mentioning, and for a time the mob held possession of the town.

In 1876 another of our strange elements—the Bohemian lumber shovers—terrorized the timber section of the city, set fire to saw and planing mills, and threatened to destroy property to the value of millions of dollars. The police force at this time numbered scarcely 300 men, there was no patrol signal service to draw upon, and the rioters had their own way until they cooled down, although the police who were assigned to the duty of preserving order behaved bravely in every instance. In 1877 the municipal authorities dilly-dallied with the mobs that sprang into existence in every quarter of the city, vacillated in their policy, and showed such weakness for a time that it was only by a miracle that the city escaped a bloody and destructive conflict. Again at Ogden's Grove, where Anarchy showed its teeth for the first time in Chicago, one Sunday afternoon, the rioters and assassins were treated with undue consideration.

All these occurrences had made deep impressions on the mind of Frederick Ebersold. He saw the dangers which threatened the city every time the lawless elements asserted their contempt for authority. He saw nothing but evil results from the unwise policy of even seeming to palliate mob rule. He saw that eventually the cost would be great in life and property, if the ignorant, the headstrong, the criminal, the incendiary classes, were permitted to defy the law with impunity. He determined to put an end to riots in Chicago, and during his administration wherever the mob has shown itself it has been hammered on the head and knocked senseless.

The part he played in the Haymarket riot and the troubles which preceded it, have been described in the proper place. For the present let us glance over the career of this distinguished citizen.

He first saw the light in the little town of Ixheim, in the district of Zweibruchen, a province of Bavaria on the Rhine. That was over forty-six years ago—March 30, 1841. A terrible shadow fell upon his life, when little more than a lad, his father and mother dying in a single night. There being little left now to bind him to his native land, the doubly orphaned boy determined to seek his fortune in the New World. His only capital when he arrived in New York, in 1856, consisted of a stout and honest heart and a good common school education. He found some friends on landing, but he decided to push into the interior, and he arrived in Chicago in February, 1857, where he apprenticed himself to the varnishing trade with J. J. West, at 197 Lake Street. Shortly afterward, or in 1859, young Ebersold moved to Mendota, Ill., where he engaged in the grain business, then becoming an important pursuit in this State. He was prospering fairly when the first gun at Sumpter reverberated throughout the land. Five days after that event, on May 19, 1861, he enlisted at Mendota, as a private soldier, in the Twelfth Illinois Infantry. His name was the third or fourth on the list.

He was made corporal in Company B. The regiment was assigned to duty at East St. Louis and afterward at Cairo, and before his time was out, Corporal Ebersold became very ill and was compelled to lay up in a hospital for some time. This illness told upon him so that when he sought to re-enlist he was rejected. He immediately returned to Mendota, very indignant over his rejection, thence to Chicago, and before calling on his friends in the city, proceeded to Camp Douglas and enlisted for three years as a private in the Fifty-fifth Illinois Infantry For this regiment he himself recruited thirty-eight men. On the organization of the regiment he was made fourth sergeant, and shortly afterward, at Paducah, Ky., was promoted to second or first duty sergeant. On the eighth or ninth of April, 1862, after Shiloh, he was made orderly sergeant, which position he held for eleven months. At the battle of Chickesaw Bayou, on Sidney Johnston's plantation, he was made second lieutenant, but did not receive his commission till the following April. During the war he served continually under Gen. Sherman, except while in the three months' service, when he was with Gen. Prentiss.

He has the honor of being a survivor of the famous battle of Shiloh, in which his regiment suffered a loss of one officer and fifty-one enlisted men killed, nine officers and one hundred and ninety men wounded, and twenty-six men captured—a greater loss than was suffered by any other Federal regiment in that dreadful combat, and heavier than the loss sustained by some brigades. The regiment had taken part in the expedition to Columbus, Kentucky, to test the question of its evacuation immediately after the capture of Fort Donelson, and on March 8, 1862, it embarked on a steamer to take part in the movement up the Tennessee river which resulted in the terrible affair at Shiloh. On March 15, with other troops, the regiment disembarked at a point

several miles above Pittsburg Landing, and was prevented
from cutting the railroad in the interior by high water.
Dropping down to Pittsburg Landing the Fifty-fifth went
into camp on the front line. Here Col. D. Stuart took command of a brigade formed from the Fifty-fifth Illinois, and
the Fifty-fourth and Seventy-first Ohio. This brigade was
then known officially as the Second of the Fifth (Sherman's)
Division, but more popularly known as Stuart's. Although
belonging to Sherman's Division, says the authorized history of the regiment, it was located about two miles east of
the other three brigades of its division, being in point of
fact the extreme left of the army, which met the rebel
attack. Prentiss' Division was next to its right and front,
though about one mile away. The Fifty-fifth with its companion regiments was encamped upon the road leading from
Pittsburg Landing to Hamburgh Landing, and near a small
branch of Lick creek. On the morning of the battle of
Shiloh, says the report alluded to, the Fifty-fifth, like all
other troops upon the field, had no premonition of the fearful conflict to follow, until the report of fire-arms further to
the right gave evidence of that fact. The regiment under
the immediate command of Col. O. Malmborg formed the
center of the brigade, the Seventy-first Ohio being on its
right and the Fifty-fourth Ohio (Zouaves) upon its left.
After forming line in several localities contiguous to its
camp, during which time it was not engaged except in skir-
mishing, though under the fire of Gage's rebel battery,
position was taken to the left of its camp and about sixty
yards in its rear along the south edge of a precipitous ravine.
During the evolutions resulting in this formation, the Seventy-
first Ohio (excepting eighteen men) retreated. The position of the regiment at this time was with its right resting
at a point precisely five hundred yards east of Col. Stuart's
headquarters, with the Fifty-fourth Ohio upon its left. A
full half-mile of space unoccupied by troops existed to its
right. This dangerous interval had been in part caused

by the retreat of the Seventy-first Ohio. No artillery was upon this portion of the field to assist the federal troops. The Fifty-fifth Illinois had exactly five hundred and twelve men in line, and the Fifty-fourth Ohio from three hundred and fifty to four hundred. In this position it was finally attacked by Chalmer's and Jackson's brigades of Bragg's corps, which had been placed in position at this point under the personal supervision of Gen. Albert Sidney Johnston, the rebel commander-in-chief. The main attack commenced here about noon, and this position was held until between two and three o'clock P. M. by the two isolated regiments above named, and was of incalculable value to the ultimate success of the Union army, inasmuch as it defended the extreme left during a vital period from a flank movement contemplated by the rebel order of battle, and vigorously attempted at the period spoken of. After being nearly surrounded and suffering terribly, the regiment retreated from point to point and took its position, with its organization still complete, in the last line formed in the evening near the landing. It participated in the battle of Monday, acting on the right, and suffered some loss. This was the first engagement in which the regiment had taken part, and that the men bore themselves with most admirable discipline and bravery, in the face of terrible slaughter, is evidenced by the record they made on those two awful days.

During the campaign before Vicksburg, Ebersold was one of the officers who had charge of the saps of the rebel works—a position that calls upon all the bravery that the pluckiest of men possess. For hours he worked with his men in a narrow trench, under constant fire from the enemy above. They were to dig a trench sufficiently large to cover the advance of five men abreast, and while engaged in this perilous undertaking, the rebels on the bluffs overhead rolled hot shell down upon them. It was a desperate position, an awful position to be placed in, but the work had to be done, and Ebersold set about accomplishing it with such a will, that at the surrender of this great rebel stronghold he had succeeded in excavating a sap within eleven feet and three inches of the rebel works, and had undermined them twenty feet.

In the same fall, after the occupation of Vicksburg, Ebersold was promoted to a first lieutenantcy, and started from Vicksburg to Mission Ridge, and to the relief of Knoxville.

In the spring of 1864, his three years of service having expired, he re-enlisted and was unanimously elected first lieutenant by the company. During the Atlanta campaign he was in charge mainly of "A" and "E" companies. On account of Gov. Oglesby's order that no man in one company should be promoted to a captaincy in another, he was kept eleven months out of this advancement. Finally, owing to the promotion of Capt. Andrews of "I" company to a lieutenant colonely, he was at length made captain, to fill the vacancy.

About this time Capt. Ebersold had some practical experience in warfare, and not always of a pleasant character. At Shiloh, April 6th and 7th, 1862, he was wounded in the left hand and across the shoulders. On the Monday of that celebrated fight he was blown up by a shell near Shiloh Chapel, but escaped unhurt. That afternoon (the second day of the fight), he was struck by a piece of shell in the right arm, and had to be taken off the field. This shell crushed accross the left breast, and he feels the effects of it to this day.

The Fifty-fifth Illinois Infantry had an eventful career during the war, and in every skirmish and battle in which it was engaged, Ebersold was with it. Its record stands as follows:

Battle of Russell House, front of Corinth, May 17, 1862.
Siege and capture of Corinth which followed, May 30, 1862.
Battle of Chickesaw Bayou, Dec. 27, 28 and 29, 1862.
Battle of Arkansas Post, July 10 and 11, 1863.
Fight at Champion Hill, May 17, 1863.

Siege and capture of Vicksburg, under fire for forty days.

Siege and capture of Jackson, from July 10 to July 16, 1863.

Fight at Tuscumbia, Aug. 27, 1863, when the regiment went up to Chattanooga to reinforce Rosenkranz.

Battle of Mission Ridge, Nov. 24 and 25, 1863.

Battle of Kenesaw Mountain, June 27, 1864.

Battle of Decatur, July 22, 1864, and battle of Ezra Chapel, July 28, which resulted in terrible slaughter of the rebels.

Fight at Jonesboro, Aug. 31, 1864, when Capt. Ebersold took and held the hill where the main battle was fought.   The capture and holding of this position gave the army the main road to Macon the next morning. It was a daring stroke on Ebersold's part, and was considered an admirable manœuver at the time by commanding officers.

From there the Fifty-fifth went into camp at East Point, then followed Hood to Gainesville, then returned to Vining Station, and then joined Sherman in his famous march to the sea.

The regiment's next engagement was at the capture of Fort McAllister on the coast, which opened the " cracker line " for the commissary department.

Next it engaged in some warm work at Beaufort, S. C., and on Feb. 9, 1865, went into a fight at South Edisto River, and for the good work it did in cutting off communication, was allowed to put " Charleston " on its banner.

Was at Columbia, S. C., Feb. 15 and 16, with the advance in crossing the river; next at Bentonville, N. C., March 20 and 21, and finally at Johnson's surrender near Raleigh.

The regiment was 120 days under fire in all; travelled 12,065 miles, of which it marched 3,340.

After the grand review and muster out at Washington, Capt. Ebersold returned to Chicago.   He had contracted malaria in the Southern swamps, but the excitement and activity of army life had kept him on his feet.   No sooner had he reached Chicago however, than he succumbed, and for two months and a half he was laid, to use a familiar expression, on the flat of his back.   He continued to suffer from the effects of his army life, and to be sickly for seven or eight years after the close of the war.   Even now he is afflicted with malaria, and he never expects to be actually rid of it.   In addition to his sickness he was destined to undergo other troubles almost equally annoying, and even more discouraging.   He had money when he went into the army, and saved money while soldiering.   As soon as he was able to turn his attention to business, he entered into a partnership and opened a flour and feed store on Canal street.   In this enterprise he lost every dollar he possessed. He was a poorer man than he was the day he went into the army, and he had to turn his attention to some means of making an honorable living.

On July 9th, 1867, Jacob Rehm being at the time super-intendent of police, the name of Frederick Ebersold was first entered on the rolls of the department as a patrolman. He was assigned to the old Armory police station, corner of Franklin and Adams streets.   He traveled post till the next April, when he was assigned to the day squad at the Central station, and appointed to duty at Rush street bridge.   When navigation closed and the squad was broken up in the winter, he was sent back to the Armory and traveled beat till the following May, when he was again placed on the day squad and assigned to duty at the Washington street tunnel for eleven months.   On acount of the dampness of the place he became sick, and was assigned to the Randolph street bridge, then at Lake and Fifth avenue, then was assigned to head-quarters where he acted as interpreter and operated the old time dial telegraph machine, which sank into inocuous disuetude on the introduction of the telephone.   He did the work usually performed by station-keepers, until May 4, 1872, when he was promoted to a sergeantcy and assigned to the Twenty-second street district.   He remained there till 1873, when he was assigned to the new Armory, Harrison street and Pacific avenue, and, when the rank was established in the department, was created a lieutenant.   On August 1st, 1879, he was appointed captain, and remained in charge of the Harrison street precinct till August 1st, 1881, when he was transferred to West Twelfth street.   This was at the time there was so much shooting of policemen going on in the " terror district."   He was accompanied by Lieutenant (now Inspector) Bonfield, and remained at this post till Dec. 1st, 1880, when on the promotion of Capt. McGarigle to be superintendent of police, he was assigned to the **Madison** street district, from whence (August 1st, 1881,) he was transferred to the Central station and placed in charge of the central detail. Here he remained two years, when he was sent back to the Armory, the point from which he started; from this assignment he was raised to the Inspectorship in August, 1885, and two months later was named by Mayor Harrison, general superintendent of police. He was re-appointed by Mr. Roche, after the election of that gentleman to the mayoralty.

What a history! What a struggle! What ups and downs—what a hard battle for success, what a well-earned triumph over difficulties at last! To-day a sapper, digging beneath the breastworks of the enemy. To-morrow a captain leading a mixed picket to the capture of a prized position. To-day marching at the head of a company that had seen service under 120 days of fire. To-morrow shaking with malaria as a common patrolman in front of a damp and ill-smelling Chicago tunnel. To-day tossed around from pillar to post, and from post to pillar, to-morrow chief of the force which he entered in the humblest capacity! Surely there is material for a romance in such a life as this!

He was a lieutenant when the riot of 1877 broke out, and during that disturbance he acted as quarter-master. He dispersed the mob in the stone-yards, and at the burning of the planing mill at Van Buren and Franklin streets, he took vigorous measures against the rioters and laid them low by the liberal use of the club. He arrested Charlie Allen who shot Beattie, and came near losing his life in the transaction. In a midnight fight on Fifth avenue, between Harrison and Polk streets, in 1875, in which stone-cutters and sailors were the participants, he ran into the midst of the combat. The sailors ran away and the stone-cutters surrounded him. In a minute or two it seemed as if all was up with him. He had to use his pistol and did some terrible execution. Single handed and alone he brought in two of the fighters to the station, and left five or six more unable to move until he called for them. As for himself he had been beaten so badly that he was black and blue for a month afterward.

In June, 1875, when the notorious Ed. Burns was shot, Ebersold ran after him, thinking that he (Burns) had done the shooting. Burns pointed out the notorious Charlie Powers as his assailant, and when Ebersold ran toward Powers, the latter turned upon him and sent a bullet whizzing through his clothing.

Later when he arrested "Cranky Bill," a desperate character, he felt in his pocket for a pistol but found none. On the way to the station Bill turned upon his captor and pointing a pistol to his face blazed away. The ball missed. Cranky Bill had concealed the weapon in his coat-sleeve.

Superintendent Ebersold is recognized as one of the ablest commanding and executive officers that has ever filled the Chief's chair in the police department. Elsewhere in this volume the story of his management of the force during the riots of 1886, is given in detail. The manner in which he handled his men during the perilous days preceding the Haymarket explosion, was so skillful as to elicit the unqualified admiration of citizens generally, and military authorities in particular.

CHAPTER XVII.

JOHN BONFIELD—AN ADVANCED MEMBER OF THE NEW SCHOOL OF
POLICE OFFICERS—A MAN WHO NEVER SHIRKED A DUTY—THE
USE OF THE CLUB DURING THE STREET CAR RIOT—WHY HEADS
WERE DAMAGED—THE RESULT JUSTIFIED THE PROCESS—BON-
FIELD IN PRIVATE AND POLICE LIFE—HE PROVED A FAILURE IN
COMMERCIAL LIFE—FROM PATROLMAN TO INSPECTORSHIP.

A man who has never shirked his duty, who has never
apologized for doing his duty, who has done his duty in the
teeth of the most bitter and violent opposition, who has never
mistaken his duty, who has not paused to consider consequences when he had a duty to perform—such a man is John
Bonfield, Inspector of Police.

In the strong light cast upon the character and qualifications of Inspector Bonfield by recent and well-remembered
events, any attempt on the part of his biographer to defend
his career against the malignant attacks made upon it, would
be considered wholly superfluous by the average citizen. As
the plain record of the man is laid bare the necessity for
either a defense or explanation of his acts becomes unnecessary.

Elsewhere in this history, the name of John Bonfield
figures, as a matter of necessity, most conspicuously. He
belongs to the modern school of police officers—that class
of men who have made the police force of Chicago
famous for its discipline, efficiency and bravery throughout
the nation. The ability which he displayed in organizing
our present admirable Police Patrol system—a system which
has been or is being eagerly copied by every large town and
city on the continent—would entitle him, were his record to

FREDERICK EBERSOLD,
General Superintendent of Police.

JOHN BONFIELD,

Inspector of Police.

reach no farther, to the lasting gratitude of our people. The discretion, the valor he has displayed in the face of frenzied rioters, on more than one occasion, checking almost single-handed and by the most heroic example, tumults that threatened to culminate in public disaster and bloodshed, entitle him and his acts to the highest popular esteem.

Of all his conspicuous exploits perhaps the one that has called down upon his head the most unmerited abuse and villification, was his daring conduct during the street car disturbance of July, 1885. That episode in his career stands out in bold relief in the memory of the reader, for it has received more attention than any similar event in the history of this city. Even those who profess to be his friends, and who have not forgotten, and cannot forget, his admirable conduct on other occasions, at this late day shake their heads gravely and sigh audibly when that, to them, very unfortunate occasion is mentioned.

Neither as Captain nor Inspector, has John Bonfield ever offered to the public any defense, much less apology, for his conduct on this occasion. He has simply allowed the result of his work to speak for itself. The result was the extinguishment of a dangerous public tumult, the crushing out in its incipiency of what gave unmistakable signs of becoming within a very few hours, a bloody and destructive riot.

These disturbances are dealt with fully in the proper place. Let us simply take a glance at the situation:

The street car company had openly violated an agreement with its employes. That was a fact so palpable that the public could not fail to see it. It was a corporation never popular, and never so unpopular as in July, 1885. The employes were known to thousands of citizens, and looked upon as faithful, conscientious, overworked and underpaid men. Popular indignation ran high against the company, and the strike which followed met with undisguised and even demonstrative and practical public approval. The people of the West Division were almost a unit in their desire that full

The morning af

STOVES

justice should be done the company's employes. Men and women walked to and from their places of business uncomplainingly or rode in express wagons, hacks or broken-down omnibuses cheerfully, in order that the strikers might gain their point.

Even the policemen sympathized with the struggling car men, for a blue blouse or a helmet does not change a man's nature, and he is just as apt to entertain the same opinions, sentimental or otherwise, after putting on his numbered star as before. His neighbors, friends—his fellow citizens without regard to station—were in sympathy with the strikers, and why not he? How could he be otherwise? Besides he was, more than likely, a member of the society to which a great majority of the men belonged. And then, again, he had a bowing, a speaking, and, may be, a familiar acquaintance with a large number of the men engaged in this fight against a grasping corporation and cold-blooded monopoly! At any rate he was with them at heart and it would go hard with him should he be compelled to place a straw in their way.

In the meantime, the strike, which started fairly enough, and peaceably enough, is assuming threatening phases. The company engages men who are willing to take the places of the strikers. They are beaten or stoned and compelled to fly for their lives. Street cars are overturned, and the company's property is damaged or destroyed. The conductors and drivers who struck against the injustice of the company, have, with very few exceptions, taken the advice of the press and all right-thinking men, and discouraged these violent measures. Most of them have gone quietly to their homes. Their places are filled by roughs, toughs, hoodlums, criminals, socialists and anarchists, who will not let this opportunity for a riot slip by if they can help it. Business men along West Madison street are frightened. They see a peaceable strike rapidly transforming before their eyes into a menacing riot. They are fearful of the results. They demand police protection.

The street car company notifies the Mayor that it is prepared to run its cars, but is prevented from doing so by a mob. It demands police protection.

Citizens generally who sympathize with the strikers but have no sympathy for disturbers of the peace, for rioters or anarchists, call upon the Mayor to break up this dangerous and disgraceful mob. They demand police protection.

John Bonfield is captain of the third precinct, in which this disturbance is occurring and hourly assuming more threatening proportions. His superiors send for him. He is ordered to see that the street car company is protected in its right to transact business. He is also ordered to preserve the peace. He is informed that assistance will be given him from other precincts. He maps out the plan of his campaign. The street cars must be permitted to run if the company has men enough to run them. That is settled.

He brings the patrol service into play. At intervals along the route his wagons loaded with men are stationed. He proceeds with a force of "blue-coats" to Western avenue. He finds assembled there, and stretching for blocks around, a howling mob bent upon mischief, regardless of any principles involved, and utterly careless as to the main question at issue. At his request the company starts a car down the street. It is heavily guarded by policemen, who are ordered to see that the non-union conductor and driver are protected. Scarcely has it moved half a block before the driver is pulled off the car, and threatened with summary punishment by the mob. Bonfield, indignant that the policemen should have permitted this, rushes into the mob, cuts a passage through it and takes the driver by the arm.

"Do you want to drive a car for the company?" he asks.

"I do, if I'm protected," replies the driver.

"Well, then come with me—you'll be protected!" says Bonfield, and he marches his man through the midst of the howling, cursing, blackguarding, angry mob.

He plants his man on the front platform of a car. "Drive!" he says.

Just then a big fisted thug comes up and yells at Bonfield, "That feller aint a goin' ter drive—ye'd better let this thing alone," at the same time moving toward the captain in a menacing manner.

Policemen are standing by. They appear to be confused in their minds as to their duty. They do not realize that the struggle is now between the lawful authority of the city and the lawless mob. Bonfield sees that a terrible emergency has sprung up. If he weakens now, in the presence of his men and in the presence of the rioters, all is lost. The police of Chicago will have acknowledged their inability to preserve the peace, and protect the property of citizens. Moreover, the police require that they should be brought to a sense of their duty. They have permitted their friendships, their sentiments and their prejudices to blind them. They have momentarily forgotton their allegiance to the public. And yet there is another consideration paramount to all these. If the police fail to stifle this tumult, the result will be a general riot—the times are ripe for it—*the militia will be called out and hundreds may be killed.* Something must be done and done quickly. All this flashes through Capt. Bonfield's brain while the thug, followed by hundreds of his kind, are approaching him. His club is lifted, and the ruffian lies at his feet.

That was the first blood. It not only disabled the thug, but it hammered a sense of duty into the minds of the police. They saw their way at a glance.

The company furnishes drivers and Capt. Bonfield arranges the strangest procession that has ever appeared in the streets of Chicago. First comes an open car loaded with forty policemen facing forward, then a closed car to be used as a prison van, or ambulance, containing twenty men; then another open car with twenty blue-coats, facing backward. The three cars are started together in a block. As these move away three more cars are arranged in the same manner, and then three more until there are about seventy-five cars in line.

Bonfield with a platoon marches ahead. Obstructions are met with at every step. Building material is thrown across the track; perfect barricades are erected; the mob follows, howls, curses and throws stones; Bonfield and his men keep the track clear; clubs are used freely, and none more frequently than Bonfield's; it is a constant fight from Western to Ogden avenues, and many a head and shoulder is left to ache, but the street cars move on and the backbone of the riot is broken.

So called innocent men are hurt, some badly. But warnings enough had been given. Time and again Capt. Bonfield had commanded the crowd to disperse. Innocent men were cautioned to get out of the way. It was no time to decide by a man's appearance whether he was innocent or not. Stones and other missiles were being constantly hurled at the platoon and into the cars. The men had been ordered not to fire. Innocent looking men stood in the front ranks of the mob and allowed thugs to use them as shields or breastworks while they hurled stones over their shoulders. If innocent men were injured, the lives of hundreds were saved; for, had it become necessary to call out the militia, that organization would never have submitted to the insults and outrages heaped upon the police, but would have replied with volleys.

It was Capt. Bonfield's aim to prove to the people of Chicago that the police force, in its own way, could protect the lives and property of citizens, could suppress rioting and preserve the peace, and his aim was successful.

Whether it is looked upon as an honor, or whether by tacit agreement, the injured ones determined to lay their united grievances upon his shoulders, certain it is that every man clubbed that day is prepared to swear that Capt. Bonfield did the clubbing, although the Inspector is perfectly willing to acknowledge, and does acknowledge most cheerfully, that every officer in his advance guard performed his duty faithfully and bravely, and wielded his club effectively.

That the sober second thought of the public has applauded rather than condemned Bonfield for his conduct on that day, is now a matter of fact; that the good judgment of the best citizens endorsed his conduct at this time, is also a matter of fact. The efforts made to injure him in the estimation of his superior officers and the public, have, one after another, fallen flat. While discussion over this occurrence was still warm, and while criticism of his acts was in its most violent stage, Mayor Harrison rewarded him with a handsome promotion. Since then, Mayor Harrison's successor, Mayor Roche, a man of another political party and representative at once of the employed and employing classes, has endorsed that promotion with his official sanction.

John Bonfield is the son of a County Clare Irishman. His father was a staunch supporter and warm admirer of Daniel O'Connell, and participated in many an election that returned, and many a demonstration that honored, the great Irish Parliamentary leader. Much as was expected from the efforts and final successs of the great Kerry statesman, the elder Bonfield, like many another honest Irishman who had preceded, and many who have followed him, felt that for his own good and the good of his little family he must leave his native country. He emigrated to New Brunswick, leaving a part of his family, to be sent for later, behind him. At Bathurst in that province of her gracious Majesty, in the month of April, 1836, his son, John, first saw the light of day. The family moved from New Brunswick to Buffalo, N. Y., in 1842; and in the summer of 1844 settled in Chicago.

John attended the best common school the place afforded in those days, and received a thorough elementary education. Leaving school ten years later, in 1853 or 1854, he became apprenticed to the machinist's trade, and after mastering this art, took charge of stationary engines, first in the packing house of O. S. Hough and afterwards in the glue works of Wall Brothers.

In 1858 he determined to become a locomotive engineer and in order to fulfill the requirements of that trade, served six months as a fireman on the Chicago & Alton, when he was placed in charge of an engine. Although in narrating the events of his career, he passes hastily over this period, those who knew him at the time say that he was one of the best locomotive engineers that ever pulled a throttle open or blew a whistle. He remained on the road for ten years, making his daily runs with regularity, and to the entire satisfaction of the corporation, and in 1868, having saved some money and being tired of the hardships of an engineer's life, he determined to try his hand at a commercial pursuit. He opened a grocery store on Archer avenue, expecting to retire as a millionaire merchant in a few years; but like his friend Ebersold, he gave too much credit and failed after two years' experience. The Bonfield family at that time consisted of his father, Thomas and Catherine, born in Ireland; John, Susan, Michael and Joseph, born in New Brunswick; James H., born in Buffalo, and Martin L. and youngest sister, Maria, born in Chicago. Of these, Joe was, perhaps, the best known, and, while he lived, the most popular. He studied and practiced law in this city, and was considered a young lawyer of remarkable ability. He was appointed corporation counsel by Mayor Heath, which position he held with credit to himself and with entire satisfaction to the city, until a change of administration turned the position over to Frank Adams. He died shortly afterward of a long standing disease of the stomach, and his death was very generally regretted by the community. Susan Bonfield is now Mother Agatha of St. Xavier's Academy in this city. Michael W. is an undertaker on Archer avenue. James H. is on the city detective force. For several years he was deputy jailer. Martin L. is connected with the Union Iron & Steel Works. His youngest sister, now deceased, was the

wife of John O'Malley, one of Chicago's heaviest pork pack-
ers.   The father of this family died in 1885.

After failing in the grocery business John, who had been
a Douglas man till Lincoln's first election, when he became
a republican, was appointed Inspector of Customs by President Grant.   This position he held till 1875, when in
partnership with his brother Joe and Mr. James T. Healy,
he went into the manufacture of fertilizing material. He put
all the money he had into this enterprise and before it was
able to pay dividends, a fire swept all the tangible property
possessed by the company out of existence, and left him
almost penniless once more.

It was after this misfortune that he turned his eyes toward the police department.   In the spring of '77 he was
sworn in as a patrolman and assigned to the Twenty-second
street station for duty.   There he served about two years.
He was then transferred to the Central station, and placed
upon the detective force where from the very first he did excellent work.   After the resignation of Supt. Hickey and the
appointment of Supt. Seavey he was promoted to a Lieutenancy and placed in command of the Twenty-second street district.   Shortly after the first election of Mayor Harrison, he
was transferred to the old Union street station (now Desplaines) and after a year was ordered to the West Twelfth
street, then known as the "terror" district. It was while serving
in this district that the organization of the patrol service was
placed in his hands.   Six months after this latest transfer,
he was made a captain, with headquarters at Central station.
Here he served until Captain Ebersold was promoted to the
Inspectorship, when he was placed in command of the third
precinct, with headquarters at the Desplaines street station,
and once more, on Inspector Ebersold's promotion to the
Superintendency, he was selected to succeed him.   The duties of the Inspectorship embrace also those of the Secretaryship of the Police Department.   The Inspector has entire
control of the purchase of supplies, the equipment of the

men, the management of the patrol service, etc. He is at once the auditor, quarter-master, commissary commander, of ·the force, and aid-de-camp to the Superintendent, with the supervision of the detective force under his special charge.

In this sketch of Inspector Bonfield's career, several important events connected therewith have been omitted. They are, however, covered under other heads.

CHAPTER XVIII.

THE YEAR 1887—JOHN A. ROCHE, MAYOR OF CHICAGO—THE POLITICAL REVOLUTION THAT BROUGHT ABOUT HIS ELECTION—A MAN OF STERLING QUALITIES—THE POLICE STAFF OFFICERS—CAPTAIN HUBBARD OF THE CENTRAL DETAIL—CAPTAIN BUCKLEY OF THE FIRST PRECINCT—CAPTAIN O'DONNELL OF THE SECOND PRECINCT—CAPTAIN LEWIS OF THE THIRD PRECINCT—CAPTAIN HATHAWAY OF THE FOURTH PRECINCT—CAPTAIN SCHAACK OF THE FIFTH PRECINCT.

The election of John A. Roche to the mayoralty of Chicago marked an epoch in the city's history. The circumstances surrounding his nomination by the republican party and election by the people were peculiar. A man of approved business standing and no little political experience, he was not popular, because unknown to the vast majority of the voters. His business, conducted in the Lake street wholesale district for eleven years, was not such as to bring him into actual contact with the people, and when his name was mentioned in connection and competition with those of E. Nelson Blake and Graeme Stuart as a suitable man with whom to fight Carter H. Harrison, the friends of the latter asked, "Who is Roche, anyhow?" Harrison had enjoyed four terms of encumbency, and his declaration that he wanted no more was not taken as being made in good faith. DeWitt C. Cregier was nominated by the democratic convention, but declined. Then Mr. Harrison had an opportunity to make a pyrotechnic display in declining a nomination that meant certain defeat. His following had disappeared, and he was only named as a last resort by the now desperate democracy. The causes leading to his decadence would be improper to discuss here. But the result was a reminder of Æsop's fable of the dying lion. The nominee of the republican party was really a people's candidate.

He represented opposition to the methods which had tolerated the anarchistic harangues on the lake front and elsewhere, that led to the Haymarket riot, and the practical suspension of the ordinances against gambling and other forms of public vice which flaunted themselves with the impudence born of long immunity. He, moreover, represented an element of his own party opposed to what was known as the "silk stockings." He had not been nominated a week before plans were put forth to have him withdrawn. But he developed a force of character little suspected by those who had not known him, and his veto to such a proceeding was no less effectual than the staunch support of his friends. He stayed on the ticket and was elected by votes from all parties but the socialist, and on a distinctly reform platform of personal pledges, outside of mere convention rhetoric.

In the effort of his opponents in his own party and the opposing forces arrayed against him to belittle his personality, it was stated among other things that he was merely a small agent for a small boiler-making concern, a sort of salesman and erector combined. The impression was created that his trade was, as like as not, to canvass the business houses for orders which, when received, he would personally see to the execution of, so far as to superintend the placing of the boilers in position. The truth is, and was, that Mr. Roche began the large machinery business, of which he is the head, as agent for Fay & Co.'s goods, but soon branched out into handling all classes of wood and iron working machinery At the start he had a small single store on Lake street, between Franklin and Market. The expectations of his principal would have been more than realized if he and his associate, Mr. Wood, had done a business aggregating $40,000 a year. Four times that amount was soon exceeded, and other lines added, which more than doubled the receipts from the original source, until now it is one of the largest houses of the kind in the United States. The remarkable results of those eleven years have been largely due to Mr. Roche's energy and push. There was never any of the mugwump about Mayor Roche. He is a positive man in his political opinions, and not at all backward in declaring his intentions. He is liable to act on first impressions, and that quickly; a good friend, and an equally good hater, though he is of a forgiving disposition and has never been known to harbor resentment long.

Mayor Roche, upon assuming the duties of his office, wisely decided to make but few changes in the department of police. He almost immediately reappointed Frederick Ebersold to be general superintendent, and John Bonfield to be inspector and secretary of police—an act which at once won over to him the confidence of all law-abiding people, regardless of party. For reasons which need not be referred to here, it became necessary to make a change in the captaincy of one of the precincts, a change regretted by all who knew the deposed commander, but nevertheless one which the interest of the force demanded. Some minor changes were also made, and some promotions, all of which are mentioned in their proper place. The careers of the superintendent and inspector are reviewed in the preceding chapters. It is fitting that something should be said regarding the staff or precinct officers:

George Washington Hubbard, captain of the Central detail, was born at Cambridge, Maryland, on the birthday of his namesake, the Father of his Country, in February, 1848. He was the second son of Thomas Hubbard, who came from Connecticut and settled in Maryland early in the '40's. There were ten children of them, seven sons and three daughters. George Washington went to school at Cambridge until he was 17 years old, and then took a course at Bryant & Stratton's business college, in Baltimore. In 1866 he came west, his first stop being at Alligan, Mich., where he worked for a year in a shingle mill as receiving and shipping clerk. The next work he did was in the office of Root, the ice merchant, at Kalamazoo. From this avocation he drifted into public life as clerk in the American Hotel there. He occupied confidential relations with the proprietors, succeeding to the duties of one of them when he left.

In the spring of 1871 he came to Chicago, and secured a position with Dawson & Shields, confectioners, on South Clark street. The fire destroyed this business, and Hubbard then worked on the tug "Shields" for a season. From this he passed to the employ of the South Division Street Railroad Company, remaining with it until 1872, when he went to St. Louis. The epizootic was raging there, and men were more valuable as draught animals for a time than in almost any other capacity. For twenty-eight days he formed one of a team of thirty men that pulled a fire engine to its scene of operations on occasion.

Back again to Chicago he came, and on July 25, 1873, he was appointed as a patrolman on the police force, being attached to the Deering street station. He faithfully traveled a beat for a year and a half, except a portion of the time, when he acted as station-keeper. He was finally made station-keeper, and "held the fort," with the exception of one occasion, until 1877. The exception was on the occasion of the West Side railroad riots. A mob attacked the station, and as Hubbard was the only living soul in the building, he made a virtue of necessity, and surrendered at discretion. The mob took possession, but found nothing upon which to lay hands, violent or larcenous, and left. The station-keeper locked up his violated fortress, and also took a walk. He was transferred to Union street in September, 1877, and acted there as station-keeper until 1880, when Capt. Simon O'Donnell took him to West Twelfth street, where he traveled a beat for twenty-two days. He drove the first (experimental) patrol wagon in the service, in 1881, and when West Lake street was made a patrol station he was put in charge. In April, 1882, he was transferred to the Desplaines street station and made desk sergeant, a position he held until October 20, 1883.   He was appointed a lieutenant in the spring of 1884 and transferred to the Central station, where he had charge of the day squad.   The first day of the present year (1887) he was given the full rank and pay of captain; he had enjoyed the rank but not the pay for months.

As a lieutenant, Captain Hubbard, with Sergeant Fitzpatrick, led the last two companies on the night of the Haymarket riot.   His career has been signalized by few brilliant feats of detective work, or remarkable experiences with the rougher class of criminals, in the way of arrests. He has had his full share of the ordinary run of " cases." and has acquitted himself creditably in every instance.

In the organization of the patrol service, he rendered very important assistance to Inspector Bonfield, then a lieutenant, and Chief Doyle.   He furnished the plans for the quarters for the wagons, etc.   His mechanical talent has enabled him to invent many very useful appliances, by which the time of getting out on a call has been shortened, and the service generally much benefited.

A man of marked intelligence, and much above the average in education, he has found his vocation in lines to which these qualities fitted him.   His fine executive ability and good address have caused his selection, since he has been captain, to manage the police part of parades, processions and demonstrations.   The detail at the Central station is regarded as a "fancy" one, the captain there having charge of 156 men, who are the flower of the force—the "Broadway squad" of Chicago.

Captain Hubbard's year and a half of patrol duty was crowded with lively experiences.   He had only been on the street a month or two, when, early one morning, he met four burglars hurrying away from Egan's grocery store, on Lyman and Farrell streets.   He made for them, and caught one, who gave the name of Henderson.   It was very cold, and snowing hard, and the burglars had no shoes on.   A moment later, a voice heard in the distance, calling murder,

GEORGE W. HUBBARD,
Captain, Central Detail.

WILLIAM BUCKLEY,

Capt. Comdg. First Precinct.

materialized in the form of Egan, dressed in one short garment. He had heard the burglars in the store from his room in the rear, and found they had stolen all his clothes. The latter were found in a bundle near by, and Henderson's shoes were in the store. Henderson went to Joliet for eighteen months.

Another time, Alderman Pat Rafferty's plumber's store, on Blue Island avenue near Twenty-second street, had been robbed, and, this being Hubbard's beat, he was feeling badly about it. He kept his eye on the place, and a few nights later, caught two men rifling the place again. One of the men was a son of a leading politician, and Rafferty refused to prosecute.

The first beating Hubbard ever got was in protecting a woman named Murphy, who lived on Emerald street, near Thirty-seventh, from her brutal husband. He had pulled the fellow off, and was struggling on the floor with him, when the wife deliberately locked the door, put the key in her pocket, and then, seizing a heavy stove-lifter, began beating the officer over the head. The arrival of the man on the next beat, Murphy by name, alone saved Hubbard's life.

An amusing, and yet, at the time, rather serious, incident of Captain Hubbard's career as a lieutenant, was the exposure and arrest of Dr. O'Shea, a fraudulent spiritualist medium. Captain Bonfield engineered the matter, and, telling Hubbard the fellow was sixty years old, and weighed about 140 pounds, left him to seize the "materialized spirit." "Dr." O'Shea was an athlete, weighing 240 pounds, and when the police broke in, he and Hubbard were on the floor in a catch-as-catch-can wrestle. O'Shea had all of his clothes torn off, except his collar and socks. "Sixty years old, and 140 pounds!" gasped Hubbard, as Bonfield came in, adding an impolite expression that would have caused him to be court-martialed in the army. But Bonfield forgave him.

Captain William Buckley is as plain and unostentatious as his name. There are no pyrotechnics in his make-up or career. Simple but zealous performance of duty has characterized his official life. For twenty-two years he has had charge of the most turbulent precinct in the city. A purification of it would have been not only a more hopeless task than the cleansing of the augean stables, but disastrous to the rest of the city, where the denizens of a portion of the first precinct would be scattered, if driven from their chosen haunts. Captain Buckley was born in Waterford county, Ireland, in 1832, but bears his years lightly. He was a well-to-do farmer's son, and went to school up to the time he came out to this country, in 1852. He landed in New York City, and worked in an iron foundry for the first year after his arrival. Then he spent a year or two on a Long Island farm, and came to Chicago in the spring of 1857. Here he entered the employ of Col. R. J. Hamilton, the step-father-in-law of Judge Tuley, having charge of a coal-yard for that gentleman, where the Sibley building now stands, at the Clark street bridge. He afterward worked for Law & Strother, another coal firm, and in 1859 helped inaugurate the first street railway, begun in that year by the Chicago City Railroad Company, which operated both South and West Sides. He drove one of the four cars on Madison street, when five were sufficient for the traffic on Randolph and seven on State street. Two years he braved the weather on the front of the car, and was then made a conductor. He collected fares—without a punch—until 1865, joining the police force in April of that year. He was first attached to the old Armory station, on Franklin street, and served there as patrolman until 1867, when he was made a roundsman, and given charge of the territory now comprising the Twenty-second street district. After a year at this responsible work, in which he acquitted himself so well as to attract the favorable attention of his superiors, he was brought down to the Armory again by Captain Jack Nelson, and made desk sergeant and lock-up keeper. He was promoted to a lieutenancy by the board in 1870, and in 1873, he was recommended to succeed Captain Hickey, removed, by Chief Elmer Washburn, appointed by Mayor Medill, and confirmed by the council unanimously. A personal feeling between him and Chief Hickey, caused Captain Buckley's removal in 1877, but Mayor Harrison promptly restored him to the force when he took office in 1879. He was a lieutenant again, and a short period of detail at Twenty-second street led to his complete reinstatement to his old position as captain of the Armory precinct, December 18, 1880. Four years later he was transferred to the East Chicago avenue precinct, making way for Captain Ebersold, the present chief, who, with Inspector Bonfield, served at one time as patrolmen under him. A little over a year saw him back again, upon Captain Ebersold's promotion, and he has served with satisfaction to the public, his superior officers and himself, ever since.

Captain Buckley's career has been so full of the rough and tumble of police work, that there has been little room for brilliant episodes. Some of the earliest experiences to develop the sturdy personal courage of the man, occurred in the spring of 1865, when the police were largely employed in corralling soldiers and returning them to their regiments. But this work was discounted by the period after the war, before Grant ordered that no liquor should be sold to discharged soldiers on their way home. The returning heroes several times seemed about to take possession of the city, and few of the police officers of that day escaped numerous beatings at the hands of the disbanded blue-coats, while the latter were spending their battle-earned money in bad whisky. Captain Buckley had a dozen men's share of pounding, because he was in the thick of every fight, and had a way of running his men in, despite any amount of punishment. But he miraculously came out of it all without permanent injury, though more than once given up for dying.

A notable encounter, in which he came out victorious, after a terrific battle, occurred during the progress of the sanitary fair on Dearborn park. While on the corner of Madison and Clark streets, at midnight, on this occasion, he saw a disorderly crowd in a hack. He endeavored to quiet the riotous riders, when the hackman dismounted and attacked him in the rear. A rough and tumble fight took place, and Buckley was terribly punished, but succeeded in landing the whole cargo at the station.

The murder of McKeever by Hickey, at the old driving park, then located between Thirty-first and Thirty-fifth streets, and State street and Indiana avenue, in 1866, led to another notable episode. He came upon Hickey and his brother in a room on Sherman, near Van Buren street, at one·o'clock in the morning. Both drew revolvers, but Buckley succeeded in taking the murderer, a giant and athlete, to the station. The fellow had but a single garment on when the fight began; when it ended, that had been torn to shreds. But there was no time for toilet making, and the prisoner was taken to the station, with no more on than he was born in.

The rolling mills safe robbery, in 1881, gave Captain Buckley an opportunity to show his paces both as a detective and thief taker. He worked the case up successfully, with scarcely a clew worth speaking of in sight. When he arrested Alexander McKay, the principal, the safe-blower had his hand on his pistol and was walking on the lake front. He and his pistol were soon in the custody of the captain, and the thief and several others were safely lodged in Joliet.

Among the newspaper men who, as reporters, Captain Buckley made firm friends of, are recalled M. G. Russell, W. K. Sullivan, C. A. Snowden, M. E. Stone, Billy Taylor, Sam. Medill, Fred. Hall and Joe Dunlap.

Simon O'Donnell, captain of the second precinct, was born November 23, 1836, in County Clare, Ireland, and came to this country when thirteen years of age. April 7, 1862, was the date of his advent on the scene as a Chicago policeman. He served first attached to the old Armory, corner of Franklin and Adams streets. He was in the Lake street squad in 1863, when Lake and Clark streets were the only paved thoroughfares in the city. He was stationed for six years on the corner of Lake and Clark streets, and was accounted the most popular man on the force. He was young and handsome, and several pounds lighter than now. He was made a sergeant in 1869, a rank about equal then to a lieutenancy now, and was stationed in the Twelfth street district, which was covered by only seventeen men, and no patrol wagons. The men had to carry helpless "drunks" on their shoulders to the station then. The same district is now occupied by four stations, and patrolled by 212 men, who have wagons at call. Then it was infested by thieves of the worst class, and many a time has O'Donnell been for twenty-four hours on his feet. He was transferred to Harrison street April 24, 1877, when Mayor Heath was in office, and was promoted to be deputy superintendent of police August 4, 1879, and was made general superintendent December 15, 1879, *vice* V. A. Seavey. He resigned this position, of his own accord, the following November, and took the captaincy of the Twelfth street district.

While in this position, he broke up more gangs of thieves than any three men on the force. He was indefatigable in the performance of his duties; of strong constitution, herculean strength, and undaunted courage, he soon became a terror to evil-doers.

One of his notable exploits was the capture of Con. Brown, the notorious desperado, who, between 1865 and 1868, had escaped six times from Joliet. He had nearly killed Officer Stimpson, when O'Donnell came up, and knocked him down with a blow that would have rattled an ox, put his foot on the ruffian's neck, and made him plead for mercy. After that, O'Donnell was always called upon when Brown was to be captured, until the latter was shot, down near Lemont.

The Patterson murder, some fifteen years ago, also added a leaf to the gallant captain's laurel wreath. Jack Patterson and Thomas Hurley were rivals for the affections of the same girl, and Patterson was shot at 3 o'clock one morning, in a low resort, corner of Canal and Twelfth street, and the murderer escaped. The wounded man was taken to an adjoining drug store, and, though dying, refused to tell who had shot him, saying: "It would do no good now. I'm dying, anyhow." The proprietor of the place could only say that the murderer had three fingers off one hand.

"I'm going after that man," said Simon O'Donnell, and started for the saloon kept at Seward and Eighteenth streets by old Hurley. "The night is cold," said he, in Irish, as he knocked at the door; "let me have a drop of that which is warm." "Musha, failthe," replied Hurley, senior, as he opened the door. "How's all here?" "Well." "And Tommy?" "Just gone to his bed this half hour." Tommy was found asleep, with the fatal pistol under his pillow, but denied knowing Patterson or having a pistol, until O'Donnell showed it to him, and took him into the dying man's presence. "You've got the man," said Patterson. "Yes, I did it, and you deserved to be killed long ago," blurted out Hurley, suddenly. Patterson died in three hours, and Hurley went to Joliet for eighteen years.

Then Captain O'Donnell broke up a gang of bank robbers, by arresting Paddy Guerin, Jimmy Carroll and Billy Burke, who had robbed the Galesburg bank of $12,000. The first went down for three years, but the others jumped their bail. They had all fixed up a beautiful alibi, by means of a farmer's boy, but the captain saw through the trick, and turned the countryman to good account in identifying the fellows.

While at the Armory station, O'Donnell cleaned out a gang of professional bondsmen and bribery go-betweens, in the face of an offer by George Eager, chief of the gang,

SIMON O'DONNELL,
Capt. Comdg. Second Precinct.

LYMAN LEWIS,
Capt. Comdg. Third Precinct.

of $10,000 a year to keep his mouth shut. The same fellow, later, offered the genial captain half of the money stolen from a man named Tolquiss, to keep quiet. "Arrest this man," shouted O'Donnell to one of his own officers; "he's trying to send me to Joliet." Eager was sentenced to two years for attempted bribery, and one year for receiving stolen goods, but died before he went down the road. The captain's good nature was never again mistaken for a sign of accessibility with corrupt propositions.

The Twelfth street district was infested with anarchists. One shoemaker hung out a red flag. Captain O'Donnell ordered it down, saying: "The stars and stripes are good enough for any Bohemian 'bosthoon'." On one occasion, when Charlie Reed was state's attorney—to go back a few years—three toughs set upon and beat a policeman in Captain O'Donnell's precinct. One of the fellows was captured, a month or two after, and locked up. The captain was sitting in front of the station one night, when he heard groans from the cell-room. Rushing down stairs, he caught the officer who had been beaten cruelly abusing the prisoner. Seizing the blackguard in blue, the captain hurled him out of the cell, and against the opposite wall, nearly knocking him senseless. "You coward!" he exclaimed; "I've a notion to break your neck!" The officer begged his captain not to say anything about it, or to deny it. "I'll not perjure myself for the whole police force, but I won't volunteer evidence, if not asked for." He was asked, and told the story in court. But there is no more beating prisoners in cells at Twelfth street.

Lyman Lewis, the captain of the Desplaines street precinct, was born November 20, 1844, at Norwich, Conn., of American parents. His father was a general merchant, and Lyman worked in the store until he was 19 years old, receiving in the meantime a good common school education. His first venture away from home was at White River Junction, Vt., where he was clerk in a hotel for five years. He married Miss Clara T. Worth, of Bradford, before coming West, and the young couple arrived in Chicago in 1868. Lewis went to work for J. H. Smalley in the latter's butcher shop at 44 East Chicago avenue, where he remained for a year. Then he began business for himself in the same line, remaining on the same street, and prospering moderately until the fire came. Then he lost everything, with hundreds of others. He went to work again for Mr. Smalley, and would be a rival of Armour, Swift and Morris to-day had he not, on March 18, 1872, joined the police force. His first detail was at the Dearborn avenue station, in the fifth precinct. The station house was then temporarily established where the Babcock fire engine house is now, between Superior and Huron streets. The station was moved in the following year to the present site on East Chicago avenue. From this point he faithfully traveled his beat for four years. Then he was transferred to the Twenty-second street station, where he acted as patrolman, and also served as desk sergeant. He drew patrolman's pay, however, until October 26, 1885, when he was made patrol sergeant at the Twenty-second street station. He lost his first wife in 1883, and was married to Miss Annie L. Hoye, Syracuse, New York, in July, 1885.

Lieutenant Lewis, of the Stanton avenue station, was his designation from June 19, 1887, to the date of his last promotion.

He was so well thought of that, when, in September of the same year, there was a "shaking-up" of the department, after Mayor Roche's visit to eastern cities, his name was suggested to the chief magistrate as that of a good man for captain. The mayor said nothing, but drove out to the station one afternoon and had a talk with the broad-shouldered, black-moustached lieutenant. The result was satisfactory. This was the man to carry out Captain Schaack's rigorous reform movement on the West Side, and he was appointed captain.

Captain Lewis is so modest that it was by no means easy to make up his police record, though he has taken an active part in all the great riots of his day, except that at the Haymarket, and including the street-car troubles on the West Side. He has sent his share or more of criminals to Joliet, but was fortunate in never having been wounded or even the target for a bad marksman. He has had no hair-breadth escapes or startling adventures, or if he had he has forgotten all about them. His police life was apparently one of duty-doing, without ostentation or flourish. When he took charge of the third precinct the disreputables held an orgie to celebrate the departure of Captain Schaack and the advent of a supposedly less zealous officer to the command. But when they all appeared in court the following morning and were fined, it did not need the magistrate's warning to make them understand that Jupiter had not reversed the fable and removed King Stork to make room for King Log. His promotion was entirely unexpected, but he seems to have devoted himself to an earnest effort to demonstrate the wisdom of the mayor's choice, in which he is eminently successful, to all appearance.

Captain Lewis was a patrolman in the Twenty-second street precinct when Inspector Bonfield was a lieutenant. "He was the best patrolman I ever knew," said the inspector, in referring to his brief personal contact with the present captain of the third precinct, "and so far as the indications point he will make one of the best captains on the force. He was conspicuous for courage and coolness in the railroad riots in 1877, and the street-car troubles later."

The first recognition Lewis received was for an act of bravery which came under the notice of Superintendent Ebersold. It was during the street-car troubles. A car had been taken from the men in charge of it, including an officer, when Officers Lewis and Ptassec, two of the smallest men in the second precinct, came along. They charged the mob, captured the car and set it running, and then chased and arrested the ringleader in the riot, the latter being Lewis' work, and he had to fire a shot to bring his man to his senses. Each one of the men were promoted, the others to desk sergeantcies, and Lewis to be patrol sergeant. He had served under Mr. Ebersold while the latter was sergeant at the Twenty-second street precinct, and was well known to be very efficient as a patrolman.

Amos W. Hathaway, captain of the fourth precinct, was born May 29, 1839, at Providence, R. I., but owing to the death of his mother when he was an infant, his grandmother took charge of him until he was eleven years of age, bringing him up on her farms near Oswego and Jefferson, N. Y. He made up his mind about this time that he ought to be making his own living. Earning enough money to carry him from Jefferson to Oswego, by picking cranberries, he started out to the latter city to seek his fortune. There he soon found employment in Smith & Kind's machine shop, where for three years he worked, learning the trade. Then he ran a stationary engine for W. H. Wheeler; leaving this for the life of a lake sailor, his first vessel being the W. H. Wheeler, sailing to Chicago. He "followed the lakes" until navigation closed for 1855, when he determined to settle in Chicago, after working for awhile on a LaSalle, Ill., farm and driving a team. With Col. "Jim" Lane he spent a portion of 1857 and 1858 in the neighborhood of Lawrence, Kas., having been taken with an attack of western fever. While in this, then, border country, he was a participant in many a stirring adventure, but returned to Chicago in the fall of 1858. He worked on a farm in Palatine for awhile, locating permanently in this city in 1860, securing the position of foreman of the mechanical bakery of Henry C. Childs, which had a contract for army hard-tack, supplying all that was used during the early days of the war. As many as one hundred barrels of flour were worked up into soldier bread in a day, the establishment running continuously, night and day, to meet the demands of the commissary department. He remained in this place for three years, when his health gave way under the strain, and he was compelled to take to the lakes again, spending several months in a recuperative ramble on shipboard, in 1863.

During this period of activity he found time to court and marry Miss Rosalie R. Russell, the auspicious event taking place in 1862. They have had nine children, four girls and three boys surviving.

He joined the Chicago police force in 1864, being first attached, as patrolman, to the old North Market hall, where he remained for three years. By this time he was 25 years of age, and he became impatient of the comparatively small pay and slow promotion on the police force, and resigned to engage in more remunerative business. Within the year, however, the old life proved again attractive, and he joined the force as sergeant in charge of the Huron street station, a position equal to a lieutenancy to-day. The name of the office was, in fact, changed about this time, under Elmer Washburn's administration, and Sergeant Hathaway became Lieutenant Hathaway without a promotion. He continued in charge here until August 1, 1879, when he was promoted to be captain, being assigned to the fourth precinct. The headquarters were then at the East Chicago avenue station. April 22, 1884, he was transferred to the West Twelfth street station, the precinct being still the fourth, though the headquarters and district embraced were different.

The major portion of Capt. Hathaway's police experience was on the North Side, but save for being shot through the body when trying to arrest four burglars all by himself on Kinzie street and LaSalle avenue, in 1868, he has had few startling experiences with the criminal classes, though his record is one of the best in the city as an efficient executive officer and detector of crime. His respective superior officers during his subordinate career, Captains Gund, Miller, Shannon, Fox, and Gund again, all have from time to time expressed the greatest admiration for his sterling qualities, and his lieutenants are no less pronounced in their warm regard for him as a man and officer.

Among the cases in which he has taken part in the detection or arrest of the criminals, are the Mulkowsky murder, the arrest being made in the precinct by Officers McNulty and Johnson, and the Herman Mocade murder on Ashland and Milwaukee avenues, about five years ago. Capt. Hathaway and Lieutenant Quinn started out without a clew to find out the slayer of Mocade, who was found dead on the street with a bullet hole in him, but no witnesses to the infliction of the wound or what led to it. They finally found that two men, brothers, had been quarrelling with Mocade a few days before. It was at midnight when this clew was secured. Over thirty houses were searched before the brothers were discovered. One opened the door. He said his brother was asleep in bed. Seizing him the officers went to the sleeping man and shaking him violently demanded what he had done with the pistol. "Threw it away," said he, blinking at the bright light. "What did you shoot that man for?" "He hit me first." Subsequently, evidence in corroboration was obtained, but self-defense being set up, the man's life was saved.

As an instance of his integrity and qualities as a disciplinarian it is related that when a lieutenant at the Huron street station, under Capt. Fox, when a patrolman with political influence was to be brought down to his duty, he was always put in Hathaway's platoon. Others might be afraid to report a man who was a power in the ward, but Lieutenant Hathaway was never known to inquire who was behind a wrong-doer. An experience with Mr. Ebersold, before he became superintendent, convinced the latter of Hathaway's courage and coolness in danger. Together they faced and dispersed an angry and dangerous mob at a Bohemian picnic, an achievement of no small danger and difficulty.

Michael John Schaack, whose management of the police

AMOS W. HATHAWAY,
Capt. Comdg. Fourth Precinct.

MICHAEL J. SCHAACK,
Capt. Comdg. Fifth Precinct.

end of the anarchist prosecution has given him a national
reputation, was born in the Grand Duchy of Luxemburg,
April 23, 1843, leaving the little frontier independency
whe   thirteen years of age, after receiving a common
school education.   His first dollar was earned in a furniture factory where he thought he was getting rich fast
on three dollars a week.   Next he worked in a brewery,
and then sailed the lakes for seven years as second mate of
various steamers hailing from Chicago.   Several of the
vessels were lost, but "the little cherub that sits up aloft looking after poor Jack," looked after him so well that he always
managed to change ships just before the fatal voyage.   After
three more years spent in a brewery and two on Ludwig &
Co.'s private detective force, he joined the police department,
June 15, 1869, as patrolman, attached to the old Armory—that
cradle of Chicago's best officers, and served under Capt.
Hickey.   He was not new to the rough side of police duty,
when he was enrolled, having had some severe experiences as
a "special."   He had the good fortune, for instance, to
reach Dewey & Co.'s place, at 27 Kingsbury street, on his
rounds, just as their safe was blown out.   There were four
burglars inside, but he rushed in and was trying to see
through the smoke, when one of the two men who had jumped
out of the window, leaned in and fired at the intruder as the
latter seized one of his comrades.   A long dagger drawn by
the burglar was met and matched with a heavy billy, but
the revolver Schaack carried refused to explode.   This man,
Charles Johnson, and a comrade, were "sent up" for five
years, the other two escaping.   The next two desperate
encounters were at Bogel's store and Peterson's tailor store
on Kinzie and Kingsbury streets, in which shots were fired,
but Schaack again proved to have a charmed life.

He was detailed for special detective work soon after his
appointment, and was made a patrol sergeant in 1872, serving during Chief Washburn's term.   Then he was made a
regular detective, and in the next five years had made 865

arrests in serious criminal cases, such as murders, burglaries, robberies and other penitentiary offenses. His partner in making this remarkable, and indeed unparalleled record, was Michael Whalen, now a detective.

After joining the regular force, one of the first feats which showed the qualities that were afterward to be so highly appreciated, was in a burglary case. While he was patrolling that beat Alderman Kehoe's place, on North Clark street, was entered. This was bad for the man on the post unless he turned in the burglars, and Schaack felt worried, until one night he saw a suspicious-looking hack halt where the present Clark street viaduct is and turn into a dark alley, near a one-story jewelry store. He climbed up, leaned over the eaves, and listened. He heard one of the passengers instruct the driver to be ready to move off rapidly when they had the "stuff" in. Schaack got down and watched. There was Alderman Kehoe's cigars and liquor being loaded into the hack. Cautioning the driver not to move at his peril, he awaited the last trip out, and then grabbed the biggest burglar, who was much larger than his captor. The fellow fired two shots, and his partner threw Schaack to his knees. The big man then made for a marble yard, and the half-stunned officer after him. The pursuer hurt himself seriously by striking a marble block in the road and then stuck fast in the fence, when the burglar fired at him. But the chase was taken up by Officer Dolan, and Charles McCarthy captured. He was an old freight robber, and he and his partner gave the railroad company some valuable information, and escaped, at the intercession of the corporation, with one year at Joliet.

The capture of Tommy Ellis, who killed David O'Neil, the yardmaster of the Northwestern road, on the Erie street bridge, in 1877, was a desperate adventure. The murderer had to be shot twice before he consented to be arrested.

The capture of the leaders of the Murphy gang, while robbing Kobletz's merchant tailor store, on Clark street, was another daring piece of police work. James Strong and George Harris were sent up for five years.

In August, 1879, he was made a lieutenant, and attached to the Chicago avenue station. He was transferred to the Armory for awhile, but soon returned to the North Side again. While in the levee district he was shot at twice, but his wonderful luck or Providence preserved him. On one occasion, while arresting a gang of roughs on Pacific avenue, a bullet passed through his clothes, close to his abdomen, and then entered the trousers' pocket of his partner, but harmed neither. A falling out with the Armory justice (Foote) led to his transfer back to Chicago avenue. The magistrate excited the zealous officer's ire by certain rather extraordinary decisions, and received the benefit of a free and forcible expression of opinion upon his conduct in open court.

In August, 1885, he was made a captain, and two days afterward Mulkowsky murdered Mrs. Kledzic. This case is one of the most remarkable in the criminal annals of Chicago and created a sensation over the whole country. But the manner in which it was worked up was only less remarkable. Mulkowsky had come over here from Poland after serving the twenty-two years, which constituted a "life sentence" there for murder, and which is scarcely ever survived. He came to Chicago under the name of Brunofski, and was not recognized by the Kledzic family, whom he had known before his crime and imprisonment. He remembered them, and now cultivated their acquaintance. He learned of some savings they had invested and the shape of the vouchers therefor. Coming behind the wife while she was alone in the house and bending over a wash-tub, he crushed her skull with some heavy weapon, ransacked the rooms, ravished her finger of its wedding ring and fled. Capt. Schaack first got a complete history of his family and friends at home and here from Kledzic, who incidentally referred to Mulkowsky's supposed fate in prison, and also mentioned

Brunofski, whom he suspected of being other than he represented himself. In three days Capt. Schaack had the murderer in custody and circumstantial evidence upon which to hang him. Some burnt paper in the stove of the murdered woman's room gave the first clue. It was the remains of letters relating to the release of Mulkowsky. From a sister of the latter, whom he much resembled, Schaack learned of the identity of Mulkowsky and Brunofski, and by means of photographs of the sister he was arrested. The watch of the murdered woman and her jewelry were traced to the prisoner, who was also found to have washed his clothes in the river at midnight and his hat was stained with what Dr. Bisfeldt swore was human blood. This completed the chain, and the jury was out only twenty minutes before convicting him.

Capt. Schaack's crowning exploit, the conviction of the anarchists, is too fresh in the public mind to need any extended reference here. It is enough to say that, taking up a case which was out of his own district and conducting the investigation independently of any aid or suggestion from his superiors, he found clews of which no one else suspected the existence, and following them with a zeal and intelligence that almost surpass credence, he forged a chain, link by link, that completely encircled the conspirators.

The Krug case, of more recent date, was remarkable for the fact that the prisoner was convicted and is now in Joliet, serving what will doubtless prove a life sentence, after the coroner had once released him on the testimony of the county physician that the fellow's last victim died, not by poison, but well-defined natural causes.

CHAPTER XIX.

THE DETECTIVE FORCE—A HISTORICAL REVIEW OF THIS BRANCH OF
THE SERVICE—ITS CHIEFS FROM THE BEGINNING—DETECTIVE WORK
IN CHICAGO—LIEUTENANTS STEELE AND SLAYTON—THEIR RECORDS—
THE MEN WHO COMPOSE THE DETECTIVE FORCE AT PRESENT—
MANY ONCE FAMILIAR CRIMES RECALLED—A COMPLETE ROSTER OF
THE SECRET SERVICE OF THE CITY.

Until 1860 there was no such thing in Chicago as a
detective department. During the years before that date,
when there was anything to be done in the line of detective
duty, the marshal picked out the men he wanted from the
general force, and set them at work. While this sort of
thing was all right for that time in the history of Chicago,
the Prairie City was growing, and something of a more
pronounced character was wanted. And so, under Bradley, and after the Metropolitan Police Bill had become a
law, a detective department was organized, Charles Storer
in charge, with the rank of sergeant. In those days there
were no lieutenants. There were only half a dozen men on
the detective force then—Asa Williams, Ike Williams,
Henry Kauffmann, Joe Dixon, and Horace Elliott. These
were the early stars in the profession. Storer was succeeded by Thomas Moore in 1865, and matters ran along
then—running themselves, some people were unkind enough
to say—and without making anything of a record until the
fire had cleaned things out, and Elmer Washburn had
taken hold of the position of chief. He started in by putting Samuel A. Ellis at the head of the detective department, and making William J. McGarigle clerk. In 1874,
Ellis was promoted to the position of captain of a West
Side precinct, and Joseph Dixon was made chief of detectives. He stepped out to become deputy superintendent

of police, and Charles A. Rehm became sergeant of detectives.   In 1876, late in the year, William J. McGarigle
was made lieutenant of detectives, and in his hands the
department remained till 1878, when Edward J. Steele was
appointed to take McGarigle's place.   He was succeeded by
Edward J. Keating, in 1879, and Keating, in 1880, by
Thomas H. Currier.   Currier was at the head of the department until 1882, when he was succeeded by John Shea and
Joseph Kipley, who, with the rank of lieutenant, ran the
department jointly.   They held until the election of Mayor
Roche, in the spring of 1887, when they were transferred
to and given separate stations, and Edward J. Steele was
called in to take charge of the office.   With him was appointed Lieutenant Reuben Slayton.

Chicago has been free from great crimes, and, while
there have been a number of mysterious and daring crimes,
which furnished the department material upon which to
work and display its ability, this city has never been able to
boast of a Nathan murder or a Manhattan bank robbery.
Chicago, it is true, has given to the rest of the world a great
many criminals, who have held exalted positions in the
circles in which they moved, but it seemed that the Chicago
crook emigrated just as soon as he found that he could do
better elsewhere—that other towns were "softer," to use
his expression.   When the Habitual Criminal Act was
passed, and one or two professional crooks had been sent
down for fourteen years or more, the other members
of the fraternity began to clear out, and, as a result of
this, there has not been an important piece of "work"
done by professional criminals in this city for eight years.

Banko or "bunko" games, which abounded in Chicago
in the period immediately preceding and following the fire,
are no longer known.   Confidence operators, who once flourished, have been taught that the climate is unhealthy, and
have sought other regions, remote from that under the protection of the Chicago detective department.   This was

brought about by the practice inaugurated by Lieutenant Currier, of "vagging" a known "con" man as soon as he was spotted on the street. A series of heavy fines, with no opportunity to recoup himself, made the smoothest operator hesitate to tarry for any length of time in this city; and it naturally followed that the granger population could come to Chicago with greater security to its pocket-book than in any other large city.

The men chosen for the detective branch of the service are, as a rule, those who have served some time as patrolmen, and have exhibited a peculiar fitness for the position. True, some of the officers attached to Lieutenant Steele's force were appointed without having served a day on the general force; but there was always some good reason for such an appointment, and the ability of the appointee to discharge the duties of the office with credit has been demonstrated to the satisfaction of their superior officers. Under Mayor Roche's administration all appointments of this character were discouraged, the mayor holding that the detective force should be a goal toward which the clever members of the general force might look as a reward for faithful and able work while in uniform. He held that it was a bar to the best of work among the patrolmen if they saw nothing ahead of them—no chance for places on the detective force— a department which contains the very flower of the service, and he determined to demonstrate that there was good material for that branch of the service among the men of the general force, and that it would be developed by encouraging this system of promotions. The wisdom and correctness of this view is now acknowledged by the oldest and best officers in the department.

The force at the Central station, under Lieutenants Steele and Slayton, was not limited as to number. There might be as many men as the exigencies of the hour demanded. As a rule, it averaged twenty-five men. These, while they bore the rank of patrolmen, were paid $1,213 per annum, as against $1.000 a year to the patrolmen on beat. The Central station force, as a whole, comprised the two lieutenants in charge, twenty-eight patrolmen, and two inspectors of pawnshops. Of the twenty-eight men thus attached to the force, three were engaged in clerical work a large portion of the time, but were men fully able to discharge the duties required of the detective department. Most of the men had specialties in the line of which they were most valuable. Some had a wide acquaintance among the colored denizens of "Cheyenne;" others had confidential relations with members of the sporting fraternity, who might be relied upon for valuable information; others, by long years of service in all branches of the department, were familiar with all the more noted criminals who had "worked" Chicago in earlier years, and were able to spot them if they turned up and attempted to do anything in this city; others, trained in the districts from which the criminal population of Chicago is most largely recruited, were thoroughly familiar with the younger generation of thieves and pickpockets, from whose depredations the public was the greatest sufferer.

While Chicago has been troubled little by gangs of shrewd and desperate burglars and safe-blowers, it has had more than its share of brutal murders. The average detective, as a matter of fact, has had much more experience solving murder mysteries than getting at the bottom of lesser crimes; and while capital offenses are more difficult of solution than the ordinary run of offenses against property, so capable have the detectives been that Chicago has far less than its proportion of unsolved mysteries. The Wilke murder, the Jacobson murder, the Amelia Olson murder, and less than half a dozen others, are the only ones that have baffled the skill of the department in the twenty-six years of its existence.

It is not necessary here to attempt to give in detail the stories of all the important cases which have been handled by the detective department. It will be found in reading the sketches of the men, that most of the sensational crimes of which Chicago may boast, have been worked with varying degrees of success by officers who are yet young and still connected with the force. It will be observed, too, that in addition to the attributes of shrewdness which every successful detective should possess, an unusual degree of courage is demanded of the detective who would make a success in Chicago. The criminals of the Garden City are noted for their recklessness. They shoot quicker and with less provocation than in any other city, and the detective who pits himself against these desperadoes and hopes to come out with a whole skin, must be nervy to a degree and as quick as chain lightning in handling a "gun."

Detective work in Chicago is rendered peculiarly difficult. There are in various sections of the city great stretches of territory inhabited by foreign elements. There are the Polish, the Bohemian and the Italian quarters where one might travel all day and never hear a word of English. In certain of these localities mysterious assaults are of frequent occurrence. A foreigner is found bathed in blood and at the point of death; he dies refusing to make any statement incriminating anyone, and it becomes the duty of the detective department to fathom the mystery of his death. On every hand the officer is beset with difficulties that would speedily discourage an ordinary detective. These settlements of foreigners are clannish to a degree. Every effort is made to deceive the police, to throw them off the scent and to cover the tracks of the criminal, who, as such, is known to hundreds of his acquaintances. Everywhere the detective is met with protestations of ignorance, and nowhere is he able to find one willing to comprehend a three-word sentence of English. Even to officers of their own nationality these secretive people will divulge little; but, and it is to the credit of the police department, a remarkably small percentage of crimes in the foreign settlements go undiscovered and unpunished. The Caruso murder in an Italian district and the Kledzic murder in the Polish settlement, the perpetrators of both of which paid the penalty with their lives, are conspicuous examples of the ability of the Chicago detective department to achieve success under the most discouraging circumstances. These crimes will be found treated somewhat in detail in the sketches of the men who were instrumental in bringing the murderers to the gallows.

LIEUTENANT EDWARD J. STEELE: Clear-eyed, keen, with a mind capable of thoroughly grasping the most complicated situation and acting on the instant, courage and determination, which no combination of circumstances can affect, the physique of a giant, a reputation for honesty that he values above all else—this is Edward J. Steele, senior lieutenant in charge of the detective department of the city of Chicago. Lieutenant Steele was born at Lowville, N. Y., in 1839. His father was a justice of the peace and farmer. When Edward was five years old the family removed to Ontario. There the lad grew up on his father's farm and learned the trade of carpenter. When he was 24 years of age he married Mary Parker, and a few years later cut loose from Canada and struck up into Minnesota, where he farmed till 1869, when he removed with his wife and children to Chicago. Here he followed his trade for two years, and then accepted a position on Hamblen's Merchant Police. Here he remained for a year, leaving it to go on the regular police force, to which he was appointed in 1872, and assigned to the old Madison street station. For three years he traveled a beat, and was then assigned to the day squad and stationed at State and Washington streets. He was not content to do nothing but pose and help the ladies across the street: the spirit of the detective was there, and he was ever on the lookout for a chance to do some creditable police work. This came in time. He received a pointer in reference to the perpetrators of a number of church burglaries, cases in which Catholic places of worship had been entered and stripped of everything in the way of silver and valuables. He received permission to work the case up, and within a few days pulled into the station Blibley and Yorke, a pair of clever house-breakers. He made his case on them, they went to the penitentiary, and he was assigned to the Central station detective force, where he would be of more value to the city than on a crossing. After a year there he was transferred to the Harrison street station, still in citizen's clothes. While there he arrested Edward Stevens, the robber who gagged and bound old Mrs. Noonan, at No. 160 Fourteenth street, and got away with $170 of her money. The case was worked up from a very slight clew, and Stevens went down for ten years. His success in this case

EDWARD J. STEELE,
Comdg. Detectives Central Station.

REUBEN SLAYTON,
Lieut. Comdg. Detectives Central Station.

caused the authorities to turn over to him another even more difficult. A woman named Marshall, living near the rolling mills on
the South Side, had been held up in her house by masked men and
her money taken. There was absolutely no clew that offered a
hope of success. But that was the sort of case that he liked most;
and taking with him Detective Stewart, he started out to see what
could be done. While working about in the neighborhood of the
place where the crime was committed, Steele ran across an old
woman named Cavanaugh. She was tipsy, and foolishly volunteered the remark that "it couldn't have been Clipper Flynn and
Conny Mahoney, for they were both in the house the night of the
robbery." This was considered a good tip, and one of the thieves
was arrested and locked up. Steele was put into the same cell
with him, represented that he was the nephew of a prominent man,
and was soon to get out. On the strength of this, the thief asked
him to carry a note to a friend of his, and furnished him with a
letter to Mahoney. He was arrested, and they were given five
years apiece. Bermont, alias Ro and, the Chambersburg, Pa.,
bank robber, was one of the noted crooks who was rounded up by
Officer Steele and sent down. Roland was a thoroughly desperate
man, and was waiting for the officer with two revolvers and a dirk
knife handy; but Steele got the drop on him and took him in without a struggle. He was given seventeen years. In 1878, Officer
Steele was placed in charge of the detective force at the Central,
where, after ten months' service, he was given a lieutenant's commission and assigned to the Harrison street station. From there he
was transferred to the West Lake street station, and then to the
West Chicago avenue station, where he remained till his appointment as chief of the detective force, in the spring of 1887. His
company at the Haymarket riot led the column of police
up Desplaines street to where the speeches were being made.
The lieutenant was prostrated by the force of the explosion, and received a number of pistol balls through his clothing.
He broke his wrist using his pistol as a club, but otherwise escaped
injury. Nine out of twenty-four men in his company were seriously injured by fragments of the bomb. Lieutenant Steele has
five children, Freeman, his eldest son, being connected with the
detective force under his father.

LIEUTENANT REUBEN SLAYTON, associated with Lieut. Steele in
running the detective department, is in every way qualified for the
position. He has had, first of all, the thorough discipline that
comes of long service in the army, and then an admirable training
in the police and detective department of the city for a dozen years.
Of courage, ability, determination and all the other elements that
go to make up the successful officer, he possesses his full share. He
was born at Mt. Pleasant, Mass., Oct. 18, 1839, upon a farm, and

with his parents removed while a youngster to Monroe county, Mich., where he remained till 14 years of age. Then he started out for himself, striking up into the pineries, and going from there to Mackinaw, where he remained till 1860. That year he came to Chicago, and in 1862 enlisted in Co. E, 39th Illinois Volunteers, and went to the front. He was in a number of engagements with his regiment, but was wounded at Drury's Bluff and sent to the rear. He went first to Fortress Monroe and afterward to the general hospital at Newark, and was transferred to Bedloe's Island, where he was in the quartermaster's department till mustered out in 1865. Returning to Chicago, he went to work for the West Division Street Railway, and in 1866, Aug. 3, was appointed on the police force and assigned to the old Armory at Adams and Franklin streets. The following year he was made roundsman by "Jack" Nelson, this being the first appointment to that rank. As roundsman he looked after affairs in his district till after the great fire, when he was transferred to the Central, where he remained till 1879, resigning on a change of the administration. April 19, 1886, he was reappointed to the force, and May 10, 1887, was promoted to the lieutenancy he now fills. While at the Central he did a great deal of creditable work. Perhaps the most celebrated case he ever handled was that of the burglars Collins and Herman. These men were the smoothest of their class, and brought themselves to the notice of the police at the Central in 1878 by carrying away $1,800 worth of silk linings from Cahn, Wampold & Co.'s place. They concealed their identity with great success, and covered their tracks well. They lived in a respectable part of town and nothing criminating could be found against them, although they were suspected. Slayton had got the case along to a point where he could swear that they were the men, but he couldn't prove it. A detective took up quarters as a roomer in the same house, but just at this juncture a green policeman arrested the pair for vagrancy. Slayton took before them a man whom he had instructed to say loudly that they were not the men, and hoped thus to throw them off their guard. The scheme worked all right and they were turned loose with an apology. They went right back to the place where they were hanging out and the next day were caught handling the stolen goods. Nine other burglaries were proven against them and property to the amount of $10,000 recovered. On the trial they got ten years each. Collins went down, but Herman fought for a new trial. He got it, and after having spent a year in jail waiting for it to come off, was given twelve years. Of cases like this and of less importance, Lieut. Slayton has had his share, and he has every reason to be proud of the record he has made for himself as a police officer.

MICHAEL J. GRANGER first saw the light in Chicago, January 11, 1852. In 1879 he entered the service of Allan Pinkerton, and August 6, 1881, was appointed to the police force, and assigned to the Harrison street station. Within six months, Officer Granger had demonstrated the fact that he was a clever man in citizen's clothes, was assigned to special duty, and in May, 1883, was permanently connected with the detail at the Central station. He made a great many important arrests, first attracting attention by bringing in single-handed the notorious Ed. Milligan. It had been the custom to send a squad of men after Milligan when he was wanted for anything, and it took Officer Granger the better part of an hour, and cost him a new uniform and a pair of black eyes, to get Milligan in ; but he got him. That was a sample of his nerve. The arrest of Murray and Rice, the noted climbing thieves from St. Louis, whose work in Chicago for two months, during the winter of 1881–2, netted them $12,000 in plunder, was by Officer Granger, and most of the stuff recovered. Murray got fifteen years. Wilson, Ryan and Howard, the Amboy safe-blowers, were arrested and sent down by Officer Granger. Granger and Bonfield did a great deal of work on the election fraud cases of 1880, and they together arrested "Dutchy" Keefe for the theft of a Third ward ballot-box. Hundreds of cases of almost as great importance have been successfully handled by   energetic officer. He was wounded at the riot at Eighteenth street and Center avenue, May 4, 1886.

HERMAN SCHUETTLER is one of the young men of the detective force, having been born in Chicago in 1861. In addition to being about the youngest man on the force, he is the tallest. He was appointed to the force June 8, 1883, and was only kept in uniform a short time. So clever an officer was more valuable in citizen's clothes. In connection with Detective Officer Stift, Officer Schuettler worked up the case of Lorenz Krug, who was charged with poisoning Lucy Heidelmeyer, and Krug was convicted. It was the first conviction in a poisoning case ever secured in Cook county. Klein and Tiedeman, the highwaymen, were brought up with a sharp turn by this young officer, and treated to eight years each in the penitentiary. William Heller, an expert burglar, who had gone through most of the fine residences in Lake View, was run down, and sent to Joliet for three years. Over fifty cases were developed against him after he had gone down, and when he was released, in the summer of 1887, he was rearrested and given twenty years. Officer Schuettler was a valuable aid to Captain Schaack in the working up of the Kledzic murder mystery, for which Mulkowsky was arrested and hanged. But his widest reputation was gained during the anarchist troubles. He it was who tracked Lingg, the bomb-maker, to his hiding place on the South Side, and there bearded him in his den. Lingg made a desperate resistance, trying his utmost to kill the officer with a knife or revolver ; but Schuettler, being young and strong as an ox, overpowered him by main strength, and made him a prisoner.

BARTHOLOMEW FLYNN is a native of County Meath, Ireland, where he was born Aug. 14, 1842. When 20 years of age he came to Chicago, and six years later joined the police force. He served at the old Armory at Franklin and Adams streets, and after the big fire was sent to the West Side, and finally to the Harrison street station. From there he was transferred to the Central. The best work he has done on the force was the running down and capturing of the clever counterfeiter, Walter P. Carter. Carter had rented rooms from an old policeman on the West Side, and in these rooms had concealed one of the finest and most complete counterfeiting outfits that a man could wish. His hiding place was discovered, and so clear a case made on him that he pleaded guilty and took a five-year sentence. Officer Flynn has handled scores of important cases in his time. He resigned from the force in 1879, and was reappointed to the detective force in 1886.

MARTIN D. RINGROSE was born in Ireland Nov. 11, 1850. He came to Chicago in 1865, and in 1873 was appointed to the police force and assigned to the old Madison street station. Here he served through the riots of 1877, and while traveling a beat was shot at by Doc. Fitz, alias James Fitzpatrick, who had shot Officer Keefe a day or two before. Officer Ringrose grappled with him and landed him at the station. He saw him go down for ten years for the assault on Keefe and a case of robbery. Mike Sullivan, highwayman, Cusick, Elligott, Scully, and Healy, burglars, and a score of less noted criminals, were sent to Joliet by this officer. He was assigned to the force at the Central station in July, 1887.

JAMES MORGAN is one of the veterans of the detective force. He entered it in 1861, when he was thirty-three years of age, and has served continuously ever since. He is a native of Ireland, but has lived in Chicago since he was a mere baby. His specialty in the detective department is the running down of horse thieves. He has a personal acquaintance with every animal of note in the Northwest, and can identify a horse on the darkest night that ever grew. He has broken up more gangs of horse thieves than any other man in the country. His methods are peculiarly his own, and he never "gives anything away." From early in 1875 he has devoted himself to this one class of cases with a success that has been almost phenomenal. In 1879 he broke up a gang of which Harry Smith, Dempster, Cass Lyons, Bates, and Pierce were the shining lights, and who, with twenty-five or thirty others, were getting away with a great deal of horse-flesh through Wisconsin and Illinois. The Knights gang, with which Bill Mead was connected; George Gay's gang, with Sarah Wheeler and the Hickson brothers; George Craig, Burdy, Nash, and True—these are some of the illustrious names that adorn "Jim" Morgan's note book as victims of his relentless hatred for the being who would steal a horse, and most of them have caught a glimpse of Joliet as a result of his good work. During the twelve years he has devoted himself to this specialty he has recovered more than one thousand horses, whose combined value would reach close to $325,000.

TIMOTHY McKEOUGH is one of the youngest detectives in the department, but he has succeeded in making for himself a reputation that a much older officer might envy. He was born at Saratoga Springs, N. Y., in 1860, and came to Chicago when he was seven years of age. February 17, 1883, he first entered the department as a patrolman in uniform, but it was only a short time before he showed so much ability that his superior officers ordered his transfer to the detective force at the Central station. June 23, 1885, he arrested the notorious Pennsylvania outlaw, Ike Buzzard, and turned him over to the authorities of the state where his depredations had made him the terror of half a dozen counties. It was Detective McKeough, too, who succeeded in breaking up a troublesome gang of colored thieves which had given a deal of annoyance to the down town merchants. Inviting-looking display windows were broken at night and large quantities of fine goods carried away. This work, which went on for several months, was finally stopped by Detective McKeough, who corralled the gang, Johnson, Wise, Muller, Turner, and Wheeler, who went down for terms of from one to six years.

MICHAEL H. MARKS is another of the young men on the Central station force, having been born in New York City in 1860. He first came to Chicago in July, 1878, and six years later was appointed to the police force. He served as patrolman at the Cottage Grove station, and three months later was transferred to Harrison street, where he traveled a beat and worked in citizen's clothes till February 1, 1886, when he was detailed on the force at headquarters. He has, on many occasions, shown the possession of detective ability of a high order, but is too modest to have anything said about it.

WILLIAM B. THORPE is one of the most valuable men attached to the detective force. He is a Canadian by birth, having been born at Hamilton, Ont., in 1842. When he was 20 years old he came to Chicago, and, after following his trade for a number of years, applied for and obtained an appointment on the police force. He served in uniform at the West Lake and old West Madison street stations, and at the latter station while working in citizen's clothes did his first "fly" duty. Since 1885 he has made a specialty of the pawnshop work, but this has not prevented him from rendering excellent service outside of his specialty. Through his efforts, aided by his then partner, P. B. Tierney, Thorpe was the means of breaking up the Proctor gang of safe-blowers. Proctor and his partners, Johnny Murry, Manion the "Scout," Tom Fitzpatrick, Jack Edwards and Jim Donavan, had done a good deal of clever safe-blowing during 1885. Over twenty establishments had been visited and the plunder secured had amounted up into the thousands. Thorpe and Tierney spotted Manion in a restaurant with a couple of partners, at No. 258 State street, and Manion, who was a desperate fellow, had a revolver up his sleeve ready for use. The officers stepped in with their hands in their overcoat pockets. Each held in his right hand a revolver with which he covered one of the party. The crooks, appreciating the situation, made no resistance, and were soon under lock and key. With Manion as a starter, it did not take long to corral the whole gang. Detectives James Bonfield and Reinhold Meyer were assigned on the case with them and aided in bringing the matter to a successful issue. Every one of the gang was captured, the tools and a lot of dynamite recovered from an ash heap in the rear of No. 130 Brown street, and so complete a case made against them that every one went down for a term of years. Their stealings in two months exceeded $30,000.

SAMUEL A. ELLIS, detailed on the pawnshops, is one of the oldest officers in the department. He was born in London, England, in 1834, and came to this country when but five years old. His parents came to Chicago, and here he lived until he was man grown, when he joined the police force. This was in 1856, and Chicago then was not much of a city. John M. Donnelly was city marshal and the force did not consist of more than a dozen men. Ellis was assigned to the old Market Hall where Mike Finucane was in charge, and there he remained till the breaking out of the war, when he responded to the call of the country he had learned to love. He enlisted in the Eighty-ninth Illinois Infantry, Co. C, of which he was made lieutenant, and with it he remained till wounded at Stone. River, when he returned to Chicago. For two years he was laid up, but as soon as he got well he returned to the police force, and was assigned to the old Huron street station, where he remained in charge until the time of the great fire. After that calamity he was transferred to the City Hall, where he served as a detective under Thomas Moore. This position he held until 1873, when Elmer Washburn made him chief of detectives. A little later he was made a captain and given charge of the second precinct, where he had command of the police during the memorable lumber riots of 1875. In 1876 he was returned to the Central station with the rank of detective, and there he remained till transferred to the West Madison street station as desk sergeant in 1880. In 1886 he was transferred to the Central station again, and in 1887 was looking after the pawnshops. As patrolman, commanding officer and detective, Officer Ellis has had some strange experiences and done some clever work. He did a great deal of important work on the Gumbleton mystery for which others got the credit. This was the case where a stranger named Gumbleton was found dead on the lake shore, where he had been murdered. His murderer was supposed to be a companion with whom he had been seen. This man's name, it was learned, was Zeigenmeyer, and he had disappeared after the crime. He was located in Germany, arrested, extradited, brought home, tried, convicted and sentenced to the penitentiary, where he died afterward. In the stories of the work on the case that have appeared since, Officer Ellis received but a small share of the credit that really belonged to him. His arrest of the clever forger, Livingstone, who made two attempts to kill the officer after his capture, won him a wide reputation. Commodore Vanderbilt, whose name Livingstone had forged for $75,000, sent Ellis an annual pass over his lines, and the bank from which the money had been obtained sent him a check. These are only two of the hundreds of cases that have made "Sam" Ellis one of the best known officers in the West.

ANDREW ROHAN first saw the light in the little town of White Gate, county Galway, Ireland, and when nineteen years of age came to this country and Chicago. March 27, 1874, he joined the police force, serving as a patrolman until November 18, 1882, when, in recognition of his excellent services in running down the murderer of Officer John Huebner, of the West Chicago avenue station, he was appointed on the detective department. This was one of the mysterious crimes of the day, and for a long time it seemed that it would never be cleared up. But Detective Rohan, assisted by Officer John Stift, ran the murderer down. The man was James Tracy, and so complete was the chain of evidence against him that he was convicted and paid the penalty on the gallows, September 15, 1882. In connection with Detective Reinhold Meyer he spotted and arrested the murderer, Luke Phipps, who killed his wife on a ferry boat running between Detroit and Windsor. He had been arrested, and escaped from jail, going to Roseland, Ill., where he opened a billiard hall. There he was arrested and turned over to the Canadian authorities, by whom he was hung. Detective Rohan rendered valuable service in the solving of the mystery surrounding the murder of Phillipo Caruso, the Italian, for whose killing three men were executed. Charles Mitchell, a colored murderer, was arrested by Detective Rohan and turned over to the Louisville authorities. The noted Page gang of robbers, whose depredations were the talk of the day, was broken up and its members convicted through the efforts of Detective Rohan. Frank Boyle, Harry Bennett and John Valentine were sent to the penitentiary for terms ranging from eight to seventeen years. Of cases of lesser importance he has handled as many as usually fall to men in his position, and success has almost invariably attended his efforts.

REINHOLD MEYER is a Chicago boy, having been born in this city September 10, 1859. He was appointed to the police force June 1, 1882, and assigned to travel a beat in the Harrison street district. There he remained till October 1, 1883, when the aptitude he had shown at detective work caused the authorities to transfer him to the Central station, with which force he has been since connected. Most of the time he was associated with Detective Rohan, and with him shared the credit of locating and arresting Luke Phipps, the Canadian murderer Though his efforts the Thomas Dowd gang of postoffice burglars, who bound and gagged the postmaster at Mt. Forest, Ill., and stole all of value about the place, was broken up and its members arrested. They were sent to Joliet for long stretches. He was associated with Detectives Thorpe, Tierney and Bonfield in the breaking up of the Procter gang of safe-blowers, his share of the work being a clever demonstration of what a good detective can do.

JAMES H. BONFIELD is, probably, better known to the public than almost any other man on the detective force—at least by name. His prominence in the anarchist trials, as an assistant to Messrs. Grinnell and Furthmann, accounts for this. He is a younger brother of Inspector John Bonfield, and was born at Buffalo, N. Y., December 25, 1842, and he came to Chicago, with his parents, when a baby. As a young man, he was deputy South Town assessor, and from 1877 to 1879 was a bailiff in the Criminal Court, under Sheriffs Agnew and Kern. In 1879 he was made an assistant jailer under Sheriff Hoffman, and in 1881 was appointed to the detective department, and assigned to the Twenty-second street station. For failing to work for McGarigle when he ran for sheriff, Officer Bonfield was reduced to the rank of patrolman, and made to travel a beat for seven months. Austin Doyle restored him to the rank of detective, and transferred him to the Central station in 1882. Perhaps the best work he has done was in the Caruso murder case, upon which he was engaged with his partner, Officer John McDonald. Phillipo Caruso, a young fruit vendor, was murdered in his room, at No. 96 Tilden avenue, in the midst of an Italian settlement, his body forced into a trunk, and shipped away to Pittsburg. Here it was discovered, and the only clew upon which the officer had to work was a money order bearing the names of Phillipo Caruso and another Italian, and which had been issued at the Chicago postoffice. With this as a starter,

Bonfield and his partner set to work. They found the second Italian, whose name was on the order, and he explained that Caruso had got him to forward some money to the old country, just as others of his countrymen had done. From him they learned the address where Caruso had lived, and the house was watched. A letter was intercepted from one Gelardi, who, it appeared, had started for Italy *via* New York, and Inspector Byrnes was telegraphed to look out for him. As the baggageman (Reardon) who had handled the trunk could identify the man who had checked the trunk, Detective Bonfield took him with him, and started for New York. When he got there, he found that Gelardi had been arrested, and the prisoner was picked out of a party of prisoners by Reardon. With his prisoner, Bonfield returned to Chicago. Then No. 96 Tilden avenue was pulled, and all of the occupants locked up. Among them was an old man named Bovo, who, after a day or two in the lock-up, was prevailed upon to make a statement, from which it appeared that there had been a regular conspiracy to kill Caruso. Gelardi, with two companions—Sylvestri and Azari—were the conspirators. They prepared a rope, and, one morning, while Caruso sat in a chair, expecting that he was to be shaved by one of them, the rope was thrown about his neck, and he was strangled. Then they took what money he had, and shipped the body away. The murder was committed in Bovo's presence, but he was afraid they would kill him if he informed. One of the prisoners confirmed Bovo's story, and, with very little more work, so complete a chain of evidence was forged that all three of the principals were executed for the crime. Officer Bonfield arrested Spies and Schwab, the anarchists, in the raid on the *Arbeiter Zeitung* office, and made numerous other arrests in the case He was the officer who worked up the cases against the burglars, "Boody" Mason and "Bat" Shea, who had been cleaning out houses all over the West Division. The result was the arrest of fourteen people—pawnbrokers, middlemen, and so on—and the recovery of $6,000 worth of stuff. Of the fourteen arrested, eleven went to the penitentiary—three for twenty and one for fifteen years; two (the pawnbrokers) jumped to Canada, and one was acquitted. Officer Bonfield is a veteran soldier, having enlisted in Troop "B" of McClellan's Dragoons in October of 1861, and acted as body-guard to "Little Mac" till he was relieved of command. At Williamsburg, after the evacuation of Yorktown, while riding alongside the Prince de Joinville, who was on McClellan's staff, Bonfield was shot in the mouth by a glancing bullet, losing a part of his jaw and several teeth. He was in the second Bull Run, Gettysburg, and Fredericksburg, and afterward went up the Red River with Banks. At Bayou Lafouche, while scouting, in 1863, he was captured, with some other men of his regiment, by Captain Farrell, of a Louisiana regiment. They were being closely pressed by the Federals, and

Farrell ordered Bonfield, who was riding a splendid animal, to change with him, as his mount was a badly blown pony. They had taken Bonfield's carbine away from him, but had overlooked his revolver. Farrell and he had dropped a little behind the body of his command, and while pretending to be willing to comply with the captain's order, shot his captor dead, turned his horse, and in half an hour was within the Union lines, having been a prisoner about two hours. His carbine was recaptured by Captain Hasbroucke Davis, who had it engraved with the dates of capture and recapture, and presented it to Officer Bonfield, whose home it now adorns.

WILLIAM A. HARTMAN is a native of Canton, O., where he was born March 31, 1856. He came to Chicago when two years old, and in 1877 was appointed on the police force and assigned to Deering street station. The railroad riots of that year occurred while he was putting in his time and those sixty days were marked by some very lively experiences. The new policeman was shot at, and became mixed up in numerous rows with gangs of toughs bent on mischief during the excitement. Officer Hartman resigned after the riots were over and went West. In 1884 he returned to Chicago and was appointed with the three hundred men put on in December of that year. He was assigned to the Cottage Grove station where he remained till transferred to the Central July 8, 1887. A curious case in which Officer Hartman was interested is worth recording. One night while traveling a beat a resident of the neighborhood complained to him that his house had been entered by thieves and a great deal of valuable stuff taken. He had no idea who the crooks were. Hartman said he would report it and started toward the patrol box to telephone to the station. Just as he approached the box a Cottage Grove avenue car rolled by and standing on the step, as if ready to alight, were two negroes, one of whom had a big bundle in his arms. When they saw the officer they drew back into the car. This aroused Hartman's suspicions, but the car was too far gone for him to catch it. He noted the number, and then stepping into the patrol box telephoned to the station for the sergeant to board car No. 182 and see what the negroes had in the bundle. The car had just reached the station when the message was received, and the sergeant hopped aboard, collared the negroes and took them into the station, where it was found that they were loaded with stolen goods, among them the things of which the gentleman had notified Officer Hartman. They went to the penitentiary for ten and two years each.

WILLIAM H. JONES is a native of England, where he was born Sept. 23, 1848. He came to Chicago in May, 1866, and for a short time followed his trade as machinist. After the great fire he was appointed to the police force and assigned to the Twenty-second street station. He traveled a beat for four years and then was put into citizen's clothes and assigned to special duty. While on this he was unfortunate enough to kill a notorious character, "Kid" O'Brien, and thirteen months afterward O'Brien's friends succeeded in getting the officer removed from the force. It was only for five months, however, and in 1879 he was reappointed and placed at Deering street station. Here he worked in citizen's clothes with Officer Enright, and in the three years he was there he and Enright arrested and sent to the penitentiary more men than had been sent down by all the other men in the station combined since the station was opened. Among other cases that they worked up successfully, although others got much of the credit, was the robbery of the rolling mills office at the corner of Archer and Ashland avenues. Two brothers, named Cavanaugh, and Alexander McKay, an expert safe-blower, went to the penitentiary for this job, and nearly all the $11,000 that was taken was recovered. He was detailed on the force at the Central station in 1884.

JAMES T. O'DONNELL was born in Chicago March 23, 1860. In December, 1884, he was appointed to the police force, and assigned to the East Chicago avenue station, where he traveled a beat but four months before he demonstrated that he could do excellent work in citizen's clothes. He spent two months working on the Kleidzic murder mystery with Officer Lowenstein, and together they secured the bulk of the evidence upon which the murderer Mulkowsky was hanged. The victim of the case was the wife of a poor laborer named Kleidzic. The little home was invaded one day by a stranger, who, without a word of warning, struck her dead as she was at work at her household duties. With her died her unborn child. The little home was rifled of a small sum of money and a number of pieces of jewelry which had been given to Mrs. Kleidzic by her parents and friends in the old country. The case was a very blind one for the police, for no one had been seen to enter the house, and the people who lived downstairs under them had heard no unusual noise. But a man had asked some questions about the house and inmates a few days before, and the search began for this man. Capt. Schaack, in whose district the murder had occurred, took an active interest in the affair and pushed it in every possible way. All the men he could spare were detailed upon it, but it fell to the lot of Officer O'Donnell and his partner to find the jewelry that had been stolen and which had been given away by the murderer, Frank Mulkowsky. His arrest followed, and then conviction on the strongest case of circumstantial evidence ever taken into court, and the extreme penalty of the law was imposed. Officer O'Donnell also did excellent work in unearthing the conspiracy in the anarchist cases. He was detailed on the force at the Central Aug. 15, 1887.

HENRY PALMER is one of the most valuable men on the detective force. He was born in New York City Sept. 21, 1836, and moved West in 1849. He first went to Milwaukee, and came to Chicago in 1853. From 1877 to 1880 he was in charge of the detective department of the Milwaukee & St. Paul Railway Company in Chicago, and in 1880 was attached to the city detective force at the old Rookery. He has made a specialty of pawnshop work, and through him there were convicted and sent to the penitentiary two notorious pawnbrokers—something that had never been done until he accomplished it. One of them was the notorious "Original" Andrews, who went down for eight years for receiving stolen property. He had staked an ex-convict named Billy Murray and then picked out places for him to "work." Murray, being an expert "pennyweighter," or jewelry thief, was able to bring Mr. Andrews a great deal of plunder, but Palmer nipped him one day stealing diamonds at Giles Bros. Murray "gave away" Andrews, and they both went to the penitentiary. Emanuel Isaacs was another "fence" who was sent down, and he went only after he had taken his case to the Supreme Court. One of the most interesting cases with which Officer Palmer was connected was that of Steele and Carson, the burglars. They had been working all over the West Side and were unknown to the police. Palmer picked up Carson one day by chance, and, suspecting from his description that he was one of the men wanted, he was put in the "sweat box." Here he remained for two days, but finally "squealed" on his partner, whose name he said was Steele, and who lived on Fifth avenue near Polk street. It was no use going after him, Palmer was told, because Steele's wife always came to the door, and the man was off at the slightest warning. Palmer thereupon had Carson write a letter at his dictation and strolled down to Mr. Steele's home. Mrs. Steele came to the door. No, her husband was not at home, she said; he was at work. Mr. Palmer was very sorry. He was a lawyer named King, and he had come from a young man named Carson who was in a little trouble, and had a note for Mr. Steele. Mrs. Steele was interested. If he'd come in she would see if she could find her husband. Steele turned up within two minutes, all of a flutter. Palmer explained that Carson was arrested for carrying concealed weapons, and that they must get him out and away before the police could "get onto" him. If Steele had the money they could go around to the station and deposit $25, and then Carson could "skip." Steele said he could raise the money, but he didn't want to go to the station. He had heard that Palmer, the pawnshop man, had a description of him, and he feared arrest. Palmer told him there would be no one at the station then, for it was about noon. Steele finally agreed to go, but before he did so he shaved off a heavy moustache and covered his fair face with a preparation that turned him as brown as a berry. Then, with a slouch hat on the back of his head, he looked as perfect a farm-hand as ever traveled behind a plow. They started for the station. Palmer had Officer Tierney "planted" in a neighboring alley and had told him to arrest Steele as they were passing by. But Steele's appearance was so totally different from Carson's description that Tierney failed to recognize him. He followed along over to the station, however, and got the tip from Palmer that this was the man. He was very much surprised, but not half so much as Steele when the officer tapped him on the shoulder and told him to consider himself under arrest. He was obliged to admire Palmer's work in spite of the fact that he was the victim, and shook hands with the officer on the strength of it. About $6,000 worth of stuff was recovered, and the men went down to Joliet, Steele for five and Carson for three years.

FREEMAN STEELE is the youngest officer at the Central station. He was born January 22, 1864, and is the eldest son of Lieutenant Edward Steele. He came to Chicago with his parents and entered the force as a patrolman, under his father, at the West Chicago avenue station, September 11, 1885. June 9, 1887, he was transferred to the Central station. He is a young man of great promise. He proved the possession of unlimited courage in a struggle with a desperado named "Tommy" Smith in the West Chicago avenue district. Young Steele and his partner, Officer Loftus, caught Smith as he was coming out of a house, and the desperado at once drew his revolver and tried to put an end to the younger man. Loftus grabbed the sleeve of the right arm and pushed the weapon to one side, whereupon Smith so twisted the pistol that he had a drop on Loftus. Just as he pulled the trigger, Steele thrust his finger in between the hammer and the cartridge, and before their man could make another move they had him overpowered. He was a member of Lieutenant Quinn's company at the Haymarket riot, and was shot in the side. The ball followed a rib around to the spine, tearing the flesh loose from the bone, and it was four months before he was able to get out again.

WILLIAM STEWART is a native of Pennsylvania, and was born January 9, 1842. He came to Chicago in 1857, and in 1872 was appointed to the police force. For five years he served at the Harrison street station, and was then transferred to the Central, where he remained till 1879, when he resigned. He was reappointed in May, 1887. He worked with Lieutenant (then detective) Steele on the "Clipper" Flynn-Mahoney robbery case, where the two young fellows were neatly trapped and sent to the penitentiary, where they could do no harm. He arrested Crawford, for the murder of old man Shandley, and sent him to the penitentiary for seventeen years. Stewart is one of the old reliables on the department, and has handled hundreds of good cases in his time.

DENNIS SIMMONS is a native of Queens county, Ireland, where he was born September 22, 1832. He came to America with his parents while a boy, and after a few years in Connecticut, came to Chicago. March 7, 1861, Dennis was appointed to the police force— a force which was at that time a very small one. He was on duty as patrolman at the old West Market hall for a short time, and then was transferred to the old Chicago & Alton depot, where he was on duty four years. When the day squad was organized under Officer William McAuley, Officer Simmons was one of the first men appointed to it. He held a crossing for five years, and then was made a detective and assigned to headquarters in the old west wing of the court house. Since 1882, Detective Simmons has been detailed especially on the banks. His familiarity with bank sneaks renders this position an appropriate one. In his day he has handled some of the most important cases that have been entrusted to the force at the Central station. The Reid and Pierson gang of burglars was broken up by him. The story is an interesting one. Pierson had gone up to St. Paul to lay out a plan for a little safe-blowing expedition. While there he stepped into a dry goods store to buy a paper collar, and was at once struck by the favorable location of the place for a burglary, and he accordingly telegraphed to his partner in Chicago, a fellow named Reid, to join him. Together they got into the place and selected the choicest silks and satins in stock, carrying away with them about $15,000 worth of property. This they put into a Saratoga trunk, got into a skiff, and floated down as far as Winona, where they took the next train for Chicago. The Chicago police were notified, and Detective Simmons, among others, went to work on the case. At the Milwaukee & St. Paul depot he found an old expressman who remembered a couple of "traveling men" with a heavy trunk—so heavy that in handling it he had got a "crick" in his back. They had given him five dollars, telling him they would do their own driving, and would return his wagon within a very little time. He let them have it, but followed them to see where they went, and this information he imparted to the officer. The men were arrested in their room at the corner of Jackson and Desplaines street; and were taken back to St. Paul, where they got four years each. The property was recovered. Another case ante-dating the Reid-Pierson matter was that of the Landgraf-Mott gang of "kid" burglars, that worked so successfully in Chicago in 1873–4. One night they went into the lace store of a man named Mendelson, on Washington street opposite the old Field & Leiter establishment, and took out $18,000 worth of the finest kinds of laces. Landgraf and Mott had two partners, Corley and Hermann, and all of them were under eighteen years of age. By the hardest kind of detective work, it was developed that the thieves were probably these boys, and they were finally located and arrested. In addition to most of the Mendelson plunder, the officers found fine cutlery and stationery that had been stolen from other places. Altogether $12,000 worth of property was recovered. All the prisoners were too young to go to the penitentiary, and were given eighteen months each in the house of correction.

JAMES WILEY was born in Syracuse, N. Y., February 14, 1844. He came to Chicago in 1857, and was appointed to the police force September 28, 1873. He served first at the West Chicago avenue station, where he traveled in uniform, and he was afterward transferred to the Harrison street station, where he was promoted to the rank of detective, after having traveled a beat for ten days. He has been at the Central since, and has done his share of the good work credited to the Chicago detective force. Among others, he worked in the case of the notorious Harry Myers, alias "Muldoon," a desperado who had robbed a farmer named Fairbanks, near Wheaton, Ill. Myers was given fourteen years.

STEPHEN B. WOOD was born at Binghampton, Ill., April 12, 1855. He went to Milwaukee when a boy and for twenty years was in the employ of the St. Paul road in various capacities. He started in as a news agent in 1867, was made a train hand in 1870, and in 1876 was attached to the police department of the road. In 1880 he left the company for ten months, during which he was in the employ of the city of Milwaukee, in charge of the detective department. When Detective Palmer left the position of chief of the railroad detective force at Chicago, Officer Wood was transferred to Chicago and put in charge. From 1881 to 1887, when he became attached to the city detective department, Detective Wood made his name a terror to the men who make a specialty of "working" railway trains. He knew every confidence operator who worked in the West, and the moment he showed up on a Milwaukee & St. Paul train that moment he was in danger. He made it so dangerous for these fellows, in fact, that they let the road entirely alone. Wood had eighty men under him, and he kept them all busy. O'Donnell, the Irishman, who afterward killed Cary, the informer, was on his way from Montana to Philadelphia, en route to Ireland, in 1883, when he dropped $2,500 to Snell, Allen, and Devine, a trio of three-card monte sharks. The robbery occurred at Red Wing, and Detective Wood got the thieves when they reached LaCrosse. They spent eight months in jail and then "squared" it with O'Donnell who, having got his money, left the country, and there could be no prosecution. They fought shy of the Milwaukee & St. Paul after that, however. Among other noted operators who have learned to dislike this young officer, are "Tommy" O'Brien, Traylor, "Doc" Baggs, "Ed" Hayes, "Jim" Tripp, Fred Olley, George Post, "Rebel" George Knowlton, and a score of others equally as accomplished in the way of "skinning suckers." After Officer Wood had cleared the road of these characters, he spent the last two years with the company looking up litigation cases. He is a valuable man on the city force.

WILLIAM BOYD is a native of New York City, where he was born August 6, 1840. When 14 years of age he came to Chicago, and in October, 1874, joined the department. He was first assigned to the Hinman street station when it was opened and traveled a beat there for three years. He was then transferred to the Union street station where he remained as patrolman till the patrol wagon was put in service, when he was assigned to drive it. This position he filled until 1884, when he was transferred to the Central station detective force and made a partner of James Morgan, with a specialty of looking after horse thieves and their work. In this branch of the service he has been very valuable to the department.

LOUIS HAAS was born in Chicago in 1844 and was appointed to the police force in 1881, being made a member of the detective force after a short time traveling a beat. He has handled a great many cases during the time he has been with the department, and numbers of tough people are in Joliet as a result of his good work.

WILLIAM E. TURNER is a native of Philadelphia, where he was born in 1839. He came to Chicago in 1869, and entered the force April 21, 1885. His position is a clerical one, as he looks after the records of the department with which he is connected.

WILLIAM F. SMITH is a colored detective who has been connected with the department since July 11, 1882, when he was assigned to special duty at the Desplaines street station. He was born in Western Ohio June 6, 1856. He came to Chicago directly after the great fire, and after he had joined the department quickly showed that he was a good man. He was accordingly transferred to the Harrison street station in November of the year he was appointed, and has been connected from that time as a regular member of the detective force. During the latter part of 1885 and the early months of 1886 he sent thirty-five criminals to the penitentiary. He was interested in the capture of Major, the colored diamond thief of Washington, wherein several thousand dollars worth of diamonds were recovered. Of the thirty-five men he sent down in the short space mentioned, six were for twenty years under the Habitual Criminal's Act.

HORACE M. ELLIOTT is one of the veteran detectives of the force, and ranks very high as a clever man in his business. He was born in New Hampshire May 24, 1841, and in 1859 came to Chicago. After an attempt to "reach Pike's Peak or bust," which resulted in a clear case of "bust," he took up his residence in Chicago and turned his attention to private detective work for railways, and in 1861 was appointed to the detective department under C. P. Bradley, at the old court house. When Col. Hickey was made chief of police, Elliott resigned, and was off the force for two years, but when Seavey came in he was reappointed at the Twenty-second street station, where he put in sixty days in uniform. In 1878, he was transferred to the Harrison street station, where he served as a detective until he was transferred to the Central, under Simon O'Donnell, in 1879. One of the earliest and most important cases that Officer Elliott handled was that of the forger J. B. Cross, whose cleverness with a pen caused no end of trouble through the Western part of the United States early in 1870. He made a specialty of checks, and was so clever an imitator of peculiar writing, that in many instances the business man whose name was signed could not tell whether he wrote it or not. Elliott followed the young man up, arrested him, and sent him down for six years. His partner, a man named Steele, was also captured and sent to the penitentiary for thirteen years. Officer Elliott, with Officer Wiley, convicted the notorious desperado, Harry Myers, alias "Muldoon," to fourteen years for the Fairbank robbery. Wilson, the Englishman who scattered a lot of bogus £50 bank of England notes through the West, was run down and located by Detective Elliott. He was arrested and taken to the Desplaines street station, where, after being confined for two days, he bribed a tramp in the cell corridor to unlock his door, and together they escaped. Wilson went to Canada, where he was arrested and sent to the penitentiary for a term of years. Jo Parish, alias "Sealskin Joe," was arrested by Detective Elliott and sent back to New York state, where he was convicted and sent to the prison at Auburn for a number of years. These are only a few of the hundreds of cases Officer Elliott has handled. In addition to the work he has done for the city, he was for a number of months in the employ of the government, in the postoffice department, under Postmaster Ike Cook, and there he did a great deal of good work for Uncle Sam.

BERNARD P. BAER was born at Port Washington, Wis., May 27, 1859. He came to Chicago in 1877, and was appointed to the police department May 3, 1882. He traveled a beat in the East Chicago avenue district for a little over a year, and then was made acting desk sergeant. This place he filled from October, 1883, to April, 1884, when he was transferred to the Central station, and made chief clerk of detective's department, where he remained from April 17, 1884, to Aug. 1, 1885, when he was appointed to the detective department. He was detailed to break up the policy shops which had been running wide open for a number of years, and did his work speedily and well. He has handled a great many cases of importance, among them the following: James Geohegan, burglar; Minnie Daly, the notorious female thief; Dr. Meyer, the Ruscher-Grief shooting case; Harry Roberts, the noted climbing burglar; William Hamilton, the furnished room worker, who was sent to Joliet on fifteen charges of larceny; Thompson Adams, the burglar whom he sent back to Meadville, Pa.; Melina McShane, the female room worker, who was arrested, sent back to Ireland, and afterward to New York, where she was arrested and sent to Sing Sing; George Williams, the hotel thief, arrested at the Palmer House, and the Parkinson-Gray-Thornton gang, which had gotten away with $2,500 worth of diamonds from Mrs. Sherman of Broadhead, Wis. There were hundreds of other cases in which he played a more or less prominent part, but these were the most noted.

PATRICK D. TYRRELL is one of the best known officers in the country, his record while in the secret service, attached to the treasury department, having been an unusually brilliant one. He was born in the city of Dublin, March 13, 1835, and came to this country when he was three years old. His family settled in Buffalo, and there he remained until he was of age, having in the meantime learned the trade of shipwright. In 1869 he made his way west to Chicago, where he began to do some private detective work on patent cases. This sort of work he kept at until after the fire, when he joined the police department, doing some private work for the police board for a time, and finally, at the suggestion of Mancel Talcott, who was then president of the board, he was put on one of the greatest mysteries that ever puzzled the police department. It was known as the Winnetka case, and was the killing of an old Irishman named Higgins, who was found dead one Sunday morning with a bullet hole in his body that plainly showed how he met his death. There was absolutely no clew upon which the officers could work. Several men were working on the case when Detective Tyrrell started in, and within a few weeks landed at the Central station one William Swigart, against whom he made a perfect case of circumstantial evidence, and he was sent down for life. Only a little while afterward he worked to a successful issue the Shotwell bond robbery case. This was where Mrs. Charlotte Shotwell had been robbed of $52,000 in bonds. It was thought at first that the bonds had been taken from her trunk at the Tremont House, but Officer Tyrrell's investigation showed that the work had been done at Detroit. There he found that the bonds, in an express package, had been shipped to an address in New York, and on going there he found and arrested George A. Everett. He was brought to Chicago and held to the grand jury in bonds of $75,000 by Justice Banyon. He was indicted, but the case was never tried, and it was intimated that there was crookedness somewhere in the state's attorney's office at that time. As a city detective, Officer Tyrrell broke up a gang of burglars that had been stealing goods from the Star line of freight cars, and solved the mystery that surrounded the theft of $21,000 from Isaac Mills, a guest at the Tremont house. J. R. Barron was arrested for this and the Star line cases, and was sent down for seven years. In December, 1874, when Elmer Washburn was made chief of the secret service department, Officer Tyrrell was appointed the head of the Chicago force, as an agent of the treasury department. He arrested Rittenhouse, the counterfeiter, and sent him to the penitentiary; broke up Tom Ballard's famous gang; stopped the work and arrested the principals of the Wolsey gang, of Clear Lake, Iowa; but the most famous counterfeiting case he handled was that of the Driggs and Ben Boyd gang. These people had been working in the West, and had flooded the country with some very excellent bills. Washburn told Tyrrell one day in February, 1885, that if he could get onto the Ben Boyd people, and get them "dead to rights," that he would break the back-bone of counterfeiting in the United States. Tyrrell devoted himself to that one matter for nearly a year, and at the end of that time had Driggs, Boyd, and seven others more or less mixed up in the shoving of the queer, $132,800 in counterfeit money, seventeen sets of plates, which included fourteen different kinds of five dollar bills on banks in Illinois, their presses, and everything else pertaining to the business. Driggs got fifteen years and a fine of $5,000, and Boyd ten years, and the others shorter terms in the penitentiary. From the Tom Ballard gang he got $36,000 in bogus money, and from the Wolsey gang, five sets of plates. Out of the sixteen counterfeiting cases, considered of great importance, which were worked up in the United States by all of its officers, and which are mentioned in the government blue book, Officer Tyrrell is credited with four. He ran the Chicago and St. Louis divisions of the secret service for fifteen months, has had charge of the St. Louis office three times, and Pittsburg once, did a great deal of work in the Lincoln monument plot, and has handled hundreds of minor counterfeiting cases. He resigned from the government office March 13, 1886, and in October, 1887, was assigned to his old place on the detective staff at police headquarters.

MICHAEL WHALEN was born at Spencer, Mass., Aug. 15, 1847, and came to Chicago in 1866. Sept. 16, 1873, he was appointed to the police force, and the first four weeks he put in were at the Hinman street station. Then he was transferred to the East Chicago avenue station, where he traveled a beat until May, 1875, when he was detailed in citizen's clothes, and from that time on he did detective work, sometimes at that station and again at the Central station. He has handled a great many important cases, and for a number of years worked with Detective, now Capt. Schaack. He sent Tom Ellis down for life for the murder of Jake O'Neill, and Luther Ross, a colored steward, for twenty years for the killing of a companion at the Owl Club. He did a great deal of work in the Mulkowsky case, and he also assisted in the conviction of Jacobson for the murder of George Bedell, the North Clark street carpet man. At the time John Keenan was being tried for the murder of a West Side resident named Hensley, he set up an alibi as a defense, and this was successfully broken by Officer Whalen, Keenan going down for life. With Detective Schaack he arrested a crook named Garry, alias Sheppard, and secured what was conceded to be the finest set of burglar's tools ever seen in the West. He was of material assistance to Capt. Schaack in working out the details of the anarchist conspiracy, and he it was who broke in the door to Linng's room, where so much of the dynamite and the loaded bombs were found. In five years of duty in plain clothes, Officer Whalen handled over nine hundred cases. That he does not want for pluck is shown by his conduct in a single case. Harry Bennett and two other burglars entered the residence of Mr. Roseboom, at 107 LaSalle avenue, one night in 1882, and had the man of the house at the point of their revolvers when Officer Whalen showed up on the scene, and, though it was three against one, made so determined a "bluff" with his revolver that he captured the trio, and had the pleasure of seeing them go to the penitentiary.

WILLIAM B. GREEN is one of the colored detectives employed in the city. He is a bright young man. He was born in Lexington, Ky., January 15, 1854, and came to Chicago in 1881. He was appointed to the police force in November, 1886, and assigned to special duty in citizen's clothes at the Harrison street station, but is under the control of the officers commanding the force at the Central station. The cleverest capture that he made was that of the colored thief, Charles Majors, who had been a bell boy in a Washington hotel and had robbed one of the lady boarders of $15,000 worth of diamonds. A large part of the plunder was recovered and Majors was sent back to Washington, where he tried and convicted for his crime.

JOHN REID is a native of County Meath, Ireland, where he was born Aug. 15, 1830. In April of 1862, he came to Chicago, and went from there to Joliet, where he put in nearly a year as guard at the penitentiary. In 1863, he enlisted in the Eleventh Illinois Infantry, Co. K, and served clear through to the close of the war. When mustered out, he returned to Joliet, and for two and a half years was at his old post as guard. Then he came to Chicago to live, and was employed in Crane's foundry till May 8, 1880, when he joined the police department, and was assigned to the Union street station. After the fire he was detailed in citizen's clothes for special duty, and from that time on did detective work. The night of the Haymarket riot he was in uniform and with Lieut. Bowler's company. He was wounded in both legs, in one with a piece of shell, and in the other with a bullet. Oct. 5, 1887, he was transferred to the Central station permanently. He arrested an old Italian, named Pierre, who, in a trifling dispute about a pane of glass, had stabbed to death two men named Reedy and O'Brien. On one of the cases he was sentenced to a life imprisonment, and in the other to be hanged. The death sentence was suspended, and he went to Joliet to serve out his life sentence, but was pardoned, after having served three years and a half.

CHARLES AMSTEIN is a native of Germany where he was born Sept. 22, 1850. He came to Chicago early in the 60's and in 1874 was appointed to the police department and traveled a beat in uniform for six years at the Harrison street station. Then he was transferred to the Central station detail where he has proved himself a careful, reliable officer. He it was who arrested Herbert T. Thiers, the noted Kenosha land swindler, who, after getting hold of over $100,000 of the funds of Kenosha investors, fled the city. Officer Amstein arrested him and received a reward of $500 for the job. "Bob" Stratton, who murdered a woman in a disreputable resort on West Kinzie street and then attempted to conceal himself, was arrested by Officer Amstein. He traced up and brought back from Canada the diamond thief, Joe Harris, and also arrested and sent to the penitentiary for fourteen years the colored murderer, George Smith, who killed a colored companion on Fourth avenue near Polk street. He has assisted in the development of many of the most important cases handled by the detective department, and always with credit.

CHARLES REHM was born at Naperville, Ill., March 15, 1842. He caught the gold fever in 1866, and went to California, where he spent two years, and then came to Chicago, where he settled down. He was appointed to the police force in 1868, and assigned to the Huron street station, where he traveled a beat for four months, and was then made station-keeper, and transferred to the North avenue sub-station, which afterward became the Larrabee street station. After two years there, he was promoted to the rank of sergeant, and sent back to the Huron street station. While there he did some work on the Gumbleton mystery, and went to Germany with Joseph Dixon to bring Ziegenmeyer, the murderer, back to this country. In 1874 Sergeant Rehm was given charge of the day squad, which had been abolished under Washburn, and reorganized it. Then he was made chief of the detective department, and after a year's service there resigned. He was in the sheriff's office under Agnew and Mann, and for a short time filled a position in the postoffice. In 1882 he was reappointed to the police force, and assigned to the Larrabee street station, where he traveled in citizen's clothes, and did detective work with Officer John Stift. He was transferred to the Rookery in·1883, in 1884 was sent to the East Chicago avenue station, and in 1887 was detailed permanently at headquarters.

JOHN STIFT is one of the officers whose steady advancement in the department has been wholly due to merit, few men being able to show as many important cases to their credit as he. His parents were Germans, but were living in Havre, France, when John was born, September 5, 1847. He was the first of sixteen children, twelve of whom still live. When he was a year old, his parents came to America and settled in New York, removing to Chicago two years later. Here the young man grew up, and the year following the fire he was appointed to the police force, being assigned to the East Chicago avenue station, under Captain Gund. His careful attention to the details of his duty attracted the attention of his superiors, and when, in running down the murderer of Officer John Huebner, he demonstrated that he was too valuable to travel a beat, they assigned him to the detective branch of the service, where he has done excellent work. In addition to the Huebner case, he did a large share of the important work that·ended in the hanging of Mulkowsky for the murder of Mrs. Kleidzic, was Captain Schaack's right hand man in unearthing the details of the anarchist conspiracy, and has unraveled many of the lesser mysteries that are turned over to the police for solution.

CHAPTER XX.

THE PATROL SERVICE — PECULIAR ORIGIN OF A SYSTEM NOW ADOPTED
BY EVERY WELL-GOVERNED AMERICAN CITY — AN IDEA PUT INTO
EXECUTION — OPPOSITION OF MANY OF THE MEN — CAPT. BONFIELD
PLACED IN CHARGE — THE DEVICES OF A YOUNG NEWSPAPER MAN
SOLVE A PROBLEM — GROWTH AND SATISFACTORY WORKING OF
THE SYSTEM — ITS APPLICATION TO THE 12TH STREET DISTRICT.

Some years ago, a writer in a New York paper had an
entertaining article on the possibilities of a great crime in
that city.   He pointed out the fact that it would be the
easiest thing in the world for three or four men to clean out
any banking institution in the city in broad daylight.   How
easily it could be done! Two determined men go inside and
make a sudden attack on the cashier and his assistants,
while the other two, with drawn revolvers stand on the sidewalk in front of the place and keep everybody moving.
"Supposing," he asked, "supposing some one carried information to the nearest station, say a quarter of a mile away?
And supposing a number of officers started for the place on
a keen run, what then?   Either the thieves would have
finished their work before the officers arrived, or the policemen when they reached the ground would be so blown by
their long run, that they would be no match for the cool and
desperate men who were awaiting their coming, and the
chances are that the robbers would get away."   That was as
it might have been ten years ago.

Let us suppose that this were attempted to-day in any
large city.   At the first appearance of the desperadoes,
some-one about the place would jump to a small, dial-faced
box against the wall, turn a pointer on the dial to a division

marked "thieves," and pull a little lever on the side of the box. Within a half a minute there would dash up to the door a wagon loaded to the guards with blue-coats, and the

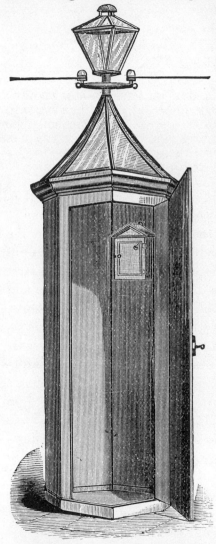

chances are that within two minutes the four bold bank robbers would be on the way to the station or the morgue. This is the result of the introduction of the Police Patrol and Signal Service which had its origin in this city about 1880.

This valuable branch of the Chicago Police Department has been in existence for about six years, and to it is entirely due the fact that Chicago to-day is able to get along with a smaller police force in proportion to its size than any other city in the world. The system was practically the creation of a single night. One day in the summer of 1880, while attending a society picnic, Mr. Harrison, at that time Mayor, and Austin J. Doyle, then Secretary of the Police Department, dropped into a chat, in the course of which it was suggested that it would be a great thing for

PATROL BOX—OPEN.

the department if there could be some means devised whereby the men on beat could communicate with the station at any time they desired to do so. It struck both parties to the conversation that this should be a simple matter, at least in the hands of an electrician. Upon returning to the city that evening Secretary Doyle saw Prof. Barrett, superintendent of the Fire Alarm Telegraph, and detailed to him the talk he had had with the Mayor. It was then suggested that a system somewhat similar to the Fire Alarm Telegraph might work in the Police Department, wagons could be located at cen-

SIGNAL INSIDE BOX—CLOSED.

tral points in the various districts, and that they could respond as the steamers did to an alarm. The Professor thought it over during the night, and the next morning presented for the inspection of the Mayor and Secretary Doyle, a plan which provided for the system as it exists to-day, with the exception of a few minor changes in the electrical features. The plan was approved and the electrical department was set at work on the manufacture of the necessary instruments.

The plan proposed by the Professor was in brief, that there should be scattered through the districts a number of call boxes suitably protected from the weather, and in electrical connection with the station. In each of the boxes there should be in addition to the calling mechanism, a telephone through which the man on beat might talk with the operator who would be at the station. The necessary apparatus at each calling point could be enclosed in a sort of a sentry box, and that could be kept locked, while keys could be distributed to residents in the neighborhood, and a means of calling assistance from the station thus placed within the reach of everybody. It was thought that there should be a wagon drawn by two horses and well manned at the station to respond to the calls from the boxes. It was also suggested that there should be at each station an alarm bell which might be rung in case it was desirable to get information to the men on beat in the shortest possible time, the idea being that the men on hearing the bell would immediately report at the nearest box and there receive the necessary orders. The alarm bell feature of the plan is the only one that was not carried out.

In the course of a few days, rumors of the intended innovation spread through the department, and there was developed among the men as a whole, a most amazing opposition to anything of the kind. One would naturally think that the men would be glad to see a system introduced which should lighten their labors as this was intended to do; but they understood in a general way that it was something that would insure regular reports to the station from the men on beat during the night, and as this meant that there could be no shirking of duty, a great many of the men swore they would do all in their power to make the thing a failure.

This opposition on the part of some of the men lasted till long after the system had been introduced, and was so pronounced as to attract public attention. The matter was taken up in the newspapers and freely discussed, and a number of poems on the subject were published. About the best of these was an anonymous one which appeared in *The Tribune:*

"Say, what is the manin'," says Patrick to Murphy,
" Of all the blue boxes I see on the street,
That's standin' like sentries, but barrin' the sogers
To tramp up an' down in the shnow and the shleet?"

Says Murphy to Patrick, " Thim same is to bother
The boys wid the sthars, and to keep them awake;
An' iv'ry half hour they must give up their freedom
To give the alarm, and their shlumbers to shake.

"And inside there's a box, wid a divil's tail hangin';
Ye jist pull it down, aisy-like, don't you see?
An' it tells to the station yer there at yer duty,
As plain, Paddy, now as I'm spakin' to ye.

" Inside of the box there's a tillyfone waitin';
Ye shpake to an inkstand—the Captain hullos;
And thin, mind yer eye, if ye shpake to the Captain,
Ye'd better braithe aisy, and not be too close.

" Thim tillyfone chaps that McGarigle's usin',
They shmell iv'ry dhrap ye've been tastin' the night,
Git on to yer sthyle, and they see where ye've bin to,
And ain't takin' stiffs, though they be mighty bright.

" O but I'm mighty glad that I'm not on the force now—
I couldn't in honor keep frinds wid thim things.
Karacters is busted, and gone to the divil,
Since lightnin' is doin' sich work for the rings,

" Wid these, sir, the boys can't get up half a shindy
Before the alarm brings the wagon aroun';
An' bedad, sir, they'll gobble the whole of a party
Before the first man's fairly laid on the groun'!

" Ah! onct I was proud of my sthar and my billy!
I walked like a turkey-cock, happy and free;
But now, sir, I wouldn't be under McGarigle;
No, sir, I thank ye—not any for me.

"They say out in Leadville there's freedom in plenty.
Say, Pat, let's go West and grow up wid de noise—
For here, where a street is patrolled by a shanty,
The force is a-gittin' too fly for the boys!"

In addition to this opposition on the part of the men,
there was no money available for the purpose of experiments,
and the immediate success of the idea was far from clear
when it was proposed.   The only thing to be done was to
take a part of the unexpended balance in the Secret Service
fund, and then, by scrimping some of the branches of the
Department, there was found to be available a few thousand
dollars, and they had to do the best they could with that.

From that time on the system grew rapidly, being extended to· all parts of the city as fast as the call boxes and
electric registers for the call stations could be provided.
Now there are a score of wagons in service, and an immense
amount of work is done each year by the officers detailed
for that branch of the service.   Take for instance the last
annual report of the Superintendent of Police, and examine
the record made by the detail, say at the Central station,
covering the district bounded by the river on the north and
west; by the lake on the east, and Van Buren street on the
south:

Reports received from policemen in districts	101,956
Alarms responded to	3,001
Arrests made	2,899
Fires attended	112
Miles traveled	7,172
False alarms	39
Sick and injured persons taken to hospitals	126
Sick and injured persons taken home	77
Sick and injured persons taken to station and cared for.	53
Dead bodies taken to the morgue	46
Dead bodies taken to residence	10
Disturbances suppressed without arrests	140
Insane persons cared for	21
Destitute persons cared for	21
Prisoners taken to county jail	178
Prisoners taken to division police courts	794

Packages of stolen property recovered................. 2
Lost children taken to parents....................... 30
Mad or crippled animals killed...................... 1
Runaway horses overtaken and stopped............... 1
Stolen horses recovered............................... 1
Abandoned children taken to the Foundling's Home.... 6
Persons rescued from drowning...................... 4
Inebriates taken to the Washingtonian Home.......... 6
Destitute persons taken to Home of the Friendless..... 1
Miscellaneous and incidental runs................... 100

In 1881 a radical change was made in the form of the patrol boxes. They were at first constructed in the simplest form possible—of pine, 36x36 inches on the ground and six feet high with a slant roof. While these served their purpose admirably they were anything but ornamental, and for this reason a hexagonal box was adopted which should take the place of a lamp post at the corner where it is located. The top is made of heavy glass so that the lamp may illuminate the interior at night. As will be seen by the cut the complete box is tasteful in form, and rather an ornament to the corner upon which it is placed. The alarm box with its interior arrangement of telephone, etc., is shown. It was devised entirely by Prof. Barrett, and is remarkably compact and strong. The public may only open the outer door of the big box, and all that is necessary to summon the wagon and officers is to pull down the small hook which projects from the side of the small box. This acts on the same principle as the contrivance by which American District Telegraph boys are called, registering upon a narrow band of ribbon at the station an arbitrary signal. Each box having a different signal it is easy to see that there is no difficulty for the operator in locating the box from which the call has been transmitted. In addition to the public boxes on the street corners it was provided in 1881 that private boxes might be set up in any residence or store on payment of $25, and about four hundred of these boxes were set up in various parts of the city.

Inspector Bonfield, then a Lieutenant at the West

Twelfth street station, was called into service to assist in the working out of the details of the system. While Prof. Barrett had provided everything pertaining to the electrical part of the problem, there still remained much to be done. What sort of wagons should be used? How should wagons be manned? Where should they be kept? What system of reports would be the most effective? and so on. It was

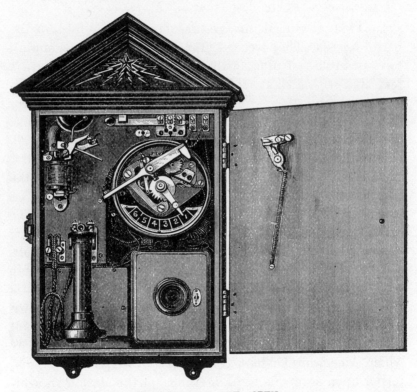

SIGNAL INSIDE BOX—OPEN.

early determined that the system should provide for an ambulance service, but it was desirable to avoid having a wagon and an ambulance in service, and so the question arose: How can we get a wagon that shall serve both as a conveyance for officers to a scene of riot or murder, and at the same time have it available for use as an ambulance in case it should be required? There was not much money available for the purposes of the projectors of the scheme, and whatever they had must be in the way of a wagon so simple that a supply wagon that had been used by the department could be easily converted to answer the purpose. This question was solved by a young newspaper man, John E. Wilkie, at that time a police reporter on the *Times*. He drew plans for a wagon and a simple stretcher arrangement that answered the requirements so well that it was instantly adopted, and this is the one in use by patrol wagons everywhere.

In the meantime Lieut. Bonfield had been busying him-

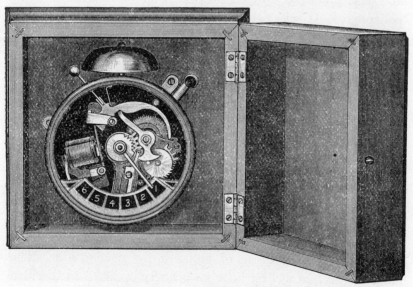

POLICE STATION ALARM PATROL SIGNAL.

self in working out the details of the application of the system, the plans of the quarters where the wagons were to be located, and so on, and the completeness and thoroughness with which this was done is witnessed by the fact that there have been no changes in the system he then outlined. It provided for hourly reports from the men on beat, the posts traveled by the men being so arranged that there should be two or more boxes to be reported from by each officer. These things having been satisfactorily arranged, it became necessary to select a district in which the system might receive its test before it could be generally introduced in the Department. At that time the toughest district in the city was in the second precinct—the West Twelfth street district, embracing that part of the city lying between Harrison street on the north, Eighteenth street on the south, the river on the east and Centre avenue on the west. Within this area there existed the worst elements in the city. Gangs of young hoodlums frequented the corners and held up and beat passing pedestrians "just for the fun of the thing," and even made so bold occasionally as to attack a solitary policeman. It was believed that here was the place to test the new system. If it should succeed here it would be a success anywhere, and so it happened that in the fall of 1880 the wires were strung through the district, boxes set up, an electrical plant consisting of the automatic recording instruments and so on being placed in the station, and a wagon drawn by one horse and manned by a sergeant, a driver and a patrolman established in temporary quarters near the station.

It was an instantaneous success. The citizens of the district who had for years been terrorized by lawless gangs and had been unable to obtain police assistance when it was most wanted, were reassured by finding that they had had at their elbows a means of summoning needed aid. The officers who had at first been so bitterly opposed to the idea discovered that they were saved miles of weary walking. Before the system was introduced a policeman travelling a beat at a point remote from his station was obliged, whenever he made an arrest, to escort his prisoner all the way there; and that, oftener than not, meant a running fight for the mile or more it might be to the station. Sometimes the prisoner, assisted by his friends, managed to overpower the officer and make his escape, and many a tale of awful struggle under these circumstances can be told by the men who travelled in the Twelfth street district before the introduction

of the patrol system.   After it came all this was changed.
The officer who saw any signs of disturbance on his beat
had but to step to the corner and send in a call for the
wagon.   When it arrived the assistance it brought him was
sufficient to enable him to make any arrests demanded by
the circumstances, and the prisoners were escorted to the
station by the wagon.

One might imagine that there would be a large proportion of false alarms where the call boxes were accessible to
the public generally, but this was provided against by a
very simple arrangement.   Keys furnished to citizens were
numbered and registered at the station.   Each box was provided with a trap lock which held fast any key that was used
to open the door.   Each policeman carried a master key
which enabled him to release the citizen's key upon arriving
at the box; so that, if on reaching there, it was found that
there was no trouble, it was a simple matter to release the
key, and by referring to the register at the station to learn
whose key had been used, and if an investigation showed
an abuse of its possession, it was withheld.

CHAPTER XXI.

THE PATROL SERVICE—THE PRACTICAL UTILITY OF THE SYSTEM DEM-
ONSTRATED BY THE CELEBRATED BILL ALLEN CASE—HISTORY OF
THAT SENSATIONAL EPISODE—THE KILLING OF OFFICER CLARENCE
WRIGHT AND WOUNDING OF OFFICER PATRICK MULVIHILL—THE
SEARCH FOR THE DESPERADO—HIS FINAL CAPTURE AND DEATH—
REMARKABLE EXHIBITION OF PUBLIC FEELING—FURTHER PRO-
GRESS OF THE SYSTEM.

One of the most valuable features of the patrol wagon
service is the rapidity which it permits in centralizing a
large number of men.   Each district covered by the service
is separate from all the others, and is complete in itself; but
as all the stations are connected and in communication with
each other it is easy to see that trouble in one of these districts may be instantly reported to all the others, and any
required force thrown in on the scene of the difficulty.   This
was demonstrated for the first time late in 1882.   Bill
Allen, a colored desperado, had killed a colored man, nearly
murdered another, shot and killed Officer Clarence Wright,
who was sent to arrest him in a shanty at the corner of
Washington and Clinton streets, and shot and seriously
wounded Officer Patrick Mulvihill, who tried to capture him
two days later.   Allen had done most of his dreadful work
on the afternoon and evening of Nov. 30.   All day Friday
and Saturday the police searched high and low for him, but
failed to find him.   Sunday, Dec. 3, in the afternoon, Officer
Mulvihill was told that the man he wanted was in the basement of a negro resort on North Halsted Street.   He attempted to enter the house but was shot through the window
by Allen, who had watched his approach.   The Desplaines

Street patrol wagon was called to carry Mulvihill to the station, and word was sent at the same time that Allen was hiding somewhere in the neighborhood.   An order was transmitted to the stations to get all the spare men to that point with all possible speed.   Within ten minutes there were 200 policemen on the ground, and they were so disposed as to entirely surround the locality where he was secreted.   It was known that Allen was armed, and that he was desperate and a good shot.   It was therefore to be expected that when he was found there would be trouble.

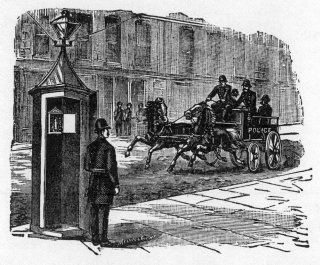

THE SIGNAL ANSWERED.

Reports of the fact that Allen was in hiding had spread all over the city, and it was not long before upwards of 10,000 people armed with all sorts of weapons, from pocket pistols and pitchforks to rifles, were assisting the police in the hunt for this negro desperado.   It was a wild and peculiar scene. One might have expected to see something of the sort in a frontier town, but in a city of half a million or more, it was doubly strange.   The search had proceeded for half an hour before the man was found, and the manner of his discovery and death was graphically detailed at the time by Signal

THE POLICE WAGON IN FULL MOTION.

From an instantaneous photograph, taken in front of Studebaker's Carriage Repository, on Michigan Ave., by the Police Photographer.

Sergeant John Wheeler, of the Desplaines Street patrol.
Said he:

"It was our day to change watch at the Union Street patrol barn, it
being the turn of our squad to go on day duty, and we had been on from
6 o'clock Saturday evening until noon. At 12 o'clock I left the barn
and went over to my boarding-house, on North Union Street, where
I had dinner. Officer Mulvihill boards there, too, and at the close of the
meal as I was passing him, I pulled his hair in a joking way and said something about getting the nigger after dinner, and then went out. I went
from the house over to Murdock's cigar store on Milwaukee avenue,
bought a cigar, stood around a little while, and then walked along Milwaukee avenue to the corner of Hubbard Street, where I saw the wagon
from our station standing at the box while the boys were helping Officer
Mulvihill into the wagon. His face was covered with blood, and when I
asked what the matter was they told me that the nigger had shot him
and run over the viaduct to Green Street. I went west a short distance,
and met a number of policeman who had been sent out to hunt for him.
The boys were all hurrying west, going beyond Green Street, but as I
felt that he wouldn't go very far, I tried to get some of them to stay with
me. I finally got Officers Roach and Stahl, and with them and a young
man named Fred Lang made a search of the cars along Kinzie Street
between Halsted and Green. We didn't find him there, but got a pointer
that he wasn't very far away, and so kept on, confident of striking him
sooner or later. We finally came to this place, No. 182 West Kinzie
Street, and like every other place we came across we started in to search
that. The house faces north. The yard is about ninety feet deep, I
should say, and in the southeast corner of the yard is a coal-shed six or
eight feet in height and about twelve feet long. The entrance to this is
through a door on the north side at the west end. Officers Roach and
Stahl stood at the door outside, and Lang and I went inside. We turned
over some barrels, and nests, and one thing and another, and then Lang,
who was in the southeast corner of the shed, tried the lid of a feed-box
about two feet square, I should think, and jumped back, saying excitedly:
'There's something in there, John, sure.' I didn't think there was anything there, to tell the truth, but I walked over to have a look at it. The
box had a lid on it that was hinged at the back, which was toward the
north. There was a ring in the north end of the lid, and I took hold of
this to raise it up. The lid didn't come, but a strip about four inches
wide broke off, and through this opening I saw the head, shoulders, and
arms of a negro. When I saw him I yelled: 'Here's your nigger; get
some help!' and Roach, Stahl and Lang ran off after more officers.
There was but one way to get out of the place, and that was through the
door, and so I jumped for that, got outside, closed it, and put my left
shoulder against it. I heard Allen get out of the box and come toward
the door, and through a crack I saw him approach, and then he put his
right shoulder to the door and began to push to get out. I yelled for

help, for he had the best footing, and was getting the better of me, and when I couldn't see any one coming I felt that something would have to be done, and that right quick. My revolver, a self-cocking Smith & Wesson, 38-calibre, was in my right-hand coat pocket, and I took it out. Right on a level with my head and just over where Allen stood was a pane of thick blue glass about six inches square. Reaching up I put the gun against that and fired a shot to break it, and then shoving my hand through the hole and pointing the pistol down I fired the remaining four shots very rapidly. The pressure on the door let up then, and after waiting a few seconds I partly opened it just as Officer Reid of the Lake Street district jumped over the back fence and came to where I stood. I had opened the door then two or three feet and we could see the negro leaning up against some barrels just east of the door. He made a threatening move with his hands and Reid shot at him, after which he threw up his hands, said 'I give up,' and within a minute and a half was a dead man. We found a 32-calibre Smith & Wesson revolver fully loaded and about twenty extra cartridges in his pockets. Reid, Roach, Stahl and I then picked him up and carried him through the yard to where the Thirty-fifth Street patrol wagon was standing, loaded him in, and drove him here to the station on the run. Now that it's all over, there's only one thing that puzzles me."

" What is that?"

" Why, that with a loaded gun in his pocket and only one policeman between him and a few minutes' more liberty he didn't shoot me through the'door, as he had ample opportunity of doing. I tell you I consider myself a lucky man."

About 2 o'clock, when the news of the pursuit and shooting of Mulvihill first began to be circulated, an immense crowd gathered about the Desplaines Street station. They were quiet and orderly, and seemed to be mere curiosity-hunters. They laughed, chatted, and made inquiries of the police in a careless way. All of a sudden, at a quarter of 3, there was a terrific shout, "There they come," and a patrol wagon was seen turning the corner. In an instant the mob changed front and showed its teeth. The wagon was surrounded by a struggling mass of humanity, perfectly wild with rage. The body of the negro lay in the bottom of the wagon. The crowd pressed eagerly forward, shouting, "Lynch him," "String him up," "Bring a rope." The rope was soon ready, and the crowd made a determined rush for the wagon. Half a score of officers were on the seats, but they could do nothing. Following in a buggy was Capt.

Bonfield, who quickly appreciated the situation. He stood up and drew his revolver, ordering the men to do the same. They cocked their weapons, but refrained from firing, for the mob by that time was beyond all control. It was impossible to take the body from the wagon, and so a flank movement was decided upon. The wagon was rapidly wheeled and driven into the alley. Before the crowd knew what was up the body was quickly shunted through a window in the rear.

The crowd, thus balked of its prey, became frenzied and

REAR OF WAGON—AMBULANCE STRETCHER.

threatened to tear down the station. Threats and promises were all in vain, and a serious riot seemed inevitable. Chief Doyle mounted the wagon and assured the crowd that the negro was really dead. They hooted and yelled, shouting that the police were concealing the man, and encouraging each other to break in the windows of the station. Meanwhile the body of the dead murderer lay on the stones in the basement, surrounded by a wondering crowd of detectives, officers and reporters. The man was hastily stripped and a cursory examination made of his wounds. One bullet had glanced on his right arm and buried itself below the armpit. Another had pierced the muscles of the arm and buried itself within an inch of the other. Still another bullet had pierced the left muscle and buried itself in a similar position under the left armpit. A fourth bullet struck the negro in the left side just below the short ribs, and would of itself have caused death. The fifth bullet was buried in the left thigh. The mouth was full of blood, and

AMBULANCE ATTACHMENT—COVER WITHDRAWN.

the tongue seemed torn, which gave rise to the belief that he had swallowed still another leaden pellet.

The body was not long left in peace, however, for the crowd outside was growing more and more unruly. To quiet them down, Chief Doyle had the naked body laid on a mattress, supported by ladders, and placed in front of a grated window, from which it could be seen from the alley. In an instant there was a shout of triumph from the crowd, and then a strange scene was enacted. A line was quickly formed, reaching up the alley and across Desplaines Street.

The crowd passed in eager procession and were satisfied by a simple glance at the dull, cold face. The scene from the steps of the station was a most remarkable one. All the afternoon that line moved steadily along, and the officers were busily occupied in keeping it in order. The crowd increased rather than diminished, and until darkness settled down they were still gazing at the dead murderer.

After dark a flaring gas jet at the head of the body brought it out in strong relief, and all night long the line of curious people filed by for a glimpse at the dead. For forty-eight hours his body was on exhibition, and was viewed by thousands. This was one of the most remarkable incidents in the history of the police department.

In December, 1880, when Capt. McGarigle was appointed Chief of Police, he determined that the new system which had proven a success beyond the hopes of the originators should be introduced throughout the department with all possible speed. At that time there were only 502 officers in the department; of that number not over 300 were available for duty as patrolmen proper, so that it was equivalent to one policeman for every 1,680 of population. There was a demand on all sides that the force should be increased by the addition of several hundred men, but the new superintendent took the view that a well manned signal service branch in the department would make it far more effective than 200 new men. It was for this reason that in his annual report covering the year 1880, and looking to the needs of 1881, he said:

"It seems proper for me in this report to make some reference to the police alarm telegraph system, recently introduced in this department, and now in operation and rendering excellent service in the West Twelfth street district. The telegraph is the one thing that thieves and evil-doers dread; for it circumvents all their skill and their cunning. This fact being so well recognized, it becomes an important question as to how it can be still further utilized in aiding the officer in his work. We already have the telegraph connection between cities and between stations and sub-stations but this is not sufficient for police purposes, under all circumstances. With the introduction of the new system of telephone boxes, however, instantaneous communication is established between the station and every patrolman on beat in the district. This is no longer an experiment, but an actual accomplished fact, and as its value for police purposes can hardly be over-estimated, it is hoped that our city council will provide for its general use in the department."

The report then explains the box system now in use in the west division, giving cuts and diagrams of the instruments, telephones, dials and patrol wagon, and then goes on to say:

"I am so impressed with the usefulness and manifold advantages of the system that I thought it proper, and for the best interests of the city, to include in my estimates for the department for this year the probable cost of introducing it, viz., $58,120, exclusive of wire and telephone boxes, which would probably bring the aggregate cost of the outfit up to $100,000. This amount may appear large; but it must be remembered that when once established, there is no further expense to be incurred in connection with the system, beyond the ordinary expense of running it. I feel certain that the lasting benefit in the increased security to life and property which the people will draw from its use, will more than compensate the expense of its introduction and maintenance."

"I presume it is unnecessary for me to remind our honorable city council that the city has outgrown its police force beyond all reasonable proportion. If the use of the police alarm telegraph is provided for, it will probably supply immediate necessities; if not, the police force must soon be largely increased. The fact that our present force is numerically insufficient to discharge the constantly increasing amount of service required, is too well known to call for any argument here. This matter has so often been referred to that all there remains to say now on the subject is the plain statement that the city of Chicago needs, to-day, not less than one thousand policemen. It is difficult to imagine how three hundred and ninety patrolmen, the number at present employed, can reasonably be expected to perform the work that should more appropriately be allotted to the larger number."

The amount asked for by the chief was included in the appropriation bill the following February, and during 1881 work on the system was pushed with such energy that the close of the year saw eight districts under the protection of this branch of service. It was during this year that the necessity was recognized for giving the men in charge of the wagons, some instruction in surgery. The ambulance feature of the system was getting to be generally appreciated and scarcely a day passed without a half dozen calls for the patrol wagons in cases of accident. The men detailed for duty on the wagons were the flower of the force, an unusually intelligent lot of officers, and it was a comparatively easy matter for them to acquire the necessary information. Dr. Henrotin, the Department Surgeon, devoted several hours of each day to classes of the Signal Service men, and in the course of a month, the officers were prepared to handle almost any sort of simple surgical case. Each wagon was equipped with a "chest" which contained bandages, carbolized gauze, one, two or three sorts of stimulants, a tourquinet an elastic bandage to be used to stop the hemorrhage in mangled limbs, two or three varieties of splints and so on. A phamphlet embodying the points made by the doctor in his lectures to the men was printed and circulated among the officers, who were quizzed at intervals by the Doctor. It covered the procedure in case of sunstroke, epilepsy and the Howard method for the resuscitation of drowned persons, as well as points on the treatment of poisoning from narcotics.

418 THE CHICAGO POLICE.

CHAPTER XXII.

THE PATROL SERVICE—CHARACTER OF THE MEN EMPLOYED IN THE
SIGNAL DEPARTMENT — WHY THE BEST OFFICERS ARE USUALLY
SELECTED FOR WAGON DUTY—THE WORK EXACTING IN ITS NATURE—
PRESENT COMPOSITION OF THE FORCE — SOME SPLENDID RECORDS
MADE BY THE MEN—MANY GREAT CRIMINAL CASES IN WHICH THEY
HAVE PARTICIPATED.

The men selected to serve on patrol wagons are not surpassed by any body of officers in this country. They form
the flower of the force. They are the most intelligent and
the most reliable that could be selected from the department. The fact that a man is serving on a patrol wagon is
evidence that his superior officers think well of him; indeed,
ever since the patrol branch of the service was organized,
the men have regarded appointment to it as rather in the
line of promotion. The position of these officers is a peculiar one. The variety of duty they are called upon to perform in the course of a year, demands that they shall be
thoroughly "up" in everything pertaining to police matters.
They have a great many bits of delicate work to do; cases
where some knowledge of law is required. They are called
upon to quell all sorts of disturbances, from a family dispute,
which may be settled by a little good-natured advice, to a
riot of formidable dimensions, where courage and firearms
must be displayed. They are often first in at fires, and must
have their wits about them for emergencies of all sorts.
Men traveling a beat must needs possess some of the attributes of the wagon men, but as the patrol wagon crews are
called upon to act a dozen times a night while the man on
beat is given the opportunity but once in a week or a month,
it follows that the men on the wagons must be an improvement on the ordinary officer on beat.

The electrical features of the patrol system have challenged the admiration of electricians all over the country,
Professor Barrett, the head and front of the working electricians of the West, found, that in carrying out the details
of the system he had outlined in his original plans, his
pathway was anything but an easy one. The field of invention in the way of electrical appliances, such as would be
called into service in arranging a patrol system, was pretty
thoroughly covered by patents, and there was no way he
could do but go to work and devise a combination of instruments that would not infringe on any of the thousands of
patents already in the field, and yet that should excel any
of them. This, after a few weeks of hard work, he succeeded in doing, but while waiting for the issuing of the
necessary papers, he fixed up a temporary arrangement that
answered the purpose for the first year that the system was
in service. He fixed up at the receiving points a number
of the "registers" used by the fire-alarm telegraph. These
were open to but one objection: the record had to be made
rather slowly, and in a system like this, the saving of a few
seconds was a matter of great importance. The receiving
apparatus which he invented, and is now used wherever the
patrol system has been adopted, is the most compact thing
of the kind ever constructed, and works so rapidly that it is
impossible for two boxes on the same line to be pulled, or
the signals so sent in that the record will be mixed. The
great objection to the slow working registers was that it
often happened that two alarms turned in almost simultaneously would be so blended on the register tape, that it was
impossible to tell what signal had been sent in.

In arranging the electrical plant of a district, three loops
of wire are so strung as to cover the points at which it is
desired to locate the boxes. Upon each one of these loops,
from eight to ten call and telephone boxes are connected.
At the station there are three registers, one for each of the
lines. A "running card" or list of the numbers of the

boxes with their location is close at hand.   An operator is constantly on duty.   The number of a box is expressed by a series of dashes separated by spaces.   In registering number 35, for instance, there would be printed on the tape three dashes, then a short space, and then five dashes, thus: — — — — — — — —.   That would indicate that the wagon was wanted at Box No. 35.   The operator, comprehending this, would push an electric button connected with the quarters of the wagon crew.   Pushing the button starts an electric current at work; a weight is dropped, pulling the bolts to the doors of the stalls of the horses; the animals step out to their places and are hitched up; the officer in charge moves to a telephone connecting him with the station, and receives from the operator the location of the box, and they are off.

In case a policeman goes to the box to report to the station, as he is required to do every hour, he moves the pointer on the dial of the call box one space, and then pulls the lever.   The record Box 35 makes in this case is: — — — — — — — — —.   The one additional dash means "telephone" to the operator, and he accordingly moves a switch which connects a telephone at the station with the one in the box.   The officer gives his name, receives any instructions there may be for him, a record is made of his report, and the report sheet is filed with Inspector Bonfield the next day.   By this means it is possible to learn where any particular patrolman was at any specified hour at any date— something that often proves of value in a police department.   In the preparation of plans for the quarters occupied by the men and the wagons, Captain Hubbard, who, at the time the system was being introduced, was a patrolman in the West Twelfth street district, made a great many valuable suggestions.   In fact the quarters for the wagon and the men are still built on his plans.   He introduced a simple and ingenious contrivance for the automatic opening and closing of the big double doors of the houses.   They open when the alarm comes in, and after the wagon has been run out close and lock.

The following is the roster of the patrol service:

FIRST PRECINCT.

CENTRAL STATION DISTRICT.—The quarters of the patrol wagon in this district are at the north end of the Exposition building in a part of what was once the First Cavalry Armory. The men respond to alarms within the district bounded on the north and west by the river, on the east by the lake and on the south by Van Buren street.

MICHAEL MANNING, patrolman, in charge of one of the details; born at Dublin, Ireland, August 17, 1855; came to this country early, and to Chicago, May 10, 1872; in June, 1883, was made a member of the police force, and assigned to the Harrison street station; while there he had a sensational fight with a female maniac on Fourth avenue in which he had his right shoulder broken; was one of the relief squad sent to the scene of the McCormick riots just before the Haymarket horror; April 26, 1887, was detailed in charge of the Central wagon.

DENIS H. HARRINGTON, patrolman; born at Chatham, New Brunswick, February 1, 1846; came to Chicago in 1867, and July 14, 1883, was appointed to the police force; traveled a beat in the Desplaines street district for a time; served at the West North avenue station, and on the Central detail; in October, 1885, was assigned to the patrol service, on the Central wagon; was one of the reserve force sent in to the scene of the Haymarket riot, after the bomb was thrown.

ANCEL D. NORCROSS, patrolman; driver of the Central wagon; is a graduate of the fire department; was born at Fort Miller, N. Y. thirty-nine years ago; came to Chicago immediately after the great fire; was a member of the fire department from 1874 till 1881, serving on engine companies No. 12 and 24; in September, 1881, the Harrison street wagon was put in service, and as an experienced and careful driver he was wanted on this the first two-horse wagon; remained there for two years; in 1883 was sent out to drive the West Lake street wagon, and in 1885 was transferred to the Central; made remarkably fast time with a load of officers from the Harrison street station to the Haymarket, and all through that night was busy hauling the wounded officers to their homes or the hospital.

MICHAEL J. COSTELLO, patrolman, in charge of one of the Central station wagon details, is one of the best known officers in the department; born at Rutland, Kane county, Ill., January 24, 1850; came to Chicago while a lad with his parents, and became a police officer March 12, 1873; as patrolman and detective, served at the Madison (Union) street, and Hinman street stations, and on the Central detail; did much creditable work as a detective at the Madison street station, and made a reputation as a brave and determined officer in many a struggle with the desperadoes of that district; arrested and sent down for 35 years, Tom Welch, the wife murderer, and in 1847 shot "Fat man" Burke in a desperate fight on West Indiana street; had charge of a company of men under Captain Seavey, in the railroad riots, and with them went to the relief of a little squad of officers, who had been cut off from their companies, and surrounded by a maddened mob were being pounded and shot to pieces at Halsted street bridge; was assigned to the Central wagon February 17, 1886.

WILLIAM BUTCHER, patrolman on the Central wagon; born in Toronto, Canada, October 24, 1846; came to Chicago in 1863; August, 1874, was appointed on the force, and sent to the Rawson street Station; afterward was transferred to the Webster and last to the Chicago avenue station; February 17, 1886, was assigned to the Central station wagon.

FITCH A. TAYLOR, patrolman, driving the Central station wagon; born at Pleasant Prairie, Wis., July 1, 1849; first came to this city in January, 1872, and July 18, 1873, was appointed to the police force, and assigned to the West Twelfth street station 'under Sergeant Simon O'Donnell; served there three years, then went to the Union street station; was at the Lake street station for a time, and in 1881, went on the day squad or Central detail; November, 1885, was assigned to the Central wagon; during the railroad riots of 1877, was one of a squad of 29 men which became cut off from the general body of police at the Halsted street bridge, and surrounded by the mob, was almost annihilated before assistance arrived; was shot on this occasion and was seriously injured by missiles thrown by the infuriated mob.

HARRISON STREET DISTRICT.—The patrol wagon at the Armory was placed in service in July, 1881. It was the first wagon built for the service and fully equipped as a patrol wagon, and drawn by two horses. It responds to alarms within the district bounded on the north by Van Buren street, on the east by the lake, on the south by the

Union Railroad tracks, near Sixteenth street, and on the west by the south branch.

THOMAS POWERS, patrolman in charge; born in Chicago, March 25, 1856; was appointed to the police force in 1879, and detailed at the Twenty-second street station, serving two years as a patrolman; was then transferred to the Harrison street station, where he was given charge of one of the details; in this position he has frequently distinguished himself, but never more than in an accident at the Polk street bridge. A carriage load of people had been thrown into the river, an alarm summoned the Harrison street wagon, and Officer Powers was in the nick of time to save one of the women of the party, who was about sinking for the last time; his coolness and judgment at critical times have often proven of value to his companions on the wagon.

WILLIAM GILLARD, patrolman in charge; born in Franklin county, N. Y., April 16, 1847; came to Chicago early in 1856, and was made a member of the department October 8, 1873, being assigned to the Harrison street station, where he has remained ever since; has been in charge of a wagon detail for about two years, though he was assigned to that branch of the service in December, 1882.

JOHN MOORE, patrolman; born at Libertyville, Ill., April 30, 1857; came to Chicago January 1, 1877, and joined the police force in December, 1884, being located at the West Twelfth street station, where he traveled a beat till January 1, 1885, when he was transferred to the Harrison street station and assigned to the wagon June 1, 1887; Pete Campbell a notorious burglar, now serving a term at Joliet, owes his confinement to Officer Moore, who captured him and sent him down.

DANIEL DONAVAN, patrolman; born in Ireland twenty-nine years ago; came to Chicago in 1868, and was appointed to the force September 15, 1884; has served all of the time at the Harrison street station, and, since 1886, on the wagon.

DAVID BARRY, patrolman and driver, is a native of Tipperary, Ireland, where he was born March 19, 1834; came to Chicago in 1868, and in November, 1871, just after the great fire, was made a member of the force; served first in the Union street station, putting in ten years there; in 1881 was transferred to the Central station, in the old Rookery, where he drove the little single-horse wagon that used to run out of there, and in March, 1886, was given a place on the Armory wagon; has been through all the riots since the fire, and has seen much hard service, but was never seriously wounded.

DANIEL DOHNEY, born in Ireland in 1851; came here when he was ten years of age, and joined the police force September 15, 1884; since his appointment he has divided his time between traveling a beat and driving the wagon.

TWENTY-SECOND STREET DISTRICT.—A patrol wagon was placed in service at the Twenty-second street station late in 1881, and responds to alarms within a district one and five-eighths miles in area.

ANDREW BARRETT, patrolman in charge; born in County Cork, Ireland, July 20, 1848; came to this country at the age of five years, reaching Chicago in 1861; was connected with the Western Bank Note Engraving Company for four years and first joined the police force August 20, 1870; served at the West Twelfth street and Armory stations before being assigned to the Twenty-second street station, where he has been since the fire; was the first man appointed to a wagon when the patrol was introduced at the Twenty-second street station; as a patrolman on beat, convicted a number of criminals and served in all the riots except the Haymarket, being in San Francisco on a furlough at the time the bomb was thrown.

JOHN W. DUNNE, patrolman; born in Dublin county, Ireland, August 15, 1846, and came to the United States in 1860; after a few years of farm life in New York and Pennsylvania, came to Chicago; followed his trade in a blast furnace till 1874 when he joined the force, April 2; has been at the Twenty-second street station ever since his appointment, and was assigned to the wagon in 1882; had a narrow escape from death when shot at by Mike Muldoon Madden, and was fearfully assaulted in Bridgeport in the spring of 1875; was in the riots of 1877 and at McCormick's; arrested McLain at Thirtieth and Clark streets, with $2,600 in stolen money in his possession; McLain pleaded guilty and took a year in the penitentiary; traveled as a "fly" in citizen's clothes for several years, and made an excellent record.

THOMAS CULLEN, patrolman and driver; born in Dublin in 1852; came to Chicago when he was sixteen years of age; teamed it, drove a street-car, drifted around the country and finally came back to Chicago, going on the fire insurance patrol as driver in 1872; the following year went into the fire department, where he remained till 1879; drove three years for the American Express Company, and went on the police force in 1882; served at Desplaines street for a few months and then went to the Twenty-second street station where he has remained; went on the wagon as driver in March following his appointment; made a good record as patrolman on beat, and handled his team well in the West Side street-car riot and the trouble at McCormick's.

WILLIAM FLYNN, patrolman in charge, is a Limerick man, born in that county, March 24, 1843; his family came to Chicago in 1852; became connected with the force October 1, 1874; served at the Union street station and at West Twelfth street before going to Twenty-second street; made one of the first crew detailed at the Twelfth street station; was assigned to the Twenty-second street wagon when it went into service; was in the riots of 1877, West Side street-car riot, at McCormick's and the Haymarket, his crew doing noble work caring for and hauling the wounded; has had a number of thrilling experiences in dealing with the toughs of the West Twelfth street district; shot at by Ed. Fitzgerald, in 1877, and shot his assailant in self-defense; Fitzgerald had previously shot Officers McInerney and Kelly, Kelly being in an insane asylum now from the effects of the wound; in 1884, an insane prisoner, named Miller, cut Officer Flynn in twelve places, one cut reaching to the lung, but a strong constitution saved him.

STEPHEN KELLY, patrolman; born in Tipperary county, Ireland, December 24, 1851; came to Chicago with his people in 1865; was on the fire department from 1874 till 1883, serving as driver of Truck No. 4, and Engines Nos. 6, 7 and 23; in 1884, joined the police department; was assigned to the Twenty-second street station and to the wagon in May, 1885; was in the street-car and Haymarket riots.

THOMAS MAHER, patrolman; born at Willow Springs, Ill., June 11, 1849; made Chicago his home in 1863, and joined the force August 26, 1873; served at Union street and Hinman street stations before he was sent to the Twenty-second street station; was among the first assigned to the wagon, and with Officer Flynn was cut by the insane man Miller, in 1884; while at the Union street station, on his way in with a prisoner named Haggerty, was assaulted by a rescuing party, shot twice and fearfully beaten, but he hung to his prisoner and got him to the station; served through all the riots, and in 1884 sent Dunkle, Schultz and Long, counterfeiters, to Joliet for three years, each; they had $1,700 in counterfeit silver certificates at the time of their arrest.

COTTAGE GROVE AVENUE DISTRICT.—The Cottage Grove avenue patrol was established May 22, 1882. The district contains many of the finest residences in the city, extending as it does from Twenty-second street south to the city limits, and from the lake to State street. There are about two square miles in the district, with a population of about 70,000.

MICHAEL OTTO, patrolman in charge; born in Putnam county, Ill., October 8, 1842; came to Chicago at the close of the war; during the Rebellion, served as a private in the Eighteenth Illinois Infantry, Co. G.; was at Pittsburg Landing, Donelson, Missionary Ridge, Lookout Mountain and Johnsonville. At Pittsburg Landing was slightly wounded; joined the police force in 1870, serving first at the Union street station; in 1872, went to the West Twelfth street station, where he stayed till 1880, since when he has served at the Twenty-second and Cottage Grove station, doing duty on the wagons at both stations; has been in his present position for two years; shot Henry Jones a colored desperado who had stabbed a man and was trying to get away in 1873; in 1871, arrested Johnson, the wife murderer, at Polk and Clark street, and had the satisfaction of seeing him swing for it; has sent to the penitentiary a number of men whose combined sentences aggregate fifty-two years.

MORRIS WHEELER, patrolman; born at Naperville, Ill., January 8, 1851; joined the force in December, 1884, and has been at the Cottage Grove station all the time, going on the wagon in July, 1886; has made an excellent record, and participated in all the riots that occurred after he became a policeman.

JAMES E. FARRELL, patrolman; born at Oswego, N. Y., June 4, 1841; came to Chicago in 1844; followed railroading till he joined the force September 18, 1874, serving at the Webster avenue station two months, and then going to Cottage Grove; was assigned to the wagon in June, 1882, and has served upon it continuously since; convicted his share of the men who are now in Joliet, and was in all the riots.

OWEN BOWEN, patrolman in charge; born in County Letram, Ireland, on Christmas, 1842; came to the United States in 1867, and to Chicago shortly afterward; worked at the North Side rolling mills, and for Allan Pinkerton, from 1868 to 1873, and joined the police force under Washburn; served at the old temporary station on Dearborn avenue, and at the East Chicago avenue station when it was built, afterward at the Armory and Cottage Grove, making the last change in 1882; was interested in the work that broke up the Williams gang of body snatchers, Dr. Williams being shot in attempting to get away from the officers; in trying to arrest Mike Madden on a state warrant, in 1878, Bowen met with resistance, and shot him dead; secured admission to the penitentiary for a number of people who were preying on society; has been in all the riots since he joined the force.

PATRICK MAHONEY, patrolman; born in Clare county, Ireland, February 13, 1844; came to this country, and direct to Chicago, in 1863; joined the force ten years afterward; put in eight years at the

Deering street station, and was then transferred to the station with which he is now connected; was assigned to the wagon when it was first placed in service; was stabbed in the breast by James Furlong in 1878, while trying to eject him from a dance hall at Wood street and Archer avenue; Furlong got off with a $25 fine; was shot at by Bob Sheridan, whom he was trying to arrest for the gas house robbery; Mahoney had him but a gang rescued him, and revolvers were freely used; the bullet intended for Mahoney struck Sergeant (now lieutenant) Shepard in the shoulder; served in all the riots.

THOMAS S. BRADY, patrolman; born at Carbondale, Pa., December 25, 1848; came to Chicago in 1852; enlisted in the One Hundred and Fifty-sixth Illinois Infantry when sixteen years of age, and served a year; before his enlistment he was connected with the *Cleveland Leader*, and all the other pressmen but him were called out for three months; Brady who was then but a lad, worked the presses alone for three issues; before coming to Chicago had vainly tried to enlist at half a dozen points, but was refused on account of his youth; finally got in with four sailors who took him to Camp Fry and there he was accepted; joined the police force June 13, 1883, and was sent to Cottage Grove, after putting in sixty days at the Harrison street station; July 20, 1886, was assigned to the wagon; has convicted a number of tough people and saw service during the street-car, McCormick, and Haymarket riots.

THIRTY-FIFTH STREET DISTRICT.—The detail at the Thirty-fifth street station has one of the hardest districts in the city to cover, adjoining the stock yards as it does and being populated in certain parts by an exceedingly tough class of people.

GEORGE D. MEAD, patrolman in charge; born in Lee county, Ill., October 31, 1844; served with the Thirty-fifth Illinois from 1861 to 1865, and at the close of the war came to Chicago, and joined the force April 7, 1873; served at the Harrison street station till 1880, when he was transferred to the Central detail, where he put in three years; in August, 1884, was assigned to the Thirty-fifth street station, and given charge of one of the details; was through the riots of 1877, and was at the Haymarket with his detail.

RICHARD F. CRONIN, patrolman; born in Ulster county, N. Y., February 8, 1849; in 1865, came to Chicago, and in December, 1884, was appointed to the police force, and assigned to the Twenty-second street station; remained there till June, 1887; transferred to the Thirty-fifth street station; was at the Haymarket as a member of Lieutenant Rehm's company, but was not wounded; has handled his share of criminal cases, and is detailed as driver for one of the crews.

DENNIS QUINLAN; born in Ireland July 23, 1845, and came to Chicago in 1869, after five years spent in other parts of the country; October 8, 1873, was appointed to the police force, and put in nine years at the Twenty-second street station; in 1882, was transferred to the Harrison street station, where he remained for two years; then was sent to the Thirty-fifth street station, and August 7, 1887, was assigned to the wagon; was shot by a burglar named Frank Brodie, and was through the riots of 1877, and was at McCormick's; while traveling a beat at the Harrison street station, Officer Quinlan ran against a bartender named John Weaver with whom he was acquainted, and was at once struck with the unusual fineness of his clothes, and the bigness of his watch chain. He told Quinlan that he had just received a check from his aunt in the old country, and was going to leave for Ireland that night. Quinlan invited him down to say good-bye to the captain, and forced him to go along. When they got there they found a Scotchman who exclaimed as they entered the door, "That man has got on my clothes." He had been robbed of his clothing, $186 in cash and a check for 800 pounds sterling. Weaver was sent to Joliet, and died there. Billy Jourdan, who killed a companion in a quarrel, and Fred Ray, who kicked his wife to death, were sent down by Officer Quinlan for fifteen years each.

WILLIAM BOWE; born in Tipperary, Ireland, November 28, 1846; came to the United States in 1859, and in 1860 to Chicago; enlisted in the Thirty-sixth Wisconsin Volunteers, and served for nine months; then came to Chicago, and remained here; joined the force in June, 1883, and served at the Desplaines street station till October of that year, when he was transferred to the Thirty-fifth street station, and was assigned to the wagon; was driving the wagon in response to a call one night in 1886, and at one of the railway crossings was run into by a fast mail train; both horses were killed and the wagon reduced to kindling wood, but no one was injured seriously.

JAMES DONLIN; born in New York City November 14, 1847, and came to Chicago in October, 1860; was appointed to the force June 13, 1883, and assigned to the Harrison street station where he remained till transferred on the Thirty-fifth street station, November 1, 1884; was appointed on the wagon August 1, 1887; was present at the Haymarket as a member of one of the companies sent in after the bomb had been thrown.

MICHAEL McGRATH is a native of Waterford county, Ireland, where he was born December 25, 1854; came to Chicago in 1872, and joined the police force in December, 1884; was assigned to the Thirty-fifth street station, and in March, 1885, was detailed on the wagon; was in the McCormick riots, but was not wounded.

STANTON AVENUE DISTRICT.—The Stanton averue station was opened June 11, 1887, and a wagon placed in service there covering the district lying south of Thirty-first street between the lake and State street.

ANTHONY PAYTON; born August 4, 1862; came to Chicago in 1880; in December, 1884, was appointed to the police force and sent first to the Larrabee street station; was there for about a year and a half, and at West Thirteenth street a year, and a short time at the Cottage Grove avenue station; when Stanton avenue was opened was given charge of one of the details; during the anarchist troubles was at the Haymarket, and at the corner of Division and Halsted streets in April, 1886, was assaulted by a gang of toughs and nearly killed, and it was in the Larrabee street district that he arrested Robert Zimmerling and sent him to the penitentiary for assaulting his wife.

CHRISTIAN HIORTH, patrolman in charge, is a native of Sweden, where he was born October 8, 1844; came to the United States October 8, 1868, coming direct to Chicago; was appointed to the police force in 1877; put in all his time at Cottage Grove avenue station until Stanton avenue was opened, when he was placed in charge of one of the wagons there; has handled a number of good cases, fully his share of those that fall to the patrolman, among others sending the burglar Frank Rush to the penitentiary.

JOHN COSTELLO, patrolman, was born in Ireland May 21, 1851, and coming to this country when an infant, grew up in Chicago; was appointed to the police department in July, 1885, and assigned to the Harrison street station, where he traveled a beat until he was transferred to the Stanton avenue station when it was opened; he is second in rank on the wagon.

JACOB A. WEST; born in Oshkosh, Wis., April 8, 1859; came to Chicago in 1879; August 15, 1885, was appointed to the police force at the Hinman street station, where he served two years, then was transferred to the Stanton avenue station, where he was made driver of the patrol wagon; while at the Hinman street station the McCormick riots occurred, and he was one of the officers who had been sent to the works to see if there was to be any trouble; was standing at the big gate leading to the works when the charge of the mob was made on the workmen as they left the place, and Officer West turned in the alarm for the wagon from Hinman street station; there was a lively time for an hour or so, but he escaped without injury.

FRANK LAWSON, patrolman, was born in McHenry county, Ill., December 11, 1858, and came to Chicago in 1881; January 10, 1887, he was appointed to the police force, and assigned to the Thirty-fifth street station, from which he was transferred to the Stanton avenue station when that was opened; drives one of the details, and is a careful and reliable man.

SECOND PRECINCT.

WEST TWELFTH STREET DISTRICT.—The West Twelfth street police district has probably seen the development of more thieves and thugs than all other parts of this city combined, and to the officers of the West Twelfth street station has fallen the lot of keeping an eye on the rising criminal generation. A few years ago it seemed as if nothing could protect the respectable people of the district against the depredations of the gangs and hoodlums that infested every corner. A single policeman had no terrors for the young desperadoes, and it was as often an officer who was tackled as a belated citizen who was attacked. They shot, slugged and stabbed at the slightest provocation, and generally managed to get away Scot free. It was in this district that the patrol system received its first trial, and the change wrought by the introduction of the blue boxes and the dashing wagons was almost miraculous. The patrol service, more than anything else, brought about the improvement of the district, and has made it a pleasant section to live in.

THOMAS R. SHANLEY, patrolman in charge; born in County Leitrim, Ireland, in 1842; came to this country and Chicago in 1856; became connected with the force September 3, 1874, and served through the thick of the '77 riots; served three years in plain clothes and sent a great many deserving young men to the penitentiary for their misdeeds; was at the scrimmage between the mob and the police at McCormick's, and at the riots at Center avenue and Eighteenth streets; has never been reprimanded.

MICHAEL McMAHON, patrolman; born in County Limerick, Ireland, April 24, 1839, and came to Chicago June 28, 1848; January 23, 1872, joined the police force; served till August, 1883, when he resigned; was reappointed in March, 1885, and in July, 1886, was assigned to the wagon; made an excellent record as a patrolman, and did splendid service in the riots of 1877 at the McCormick works, Eighteenth street and Center avenue and at the Haymarket; has never had charges preferred against him.

JOHN GARA, patrolman and driver; came from Roscommon, Ireland, where he was born in 1845, to Chicago in 1866; joined the force in the spring of 1871; as a patrolman on beat was faithful and efficient, as the records of the criminal court will testify, and when the wagon was placed in service was one of the first to be selected as a driver; has seen service in all the riots since becoming connected with the force.

HENRY CARRAGHER, patrolman in charge; born in County Monahan, Ireland, in 1844, but left Ireland to come to America and Chicago, in 1867; for six years found employment in the wholesale groceries, and in September, 1873, secured a position on the force, being assigned to the West Chicago avenue station; since his appointment has served at the West Madison and Hinman street stations, but for the last ten years has been at the West Twelfth street station; was placed in charge of the wagon November 1, 1886.

MICHAEL KENNEY, patrolman; born in County Clare, Ireland, in 1849; when eight years of age came to the United States, and a year or two afterward came to Chicago; August 9, 1874, was appointed to the force, and assigned to the West Twelfth street station; was attached to the Hinman street station during the riots of 1877, after which returned to the West Twelfth street station, where he has since remained; was appointed to serve on the wagon in 1882.

PATRICK SULLIVAN, patrolman and driver; born in County Clare, Ireland, in 1850, and came to Chicago with his parents in 1852; was a teamster till he joined the police force in January, 1877; served first at Deering street station, and then went to the Twelfth street, where he had served two months; when the wagon was introduced he was made driver; during the two months he traveled post he convicted two men, "Fixy" Fritz, who shot Mrs. O'Brien, and Breckenridge the burglar; was the first driver of a patrol wagon in the city; as a patrolman he served through the riots of 1877, and since going on the wagon has taken part in the disturbances at McCormick's at Eighteenth street and Center avenue, and drove a load of twenty-five men to the Haymarket riot in remarkably short time.

CANALPORT AVENUE DISTRICT.—The patrol wagon of this station covers the area bounded on the north by west Sixteenth street, on the south and east by the rivers, and on the west by Loomis street. It contains about one square mile, and has a population of about 20,000.

FRANK REHM, patrolman in charge; born at Baltimore, Md., May 22, 1857; lived there till he was fifteen years old, when he removed to Chicago and followed the trade of boxmaker till January 13, 1883, when he joined the police force and was assigned to the West Twelfth street station; after serving two months at that station was transferred to the Harrison street station, where he remained till the opening of the Canalport station, when he was transferred and placed in charge of the wagon in September, 1886; was through the McCormick and street-car riots, and has a number of creditable convictions on his record.

JOHN BECVAR, patrolman; born in Austria, May 18, 1859; at four years of age came to this country and worked as a teamster till he joined the force July 18, 1886; was at Twelfth street first, but afterward was sent to the Canalport avenue station, and January 20, 1887, was assigned to the wagon; Officer Becvar was with Officer Walsh when the latter was shot by Geise, and it was Becvar who arrested Geise, and saw that he was sent to the penitentiary for nine years.

JOHN M. SISK, patrolman and driver; born in County Limerick, Ireland, March 8, 1850, and when five years old came to Illinois with his parents; when eleven, came to Chicago and followed the trade of brickmolder till he joined the force in 1883; put in three years at the West Chicago avenue station, and was transferred to Canalport avenue when that station was opened; was attached to the wagon at once; served at the Haymarket and the West Division street-car riots.

JOHN O'DONNELL, patrolman in charge; born in County Clare, Ireland, June 22, 1851, and came to Chicago in 1869; followed his trade as heater in a rolling mill till June, 1883, when he was made a member of the force; was at the Harrison street and Deering street stations till the Canalport avenue one was opened, when he was transferred and placed in charge of the wagon; was in all the riots, great and small, that happened after he had joined the force, and he has a number of toughs stopping at Joliet through his efforts.

PATRICK FARLEY is from County Meath, Ireland, where he was born December 5, 1854; when fifteen years old he came to Chicago, and June 1, 1882, secured a position on the police department; when the Canalport avenue station was opened, was transferred from Hinman street, where he had been on the wagon, and set at driving the one at the new station; was handling the lines the day of the McCormick riot, and ran twelve men in on the scene; they were the first on the ground, and had a hot time of it till reinforcements arrived.

HINMAN STREET DISTRICT.—There is in this district an area of about four and a quarter square miles to be covered by this wagon. The system was introduced in the district July 7, 1883, and the wagon responds to alarms between Sixteenth street and the river, and Loomis street and the city limits.

JOHN MONAGHAN; born in County West Meath, Ireland, February 27, 1852; in 1869 came to Chicago, and in September, 1885, was put on the force; served at the Thirty-fifth and West Thirteenth stations before going to the Canalport avenue station, and was assigned to the wagon in August, 1886; was present at the Haymarket affair, but escaped uninjured.

WILLIAM MAYWORM, patrolman in charge; born at Olpe, Germany, January 5, 1842; came to the United States when three years old, remained at Detroit till sixteen years old, when he came to Chicago; in 1874 was appointed to the police force and assigned to the Union street station, where he served four years, till the Hinman street station was opened, when he was sent there; was assigned to the wagon January 12, 1883; was in all the riots that have occurred since he joined the force, and has stowed a dozen crooks away in Joliet.

PATRICK McCARTHY, patrolman; born in County Clare, Ireland, August 15, 1853; came to Chicago, 1871, and February 2, 1880, was appointed to the police force; served first at the West Twelfth street station, but after three months was sent to Hinman street; has been on the wagon, with the exception of one year, since 1883; was at the McCormick and street-car riots, and has sent two men to the penitentiary for long terms.

MYLES DOLAN; born in County Leitrim, Ireland, June 2, 1853; came to this country and Chicago in 1869; for several years was connected with one of the City Hall departments, and May 9, 1882, was appointed to the police force; was at Desplaines and West Twelfth street for three years before being assigned to Hinman street; was detailed on the wagon in June, 1886; was in the McCormick troubles, and has to his credit the usual number of good police cases.

LAWRENCE BIRMINGHAM, patrolman in charge; born in County Limerick, Ireland, February 28, 1847. When he was nineteen years old, came to Chicago, and January 28, 1882, was appointed to the police force; was assigned to the Hinman street station, and was never transferred; was given charge of the wagon crew in May, 1885, and has shown considerable ability in the discharge of his duties; was through the McCormick and street-car riots.

WILLIAM P. COLEMAN, patrolman; born in County Sligo, Ireland, March 10, 1839; in 1861 struck out for himself, coming to the United States and obtained employment in A. T. Stewart's store, where he remained till 1870, when he moved to Chicago; here he joined the police force in February, 1874, putting in his sixty days at the Deering street station; put in six years at the old Madison street station, and after fifteen months at the Rawson street station, was sent to Hinman, and assigned to the wagon in July, 1886. Two years ago, Officer Coleman tried to arrest "Speckled" Colvin, who had killed a policeman in Ohio, and broken jail. Colvin and several of his companions resisted the officer and then assaulted him, but he managed to get his man to the station. He has been shot at often, but seems to bear a charmed life; was in the riots of '77 and all of importance since that time.

JAMES MERNEN, is a native of County Clare, Ireland, where he was born April 5, 1850; when fourteen years old, came to New York, and finally to Chicago in 1868; in September, 1880, was appointed to the force, and sent to Hinman street after a month at West Twelfth street; was assigned to the wagon when it was put in service in 1883, and was in all the riots that occurred after he joined the force.

DEERING STREET DISTRICT.—The Deering street station patrol wagon was placed in service July 4, 1884, and owing to the heavy roads and the tough character of certain districts there, the men on the detail have anything but a rosy time of it.

JOHN J. MEANY, patrolman in charge; born in Burlington, Vermont, June 15, 1850; came to Chicago in 1868, and August 25, 1875, was appointed to the police force, and sent to the Deering street station; was through the riots of 1877, and the street car troubles of late years, as well as at McCormick's and the Haymarket; as a patrolman on beat, did a great deal of creditable work in connection with the other offices of the station; helped work up the evidence which sent Burk, Kennfrick and Steve Rogers to the penitentiary for burglary in 1881, and Sam Gaskin was another desperado whom he helped place within the walls of Joliet.

MICHAEL NAGLE, patrolman; born in Ireland, December 24, 1853, and came to the United States in April, 1876; September 19, 1882, was appointed to the police force and detailed at the Twenty-second street station, where he remained until November, 1883, when he was transferred to the Deering street station and assigned to the wagon in September, 1886; was in the McCormick riots, but was not injured; arrested Riley and Harrison, the burglars, and sent them to the penitentiary for a term of years each.

JOHN P. NOLAN; born in Chicago, April 8, 1851, and was made a member of the force, October 26, 1875; for four years he served at the Union street and Hinman street stations, and was then transferred to Deering, where he was assigned to the wagon when it was put in service; worked in connection with Officer Meany in settling the Rogers-Burke-Kennefrick gang of burglars, and has done his share of good work in putting away the toughs of the district.

JAMES D. FITZMAURICE, patrolman in charge; born in Ireland in 1840, and came to the United States in the fall of 1866. In 1873 was appointed to the police force, and after being shifted about for a time was assigned to the Deering street station, where he was detailed on the wagon when it was started; has participated in all of the riots since becoming a member of the force; sent down to Joliet the notorious John Welch, and, with Officer Meany, "settled" Sam Gaskin, burglar and highwayman.

MICHAEL CONROY; born in Ireland in February, 1859, and came to the United States and Chicago in 1877; in June, 1883, was appointed to the police force and assigned to the Deering street station; in 1886 was detailed on the wagon; was at the riots at Center avenue and Eighteenth streets, and was lucky enough to get away unhurt; arrested and sent to the penitentiary James Crotty and Mike Nicholson for burglary, and also sent the notorious Dan Cavanaugh, one of the Cavanaugh brothers, down for ten years.

JAMES BERGEN; born in Ireland, in 1846, and when he was seven years old came to this country; in 1855 came to Chicago, and August 18, 1870, was made a member of the force; served first at the old Armory, corner of Adams and Franklin streets, and a few months each at the Twenty-second, Deering, and Hinman street stations, before settling down permanently at the Deering street station; when the wagon was placed in service was assigned to drive it; was in the lumber yard riots of 1874; in 1872 was shot by a man named Coughlin; and in 1873 was again shot, this time by the notorious "Dicky" Burns; was at the Halsted street viaduct during the railroad riots of 1877, but, beyond a few scratches, escaped unhurt. It was the crew with which he is connected for whose benefit a mob stretched a telegraph wire across the street at a height that would catch the men in the wagon about breast high as they were dashing along, and the expectation was that it would sweep them all from the vehicle. The plot was discovered in time, and a citizen cut the wire a few minutes before the wagon appeared, in response to an alarm from the neighborhood of the

McCormick works, where rioting was going on. He sent Jeff Keating to the penitentiary for life, for the murder of James Townsend.

WEST THIRTEENTH STREET DISTRICT.—The West Thirteenth street wagon was placed in service when the station was opened May 1, 1886, just in time to become valuable during the labor and anarchistic troubles of that month.

ANDREW J. PENNELL, native of Burlington, Vt., where he was born November 27, 1829; came to Chicago in 1847, and at the breaking out of the war ·enlisted in the Fourth Michigan Cavalry with which he served till mustered out in 1864; returned to Chicago, and September 15, 1865, was appointed to the police force; served at the old Armory till 1866 when he went to Twenty-second street; two years later was sent to Cottage Grove; went back to the Armory in 1870; was made a member of the day squad in 1872, and in 1882 was sent to the Twelfth street station, where he remained till he was sent to the West Thirteenth street station, and assigned to the wagon May 1, 1886; participated in all the riots that occurred after he joined the department, and has done his share of good police work.

PHILLIP G. MILLER, born in Germany October 21, 1838, and came to Chicago in 1864; was made a member of the police force in July, 1873, and after putting in nearly two years at the Cottage Grove station, was sent to the West Twelfth street station where he remained till assigned to West Thirteenth street, and the wagon May 1, 1886; sent Pat Kelly to the penitentiary for three years for robbery, and served in the riots of 1877 and 1886.

JOHN McDERMOTT, born in Ireland in 1853, and came to Chicago in 1870; was made a member of the force June 15, 1883, and assigned to the West Twelfth street station, where he remained till the West Thirteenth street station was opened; was detailed on the wagon September 15, 1886, and has shown himself to be a good officer; sent Henry Flannery to Joliet for eight years for robbery in 1883, and August Zinc for one year for assault with intent to kill; took part in the riot of 1886, but was not wounded.

JOHN H. DUNN, patrolman, born at Dubuque, Iowa, in 1845; came to Chicago in 1876; was appointed to the force May 8, 1882, serving first at the West Twelfth street station where he remained till May 1, 1886, when he was sent to the West Thirteenth street station; was appointed to the wagon when it went into service; was in the Haymarket riot, and other disturbances of 1886, escaping, however, without any injury.

JAMES HARTIGAN, born in Ireland in 1850; came to Chicago in 1866; was made a member of the force in 1884, being detailed first at The West Twelfth street station, where he remaind till the West Thirteenth street station was opened in May, 1886, when he was transferred, and made a member of the wagon detail, September 15, 1886; was at the McCormick and Haymarket riots, through which he passed safely; sent the burglar George Jennings to the penitentiary for a year, and has done other good work.

JAMES BRADY, born at Holy Cross, Iowa, in 1859, and came to Chicago in 1872; was appointed to the force in May, 1883, at the West Twelfth street station, and remained there till transferred to West Thirteenth street, when the station was opened; was present with other members of the detail at the riots of 1886, and has been on the wagon since May 1, 1886.

THIRD PRECINCT.

THE DESPLAINES STREET DISTRICT.—This is one of the most important districts in the city. While it embraces a large territory devoted to manufacturing, it also takes in a large section of the disreputable houses. There is within it a large criminal population demanding the constant attention of the officers. The wagon at this station does a great deal of running in the course of the year. The presence of the lodging house element and barrel-house habitues is always a menace to the public peace, and were it not for the knowledge that the blue wagon, with its little crew of determined men, is within call of everybody, there is no telling what disturbances there would be. As it is, the detail on this wagon have probably been called on more murders than any other in the city.

JOHN WHEELER, patrolman in charge, is probably one of the best known and most efficient man in the service. His connection with the Bill Allen case, referred to at length elsewhere, in which he shot and killed that desperate negro murderer, only gave general publicity to the fact that he was a nervy and courageous officer. He was born at Wheaton, Ill., February 8, 1851; came to Chicago in the fall of 1877, and October 24, 1878, was appointed on the police force and assigned to the Union street station; here he showed that he was a man to be depended upon in a pinch, and when the patrol wagon was put in service, he was given charge of one of the crews; his detail has caught most of the sensational work of the district; when Jim Dacey murdered Alderman Gaynor on Halsted street, it was Wheeler's crew that responded and arrested the murderer; the night of the Haymarket tragedy the officers of this detail rendered valuable services; they dressed and bandaged up the wounds of half a score of men, saving the lives of some of them by the prompt application of surgical appliances, and thirteen of them were taken to the hospital in this wagon; the record of his crew is one of which Officer Wheeler may well be proud.

DOCTOR F. SAYLOR, patrolman; born in Maryland, February 12 1847; enlisted in the regular army and served through the war in the Seventeenth Infantry under Major Andrews; was at the Wilderness, Cold Harbor, Chapin's Farm, and Petersburg; at Weldon Station was wounded in the shoulder and spent six months in the hospital, and six months more as nurse; was mustered out in 1865 and came to Chicago in the spring of 1871; donned his star as policeman January 15, 1879, and put in his sixty days at the West Chicago avenue station, was afterward at the West Lake street station, and was finally sent to the old Union street station, where he remained until assigned to the wagon in April, 1884; was with Officer Wheeler at the Dacey arrest, and was also present when the crew chased and arrested McLain and Caters for the murder of Sam Booth in 1885.

JAMES BYRNES, driver; born in McHenry county, Ill., September, 1860, and took up his residence in Chicago, November 1, 1876; June 13, 1883, was appointed to the police force, and at the Desplaines street station put in all his time for two years, being assigned to drive the wagon in June, 1885; while traveling a beat he made a number of important arrests, Billy Felton and George Lamont, colored thieves, George Wilson, alias Walsh, against whom he had seventeen charges of robbery and larceny, George Kelly, Pat. Carroll, John McKenna and John McNamee, being among the more noted criminals he has sent to the penitentiary.

JAMES S. LIBBY, patrolman in charge; born at Cape Elizabeth, Maine, November 9, 1842; enlisted in the Sixth Maine, which joined the Army of the Potomac, Hancock's Brigade. After two years and a half in the army, shipped in the navy and put in two years with the East Gulf Squadron stationed most of the time at Key West; came to Chicago in 1870, and two years later joined the police force; was assigned to the old Union street station which was afterward removed to Desplaines street, and was never transferred thereafter. January 7, 1881, when the wagon was placed in service, was put in charge of one of the crews; within a month afterward he was thrown out of the wagon while responding to an alarm and had his shoulder broken; has had the usual experiences of old policemen in being shot at and having numerous desperate struggles, but he always escaped luckily.

JOHN HICKEY, patrolman; born in Limerick in 1839; came to Chicago in 1864, and September 12, 1868, was appointed to the police force and assigned to the Union street station with which he remained until it was removed to Desplaines street, when he changed also; was assigned to the wagon with Officer Libby when it was first introduced; served with Libby through the riots of 1877, and the other minor difficulties, but was off watch when the Haymarket affair occurred and therefore missed that.

MICHAEL HENNESSY, patrolman, native of Illinois, was born at Rutland, Kane county, December 8, 1854; in November, 1869, came to Chicago, and June 13, 1883, was appointed to the police force, being assigned to the Desplaines street station; May 8, 1885, was transferred to the wagon of which he is the driver.

WEST LAKE STREET DISTRICT.—A patrol wagon was placed in service in the West Lake street district in December, 1881. It covers the territory lying between Kinzie and Harrison streets, and between Hoyne avenue on the west and Ann street and Centre avenue on the east. It is chiefly a resident district, some of the finest homes in the city being within its precincts.

THOMAS GRADY, patrolman in charge; born in Ireland on January 1, 1830, and came to America in 1848, came to Chicago 1849, and in June, 1866, became attached to the police force; was detailed at the West Lake street station where he has served continuously ever since; the position of officer in charge of one of the details has been filled by him off and on since the wagon was placed in service, has handled a number of important cases in his time and is particularly successful in working in the district where he has served so many years; is known by about every man, woman and child in the precinct.

JOHN O. DOWD, patrolman; born in Ireland in 1846, January 7, and was brought to this country when four years old; in 1864 he made Chicago his home, but it was not till June, 1883, that he became connected with the force; was then assigned to the Desplaines street station and after a month there was transferred to the West Lake street station where he has been ever since; April, 1884, he was assigned to the wagon; saw what there was to be seen, after the first awful outbreak, at the Haymarket.

MARSHAL N. WALTON, driver, is a veteran of fifteen years' service;

born in Dupage county, Ill., September 11, 1846, came to Chicago in 1861; in the spring of 1872 became a member of the police force, being first assigned to the temporary station on Huron street; in 1874, was transferred to the Union street station, and there he remained till January, 1881, when he was sent to the Central detail and assigned to drive the single-horse wagon that then ran out of the Rookery; held the position of driver on the Central wagon until March, 1886, when he was transferred to the West Lake street station; his wagon was present and rendered efficient service at the Haymarket riot; smelled powder and saw blood during the riots of 1877, as he was one of the few policemen who had to fight for their lives at the Halsted street viaduct; when Officer Fitch Taylor went down under a bullet from a rioter, Officer Walton was by his side, and fought his way out with the wounded man; as a patrolman, he handled a large number of important cases and half a score of desperate highwaymen and burglars now serving their time in the penitentiary attest the successfulness of his labors; the most widely known of these was "Nibsy" Wilson, the old time burglar who is doing a seventeen-year stretch.

MICHAEL C. SLAVIN, patrolman; born in Nova Scotia, February 4, 1837; came to Chicago in 1844, and was made a member of the force October 20, 1865, being assigned to the old Union street station, which was then new; was there three years and then resigned; went into the lumber business for three years; was elected constable and spent five and a half years at that, and then was made an inspector in the health department for two years; the next year was passed doing guard duty in the shops at the Bridewell, and then he returned to the police department; was at Union street for a year and then was transferred to the West Lake street station, where he was assigned to take charge of the wagon August 14, 1881; was in the street-car riots of 1885, and faithfully discharged the duties imposed upon him by the regulations of the department.

JOSEPH NORMAN, patrolman; born in Chicago, April 24, 1860; in 1884 was one of the three hundred men added to the force, and was assigned to the West Lake street station; was one of Lieutenant Stanton's company at the Haymarket, and had part of his left hand and his left heel torn off by pieces of the infernal shell; was in the hospital for a year, and as soon as he recovered was detailed on the wagon; was at the Eighteenth street disturbances the night before the Haymarket affair, and at the street-car riots.

JOHN T. O'HARA, patrolman, is a native of Ireland, where he was born June 4, 1850; came to Chicago in 1865, and went on the police force January 9, 1879, at the West Chicago avenue station; in 1881 was transferred to the West Lake street station and detailed as driver of the wagon; has shown himself to be a perfectly trustworthy man, and his superior officers have reposed great confidence in him.

WEST MADISON STREET DISTRICT.—The patrol wagon of this station covers the territory bounded by Kinzie street, Hoyne avenue, Harrison street and the city limits. It has an area of two and one-fourth square miles. The wagon was placed in service in January of 1881.

LUMAN BARKLEY, patrolman in charge, was born at Dundass, Canada, January 17, 1839; came to Chicago in 1865; followed his trade as baker at Woodman's bakery for a number of years, finally joining the police department July 18, 1873; served at the Twelfth street and Union street stations till 1876, when he resigned and went into business; in March, 1881, re-entered the force, and September 1, 1886, was placed in charge of the wagon.

HURON C. SCOTT, patrolman and driver, is a native of Plymouth, N. Y., where he was born August 1, 1845; at the breaking out of the war, enlisted from Norwich, N. Y., in the Twenty-second New York Cavalry, and was with that organization through all its engagements—Malvern Hill, White Oak Swamp, Cold Harbor, on Wilson's famous raid, and so on; came to Chicago and took up a residence here in 1873, and four years later joined the police department; while putting in his sixty days at the West Twelfth street station, the railroad riots broke out, and his first experience as a policeman was very lively; was transferred to the West Madison street station when it was opened in 1881, and assigned to the wagon; Maurice Kelly, one of the most desperate men who ever preyed upon the public, was arrested by Officer Scott in 1882; Kelly was a safe-blower and a thoroughly reckless character, and when he saw the officer approaching him he made for his gun, but his finger slipped, and before he could recover his grip, Scott had him covered and he was soon on the way to the station; several crooks of distinction were put out of the way, in the penitentiary, by Officer Scott while he was at the Twelfth street station; he is an animal trainer of no mean ability, and his team on the patrol wagon can do everything but talk.

NATHAN A. BRISCOE, patrolman in charge, was born at Kingston, Canada, April 1, 1826; came to Chicago in 1856 and in 1863 was made a member of the police force; was assigned to the West Market Hall, when Captain Turtle was in charge, and there were fourteen patrolmen; this was then known as the second precinct and the officers attached to the station looked after the whole West Side; he had traveled beat but a few months when he was promoted to the rank of sergeant, and in 1865, when the West Twelfth street station was opened, he was placed in charge of it; was afterward shifted to the West Madison street and West Chicago avenue stations, and held the rank of sergeant and lieutenant until 1879, when he resigned and was out of the department for three years; went back on the force as a patrolman at the West Madison street station, and was placed in charge of the patrol wagon; was through the lumber riots of 1874 and all the '77 railroad troubles; has had many narrow escapes in the years he has been a member of the force, and has sent his share of men to the penitentiary.

MARTIN CARLSON, patrolman; born in Norway, December 14, 1835, and came to the United States in 1860; ten years later was appointed to the police force and attached to the Union street station, where he remained for three years, when he resigned; in 1877 re-entered the department and served two years at the West Chicago avenue station when he again resigned; in 1882 returned to the department, this time being assigned to the West Madison street station which had been opened but a short time, and in June of that year was assigned to the wagon; was in the McCormick and Eighteenth street riots but escaped injury.

MICHAEL J. HORAN, patrolman and driver, one of the men who suffered from the bomb of the anarchists at the Haymarket horror; was born in Buffalo, January 24, 1849; came to Chicago when two years old; in 1882 was made a member of the force and assigned to the Lake street station; the night of the Haymarket riot was detailed under Lieutenant Stanton for special duty, and was in the fourth company that marched to where the speeches were being made; when the bomb exploded he fell wounded in four places, the most severe injuries being in the right knee, left arm and wrist; was laid up for nearly a year and will never fully recover the use of his leg; in January of 1887 was so far recovered as to be able to drive a team, and was assigned to the wagon at this station; bears the reputation of a careful and conscientious officer.

FOURTH PRECINCT.

WEST CHICAGO AVENUE DISTRICT.—June 17, 1883, the patrol wagon at the West Chicago avenue station was placed in service. It responds to alarms within the district bounded on the north by Augusta street, south by Kinzie street, east by the river and west by the city limits. It embraces an area of about three-fourths of a square mile.

JEREMIAH D. DONAHUE, patrolman in charge; born in Ireland, April 22, 1857; came to Chicago in the summer of 1873; in June, 1880, was made a member of the police force, assigned first to the Hinman street station, he served there and at the North avenue station, being transferred to the West Chicago avenue station in August, 1887; in 1885, early in January, arrested John Schultz, alias Wagner, a desperate burglar, and sent him to Joliet for five years; Johnson and Eddie Harper, notorious criminals, are also serving terms in the penitentiary through the good efforts of this officer.

ROALD LUND, patrolman; born in Norway, August 29, 1845; came to Chicago early in 1866, and followed his trade till 1873, when he was appointed to the force and detailed at the West Chicago avenue station, afterward served a short time at Rawson street station, but when the West Chicago avenue wagon was put into service, was detailed upon it; was actively engaged during the riots of 1877, and at the Haymarket the detail with which he is associated did excellent service in removing and caring for the wounded.

MICHAEL CONNELLY, patrolman in charge; born in Ireland, July 19, 1857; came to Chicago in 1873, and in 1881, early in April, was appointed to the force and detailed at the West Twelfth street station where he served till 1883, when he was transferred to the West Chicago avenue station and assigned to the wagon; during the McCormick riots was at the scene of the difficulty, and went through a great many lively experiences; has had a number of important police cases during his connection with the department.

WILLIAM LAVE, patrolman; born in Chicago, December 19, 1859; November 15, 1884, was appointed to the police force, and assigned to the Chicago avenue station, where he has served all his time; was detailed on the wagon in November, 1885; was present at McCormick's and the wagon with which he is connected is the one that participated in the rescue of Officer Casey from a mob of howling anarchists.

THOMAS F. MAHER, patrolman and driver; born in Ireland, February 13, 1860; came to Chicago in 1879; in December, 1884, was appointed to the police force and assigned to the West Twelfth street station, afterward served at the Hinman and Canalport avenue stations, driving the wagon at the latter place till transferred to the West Chicago avenue station and detailed on the wagon there; was in the McCormick riots.

CHARLES H. ROCHE, patrolman and driver; born in Dupage county, Ill., July 25, 1861; May, 1882, was made a member of the police force, being detailed at the Desplaines street station; in Septem-

ber, 1883, was transferred to the West North avenue station,
where he served for a year and then was sent to the West Chicago
avenue station, where he was made driver of the wagon.

WEST NORTH AVENUE DISTRICT.—August 21, 1883,
the West North avenue district was established, and a
wagon put in service there. The boundaries were fixed at
Armitage road, Ashland avenue, Augusta street, and the
city limits. There are something like two square miles
covered by the lines of the patrol system.

GEORGE W. H. ROYCROFT, patrolman in charge; born in Cork,
Ireland, March 13, 1847; came to Chicago, 1866, where he followed
his trade as a tanner until August 12, 1873, when he was appointed
to the police force and assigned to the Rawson street station;
after four years' service left the department to try farming in New
York and Texas, and after the grasshoppers had eaten him out of
house and home in Texas, returned to Chicago, and in June, 1880,
went back to his beat in the Rawson street district; served there
and at the West Lake street station and on the Central detail;
was detailed at the West North avenue station, and placed in
charge of the wagon there when it went into service; he took part
in the riots of 1877, and it was his wagon that took from the
station to his home the body of Officer Mathias Degan, the first
of the Haymarket victims; other officers wounded on that memorable night were aided by the crew of the wagon in charge of this
cool-headed officer.

ELEF DANIELSON, patrolman, born in Norway, August 22, 1834,
and in 1861 came to the United States; followed the sea for a
number of years, but finally came to Chicago where, in 1873, he
became a member of the police force, putting in his sixty days at
the old station at the corner of Madison and Union streets; saw
the thick of the fight during the railroad riots of '77.

MICHAEL BURNS, driver; born in Ireland in 1860, and came to this
country when he was six years old; June, 1883, was appointed on
the police force and assigned to the Desplaines street station;
served here but thirty days being transferred at the end of that
time to the West North avenue station, where he was made driver
of the patrol; has established a reputation as a skillful handler of
the ribbons in fast driving.

JOHN HANRAHAN; born in Ireland September 30, 1834; came to
Chicago in April, 1851; was appointed to the force in October,
1870, serving first at the Union street station, and later going to
the West Chicago avenue station, from which he was transferred

to the West North avenue station, and assigned to the wagon, September 1, 1887; took an active part in the suppression of the riots of 1877 and the anarchist troubles of 1886, and was once wounded in discharge of his duty; was shot through the wrist by a thief in 1881, but soon recovered from the effects; is a careful officer who enjoys the full confidence of his superiors.

JOHN C. GUNDERSON is one of the men who have passed a decade or more in the service of the city; was born in Norway, March 15, 1845, and came to Chicago when he was but three years of age; in 1876 was appointed to the police force and sent to the Union street station, from which he was transferred to the West Chicago avenue station in 1881, and when the West North avenue station was opened was sent there, being detailed on the wagon in June, 1883 ; he was at the Haymarket riot after the bomb had been thrown; as a patrolman he has made an excellent record.

JOHN R. LOOBY, was born in Milwaukee, Wis., July 14, 1842, and came to Chicago in the spring before the fire; July 11, 1882, he was appointed to the force, being sent first to the West Chicago avenue station, and remained there till September, 1883, when he was transferred to the West North avenue station, and assigned to the wagon of which he is the driver.

RAWSON STREET DISTRICT.—The Rawson street district embraces an area of one and a quarter square miles, and is in what is known as the "rolling-mill district" of the city— the extreme northern portion west of the river, extending to the west as far as the city limits. Much of the work, owing to the poor roads in the district, is of the heaviest character, and the stock in this district has harder work than in any other part of the city.

MATTHEW FOLEY, patrolman in charge; born in Ireland in 1843; came to Chicago in 1866, where he followed his trade till August, 18, 1875, when he was made a member of the police force; his arrest of George Anderson for murderous assault April 12, 1885, was followed by the conviction of the prisoner and a sentence of three years in the penitentiary.

MAX HEIDELMEIER, patrolman in charge; born in Bavaria August 22, 1845; came to America in 1867, and in 1869 to Chicago, where he followed his trade of tinner until March 27, 1874, when he was appointed on the force, being sent to the East Chicago avenue station under Captain Gund; was there four years, at Larrabee street station a little over three, then at the Harrison street station nearly three years, serving about a year on the wagon there; back to Larrabee street in 1883, where he was on the wagon

for a time; then to the Central detail, where he was put on a
crossing for a few months, and finally, when the Rawson street
wagon was put into service, was detailed there, and has been there
ever since; the most important case he has been connected with
was the poisoning exploit of Lorenzo Krug. [Krug married one
of Officer Heidelmeier's sisters, and a niece named Lucy Heidelmeier lived with them; Krug had them both insured in the mutual
benefit organization known as the Knights and Ladies of Honor,
and when Mrs. Krug died, after a somewhat lingering illness,
collected the money. A little later Lucy Heidelmeier was taken
mysteriously ill, and she, too, died. Then Officer Heidelmeier
suspected poison; a post mortem and subsequent chemical analysis
showed that both the women died from the effects of arsenic.
The case caused a good deal of sensation at the time of Krug's
arrest, and Officer Heidelmeier deserves considerable credit for
the manner in which he pushed the prosecution of the case, Krug
getting an eighteen years' sentence in the penitentiary.]

SIMON KLIDZAS, patrolman; was born in Poland twenty-nine years
ago; came to Chicago in 1881, and December 15, 1884, joined the
police force; as there are large Polish settlements in the Rawson
street district, Officer Klidzas' services are almost absolutely
necessary to the successful handling of cases there.

WILLIAM LOHMEYER, patrolman; born in Germany in 1842; came
to Chicago in 1863, and after a residence of twelve years here
became a member of the force; since 1875 has been in continuous
service, and has acquitted himself with credit on many occasions.

JULIUS L. SIMONSEN, patrolman, born in Denmark twenty-nine
years ago; came to Chicago when only ten years of age, and
December 15, 1884, obtained an appointment to the police department; has made something of a record for himself as a careful and
successful officer; his capture of Tom Honors and Mike Reilly
about a month after he came on the force, and the successful
prosecution of those desperate highwayman, sending them down
for four and five years respectively, was a plucky and clever piece
of work; has had a number of other cases of a similar character,
and equally important.

JOHN BOYD, patrolman and driver, is a shrewd and experienced
policeman; he is a "Troy boy," having been born in that well-known
New York town forty years ago; has been a resident of this city
since 1865, and a member of the force since 1881; served first at
the West Lake street station, and was later transferred to the
Rawson street station, where he has made an excellent record as
a driver and an officer; in 1883, December 5, arrested a pair of
desperate burglars, Burke and Santry, and got each of them a
three-years' stretch in the penitentiary.

FIFTH PRECINCT.

EAST CHICAGO AVENUE DISTRICT —The wagon and crew at the East Chicago avenue station were put into service in April, 1883. The wagon responds to calls within the district bounded on the north by Division street, south by the Chicago river, east by Lake Michigan, and west by the north branch of the Chicago river. The district contains one and one-fourth square miles.

JAMES D. COOK, patrolman in charge; born in Auburn, N. Y. November 20, 1839; when the war broke out he was one of the first to enlist, choosing the naval branch of the service; shipped on the Ottawa under Admiral Dupont, and on the Ottawa and the Norwich served his country from '61 to '66 in the South Atlantic blockading squadron; at the close of the war came West, and March 9, 1867, was appointed on the police force and assigned to the old Huron street station under Captain Wells Sherman; after the great fire was transferred to the Webster avenue station; later to the temporary station on Dearborn avenue near Superior, and when Washburn took hold of the department, was made a sergeant at Larrabee street; was in charge of a squad of men sent to relieve the little band of officers fighting for their lives at the Halsted street viaduct in the railroad riots of 1877, and rendered excellent service; afterward served a short time on the Central detail, and in April, 1883, was detailed on the wagon where he is now serving.

CHARLES A. STRAIL, patrolman in charge; born at Syracuse, N. Y., June 21, 1843; his family first came to Chicago, in 1852, but after remaining for a short time returned to Syracuse, where they remained till 1871, after the great fire, when he came here again; was appointed a member of the police force in 1882, and assigned to the East Chicago avenue station; February of 1884, was given charge of the detail in his present position where he has discharged his duties to the satisfaction of his superiors; his wagon loaded to the guards with officers was one of the first to dash in at the Haymarket after that memorable riot.

DAVID E. LITTLE, patrolman; born in Troy, N. Y., December 25, 1842; he came to Chicago just before the war and when trouble broke out enlisted in Company E 95th Illinois Infantry; took part in nearly all of the battles of his regiment; was at the Siege of Vicksburg, and in the Red River Expedition; was mustered out in August, 1865, as well as when he went in, except that he left a finger at Vicksburg; was appointed to the police force April 13, 1874, and sent to the East Chicago avenue station under Captain

Gund; with the exception of one year at the Larrabee street, has been all the time at this station and has been on the wagon since it went into service April 23, 1883; went through the riots of 1877 and the Haymarket without injury.

WILLIAM GRIFFIN, driver, is reckoned one of the best in the department; since April, 1883, when he was detailed for the work, he has never had the slightest accident to his apparatus or stock; was born at Cold Spring, Wis., November 15, 1855, joined the force May 8, 1882, and was assigned to the Chicago avenue station where he has remained.

PETER SCHAUS, patrolman, born in Luxemburg thirty-five years ago. He came to this country when 17 years of age and December 15, 1884, was sworn into the police force, being assigned to the East Chicago avenue station from which he has not been moved.

WILLIAM W. CUDMORE, patrolman and driver, born in Chicago in October, 1868; in 1884, he became a member of the police department, detailed at the East Chicago avenue station, and was assigned to the wagon in May, 1888.

LARRABEE STREET DISTRICT.—At the Larrabee street station the patrol system was introduced early in 1883, and covers two districts, taking in calls from boxes in both the Larrabee and Webster avenue stations. The force therefor covers that part of the North Division bounded on the south by Division street, on the north by the city limits, on the east by the lake, and on the west by the river.

NATHAN J. YOUNG, patrolman in charge; born at Portland, Me., August 10, 1839; came west while a lad and at the breaking out of the war, enlisted in the first Illinois Light Artillery, going to the front and making a record for himself as a member of Taylor's famous battery; was honorably discharged in 1864, and August 19 1869, became a member of the police force, being first assigned to the old Huron street station, then after the fire to the Dearborn avenue station, and when the Chicago avenue station was built went there; in 1879, was transferred to the Larrabee street station and when the patrol system was introduced took charge of one of the details; went through the riots of 1877, and every other disturbance of any importance except the Haymarket, which he missed by a few minutes.

BERNARD DEMOLING, patrolman; born at Waxweiler, Germany, November 2, 1842; came to this country in 1864, and eleven years later—August 19, 1875, joined the police department; was assigned to the Larrabee street station; was transferred to Chicago avenue where he served seven years, and in May, 1883, was detailed on the wagon at Larrabee street; saw some desperate fighting during the riots of '77, and took part in a good many scrimages, but escaped unharmed.

THEODORE DUDDLES, driver; born in Lincolnshire, England, February 27, 1850; when two years of age came to this country, and as he grew up he learned the trade of mason which he followed till June, 1883, when he secured an appointment to the force; was assigned to the East Chicago avenue station where he traveled a beat until August of the same year and then was transferred to the position he now fills.

JOHN K. SOLLER, patrolman in charge; born in Erie County, N. Y., February 16, 1853; coming to Chicago in the spring of 1861, he went to school here and followed a trade till 1876, when he was made a member of the police force; that year he was caught in the center of a small tornado, and with a section of wooden sidewalk was lifted into the air and thrown nearly a hundred feet; lockjaw ensued and it was several months before he was able to be out; when he recovered he did not go back on the force, but in 1883, January 6, was sworn in again, and February 17, 1884, was assigned to the Larrabee street wagon; the detail with which he is connected was kept busy the night of the Haymarket looking after the wounded.

OTTO SCHIFTER, patrolman; born in Chicago, February 6, 1850. October 1, 1881, was appointed to the police force, and February 17, 1884, was assigned to the wagon at Larrabee street; at the Haymarket had charge of 26 men of the reserve that was summoned after the bomb had been thrown and was detailed to keep the intersection of Randolph and Desplaines streets clear; in the discharge of this duty he saw some lively times, but was able to bring himself and his men out without injury.

Upon the bright young men who manipulate the various pieces of electrical apparatus at the stations, much of the success of the system depends. The veteran of the force of police telephone operators is Eugene Fitzpatrick, of the Central station, who was the first operator employed, and who received the first alarm over the first circuit built in the West Twelfth street district. Following is a complete list of the operators, including the linemen and repairers:

Central Station—Eugene J. Fitzpatrick, Edward Gleason, C. W. Thomas. Harrison Street Station—Thomas Joyce, Mich. K. Mahoney, George Oakey.

Twenty-second Street Station—William Sheridan, Patrick Davenport.

Cottage Grove Avenue Station—J. J. Amstein.

Thirty-fifth Street Station—William Sheridan, Wm. Flanagan.

Stanton Avenue Station—W. P. O'Meara, John N. Talbot.

Desplaines Street Station—Frank O. Byrne, Wm. Clare, Joseph E. Dargan.

West Twelfth Street Station—Phelim Deavitt, Fred C. Hahn, Archie Shannon.

Canalport Avenue Station—Michael Callahan, John Lardner.

West Thirteenth Street Station—Eugene Carroll, Chas. Ludington.

Deering Street Station—M. J. Dunne, Joseph H. Tirado.

Hinman Street Station—Daniel Curran, John Barrett.

West Madison Street Station—J. T. Troy, Frank D. Crosby.

West Lake Street Station—Alexander B. Cameron, R. A. Brown.

West Chicago Avenue Station—John Lynch, Wm. Haag, Chas. Boettger.

West North Avenue Station—Edward Kelly, John Quinn.

East Chicago Avenue Station—Jacob Baer, D. B. Hart, John McFighne.

Webster Avenue Station—Hans Boecklin, E. N. Dickson.

Rawson Street Station—Adolphe Doroche, Charles Schilip.

Larrabee Street Station—Frank Rosa, Usher L. Wilkinson.

Repairers—Burton E. Thompson, William E. Foltz, Wm. J. Cronin, James P. Crowley, Edward Carroll.

Batteryman—Edward J. Barrett.

Following are the signal service stations, showing number of men and horses employed, according to Veterinary Surgeon Leamy's last report:

STATIONS.	No. of Men.	No. of Horses.
Central	6	4
Harrison	6	9
Twenty-second Street	6	4
Cottage Grove Avenue	6	4
Stanton Avenue	6	4
Thirty-fifth Street	6	5
West Twelfth Street	6	4
West Thirteenth Street	6	4
Hinman Street	6	4
Canalport Avenue	6	3
Deering Street	6	3
Desplaines Street	6	9
West Lake Street	6	4
West Madison Street	6	3
West Chicago Avenue	6	4
West North Avenue	6	3
Rawson Street	6	3
East Chicago Avenue	6	8
Larrabee Street	6	4
Total	114	86

CHAPTER XXIII.

THE POLICE DEPARTMENT IN THE AUTUMN OF 1887—COMPOSITION OF THE
FORCE — ITS OFFICERS — THE MAYOR, THE SUPERINTENDENT AND
HEADQUARTERS STAFF—THE INSPECTOR AND HIS ASSISTANTS—CAPT.
HUBBARD AND HIS LIEUTENANTS—THE "LAKE STREET SQUAD"—
ROSTER OF THE DAY FORCE—SOME SPLENDID RECORDS—BIOGRAPH-
ICAL SKETCHES OF THE MEN.

The police department of the city of Chicago, in the
autumn of 1887, was constituted as follows: One general
superintendent, one inspector and secretary; six captains,
26 lieutenants, 41 sergeants, 1,167 patrolmen; the total force
mustering 1,242 men. Every man connected with the government of the force, from superintendent down to desk
sergeant, has risen from the rank of patrolman. There
have been no appointments to high positions in the department from the outside since Colvin's administration. Experiments of that kind, whenever attempted, have proved
dismal failures. It has now become an unwritten law that
by promotion alone, and slow promotion, too, can any man,
no matter how ambitious he may be to govern, hope to
reach executive positions in the Chicago police force. The
young man who feels that he might win distinction or rank
as a Chicago police officer, must begin at the bottom round
of the ladder, and by his own exertions alone, can he hope
to ascend. Before stepping on the round it is essential to
file the following application and affidavit. To simplify the
matter we will fill it out with fictitious names, addresses, etc.,
in *italics:*

I HEREBY MAKE APPLICATION FOR APPOINTMENT, and do declare
upon my oath, that the statements by me subscribed herein are each and
every one of them true, to the best of my knowledge and belief. I reside at No. *1797 Madison* street, in the city of Chicago. I was born on
the *10th* day of the month of *September,* A. D. *1850,* and am between
37 and 38 years of age. My occupation is that of *carpenter.* I have

been employed during the past five years as follows: *With Johnson, Thompson & Co., builders, 17 Washburne avenue, two years; with Jones, Brown & Co., 38 Parker street, two years and a half, and have been engaged in business for myself during the past six months at 976 McPherson street.* I am temperate in my habits and have no illness or disease which will shorten my life; am now in good health. In the event of my appointment as a regular member of the department, I agree to become a member of the Benevolent Association, and the Police and Firemen's Relief Fund Association, and to make punctual payments of all dues and assessments for which I may become liable. I do not owe to exceed the sum of *one hundred* dollars ($100.00).

John P. Smith.

The applicant must then answer the following questions:

What is your full name? Where were you born? [If foreign-born, the following, which are omitted if native-born: In what year did you arrive in the United States? At what age did you arrive in the United States? Are you naturalized? Where did you declare your intention to become a citizen? In what year did you make such declaration? When did you receive final papers of naturalization? In what year did you receive such final papers?] How long have you resided in Chicago next preceding this date? Have you ever been convicted of any crime? Can you read and write the English language understandingly? Are you married? What family have you? Have you ever been a member of any police or fire department, and if so, when? If you answer yes to the last question, state the cause of your leaving such force. Have you ever paid or promised to pay, either directly or indirectly, through yourself or any other person, any money or other valuable thing to receive the appointment which you now seek?

The applicant must then undergo a surgical examination, similar to that which is imposed by life assurance companies. His height must not be less than five feet eight inches, and his weight and circumference of chest must not be below that marked as the minimum accompaniment of height in the following table:

HEIGHT.	MINIMUM WEIGHT.	CIRCUMFERENCE OF CHEST. (QUIESCENT).
5 feet 8 inches	140 pounds	34 inches
5 feet 9 inches	145 pounds	34½ inches
5 feet 10 inches	150 pounds	35 inches
5 feet 11 inches	155 pounds	36 inches
6 feet	160 pounds	36½ inches
6 feet 1 inch	165 pounds	37½ inches
6 feet 2 inches	170 pounds	38 inches
6 feet 3 inches	175 pounds	39 inches
6 feet 4 inches	180 pounds	40 inches

If the applicant is accepted he is given preliminary instructions in the inspector's office, placed in charge of Officer L. J. Van Pelt, Inspector Bonfield's clerk, informed
regarding his uniform, provided with department cloth for
the making of the same, is instructed in the rules, and for
sixty days after entering the force is compelled to serve an
apprenticeship at one of the stations, in which time it is expected that he will have developed into a full-fledged policeman. During this apprenticeship he is usually accompanied
by an old and experienced officer, who "breaks him in."
After the sixty days have passed he is either transferred at
once or remains at the station of first assignment for regular
duty. It is customary in the department, however, to the
end that the men shall become acquainted with all localities,
and with all classes, that they shall be frequently transferred during the first four years of their service. If the officer proves to be a man of education, tact, skill, discretion
and bravery, promotion is sure to come, although, as before
stated, it is slow, and every inch of progress must be gained
by untiring energy. Honesty, sobriety, obedience are the
three cardinal virtues of the policeman. With these, if he
be a man gifted with a fair share of brains, education and
nerve, he may rise steadily. Without them all other qualifications count as naught. The present force is one of the
best Chicago has ever had. Strict discipline has been maintained for at least six years, and nearly all the rotten timber has been thrown out. In such a large body of men it is
not possible that all should prove trusty and efficient. Dis-
honest characters, drones and unreliable men find their way
into the ranks in spite of every precaution, but they are
quickly discovered and stripped of their uniforms.

For a number of years the question of dealing with
female prisoners at the several police stations had attracted
considerable attention, and caused a great amount of discussion, and the impropriety of having them placed in charge
of men was, on several occasions, brought prominently be-

fore the public, when, at length, April 30, 1885, Superintendent Doyle issued the following—an order which has been rigidly enforced ever since by his successor:

1. Provision having been made in the appropriation ordinance of the current year for ten matrons for police stations, two of such matrons will be assigned to each of the five precinct stations, to-wit: The Harrison street, West Twelfth street, Desplaines street, West Chicago avenue and Chicago avenue stations. One matron shall remain on day and one on night duty alternately at each of the stations mentioned, relieving each other at designated hours, so that one at all times shall be present at the station.

2. Hereafter all females arrested by members of the force for any offense whatever, shall, if bail is not at once furnished, immediately be brought to and booked at the principal station in the precinct where arrested, and under no circumstances shall any female be held for any length of time at any sub-station or elsewhere in custody of the department except at the places designated in section 1 of this order.

This was hailed as a genuine reform, and gave very wide satisfaction. At best the management of female prisoners is a very delicate matter, and though no charges reflecting upon the morality of the force in this particular were ever sustained, the officers in attendance were always liable to gross calumny and the vilest species of blackmail. The matron system has removed all possibility of scandal from the stations. The women selected as matrons must be intelligent, patient, and above all, of irreproachable character. The matrons at present on the force are as follows:

FIRST PRECINCT STATION (Harrison street), Sarah J. Littell and
    Mary A. Kelly.

SECOND PRECINCT STATION (West Twelfth street), Mary Ann
    Murphy and Mary Heelan.

THIRD PRECINCT STATION (Desplaines street), Mary Stewart and
    Catherine S. Dodge.

FOURTH PRECINCT STATION (West Chicago avenue), Annie
    Dwyer and Mary A. Mayer.

FIFTH PRECINCT STATION (East Chicago avenue), Mary Eager
    and Annie Mohrman.

The Chicago police department boasts of the most perfect "rogues' gallery " of any city in the United States, and its perfection is due to the admirable mangement of

Michael P. Evans, removed in September last. Whatever may have been the causes which led to the change, it is undoubtedly a fact, that Mr. Evans accomplished wonders for the department during his term of office, in the way of bringing about the identification of criminals, and in aiding the detectives of this and other cities in running down exconvicts and notorious crooks when they were "wanted." A perfect record of every person held for crime by the grand jury, for a number of years past, with their photographs, bodily marks, and descriptions of the most minute character, is preserved in the Chicago rogues' gallery. The gallery is located at the top of the Armory police station. In order to give an idea of the amount of work performed here, the following is appended:

Feb. 10, 1887.

FREDERICK EBERSOLD, ESQ., *Gen. Supt. of Police.*

Sir:—The following is a statement of work performed in this department for the year ending 1886:

FOR ROGUES' GALLERY.

Negatives taken	624
Negative holder addressed and numbered	624
Descriptions taken	624
Descriptions printed	17,430
Pictures printed	13,200
Names and numbers printed on pictures	13,200
Pictures placed in albums before being sent to stations. (This includes all pictures for 1885)	9,350

FOR POLICE HEADQUARTERS AND DETECTIVE DEPARTMENT.

Negatives taken	70
Negatives addressed and numbered	70
Pictures printed	4,053
" " scene of riot	29
" " of bomb experiments	29
" " of patrol wagons	30

In addition to the above, there were the indexing of criminals in the general index, the reports from the clerk of the Criminal Court, also penitentiary reports, until such time as they (the reports) were called in by the general superintendent. Yours respectfully,

MICHAEL P. EVANS,
Official Photographer.

The rosters of the detective and of the patrol or signal

service have already been given.   In the following chapters
the "Roster of the Force," aside from these two branches,
is presented as nearly complete as it is possible to make it.
It has been the aim to give every man who has distinguished
himself in any way, full credit, and if there is any short-
coming in this respect, it is due to the unwillingness of the
men themselves to communicate the desired information.
The following is the roster:

JOHN A. ROCHE, mayor of Chicago and commander-in-chief of the police force, was born in Utica, N. Y., in 1844, graduated from a high
school in Massachusetts at the age of 17; an apprentice to the Allen
Machine Works, New York City; removed to Boston at the age of
21, serving as draughtsman and superintendent of steam engine
building; came to Chicago in 1867, and entered into engine and
boiler business; invented and patented new devices in the construction of machinery; became a member of the firm of James,
Roche & Spencer; burned out by the great fire of '71; afterward
entered business alone and up to his election was manager for J.
A. Fay & Co., manufacturers and dealers in machinery; in 1876 was
elected as a republican to the House of Representatives of the Illinois
legislature; voted for John A. Logan in the memorable contest of
1877; was elected mayor of Chicago on the republican ticket in
March, 1887. As mayor, he controls, with the advice and consent
of the city council, the entire police establishment of the city, and
may at any time, at his option, assume personal command of the
force. [See 1887].

FREDERICK EBERSOLD, general superintendent of police, was born
at Ixheim, District of Zweibruecken, a province of Bavaria, on the
Rhine, March 30, 1841; arrived in New York in 1856; came to Chicago in 1857; moved to Mendota in 1859; entered the Federal army
as a private soldier on May 19, 1861, and served till the close of
the war, attaining the rank of captain; went into business in Chicago after being mustered out; joined the police force under Jacob
Rehm in 1867, and rose gradually from patrolman, through all the
grades, to the superintendency, to which position he was appointed
by Mayor Harrison, August, 1885, and reappointed by Mayor
Roche, shortly after the latter's election. [See biography].

JOHN BONFIELD, inspector and secretary of the police department, a
rank created in Chicago by Mayor Harrison, to take the place of
the deputy superintendency previously existing; was born of Irish
parents, at Bathurst, New Brunswick, in April, 1836; came to Chi-
ago when a mere lad in 1844, and received here a common
school education; in 1853 or 1854 became apprenticed to the

Desplaines Street Police Station on Night of May 4, 1886.

MICHAEL BRENNAN,
Chief Clerk, Police Department.

machinist's trade; afterward took charge of a stationary engine, and later on became a locomotive engineer on the Chicago & Alton railroad, serving in this capacity for ten years; went into business on Archer avenue and failed; was appointed inspector of customs by President Grant, as an acknowledgment of his services to the republican party; held this position till 1875, when he again entered into business and met with disaster once more, this time through fire; was sworn in as a patrolman in 1877 and rose from this rank steadily until he reached his present position, being appointed inspector by Mayor Harrison, and reappointed by Mayor Roche. The three most prominent events in the police career of Inspector Bonfield are: the successful organization of the patrol service, under his immediate charge; the suppression of the street-car riot in 1885; the stifling of anarchy in Chicago in 1886. [See biography].

MICHAEL BRENNAN, lieutenant of police and chief clerk of the police department, office of the superintendent, was appointed to his present position by Superintendent Washburn, August 15, 1873; and has acted in the same capacity through all the changes of superintendents and marshals up to the present time. He is probably more familiar with the history of the department and all the intricate details of the service than any man on the force, and is looked upon as an authority at headquarters. Lieutenant Brennan was born in Ireland and is now 46 years of age. He arrived in Chicago in 1862 and entered the force as a patrolman in 1870. After serving for some time as patrolman at the old Huron street station, north division, he was appointed in May, 1872, desk sergeant, and transferred to the Larrabee street station. Later he was transferred to the Dearborn avenue station where he served as desk sergeant under Captain Frederick Gund, and was then selected by Supt. Washburn as chief clerk. His duties from that day to this have been arduous and exacting. He is the private secretary of the commanding officer. The business of all visitors, whether civilians or public officers, is usually communicated to him, before it reaches the superintendent. He decides hundreds of questions for the chief, and directs the enquirer, who seeks the superintendent, to some subordinate officer, who may be better qualified to give the sought-for information. He is the middle man between the citizens and the police force, dealing with the multitude who daily flock into the superintendent's quarters with complaints, reports, requests, etc. Of a courteous disposition and equable temperament he manages to get through his daily labors with less friction than one would suppose, and not the least of the excellent qualifications which eminently fit him for the position, is the shrewd discernment with which he penetrates the motives of callers, and by which he determines whether or not the matter under consideration is one that must be settled by the superintendent, by the inspector, by one of the captains, or by himself. Thus he prevents the confusion and annoyance which would follow were he not at the wicket, ever ready to skillfully turn the footsteps of the visitor in the right direction. All of the superintendent's official orders and correspondence pass through Lieutenant Brennan's hands.

JOSEPH B. SHEPARD, who, as chief clerk to the department, does the bookkeeping by which the pay rolls for the twelve or thirteen hundred employes are kept straight and the $1,225,000 appropriated for salaries get to the right men, has been in the department since 1873. He was then appointed clerk by the board which, at that time, under Mayor Medill, regulated the destinies of the force. Mr. Shepard looks about 45, but confesses to having been born in Onondaga county, New York, sixty-two years ago. In 1849 he started for the great West but did not journey so far as the gold-seekers who moved across the desert for the slope at that time. Reaching the promising little town of Chicago he took service on a line of packets running between the future Western metropolis and Peru, Ill. Three seasons satisfied him with this and in the fall of 1851 he became an express messenger for the American Express Company, his route being from Chicago to St. Louis. Robberies were then rare, and though he carried millions of dollars by stage, boat and pony, he never lost a dime in any way. In 1853 he was appointed a conductor on the newly opened railroad and ran the first mail train into Rock Island. Seventeen years of railroading caused him to long for a settled place of residence and he became attached to the old Michigan avenue hotel, but the confinement made him fall sick, and then he took a two years' rest, after which he entered upon his police career. Here his varied experiences have enabled him to so systematize his work as to reduce the whole business to a science. In addition to the financial and bookkeeping work of the department Mr. Shepard has to manage the distribution of supplies. He is universally liked by the men.

LORING J. VAN PELT, clerk to inspector, ranks as patrolman, but is in reality one of the most valuable officers connected with the entire department. He was born in New York City in 1852, and comes of the old Dutch stock of the Empire state. He came to Chicago in 1865, entered the force on Dec. 8, 1873, and, having resigned, re-entered it Dec. 1, 1884. From Nov., 1880, to Dec., 1884, he was a member of the insurance patrol, and filled the position of inspector of buildings and clerk to the late B. B. Bullwinkle, who was the superintendent of the patrol. In February, 1886, after re-entering the police department, in company with Officer Fairchild, he recovered about $2,000 worth of stolen property in the town of Cicero. The same year he broke up Mrs. Huntington's baby farm on Wood street, near Twelfth, and brought the frightful condition of things existing there to the attention of the

JOSEPH B. SHEPARD,

Assistant Secretary.

LORING J. VAN PELT

public. Some children under Mrs. Huntington's charge had died of starvation and exposure. In a brief period of time he accomplished such excellent work as to attract general attention, making numerous important arrests. It was discovered by Superintendent Austin J. Doyle that Officer Van Pelt was an architect of remarkable ability, and he was called from Hinman street station to headquarters, when he was placed in charge of the architectural work of the department. Since then he has drawn plans for new police stations, patrol quarters, and a photograph gallery and a construction shop, demanding an outlay of over $40,000, and so close were his designs and specifications drawn up that the actual cost of the structures he had planned did not exceed those estimated by him by over $360. In addition to this work which comes under the supervision of the inspector, he is also private secretary or clerk to Inspector Bonfield, issues all cloth for police uniforms, and keeps account of such supplies as do not properly come under Assistant Secretary Shepard's charge. The large memorial picture of Co. A of the Desplaines street station (the company that suffered such dreadful decimation in the Haymarket massacre), presented to the station by Inspector Bonfield, was arranged and engraved by Officer Van Pelt. It is an elegant souvenir of one of the saddest events in the history of the department. Officer Van Pelt is an educated and courteous gentleman, who performs every duty assigned him quietly and faithfully.

JAMES RAY, attached to inspector's office, superintendent of construction department, ranks as patrolman. He has a splendid record as an officer. While sitting on the front steps of his residence, 68 Rebecca street, being off duty, and conversing with a friend, on the evening of August 1, 1881, his attention was called by the sound of a pistol shot at No. 50 of that street. Officer Ray quickly went to the scene of the shooting, and on his way saw one Christ. Dixon, who lived in the immediate vicinity, running out of the yard into the alley. Ray stopped him and enquired what he was running for; he stated that Thomas Cahill, of No. 50 Rebecca street, had just shot and tried to kill him on account of some trivial dispute which they had some time previous. Upon examination the officer found a pistol shot wound in Dixon's thigh, and, therefore, being satisfied of the truth of the statement, he went into the house where Cahill's parents reside, and found Thomas Cahill concealed in a bedroom upstairs, young Dixon following the officer. Cahill was asked by Officer Ray what he shot Dixon for; he denied having fired any shot, and asked to be confronted with Dixon, who immediately appeared from behind the officer and charged Cahill with the shooting; no sooner had the accusation been made than Cahill struck young Dixon a blow in the face, knocking him down the steps in the presence of Officer Ray. The officer then placed Cahill under arrest and young Dixon ran away, leaving Officer Ray alone with the Cahill family. Cahill resisted arrest and was assisted in such resistance by the whole family present, consisting of his father, mother and brother, all of whom used great violence toward Ray. However, after a severe struggle, Officer Ray succeeded in getting the door open and dragged the prisoner outside on the top of a stairway leading to the second story in rear of the house, and, in trying to get him down stairs, the prisoner's undershirt which the officer held severed in the back, leaving one-half in the officer's hands. By reason of the sudden give-away, Officer Ray fell down the steps some distance, and by the time he regained his footing the prisoner had returned into the house and locked all doors. Some one in the neighborhood turned in the alarm for the police wagon, which soon appeared on the scene with Capt. O'Donnell and five police officers. Acting in obedience to orders from the captain, then present on the ground, Officer Ray went to the door, and, knocking at the same, asked for admittance, stating that he was a police officer. Cahill refused to open the door; Officers Ray and O'Brien put their shoulders to the door and forced it open a few inches, when Cahill put his revolver into the aperture and fired several shots, wounding Officers Ray and Hefferman slightly and O'Brien fatally. Cahill was subsequently arrested by Officers Kelly and Flynn, and received a life sentence at Joliet. After being confined three years he died of consumption. Pete Stevens, who murdered his wife Mamie, and who was lately discharged from the Joliet penitentiary, was also arrested by Officer Ray, who is now detailed as superintendent of new constructions and is a first-class mechanic in every respect. It is to his credit and his co-laborer, Officer Van Pelt, that the police department has saved hundreds of dollars by their planning and constructing of new police stations and other work, without extras.

NICHOLAS SHANNON, patrol sergeant, was born in Ireland in 1835; came to Chicago in June, 1852, and entered the force in May, 1868; traveled beat a number of years and made many important arrests; appointed desk sergeant by Supt. Doyle. Has charge of construction shop and mechanics (policemen) employed in repairs, etc.

WILLIAM H. CARMAN, acting clerk of secretary's office, with rank of patrolman, was born in New Brunswick, N. J., 58 years ago; came to Chicago in 1860 and entered the police force in 1862; was appointed patrolman on March 18th, 1882, and traveled beat two years; was made station-keeper and afterward acting clerk in the old headquarters, Washington and LaSalle streets; in 1868 was appointed custodian of stolen property, which position he held until July 31st, 1879, when he was again appointed patrolman; has since filled his present position with general satisfaction. Mr. Carman has served under every general superintendent since the organization of the department.

PATRICK LEAMY, veterinary surgeon of the patrol service and attached to Inspector Ebersold's staff, was born in the County Tipperary, Ireland, in 1843. He has been a resident of Chicago for thirty-two years, where during the early years of his manhood he engaged in teaming; was connected with the fire department for five years and drove Engine 170 in the great fire; afterward entered again in the teaming business, being employed by several large wholesale houses; after eight years he was engaged to drive the police department supply wagon, and when John Bonfield was made inspector, was given charge of the police department horses. "Doc" Leamy, as he is called in the force, has been wonderfully successful in his management of the stock. During his supervision he has lost but two horses—one of which dropped dead going to a fire, and the other had a leg broken by accident. He is a careful buyer, a splendid veterinary surgeon, and a popular man in the department. [See Patrol Service.]

THE CENTRAL DETAIL.

CAPTAIN GEORGE W. HUBBARD, COMMANDING.

In years gone by a special detail of the best looking men on the police force was assigned by the department to street crossing duty on Lake street, which was, up to October, 1871, the fashionable retail thoroughfare of the city. This detail became familiarly known as "the Lake street squad," and numbered from thirty-five to forty men. After the rebuilding of the burnt district, the retail center was shifted, and the growth of population soon demanded the various changes which have contributed to the organization of what is known now to the public as the Central detail, and to policemen as "the squad." The headquarters of the Central detail are located in the City Hall, and this branch of the service must not be confounded with the Central station, also located in the City Hall, and described elsewhere in connection with the detective force. The jurisdiction of the Central station extends over all the territory comprised between Van Buren street on the south, the river on the north, the lake on the east, and the river on the west, during the day time. It also covers all the railroad depots, steamboat landings, public halls, newspaper offices, etc., and it is relieved at night by the force of the first precinct or Armory station, commanded by Captain Buckley.

GEORGE W. HUBBARD, captain of police, Central detail, was born at Cambridge, Maryland, February 22, 1848; was educated at Baltimore, came to Chicago Sept. 10, 1868, and entered the police force on July 29, 1873; was promoted to desk sergeant on Auugst 5, 1875, lieutenant Nov. 20, 1882, and captain January 1, 1887. [See biography].

MICHAEL BISCHOFF, lieutenant of police, was born in Germany in 1830; came to Chicago 1844, and entered the force March, 1857. His early record appears throughout the history of the force, and he has ranked high in the estimation of his superiors always. He commanded a company of 50 men on July 26, 1877, at the Halsted street viaduct, and when the mob drove the force engaged back, Bischoff and his men came to the rescue, charged the rioters and drove them across the bridge. In this charge three of the rioters were killed and a number wounded. [See "Riot of '77."] Lieut. Bischoff has participated, always actively, in all the great riots and strikes that have occurred in this city. He is a brave man, an efficient police officer and a good citizen.

JOHN E. FITZPATRICK, drill master and lieutenant of police, is one of the bravest and best officers of the police department; as such he is recognized by his superiors and associates. His connection with the Haymarket affair, which was of such a character as to win for him the respect and esteem of all citizens and a speedy promotion, is mentioned elsewhere. He is at present drill master of the force, and attached to the Central detail. He was born in Johnstown, Penna., in 1852, and was reared in that vicinity, entering a rolling mill when he arrived at suitable age. In 1878 he came to the West and established a rolling mill at Carondelet, St. Louis; in 1873 he became assistant superintendent of the rolling mills at Springfield, Ill., and shortly afterward became superintendent of the mills at East St. Louis. In 1879 he came to Chicago, and was employed in the Bridgeport Wire Works until that concern shut down in 1882. He had been instrumental in organizing the Johnstown Zouaves, and was head and front of the Sherman Guards at Springfield. He also became connected with Battery "D," I. N. G., at Springfield. This taste for military matters was strongly developed in the young man, and he became a most proficient organizer, drill master and disciplinarian before he entered the Chicago force. He became a patrolman on January 13, 1883, and was detailed at Harrison street. His well-known fitness for the

PATRICK LEAMY,
Veterinary Surgeon, Police Department.

JOHN E. FITZPATRICK,
Drill Master and Lieut., Central Detail.

place induced Superintendent Ebersold to make him drill master, which position he entered in 1885, and has discharged its duties ever since with skill and satisfaction. He was appointed lieutenant immediately after the Haymarket explosion.

DEXTER CODMAN, sergeant, Central detail, was born in Ontario county, New York, and is now 63 years of age; came to Chicago July 10, 1852, and entered the force on June 10, 1866. Sergeant Codman was at one time the agent of a line of boats plying between Chicago and St. Louis. After joining the force he traveled beat for a short time from the old Market street station, but was soon appointed station keeper. He was bailiff at the county jail for a time, and afterward assigned to the Armory. He was appointed to his present position under Mayor Harrison.

MICHAEL LANGAN, sergeant, was born in Ireland in 1842; came to Chicago in May, 1863, and entered the police force on February 12, 1869; patrolled post five years and was appointed desk sergeant February 2, 1874, and served as such at the East Chicago avenue station for over eight years; transferred to Central station February 2, 1882. During all these years Sergeant Langan has never been charged with violating any of the rules of the department, and has never been reprimanded by a superintendent.

JOHN POST, sergeant, Central detail, was born in New York state in 1845; came to Chicago in 1865, and entered the police force in 1874; served for some time at West Madison street station and was transferred to the Central detail on Sept. 9th, 1887.

PATRICK J. GIBBONS, patrol sergeant, born in Ireland, 1850; came to Chicago 1854; entered the force January 30, 1880.

JOHN E. MAHONEY, desk sergeant, was born at Toronto, Canada, and is at present about 45 years of age; came to Chicago in 1869, and entered the police force August 23, 1870; was first stationed at the old Armory; was made station keeper at Harrison street after the fire, and later was assigned in the same capacity at Cottage Grove avenue; was made desk sergeant first at the 22d street station, then at Cottage Grove, and in February, 1884, took his present position.

FRANCIS O'NEILL, patrol sergeant, was born in the town of Bantry, County Cork, Ireland, in 1848; came to Chicago in 1867, and entered the force July 17, 1873; was shot in the left breast by the burglar John Bridges, whom he arrested Aug. 17, 1873, just one month after joining the service; was appointed regular patrolman by the police board on the following day for meritorious conduct, and stationed at the Armory; was appointed desk sergeant at Deering street in August, 1878, and transferred to general superintendent's office in February, 1884; was classed as patrol sergeant on January

1, 1887; has never been fined, suspended or reprimanded while connected with the police department.

CHAUNCY M. BARTTELL, patrolman, was born in the village of Geneseo, N. Y., of American parents, in 1842; brought west with his family, who settled near Elgin, in 1843; has resided in Chicago for twenty years; entered the force June 16, 1883; was detailed for duty at the Maxwell Brothers and McCormick strike; has made many important arrests; was with first company of the 4th precinct in the Haymarket affair; since, assigned to Central detail.

WILLIAM BOYD, patrolman, was born in Scotland in 1840; came to Chicago in 1858 and entered the force in September, 1874.

THOMAS BIRMINGHAM, patrolman, was born in Joliet in 1861; came to Chicago in 1879; joined the police force in 1884. Has been an efficient officer.

JAMES BRENNAN, patrolman, and one of the best men on the force, was awarded the medal for bravery, on March 4, 1887, at the recommendation of Captain Hubbard, on the following presentation of facts: On or about July 21st, 1886, at 3:25 p. m., while at his post of duty at the west end of Lake street bridge, the bridge bell rang, and he immediately halted a number of teams approaching the bridge on West Lake street. When the bridge had partially turned, so that its northern section was about the center of the street, the escaping steam and noise of an engine passing under the viaduct so frightened a horse, then standing on the east end of the viaduct and attached to a two-seated carriage, occupied by Mrs. Barry and little son, and Mrs. H. C. Stover, with her little boy, that it became unmanageable, and rushed at a great rate of speed down the steep incline toward the river. He was just then near the bridge, and sprang forward and caught the horse by the bit, about half way between the bridge and where he first started. The horse was a large twelve or thirteen hundred pound animal, powerful, vicious, and badly frightened, and in his mad fury to escape the object of his fright, reared, pitched and plunged right and left; and, although Brennan is a strong, heavy man, he actually lifted him from his footing, threw him upon the pavement, trampled on him, and dragged him in various directions. The officer clung to him, regained his footing, and with great effort pulled him to the right, just as he had reached the abutment exposed by the turning of the bridge, when one more bound would have landed them in the bottom of the river. The bridge had then stopped turning, leaving a space accessible between the abutment rail and the northern upright of the bridge of about three feet wide; and with one more seemingly superhuman effort, amid the shrieks of the persons in the carriage, adding fright to the already savage beast, goaded to desperation with terror, Brennan forced him upon the end of the bridge. A crash followed. The carriage was cut in two. The policeman released his hold on the horse, and grasped the lady and little boy occupying the front seat, just as they were tottering with a part of the carriage over the embankment, and landed them safely on the bridge, while that part of the carriage in which they had been seated tumbled into the river. The other two occupants of the carriage had, during the excitement, scrambled from the rear end and escaped. The horse ran part way across the bridge, and was stopped. Thus life and property were preserved. During the struggle, Brennan's blouse and pants were completely riddled, and his flesh was badly bruised and lacerated, and he was otherwise severely hurt, so that he was unable to perform his duties for several days thereafter.

JAMES BELL, patrolman; born in Ireland 1839; came to Chicago August, 1863; entered the force 1872.

JAMES BOLYER, patrolman; born in Ireland 1854; entered the force December 15, 1884.

BERNARD BOESEN, patrolman; born in Germany 1853; entered the force December 15, 1884.

MAURICE BOWLER, patrolman; born in County Kerry, Ireland, 1847; came to Chicago July 8, 1872; entered the force January 15, 1881.

JAMES BURTON, patrolman; born in Dublin, Ireland, 1847; came to Chicago 1866; entered the force 1872.

DANIEL BURNS, patrolman; born in Ireland 1841; came to Chicago 1859; entered the force May, 1867.

THOMAS D. BECK, patrolman; born in Germany 1841; came to Chicago 1866; entered the force Oct. 1, 1874.

EDWARD BURKE, patrolman; born in Ireland in 1854; entered the force December 15, 1884.

DANIEL CONSIDINE, patrolman; born in Ireland 1844; came to Chicago 1867; entered the force March 27, 1871.

CORNELIUS W. CROWLEY, patrolman, was born at East Stoughton, Mass., October 13, 1849; came to Chicago June, 1869, and entered the force September, 1873.

JAMES CAHILL, patrolman, was born in Ireland in 1842; came to Chicago in 1866, and entered the force in the autumn of 1873.

JOHN CRAMER, patrolman, was born in Wisconsin in 1848· came to Chicago in 1870, and entered the force in 1873.

HENRY COX, patrolman, was born in Nottingham, England, in 1831; came to Chicago in 1861; entered the force September 15, 1867;

after the Chicago fire was assigned to the "Lake Street Squad;" since 1876 has been bookkeeper at the Central station.

LUKE P. COLLERAN, patrolman; born in Sligo, Ireland, March 17, 1860; entered the police force in 1883; was assigned to duty at Larrabee street; in March, 1884, at the corner of North avenue and Wells street, was shot by John Murphy whom he had under arrest, but was not seriously wounded; was transferred to the Central detail in April, 1886, and was under command of Lieutenant (now captain) George W. Hubbard on the night of the 4th of May; escaped injury except the loss of his uniform which was torn by flying fragments from the bomb.

JOHN W. COLLINS, patrolman; born in Ireland in 1861; came to Chicago 1878, and entered the police force 1883; was assigned to the second precinct for fifteen months, where he made many important arrests; was in the Central detail company on the night of May 4th, which participated in the Haymarket affair.

MARTIN COLEMAN, patrolman; born in Ireland 1849; came to Chicago April, 1869; entered the force in 1881.

HENRY H. CLUETT, patrolman; born in England 1849; came to Chicago 1856; entered the force April, 1873.

MICHAEL J. COSTELLO, patrolman; born in America 1856; came to Chicago 1850; entered the force March 11, 1873.

THOMAS M. CURTAIN, patrolman; born in Ireland; entered the force December 13, 1876.

NICHOLAS CROSBY, patrolman; born in Ireland 1848; entered the force March 24, 1881.

JOHN CASEY, patrolman; entered the force Oct. 18, 1872.

GEORGE J. DEWEY, patrolman; age 61; in charge of newsboys at the *Daily News, Mail* and *Herald* offices, is one of the oldest and best known members of the force. In a recently published sketch of his life, in which his affection for the newsboys and his regard for their welfare was commented upon, it is said that he is one of the very few men who is capable of handling the "city children"— the newsboys and bootblacks—the waifs. "He is their court of last resort." It may, therefore, be imagined how valuable his services are. He arrived in this city forty-two years ago. He fought in the Mexican and civil wars and attained the rank of captain. After the war he was connected with the American Express Company until 1868, when he entered the police force. He is an American by birth and strictly regardful of morality. For six years he has been thrown into constant contact with the newsboys of the city, and his kindly disposition and benevolent countenance has won from them that which they seldom extend to any one—respect.

He has been one of the principal organizers of the Waif's Mission in this city, a most commendable charity; he is never tired of planning to make the boys better and happier; has taken a leading part in all movements calculated for their betterment; has headed the noisy army toward picnics and excursions, and has kept them in such control that the newsboys of the present day are angels in comparison with what they were a few years ago. Captain Dewey does not stop at providing moral instruction for the boys. To him, as much as to any other one person in the city, is due the fact that for several winters past the waifs of the city have been properly shod and clothed. Captain Dewey has the confidence of the newspaper publishers, and all recognize the valuable services which he has rendered and is still rendering them, in pulling the rein tight enough to curb the Arab, without breaking his spirit.

FLORENCE DONOHUE, patrolman, was born in Ireland in 1842; came to Chicago in 1863, and entered the force in 1869; arrested the colored highwayman, Geo. Carroll, who robbed Andrew Steinmetz, May 8, 1872, and sent him to the penitentiary for five years inside of thirty-eight hours from the time of his arrest. Was shot in Mike McDonald's gambling house on the night of November 23, 1878, the ball passing through his clothing; was in the company of men from Central detail under Captain Hubbard and Lieut. Fitzpatrick at the Haymarket massacre, and has had many hairbreadth escapes from injury and death while connected with the force.

THOMAS DOOLEY, patrolman; born in Ireland 1847; came to Chicago 1867; entered the force December 3d, 1872.

WILLIAM DOLLARD, patrolman; born in Chicago 1848; entered the force April 8, 1879; has convicted several bad criminals for various crimes; among them John Oliver, alias Orr, murder; penitentiary for life; William Taylor, for the killing of Robert McCaw; Charles Hawkins for the killing of Gus Lee, and several burglars, many of whom have been convicted.

JAMES DERRIG, patrolman; born in Canada 1858; came to Chicago 1870; entered the force June 1, 1877; has made several important arrests, chief among them that of Frank Felker for robbery; Thomas McGinnis, for assault to commit murder; Harry Haxwell for assault to kill; the notorious abortionist Dr. Earll, for murder, and Andrew Nelson for murder; he has sent his share of dangerous characters to Joliet.

GEORGE DEMAR, patrolman; born in Germany 1851; came to Chicago 1868; entered the force April 11, 1876.

GEORGE DETTINGER, patrolman; born in Germany 1846; came to Chicago 1859; entered the force October, 1870.

FRANK DOLAN, patrolman; born in Ireland 1827; came to Chicago 1850; entered the force May 2, 1867,—one of the oldest men in the department. In 1869 he arrested George Harris, James Wade, alias Brewster, Andrew Gilmartin and one Brennan for burglary at the residences of Judge Wait, Mr. Kerfoot, ex-Alderman Kehoe, and for robbing several railroad cars. All were convicted and sent down with sentences of from four to eleven years each. In this case he recovered property amounting in value to $16,000. Brewster and Gilmartin he arrested while they were attempting to rob the residence of John P. Calhoun, 101 Pine street. He has done a great deal of good work since then, and is still one of the most active men on the force.

GARRETT H. DOYLE patrolman; born in New York 1862; entered the force June 13, 1883.

THOMAS DOOLEY, patrolman; born in Ireland 1844; entered the force Dec. 2, 1872.

JOHN DUFFICY, patrolman; born in Ireland; entered the force Sept. 28, 1878.

PATRICK DOUGHERTY, patrolman; born in Ireland 1838; entered the force Sept. 1, 1869.

WILLIAM H. DARROW, patrolman, born in America 1856; entered the police force March 21, 1881.

JACOB EBINGER, patrolman; born at Niles, Cook county, 1842; came to Chicago when an infant; entered the force 1870; enlisted in the army as one of McClellan's Body Guard in 1861; served until November, 1865; returning from the war entered the special police service in Chicago and served in that capacity till he joined the regular force; participated in the Haymarket riot, receiving a slight shell wound in the left hand, but was soon able to attend to duty.

MILLARD ENSWORTH, patrolman; born in Michigan 1833; came to Chicago 1847; entered the force 1862; is one of the veterans who has done excellent service during the past twenty-five years.

PETER EBERSOLD, patrolman; born in Germany 1832; entered the force 1865; another veteran.

DOMINIC FEENY, patrolman; born in Ireland 1856; came to Chicago May, 1873; entered the force October, 1882; was transferred from Cottage Grove station to the Central detail July 12, 1887.

DENIS J. FOLEY, patrolman, was born in Ireland in 1848, came to Chicago in 1871, and entered the force September 14, 1873.

STEPHEN W. FAY, patrolman; born in Ireland 1855; came to Chicago May 4, 1873; entered the force June 13, 1883.

PATRICK FALLEN, patrolman; entered the force April 25, 1886.

HENRY N. FECHTER, patrolman; detailed at the Chicago & Northwestern passenger depot; born in Luxemburg Jan'y 25, 1839; came to Chicago 1853; entered the army in 1861, being attached to B Company, 10th Illinois Veteran Volunteers, Infantry, and remained in the service till July 4, 1865; served under Halleck's, Pope's and Sherman's commands; was engaged in the fights at "Island No. 10," at New Madrid, Mo., Corinth, Miss., Chickamauga, Mission Ridge, and through the campaign from Chattanooga to Atlanta and from Atlanta to the sea; in the Carolinas from Savannah, and his last taste of war was at Bentonville on March 17, 1865; came to Chicago at the close of the war and entered the police force in August, 1865, being assigned to the old Market Hall on the North Side, where Wells Sherman was sergeant; did patrol duty on the North Side till the fire of 1871; was then transferred to the West Side, where he remained six months, then to the South Side, and placed in the Central detail, and has been connected with the day squad ever since. In March, 1867, an officer named Grief was assaulted by a man named Henry Bluchbaier, who used a knife. Fechter came to the assistance of Grief, and when Bluchbaier turned upon him Grief fled. The struggle was a terrible one for a few minutes. Bluchbaier plunged the knife into Fechter's breast and hand, but before he could inflict fatal injuries the officer shot him. He had another terrible conflict on January 29, 1870. A man named Moore went into Joseph Daqua's restaurant to take some refreshments. When he had finished, the barkeeper demanded his pay. Moore, instead of paying, presented a bill for two dollars which he had against Daqua. After some angry talk the bartender cut Moore's skull open in two places with a beer mallet. Officer Fechter was at the Chicago & Northwestern depot at the time and was called to his assistance. He picked Moore up at the corner of Wells and Kinzie streets, and asked him to point out his assailant. He pointed out the bartender, and Officer Fechter immediately placed him under arrest. Daqua, who was present, demanded the release of his employe, insisted that the officer should have a warrant, and attempted otherwise to interfere. Fechter told Daqua to keep off, as he was determined to arrest the barkeeper. Daqua then pulled a revolver and shot the officer, the bullet striking near the spinal column, where it still remains, and followed it up with another which sent a ball into Fechter's collar bone, and another which wounded him in the arm, another through his clothing. Fechter now opened fire, shooting Daqua through the thigh and breast. The latter had fired six shots in all, and had the revolver pointed at the officer's head for the seventh and last shot, when it was snatched away from him. He died in ten minutes. Under Wells Sherman's administration the North Side was infested with

burglars. Hardly a night but some of the best residences were
broken into and robbed of silver, jewelry, etc. One night in April,
1867, Fechter came across four burglars and watched them until
they had entered a house at the corner of State and Indiana streets.
When they were inside he whistled for assistance, and with the
whistle in his left hand and a revolver in his right he approached
the house. The burglars knew the alarm and three of them left the
house hurriedly and escaped. The fourth one was at the second
story window ready to jump when Fechter fired at him, when he
made his way to a window on the same floor in the rear, from
which he jumped into the yard, just in time to fall into Fechter's
arms. When taken to the station he claimed to be a barber. He
had a razor in his pocket. He said he came from Cincinnati where
he had sold a house and lot and now had $5,000 in money. On
Thanksgiving day, 1875, in the St. Elmo restaurant, Wieland, the
keeper, was murdered by Hank Davis, a gambler. Fechter was at
State and Madison street at the time, and was called upon to arrest
Davis. It was 6 o'clock in the evening. Davis had barricaded
himself behind the ice-box in the restaurant, and had a loaded bull-
dog revolver in hand, ready to commit any act rather than be
taken. Fechter, however, approached Davis coolly; the latter fired
at him, but he was soon disarmed and taken to the Harrison street
station. He was afterward sent to the penitentiary for twenty-one
years. In the riot of 1877, Fechter saw some good service under
Lieutenant Gerbing.

J. PATRICK GAVIN, patrolman, was born in Ireland in 1832; arrived
in Chicago May 13, 1847; entered the force February 11, 1868;
arrested burglars who robbed John McEwan's residence on La-
Salle avenue, and helped them into the penitentiary for five years;
captured Cunningham, "the diamond thief," and found him in possession of the plunder; Cunningham was sent to jail pending
trial, but escaped by walking out with his lawyer; later was sent
to Sing Sing penitentiary for five years.

JOHN F. GIBBONS, patrolman, was born in Chicago in 1858; entered
the force on December 15, 1884. Was in the Haymarket riot.

JACOB GROSS, patrolman, was born in Baden, Germany, February 16,
1845; arrived in Chicago 1854, and joined the police force May 15,
1875; arrested Gahgaren, who shot and killed Joseph Weeks at 142
Cornelia street, October 21, 1876; was engaged in the Haymarket
riot.

LOUIS GOLDEN, patrolman, was born in Cohoes, Albany county, N.
Y., July 18, 1859; came to Chicago in 1876; joined the force on
June 13, 1883; served under Captain Hubbard in the Haymarket
riot.

JOHN GALLAGHER, patrolman; born at Libertyville, Lake county, Ill., 1842; came to Chicago in 1861; entered the force 1872.

JOSEPH A. GILSO, patrolman; born in New York 1849; entered the force Dec. 15, 1884.

PATRICK A. GARRITY, patrolman; born in Ireland 1857; entered the force Dec. 15, 1884.

GEORGE W. HUNT, patrolman; assigned to duty at the comptroller's office, the one-armed veteran and hero of the lager beer riot, was born in Troy, Vermont, August 10, 1824. He came to Chicago in 1853, and entered the police force in the spring of 1855, being now in his thirty-third year on the force. He was a railroad man in his younger days, running on the Boston & Maine road for six years, and on the Rutland & Burlington three years. When he first entered the force there were but 31 men in the department, and he carried the hickory club and wore the leather badge until the city attained metropolitan proportions. In this history the various transfers which he has undergone, his promotions, and his gallant conduct in the lager beer riot are referred to under proper dates. He has filled his present position in the comptroller's office as long as anybody now on the force can remember. He is still a robust man, and capable of the best of work. [See lager beer riot.]

THOMAS J. HOWARD, patrolman, was born in Ireland in 1857; came to Chicago in 1865, and entered the force in April, 1887.

WILLIAM A. HARTMAN, patrolman, was born at Canton, Ohio, in 1856; came to Chicago in 1861; entered the force December 15, 1884; was detailed at Cottage Grove station until July 8th, 1887, then transferred to Central station.

MICHAEL HOFFMAN, patrolman, was born in Chicago in 1855; entered the force on May 24, 1881.

JOSEPH T. HARNOIS, patrolman, was born in Montreal, Canada, July 9, 1842, came to Chicago in 1847; entered the police force September 8, 1877.

JOSEPH A. HILLIER, patrolman; born in Ohio 1849; came to Chicago 1853; entered the force 1880; served in the army toward the close of the war; was at the battle of Atlanta, and with Sherman in his march to the sea; was with Company I of the 30th Illinois Infantry, First Brigade. Officer Hillier carries the gold star as the champion rifle shot of the police force.

THOMAS HAYS, patrolman; born in Ireland 1851; came to Chicago June 24, 1874; entered the force June 13, 1883; arrested William McMahon Sept. 7, 1886, for killing John Maher at the corner of Peoria street and Carroll avenue; prisoner attempted to shoot; was afterward sent to the penitentiary for ten years.

JOHN HOOLEY, patrolman; born in Ireland 1845; came to Chicago 1863; entered the force March 31, 1873.

DANIEL HOGAN, patrolman; born in Ireland 1846; entered the force Aug. 27, 1873.

SAMUEL HELZE, patrolman; born in Norway 1854; entered the force Dec. 15, 1884.

CARL EDWARD JOHNSEN, patrolman, was born in Gottenburg, Sweden, January 5, 1852; came to Chicago in 1868, entered the police force December 15, 1884, and was assigned to duty at the West Chicago avenue station, where he remained till 1886, when he was transferred to the Central detail; was fired upon in a row at a dance hall, at Indiana and Paulina streets, by a young rough named Edward Orr, whom he afterward seriously wounded; was badly beaten by a crowd of roughs on Erie street near Ashland avenue, Sept., 1885, when an unsuccessful attempt was made to rescue prisoners whom he had under arrest; was in the company under command of Lieut. Quinn on the night of May 4, 1886, at the Haymarket, and was one of those who charged the mob after the bomb explosion; was wounded in the left arm by a piece of the bomb; was transferred from West Chicago avenue to the Central detail in September, 1886.

WILLIAM F. JICHLING, patrolman, was born in the town of Lynn, Norfolk, England, on the 7th of March, 1833; was brought by his parents to Canada at the age of 3; learned the carpenter's trade and followed it in Canada till 1859; came to the United States and located at Richland, Mich.; enlisted as a private in the Federal army and was assigned to the 44th Illinois Infantry upon his arrival in Chicago; remained in the army till the close of the war; was promoted four times, and participated in some of the bloodiest battles of the rebellion; was shot in the neck and right knee at the Battle of Stone River, from whence he was taken by the rebels to Libby prison, where he was confined twenty-three days; was paroled and afterward rejoined his regiment; was shot in the left hand at Mission Ridge, and in the head at Chickamauga; came to Chicago in 1865, resuming his trade; joined the police force in 1873, served through the riot of '77, and all the subsequent riots and strikes.

PETER J. JOYCE, patrolman, was born in the west of Ireland, April 24, 1847; came to Chicago August 8, 1878; entered the police force July 23, 1883.

WILLIAM S. JOHNSON, patrolman; born in Indiana 1848; entered the force June 19, 1877.

HERMAN F. E. KRUGER, patrolman, was born in the village of Laase, in the province of Pommerania, Germany, on Dec. 19, 1858; came to America in 1865, and resided in Chicago until 1876;

enlisted in the 16th U. S. Infantry, Company "K," and served five years in the Indian Territory and Texas; was discharged September 13, 1881; returned to Chicago and entered the police force on Dec. 15, 1884; was assigned to duty at the West Chicago avenue station; was wounded by the Haymarket explosion and disabled till October, 1886; was on duty at the Central station till March 30, 1887, and transferred to the Central detail May 5, 1887.

PAUL KALLOCH, patrolman, was born in the village of Gross Stanisch, Upper Sileisa, Prussia, in 1852; came to Chicago in 1866; appointed to the force December 4, 1876; performed duty at West Chicago avenue, Rawson street and West Lake street stations; was transferred to Central detail in 1882.

PATRICK KENEFICK, patrolman; born in Ireland 1837; came to Chicago 1864; entered the force September, 1870; has been engaged in all the riots since 1877; has never been reprimanded.

JOHN J. KELLY, patrolman; assigned to duty as vehicle inspector; was born in America 1854; entered the force March 14, 1881.

PETER KELLY, patrolman; born in Chicago 1857; entered the force Dec. 15, 1884.

JOHN C. KEENAN, patrolman; born in Illinois 1857; entered the force December 15, 1884.

JAMES LENNON, patrolman, was born in Brockville, Ontario, Canada, in 1837; came to Chicago in 1854, and entered the force in 1872.

PATRICK LAVIN, patrolman, was born in Ireland March 10, 1843; came to Chicago May, 1868; entered police force in March, 1875; was in the fight on the Halsted street viaduct in the riot of '77; also in the Haymarket affair.

WILLIAM LYONNAIS, patrolman; born in Montreal 1851; came to Chicago March 17, 1866; entered the force August 1, 1882.

HERMAN MEYER, patrolman, was born in Germany in 1840; came to Chicago in 1857, and entered the force March 4, 1872.

PATRICK McGOVERN, patrolman, was born in Ireland in 1851; came to Chicago June, 1859; entered the force April, 1880.

SIMON McMAHON patrolman, was born in the County Clare, Ireland, on August 15, 1850; came to the United States with his parents in 1853; lived in the state of New York till 1857, when the family moved to Palos, Cook county, Illinois; educated in a district school; came to Chicago at the age of 16, and worked in the North Chicago rolling mills for 15 years; went into the grocery business on North Ashland avenue, and sold out in 1884; entered the force in December of that year, being assigned to the North avenue station; served under Lieut. Quinn at the Haymarket riot, receiving wounds which disabled him for three months; carries three pieces of lead in his limbs yet, as a result of the fusilade on that night; was transferred to the Central detail, and is assigned to duty at the intersection of Lake and Canal streets and Milwaukee avenue; has made many important arrests and is looked upon as a most efficient officer.

G. H. McHUGH, patrolman, was born in Ireland in 1844; came to New York in 1862 and joined the U. S. navy, serving for one year; came to Chicago in 1864, and entered the force in November, 1872.

MICHAEL McKAY, patrolman; born in the County of Tipperary, Ireland, 1856; came to Chicago in 1880; entered the force December, 1884.

JOHN C. MORRIS, patrolman; born in Oneida Co., N. Y., 1846; came to Chicago July, 1874; entered the force February, 1882; was assigned to duty at 22d street and remained there until transferred to the Central detail; was in the Haymarket affair, under Lieut. Hubbard; was slightly wounded and had uniform torn.

BERNARD J. MURPHY, patrolman; born in Ireland 1857; came to Chicago 1884; entered the force Dec. 15, 1884; was in the second company at the Haymarket riot, and was shot in the right side of the head, over the temple; a piece of the shell entered his right thigh, and he was wounded also by a fragment in the chin.

PETER MURPHY, patrolman; born in Kingston, Ontario, 1847; came to Chicago 1866; entered the force 1883.

MICHAEL MURPHY, patrolman; assigned to duty as inspector of vehicles; born in Ireland 1835; came to Chicago 1850; entered the force March 12, 1867.

MATTHEW H. McGUIRK, patrolman; born in Scotland 1843; came to Chicago August, 1868; entered the force March 12, 1873.

MICHAEL MADDEN, patrolman; born in Illinois 1860; came to Chicago 1875; entered the force December 15, 1884. Officer Madden met a leading anarchist named August Krueger the evening after the Haymarket riot, about 6 o'clock p. m., on the corner of Fulton and Desplaines streets. Krueger fired a shot and entered Schroeder's saloon at the above corner. Officer Madden followed him into the saloon and asked him about the shooting. Krueger, without saying a word, fired again, shooting Madden through the left breast under the collar bone. Although seriously wounded Madden took hold of Krueger and brought him out on the sidewalk where a desperate struggle ensued. Krueger made ready for another shot when Madden discharged a pistol, the ball of which entered Krueger's left breast. Both were taken to the county hospital. Krueger died three days later. Officer Madden slowly recovered, but carries the bullet in his breast now.

JAMES MITCHELL, patrolman; born at Fox Lake, Illinois, April 7, 1859; came to Chicago October, 1870; entered the force June 13, 1883; assigned to duty at Desplaines street, remaining there until May 1, 1886, then was transferred to the Central detail; participated in the Haymarket riot.

PETER McCORMICK, patrolman; born in New York 1850; entered the force December 15, 1884.

DENNIS McCORMICK, patrolman; born in Massachusetts 1848; entered the force June 30, 1883.

JOHN J. McNULTY, patrolman; born in Chicago 1859; entered the force December 15, 1884.

THOMAS MURPHY, patrolman; born in Ireland; entered the force June 19, 1867.

JOHN MORNEISER, patrolman; born in Germany; entered the force Sept. 18, 1877.

MICHAEL MANNING, patrolman; born in Ireland 1853; entered the force June 13, 1883.

THOMAS NOONAN, patrolman; born in Ireland 1850; entered the force April 2, 1872.

JOHN J. O'DONNELL, patrolman; born in Chicago 1852; entered the force December 15, 1881.

JAMES T. O'DONNELL, patrolman, was born in Chicago in 1860; entered the force in 1884.

JAMES O'BRIEN, patrolman; born in Ireland 1844; came to Chicago 1871; entered the force December 14, 1874.

DENNIS O'CONNOR, patrolman; born in the County Tipperary, Ireland, 1858; came to Chicago 1878; entered the force December 16, 1884.

WALTER O'DONNELL, patrolman; born in Ireland 1851; entered the force July 19, 1883.

MICHAEL O'DONNELL, patrolman; born in Ireland 1849; came to Chicago 1870; entered the force June 2, 1882.

MICHAEL O'HALLORAN, patrolman; born in Ireland 1851; came to Chicago 1869; entered the force 1881.

PATRICK O'REGAN, patrolman; born in Ireland 1845; entered the force January 18, 1876.

JOHN O'CONNOR, patrolman; born in Ireland 1859; came to Chicago 1876; entered the force 1884.

OLIVER PETERSON, patrolman; born in Sweden 1848; came to Chicago 1868; entered the force Sept. 13, 1873.

GEORGE PERRY, patrolman; born in America 1851; entered the force October 15, 1884.

B. H. REED, patrolman; born in South Durham, Canada East, 1859; came to Chicago April 7, 1879; entered the force December 15, 1884; served in the West Side street-car riot, the McCormick troubles and the Haymarket riot.

EDWARD J. RYAN, patrolman; born in Chicago 1847; entered the force 1867.

CHARLES P. REVERE, patrolman; born in California 1859; entered the force December 15, 1884.

J. REARDON, patrolman; born in Illinois 1848; entered the force December 21, 1884.

MARTIN RINTZ, patrolman, was born in Bavaria in 1842, came to Chicago August 15, 1860, and entered the force December 16, 1876.

JOHN RICHARDSON, patrolman, was born in Odeltown, Canada, in 1839; came to Chicago in 1851, and entered the force March 29, 1871.

MARTIN D. RINGROSE, patrolman, was born in Ireland in 1850; came to Chicago in 1855, and entered the force in October, 1873.

JOHN M. SCOTT, patrolman, was born in Plymouth, N. Y., in 1850; came to Chicago in April, 1871; entered the force October 4, 1873, and went on duty at the Union street station, serving there for eighteen months; was transferred to Central station, and resigned July 31st, 1879; re-entered the force May 10, 1887.

WILLIAM STENERNAGEL, patrolman, was born in Germany in 1838; came to Chicago in 1852; entered the force September 12, 1875; arrested Isaac Jacobson, murderer of George Bedell, on April 29, 1884.

FREEMAN STEELE, patrolman, was born in Canada in 1864; came to Chicago in 1869; entered the force September 11, 1885; was wounded in the Haymarket riot May 4, 1886; supposed to be youngest man on the force.

SOLOMON C. STEELE, patrolman; born in Orange county, N. Y., January 5, 1848; joined the 8th Iowa volunteers in 1865; came to Chicago in 1874, entered the force in May, 1882; was in the Haymarket riot.

C. A. SPENCER, patrolman, was born in England in 1842; came to Chicago in 1863; entered the police force in 1870

WALTER A. SARGEANT, patrolman; born in America; entered the force April 29, 1872.

NICHOLAS H. STAHL, patrolman; born at Galena, Ill., 1858; came to Chicago September 15, 1872; entered the force October 18, 1879.

Assisted in killing the notorious desperado, Bill Allen, who murdered Police Officer Wright; also participated in the Haymarket riot.

FREDERICK SOMMER, patrolman; born in Switzerland 1844; came to Chicago 1865; entered the police force 1877.

BENJAMIN F. SCHNELL, patrolman; born in Chicago 1850; entered the force December 15, 1884.

MARCELI SCHOENFELD, patrolman; born in Germany 1847; entered the force September 9, 1874.

MORRIS SAUIS, patrolman; born in Germany 1841; entered the police force December 15, 1884.

CHRISTOPHER SEIBER, patrolman; born in Germany Aug. 17, 1876.

JAMES SHORT, patrolman; born in America 1842; entered the force September 24, 1872.

WILLIAM SLEETH; entered the force February 5, 1885.

PETER TRENLIEB, patrolman; born at Liban, Russia, 1832; came to Chicago 1854; entered the force June 15, 1869; was formerly a vessel captain.

D. F. TIERNEY, patrolman; born in Ireland 1859; came to Chicago 1876; entered the force 1882.

PATRICK TULLY, patrolman; born in Ireland 1854; entered the force December 15, 1884.

FITCH A. TAYLOR, patrolman; born in America 1849; entered the force July 12, 1873.

PATRICK J. WARD, patrolman; born in Chicago 1856; entered the force October 14, 1882.

JOHN A. WEBER, patrolman; born in Brooklyn, N. Y., 1855; came to Chicago 1857; entered the force December 31, 1874; has done excellent service as a crossing officer, having saved a large number of ladies and children, and even men, from severe bodily injury, and, in one or two instances, from death; was in the McCormick and Haymarket riots, and at the latter affair stood within six feet of the spot where the bomb exploded; has made many important arrests, and is looked upon as a most efficient officer.

JOHN B. WATHIER, patrolman; born in Woltz, Luxemburg, 1859; came to Chicago in July, 1865; entered the force December, 1884.

CHARLES W. WASSMUND, patrolman; born in Prussia, Germany, 1844; came to Chicago 1860; entered the force 1872.

HENRY WALPER, patrolman; born in Germany 1835; came to Chicago 1854; entered the force 1874.

CHAPTER XXIV.

THE FIRST PRECINCT, CAPTAIN WILLIAM BUCKLEY COMMANDING—THE
OLD ARMORY AND THE NEW—THE SCHOOL OF NEARLY ALL THE
ABLEST AND OLDEST POLICE OFFICERS—HISTORY OF THE STATION IN
WHICH THE LEADING POLICEMEN OF CHICAGO HAVE BEEN DEVEL-
OPED—ADVERSITIES OF THE PRECINCT—BURNT DOWN, RE-BUILT,
MOVED, REFITTED, REMOVED, BUT STILL "THE ARMORY" AND HEAD-
QUARTERS IN CHICAGO'S POLICE GEOGRAPHY—THE ROSTER.

The first precinct includes the Harrison street, Twenty-
second street, Cottage Grove avenue, Thirty-fifth street and
Stanton avenue districts, and is commanded by Capt. William
Buckley, with headquarters at the Harrison street or Armory
station. The history of the Armory station, old or new,
is traced very completely in this volume. When the fire
had swept away the Armory building on Franklin street, it
was undergoing repairs, and the South Side headquarters
were located in the old Bridewell, at Polk and Wells streets
(Fifth avenue). After the fire the headquarters were shifted
to a frame school house on the corner of Harrison street and
Pacific avenue (present location), and then moved to another
building close by, while the present structure was being
erected. The station, which also accommodates a police
court, the rogues' gallery, a drill room, armory and sleeping
quarters, is one of the largest and best equipped in the
city. It is located in the heart of a section for many years
recognized as the slums of the city—with "Biler" avenue,
Fourth avenue, South Clark and South State streets—the
"Levee" and "Cheyenne,"—contributing to police annals
about two-thirds of all the crimes committed in Chicago.
The station has always been a prominent one, being the
parent of all the South Side stations, except the Central detail, which is under command of Captain Hubbard. The

JOHN BYRNE,
Lieut. Comdg. Harrison St. District.

EDWARD LAUGHLIN,
Lieut. Comdg. Harrison St. District.

district cared for by the Central detail in the day time is covered by the Harrison street station at night.

WILLIAM BUCKLEY, captain commanding the first precinct, was born in the County Waterford, Ireland, in 1832, and came to this country in 1852; he worked in an iron foundry in New York City for a year; farmed on Long Island for a couple of years, and came to Chicago in the spring of 1857, arriving here about the time the place became incorporated as a city; after engaging in various honorable pursuits here, he entered the police force in April, 1865, being assigned to the old Armory station, and serving as patrolman until 1867, when he became a roundsman; he was then promoted to be desk sergeant and lock-up keeper; was promoted to a lieutenancy by the board of police commissioners in 1870, and in 1873 was appointed captain to succeed Capt. M. C. Hickey, who had resigned, owing to trouble with Superintendent Washburn; in 1877 Capt. Buckley was removed by the influence of officials who were at enmity with him, but he re-entered the force as a patrolman later on, and Mayor Harrison promoted him rapidly until in 1879 he had secured his old position; he was shifted around for some time, but finally landed at the Armory, with which he had been so long identified. [See biography]. See Chapter XVIII.

JOHN BYRNE, lieutenant of police, Harrison street district, was born at Oran, in the County Roscommon, Ireland, 1849; came to Chicago, 1867, and entered the force July, 1870; he was promoted to a lieutenancy Oct. 1, 1874, and assigned to duty at the West Madison street station and commanded that district for one year; was then transferred to the Armory, from thence to Deering street, at which place he remained in charge for six years, and was finally transferred back to the Armory in May, 1887. When Capt. Buckley, Sam Ellis, Fitzpatrick and others were removed from the force, under Mayor Heath's administration, Lieut. Byrne was among the number, but, like the others, he soon found his way back. He has proved himself to be a brave and spirited officer on many occasions; has had numerous hair-breadth escapes, and is one of the most popular men on the force.

EDWARD LAUGHLIN, lieutenant of police, Harrison street district, was born at Castle Island, County Kerry, Ireland, in 1843; came to Chicago in 1862, and entered the force March 1, 1872. Before entering the force he had been in the employ of the Pittsburg & Fort Wayne Railroad Company, and on coming to Chicago took a position in the freight yards of the Milwaukee & St. Paul Railroad Company. For a time he steamboated on the Mississippi; he returned to Chicago, when he entered the employment of Merritt & Bacon, 86 and 88 South Water street, as a shipping and receiving clerk. He visited California, but came back, determined upon settling down here. His police record is a long and creditable one, and he stands high in the estimation of his superiors and associates. Like all other commanding officers at the Armory, he has seen some very rough service, but has always borne himself bravely.

DANIEL HOGAN, desk sergeant, was born in the County Clare, Ireland, in 1843; came to Chicago in 1866, and entered the force September 15, 1873. Sergeant Hogan received the advantages of a splendid English education in the cities of Dublin and Waterford, and taught "the young idea how to shoot" in his native country, and afterward in this. He taught school in Lamont and Palos in this county. After joining the force, he was raised to the position of station keeper and assigned to the Cottage Grove avenue station, but was soon transferred to the Armory, where his remarkable qualifications fit him for the arduous duties which he is called upon to perform there. He is one of the most enthusiastic supporters of the Policemen's Benevolent Association, and the fact that he is the secretary of this commendable organization shows that he is held in the highest esteem by his associates.

PATRICK O'BRIEN, desk sergeant, was born in Peterborough, Ontario, 1851; came to Chicago 1859, and entered the force July, 1882. He has been a most successful burglar hunter, having sent many members of the dark fraternity to Joliet, where he has two men serving for 20 years, and almost twenty others for various terms; traveled in plain clothes for three years; arrested Hall, a Cincinnati man, for the murder of a negro; has been desk sergeant for eighteen months. Sergeant O'Brien is still quite young, and the probabilities are that he has not yet mounted as high as he is destined to reach.

CHARLES P. ARADO, patrolman; born in New Orleans 1859; came to Chicago 1859; entered the force 1884.

THOMAS BARRETT, lock-up keeper; born in County Meath, Ireland 1827; came to Chicago 1855; entered the force 1856; was police constable in 1864; in 1868 was promoted to sergeant; was two years at the old Armory, then transferred to Cottage Grove avenue station, and had charge until 1880, when transferred here and has been lock-up keeper since.

MATTHEW BLACKBURN, patrolman; born in Lincoln, Ill., 1857; came to Chicago August, 1882; entered the force July, 1885.

EDWARD BURNS, patrolman; born in Elgin, Ill., 1859; came to Chicago 1880; entered the force August 1, 1887.

JAMES H. BUCKLEY, patrolman; born in Chicago, Ill., 1858; entered the force July 1, 1876.

JOHN BROUGHTON, patrolman; born in Ireland 1862; came to Chicago 1880; entered the force July 2, 1887.

LAWRENCE BUCKLEY, patrolman; born in London, England, 1852; came to Chicago June, 1868; entered the force June, 1887.

JOHN COAKLEY, patrolman; born in Chicago 1859; entered the force December, 1885.

JOHN COLEMAN, patrolman; born in Wisconsin 1853; came to Chicago 1876; entered the force 1884.

D. J. COUGHLIN, patrolman; born in Illinois 1852; came to Chicago March 1, 1872; entered the force August 1, 1878.

LAWRENCE COOGAN, patrolman; born in Hadenville, Mass., 1855; came to Chicago 1856; entered the force July 22, 1887.

JOHN COX, patrolman; born in Ireland 1856; came to Chicago August, 1878; entered the force December 15, 1884.

THOMAS DUFFY, patrolman; born in Samsburough, Minn., 1863; came to Chicago April, 1879; entered the force December 15, 1884; in 1885 arrested the notorious highwayman, William Barry; was in the street-car strike of 1885; has made many important arrests.

DANIEL DOHUY, patrolman; born in Ireland 1849; came to Chicago July, 1876; entered the force June, 1883.

WM. J. DRIVER, patrolman; born in Chicago 1857; entered the force June 3, 1887.

DANIEL O. DONOVAN, patrolman; born in County Waterford, Ireland, 1858; came to Chicago January, 1877; entered the force June, 1883.

MARTIN FRENCH, patrolman; born in Kentucky 1853; came to Chicago May, 1868; entered the force 1882.

MICHAEL FITZGERALD, patrolman; born in Ireland 1861; came to Chicago September, 1881; entered the force December, 1884.

JOHN FOGARTY, patrolman; born in New Britain, Conn., 1856; came to Chicago March, 1874; entered the force April 15, 1887.

EDWARD FLYNN, patrolman; born in Janesville, Wis., 1855; came to Chicago 1875; entered the force April 19, 1886.

WILLIAM GANEY, patrolman; born in Chicago 1862; entered the force June 3, 1887.

EDWARD HEALY, patrolman; born in Ireland 1862; came to Chicago 1880; entered the force April 13, 1887.

PATRICK McQUAID, patrolman; born in Ireland 1862; came to Chicago May, 1878; entered the force January 1, 1885.

JAMES MADDEN, patrolman; born in England 1857; came to Chicago June, 1869; entered the force September, 1882.

EDWARD McGRATH, patrolman; born in Ireland 1847; came to Chicago May, 1880; entered the force October, 1880.

MICHAEL J. MURTHA, patrolman; born in New York City 1856; came to Chicago 1880; entered the force 1884.

PATRICK M. MURPHY, patrolman; born in Chicago 1859; entered the force 1885.

JOHN J. MULCAHY, patrolman; born in Ireland 1858; came to Chicago 1864; entered the force September 9, 1887.

JAMES McGINNIS, patrolman; born in Green Bay, Wis., 1860; came to Chicago June, 1877; entered the force December 15, 1884; September 20, 1887, arrested Thos. White (colored), for the murder of Harry Woodson, alias "Black Diamond;" September 25, 1886, arrested Harry Moherman, alias John Schroder, a confidence operator, who is now in the penitentiary.

TIMOTHY MURPHY, patrolman; born in Ireland 1860; came to Chicago November, 1876; entered the force December, 1884.

THOMAS MULCAHY, patrolman; born in County Limerick, Ireland, 1854; came to Chicago November, 1880; entered the force 1883; rescued a man from drowning in the lake; arrested two men for burglary, and one for robbery; all are serving terms in the penitentiary.

JOHN MEEHAN, patrolman; born in Ireland 1836; came to Chicago 1855; entered the force August, 1870; during the fire of 1871, rescued four persons from a building adjoining Arcade Court, one of whom he conveyed to the St. Luke's hospital, with the assistance of an expressman; in the strikes of 1877 he had some thrilling experiences with twenty-five specials at Turner Hall; in 1878, during a fire in a dye house on Michigan Ave., rescued four persons, carried an old woman down a stairway and guided a man through the smoke at the same time, the other two by encouraging them to jump from windows and he would break the fall, which he did successfully; also several people on the Lake Front who attempted suicide by drowning.

CHARLES A. PALMER, patrolman; born in Palmyra, Wayne Co., N. Y., 1826; came to Chicago 1872; entered the force April, 1879.

MICHAEL P. QUIGLEY, patrolman; born in Scotland 1859; came to Chicago September, 1872; entered the force March 4, 1884.

STEPHEN ROWAN, patrolman; born in Ireland 1839; came to Chicago September, 1862; entered the force October 1, 187⁴

JOHN T. RAFFERTY, patrolman; born in Chicago 1861; entered the force December, 1884.

JOHN STRATTON, patrolman; born in Davenport, Iowa, 1855; came to Chicago 1875; entered the force June 2, 1887.

MATHIAS J. SCHWEIG, patrolman; born in Luxemburg, Germany, 1851; came to Chicago 1855; entered the force July 1, 1886.

JOHN P. SCHUMACHER, patrolman; born in Chicago 1854; entered the force December 15, 1884.

JAMES M. SWIFT, patrolman; born in Kingston 1853; came to Chicago June 1, 1877; entered the force April 15, 1887.

MICHAEL SWAN, patrolman; born in Cork City, Ireland, 1854; came to Chicago 1880; entered the force April, 1887.

DANIEL SHEA, patrolman; born in Nova Scotia 1858; came to Chicago 1860; entered the force September 17, 1887.

WILLIAM F. SMITH, patrolman; born in Ohio 1856; came to Chicago October 21, 1872; entered the force July 11, 1882; was engaged in the street-car strike of 1885; also the Haymarket riot of 1886; was promoted to a detective in July, 1887.

JAMES SHANLEY, patrolman; born in Ireland 1837; came to Chicago 1852; entered the force March 14, 1870.

MATHIAS STEFFENS, patrolman; born in Joliet, Ill., 1864; came to Chicago 1879; entered the force March 4, 1887.

EDWARD J. TALBOT, patrolman; born in Waterford, Ireland, 1848; came to Chicago 1867; entered the force June, 1883; in July, 1884, arrested Fred Pickard for the murder of Thomas Ashley in the Pacific Block, cor. Clark and Van Buren Sts.; Pickard was sentenced to nine years in the penitentiary.

H. R. WARD, patrolman; born in Plymouth, Rock Co., Wis., 1857; came to Chicago 1881; entered the force June, 1886.

JOHN G. WALLNER, patrolman; born in Chicago 1862; entered the force March 1, 1887.

PATRICK WALSH, patrolman; born in County Sligo, Ireland, 1846; came to Chicago 1865; entered the force 1882; since 1886 has been on duty in citizen's clothes.

MICHAEL WHITE, patrolman; born in Ireland 1836; came to Chicago in 1852; entered the force March, 1868.

TWENTY-SECOND STREET STATION, corner of Wentworth avenue and Twenty-second street, is one of the oldest sub-stations in this city, its establishment dating back to the old times of the department. Its early history is referred to elsewhere. The district patrolled by the force of this station is bounded north, from Halsted street to Lake Michigan, by the south branch of the Chicago River and the Union Railroad track near Sixteenth street; on the east, from Sixteenth to Twenty-second street, by Lake Michigan, and, from Twenty-second to Thirty-first street, by State street; on the south, from Lake Michigan to State street by Twenty-second street, and from State to Halsted street by Thirty-first street; on the west, from Thirty-first street to the south branch of the Chicago River, by Halsted street. The district embraces an area of about one and five-eighths square miles, and contains a population estimated (in 1887) at 65,000.

AUGUST C. ARCH, lieutenant of police, commanding Twenty-second street district, was born January 21, 1843, in the city of Erfurt, Prussia; came to America at the age of five, and from New York his family moved direct to the state of Wisconsin, remaining there until he was 21; worked on his father's farm in Columbia county; went into the timber country, where he worked for some time, and in 1864 enlisted in Company M, 1st Wis. Light Artillery, under Col. Meserve, of Milwaukee, and was sent to join the 22d army corps; the company was sent to Fort Lyons, Va., where it remained engaged in the defense of Washington, remaining in this position until the close of the war; mustered out July, 1865, at the grand review of the army in Washington; after the war returned to the Wisconsin woods and engaged in "logging," rafting in the spring to St. Louis; came to Chicago July, 1866, but did not remain; settled here November of the same year, and entered the force September 13, 1873, being assigned to the Twenty-second street station, remaining there till Nov. 10, 1876, when he was promoted to patrol sergeant; transferred to Cottage Grove station, where he remained till Nov. 20, 1882; transferred to Central detail and remained there till May 22, 1883; transferred to Harrison street, remaining there till February 22, 1884, when he was sent to the East Chicago avenue station as acting lieutenant, vice Lieutenant Heinzeman, resigned, remaining in that capacity till April 22, when he was transferred to Harrison street and appointed full lieutenant, and on May 10, 1887, was transferred to the Central detail, where he remained till Sept. 10, 1887, when he was assigned to his present position; was actively engaged in the suppression of the lumber shovers' riot in 1876, with Sergeant Fitzpatrick; in

1877 he was detailed with twenty-five men to Twenty-second street for emergency service, and instructed to keep that district under control; met the crowd after the bridge had been swung open by the mob on Halsted street, to prevent the passage of the police, and drove the rioters from Archer avenue south on Halsted, one of the hottest fights of the week; in the fall of '77, Thanksgiving Day, spotted the notorious "Sheeney" George and recovered $6,000 worth of stuff which his gang had stolen. "Sheeney" George was confined in jail until the following August, and shortly after occurred the brutal murder of Officer Race, in which he was deeply implicated; arrested George Adams, burglar, who had terrorized the residents of the Cottage Grove district, on Nov. 25, 1879, and sent him to the penitentiary for five years; arrested members of a gang of West Side burglars and sent them to the penitentiary for twenty years under the habitual criminal's act; arrested the negro burglars of Butterfield street, and was cut over the eye by a drunken man on Clark street, Nov. 5, 1885. Lieut. Arch is one of the most intelligent men on the force, and a brave and discreet officer.

JOSEPH LEONARD, patrol sergeant, was born in Ireland in 1843; came to Chicago in 1858, and entered the force in 1873; participated in the riot in the lumber district in 1876; also in the riot of 1877; arrested Rebel George, who was taken to Yankton, Dak., where he was wanted for murder ; assisted in the arrest of Sam Fielden for complicity in the Haymarket massacre.

JOSEPH W. CARY, desk sergeant, was born at Oswego, N. Y., in 1841; came to Chicago in May, 1857, and entered the force December 17, 1874; participated in the riot of 1876 in the lumber district, also in the great riot of 1877; appointed desk sergeant at Twenty-second street station, February 11, 1879.

TIMOTHY BARRETT, patrolman; born in Ireland 1843; came to Chicago May, 1865; entered the force July 11, 1873. June, 1875, arrested John Lawlor and William Smith for burglary; they were both sent to the penitentiary for five years; was in the railroad strike of 1877; shot through the hat by a party of rioters on Halsted street bridge.

CHARLES BACHLE, patrolman; born in Germany 1859; came to Chicago October, 1881; entered the force August, 1887.

BENJ. BRACE, patrolman; born in Utica, N. Y., 1851; came to Chicago May, 1876; entered the force June 30, 1886; assigned to Harrison street station; transferred to Twenty-second street station, 1887.

WILLIAM CORCORAN, patrolman; born in Ireland 1850; came to Chicago 1869; entered the force June 9, 1885.

ROBERT A. DAVIS, patrolman; born in Canada 1862; came to Chicago 1878; entered the force July, 1886.

JOHN J. DUFFY, patrolman; born in Ogdensburg, N. Y., 1858; came to Chicago March, 1872; entered the force December 29, 1884; was in the street-car strike of 1885, the McCormick's and Haymarket riots of 1886.

MICHAEL S. FINEGAN, patrolman; born in Ireland 1850; came to Chicago June, 1867; entered the force January 3, 1883; arrested Thomas Collins, one of the leaders of the Lake Shore & Michigan Southern switchmen's strike, on November 4, 1886, for attempting to wreck a passenger train at Archer ave.

JOHN FITZGERALD, patrolman; born in Ireland 1842; came to Chicago 1870; entered the force 1877.

TIMOTHY J. FOLEY, patrolman; born in Ireland 1848; came to Chicago 1867; entered the force 1882.

MICHAEL F. GOLDEN, patrolman; born in Hartford, Conn., 1856; came to Chicago January, 1883; entered the force April 19, 1886.

HENRY GORMAN, patrolman; born in Ireland 1861; came to Chicago March, 1880; entered the force December 13, 1884.

FREDRICK HEILMAN, patrolman; born in Philadelphia, Penn., 1853; came to Chicago 1856; entered the force April 10, 1886, July 16, 1886, arrested Michael Hickey, alias Phelps, the chicken thief, and Joseph Wolfington for burglary; each were sentenced to three years in the penitentiary. July 21, 1886, arrested James Smith for burglary; on the plea of guilty the prisoner was sentenced to one year in the penitentiary.

JAMES HAYES, patrolman; born in Ireland 1850; came to Chicago 1873; entered the force 1883; arrested Charles Styles (colored) who was sentenced to five years in the penitentiary for burglary; was on duty at the Desplaines street station on the night of the Haymarket riot.

CHARLES HACHLE, patrolman; born in Germany 1859; came to Chicago 1881; entered the force 1887.

JOHN HENEBERY, patrolman; born in Ireland 1845; came to Chicago July, 1867; entered the force 1874; was through the strikes of 1877 and 1885.

DAVID M. KELLY, patrolman; born in Virginia 1855; came to Chicago 1879; entered the force May, 1887.

STEPHEN KELLY, patrolman; born in Ireland 1851; came to Chicago 1865; entered the force December 15, 1884.

THOMAS KERSHAW, patrolman; born in Cedar Rapids, Iowa, 1854; came to Chicago 1879; entered the force 1885.

MOSES LOWENSTEIN, patrolman; born in Detroit, Mich., 1863; came to Chicago 1878; entered the force July 1, 1886.

JOHN M. LAWLER, patrolman; born in New York City 1855; came to Chicago 1865; entered the force June, 1885.

ROGER MULCAHY, patrolman; born in Ireland 1856; came to Chicago 1872; entered the force 1884.

JOHN McINERNY, patrolman; born in Ireland 1844; came to Chicago May, 1864; entered the force 1872; arrested Ike Buzzard, who broke from the penitentiary at Lancaster, Penn., and liberated twelve convicts; has been shot twice in the neck while on duty.

NICHOLAS MARTIN, patrolman; American born; came to Chicago in 1863; entered the force December, 1884; was at the Haymarket riot of 1886; also at the street-car strike of 1885.

CHARLES H. MEYER, patrolman; born in Germany 1838; came to Chicago 1863; entered the force May 8, 1868.

JAMES T. MURPHY, patrolman; born in New York City 1852; came to Chicago 1858; entered the force May, 1882.

JAMES C. McNAMARA, patrolman; born in Ireland 1849; came to Chicago 1869; entered the force December, 1884.

ROBERT MACK, patrolman; born in Ireland 1860; came to Chicago 1877; entered the force 1882; July 7, 1886, arrested Freeman Canniff for shooting Alexander Bucher in barn in the rear of 1705 Michigan ave., also recovered stolen property amounting to $1,180, stolen from the same number; it was concealed on the third floor of 743 W. Madison street.

MICHAEL McLAUGHLIN, patrolman; born in Ireland 1855; came to Chicago April, 1877; entered the force June 3, 1887.

MARTIN NOLAN, patrolman; born in Ireland 1853; came to Chicago, October, 1873; entered the force December 15, 1884.

CHRISTOPHER O'SHEA, patrolman; born in Ireland 1847; came to Chicago April, 1868; entered the force May 9, 1882; August 15, 1883, was shot by Mark Davis while quelling a disturbance at Ogden's Grove.

JOHN O'BRIEN, patrolman; born in Pennsylvania 1859; came to Chicago April, 1883; entered the force December, 1884; was at the street-car strike of 1885, also at the Haymarket riot of 1886.

DANIEL O'SHEA, patrolman; born in Ireland 1857; came to Chicago 1882 ; entered the force July 1, 1886.

MICHAEL O'BRIEN, patrolman; born in Ireland 1861; came to Chicago September, 1878; entered the force April 19, 1886.

WILLIAM O'BRIEN, patrolman; born in Ireland 1857; came to Chicago 1875; entered the force September 10, 1887.

MARTIN E. PADDEN, patrolman; born in Canada 1854; came to Chicago 1873; entered the force 1884.

MICHAEL PURCELL, patrolman; born in Ireland 1860: came to Chicago June, 1879 ; entered the force April 15, 1887.

MICHAEL C. RYAN, patrolman; born in Ireland 1849; came to Chicago 1869; entered the force October 22, 1877; arrested Samuel Fielden, one of the anarchists.

JAMES REIDY, patrolman; born in Ireland, 1854; came to Chicago September, 1865; entered the force December 13, 1884; on duty at the Haymarket riot; also at the street-car strike of 1885.

CHARLES P. STRENING, patrolman; born in Chicago, Ill., 1861; entered the force 1884; at the street-car strike of 1885; also the Haymarket riot of 1886.

DENIS W. SMIDDY, patrolman; born in Chicago 1859; entere1 the force July 1, 1886.

WILLIAM STYX, patrolman; born in Prague, Ill., 1858; came to Chicago 1858; entered the force May 8, 1882.

WILLIAM SHERRETT, patrolman; born in Scotland 1845; came to Chicago 1869; entered the force September 18, 1875.

PATRICK SHANNESSY, patrolman; born in Ireland 1842; came to Chicago 1855; entered the force 1876; assigned to duty at W. Chicago Ave. station; transferred to Harrison street July, 1876; transferred to Twenty-second street station April, 1878.

JOHN SAVAGE, patrolman; born in Moyra, N. Y., 1858; came to Chicago July 1, 1878 ; entered the force 1885; arrested Walter Burns for highway robbery, sentenced to three years in the penitentiary; John Murray for burglary, whose case is still pending in the Criminal Court; was in the strikes of 1885 and 1886.

DAVID SULLIVAN, patrolman; born in Buffalo, N. Y., 1856; came to Chicago 1857; entered the force 1885; was in the strike of 1885; also at McCormick's factory in 1886.

SEVERIN C. THOMPSON, patrolman; born in Norway 1851; came to Chicago 1865; entered the force July, 1886.

AUGUSTUS J. WEBER, patrolman; born in Chicago 1860; entered the force April 19, 1886; July 16, 1887, arrested Michael Lynch for the murder of Officer Wm. Halloran.

AUGUST C. ARCH,
Lieut. Comdg. Twenty-seeond St. District.

JOSEPH KIPLEY,

Lieut. Comdg. Thirty-fifth St. District.

THIRTY-FIFTH STREET STATION.—Thirty-fifth street, east of Halsted, is one of the old sub-stations, the history of which is connected with that of the department in its early days. The district patrolled by the force of this station is bounded north by Thirty-first street, south by the city limits, east by State street, and west by Ashland avenue; the area being two square miles, and the population about 40,000.

JOSEPH KIPLEY, lieutenant in charge of the Thirty-fifth street district, was born in Patterson, New Jersey, on November 24, 1848 and came to Chicago on July 3, 1865. Here he found employment in R. B. Appleby's picture frame establishment, but was thrown out of it by the fire. He entered the police force January 24, 1872, under Superintendent Kennedy, as patrolman, and was assigned to the Union street station; transferred to the old Huron street station, to Twelfth street, and with Simon O'Donnell to the Harrison street station, where the latter was placed in command as captain. When O'Donnell became superintendent, he was made a detective, in 1879, and when McGarigle assumed the superintendency, was promoted to a lieutenancy, December 14, 1880, and assigned to Harrison street; remained there till Superintendent Doyle promoted him, with Lieutenant Shea, and placed them in charge of the detective department. This position they held until Mayor Roche removed them, Lieutenant Kipley being assigned to his present charge. The record which Kipley and Shea made while connected with the detective force would fill a volume larger than this, and the best that can be done is to take a glance at it. On August 20, 1879, Kipley arrested "Biby" Connelly for larceny; on October 8, same year, arrested George Keene for burglary, and Henry Lawrence, same charge; on October 28, same year, arrested Joseph Bennett for larceny, and Henry Vaughan for burglary; on November 15, same year, arrested William Connors, Dennis Redden, Joseph Slater, Frank Miner, and John Keenan, all fugitives from justice, and wanted at Peoria; on November 23, same year, arrested John Halpin for burglary; on November 27, same year, arrested John Meehan, now in Paris, for vagrancy, and Dick Elbert for larceny; on November 28, same year, arrested O. H. Rockfellow, alias "Dayton Joe," for rape; on December 3, same year, arrested Frank Pierson, William Reid, Al. Bieter, and William Mitchell for burglary; on December 10, same year, arrested John F. Beggs, fugitive from Cleveland, Ohio; on December 20, 1879, arrested a notorious confidence operator, Thomas O'Brien; on December 29, same year, arrested John Murphy, alias "Kid," Frank Harris, alias "Painter," and Arthur Webster, a gang of dangerous counterfeiters; on January 30, 1880, Peter Jackson, alias Harris, Edward Elliott, and others, for larceny; January 17, same year, arrested Pat Condon for robbery; February 2, same year, William and Carrie Mitchell for robbery; February 18, same year, Charles Bowman and Pat Harrity for larceny; on May 27, same year, arrested John Mitchell, Samuel Sutherland and William Morton for burglary; on May 29, same year, arrested William Needham and Charles Stansby for robbery; on June 9, same year, arrested Charles Schubert for robbery, and June 29, same year, arrested John Cronin for burglary; on August 2, same year, arrested William Crawford, Harry McCoy, Bob Breckenbridge, and John Ryan for burglary; August 30, same year, arrested James Woods for larceny; September 20, same year, arrested James Keefe for larceny; October 1, same year, arrested James Dignan, Peter Nichol and John Fitzgerald for burglary, and also Clark, Bell, Hammell, Shoemaker and Fairchild, fugitives from justice, turned over to Toledo, Ohio; November 13, same year, arrested Bert Stanley for burglary; December 1, same year, arrested John Waters for burglary; December 7, same year, arrested the safe-blower, John Burns, and turned him over to the Bloomington authorities; December 10, same year, arrested John Sweeney and George Deal for burglary, turned over to Kankakee. These were some of the hauls made by the detectives within a short space of time. In every instance the persons arrested were held to the Criminal Court, and, with a few exceptions, all were finally gathered into the penitentiary. Joseph Kipley was identified, however, with many cases of more importance, or at least of more interest, than these. He figured conspicuously in the Hensley murder case, and in the running down of Holtgren; he worked up the Lake View and Evanston burglary cases, and succeeded in breaking up the desperate gang operating in the northeastern suburbs; arrested, with Shea's assistance, Leland, the desperate character who sandbagged and robbed Brown; arrested and broke up the Murray and Rice gang, which was partly composed of women, and had succeeded in robbing South Side houses of over $8,000 worth of property, in sealskin sacques, jewelry, etc.; goods recovered. He participated in the arrest of Crawford, May 27, 1880, and McCoy, two notorious thieves, who operated partly at Sycamore, Ill., and partly in Chicago. All of the plunder they had accumulated was recovered, and the robbers were sent back for trial. John Ryan, a burglar, came here from Michigan City, and Detective Kipley was sent in search of him. He found his man at the "Bon Ton," one of the low dives kept by Jerry Monroe. Ryan pulled a revolver and fired, and the detective has, perhaps, never been as close to death's door, since or before, as he was when the bullet missed its mark. Marks' pawnshop, of this city, was robbed of $9,000 worth of jewelry. Kipley and Shea got hold of one of the burglars, and made him confess. The property was returned. Edwards, the same burglar who entered D. B. Fisk's place, was found guilty of the robbery. He was identified with the Moore and Powers case. They took wagons to Forty-second street and robbed freight cars, bringing their stuff to a fence kept by a pawn-broker named Joachim. The end of this fence-keeper was tragic. Some thieves, with whom he had done business previously, wrote him that if he would bring $8,000 to a certain point just east of the approach to the railroad bridge over the Mississippi at Burlington, he would find there, and might have in return, valuable property worth four or five times the amount. Joachim nibbled at the bait for awhile, and finally took it whole. He arrived at the place indicated, a desolate tract of territory in the bottoms by the river. The next seen of him, he had dragged himself to the railroad platform where he had alighted. Scarcely had he arrived there before he fell dead. He had been drugged, beaten and robbed by the thieves, who then left him to die in the wilderness. Lieutenant Kipley was for a long time the associate of Edward Keating. Perhaps no trio of detectives ever performed more or better work than Keating, Shea and Kipley. Keating is dead. Lieutenant Shea, like Lieutenant Kipley, is now leading a quiet life in command of an outlying station.

PETER J. BYRNE, desk sergeant; born in Ireland 1844; came to Chicago July, 1870; entered the force December, 1878.

WILLIAM J. MOONEY, desk sergeant; born in New York City 1840; came to Chicago 1870 ; entered the force 1873; appointed desk sergeant February, 1881.

FRANCIS CAMPBELL, patrol sergeant; born in Ireland 1840; came to Chicago 1870; entered the force August 12, 1873.

JOHN P. BONFIELD, patrolman; born in Chicago 1856; entered the force December 15, 1884.

PATRICK CLEARY, patrolman; born in Ireland 1842; came to Chicago 1869; entered the force July 31, 1872.

PATRICK CLOGAN, patrolman; born in Chicago 1861; entered the force June 3, 1887.

ARTHUR DILLON, patrolman; born in Ireland 1849; came to Chicago 1870; entered the force December 15, 1884.

JAMES EVANS, patrolman; born in Ireland 1847; came to Chicago 1853; entered the force 1884.

HENRY EVES, patrolman; born in Belleville, Ontario, 1854; came to Chicago 1871; entered the force June 3, 1887.

JOHN J. FLANIGAN, patrolman; born in Bedford, N. Y., 1858; came to Chicago September, 1861; entered the force June 13, 1883.

MICHAEL GAYNOR, patrolman; born in Chicago 1861; entered the force December 15, 1884.

DANIEL HARTNETT, patrolman; born in Chicago 1858; entered the force July 1, 1886.

CHARLES P. KENNEY, patrolman; born in Ireland 1855; came to Chicago 1879; entered the force June 3, 1887.

FERDINAND F. H. KURTH, patrolman; born in Germany 1850; came to Chicago August, 1862; entered the force September, 1874.

JOHN J. LEONARD, patrolman; born in Chicago 1854; entered the force June 13, 1882.

JOHN M. LAWLER, patrolman; born in New York City 1855; came to Chicago 1866; entered the force June, 1885.

MICHAEL McGRAW, patrolman; born in Chicago 1860; entered the force March 15, 1885.

JOHN MORRIARTY, patrolman; born in Ireland 1859; came to Chicago September, 1882; entered the force December 15, 1884.

JOHN H. McDONALD, patrolman; born in New York 1864; came to Chicago 1875; entered the force 1886.

DANIEL L. McCARTHY, patrolman; born in Braaher, St. Lawrence Co., N. Y., 1860; came to Chicago 1879; entered the force December 15, 1884.

PATRICK MALONEY, patrolman; born in Ireland 1850; came to Chicago September, 1866; entered the force September 19, 1874.

JAMES McMAHON, patrolman; born in Chicago 1854; entered the force December 15, 1884.

CHARLES McDERMOTT, patrolman; born in Woodstock, Ill., 1862; came to Chicago July 1, 1877; entered the force July 1, 1886.

WILLIAM O'DONALD, patrolman; born in Ireland 1862; came to Chicago 1878; entered the force December, 1884.

MICHAEL O'TOOLE, patrolman; born in Ireland 1859; came to Chicago 1878; entered the force 1884.

WILLIAM O'MEARA, patrolman; born in Ireland 1861; came to Chicago 1877; entered the force December 15, 1884.

PATRICK O'BRIEN, patrolman; born in Ireland 1852; came to Chicago August, 1876; entered the force June, 1883.

MICHAEL J. RODNEY, patrolman; born in Chicago 1857; entered the force December 15, 1884.

WILLIAM TAYLOR, patrolman; born in Weymouth, Mass., 1850; came to Chicago 1869; entered the force December 15, 1884.

THE COTTAGE GROVE AVENUE STATION. 171 Cottage Grove avenue, was built in the winter of 1866–'67, and was opened to the public June 1, 1867, Sergeant James B. Craney in command. Ten patrolmen then traveled the district from Twenty-second to Thirty-fifth street, and from State street to the lake, most of which was then a bare prairie, but is now one of the finest residence portions of the city. The district patrolled by the force of this station at present is bounded north by Twenty-second street, south by the city limits, on the east by Lake Michigan and on the west by State street, embracing an area of about two square miles and a population of about 75,000.

MADISON BEADELL, lieutenant of police, commanding the Cottage Grove district, was born in Cayuga county, New York, 1838; was educated at Utica; came to Chicago in 1858, and entered the force on August 5, 1866. Elsewhere in this history his name appears frequently. He has been for at least fifteen years a prominent figure in the department. In July, 1861, in this city, he enlisted in the 10th Illinois Vol. Cavalry, and served four years and eight months at the front, for four years of this time being absolutely under age. He served gallantly in the battles of Pea Ridge, Little Rock, Mansfield, Benton, Prairie Grove and others of more or less note. In a skirmish near Richmond, La., he was taken prisoner and confined at Tyler, Tex. After entering the force he was the first man to travel beat from the Archer road station, in the Bridgeport district; served as patrolman and desk sergeant at Twenty-second street, and was then transferred to Cottage Grove avenue, where he served till 1877, when under the Heath-Hickey regime he was promoted to a lieutenancy and was placed in charge of the Twenty-second street district; was then transferred to Deering street, and in 1880 returned to Cottage Grove, where he has been in command ever since. As a patrolman, sergeant and lieutenant, Madison Beadell has proved himself to be a faithful and brave officer. He has commanded companies in many exciting tumults, and his military education has served him well at all times. The policemen of the Cottage Grove district are well disciplined and careful officers, and the smoothness with which affairs are conducted down there is due to the painstaking methods and good tact of the lieutenant.

ALEXIS C. BURDICK, desk sergeant, was born in Indiana 1847; came to Chicago 1865, and entered the force 1882; enlisted in the McClellan Dragoons October, 1861, being at the time but 15 years of age; was wounded at Liberty, Miss., while serving as a scout for the army; mustered out in October, 1865, having served four years and twenty days; was appointed patrolman at the Central station in 1883; transferred to Cottage Grove February 22, 1884, and appointed desk sergeant in March, 1884.

MARSHALL B. ATWELL, desk sergeant, was born in Vermont 1840; came to Chicago 1869; entered the force February, 1872; served as patrolman at Harrison street station, Twenty-second street and Cottage Grove avenue; promoted to be desk sergeant June, 1887; enlisted in the 2d Vermont Volunteers in May, 1861, and served three years; participated in the first battle of Bull Run, and went through the peninsular campaign; since his connection with the department has made several important arrests, and proved himself to be an excellent officer in every respect.

GEORGE W. SANFORD, patrol sergeant, was born in Noble county, Indiana, 1845; came to Chicago in 1871; entered the force April 15, 1872; resigned April 15, 1876, and re-entered the department Nov. 5, 1878; appointed desk sergeant at Hinman street station March 1, 1879; promoted to patrol sergeantcy February 22, 1884, and assigned to Harrison street station; transferred to Cottage Grove June 1, 1884.

JOHN ASHEN, patrolman, born in Ireland 1860; came to Chicago 1876; entered the force 1884.

LEONARD BOHRN, patrolman; born in Dover, Wis., 1860; came to Chicago 1884; entered the force June 3, 1887; is a reliable and efficient officer.

WILLIAM BRENMAN, patrolman; born in County Kinsale, Ireland, 1843; came to Chicago 1867; entered the force July, 1871; April, 1872, arrested James Jones (colored) for shooting his brother.

STILLMAN BOVER, patrolman; born in Schenectady, N. Y., 1853; came to Chicago 1869; entered the force June 3, 1887.

JAMES BYRNE, patrolman; born in Ireland 1859; came to Chicago 1879; entered the force January, 1887; has arrested Frank Pierce, James Bussy, John Lee, on petty charges. Is a good, reliable man.

JOHN BONGERZ, patrolman; born in Prussia 1849; came to Chicago July, 1864; entered the force December 15, 1884; arrested John Doyle for larceny, John Reiber for assault, and Bill Price for attempted burglary; recovered the body of Charles Curtis from the lake, foot of Twenty-seventh street.

JOHN J. DUNN, patrolman; born in Chicago 1858; entered the force December, 1884.

HERMAN EHINGER, patrolman; born in Germany 1827; came to Chicago 1856; entered the force 1868.

ANDREW J. ENZENBACHER, patrolman; born in Chicago 1860; entered the force April 20, 1886.

PATRICK FOLEY, patrolman; born in Elgin, Ill., 1862; came to Chicago 1880; entered the force June 3, 1887.

JOHN FLANNIGAN, patrolman; born in Kane county, Ill., 1862; came to Chicago 1879; entered the force December 15, 1884.

PATRICK J. GLEASON, patrolman; born in Ireland 1849; came to Chicago 1867; entered the force August, 1875.

FRANK HAHENADEL, patrolman; born in New York City 1857; came to Chicago 1858; entered the force June 3, 1887.

MICHAEL H. HEILMANN, patrolman; born in Philadelphia, Penn., 1853; came to Chicago 1857; entered the force June 3, 1887.

WILLIAM A. HARTMAN, patrolman; born in Canton, Ohio, 1856; came to Chicago 1861; entered the force December 15, 1884.

PATRICK H. HARKINS, patrolman; born in Ireland 1838; came to Chicago 1872; entered the force December 15, 1884.

DAVID HAMAHAN, patrolman; born in Ireland 1859; came to Chicago 1875; entered the force 1884.

JOHN C. KALIHER, patrolman; born in Yellow Springs, Ohio, 1856; came to Chicago September, 1880; entered the force April 20, 1886; arrested Henry Moore, an ex-convict, Isaac Bennett and Geo. Buchanan, well-known thieves; rescued four persons from the burning building 171 Twenty-second street.

JOHN E. KEEFE, patrolman; born in Bloomington, Ill., 1858; came to Chicago June, 1863; entered the force December 15, 1884; June, 1886, arrested the notorious Mrs. H. Marshall as she was attempting to commit murder.

JAMES KING, patrolman; born in Ireland 1850; came to Chicago 1876; entered the force 1881; arrested Wm. Jones for burglary, who was sent to the penitentiary; also Annie Eihre for larceny.

DAVID W. McCARTHY, patrolman; born in Chicago 1862; entered the force November 15, 1884; June 29 rescued J. Laney, a seven-year-old boy, from drowning, by jumping in the lake and swimming to shore with him; also recovered the body of Frank McNamara, who was drowned while swimming with Laney.

PETER E. MARTIN, patrolman; born in Kane Co., Ill., 1855; came to Chicago 1872; entered the force July 1, 1886.

PHILIP MILLER, patrolman; born in Wisconsin 1861; came to Chicago 1878; entered the force December 15, 1884.

JOHN M. O'CONNELL, patrolman; born in Ireland 1855; came to

Chicago 1884; entered the force July 8, 1887; arrested on two occasions "Black Jack" Yattaw.

PATRICK O'BRIEN, patrolman; born in Ireland 1852; came to Chicago July, 1870; entered the force July, 1882.

JEREMIAH F. O'SULLIVAN, patrolman; born in Lawrence, Mass., 1853; came to Chicago November, 1871; entered the force June 15, 1872.

HENRY ROTTGEN, patrolman; born in Lake Co., Ind., 1858; came to Chicago 1879; entered the force December 15, 1884; arrested Albert Peterson for house-breaking; also Andrew Sullivan for carrying concealed weapons.

HENRY ROCHE, patrolman; born in Ireland 1850; came to Chicago 1854; entered the force 1884; arrested F. J. Newton for robbery; Henry Jackson, the notorious horse shark; Joseph Taylor for larceny; all of whom were sent to the penitentiary.

FRANK E. SULLIVAN, patrolman; born in Chicago 1860; entered the force 1884.

FRANK SLADECK, patrolman; born in Bohemia 1858; came to Chicago 1866; entered the force June 3, 1887; showed great presence of mind while arresting an insane man.

JAMES SWEENEY, patrolman; born in Ireland 1854; came to Chicago 1870; entered the force June 3, 1887.

EDWARD H. SMYTHE, patrolman; born in Juneau county, Wis., 1856; came to Chicago 1880; entered the force 1886.

GUY STONE, patrolman; born in West Fayette, Seneca county, N. Y., 1857; came to Chicago January, 1881; entered the force April 20, 1886.

ALFRED B. SMITH, patrolman; born in Marine City, Mich., 1850; came to Chicago 1881; entered the force December, 1884; with others, arrested Louis Rheam for the murder of Officer Cornelius Barrett.

JOHN C. SPENCER, patrolman; born in Joliet, Ill., 1857; came to Chicago 1871; entered the force June, 1887; arrested Jack Fischer, alias McDonald, Pat Dundon, alias Riely, Jack McCue, alias Brown, three South Water street thieves, who made a practice of taking wagons loaded with provisions. They were all sent to the penitentiary.

JOHN A. TOOMEY, patrolman; born in Albany, N. Y., 1842; came to Chicago 1861; entered the force October, 1877; arrested William Armstrong for larceny, and recovered $127,000 worth of property; April, 1882, arrested Isaac Teaste for burglary, who received four years in the penitentiary.

MADISON BEADELL,

Lieut. Comdg. Cottage Grove Ave. District.

CHARLES M. DAY,

Lieut. Comdg. Stanton Ave. District.

EUGENE VALLEE, patrolman; born in Quebec, Canada, 1846; came to Chicago 1864; entered the force June, 1882; arrested the notorious Frank Wilson, with many aliases, for highway robbery, who was sent to the penitentiary for three years.

JOSEPH WOLF, patrolman; born in New York City 1861; came to Chicago 1867; entered the force June 3, 1887.

CHARLES G. WILKS, patrolman; born in Brooklyn, N. Y., 1857; came to Chicago 1859; entered the force December 15, 1884.

THE STANTON AVENUE STATION, 144 and 146 Thirty-fifth street, corner of Stanton avenue, is the youngest, handsomest and most complete sub-station in the city. It was built under the direct supervision of Inspector Bonfield and his assistants, and was opened on June 19, 1887, with Lieutenant Lyman Lewis in command of the new district. He remained in charge until his promotion to a captaincy, when Sergeant Charles M. Day, promoted to a lieutenancy September 9, 1887, was assigned to relieve him. The station is a model piece of police architecture, large, commodious and convenient, with cheerful surroundings, and the force assigned here appears to be well contented with their lot.

CHARLES M. DAY, lieutenant of police, commanding the Stanton avenue district, was born at Clinton, Lenawee county, Michigan, in 1849; moved to Blue Island, this county, when a child; attended school at Marseilles, Ill., for a couple of years, and coming to Chicago when a mere lad, enlisted in Company C, 72d Illinois Infantry, the first "Board of Trade" regiment; his company was known as "Scripps' Guards," and was organized in 1862; went immediately to the front, and saw sharp service at Vicksburg and Champion Hill; after the fall of Vicksburg, went down the Mississippi to New Orleans, then to the rear of Mobile, and from Mobile to Montgomery, under Gen. Smith, and was mustered out at the latter place; after returning home, railroaded for two years on the Rock Island road, and entered the police force January 9, 1867, being assigned to the Twenty-second street station, which was then a mere shanty on Archer avenue, near the Fort Wayne track; remained there till the present Twenty-second street station was built, and remained at the new station traveling beat for two years; was here promoted to be desk sergeant, and served in that capacity until Capt. Seavey became chief, who transferred him to Harrison street; while at Harrison street the Morse telegraph system was introduced, and desk sergeants were compelled to learn it;

he mastered it, and after a few months was transferred to Central station, and promoted to be chief operator at police headquarters; remained in this position through all administrations since then, until September 9 of this year, when he was promoted to a lieutenancy, and assigned to duty at Stanton avenue. Ten years ago, when at Twenty-second street, he started out one evening to buy a hat. On his way he dropped into a concert saloon at Wabash avenue and Twenty-second street, and entered into conversation with the special policeman, named Daly. While talking, Officer Smith, of Cottage Grove avenue, also dropped in. After him came two roughs, a fellow named Burke and one Frank Murphy, both of whom had been arrested several times for highway robbery and other crimes. They walked nearly to the front of the concert room and sat down. A man sitting in front of them had his hat on, and one of the toughs snatched it off and threw it on the stage. Officer Day arrested and conducted them to the sidewalk. Officer Smith, another officer named Russell, the special policeman and Day started with the pair toward the Twenty-second street station, when it seems that Daly turned back, without saying a word of his intention to do so. In fact, Day and his prisoners had crossed Wabash avenue before he missed the special policeman, and then he heard a scuffle behind him, between Russell and one of the thugs. Murphy ran up to Day with a pistol in hand and began shooting. Day threw his arm over his head, and stooped as Murphy raised his pistol and the ball entered his right arm. Had he failed to stoop it would have entered his head. The ball, as it was, entered near the elbow and came out near the shoulder. Murphy, after firing a salute of five shots, ran toward State street, and north through an alley, between State and Wabash, followed by Officers Elliott and Wallace M. Day, who had come upon the scene. The officers fired several shots at him as he ran, one of which took effect in the calf of his leg, and another entered his heel. The tough was laid up with his wounds in the county jail for three months, and when the trial came off, a physician testified that a penitentiary confinement would kill him, and the sentence was suspended. Lieutenant Day was eighteen years a desk sergeant. He is still a young man and very popular in the department.

JOHN L. MAHONEY, desk sergeant, was born in Ireland in 1844; came to Chicago March, 1865; entered the force August, 1870; was in active service during the fire of 1871 and in the riots of 1877; traveled post on the "Levee" for several years, and made many important arrests; was appointed desk sergeant in 1878 by Chief Seavey, and assigned to Cottage Grove station; transferred to Stanton avenue June 1, 1887.

WALLACE M. DAY, desk sergeant; born at Clinton, Lenawee county, Mich., 1845; came to Chicago in 1853, and entered the force 1878; in 1879 succeeded in arresting the notorious Edward O'Toole, after a desperate struggle; was in active service during the riots, and has distinguished himself in many ways by personal bravery and skill; was appointed desk sergeant June 1, 1887.

GERALD STARK, patrol sergeant; born in Ireland 1842; came to Chicago October 20, 1860; entered the force August 15, 1877; has participated in all the riots and disturbances that have occurred in this city since that time; arrested in 1883 two notorious burglars named Miller and Wendt, after a desperate struggle; they had entered a South Side house; both were sent to the penitentiary; has arrested a large number of criminals of all grades, and has acted fearlessly and faithfully on all occasions.

GEORGE A. BINGLEY, patrolman; born in Chicago 1860; entered the force April, 1886; rescued a man from a burning building on Randolph street; was in the Haymarket riot.

NICHOLAS BECK, patrolman; born in Chicago 1864; entered the force April 1, 1887.

CHARLES BENNECKE, patrolman; born in Plymouth, Wis., 1858; came to Chicago 1870; entered the force June 13, 1883; was severely burned while rescuing a little girl from a fire.

JOHN CUMINGS, patrolman; born in Walworth county, Wis., 1853; came to Chicago 1881; entered the force May, 1887.

JAMES CONICK, patrolman; born in Oswego, N. Y., 1855; came to Chicago December, 1878; entered the force December 15, 1884; March 23, 1885, arrested the notorious "Lewey," for murder; "Lewey" was sentenced to seven years in the penitentiary.

WILLIAM CARBERRY, patrolman; born in Ireland 1842; came to Chicago 1870; entered the force November 5, 1870.

JAMES W. DUFFY, patrolman; born at Crystal Lake, Ill., 1859; came to Chicago 1877; entered the force May 10, 1884; was assigned to the Central station; while there arrested the notorious Thos. Fitzpatrick, Wm. Lee, and Fred. Regar, all ex-convicts; also Wm. Hines, alias Doc. Hart, a criminal from Boston; was one of the officers who arrested August Spies and Schwab, the anarchists.

THOMAS DOWNS, patrolman; born in Ireland 1842; came to Chicago 1865; entered the force 1872; in 1873 wounded while arresting Mike McCarthy, a horse thief.

THOMAS DUFFY, patrolman; born in Ireland 1864; came to Chicago 1864; entered the force April 15, 1887.

JOHN J. DUFFY, patrolman; born in Ogdensburg, N. Y., 1857; came to Chicago March, 1872; entered the force January 1, 1886; was in the street-car strike of 1885, the riot of 1886; arrested six burglars, and recovered much property.

JOHN FALLON, patrolman; born in Ireland 1859; came to Chicago 1876; entered the force April 15, 1887.

ALEXANDER GOODBRAND, patrolman; born in Scotland 1839; came to Chicago in 1866; entered the force December, 1875; made many important arrests.

PHILIP GREEN (colored), patrolman; born in 1856 at Baltimore; came to Chicago 1881; entered the force June, 1887; detailed in citizen's clothes at Central station; was employed a number of years by the Pullman Car Co.

WILLIAM J. GOGGIN, patrolman; born in England 1843; came to Chicago 1866; entered the force March, 1881; took part in the Haymarket riot.

LOUIS B. IND, patrolman; born in Milton, Wis., 1852; came to Chicago 1870; entered the force June 5, 1887; detailed in citizen's clothes at the Central station; was connected seventeen years with detective agencies and railroad companies; was connected with Wm. A. and Allan Pinkerton for eight years; served two years as an officer in penitentiary at San Quinton, Cal.

MARTIN C. LEYDEN, patrolman; born in Ireland 18 0; came to Chicago 1875; entered the force August 1, 1881; in 1883, arrested the notorious burglar, George Hall, the first man sent from Cook county for twenty years under the habitual criminal's act.

GEORGE R. McNEIL, patrolman; born in Westport, N. S., 1854; came to Chicago 1884; entered the force June 14, 1887.

MARTIN W. McDONOUGH, patrolman; born in Deerfield, Wis., 1862; came to Chicago April, 1872; entered the force June 4, 1887.

JOHN J. O'FARRELL, patrolman; born in Chicago 1863; entered the force August 15, 1885.

GEORGE ORR, patrolman; born in Ireland 1863; came to Chicago August, 1878; entered the force June 4, 1887.

EDWARD PETTESCH, patrolman; born in Chicago 1858; entered the force March, 1887.

WILLIAM PLUNCKETT, patrolman; born in Ireland 1862; came to Chicago 1878; entered the force December 15, 1884; during the riots of 1885 and 1886 arrested many criminals.

CHARLES J. PETERSON, patrolman; born in Chicago 1860; entered the force 1887.

PETER W. ROONEY, patrolman; born in Ella, Dodge county, Wis.,

1855; came to Chicago December, 1871; entered the force December, 1884; assisted in the rescuing of seven persons from a fire at 85 Third avenue; was through the strikes of 1885 and 1886.

JOHN RYAN, patrolman; born in Ireland, 1839; came to Chicago in 1848; joined the force October 15, 1867; resigned under Superintendent Seavey, and re-entered April 18, 1886.

TIMOTHY RYAN, patrolman; born in Ireland 1855; came to Chicago 1876; entered the force June 13, 1883.

W. L. STAHL, patrolman; born in Rochester, N. Y., 1861; came to Chicago September, 1882; entered the force June 2, 1887.

J. C. SPENCER, patrolman; born in Joliet, Ill., 1857; came to Chicago 1880; entered the force July 1, 1886.

JOSEPH H. SHREVE, patrolman; born in West Chester, Penn., 1853; came to Chicago 1876; entered the force July 5, 1882.

CORNELIUS E. SMITH, patrolman; born in Chicago 1859; entered the force March 14, 1887.

THOMAS L. TREHARN, patrolman; born in Cardiff, South Wales, 1859; came to Chicago 1861; entered the force 1880; arrested for burglary, James Alexander (colored), who received five years in the penitentiary; Charles Brown, five years; Fred Brady, two years; Peter O'Brien, brother of the notorious "Kid" O'Brien, and husband to Mollie Mott, a noted shoplifter.

HENRY THOMAS, patrolman; born at Ottawa, Ill., 1857; came to Chicago July, 1877; entered the force 1885; took part in the Haymarket riot.

CHAPTER XXV.

CAPT. SIMON O'DONNELL COMMANDING — THE "TERROR DISTRICT" OF
OTHER DAYS, NOW ONE OF THE BEST REGULATED IN THE CITY —
WHAT THE GALLANT PRIDE OF THE OLD LAKE STREET SQUAD HAS
DONE FOR IT—SIMON O'DONNELL AND HIS MEN—THE INTRODUCTION
OF THE SIGNAL SERVICE HERE—A CAPTAIN WHO HAS BEEN A SUPER-
INTENDENT AND WHO STEPPED BACK CHEERFULLY TO THE RANKS.

The second precinct includes the West Twelfth street, the
West Thirteenth street, the Canalport avenue and the Deering street stations.   Headquarters, West Twelfth street station, West Twelfth and Johnson streets.

PRECINCT STATION, West Twelfth and Johnson streets.   It
was formerly a sub-station of the old second precinct, which
embraced the entire West Side.   It is, perhaps, the oldest
station in the city, remaining where it was originally located
in 1866.   Two additions have been built to it during recent
years, and a police court for the precinct was opened in the
structure in 1882.   A patrol barn has also been added.
The station is now one of the most substantial and commodious in the city.   It is located in what used to be the heart
of the "Terror District."   Here the first patrol wagon was
put into service, under Lieut. John Bonfield.   Simon O'Donnell's good management and the patrol service have reduced
the "Terror District" to a condition bordering very closely
upon respectability.   The force of this station patrols the
district bounded north by West Harrison street, east by the
south branch of the Chicago River, south by West Sixteenth
street, and west by Loomis street; embracing an area of
about one and a half square miles, and containing a population now estimated at 50,000.

SIMON O'DONNELL, captain commanding the second precinct; born
in County Clare, Ireland, in 1834; came to Chicago in 1841; entered
the force April 7, 1862; acted as patrolman for seven years; was

AUGUST C. BLETTNER,
Lieut. Comdg. West Twelfth St. District.

FRANCIS P. BARCAL,
Lieut. Comdg. Twelfth St. District.

promoted by Superintendent Rehm to second sergeantcy and later to first sergeantcy and placed in charge of West Twelfth street substation in 1869; was promoted to a captaincy in 1877 and took charge of the first precinct, with headquarters at the Armory; was promoted to be deputy superintendent of police, vice Dixon resigned, and acted as superintendent until the death of Superintendent Seavey; was appointed superintendent of police in 1879 by Mayor Harrison; had charge of the entire department for twenty-one months: insisted upon resigning the responsibility, and was assigned to his old station (West Twelfth street) and made captain of the second precinct; served gallantly in the riots of 1867, 1877, and 1886; swept the thug element out of the "Terror District," and has arrested and convicted criminals by the score; bears the distinction of having been the last deputy superintendent appointed, and the only man who has ever held a commanding position in the department after leaving the superintendent's chair. [See Chap. XVIII.]

AUGUST BLETTNER, lieutenant of police, second precinct station; born in Germany in 1846; came to Chicago in June, 1854; entered the force July 10, 1867; after serving as patrolman for two years was promoted to the desk sergeantcy of Twelfth street, which position he held for six years; was made patrol sergeant at Hinman street, when that station was opened; transferred to Central station as clerk in the detective department; after one year was promoted to a lieutenancy and assigned to Desplaines street station, where he remained several years; was then placed in charge of the day squad of the Central detail; served here a year, and was then transferred to Twelfth street station. Lieutenant Blettner served with distinction in the riots of 1877 and 1886; has sent several criminals to the penitentiary for forgery and burglary, and ranks among the most energetic and reliable officers on the force.

FRANCIS P. BARCAL, lieutenant of police, second precinct station; born in Bohemia in 1843; came to Chicago Sept. 6, 1853; entered the force in 1877, and served as a patrolman for six years; was desk sergeant for three years, and was appointed lieutenant March 18, 1886, by Superintendent Ebersold; served with distinction during the riot of 1886, and is considered a faithful and efficient officer.

INGOMAR V. BRICTZKE, desk sergeant; born in Germany 1844; came to Chicago April 15, 1864; entered the force April 30, 1871; served as patrolman until October 1, 1874, when he was transferred to Hinman street station as desk sergeant; has since continued to serve in that capacity.

JAMES McAVOY, desk sergeant; born in Ireland in 1841; came to Chicago in 1867; entered the force February 28, 1872; served as patrolman until August 1, 1877, when he was appointed desk sergeant, which position he has continued to fill ever since.

SYLVESTER KENNEDY, patrol sergeant; born in Ireland in 1843; came to Chicago May, 1870; entered the force January 3, 1880; traveled post about one year; was appointed desk sergeant February, 1881; appointed patrol sergeant May 1, 1883; has sent several thieves to the penitentiary for burglary, and bears a good record for efficient service generally.

THOMAS R. WALSH, lock-up keeper; born in the County Mayo, Ireland, in 1842; came to Chicago 1863; entered the force May, 1870; arrested Billy Caldwell, alias "Speckled Billy," for highway robbery, in 1872, and sent him to Joliet for four years; arrested Mike Joy for robbery, the notorious Eugene Dougherty and other criminals.

HUGH BURNS, patrolman; born in Ireland in 1847; came to America at ten years of age, and remained in Baltimore till 1868, when he came to Chicago; entered the force January 18, 1875.

PATRICK CONWAY, patrolman; born in Ireland in 1854; came to Chicago in 1869; entered the force December 15, 1884.

JOHN J. CAREY, patrolman; born in Ireland in 1847; came to Chicago in 1862; entered the force October, 1875; arrested and convicted a number of criminals; served in all the riots since 1875 with credit.

MICHAEL CONNERY, patrolman; born in Ireland in 1840; came to Chicago in 1856; entered the force August 1, 1873; engaged in all the riots from 1877 to 1886; has sent three thieves to Joliet and accomplished other good service.

PATRICK CUMMINGS, patrolman; born in Ireland 1848; came to Chicago 1856; entered the force June, 1872; served in the riots of 1877 and 1886.

CHARLES DANKS, patrolman; born in Iowa 1860; came to Chicago in 1885; entered the force June 1, 1887.

MARTIN DONAHUE, patrolman; born in Galway, Ireland, 1852; came to Chicago August 4, 1877; entered the force December 15, 1884.

PATRICK DOYLE, patrolman; born in Ireland in 1854; came to Chicago 1872; entered the force September, 1882; sent Redney Flannery and James Henshaw to the penitentiary; was in the riot of 1886.

FREDERICK FOERSTER, patrolman; born at Frankfort-on-the-Main, Germany, 1858; came to Chicago 1875; entered the force April, 1886.

MALACHY FALLON, patrolman; born in County Roscommon, Ireland, in 1857; came to Chicago 1877; entered the force June 12, 1883;

arrested and convicted Tommy Fitzpatrick for robbery, and Jacob Burley for larceny, both of whom were sent to the penitentiary.

THOMAS FAHEY, patrolman; born in Watertown, N. Y., 1858; came to Chicago when six months old; entered the force December 2, 1886.

FRANK GOLDEN, patrolman; born Ireland 1858; came to Chicago 1874; entered the force January 7, 1875.

JAMES HOGAN, patrolman; born at Kenosha, Wis., November 1, 1852; came to Chicago when 1 year old; entered the force August 4, 1885.

JAMES P. HANLEY, patrolman; born at Swanton, Vt., 1862; came to Chicago July 10, 1883; entered the force June 20, 1885.

MICHAEL HALLY, patrolman; born Tarbart, Ireland, September 28, 1852; came to Chicago August 12, 1876; entered the force December 31, 1884.

THOMAS W. HAMMILL, patrolman; born in St. Lawrence Co., N. Y., 1852; came to Chicago 1879; entered the force April 19, 1886.

EDWARD HALLE, patrolman; born in Canada 1845; came to Chicago 1864; entered the force 1877; saw active service at the Maxwell and McCormick strikes, and in the riot of 1886.

JEREMIAH HOULIHAN, patrolman; born in the County Kerry, Ireland, 1835; came to Chicago March, 1861; entered the force May 2, 1867; enlisted in the Twenty-third Illinois Infantry, Mulligan Brigade, April 15, 1861; appointed sergeant Co. F in the spring of 1862, and first sergeant in the winter of 1863; was imprisoned at Danville, Va., in the winter of 1864, for seven months.

AUGUST HAMBROEK, patrolman; born Hesse, Germany, 1832; came to Chicago in 1847; entered the force June 14, 1869; enlisted July, 1861, in the Federal cavalry, and was promoted to the rank of first drill sergeant; served under Gen. Custer; took part in the battle of Pea Ridge, March, 1862; after two years was mustered out of service on account of sickness.

SAMUEL M. JEWITT, patrolman; born in Maine 1855; came to Chicago 1872; entered the force June, 1884.

CHARLES F. KAYSER, patrolman; born in Prussia 1848; came to Chicago 1870; entered the force May, 1885.

WILLIAM KING, patrolman; born at Marine City, Mich., 1854; came to Chicago 1870; entered the force May 8, 1881; arrested and convicted a number of noted criminals; served throughout the riots of 1886.

PATRICK KELLY, patrolman; born at Prince Edwards Island 1849; came to Chicago November, 1862; entered the force June 1, 1882; arrested Charles Ray Oct. 9, 1883, for horse stealing; Joe Foley

December 31, 1883, for robbery; James Shea February 16, 1887, for burglary; Charles Downs June 15, 1884, for burglary; George Stahl August 12, 1884, for burglary; Thomas Fitzpatrick November 1, 1884, for robbery; John Dutton December 9, 1884, for burglary; Charles Roberts July 4, 1884, for robbery; Henry Moore January 5, 1885, for larceny; Edward Lamontaine August 15, 1885, for burglary; all of whom were sent to the penitentiary for various terms; did service in the riots of 1886.

JOSEPH Z. LaPLANT, patrolman; born in Chicago in 1856; entered the force June 13, 1883; arrested Richard Graham and "Screw" McCune for robbery, and sent them to the penitentiary for three years; assisted in sending Thomas Touhey to Joliet for fourteen years for murder; served in all the riots since 1883.

JOHN J. MAHONEY, patrolman; born at Buffalo, N. Y., in 1858; came to Chicago when one year old; entered the force June 5, 1887; was detailed in plain clothes under instructions of Inspector Bonfield for a short time; was formerly railroad clerk and served for two years as watchman in the Court House.

JOHN MINIHAN, patrolman; born in Ireland in 1861; came to Chicago 1878; entered the force February, 1878.

THOMAS A. McGUIRE, patrolman; born in Chicago in 1859; entered the force December 28, 1884; with Officer J. O'Malley arrested and prosecuted Albert McDuff and John Montague for a burglary at 12 Miller street, and sent them to the penitentiary for four years; also arrested Thomas Fitzgerald, alias "Nibsey Fitz," September, 1886, for robbery, and sent him to Joliet for one year.

JOHN MADDICK, patrolman; born at Kenosha, Wis., in 1854; came to Chicago in 1869; entered the force December 16, 1886.

TERRENCE McGLYNN, patrolman; born in Ireland in 1858; came to Chicago 1878; entered the force April 19, 1886.

PATRICK MEAD, patrolman; born in Ireland in 1851; came to Chicago in 1871; entered the force June 12, 1883; arrested William Kennedy for larceny in 1886, and sent him to Joliet.

JAMES H. MARTIN, patrolman; born in Chicago in 1855; entered the force in 1882.

JOHN MOORE, patrolman; born in Ireland in 1849; came to Chicago June, 1870; entered the force June 1, 1882; has made several important arrests.

JAMES MURNANE, patrolman; born in Ireland in 1839; came to Chicago 1857; entered the force October, 1873; sent Sam. Mackelrath to Joliet for twelve years for the Litchfield, Ill., bank robbery; also Filo Durfee for five years for burglary; John Doyle for fifteen years for robbery of the Walton House; Ed. Roberts for twenty-five years, for killing his wife; Eugene Dougherty for life, for murder; was also active in sending Pat. Guerren and James Carroll to the penitentiary for the Galesburg bank robbery; served in all the riots since 1873.

JAMES McSHANE, patrolman; born in Ireland in 1846; came to Chicago February, 1866; entered the force in 1883.

MICHAEL NASH, patrolman; born in Ireland in 1855; came to Chicago in 1875; entered the force December, 1885.

JOHN NORTON, patrolman; born in Chicago 1853; entered the force November 4, 1886.

WILLIAM NICHOL, patrolman; born in Michigan 1849; came to Chicago 1871; entered the force April, 1886.

JOHN O'CONNOR, patrolman; born in Ireland 1848; came to Chicago 1866; entered the force 1873.

JOHN O'MALLEY, patrolman; born in the County Mayo, Ireland, 1853; came to Chicago May 18, 1873; entered the force June 5, 1882.

JAMES PIDGEON, patrolman; born in the province of Quebec, Canada, 1864; came to Chicago 1876; entered the force March 2, 1887.

GEORGE W. PEARSALL, patrolman; born in Chicago 1864; entered the force February 21, 1887.

JOHN QUINN, patrolman; born in Chicago 1859; entered the force December 15, 1874.

PETERE VINLOVE, patrolman; born in Chicago in 1850; entered the force June 1, 1883.

DANIEL G. RIORDAN, patrolman; born in Ireland in 1847; came to Chicago July 7, 1870; entered the force January 7, 1873.

JOHN RYAN, patrolman; born in Ireland in 1860; came to Chicago May 10, 1879; entered the force June 3, 1887.

MICHAEL RAFTERY, patrolman; born in the County Galway, Ireland, in 1861; came to Chicago April, 1879; entered the force June 10, 1887.

JACOB A. SWIKARD, patrolman; born near Utica, N. Y., 1847; came to Chicago 1858; entered the force 1880; enlisted in the 58th Illinois Infantry, at Camp Douglas, in 1861, served through the war and was discharged from the army in the spring of 1865; took part in the Battle of Fort Donelson, the Battle of Shiloh, and the Siege of Corinth; was taken prisoner at the Battle of Iuka, Miss., and taken to Vicksburg and paroled in 1862; was at the engagement at Fort Derusay, on the banks of the Red River, and Pleasant Hill, Marksville Prairie, and Chafilan Bayou, Louisiana.

JOSEPH SNYDER, patrolman; born at Toronto, Canada, in 1856; came to Chicago December, 1860; entered the force April 19, 1886.

AUGUST H. SCHRAGE, patrolman; born at Menasha, Wis., in 1863; came to Chicago 1881; entered the force April 20, 1886.

THOMAS SULLIVAN, patrolman; born in Ireland in 1849; came to Chicago October, 1868; entered the force December 15, 1885; arrested Thomas Moore for burglary and sent him to the penitentiary.

FREDERICK SHANER, patrolman; born in Cista, Bohemia, in 1856; came to Chicago 1867; entered the force December 15, 1884; arrested Jerry Peck and Frank Kozeli for robbery, and sent them to Joliet for three years each.

CHARLES F. STERN, patrolman; born in West Prussia, Germany, in 1860; came to Chicago in 1865; entered the force April 15, 1887.

JOHN STEWART, patrolman; born at Aberdeen, Scotland, in 1854; came to Chicago in 1875; entered the force May 4, 1887.

HINMAN STREET STATION, corner of Hinman and Paulina streets, one of the most important stations in the city, was erected in 1872, and is situated in the center of the great lumber and manufacturing district, where a majority of all the great strikes and riots have originated. It was in this district, and principally by the Hinman street men, that the great work of suppression of 1876, during the lumber shovers' strike, and in 1877, during the railroad strike and riots, was so admirably done. In 1886 the officers of this district, assisted by reinforcements from abroad, prevented the destruction of the McCormick works. So great and so diverse are the interests which center here, that scarcely a month passes which does not see a strike of some kind. The district patrolled by the force of this station is bounded north by West Sixteenth street, south by the south branch of the Chicago River, east by Loomis street and west by the city limits, an area of about four and one-fourth square miles, containing a population estimated at about 20,000.

RICHARD A. SHEPPARD, lieutenant commanding Hinman street district; born in Ireland 1849; brought to America by his family in 1860, settling in Cleveland, Oswego county, N. Y.; arrived in Chicago in 1866, and took position first as driver and then as conductor on a North Division street-car; after the fire went into business with his brother; entered the police force August 25, 1875; married Miss Mary Green, of Waukegan, in 1876; served as patrolman for a short time and was promoted to a sergeantcy in 1878, at Hinman street station; transferred to Deering street 1879; served there until raised to a lieutenancy and given charge of his present command; is a member of the Policemen's Benevolent Association, Police State Association, Kilwinning Lodge of Masons, Order of the Red Cross and Chicago Council No. 4, Corinthian Chapter; as a police officer has frequently distinguished himself, notably during the labor riots of 1877, and three years later during the great butchers' strike at the stock yards; was placed in charge of the Triennial Conclave of the Knights Templar on the lake front in 1880, and preserved order and the dignity of the gathering admirably; was dangerously shot the same year by thieves connected with the celebrated gas-house robbery, in which $4,000 was taken, and later with the rolling mills robbery, in which $10,000 was stolen; arrested the murderer McCue; had charge of the lumber district during the labor riots of 1886, during which time three thousand strikers attacked the McCormick works on the now famous Black Road; is a fearless officer, of splendid executive ability and has the confidence of superiors and citizens.

EDWARD BARTH, desk sergeant; born at Barrington, Ill., 1857; came to Chicago April, 1873; entered the force December 15, 1884

WILLIAM SENNOTT McGUIRE, desk sergeant; born at Lamont, Ill., in 1857; came to Chicago September, 1880; entered the force July, 1882.

HIRAM ALLEN EARL, patrol sergeant; born at Morristown, Vt., 1843; came to Chicago 1880; entered the force May, 1882; distinguished for his bravery during the riots of 1886; was present at the time of the bomb explosion at Haymarket square.

BENJAMIN BURNS, patrolman; born at Lawrence, Mass., 1859; came to Chicago 1877; entered the force August, 1885; exhibited bravery during the riots of 1886.

MARK BELL, patrolman; born at Yonkers, N. Y., 1855; came to Chicago 1862; entered the force June, 1887.

PATRICK BURK, patrolman; born at Florence, Ill., 1858; came to Chicago March, 1882; entered the force August, 1887.

MICHAEL CIBROWSKI, patrolman; born in Germany 1856; came to Chicago in 1868; entered the force April 20, 1886; mentioned for brave conduct during riots of that year.

JOHN CLARK, patrolman; born in Ireland 1862; came to Chicago April, 1882; entered the force April, 1887.

RICHARD CULLEN, patrolman; born in Ireland 1862; came to Chi-

cago 1877; entered the force December 15, 1884; distinguished
himself during riots of 1886.

THOMAS CULLERTON, patrolman; born in Chicago 1844; entered
the force 1874.

WILLIAM DILLON, patrolman; born in Ireland 1850; came to Chicago June, 1875; entered the force June, 1883; distinguished himself during the riots of 1886.

THOMAS F. FARRELL, patrolman; born in Madison, Wis., 1859;
came to Chicago 1877; entered the force March, 1885; distinguished
himself during the riots of 1886.

JESSE FAIRCHILDS, patrolman; born in Johnson county, Ky., 1847;
came to Chicago 1872; entered the force March, 1875; distinguished
himself during the riots of 1886.

CHARLES R. FUGATE, patrolman; born in Salem, Ohio, 1850; came
to Chicago April, 1873; entered the force March, 1880; with Officer Fitzgerald, in 1885, arrested the Italian, Michael Rosso, who
killed John Kehoe, Sept. 13, 1885, at the corner of Nineteenth and
Halsted streets; also distinguished himself at the McCormick
factory during the riot of 1886.

JAMES EDWARD FITZGERALD, patrolman; born in Fond du Lac,
Wis., 1854; came to Chicago May, 1871; entered the force Decem-
ber, 1884; with Officer Fugate arrested the Italian who killed
John Kehoe, September 13, 1885, at the corner of Nineteenth and
Halsted streets; also distinguished himself at the McCormick fac-
tory during the riots of 1886.

OWEN FOX, patrolman; born in Ireland 1860; came to Chicago April,
1882; entered the force June, 1887.

CHARLES P. FLANNIGAN, patrolman; born in Kane county, Ill.,
1864; came to Chicago November, 1882; entered the force June,
1887.

CHARLES JOHN JOHNSON, patrolman; born in Chicago, 1859;
entered the force May, 1885; in 1886, arrested Varlav Dejnek, one
of the mob who attempted to hang Officer William Casey on May
3, 1886; also arrested, in 1885, the notorious Fred Binzle, a burglar.

JAMES W. KNOWLS, patrolman; born in Elgin, Ill., 1859; came to
Chicago 1876; entered the force June, 1881; distinguished himself
during the riots of 1886.

MICHAEL KILGALLON, patrolman; born in Ireland 1860; came to
Chicago September, 1876; entered the force April, 1886; distinguished himself during the riots of 1886.

MICHAEL E. KEATING, patrolman; born in Chicago, 1859; entered the force August, 1882; in 1886, arrested James Kane, one of

R. A. SHEPPARD,
Lieut. Comdg. Hinman St. District.

JOHN REHM,
Lieut. Comdg Canalport Ave. District.

the four who, after gagging the postmaster at Mt. Forest, Ill., robbed the office of a large sum of money and stamps.

JAMES KANE, patrolman; born in Ireland 1850; came to Chicago 1865; entered the force December, 1884; on May 3, 1886, picked up a dynamite bomb, with a burning fuse attached, and threw it from the patrol wagon, where it had been placed by some unknown person, at the corner of Center avenue and Seventeenth streets, saving his own and the lives of many other officers.

J. H. LINDELSEE, patrolman; born in Germany 1858; came to Chicago 1870; entered the force April, 1886; distinguished himself during the riots of 1886.

JAMES MANSFIELD, patrolman; born in Ireland 1848; came to Chicago 1867; entered the force December 14, 1884; distinguished himself during the riots of 1886.

WILLIAM McCLELLAN, patrolman; born in Lawrence, Pa., 1853; came to Chicago December, 1880; entered the force June, 1887.

WILLIAM O'BRIEN, patrolman; born in Ireland 1853; came to Chicago May, 1866; entered the force April, 1886; distinguished himself during the riots of 1886.

JAMES PICENY, patrolman; born in Bohemia 1855; came to Chicago May, 1860; entered the force December, 1884; distinguished himself during the riots of 1886.

LOUIS F. SHANE, patrolman; born in Rochester, N. Y., 1858; came to Chicago May, 1871; entered the force December, 1884; distinguished himself during the riots of 1886, and made several important arrests; also gave great assistance to the state's attorney in 1886, in locating witnesses for the anarchist trial.

MATHEW ZEMICK, patrolman; born in Bohemia 1860; came to Chicago, September, 1870; entered the force December, 1884; distinguished himself during the riots of 1886.

CANALPORT AVENUE STATION, Canalport avenue, near Halsted street, was opened July 27, 1886, with Lieutenant John Rehm in command. The station was given a total force of thirty-three men. It was publicly dedicated by the citizens of the district August 5, 1886. It is located in the heart of the Bohemian settlement. The district patrolled by the officers of this station is bounded north by West Sixteenth street; south and east by the south branch of the Chicago River, and west by Loomis street. The area is about one square mile, and the estimated population about 25,000.

JOHN REHM, lieutenant of police, commanding Canalport avenue district; born in Baltimore, Md., in 1848, of German parents; attended school until ten years of age; lived on a farm in Carroll county, Md., until the outbreak of the rebellion; then entered the government service at Washington as a teamster; left the service in 1864, and again followed the farming pursuit for two or three years; returned to Baltimore in 1867, and learned the box-making trade, at which he worked until 1871, when he left for St. Louis, and there engaged in the bottling business; after a few months' trial, gave it up, and came to Chicago in July, 1871; resumed his trade here, and was employed by different firms in this city until September 11, 1874, when he entered the police force as patrolman; was promoted to a desk sergeantcy March 17, 1875, at Hinman street station; transferred to Union street station April 1, 1876; promoted to patrol sergeantcy August 1, 1878, and assigned to West Twelfth street station; remained there about two years; transferred to West Lake street station, remaining there seven months, and then transferred to West Twelfth street station; after two years was transferred to Twenty-second street station, at which point he was promoted to a lieutenancy, April 20, 1884, and assigned to take charge of the Thirty-fifth street station; remained there till July 7 of same year, when he was placed in charge of the Canalport avenue district; has held every rank in the department up to the one he now holds; has never been reprimanded by a superior officer. Lieutenant Rehm secured the first conviction ever obtained in this city under the "Habitual Criminal's Act," sending a notorious burglar to the penitentiary for twenty years. In this work he was assisted by Lieutenant Steele. Arrested the notorious Dr. Thomas N. Cream for abortion, who was afterward sentenced for life on a charge of murder, at Wheaton; in the street-car troubles of 1885, had charge of a company under Captain Bonfield, and took part in the celebrated "clubbing" procession down Madison street; also took an active part during the switchmen's strike; responded to the call for assistance after the Haymarket bomb explosion, and assisted in the restoration of order, the care of the wounded, etc., on the night of May 4. Lieutenant Rehm is one of the most popular officers on the force, and as discreet as he is courteous.

DENIS FITZPATRICK, desk sergeant; born at Amsterdam, N. Y., 1842; came to Chicago 1847; entered the force May 2, 1866; served four years and six months during the war of the rebellion in the Eleventh Illinois Infantry, eight and a half months of that time in rebel prisons, part of the time under the infamous Wirz, at Andersonville.

JOHN E. PTACEK, desk sergeant; born at Ottawa, Ill., 1861; came to Chicago when an infant; entered the force December 15, 1884.

JAMES FOX, patrol sergeant; born in Ireland 1844; came to Chicago 1869; entered the force September 18, 1885.

JOHN MONAGHAN, patrolman in signal service; born in Ireland 1852; came to Chicago 1869; entered the force September, 1885.

JOHN B. BAGINSKI, patrolman; born in Poland 1854; came to Chicago 1874; entered the force June 13, 1883.

MICHAEL BRUNSFELD, patrolman; born in Germany 1855; came to Chicago June, 1872; entered the force August 1, 1887.

WM. DEVITT, patrolman; born in Toronto, Iowa, 1864; came to Chicago 1884; entered the force July 1, 1886.

JAMES DIXON, patrolman; born in Ohio 1854; came to Chicago 1882; entered the force June 3, 1887.

JOHN DEGAN, patrolman; born in Chicago 1863; entered the force July 1, 1886; a brother to the late Officer Mathias Degan, the first man killed at the Haymarket riot.

JOHN J. EGAN, patrolman; born in Ireland 1849; came to Chicago 1863; entered the force in 1877, and re-entered in 1883; served four years and three months in the 3rd Virginia Cavalry during the late war; enlisted as private and came out captain; in 1883 or 1884, arrested Anderson, the murderer of Officer Pierce, of the St. Louis force; resisting, was shot through the thumb; was in the McCormick riots.

PATRICK GORMAN, patrolman; born in Ireland 1862; came to Chicago 1881; entered the force April 15, 1887.

PATRICK J. GORDON, patrolman; born in Ireland 1859; came to Chicago May 3, 1881; entered the force July 10, 1886.

PETER GOETLEL, patrolman; born in Chicago 1860; entered the force August 1, 1887.

PATRICK HOGAN, patrolman; born in Ireland 1862; came to Chicago 1880; entered the force 1886.

AUGUST KOEPPEN, patrolman; born in Chicago 1857; entered the force July 1, 1886.

JOHN McDERMOTT, patrolman; born in Ireland 1843; came to Chicago 1871; entered the force December 29, 1875; served four years on the force in Ireland, and one year in Liverpool, Eng.

JAMES J. MURRAY, patrolman; born in Virginia 1858; came to Chicago 1870; entered the force July 1, 1886.

THOS. MARTIN, patrolman; born in Ireland 1857; came to Chicago in 1880; entered the force July 1, 1886.

PATRICK McGRATH, patrolman; born in Ireland 1863; came to Chicago 1882; entered the force July 1, 1887.

JOHN McDONALD, patrolman; born in Ireland 1851; came to Chicago 1869; entered the force June 13, 1883; was in the McCormick riots.

WM. NOLAN, patrolman; born in Chicago 1855; entered the force July 1, 1886.

TIMOTHY O'MEARD, patrolman; born in Gilbertville, Mass., 1867; came to Chicago 1868; entered the force June 3, 1887.

PATRICK J. O'BRIEN, patrolman; born in Ireland 1863; came to Chicago 1879; entered the force February 20, 1887.

TIMOTHY O'CONNOR, patrolman; born in Ireland 1859; came to Chicago Augu-t, 1879; entered the force August 1, 1887.

MICHAEL W. QUINLAN, patrolman; born in Ireland 1841; came to Chicago 1852; entered the force March, 1871; re-entered June 13, 1883; was in the McCormick riot.

RICHARD F. QUINN, patrolman; born in Chicago 1858; entered the force July 1, 1886.

PETER RAGGIO, patrolman; born in Detroit, Mich., 1862; came to Chicago 1863; entered the force June 3, 1887.

JOHN R. RYAN, patrolman; born in Ireland 1864; came to Chicago 1881; entered the force February 21, 1887.

JOHN SMALL, patrolman; born in Ireland 1859; came to Chicago 1874; entered the force January 16, 1885; was at the McCormick riot.

WEST THIRTEENTH STREET STATION, West Thirteenth street, near Oakley avenue, is one of the newest of the sub-stations. It was opened May 1, 1886, with John Croak, lieutenant, commanding; Richard Moore, patrol sergeant; O. Z. Barber and Edward Watson, desk sergeants, and thirty-four men. The district patrolled by the force of this station is bounded north by West Harrison street, east by Loomis street, south by West Sixteenth street, and west by the city limits; the area is about three and one-fourth square miles, and the population in 1886 was estimated at 25,000. This section of the city, however, has been filling up rapidly of late, and the population now is estimated to be fully 30,000.

JOHN CROAK, lieutenant of police, commanding West Thirteenth street district; born in Ireland 1837; came to Chicago 1852; entered the force 1869; was appointed patrolman and assigned to

JOHN CROAK,
Lieut. Comdg. West Thirteenth St. District.

ANSON BACKUS,

Lieut. Comdg. West Lake St. District.

duty at the old Armory station, corner of Franklin and Adams streets; rendered great service to many families in assisting them to escape during the great fire; took an active part in the riot of 1877, and shortly after was appointed to the mayor's staff under Mr. Heath, which position he held till 1879; was then appointed patrol sergeant and assigned to duty on the Central detail; in 1884 was appointed lieutenant, and assigned to duty at the Thirty-fifth street station; in 1885 was transferred to West Twelfth street station; was at the McCormick riot in the spring of 1885; at the Maxwell strike in the winter of 1885-6; also at the assault upon the drug store and saloon, corner of Center avenue and Eighteenth street, when the former was almost entirely demolished; at the Mc-Cormick strike and riot on the "Black Road" in 1886; was then assigned to duty at and opened the new West Thirteenth street station, at that time just completed. Lieutenant Croak is regarded as one of the most faithful and able officers in the department.

ORVILLE Z. BARBER, desk sergeant; born in Connecticut in 1845; came to Chicago 1867; entered the force May 1, 1872; has arrested many criminals, who have been convicted and sentenced to the penitentiary; arrested the notorious burglar, John English, for burglary and attempted murder, and secured his imprisonment in the penitentiary for nine years.

EDWARD WATSON, desk sergeant; born in Scotland in 1843; came to Chicago in 1847; entered the force October, 1873.

RICHARD J. MOORE, patrol sergeant; born in Illinois 1848; came to Chicago 1873; entered the force July 18, 1873; on October 4, 1884, arrested Joe Williams, who was convicted of murder and sentenced for life; was in the McCormick riot, May 3, 1886; also at the Haymarket riot on the following evening; also did service in the riots at Center avenue and Eighteenth streets, May 4 and 5, 1886.

JAMES E. CULLERTON, patrolman; born in Chicago 1859; entered the force December, 1884; served in the Black Road, Haymarket and Eighteenth street riots.

THOMAS CURTIS, patrolman; born in Ireland 1846; came to Chicago 1868; entered the force October, 1881; was shot by George Thompson, a colored burglar, February 22, 1882; was engaged in the Mc-Cormick, Haymarket and Eighteenth street riots.

THOMAS DONOHUE, patrolman; born at Elgin, Ill., 1857; came to Chicago 1882; served in the McCormick, Haymarket and Eighteenth street riots.

JOHN DUNNIGAN, patrolman; born in Ireland 1864; came to Chicago 1880; entered the force April, 1886; served in the McCormick, Haymarket and Eighteenth street riots.

OWEN DOUGHERTY, patrolman; born in Ireland 1855; came to Chicago 1877; entered the force December, 1884; served at the McCormick, Haymarket and Eighteenth street riots.

FRANK ELLWOOD, patrolman; born in Ireland 1861; came to Chicago 1878; entered the force December, 1884; served in the McCormick, Haymarket and Eighteenth street riots.

HENRY FITZGERALD, patrolman; born in Canada 1862; entered the force December, 1884; served in the McCormick, Haymarket and Eighteenth street riots.

DAVID B. FERNS, patrolman; born in New York 1855; came to Chicago 1860; entered the force June 3, 1887.

DANIEL A. GRACE, patrolman; born in Chicago 1864; entered the force April, 1887.

CHARLES HOFFMAN, patrolman; born in Ohio 1857; came to Chicago 1878; entered the force July 1, 1886.

JOHN M. HAINES, patrolman; born in New York 1858; came to Chicago 1872; entered the force August, 1874; sent to the penitentiary Albert Emill, alias Bater, a notorious safe-blower, for ten years; was shot by the officer while resisting arrest; also Webster Pease, the notorious hotel thief, for six years; served with distinction in the McCormick, Haymarket and Eighteenth street riots.

AUGUST L. HARDER, patrolman; born in Germany 1862; came to Chicago 1868; entered the force April, 1886; was in the riots at the Haymarket, McCormick's factory, and at Center avenue and Eighteenth street.

HENRY C. KLUSMANN, patrolman; born in Germany 1849; came to Chicago 1852; entered the force July, 1886.

JOHN B. MEDRS, patrolman; born in Bloomsburgh, Penn., 1853; came to Chicago 1868; entered the force June, 1887.

THOMAS McNAMARA, patrolman; born in Tarrytown, N. Y., 1855; came to Chicago September, 1879; entered the force June, 1887.

JAMES MADDEN, patrolman; born in Ireland 1849; came to Chicago 1867; entered the force July 1, 1883; was in the Haymarket, McCormick and Center avenue and Eighteenth street riots of 1886.

PATRICK McLAUGHLIN, patrolman; born in Ireland 1851; came to Chicago 1880; entered the force September, 1885; was wounded at the Haymarket riot, 1886.

PATRICK MAGUIRE, patrolman; born in Ireland 1857; came to Chicago 1877; entered the force December, 1884; was in the riots of May, 1886.

DENNIS McCARTHY, patrolman; born in Ireland, 1861; entered the force August 7, 1885; was in all the riots of May, 1886.

DENNIS O'SHEA, patrolman; born in Ireland 1860; came to Chicago 1880; entered the force December, 1884; was in all the riots of 1886.

CHARLES O'CONNELL, patrolman; born in Illinois 1852; came to Chicago 1862; entered the force July 28, 1875; was in the Haymarket, McCormick and Center avenue and Eighteenth street riots in 1886.

CHARLES PEHLKE, patrolman; born in Germany 1859; came to Chicago July, 1871; entered the force June, 1887.

THOMAS J. ROACH, patrolman; born in Ireland 1852; came to Chicago 1871; entered the force June, 1883; was in the Haymarket, McCormick and Center avenue and Eighteenth street riots of 1886.

JOSEPH L. RIVERS, patrolman; born in New York 1850; came to Chicago 1859; entered the force December, 1884; was in the Haymarket and McCormick riots of 1886.

JOHN STOKES, patrolman; born in London, Eng., 1852; came to Chicago 1852; entered the force April, 1887.

JERRY W. SWEIG, patrolman; born in Luxemburg, Germany, 1860; came to Chicago 1865; entered the force December, 1886.

CHARLES S. TOOLAN, patrolman; born in Pennsylvania 1848; came to Chicago 1874; entered the force June 20, 1882; was in the Haymarket and other riots of May, 1886.

JOHN J. WALSH, patrolman; born in Ireland 1856; came to Chicago 1868; entered the force April, 1887.

DEERING STREET STATION, No. 2913 Deering street. This district was organized November 1, 1870, the station being then at the corner of Archer avenue and Main street, with Sergeant Edward Hood in command; succeeded by William Carberry, June 1, 1877; next by Matt. Beadell, August 1, 1878; next by John D. Shea, May, 1887, the present lieutenant commanding. The district patrolled by the force of this station is bounded north by the south branch of the Chicago River; on the south, from South Halsted street to Ashland avenue, by Thirty-first street, and from Ashland avenue west by the south city limits; on the east, from the south branch of the Chicago River to Thirty-first street, by Halsted street; and from Thirty-first street to the south city limits, an area of three and a half square miles, containing about 30,000 inhabitants.

JOHN D. SHEA, lieutenant of police, commanding Deering street district, was born in the town of Palos, sixteen miles from Chicago, in Cook county, on the 7th of February, 1848. His boyhood was spent in Palos, where he attended the district school, and received a fair education. Leaving his father's roof at the age of twenty-five, young Shea came to Chicago, and immediately obtained an appointment as patrolman on the police force. This was on the first day of August, 1873, and during Elmer Washburn's time. On the day of his appointment, another young man, with a fresh, chubby face, also from the rural districts, was measured, weighed, examined and accepted. The latter is now captain of the Central detail. Patrolman Shea was assigned to the Twelfth street station, then in charge of Sergeant Simon O'Donnell, and remained at that post about two years, or until Sergeant O'Donnell was created a captain and placed in charge of the first precinct. Following his commanding officer to the Harrison street station, he remained there about one month, when Superintendent Hickey offered him a position on the detective force—an offer which he cheerfully accepted. Clad in plain clothes, he was assigned to the Union street station, then in charge of Captain—afterward superintendent—Seavey. For some time Detective Shea traveled with Edward Lansing, now in business on Clark street, and later with Edward Keating, one of the shrewdest and best detectives Chicago ever had. Keating is dead. When Superintendent Hickey was removed, Captain Seavey was appointed to his place, but after serving a few months, he was taken with what proved to be a fatal illness. During a part of the time while the superintendent was ill, Deputy Superintendent Dixon was acting chief, but his resignation was requested by Mayor Harrison, who appointed Simon O'Donnell deputy superintendent. After Superintendent Seavey's death Simon O'Donnell was appointed general superintendent, and he transferred Detective Shea to the Central station, where he continued in the secret service. During O'Donnell's administration, Detective Shea worked with Keating a portion of the time, and then with Joseph Kipley. The trio came to be looked upon as the ablest detectives on the force. When McGarigle was made chief and Austin Doyle secretary, they sent for Kipley, Keating and Shea one day, and said to them: "Boys, we're going to do something for you; we're going to make you lieutenants." This promotion came as a surprise, as the detectives did not know how well they stood in the eyes of the new heads of the department. Lieutenant Shea was assigned to the Twenty-second street station, vice Lieutenant Buckley, transferred and promoted to a captaincy for the second time. He remained in command of the Twenty-second street station until Doyle became superintendent, when the latter offered him the position of chief of detectives. This he accepted, and held that position, associated with Lieutenant Kipley, during Doyle's administration, and under Superintendent Ebersold until the election of Mayor Roche, when he was transferred to Deering street station. Lieutenant Shea has had a most eventful and interesting career as a detective. One of his first cases was the arrest of Michael McQuade and Jim Brady, two notorious horse thieves. Their scheme was to steal horses and buggies, and take them to a small town in the interior, where they had a "fence." They would sell the horses they stole here to farmers, and then steal horses from the farmers on their way back, disposing of them in Chicago. Shea and Keating recovered thirteen head of horses, eleven buggies, sixteen sets of harness, and several wagons. Brady was sent to the penitentiary for three years; McQuade escaped on straw bail. In a little affair on Clark street with some city thugs, Shea was struck on the back of the head with a brick, and had his nose broken. He arrested Chris. Sheridan and George R. Day after robbing Mr. Johnson and wife, corner of Aberdeen and Van Buren streets; Sheridan was an ex-convict from Jefferson City, Mo.; Day was a private detective; both were sentenced to ten years. He arrested John Quinn, Thomas Bailey and Charles Williams for burglary at the residence of Mr. Chris. Hotz, and sent them to the penitentiary for nine years each. He arrested "Bull" Crane, Thomas Gafney and Edward Moran on nine charges of highway robbery. Crane was sentenced for fourteen, Gafney for nine years. He arrested the notorious Jimmy Carroll for robbing the Farmers' and Mechanics' Bank, at Galesburg, Ill., of $9,000, together with "Paddy" Guerin and Mark Davis. Carroll was a power in Chicago among his class previous to Harrison's administration. It was his custom to organize gangs of bank robbers in Chicago and make raids upon outside towns, on the "still" plan. Carroll planned the robberies, and his men executed them. His career is familiar to Chicago people, down to his final conviction at Galesburg. One of his expert "workers" was Kid O'Brien, who was shot and killed by Officer William Jones. The notorious Billy Burke was the latter's successor. The entire gang was captured by Detective Shea and his companions, and the work done by them was considered admirable. He arrested Charles Mitchell and two pals for the burglary of General Joe Stockton's residence, at Lake View. Mitchell aroused General Stockton on entering his room. The burglar started for the door, and General Stockton threw an inkstand at him. Mitchell then fired upon the general, the ball striking the wall just above his head. The fellow got eight years in the penitentiary, and his companions three years each. Detectives Kipley and Shea arrested the notorious William Reed, Charles Pearson and Al. Beader on Washington street, near the tunnel. They were preparing to commit a series of burglaries, and had in their room a satchel full of dynamite, several rolls of fuse, percussion caps, "jimmies," revolvers, and a complete set of burglars' tools. As there was no proof of any crime committed to be brought against them, they were simply driven from the city. Al. Beader afterward received a sentence of ten years for robbing the safe in Ph. Best's brewery. Reed is in the Chester (Pa.) penitentiary, and Pearson is "doing time" at Denver. Through the instrumentality of Shea and Kipley, the Italian "stranglers," who so brutally murdered Francesci Tremarco, were brought to justice. The detectives extracted a complete confession of the horrible crime from the assassins. The same detectives sent to the penitentiary for three years William Edwards (alias Elliott) for blowing open the safe of I. N. Marks, pawnbroker, in company with Charles Proctor, James Donovan and Ed. Whalen. The gang had taken $9,000 worth of jewelry. Edwards was arrested by Officers Kelly and Hurley, and taken to police headquarters, where Lieutenants Shea and Kipley, after talking to him from 8 o'clock in the evening until 4 o'clock in the morning, succeeded in making him "squeal" and tell where the jewelry was secreted. Detective James Bonfield was put on a train, and recovered the property in a New York City express office. It was brought back by Detective Bonfield, inventoried, and turned over to the owner. Elliott was the only one of the gang arrested at that time. Afterward, Donovan, Proctor, Fitzpatrick and James Murray were arrested for committing a series of safe-blowing jobs. Murray "squealed" on his pals, and Donovan afterward followed suit, and took Lieutenants Kipley and Shea to a lumber yard on the North Side, where the proceeds of most of the burglaries were planted. These were all sent to the penitentiary for two, three and five years. Lieutenant Shea was prominently identified with the West Side street-car troubles of July, 1885. He, with the present superintendent of police, took the first car out of the barn, at 5 o'clock in the morning, and it took them until 11 o'clock to run the blockade and get down town. This was before Bonfield's famous triumphal march down Madison street. Most of Lieutenant Shea's time since entering the force has been spent in detective work. Dissatisfaction with the secret service as a whole, rather than with the work of Shea, Kipley and a few others, who are acknowledged men of rare ability in their line, led to the recent changes, which have resulted in placing Lieutenant Shea on the regular force.

PATRICK MAHONEY, desk sergeant; born in Ireland in 1834; came to Chicago in 1848; entered the force July 7, 1866; assigned to duty as patrolman at the old North Market station on Michigan street; transferred to Twenty-second street station April, 1869; from thence to Deering street station Nov. 1, 1870; was promoted to desk sergeantcy July, 1873.

JAMES LAWLOR, desk sergeant; born in Ireland in 1848; came to Chicago October, 1876; entered the force October, 1880.

M. L. MILLER, patrol sergeant; born at Newburgh on the Hudson, N. Y., in 1844; came to Chicago in 1852; entered the force February 15, 1867; did special duty for one year and over at headquarters; transferred to Armory for regular patrol duty; transferred to Twelfth street station in 1869; arrested Michael Mulholland, a member of a gang of burglars, and succeeded in recovering $13,000 worth of stolen property as a result of the arrest; while making this capture Sergeant Briscoe, one of the old-time officers, mistook Miller for one of the gang, and came near shooting him; also assisted in arresting John Lee and two others for the shooting of Officers Patten and Mitchell at the corner of Polk street and Blue Island avenue; effected other important arrests while attached to the Twelfth street station; transferred to the Twenty-second street station December, 1871; did patrol duty until 1877, in which year he was promoted to the rank of patrol sergeant by Chief Hickey; arrested Burt Tyler for committing a number of burglaries in the large residences on the South Side avenues, recovering a large amount of property, (Tyler was afterward shot by Officer Crow, while out on bail); arrested Elroy, at the corner of Fourteenth street, for robbery, and in the scuffle had his right hand broken; also arrested William Ray, the horse thief, and recovered several thousand dollars worth of property; also arrested Frank Brady, for the stabbing of a man named Canty; while out on bail the latter's father was compelled to shoot him in self-defense; arrested the father for the shooting; while engaged in hunting down the murderers of McConville, Sherry and Connolly, ran against three notorious thieves, just out of the penitentiary; arrested two of them, recovered stolen property in their possession worth $2,500, and turned them over to the Indiana authorities; was transferred to Deering street February, 1881; assisted in the arrest of Michael and John Carey for the murder of McFadden; also arrested William Mitchell for the shooting of Judge Pillsbury on the Alton train at Brighton; has participated in all the riots and strikes which have taken place in Chicago during the past twenty years.

MORGAN W. O'CONNELL, patrolman; born in Chicago 1862; entered the force July 1, 1886.

MAURICE CROTTY, patrolman; born in Ireland 1860; came to Chicago July, 1875; entered the force December 15, 1884; assigned to duty at Deering street station December 15, 1884.

ELIE S. CRIMUNG, patrolman; born in Paris, France, 1836; came to Chicago 1853; entered the force November 10, 1868; assigned to duty at the old Armory; transferred to Deering street station February 13, 1873.

WILLIAM DILLON, patrolman; born at La Salle, Ill., 1855; came to Chicago 1871; entered the force December 15, 1884; arrested Solomon Bernstein for burglary and gave him two years in the penitentiary; arrested John Leahy for murder, eight years in the penitentiary; arrested, with Officer O'Donnell, George Fallon, five years in the penitentiary; arrested Michael Carey for murder, acquitted; arrested, with Officer O'Hara, Tim Grady for the murder of Officer Michael O'Brien, seventeen years in the penitentiary; has been doing patrol duty at Deering street police station since entering the force.

FRANK DIGEREN, patrolman; born in Ireland in 1859; came to Chicago 1878; entered the force 1886.

EDWARD FLAHERTY, patrolman; born at Kenosha, Wis., 1860; came to Chicago when an infant; entered the force 1884; in January, 1885, with other officers arrested a gang of robbers and captured several trunks of silks stolen in Buffalo, N. Y.; at No. 10 Boston avenue, this city, assisted in arresting and breaking up another gang of thieves which had been engaged in stealing cloth in wagons.

JAMES J. FITZGERALD, patrolman; born in Massachusetts 1854; came to Chicago June, 1877; entered the force May 7, 1882, and assigned to duty at Deering street.

MICHAEL HICKEY, patrolman; born in Ireland 1859; came to Chicago 1871; entered the force August 6, 1885.

JAMES HEALY, patrolman; born in Ireland 1852; came to Chicago 1873; entered the force May, 1882; was assigned to duty at Thirty-fifth street station, and transferred to Deering street August, 1884; arrested John Williams for robbery, penitentiary five years; Martin Bonfield for burglary, penitentiary three years.

JOHN HOULIHAN, patrolman; born in Ireland 1845; came to Chicago 1866; entered the force October 7, 1880.

JOHN J. JONES, patrolman; born in Chicago 1854; entered the force December 15, 1884; arrested August Garns for larceny, penitentiary one year; arrested John Carey for the murder of Alex. McFadden, August, 1886.

PATRICK KEATING, patrolman; born in Ireland 1847; came to Chicago 1869; entered the force 1879; assigned to duty at Harrison street station, and transferred to Deering street Dec. 20, 1880.

JAMES P. KELLY, patrolman; born at Hartford, Conn., 1862; came to Chicago January, 1884; entered the force January, 1887; assigned to duty at Thirteenth street station, and transferred to Hinman street, thence to Deering street April 9, 1887.

DANIEL KELLY, patrolman; born in Ireland 1845; came to Chicago

1864; entered the force February 7, 1872; served twelve years in the Twelfth street district; transferred to Harrison street station 1884; transferred to Desplaines street station 1885, and transferred to Deering street station 1887.

MICHAEL LEE, patrolman; born in Ireland 1861; came to Chicago 1881; entered the force June 4, 1887; assigned to duty at Twelfth street station, and transferred to Deering street August 1, 1887

CHARLES McGOVERN, patrolman; born in Ireland 1857; entered force April, 1885; assigned to duty as patrolman at Twelfth street station April, 1885, and transferred to Deering street shortly after.

JOHN J. McCULLOM, patrolman; born in Chicago 1861; entered the force December 15, 1884; convicted William Kane, alias Freeman (an ex-convict), December 24, 1885, for burglary of the Mount Forrest, Ill., postoffice, penitentiary nine years.

STEPHEN MUCHOWSKY, patrolman; born in Poland 1852; came to Chicago 1868; entered the force 1884.

JAMES W. McKENNA, patrolman; born in Chicago; entered the force December 16, 1884; assigned to Desplaines street station, and transferred to Deering street December 20, 1884.

JOHN MALONE, patrolman; born in Ireland 1849; came to Chicago June 1, 1867; entered the force June 13, 1883; assigned to duty at Twelfth street station; remained there till after the Haymarket riot, then assigned to Thirteenth street, and transferred to Deering street November 5, 1886.

WILLIAM McSHEA, patrolman; born in Chicago 1853; entered the force December 15, 1884; assigned to Deering street station.

MORGAN O'CONNELL, patrolman; born in Chicago 1862; entered the force June 1, 1886; assigned to Deering street station.

PATRICK O'DAY, patrolman; born in Ireland, 1851; came to Chicago May, 1871; entered the force December 15, 1884; assigned to duty at Deering street station.

JOHN O'HARA, patrolman; born in Ireland 1857; came to Chicago 1877; entered the force December 15, 1884; assigned to duty at Deering street station; arrested Timothy O'Grady April 3, 1887, for the murder of Officer Michael O'Brien, penitentiary seventeen years.

WILLIAM ROONEY, patrolman; born in Dodge county, Wisconsin, 1852; came to Chicago 1875; entered the force March 25, 1881; assigned to duty at Harrison street station, and transferred to Deering street February 2, 1884.

MATTHEW RYAN, patrolman; born in Ireland 1854; came to Chicago March, 1881; entered the force April 20, 1886; assigned to duty at Hinman street; transferred to Deering street June 6, 1886.

THOMAS J. SLOYAN, patrolman; born in Ireland 1855; came to Chicago June 20, 1880; entered the force July 13, 1885; assigned to duty at Twelfth street station, and transferred to Deering street November 1, 1885

CHAPTER XXVI.

THE THIRD PRECINCT, CAPTAIN LYMAN LEWIS COMMANDING—ONE OF THE OLD-TIME PRECINCTS AND THE MOST ANCIENT OF OUR STATIONS— FROM THE WEST MARKET HALL TO THE PRESENT HANDSOME EDIFICE ON DESPLAINES STREET—CAPT. LYMAN LEWIS AND HIS GALLANT MEN—MEMORIES OF THE NIGHT OF MAY 4—VAN PELT'S HANDSOME PICTURE—THE WEST LAKE AND WEST MADISON STREET DISTRICTS— BIOGRAPHIES OF OFFICERS AND MEN IN THE PRECINCT.

The third precinct includes the Desplaines street, West Madison street and West Lake street districts. Headquarters, Desplaines street station, Desplaines street and Waldo place.

PRECINCT STATION, Desplaines street and Waldo place.— Originally the station belonging to this district was located in the old West Market hall. It was then moved to No. 14 Union street, which was the headquarters of the West Division force until a new station was erected on the corner of Union and Madison streets. This was known popularly and officially as the "Union Street Station" until its abandonment. The Desplaines street station, one of the largest and best equipped in the city, is the successor of all these. Elsewhere in this history this station and its predecessors are frequently mentioned. The district patrolled by the force of this station is bounded on the east by the south branch of the Chicago River; west, by Center avenue and Ann street; north, by Kinzie street, and south, by West Harrison street, embracing an area of about one square mile, containing an estimated population (in 1887) of 85,000. In the main hall of the Desplaines street station hangs a historical souvenir of the Haymarket explosion, which occurred almost in the shadow of the building on May 4, 1886. This is a magnificent group of pictures of the men of this station who composed Company A, commanded by Lieut. James Bowler, on that dreadful night. This was the company that suffered the greatest loss in killed and wounded. The picture was presented to the station by Inspector John Bonfield, the engrossing and arranging having been done by his clerk, Officer L. J. Van Pelt, and it has been pronounced one of the most creditable pieces of work of the kind ever produced in this city.

The photographs are made by Hartley, headed by those of Captain Ward, Inspector Bonfield and Lieut. Bowler, and are followed by twenty-five patrolman, as follows: Killed— George Miller, John J. Barrett, and Michael Sheehan; died since from typhoid fever, on Sept. 7, 1886, Edward Griffin. Incapacitated for duty at that time—Adam Barber, John E. Doyle, John H. King, August C. Keller, Arthur Connolly, Patrick Hartford, Nicholas Shannon, Thomas McEnery, and Lawrence J. Murphy, half of whose foot was blown off by the bomb. Those who were wounded of this squad, but who have since returned to duty, were Michael Cordon, Louis Johnsson, James Brady, Frank P. Tyrell, John Ried, James Conway, and Hugo Aspin. The rest of the squad was uninjured and were Sergeant R. J. Moore, Thomas Meaney, John Wessler, Robt. J. Walsh and Peter Foley.

LYMAN LEWIS, captain, commanding the third precinct; born at Norwich, Vt., 1845; came to Chicago May, 1869, and entered the force March, 1872; traveled beat as a patrolman for thirteen years; appointed patrol sergeant October, 1885; made many important arrests; was in active service during the riots of 1877, and in every serious outbreak that has occurred in the city since; was appointed lieutenant in May, 1887, and placed in charge of the Stanton avenue station; was appointed captain of third precinct, vice Captain Schaack transferred to East Chicago avenue station, Sept. 9, 1887. Capt. Lewis served with Inspector Bonfield during the street-car troubles of July, 1885, and so distinguished himself that he became a prominent figure in the department. He is a bright, intelligent and brave officer; addicted to systematic business methods, and quietly dignified in his manners. At present he is the junior captain of the force.

ALEXANDER S. ROSS, lieutenant of police; born in Rosshire, Scotland, 1857; came to Chicago 1876; entered the force June 1, 1882;

ALEXANDER ROSS,

Lieut. Comdg. Desplaines St. District.

ALEXANDER BOLD,
Lieut. Comdg. Desplaines St. District.

first detailed as patrolman at the 35th street station and afterward transferred to the Armory under Captain Buckley, where he remained for three years; transferred to Central station under Captain Hubbard and made roundsman; promoted to be patrol sergeant, and was made lieutenant June 28, 1885.

ALEXANDER BOLD, lieutenant of police; born at Deahn, province Bavaria, Sept. 1, 1850; came to America at the age of 15, in 1865; worked at the cooper's trade in New York a number of years; afterward went to Worcester, Ohio, and came to Chicago in 1871; returned shortly afterward to Ohio and came here to settle in 1874; had been engaged in the meantime in conducting a tannery, acting as engineer and traveling salesman; entered the police force in 1878 and assigned to Harrison street; transferred from Harrison to East Chicago avenue, then to West Lake street, and then back to Harrison street; transferred to Central detail for detective duty, serving in this capacity for three or four years; was appointed patrol sergeant May 1, 1886, and assigned to the West Thirteenth street station, vice Lieutenant Max Kipley, transferred to East Chicago avenue. On the night of September 1, 1881, John C. Neel, of Amsterdam, Montgomery county, N. Y., while insane, shot five persons in this city. On being approached by Officer Bold, the infuriated madman snapped the pistol in his face, but he was overpowered, disarmed and afterward sent to the Elgin insane asylum. Among the important arrests made by this officer were the following: Wing Lee, the Chinaman, who murdered Charles Mansfield; arrest made June 11, 1881. The jury is this case disagreed, eight being for hanging. William Henderson, Mat. Hart (alias Talsen) and Mat. Rose, burglars, sentenced to five years each by Judge Anthony, June 17, 1881. John Burns (alias Fredericks) for burglary and assault with intent to commit murder, sentenced to twenty years, December 15, 1881. Higgins (alias Parks), six years; Merigo (alias O'Leary), six years; George Bennett, September, 1880, for shooting Henry Kaas with a 44-caliber revolver, one year; John Drake, burglary, ten years; and Mike Burk, burglary, five years, sentenced by Judge Williamson June 12, 1884. These are but a few of the many cases of importance which Lieutenant Bold has had in hand. He has been, from his entrance into the force to the present day, one of the most energetic and industrious of officers, and his indefatigable labors marked him out as a prominent subject for promotion on the accession of Mayor Roche.

JOHN H. KINNEY, patrol sergeant; born in Ireland 1840; came to Chicago 1847; entered the force 1865; promoted from patrol duty to desk sergeantcy, and transferred from West Lake street to Desplaines Sept. 9, 1887.

CHARLES H. GOODMAN, desk sergeant; born at Woodstock, Ill., 1856; came to Chicago August 10, 1870; entered the force February 23, 1882.

JOHN C. DAMMANN, desk sergeant; born in New York City 1852, came to Chicago 1873; entered the force June 14, 1883; did duty at the Haymarket riot.

HUGO ASPING, patrolman; born in Sweden 1850; came to Chicago 1876; entered the force 1884.

ADAM S. BARBER, patrolman; born in Chester county, Pa., 1847; came to Chicago 1858; entered the force June 14, 1883; crippled for life in the Haymarket riot; also served fifteen years in the fire department.

JAMES A. BRADY, patrolman; born in Bloomfield, Davis county, Ia., 1854; came to Chicago 1875; entered the force April 20, 1886; injured at the Haymarket riot, May 4, 1886, receiving five wounds— one in the thigh, one below the knee, one in the calf, and left shoe torn off, slight injury across the toes, also a bullet wound in the right groin; in company under command of Lieutenant James A. Bowler.

JAMES A. BRACE, patrolman; born in Chicago 1852; entered the force June 3, 1887.

MATHEW T. CONNELLY, patrolman; born in Chicago 1860; entered the force April 2, 1885.

THOMAS S. COWDREY, patrolman; born in Warwick, Orange county, N. Y., 1840; came to Chicago March, 1870; entered the force August, 1870; was wounded in 1874 while attempting to arrest a drunken man; in 1883 resigned to take a western trip for his health; returned in November, 1886, and re-entered the police force June 1, 1887.

PATRICK CONNOR, patrolman; born in Ireland 1858; came to Chicago 1876; entered the force December, 1884; was in the street-car strike, also the Haymarket riot.

PATRICK O. CONNOR, patrolman; born in Burnsleigh, County Tipperary, Ireland, 1857; came to Chicago 1876; entered the force December 10, 1884.

JOHN L. CASEY, patrolman; born in Chicago, Ill., 1862; entered the force October 18, 1886.

PATRICK W. CLARK, patrolman; born in Oswego, N. Y., 1859; came to Chicago April 10, 1875; entered the force June 30, 1887; on 3rd of July arrested two men, Lebaun and Sands, while robbing Murray & Baker, Nos. 8 and 10 Jefferson street.

MATHEW T. CONNELLY, patrolman; born in Chicago 1861; entered the force April, 1885; was in the Haymarket riot.

ARTHUR CONNOLLY, patrolman; born in Monaghan, Ireland, 1854; came to Chicago 1868; entered the force January 6, 1879; received four severe wounds in legs and arms at the Haymarket riot, May 4, 1886.

EDWARD COSGRAVE, patrolman; born in Ireland 1848; came to Chicago 1866; entered the force February, 1883; was detailed on pawnbrokers and second-hand stores. In 1884 and 1885, with Detective Palmer, recovered property amounting to $11,875, and sent criminals to the penitentiary whose sentences aggregated eighty years. Among them Edward Howard, who entered Mr. Mayerhoff's house, at cor. of Loomis and Hastings streets; he was arrested by description furnished from Mr. Mayerhoff, and sentenced for twenty years. "Original" Andrews, the notorious State street pawnbroker, eight years. Emanuel Isaacs, the notorious Clark street pawnbroker, of Morrow jewelry robbery fame, for two years. During the year 1886, he recovered $14,300, and sent criminals to the penitentiary whose sentences aggregated forty years. Was in the Haymarket riot, and a witness during the trial of the anarchists.

JAMES CONWAY, patrolman; born in Limerick, Ireland, 1849; came to Chicago 1880; entered the force January, 1883; was in the street-car, Maxwell's box factory, and McCormick's factory strikes; wounded in calf of right leg by shell, at Haymarket riot, May 4, 1886.

JOHN E. DOYLE, patrolman; born in Chicago 1858; entered the force December 15, 1884; received eight wounds at the Haymarket riot.

DANIEL J. DALEY, patrolman; born in Ireland 1862; came to Chicago 1867; entered the force April, 1885; was in the Haymarket riot.

JOHN J. DALEY, patrolman; born in Chicago 1853; entered the force December 10, 1884; helped to convict for burglary, John Olsen and William Byrnes, to the penitentiary for three years each; Thomas Daley for two years; Frank Bennett for four years; Hattie Smith and Charles Taylor to three months each in the county jail.

STUART U. DEAN, patrolman; born in Andalusia, Pa., 1856; came to Chicago 1877; entered the force September 10, 1887.

MICHAEL DILLON, patrolman; born in Dublin, Ireland, 1859; came to Chicago 1880; entered the force July 17, 1885; February 19, 1886, arrested John Hastings for burglary, who was sentenced to the penitentiary for three years.

DANIEL DOUGHERTY, patrolman; born in Benton, Ill., 1857; came to Chicago October 10, 1871; entered the force August 6, 1886.

T. A. ELCHINGHAM, patrolman; born in Buffalo, N. Y., 1853; came to Chicago 1872; entered the force June 4, 1887.

JOSEPH F. FISHER, patrolman; born at Lake Geneva, Wis., 1860; came to Chicago 1882; entered the force April 15, 1887.

WM. J. FREEMAN, patrolman; born in Castle Ray, Roscommon Co., Ireland, 1861; came to Chicago May 20, 1880; entered the force January 10, 1887.

DENIS FEELEY, patrolman; born in Ireland 1860; came to Chicago 1881; entered the force August 20, 1887.

PETER FOLEY, patrolman; born in Ireland 1848; came to this country 1872; entered the force June 13, 1883; made a number of important arrests; was one of the seven men of Company " A," Desplaines street police, who escaped injury in the Haymarket riot, May 4, 1886.

DENIS FITZGERALD, patrolman; born in County Kerry, Ireland, 1857; came to Chicago 1875; entered the force July 2, 1886.

B. FLEMING, patrolman; born in Ireland 1861; came to Chicago 1879; entered the force 1886.

PETER G. GREENE, patrolman; born in Cook county, Ill., 1863; came to Chicago September, 1879; entered the force June, 1886.

PATRICK GRADY, patrolman; born in La Salle, Ill., 1857; came to Chicago 1873; entered the force October 9, 1886.

EDWARD GASQUOINE, patrolman; born in Brooklyn, N. Y., 1860; came to Chicago 1879; entered the force April 20, 1886.

JEREMIAH GROGAN, patrolman; born in Ireland 1849; came to Chicago 1870; entered the force June 13, 1883.

PATRICK HARTFORD, patrolman; born in Lowell, Mass., 1851; came to Chicago March, 1853; entered the force December, 1884; wounded in the Haymarket riot, two toes cut from the left foot, shell wound in right ankle, and bullet wound in left thigh.

JACOB HILBERT, patrolman; born in Barrington, Ill., 1858; came to Chicago July 6, 1878; entered the force December 15, 1884.

FRANK T. HOFFMAN, patrolman; born in Germantown, Pa., 1862; came to Chicago September, 1882; entered the force March 7, 1887.

JAMES W. IZARD, patrolman; born in Canada 1855; came to Chicago 1867; entered the force June 3, 1887.

LOUIS JOHNSSON, patrolman; born in Norway 1846; came to Chicago 1867; entered the force June 16, 1883; injured in the Haymarket riot; shell wound in the leg and other smaller ones.

THOMAS KINDLAN, patrolman; born in Channahon, Will county, Ill., 1857; came to Chicago March 22, 1879; entered the force December 15, 1884.

JOHN H. KING, patrolman; born in Ireland 1860; came to Chicago 1880; entered the force December, 1884; received eight wounds in the riots of 1886.

GEO. S. KAISER, patrolman; born in Germany 1846; came to Chicago 1862; entered the force June 13, 1883.

PATRICK H. KEEFE, patrolman; born in New York 1853; came to Chicago 1865; entered the force June 13, 1872; helped to convict Alvin Weaver to ten years in the penitentiary for safe-blowing; Dock Fitzgerald, to five years for highway robbery; Thomas Tracey, to five years for highway robbery; Thomas Reynolds, to five years for robbery; received two wounds while making arrests.

JOHN KREUTZBERG, patrolman; born in Hanover, Germany, 1839; came to Chicago 1852; entered the force October, 1869.

JOHN KEEGAN, patrolman; born in Milwaukee, Wis., 1852; came to Chicago 1871; entered the force June 14, 1887.

THOMAS McENERY, patrolman; born in Ireland 1858; came to Chicago 1873; entered the force 1883; received eleven wounds during the Haymarket riot.

LAWRENCE J. MURPHY, patrolman; born in Ireland 1854; came to Chicago 1868; entered the force 1884; received fifteen wounds, and lost half of left foot during the Haymarket riot, May 4, 1886.

THOMAS MEANY, patrolman; born in Burlington, Vt., 1850; came to Chicago 1866; entered the force January, 1885.

EUGENE V. McWILLIAMS, patrolman; born in Racine, Wis., 1852; came to Chicago in 1874; entered the force December 15, 1884.

PATRICK NASH, patrolman; born in Limerick, Ireland, 1858; came to Chicago 1877; entered the force December 15, 1884; in the streetcar strike, also the Haymarket riot.

ISAAC ORELL, patrolman; born in Brooklyn, N. Y., 1850; came to Chicago July 6, 1867; entered the force February 25, 1875.

JOHN PLUNKETT, patrolman; born in Burlington, Vt., 1850; came to Chicago 1872; entered the force December 15, 1884; was in the street-car strike of 1885, also in the Haymarket riot of 1886.

THOMAS PRESTON, JR., patrolman; born in Chicago 1852; entered the force August 1, 1887.

ARTHUR A. PECERY, patrolman; born in Plano, Ill., 1859; came to Chicago 1880; entered the force June 3, 1887.

ADAM REINHART, patrolman; born in Chicago 1855; entered the force July, 1886.

JOHN REID, patrolman; born in County Meath, Ireland, 1838; came to Chicago 1862; entered the force May 8, 1870; wounded in both legs at the Haymarket riot in 1886.

MARTIN D. RINGROSE, patrolman; born in Ireland 1850; came to Chicago 1865; returned in 1871; entered the force 1873.

PATRICK RYAN, patrolman; born in Silver Mines, County Tipperary, Ireland, 1863; came to Chicago 1879; entered the force June 29, 1886.

PHILLIE OBINSON, patrolman; born in Fond du Lac, Wis., 1858; came to Chicago 1858; entered the force June 3, 1884.

JOHN REDDEN, patrolman; born in Chicago 1856; entered the force September 10, 1887.

TIMOTHY J. STANTON, patrolman; born in England 1845; came to Chicago 1854; entered the force June 13, 1883.

JAMES B. SHORT, patrolman; born in Lake Co., Ill., 1861; came to Chicago March 10, 1869; entered the force December 4, 1884; was in the street-car strike, also the Haymarket riot.

CORNELIUS D. O. SHEA, patrolman; born in Ireland 1860; came to Chicago April, 1875; entered the force November, 1882.

CHESTER P. SMITH, patrolman; born in O'Fallon, Ill., 1858; came to Chicago July 17, 1881; entered the force June 3, 1887.

FRANK P. TYRELL, patrolman; born in Dunkirk, N. Y., 1859; came to Chicago 1871; entered the force December 18, 1884; received two wounds in back, at Haymarket riot.

JOHN UHRIG, patrolman; born in Germany 1856; came to Chicago May, 1872; entered the force July 2, 1887.

ROBT. J. WALSH, patrolman; born in County Kerry, Ireland, 1854; came to Chicago April 12, 1871; entered the force December 12, 1884.

GUSTAVE A. WOLTER, patrolman; born in 1845; came to Chicago 1870; entered the force 1875; resigned March, 1879; re-entered June 13, 1883.

PATRICK WILEY, patrolman; born in Addison, N. Y., 1853; came to Chicago 1880; entered the force 1883.

MATHEW WILSON, patrolman; born in County Longford, Ireland, 1849; came to Chicago 1851; entered the force December 31, 1884; in March, 1885, arrested Geo. Wilson, alias Anderson, a well known crook, for burglary; his sentence was 17 years in the penitentiary.

JOHN W. WESSLER, patrolman; born in Binghamton, N. Y., 1859; came to Chicago May 25, 1876; entered the force June 14, 1883; has made many important arrests; among them, John Brennan, robbery, five years in the penitentiary; Samuel Thomas, counterfeiting, three years in the penitentiary; was one of the seven men in Company "A" who escaped injury in the Haymarket riot of 1886.

WEST LAKE STREET STATION, 609 West Lake street, was built in 1867 and enlarged in 1873. The signal service was established here in 1880. It was the first sub-station established in the West Division, being organized some time before the station at West Twelfth and Johnson streets, and in this history, elsewhere, will be found the names of the different commanding officers who, from time to time, have been assigned to it. The force on duty at this station patrols the district bounded north by West Kinzie street, south by West Harrison street, east by Center avenue, and west by Hoyne avenue—an area of one and one-fourth square miles, containing an estimated population of about 50,000.

ANSON BACKUS, lieutenant of police, commanding the West Lake street district, is one of the youngest commissioned officers on the force, having passed only his thirty-second birthday. He was born in the little town of Gaines, Orleans county, N. Y., in 1855, of very respectable parents, his father being a Methodist minister. Young Backus received a first-class education, and might have won his way in any path of life. He came to Chicago in 1879, and circumstances turned his steps toward the police department. He entered the force August 1, 1881, and was assigned to patrol duty at the station which he has now in charge. He was promoted to the rank of desk sergeant in 1882, to a patrol sergeantcy in 1885, and to the lieutenancy at a later date.

MICHAEL S. HYLAND, desk sergeant; born at West Point, N. Y., 1857; came to Chicago 1875; entered the force January 29, 1880.

EDWIN P. MANN, desk sergeant; born in Elgin, Kane county, Ill., 1849; came to Chicago 1872; entered the force May 15, 1875.

JAMES H. WILSON, patrol sergeant; born at Oswego, N. Y., August 11, 1845; came to Chicago August 2, 1846; entered the police force February 7, 1872; promoted to patrol sergeantcy 1887; has done service as patrolman, detective and signal officer; was in the riot of '77; in the great strikes, and suffered a severe wound at the

Haymarket; transferred from Central detail to West Lake street September 9, 1887.

CHARLES E. ALLEN, patrolman; born in Ohio 1847; came to Chicago 1880; entered the force December 15, 1884.

PETER BUTTERLY, patrolman; born in Ireland 1851; came to Chicago April, 1875; entered the force December 15, 1884; was in the street-car strike of 1885; in the riot at McCormick's factory; was wounded at the Haymarket riot of May 4, 1886.

WILLIAM BURNS, patrolman; born in Ireland; came to Chicago 1879; entered the force December 15, 1884; injured at the Haymarket riot, May 4, 1886.

THOMAS BROPHY, patrolman; born in Ireland 1860; came to Chicago 1877; entered the force November 1, 1885; injured at the Haymarket riot.

ADAM W. COOK, patrolman; born in Oak Creek, Milwaukee Co., Wis., 1842; came to Chicago 1865; entered the force October 28, 1875.

PATRICK CUNNINGHAM, patrolman; born in Ireland 1858; came to Chicago 1878; entered the force December 15, 1884.

CHARLES N. COFFEY, patrolman; born in New York 1853; came to Chicago 1870; entered the force June 30, 1883.

BERNARD CONLON, patrolman; born in New York 1853; came to Chicago 1867; entered the force July, 1886.

MICHAEL M. CORDON, patrolman; born in Ireland 1854; came to Chicago 1876; entered the force June 14, 1883; was at the Haymarket riot under Capt. Ward; was the second man going to work after being wounded.

TIMOTHY M. DILLON, patrolman; born in Ireland 1847; came to Chicago 1868; entered the force 1873.

AUGUST G. DELAMATER, patrolman; born in Corning, N. Y., 1851; came to Chicago 1865; entered the force September 19, 1873.

JAMES E. ENGLISH, patrolman; detailed as photographer in the rogues' gallery.

JAMES EARLY, patrolman; born in Ireland 1845; came to Chicago 1871; entered the force September 10, 1874.

CHARLES N. FINK, patrolman; born in Ohio 1856; came to Chicago 1871; entered the force December 15, 1884; injured at the Haymarket riot, May 4, 1886.

CHARLES N. GEISCH, patrolman; born in Germany 1861; came to Chicago 1865; entered the force September 11, 1874.

MICHAEL GALLAGHER, patrolman; born in Ireland 1834; came to Chicago 1847; entered the force 1867.

JACOB HANSON, patrolman; born in Denmark; entered the force 1881; lost his right leg above the knee in the Haymarket riot, May 4, 1886.

JAMES E. HAMMON, patrolman; born in Canada 1862; came to Chicago 1872; entered the force December 15, 1884.

JOHN P. HINES, patrolman; born in Lajunta, Col., 1859; came to Chicago 1881; entered the force July 1, 1886.

JOHN HARTNETT, JR., patrolman; born in Chicago 1858; entered the force December, 1884.

THOMAS HENNESSY, patrolman; born in Wisconsin 1858; came to Chicago 1879; entered the force December 9, 1884; wounded at the Haymarket riot, May 4, 1886.

THOMAS HALLEY, patrolman; born in Michigan 1857; came to Chicago 1875; entered the force June 13, 1883; injured at the Haymarket riot, May 4, 1886.

JOHN HARTFORD, patrolman; born in Chicago 1858; entered the force June 13, 1883.

ALEXANDER JAMESON, patrolman; born in Oakwell, Ill., 1831; came to Chicago 1848; entered the force July 12, 1865.

JOHN S. KELLEY, patrolman; born in Chicago 1849; entered the force July 17, 1885.

WILLIAM KELLY, patrolman; born in Ireland 1850; came to Chicago 1860; entered the force December 1, 1884; discharged August 10, 1887.

GEORGE LYNCH, patrolman; born in Ireland 1851; came to Chicago 1857; entered the force June 3, 1883.

PATRICK McMAHON, patrolman; born in Ireland 1843; came to Chicago 1865; entered the force April 2, 1874; served during the riots of 1877, also the Haymarket, May 4, 1886.

MICHAEL MORAN, patrolman; born in Ireland 1852; came to Chicago 1879; entered the force December 17, 1884.

JAMES McGARRY, patrolman; born in Minnesota 1858; came to Chicago 1860; entered the force November 7, 1886.

JOHN McWEENY, patrolman; born in Manistee, Mich., 1857; came to Chicago 1881; entered the force August 12, 1885.

FRANK J. McCOMB, patrolman; born in Chicago 1864; entered the force June, 1886.

TIMOTHY O'SULLIVÀN, patrolman; born in Ireland 1836; came to Chicago 1882; entered the force June 20, 1883; injured in the Haymarket riot of May 4, 1886.

PATRICK PRIOR, patrolman; born in Ireland 1847; came to Chicago 1879; entered the force December 15, 1884.

WILLIAM L. SANDERSON, patrolman; born in Pennsylvania 1837; came to Chicago January, 1856; entered the force August 20, 1873.

MICHAEL SHORT, patrolman; born in Illinois 1864; came to Chicago 1880; entered the force July 1, 1886.

MATHEW J. SULLIVAN, patrolman; born in Ireland 1859; came to Chicago June, 1877; entered the force April 15, 1887.

DANIEL W. SHAY, patrolman; born in Boston, Mass., 1860; came to Chicago 1862; entered the force July 1, 1886.

JOHN B. VAIN, patrolman; born in Lorraine, Germany, 1852; came to Chicago 1878; entered the force July 1, 1886.

CHARLES W. WHITNEY, patrolman; born in Naperville, Ill., 1857; came to Chicago 1877; entered the force 1885; was wounded at the Haymarket riot and unable for duty for one year.

MICHAEL WALSH, patrolman; born in Ireland 1854; came to Chicago 1879; entered the force April 19, 1886.

BEN WILLIAMS, patrolman; born in Quebec, Canada, 1852; came to Chicago 1862; entered the force September, 1878; on special duty under Inspector Bonfield.

WEST MADISON STREET STATION, west of Western avenue, originally a sub-station of the "West Madison street station," the name by which the station corner of West Madison and Union streets was for a time officially known. A great deal of confusion has arisen out of this similarity in names. Properly speaking the precinct station was the "Union street station," and the sub-station should have been called the West Madison street station. Since the change of precinct headquarters to Desplaines street, however, there is no longer any danger of mixing the stations up. The West Madison street sub-station was organized in 1881, under Superintendent McGarigle, with one lieutenant, one sergeant, two station keepers (desk sergeants), nine patrolmen and four signal service men, seventeen in all. The station in 1886 had 35 men. The present quarters are very poor, and as the

WILLIAM H. WARD,
Ex-Capt. Third Precinct.

JOHN P. BEARD.
Lieut. Comdg. West Madison St. District.

station is destined to advance in importance with the growth of the western limits, a new structure will soon be a necessity. It is believed that the West Madison street station will, inside of a very few years, become the headquarters of a new precinct. The district patrolled by the force of this station is bounded north by West Kinzie street, south by West Harrison street, east by Hoyne avenue, and west by the city limits. The territory patrolled is about two and one-fourth square miles, and contains a population of about 40,000.

JOHN P. BEARD, lieutenant of police; born at Macomb, Ill., 1850; came to Chicago 1867; entered the force Sept. 17, 1878, and assigned to Hinman street station; was detailed to draw up the annual report of Superintendent Seavey at headquarters; after completing this work, was detailed in plain clothes, to catch Lesser Friedburg, of Race murder notoriety, in illegitimate transactions; did so and had the pawnbroker punished; transferred to Harrison street and shortly afterward transferred to Union street; promoted to a desk sergeantcy and transferred to West Lake street; was appointed, at Lieut. Keating's death, acting lieutenant; appointed full lieutenant and transferred to West Madison street; has commanded companies in all the great riots and strikes which have occurred here during recent years; was particularly prominent in the street-car and Haymarket affairs; broke up several gangs of boy burglars in his present district, notably one which went by the name of the "Buffalo Bill Gang." Lieutenant Beard's connection with the street-car troubles and the Haymarket massacre is referred to elsewhere.

FRANK J. BEAUBIEN, patrol sergeant; born in Chicago 1852; entered the force October 24, 1873; assigned to the Union street station; transferred to Central detail 1878; August, 1883, was detailed for service on first patrol wagon that ever left the Central station; was appointed sergeant and assigned to West Chicago avenue station; transferred to West Madison street station September 10, 1887; is the son of Mark Beaubien, first hotel proprietor of Chicago, and frequently mentioned in the early chapters of this history, and nephew of John B. Beaubien, also a prominent pioneer settler; was instrumental in closing the concert dives of the West Side in 1874; did active work on the Halsted street viaduct in the riots of 1877; arrested Alexander Halinton and John Kelly for the killing of Patrick Tierney in the Sailors Home, on Desplaines and Lake streets; arrested George Gifford, alias Charles Dean, for forgery, three years; also Jay Dean, the notorious counterfeiter, four years; has made many other important arrests; is vice president of the Policemen's Benevolent Association, a faithful and efficient officer, and a popular man. He was transferred to his present post on September 10, 1887.

WILLIAM W. CLUETT, desk sergeant, born in the Isle of Alderney, England, August 29, 1847; came to Chicago in 1853; entered the force September 18, 1873; enlisted in the Federal Army September 24, 1861, in the 57th Illinois Volunteers, Infantry; left Chicago with the regiment February 8, 1862; participated in the battles of Fort Donelson, Shiloh, Siege of Corinth, Town Creek, Resaca, Kingstown, Allatoona Pass, Atlanta, Savanah and Bensonville. Was with Gen. Sherman in his famous "March to the Sea," and through North and South Carolina, Virginia; took part in the grand review at Washington, May 4, 1865; mustered out of the service July 6, 1865, at Louisville, Ky.; is a member of Geo. H. Thomas Post, No. 5, G. A. R., and a faithful, industrious and brave officer.

MICHAEL CALLAHAN, desk sergeant, was born in the city of New York in 1838; came to Illinois (McHenry county) with his parents when an infant; reared and educated in that vicinity, graduating at Prof. Anderson's academy in New York City; worked on his father's farm until 1854, when he left for California, by way of the Isthmus of Panama; worked on a farm near Stockton, in the Golden State, for three years, and, later, engaged in mining operations, in which he made and lost a fortune; returned to Illinois in 1865, by way of Nicaragua, and shortly afterward settled down in Chicago; entered the force May 1, 1867, as patrolman; was assigned to the old Armory station, on Franklin street; transferred to West Lake street, where he remained five years; was promoted roundsman (patrol sergeant) and transferred to West Twelfth street station; transferred back to Lake street, and made desk sergeant; resigned, and acted as bailiff at Justice Scully's court, 1872; was appointed, 1876, by Mayor Heath his only staff officer, three having been dropped; served a year in this capacity, and was appointed lieutenant, and assigned to West Twelfth street station; was lieutenant seven years, and then reduced by Mayor Harrison, with other officers, for political reasons, it is claimed; served a year at West Chicago avenue before reduction; transferred in 1884 to West Madison street station, and appointed desk sergeant, which position he has held since; served gallantly in the riot of '77. [See Riot of '77.]

JOSEPH BURNS, patrolman; born in Chicago 1855; entered the force July 1, 1886.

JOHN BROWN, patrolman; born in Schuylkill county, Pa., 1856; came to Chicago August 20, 1878; entered the force December 18, 1884; was at the Haymarket riot, May 4, 1886.

ALEXANDER BEAUBIEN, patrolman; born in Chicago 1832; en. tered the force in 1862; re-entered in 1882; was first appointed by Police Commissioners Wayman, Newhouse and Alexander Coventry, C. P. Bradley, superintendent; has made many important arrests.

PETER J. BURNS, patrolman; born in Ireland 1859; came to Chicago 1877; entered the force April, 1885; was at the Haymarket riot, May 4, 1886.

MARTIN CULLEN, patrolman; born in Ireland 1851; came to Chicago 1864; entered the force March 16, 1885; injured in shoulder and knee by shell during the Haymarket riot of May 4, 1886.

DANIEL CRAMER, patrolman; born in Wisconsin 1849; came to Chicago 1870; entered the force 1878; was wounded at the Haymarket riot.

MICHAEL CONNELLY, patrolman; born in Ireland 1857; came to Chicago 1876; entered the force 1884; was at the Haymarket riot.

PATRICK DONOVAN, patrolman; born in Clare, Ireland, 1835; came to Chicago 1865; entered the force December, 1874; joined the Ninth Mass. Volunteers June 11, 1861, and served three years in the Army of the Potomac; also a member of Col. Mulligan's Post G. A. R.

TIMOTHY DALY, patrolman; born in Ireland 1859; came to Chicago 1874; entered the force 1885.

DENIS DUNNE, patrolman; born in Chicago 1857; entered the force 1883; was at the Haymarket riot.

RICHARD ELLSWORTH, patrolman; born in Boston 1858; came to Chicago 1879; entered the force 1884; was at the Haymarket riot, 1886.

JOSEPH FULEY, patrolman; born in Ireland 1863; came to Chicago 1876; entered the force January 10, 1887.

JOSEPH FALLON, patrolman; born in Stueben Co., N. Y., 1851; came to Chicago 1871; entered the force June 1, 1882; was at the Haymarket riot.

MICHAEL M. HORAN, patrolman; born in County Clare, Ireland, 1855; came to Chicago 1872; entered the force 1883; was at the Haymarket riot.

MICHAEL KEELEY, patrolman; born in Ireland 1839; came to Chicago 1857; entered the force September, 1873.

GEORGE KERNAN, patrolman; born in Chicago 1847; entered the force August 1, 1882; was at the Haymarket riot; made some important arrests.

HUGH McNEIL, patrolman; born in Waukegan, Ill., 1854; came to Chicago 1878; entered the force December 15, 1884; was at the Haymarket riot, May 4, 1886.

JOHN MAGIS, patrolman; born in Lamont, Ill., 1850; came to Chicago 1867; entered the force December 15, 1884; was at the Haymarket riot.

W. I. NEFF, patrolman; born in Chicago 1855; entered the force December, 1884; was at the Haymarket riot.

J. F. ORCHARD, patrolman; born in Washington Co., Indiana, 1856; came to Chicago 1879; entered the force in 1886.

ANDREW O'DAY, patrolman; born in Chicago 1854; entered the force December 18, 1883; assigned to special duty with Officer Hartford. The following are some of the important arrests made: May 12, 1884, arrested Oscar Hanson and Bill Hurd for burglary, sentenced for two years in the penitentiary; July 17, 1884, arrested two men at the Gault House for burglary; December 20, 1884, the arrest of Bill Myers for robbery, four years in the penitentiary.

CHAPTER XXVII.

THE FOURTH PRECINCT—CAPTAIN AMOS W. HATHAWAY COMMANDING — THE WEST CHICAGO AVENUE, NORTH AVENUE AND RAWSON STREET DISTRICTS—WONDERFUL GROWTH IN POPULATION AND CONSEQUENT INCREASE IN POLICE AREA—THE DAYS OF SERGEANTS BEADELL AND BRISCOE—CAPTAIN HATHAWAY'S CAREER—THE FORCE ONE OF THE BEST ORGANIZED IN CHICAGO—ITS MEN AND THEIR RECORDS—HISTORY OF THE STATIONS.

The fourth precinct includes West Chicago avenue, West North avenue and Rawson street districts, and is commanded by Captain Amos W. Hathaway. Headquarters, precinct station, 233 West Chicago avenue.

PRECINCT STATION, 233 West Chicago avenue, was organized as a sub-station in the spring of 1868, with Sergeant Beadell in charge, who was succeeded in command by Sergeant Briscoe, and, owing to the rapid growth of this section of the city, the police boundaries were changed in 1875, and this was made a precinct station with Jonas M. Johnson as captain. It was then known as the third precinct, the second precinct station being located at Union and Madison streets. Capt. Johnson was succeeded in command by William J. McGarigle. In 1880 McGarigle was transferred to the second precinct as captain, and this became a sub-station once more, with Lieutenant Michael C. Callahan in command. He was succeeded by Lieutenant J. S. Barbee, and he by Lieutenant E. J. Steele. In 1884 Amos W. Hathaway was placed in command. Again the police boundaries were changed, and this once more became a precinct station, Capt. Hathaway commanding. May 10, 1887, Capt. Hathaway being transferred, Capt. William Ward was placed in command again. Sept. 9, 1887, Capt. Ward was removed, and Capt. Hathaway transferred to the command of this precinct, with a total force of 144 men, all told. The precinct station has a force of about 77 men and two matrons. The present station, one of the handsomest in the city, was completed in the spring of 1886, the old station being set aside for a court room, in which Justice Ingersoll first presided, and was succeeded by Justice Eberhardt in May, 1887. The patrol system was adopted in this precinct, and went into service in June, 1883. The precinct is, and always has been, recognized as the hot-bed of anarchism, and it is with difficulty that this disturbing element is kept under control. The force on duty at this precinct station patrols the district bounded north by Augusta street, south by West Kinzie street, east by the north branch of the Chicago River, and west by the city limits, an area of about two and three-quarters square miles, containing in 1887 an estimated population of about 100,000.

AMOS W. HATHAWAY, captain commanding the fourth precinct; born at Providence, Rhode Island, May 29, 1839; worked on a farm when a boy; learned the machinest trade at Oswego, N. Y.; was with Col. "Jim" Lane in Kansas in 1857 and 1858, and was a participant in some of the exciting border episodes of those days; came to Chicago in 1860; worked at his trade here, managing the mechanical department of an immense bakery which supplied "hard tack" to the Union army; entered the police force in 1864, being assigned to duty at the old North Market station on Michigan street; after three years' service as patrolman, resigned and returned to the cracker business; re-entered the force, and was appointed sergeant of the Huron street station in 1869; promoted to a lieutenancy in 1871; appointed captain in 1882; transferred to the West Chicago avenue station in 1884; transferred to the East Chicago avenue station in May, 1887; transferred back to the West Chicago avenue station Sept. 9, 1887. He is a man of pleasant manners, courteous and gentlemanly in his bearing, very successful as an executive officer, and reliable in every particular.

CHARLES C. LARSEN, lieutenant of police; born in Copenhagen, Denmark, 1844; came to Chicago July, 1866; entered the force September 18, 1873; assigned to patrol duty at the West Chicago avenue station; promoted to be desk sergeant April, 1881; transferred as such to East Chicago avenue station October 1, 1882; promoted to be patrol sergeant February 13, 1885, and transferred to Harrison street station, where he remained until October 28, 1885,

CHARLES LARSEN,
Lieut. Comdg. West Chicago Ave. District.

FRANCIS SMITH,
Lieut. Comdg. Central Detail.

then transferred to East Chicago avenue station; promoted to lieutenancy February 19, 1885, remaining at the East Chicago avenue station until May 10, 1887, when he was transferred to present station. In the great strike and socialistic propaganda of 1878 he was, owing to his familiarity with the different North European languages, detailed to ascertain and watch the movements of the socialistic anarchists who then numbered more than a thousand well-armed men, calling themselves the "Lehr and Wehr Verein." In February, 1879, Lieutenant Larsen was detailed to ferret out the mysterious deaths of Henry Gelderman, a well-to-do German grocer, of No. 505 Sedgwick street, and of Ida Meyer, wife of Gelderman's attending physician, which deaths occurred within six weeks of each other. After six weeks of hard labor Lieutenant Larsen succeeded in having Dr. Henry Meyer and Mrs. Ida Gelderman held for murder. It was proved beyond doubt that Gelderman and Mrs. Meyer had been poisoned, the motive being found in the fact that Dr. Meyer and Gelderman's wife were unduly intimate. By legal legerdemain both escaped punishment. Shortly afterward they were married, and moved to 333 Center street, where, on March 17, 1880, Dr. Meyer's child, a boy of two years and five months (by his first marriage), was found drowned in a bath tub half filled with water. In May, 1883, Dr. Meyer was again brought before the public, at this time charged with an attempt to poison his second wife with sugar of lead, but escaped conviction. The two were afterward divorced; he went West and she married again. Lieutenant Larsen also took a very active part in the artesian well murder case, July 4, 1880, by discovering the identity of the victim, and fastening the crime on Claus Hultgren, a friend and companion of Johansen, the victim. Hultgren was tried, but escaped conviction. On the eventful evening of May 4, 1886, Lieutenant Larsen, with a company of men from the East Chicago avenue station, was ordered to report at the Twelfth street station to Captain O'Donnell, but on arriving there the latter ordered him to report back to his own station, as everything was apparently quiet. On returning, Lieutenant Larsen ordered all his men to bed, in that they might have a good rest, and be ready for emergencies. It was then 10 o'clock at night. The men had scarcely turned in before a telephone message was received calling all the available men of the station to the Haymarket as speedily as possible. In less than three minutes Lieutenant Larsen, with two patrol wagons, manned by forty patrolmen, rushed out of the station to the scene of the explosion. The drivers allowed their horses to run at full speed, and turning the corner of Erie street the one in which Larsen was ran against the curbstone and was upset. Several of the officers were slightly injured and Lieutenant Larsen sprained his left ankle. The wagon was raised without delay, however, and with all but one man, who had his shoulder dislocated, started out afresh for the scene of the riot, arriving there seven minutes after the message had been received. The wounded officers and anarch· ists were still lying around. Inspector Bonfield ordered Lieutenant Larsen to search for and bring in the wounded, and then drive the remaining crowd away from the Haymarket and neighboring streets. Several wounded rioters were found hiding themselves in basements and cellars. These were conveyed to the Desplaines street station and cared for. While this search was going on Larsen's men were fired at several times, but none of them were injured. A few days later Lieutenant Larsen rendered valuable service in locating the Lingg bomb manufactory at 442 Sedgwick street, which led to the arrest of Seliger and afterward of Louis Lingg.

FRANCIS SMITH, lieutenant of police, was born in the Grand Duchy of Baden, Germany, in 1837; came to this country when sixteen years old, remaining in New York for about three years and learning the confectionery trade; went into the regular army, 3d Artillery, under Col. Thomas Sherman, and served in the northwest, doing border duty at Fort Snelling and elsewhere, from 1855 to 1860; went back to Germany; returning, enlisted in the 1st New York Cavalry in 1861, and went at once to the front, fighting at first under Phil Kearney, and later under Phil Sheridan, the two leading cavalry officers of the war; was in most of the battles of the Army of the Potomac, and was with Sheridan in the Shenandoah Valley; served three years and four months and was discharged in August, 1864; went into business in New York City; came to Chicago in 1867, and entered the police force in 1869; assigned to Larrabee street station; remained there eighteen years, excepting a few months at East Chicago avenue station, serving twelve years as desk sergeant; promoted to a patrol sergeantcy and to a lieutenancy fifteen days later, September 9, 1887, at which time he was transferred to West Chicago avenue station vice Lieutenant Schumacher, resigned.

EDMUND ROACH, patrol sergeant; born in Ireland 1848; came to Chicago 1857; entered the force September 3, 1869; promoted to patrol sergeantcy and assigned to West Lake street station; transferred to West Chicago avenue station September 9, 1887.

LOUIS KAISER, desk sergeant; born in Hesse Cassel, Germany, 1843; came to Chicago 1871; entered the force March, 1874; served as desk sergeant at Larrabee street station; as clerk of chief of detectives, Central station; as record clerk, and again desk sergeant at West Chicago avenue station.

ADOLPH SANDERS, desk sergeant; born in Germany 1835; came to Chicago 1866; entered the force August 19, 1870; appointed desk sergeant August 26, 1873; detailed at East Chicago avenue station; transferred to West Chicago avenue 1880; was nearly beaten to death by a mob, led by Daniel Coughlin, on Kinzie street, 1871, while in the discharge of his duty.

JOHN LYNCH, telephone operator, police department; born in Chicago 1863; entered the force April 10, 1886.

EDWARD BARRETT, patrolman; born in Ireland 1845; came to Chicago 1866; entered the force 1874; has made many important arrests; at the point of his revolver, arrested Culkins and Clark for horse stealing; was in the riot of 1877, and wounded in the Haymarket riot of 1886.

CHRISTIAN BLUXITH, patrolman; born in Norway 1842.

MARTIN BOCK, patrolman; born in Westphalia, Germany, 1854; came to Chicago August, 1875; entered the force December, 1884; was at the Haymarket riot of 1886.

WILLIAM BURKE, patrolman; born in Ireland 1855; came to Chicago 1874; entered the force June 3, 1887.

PETER BOWEN, patrolman; born in Dorset, Vt., 1853; came to Chicago March 8, 1880; entered the force July 1, 1886; before entering the force, was employed as marble worker by Davidson & Sons; has proved an efficient and faithful officer; has never as yet been reprimanded by his superior officers.

JAMES COOK, patrolman; born in Fifeshire, Scotland, 1837; came to Chicago June, 1861; entered the force May 1, 1872; arrested Christ. Johnson for the murder of a girl while drawing water at a hydrant, and was sentenced to seventeen years at Joliet; also Patsy Fagen for highway robbery, sentenced to three years; has been detailed on river police, and took active part in the riots since 1872; was at the Haymarket in 1886.

JOHN J. COLLINS, patrolman; born in Canada 1855; came to Chicago 1879; entered the force April 20, 1886; at the Haymarket riot of 1886, under Lieutenant Martin Quinn.

NICHOLAS CROSBY, patrolman; born in County Wexford, Ireland, 1855; came to Chicago April, 1871; entered the force March 25, 1881.

JOHN O. CONNELL, patrolman; born in Waukegan, Ill., 1857; came to Chicago 1868; entered the force December 15, 1884; was in Lieutenant Steele's company at the Haymarket riot.

WILLIAM J. DETERLING, patrolman; born in Germany 1863; entered the force December 15, 1884; was at the Haymarket riot of May 4, 1886.

THOMAS F. DIVANE, patrolman; born in Ireland 1856; came to Chicago 1875; entered the force July 31, 1886; arrested a young man named Mahoney, who kicked and beat his father because he would not furnish him money to buy liquor; he was sent to the Bridewell on $100 fine.

MICHAEL DENNEHY, patrolman; born in Ireland 1861; came to Chicago June, 1880; entered the force July, 1886.

JOHN H. FOSS, patrolman; born in Norway 1855; came to Chicago 1881; entered the force June 1, 1887.

CHRISTOPHER W. GAINER, patrolman; born in Cincinnati, Ohio, 1858; came to Chicago 1871; entered the force December 5, 1884; was wounded at the Haymarket riot, in the right leg, above the knee.

HERMAN GAINER, patrolman; born in Cincinnati, Ohio, 1861; came to Chicago 1878; entered the force July 1, 1886.

ALBERT GRAUTIER, patrolman; born in Richland county, Ohio, 1857; came to Chicago 1870; entered the force June 3, 1887.

WILLIAM HALPIN, patrolman; born in Ireland 1856; came to Chicago 1874; entered the force 1885; with Officer James Culkin, arrested Nicholi Daloi, who stabbed his wife at 87 Austin avenue. He pleaded guilty to manslaughter in Judge Tuley's court, and was sentenced to five years at Joliet.

CHARLES HARDIN, patrolman; born in Germany 1854; came to Chicago 1864; entered the force June, 1887.

DANIEL R. HOGAN, patrolman; born in Detroit, Mich., 1859; came to Chicago 1878; entered the force January 1, 1887.

EDWARD J. HANLY, patrolman; born in Albany, N. Y., 1851; came to Chicago 1852; entered the force 1883; had some narrow escapes from being shot while in the discharge of his duty, particularly on the night of July 5th, when he shot and killed Mitzger, a burglar and thief.

WILLIAM HAGUE, operator; born in Park Ridge, Ill., 1855; came to Chicago 1865; entered the force June 27, 1883.

JOHN JURO, patrolman; born in Germany 1854; came to Chicago 1867; entered the force December 13, 1884; made many important arrests; Thomas Harris, five years in the penitentiary for robbery; Walter Furlong, two years and six months in the penitentiary for burglary.

CHARLES JENSCH, patrolman; born in Germany 1851; came to Chicago June 9, 1872; entered the force February 9, 1873; was at the Haymarket riot.

SOLFEST L. JOHNSON, patrolman; born in Bergen, Norway, 1852; came to Chicago 1875; entered the force June 3, 1887.

MICHAEL KISSANE, patrolman; born in Ireland 1856; came to Chicago May 26, 1873; entered the force December 15, 1884; was at the Haymarket riot of May 4, 1886.

JEREMIAH KENNEDY, patrolman; born in Ireland 1850; came to Chicago 1872; entered the force December 15, 1884; was at the Haymarket riot of May 4, 1886.

STEPHEN KOLSTAD, patrolman; born in Norway 1853; came to Chicago 1870; entered the force June 3, 1887; before entering the force was letter carrier for five years.

JOHN KINSELLA, patrolman; born in Ireland 1849; came to Chicago 1851; entered the force December, 1884; was in the street-car strike of 1885, and the McCormick and Haymarket riots of 1886.

G. M. KNOWLES, patrolman; born in Kane county, Ill., 1857; came to Chicago November, 1871; entered the force April 14, 1887.

LUKE KALAS, patrolman; born in Germany 1864; came to Chicago October 7, 1871; entered the force June 3, 1887.

JAMES C. LARKIN, patrolman; born in Pennsylvania 1861; came to Chicago 1879; entered the force April 20, 1886; was at the Haymarket riot.

FRANK G. LETIS, patrolman; born in Austria 1853; came to Chicago July, 1871; entered the force February 20, 1883; at 1:30 a. m., on April 29, 1884, was fired at by Joe Honnors and James Foley, burglars, at the corner of Emerson avenue and Leavitt street, one ball struck a memorandum book in his vest pocket and glanced off, the other passed through his coat tail; these men received a sentence of nine and five years in the penitentiary; was sick for five weeks from the effects of a beating over the head with a soda-water bottle in the Aurora Turner Hall; was at the Haymarket riot, and had a very narrow escape from three different shots, one through the right sleeve of his coat, another grazed his back, and another struck his helmet.

PATRICK T. LOFTUS, patrolman; born in Chicago 1856; entered the force May 8, 1882; made many important arrests. Michael Sullivan received twenty years in the penitentiary for burglary; Geo. Barry, alias Frank Wilson, for burglary, who attempted to shoot him at the time of arrest; the case against him was dismissed by Judge Baker, upon condition that he leave the United States for Scotland.

JOHN MILLER, patrolman; born in 1831; came to Chicago 1858; entered the force August 1, 1868; lock-up keeper.

JOHN K. McMAHON, patrolman; born in New Orleans 1857; came to Chicago 1871; entered the force December 15, 1884; arrested Frank Edgar, alias "Shorty," for burglary, who was sentenced to five years at Joliet; received two wounds at the Haymarket riot, from which he is still suffering.

PETER McGUIRE, patrolman; born in Lamont, Ill., 1854; came to Chicago 1879; entered the force April 20, 1886; was at the Haymarket riot.

JAMES J. MACKEY, patrolman; born in Chicago 1859; entered the force December 15, 1884; was at the Haymarket riot of May 4, 1886.

MARTIN MATHESON, patrolman; born in Christiana, Norway, 1853; came to Chicago December 11, 1868; entered the force June 3, 1887.

JAMES F. McMANUS, patrolman; born in County Cavin, Ireland, 1860; came to Chicago 1876; entered the force July 1, 1886.

JOHN J. MURPHY, patrolman; born in New York 1858; came to Chicago 1863; entered the force 1886; was at the McCormick strike, May, 1886.

PETER McGRAIN, patrolman; born in Lake county, Ill., 1854; came to Chicago 1881; entered the force June 3, 1887; had been special policeman at the Chicago Opera House for eighteen months prior to entering the force.

P. J. MOLONEY, patrolman; born in Ireland 1848; came to Chicago 1866; entered the force August, 1871; served through the riots of 1877; has been on duty at the West Lake, West Madison, and West Twelfth street stations; was appointed clerk of detectives in 1879, which position he held until 1882; which was resigned to accept the position of deputy under County Clerk Ryan, which position he held for four years; on January 1, 1887, was reinstated on the force.

PETER McCUE, patrolman; born in Ireland 1863; came to Chicago May 3, 1867; entered the force 1881; has made many important arrests.

JOHN MULLINS, patrolman; born in Ireland 1840; came to Chicago 1850; entered the force 1869; arrested John Keegan and William Quinn, for burglary, who were sent to the penitentiary.

FRANK W. NOHREN, patrolman; born in Chicago 1859; entered the force June, 1885; was at the Haymarket riot, under Lieut. Quinn.

PETER NELSON, patrolman; born in 1853; came to Chicago May 11, 1857; entered the force January 1, 1886.

PATRICK O'NEILL, patrolman; born in County Cork, Ireland, 1854; came to Chicago May, 1873; entered the force July, 1886.

PATRICK D. OWENS, patrolman; born in Ireland 1842; came to Chicago 1863; entered the force 1878; arrested many notorious criminals; the most important were Frank Garrity, who shot him in the knee, and Pete Mallory, who died in the penitentiary.

JACOB B. REHM, patrolman; born in Lake county, Ill., 1857; came to Chicago 1877; entered the force January 3, 1887; worked for the Chicag › Rawhide Manufactory three years, then opened a tannery of his own; sold out in 1881; worked as a carpenter until installed in the police force.

JOHN L. RIVERE, patrolman; American born; came to Chicago in 1865; entered the force 1887.

WILLIAM J. RYAN, patrolman; born in Lake Co., Ill., 1858; came to Chicago October, 1878; entered the force June 7, 1887.

JOHN RYAN, patrolman; born in Ireland 1836; came to Chicago 1857; entered the force Sept. 1, 1870; has been doing detective work since 1882, in company with Officer Loftus, the most notorious ones arrested being Jas. McGrath and Pete Mallory; they each received five years in the penitentiary; Michael Sullivan, burglary, who received twenty years; John Dunn and Henry Gillespie, robbery, ten years each; John Mahoyede, murder, seventeen years; also Thos. Smith, who has served three terms in the penitentiary.

FRANK SCHNEIDER, patrolman; born in DuPage Co., Ill., 1862; came to Chicago February 14, 1881; entered the force July 1, 1886.

JOHN J. SHEA, patrolman; born in New York City 1854; came to Chicago in 1864; entered the force 1884; was in the street-car strike of 1885; the McCormick strike of 1886; arrested the notorious Annie Schimmel, victim of Newhall House fire, Milwaukee; also Harry Rivers, for obtaining money under false pretenses.

NELS O. SLOIER, patrolman; born in Holmstrand, Norway, 1849; came to Chicago July, 1872; entered the force Sept. 15, 1884; was in Lieut. Quinn's company at the Haymarket riot.

CORNELIUS SULLIVAN, patrolman; American born; came to Chicago May 16, 1885; entered the force June 3, 1887.

JOHN SULLIVAN, patrolman; born in Ireland 1859; came to Chicago 1878; entered the force 1884; arrested John DeLowery for larceny; Geo. Marks, who was sentenced to the penitentiary for two years.

HENRY J. WIENEKE, patrolman; born in Cook Co., Ill., 1857; came to Chicago 1857; entered the force April, 1886; was in Lieut. Quinn's company at the Haymarket riot, and was shot in the neck.

PATRICK WALSH, patrolman; born in Ireland 1856; came to Chicago June, 1872; entered the force December 15, 1884; was in Lieut. Steele's company at the Haymarket riot.

FRANK WELLMAN, patrolman; born in Hanover, Germany, 1848; came to Chicago 1851; entered the force December 15, 1884; machinist by trade; was at the Haymarket riot.

FRANK WESOLEK, patrolman; born in Poland 1860; came to Chicago August 5, 1878; entered the force December 13, 1884; was in Lieut. Quinn's company at the Haymarket riot.

JOHN WAAGE, patrolman; born in Norway 1862; came to Chicago 1884; entered the force June 3, 1887.

WEST NORTH AVENUE STATION, West North avenue, near Milwaukee avenue, was opened August 1, 1883. The district patrolled by the force of this station is bounded on the north by Ashland avenue, to Western avenue by Armitage road, and from Western avenue to the city limits by West North avenue, on the south by Augusta street, east by Ashland avenue, and west by the city limits. The area is about two square miles, and the population about 35,000.

FRANK PENZEN, lieutenant of police, commanding West North avenue district, was born in the city of Rosbach, province of Mecklinberg, Germany, August 11, 1838. He left his native land, as a sailor, at the age of fourteen, and remained at a seafaring life until 1868. He crossed the ocean several times, and became a proficient seaman. After coming to this country, in 1854, it was his custom to spend his summers upon the lakes and his winters upon the ocean. He first came to Chicago in 1856, and became commander of the schooner Hamlet, which plied between lake ports and Chicago. He was captain of this vessel until 1864, and of other vessels until 1868, when he retired from that mode of life. Entering the Chicago police force on August 6, 1869, he was assigned to the Union street station, and remained there three years. He was then transferred to the Central detail, and remained until 1873, when he was transferred back to Union street, and from there to West Chicago avenue, as roundsman (now patrol sergeant); remained here till 1881, and transferred to the Webster avenue station with same rank; remained here twenty months, and was transferred back to West Chicago avenue. On August 1, 1883, he was promoted to the rank of lieutenant, and placed in charge of the West North avenue district, from which he was transferred to the Desplaines street station, remaining there two and one-half years; and when Captain Ward was transferred to West Chicago avenue, he was transferred to his old station, the West North avenue, where he has remained ever since. In the riot of 1877 his left cheek bone was broken by a stone thrown from the mob; he was in charge of a company at the Division street bridge; has seen active service in the lumber shovers', switchmen's and other strikes, and was detailed for a week on the Michigan Southern tracks during the

FRANK PENZEN,
Lieut. Comdg. West North Ave. District.

VICTOR SCHUMACHER,
Ex-Lieut. of Police.

troubles on that line; was at the Desplaines street station on the night of May 4, 1886, and commanded the sixth company which marched upon the socialistic meeting before the bomb was thrown, being detailed to guard the approaches on Randolph street, and was stationed seventy or eighty feet away from the spot where the bomb fell. Only one of his company was wounded— Henry F. Smith, who received a stray bullet in the shoulder, and has recovered.

GEORGE A. BENDER, desk sergeant; born in Germany 1843; came to Chicago 1847; entered the force 1872.

JOSEPH KANDZIA, desk sergeant; born in Germany 1856; came to Chicago 1870; entered the force 1881.

PETER BERGER, patrolman; born in Chicago 1850; entered the force 1886.

JOHN J. BARRY, patrolman; born in Chicago 1860; entered the force 1886.

LOUIS BOUMAN, patrolman; born in Milwaukee 1851; came to Chicago 1869; entered the force 1884.

JAMES F. CULKIN, patrolman; born in Vermont, 1857; came to Chicago 1859; entered the force 1886.

SAMUEL COLLINS, patrolman; born in Canada 1858; came to Chicago 1881; entered the force 1884.

WILLIAM DE WALD, patrolman; born in Germany 1843; came to Chicago 1853; entered the force 1881.

C. J. FITZGERALD, patrolman; born in Chicago 1862; entered the force December, 1884.

JAMES GLEASON, patrolman; born in Chicago 1861; entered the force 1884.

JULIUS HAERLE, patrolman; born in Chicago 1850; entered the force June, 1883.

ALEXANDER HALVERSON, patrolman; born in Chicago 1858; entered the force 1884.

JAMES B. KELLY, patrolman; born in Jefferson, Cook Co., Ill., 1856; came to Chicago 1860; entered the force December 15, 1884.

JAMES KEARNS, patrolman; born in Ireland 1847; came to Chicago 1871; entered the force 1874.

JAMES W. KEER, patrolman; born in Dundee, Scotland, 1834; came to Chicago 1860; entered the force 1870.

JOHN LINDSTROM, patrolman; born in Sweden 1846; came to Chicago 1867; entered the force 1882.

JOHN J. McNULTY, patrolman; born in Peru, La Salle Co., Ill., 1861; came to Chicago 1881; entered the force 1884.

WILLIAM C. MORRIS, patrolman; born in Pittsburg, Penn., 1849; came to Chicago 1865; entered the force 1873.

JAMES B. MALLOY, patrolman; born in Joliet, Ill., 1854; came to Chicago 1882; entered the force 1884.

DANIEL P. McCARTHY, patrolman; born in 1863; entered the force 1884.

THOMAS McNAMARA, patrolman; born in Ireland 1854; came to Chicago 1868; entered the force 1884.

CHARLES L. MOORE, patrolman; born in Rock Island Co., Ill., 1858; came to Chicago 1881; entered the force 1884.

CONRAD L. NIEHOFF, patrolman; born in Chicago 1857; entered the force 1886.

PATRICK H. OWENS, patrolman; born in Ireland 1848; came to Chicago 1862; entered the force 1872.

DANIEL RYAN, patrolman; born in Lancaster, Penn., 1854; came to Chicago 1877; entered the force 1887.

GEORGE W. RAYCRAFT, patrolman; born in Ireland 1847; came to Chicago 1866; entered the force 1873.

CHARLES SPIERLING, patrolman; born in Germany 1858; came to Chicago 1865; entered the force 1884.

CHARLES SCHOEN, patrolman; born in Germany 1850; came to Chicago 1872; entered the force 1884.

JACOB TAMILLO, patrolman; born in Germany 1850; came to Chicago 1878; entered the force June 13, 1883.

RAWSON STREET STATION.—January 27th, 1879, the board of police formed a new police district in the northwestern part of the city, bounded on the east by the Chicago River, south by North avenue and west and north by the city limits, and opened a new police station termed the North Branch sub-station. There was no station house, but the rolling mill company gave the commissioners the use of a vacant office at the foot of Wabansia avenue and between the north and south mills, until such time as a station house would be built. This office was small, and there was far from sufficient room for either officers or prisoners. Into this building Sergt. James Garritty, who was transferred from 12th street station, was installed in command of the following named men: William Kaeke and Thos. E. Walsh, station keepers; Herman Nelson, Adam Bender, Wm. H. Jordon, Laurence Heelan, James Buckley, M. B. Hansen, John Delaney and Noble Hilliard—one sergeant, two station keepers and eight patrolmen. October 26th, 1871, a new frame station house having been built at No. 37 Rawson street, Sergt. Garritty took charge of it in command of the following named officers: Wm. Kaeke and Thos. E. Walsh, station keepers; Herman Nelson, Adam Bender, Wm. H. Jordon, Ed. Miller, Laurence Heelan, Noble Hilliard, Michael Murphy; Officer Delaney in the meantime having been transferred, and Officer Buckley discharged. May 21st, 1872, Sergt. Garritty was transferred to Union street station and Wm. B. Macauley was transferred from Webster avenue to Rawson street station. Also several patrolmen transferred. September 1st, 1872, Wm. B. Macauley having resigned from the force, Sergt. Frank Gerbing took command of Rawson street station, having been transferred from the Lake street squad, now Central detail, abolished at that time by Elmer Washburn, the new superintendent of police succeeding Mr. Kennedy, who had been chief from the time this station was opened. Mr. Washburn also made a change in the routine of duty, forming the men into three sections, with a roundsman at the head of each section. 1st section, three men under Roundsman Adam Bender; 2nd section, two men under Roundsman James Fisher; 3rd section, three men under Roundsman James Brennan. This system did not work well; the men were dissatisfied, and the men were changed again into two sections, under Roundsmen Bender and Fisher. On the 1st of October, 1872, Officer Wm. Patton, of the Lake street squad, was appointed roundsman, and Bender was reduced to the ranks. December 29th, 1873, Supt. Washburn having resigned, Jacob Rehm was appointed superintendent, and he abolished the system of traveling by platoons in the sub-stations. Roundsman Fisher was reduced to the ranks and Patton was retained, there being only one section on night duty. February 2nd, 1874, Sergt. Gerbing was transferred to East Chicago avenue station, and Sergt. T. D. Fox was changed from Webster avenue to Rawson street. December 21st, 1874, Rawson street district was enlarged to Division street, which was made the dividing line from the river to limits, and three additional patrolmen were transferred here July 1st, 1877. The title and rank of the officers were changed, and Sergt. Fox received the title of lieutenant, while Roundsman Patton received that of sergeant, the pay remaining the same.

December 1st, 1877, Sergt. Patton resigned from the force under charges invented by a clique of four policemen in the station, which he was unable at that time to controvert, but which he cleared himself of afterward to the satisfaction of Mayor Heath, who was then mayor of Chicago. December 1st, 1877, Officer Martin Quinn was appointed sergeant vice Patton. February 1st, 1877, Lieut. M. Bischoff was transferred to Rawson street station, and Lieut. Fox transferred to East Chicago avenue. January 16th, 1883, Lieut. Bischoff was transferred to East Chicago avenue station, and Lieut. Victor Schumacher took charge of Rawson street station, and on the 24th of June, 1883, Sergt. Martin Quinn was transferred to East Chicago avenue, and Sergt. Chas. O'Connor was transferred from Webster avenue to Rawson street. February 10th, 1885, Lieut. Schumacher resigned from the police department, and the present commandant, Charles J. Johnson, was transferred here from East Chicago avenue.

On the morning of July 26th, 1876, Officer Fred W. Koenig, who was traveling his post, had his attention called, at 4 o'clock, a. m., to five men who were walking south on Ashland avenue south of North avenue, by Thomas Gill, living on Wabansia avenue near Robey street, whose house they had just burglarized. He was following them with a shotgun, and the officer seeing him, joined in the chase. They came up to the thieves, but the officer had no sooner stopped them when one of them put a pistol to his forehead and shot him. The officer fell to the ground senseless, and Gill ran away. Sergeant Patton was walking along Noble street at the time, and on hearing the shot gave chase to the thieves, running them to North avenue bridge, through the lumber yard there, then through the rolling mills, and over the railroad bridge on Bloomingdale road, but, though he exchanged several shots with them, he was unable to catch up to them. They were subsequently arrested, but Koenig was unable to identify them to the satisfaction of Justice Scully, and they were discharged. After the shooting Koenig was brought to the station and attended by Dr. Sharpe, who inserted the probe some six inches in the wound but was unable to locate the bullet, which went right through his head from nearly between the eyes and lodged in the back part of the skull, where it still remains. Officer Koenig was taken home, and lay on his bed for months, hovering between life and death, but he finally recovered, though the state of his head would not allow him to resume police duty, and he was subsequently discharged from the force. At present he is in poor circumstances, and barely able to earn a living for himself and family.

On the 12th of August, 1879, about 10 o'clock in the evening, Sergeant Martin Quinn was cut with a razor in the hands of an infuriated wretch named Martin Blake, living at No. 34 Rawson street. Blake had beaten his wife, and put her and her child out of the house. The woman, in her flight, had left a younger child, three months old, behind, and the inhuman wretch threw this child on the street, almost killing it. Sergeant Quinn, learning how affairs stood, proceeded to Blake's house to investigate the cause of the trouble. On arriving, Blake, himself, opened the door, and, without speaking, drew a razor, and slashed Quinn on the abdomen, inflicting a slight wound; he then made another lunge and cut the sergeant on the right arm, cutting the cords, and rendering the member useless. Blake was arrested, and served one year in the penitentiary.

Notable Arrests: September 3d, 1871, a fugitive from justice, named Robert J. Brown, a murderer, was arrested by Officer Ed. Miller, and turned over to the authorities of Newcastle, Penn. June 10th, 1871, John Koch arrested by Officer P. Hussey, on the charges of horse stealing and assault; five years in state's prison. August 26th, 1875, Julian P. Kelly was arrested by Officer Robert C. Montgomery, on the charge of cattle stealing, and was sentenced to the penitentiary for two years. This man dressed well, represented himself to be a physician, drove a horse and buggy, resided in the district, and was in the habit of coming around the station and fraternizing with the officers, who never suspected him of being a thief. On the evening before he made his last haul of cattle from the country, he drove to the station and borrowed a revolver, saying he was going to the country to see a patient, and wanted to protect himself. Next morning he was followed by farmers to where he had driven four cows to Benzow's slaughter house, and they called on the officer, who arrested him. He was sent to state's prison, a second time, for passing counterfeit coin. February 26th, 1876, James Quirk and John Cotter, well-known thieves, were caught in the act of burglarizing a house on Clybourn place, and were arrested by Sergeant Patton and Officer Keller. They were sentenced to the penitentiary for two years. July 27th, 1877, Horace B. Sturges, a U. S. soldier, camping at the corner of North avenue and Holt street, was arrested for rape on the person of Hilda Berg, 12 years old, by Sergeant Patton, and he was sentenced to five years in the penitentiary. The soldiers were camped here during the riots at the lumber yards, and had just returned from the plains. They were an unruly lot. October 23d, 1879, August Asciach was arrested by Officer August Keller, for assault

DANIEL J. DUFFY,
Ex-Lieut. of Police.

CHAS. J. JOHNSON,
Lieut. Comdg. Rawson St. District.

and robbery; five years in the penitentiary. February 14th, 1880, John Rumvask arrested for rape by Officer Foley; two years in the penitentiary. June 19th, 1882, William Thomson and John McCauley arrested for rape by Officer Foley; held in $1,500 to the Criminal Court. December 5th, 1883, Joe Burke, alias Sandy, was arrested for burglary by Officer John Boyd; three years in the penitentiary. October 21st, 1884, William Gilow was arrested for rape by Officer William Coleman; one year in the penitentiary. April 12th, 1885, George Anderson was arrested for murder by Officer Mat. Foley; three years in the penitentiary. August 25th, 1885, Frank Mulkowski was arrested for murder by Officers McNulty and Johnson; hanged March 26th, 1886. January 8th, 1885, Robert Knight was arrested by Officers Johnson and McDonald, on eight charges of forgery. He was a young man of respectable connections, and through the pleading of his mother he escaped with a light sentence of one year.

The district patrolled by the officers of this station is bounded on the north by Fullerton avenue, on the south, from Western avenue to North Ashland avenue, by Armitage road, and from North Ashland avenue to the Chicago River, thence southeasterly along said river to its intersection with the north branch canal to North avenue, and from North avenue to the city limits by the north branch of the Chicago River; on the west, from Augusta street to Armitage road to the north city limits, by Western avenue. This district has an area of one and one-half square miles, and contains a population of about 35,000.

CHARLES J. JOHNSON, lieutenant of police, commanding Rawson street district, is a native of Sweden, where he was born in 1846. He came to Chicago in 1851, and entered the force in February, 1872. He enlisted in Battery H, First Illinois Artillery, January 22, 1862, for three years or during the war. He re-enlisted as a veteran in the same battery, February 27, 1864, and was mustered out of the service at Springfield, in this state, on June 14, 1865. The same month he engaged in business at Miller

Bros.' ship yards, and remained in that company's employ until he entered the force. He was appointed patrol sergeant December 14, 1880; acting lieutenant, November 18, 1882; and full lieutenant, January 1, 1883. During the war he saw much hard service in the field, and acquitted himself always with the greatest credit. In this history his name appears prominently in connection with several important events, notably the riot of '77.

WILLIAM PATTON, desk sergeant, was born in the province of Ulster, Ireland, 1837; came to Chicago 1865, and entered the force August, 1870. In July, 1871, he was shot and seriously wounded by John Lee, while placing him under arrest, with some other tough characters, who had committed burglary in a hardware store some time before; served two years at the Twelfth street station, two years on the day squad, at crossings and bridges, one year as sergeant, and has been desk sergeant eight years; was on duty under Sergeant (now captain) O'Donnell during the great fire of 1871.

MILO M. WHEADON, desk sergeant, was born in Vermont 1850; came to Chicago 1864; entered the force June 9, 1877; was appointed desk sergeant July 24, 1883.

JAMES T. JOHNSON, patrolman, on detective duty; born in Norway 1850; came to Chicago 1866; entered the force December 15, 1884; arrested Frank Mulkowski, August 25, 1885, who was hanged March 2, 1886; January 8, 1885, arrested Robert Knight on seven charges f forgery; received one year in the penitentiary; April 16, 1887, arrested Ed. Patterson, James Nolan and James Murphy for burglary; five years each in the penitentiary.

PATRICK FLANIGAN, patrolman; born in England 1860; came to Chicago 1876; entered the force December 15, 1884.

THOMAS D. FOX, patrolman; born in Ireland 1832; came to Chicago 1854; entered the force April, 1856; was appointed sergeant in 1865; as captain in 1868, resigned. In 1872 was appointed sergeant; in 1877 was appointed lieutenant; August 1, 1879, resigned; in 1882 joined the force as patrolman.

THOMAS GRIFFIN, patrolman; born in Ireland 1847; came to Chicago 1871; entered the force June 14, 1883.

WILLIAM HAERLE, patrolman; born in Germany 1846· came to Chicago 1855; entered the force July 19, 1873.

JOHN G. HENNING, patrolman; born in Prussia 1853; came to Chicago 1862; entered the force June 3, 1887.

JOHN KOCH, patrolman; born in Germany 1837; came to Chicago 1856; entered the force June 20, 1875.

LOUIS KROLL, patrolman; born in Germany 1859; came to Chicago 1872; entered the force June 4, 1887.

MIKE KORZIEWSKI, patrolman; born in German Poland 1856; came to Chicago 1872; entered the force December 15, 1884; November 25, 1885, arrested John Publeski on the charge of larceny; sentenced one year in the penitentiary.

JOHN LEMLKE, patrolman; born in Germany 1857; came to Chicago 1864; entered the force June 4, 1887.

PATRICK J. MURPHY, patrolman; born in Ireland 1852; came to Chicago 1877; entered the force August 1, 1882.

ALEXANDER McDONALD, patrolman; born in Little Washington, Penn., 1850; came to Chicago 1883; entered the force December 14, 1884; detailed at Central station in citizen's clothes under Inspector Bonfield; before entering the force, was employed by Springfield and North Chicago Rolling Mill companies; also by Pinkerton's National Detective Agency; has had many important cases.

PATRICK E. McNULTY, patrolman; born in Ireland 1850; came to Chicago 1876; entered the force May, 1880; was injured and crippled permanently while on duty at the Haymarket riot of 1886; was with Officer Johnson when Mulkowski was arrested.

WILLIAM MARSH, patrolman; born in Germany 1853; came to Chicago 1856; entered the force December 15, 1884.

WILLIAM H. OUTHAUK, patrolman; born in Waukegan, Ill., 1857; came to Chicago September 12, 1876; entered the force August 10, 1885.

CHARLES F. OUTHAUK, patrolman; born in Will county, Ill., 1860; came to Chicago 1881; entered the force December 15, 1884.

JOSEPH PALCZYNSKI, patrolman; born in German Poland 1863; came to Chicago 1874; entered the force July 18, 1885; August 27, 1885, arrested William Smith for burglary; sentenced one year in the penitentiary.

GEORGE H. RUGER, patrolman; American born; came to Chicago 1880; entered the force June 3, 1887.

MATHEW REGAN, patrolman; born in Ireland 1851; came to Chicago 1871; entered the force December, 1884.

CHARLES F. WENDT, patrolman; born in Germany 1856; came to Chicago 1867; entered the force December 15, 1886.

CHAPTER XXVIII.

THE FIFTH PRECINCT—CAPTAIN MICHAEL JOHN SCHAACK COMMANDING—
EARLY DAYS OF POLICE LIFE IN THE "NORD SEITE"—THE OLD NORTH
MARKET HALL AND HURON STREET STATIONS—MAX KIPLEY AND
MARTIN QUINN—LIEUTENANT BAUS AND THE BAVARIAN HEAVEN—
LIEUTENANT LLOYD AT WEBSTER AVENUE—THE CAREERS OF A
BATALLION OF GOOD MEN—SPLENDID RECORDS.

This precinct includes the Chicago avenue, Larrabee
street and Webster avenue stations, with headquarters at
Chicago avenue.

CHICAGO AVENUE STATION was built in 1873. Before
the great fire of 1871, the station was located on Huron
street, between Dearborn avenue and Clark street, and was
known as the Huron street station. Here many of the ablest
officers of the force at the present time received their police
education, and here Wells Sherman was sergeant and afterward captain, followed by Gund and others whose names are
indelibly connected with the early history of the Chicago
police department. The force on duty at this station now
patrols the district bounded, north by Division street, south
by the Chicago River, east by Lake Michigan, and west by
the north branch of the Chicago River to its intersection
with the north branch canal, thence along said north branch
canal to Division street. The district contains an area of
one and one-fourth square miles, with a population estimated, in 1887, at 50,000. The force at this station, all
told, numbers 75 men.

MICHAEL JOHN SCHAACK, captain commanding the fifth precinct,
was born at Saptfountaines, Luxemburg, Germany, April 23, 1843;
in 1853 came with his family to America; came to Chicago and
remained a short time, locating later on a farm near Port Washington, Wisconsin; at the age of fifteen went to Cairo, Ill., and
found employment in a brewery, where he remained three years;

returned to Chicago, and engaged upon lake vessels; became connected with Ludwig's night and detective force and entered the
regular police force June 15, 1869, being assigned to duty at the old
Armory as a patrolman; was transferred after six months to the
North Division, where most of his police service has been centered;
after serving as roundsman, sergeant and detective, in 1879 was
promoted to a lieutenancy, and on Nov. 1 assigned to duty at
the Armory, where he remained for a year; August 17, 1885, was
promoted to a captaincy and placed in charge of the fifth precinct,
where he remained until a short time after the Haymarket riot
when he was transferred to the Desplaines street station and remained there until the changes of September last, when he was
transferred to his old precinct, greatly to the satisfaction of North
Siders. His career as a police officer has been a brilliant one. (See
Chapter XVIII).

MAXIMILLIAN KIPLEY, lieutenant of police, was born at Patterson,
N. J., in 1843, where he was reared, and attended school. In his
boyhood days he worked in cotton factories and machine shops,
and in 1866 came West, engaging in the railroad business; entered
the Chicago police force on June 8, 1870, under Superintendent
Kennedy; was about one and a half blocks away from the historical
O'Leary barn, when the fire broke out in 1871; was the first policeman present and stayed with the fire until it had done its dreadful work; was at the Twelfth street station with Simon O'Donnell,
and remembers, with peculiar pride, that it was Mark Sheridan,
then a member of the police board, who put him on the
force; remained at the Twelfth street station for a few months
after the great fire, when he was transferred to the Armory,
under Capt. Hickey and Lieutenant Buckley; at that time there
was nothing north of Harrison street but the ruins, and the district
surrounding the Harrison street station was the roughest in
the city; traveled beat in this district, between Taylor and
Twelfth streets, Third avenue and the river, for a year and a half,
and had some of the roughest experiences of any man on the force;
the rabble, the thugs, and the bad element of the city generally, were
gathered here, and here remained until the city was rebuilt and
they became scattered; was given nearly every new man that was
assigned to the station in order to "break" him in, and he "broke
in" many of the men who afterward became able and efficient officers, among them John Gallagher, now at the Wabash depot, Tim
Madigan, now dead, Dennis Mahoney, dead, Andrew Carey, still
alive and on the force, Martin Hayes, who became a lieutenant, and
many others; was transferred to the Twenty-second street station
when Washburn became superintendent and many changes occurred in the force; was again transferred to Harrison street and promoted to a desk sergeantcy, remaining in that capacity nine years;

again transferred to Twenty-second street as desk sergeant, but was permitted to do patrol duty on account of delicate health caused by long confinement in the station, and was detailed with Officer Jones, still holding the rank of desk sergeant; while traveling beat sent twenty-one persons to the penitentiary, and the first one ever sent for twenty years from that station; the records of the department show that he did splendid work in breaking up the gang of thieves which infested the Twenty-second street district, and for a time terrorized it; was in the troubles at the lumber district in 1876, under Sergeant Dennis Fitzpatrick, who won promotion; was with Lieut. Ebersold in the riot of 1877, taking a company over to the Halsted street viaduct and acting under Deputy Superintendent Joseph Dixon; was transferred to Central station and was appointed detective, working with Detective Shea, and Joseph Kipley; was transferred to Cottage Grove avenue and appointed sergeant. At 8:30 o'clock on the morning of March 13, 1881, William B. Simpson, of No. 1209 Michigan avenue, and George McBride, his hired man, were in Addison Sneel's saloon at No. 542 Wabash avenue. Simpson, McBride and a man named Harry Gilmore were all drinking at the bar when a quarrel arose between the latter two, and McBride challenged Gilmore to the street to settle their difficulty, and started for the door; at the same time Gilmore was handed a revolver by the bartender a man named Cook, and with this in hand Gilmore jumped at and grabbed McBride by the back of the neck and fired one shot which took effect in the head, killing McBride instantly; he fell to the sidewalk, where the body was found and removed to the morgue. Gilmore made his escape and was never seen in Chicago by any of the officers who knew him, until the night of Nov. 6, 1886, when he was recognized in a saloon by Max Kipley, who arrested him. He denied his identity, but it was fully proved, and he was sentenced to 30 years in the penitentiary at the January term of court, 1887. Sergeant Kipley was promoted to a lieutenancy May 9, 1887, and transferred with Capt. Schaack to Desplaines street, going with him to Chicago avenue last September. Lieutenant Kipley married Miss Anna Kolman in 1866 and is the father of nine children, one of his daughters being the wife of a resident of St. Paul. He is a member of the old fashionel, robust school of police officers, and one of the most competent men in any capacity on the force.

MARTIN QUINN, lieutenant of police, was born in the County Clare, Ireland, 1847; came to Chicago 1851, and entered the force in 1870; commanded a company of twenty-five men from the commencement of the McCormick strike until the bloody ending at the Haymarket, May 4, 1886. His company lost two men in killed and thirteen wounded in the massacre. He proved throughout that most exciting and exacting period in the history of the

MAX KIPLEY,

Lieut. Comdg. East Chicago Ave. District.

MARTIN QUINN,
Lieut. Comdg. East Chicago Ave. District.

Chicago police force, to be a brave, skillful and faithful commanding officer, and won well-merited praise on all sides. Lieut. Quinn
had served in the United States army during the war, and his military education has always served him well as an officer of police.
He was honorably discharged from the army after serving at Nash-
ville and other points, in 1864; received employment with the
United States Express Company in 1865, and remained until 1868
as collector and delivery man; went into the teaming business and
contracting. After entering the force was for seven years a
patrolman, and for eight years a patrol sergeant. In this time he
distinguished himself by making many important arrests, and no
man on the force has the confidence of the department and the
public to a greater extent than he.

WHEELER BARTRAM, patrol sergeant; born at Madison, Lake county,
Ohio, April 14, 1843; came to Chicago March, 1858; entered the
force February 13, 1868; served as patrolman at Huron street and
Larrabee street stations; appointed roundsman at Webster avenue
February 10, 1871, and desk sergeant March 1, 1871; served as
such at Webster avenue and Larrabee street, and appointed patrol
sergeant Nov. 1, 1878; transferred to Webster avenue Oct. 1, 1882,
to Central detail June 20, 1882, and to Chicago avenue May 10,
1887; in January, 1869, saved two men from drowning at Chicago
avenue bridge; was instrumental in reorganizing the Policemen's
Benevolent Association in '76 and '77; was elected president and
re-elected until January, 1887; had charge of the special relief for
the officers injured at Haymarket riot May 4, 1886; was in the riots
of 1877; suppressed the *Pall-Mall Gazette* and other obscene literature during 1885; enlisted in Co. G, 29th Indiana Volunteers, at
Laporte, Ind., Aug. 5, 1861; re-enlisted in same regiment January
1, 1864, and served to the end of the war; mustered out at Marietta,
Ga., as 1st sergeant, Dec. 2, 1865; was in the battle of Liberty
Gap, Tenn., and Chickamauga, Ga., the Siege of Chattanooga,
Tenn., and several skirmishes; was captured and paroled by Gen.
Morgan at Pulaski, Tenn., May 1, 1862; exchanged January 9, 1863,
and returned to duty.

ROBERT C. MONTGOMERY, desk sergeant; born in Ireland 1840;
came to Chicago 1865; entered the force July, 1872.

CHARLES J. KOCH, desk sergeant: born at Hessen, Germany, 1847;
came to Chicago August 15, 1865; entered the force October 9,
1872; was detailed at Deering street as patrolman; seriously
wounded in a fight with six roughs at Halsted and 37th streets
March 7, 1873, and shot three of them, the McVeigh Brothers, two
of them dying next day; same year arrested the two notorious
burglars, Edward Bush and Pat Hannahan, on six different charges,
both being sent to the penitentiary for long terms; was transferred

at his own request to Chicago avenue station; has arrested a number of burglars and thieves in this district, shooting one while chasing him; while arresting a rough named Burke, corner of Wells and Indiana streets, had a hard struggle with a crowd of thieves and was stabbed in the hand; did service during the fire in 1874; was injured internally corner of Pine street and Delaware place in 1876; was in active service during the riots and at the Halsted street viaduct fight in 1877; was appointed signal sergeant March 15, 1883, and was appointed desk sergeant February 13, 1885; rescued a boy and a man from drowning at Wells street bridge, summer of 1880.

PATRICK J. ARCHIBOLD, patrolman; born in Ireland 1853; came to Chicago 1866; entered the force April 18, 1886.

JOHN P. BERWICK, patrolman; born in Luxemburg, Germany, 1844; came to Chicago March 23, 1868; entered the force October 1, 1881; was detailed for duty at the old Union street station; has made several important arrests; was shot at by a burglar, narrowly escaping with his life, at the corner of Carpenter and Lake streets, March, 1882; May 1, 1882, was transferred to the East Chicago avenue station.

RICHARD BARTLETT, patrolman; born in Ohio 1842; came to Chicago 1867; entered the force July, 1873.

THOMAS B. BAYNES, patrolman; born in Ireland 1844; came to Chicago March, 1867; entered the force March, 1872.

ALFRED M. CLARK, patrolman; born in Lorrain, Jefferson county, N. Y., 1855; came to Chicago March 2, 1885; entered the force April 3, 1887.

DANIEL CAUGHLIN, patrolman; born in Hancock, Mich., 1859; came to Chicago April, 1879; entered the force December 15, 1884.

WILLIAM EVERS, patrolman; born in Chicago 1858; entered the force June 14, 1887.

JOHN T. FINN, patrolman; born in Chicago 1859; entered the force December, 1884.

JOHN FLEMING, patrolman; born in Ireland 1855; came to Chicago 1878; entered the force December 15, 1884.

JOHN J. GARRIGAN, patrolman; born in Chicago 1860; entered the force April 1, 1887.

PAUL HOEFIG, patrolman; born in Germany 1852; came to Chicago 1879; entered the force June 14, 1883; served one enlistment in Troop "I," 7th U. S. Cavalry (Gen. Geo. A. Custer), as a sergeant; participated in the fights against hostile Sioux, Nez-Perces and Cheyenne Indians, in Montana and Nebraska, 1876 and 1878.

HARVEY HUGHES, patrolman; born in Louisville, Ky., 1849; came to Chicago June, 1872; entered the force December 15, 1884.

JOHN HARTMAN, patrolman; born in Germany 1827; came to Chicago July 4, 1855; entered the force April 19, 1868; served eighteen years as patrolman; is at present lock-up keeper.

GEORGE W. HESS, patrolman; born in Washington, D. C., 1862; came to Chicago 1881; entered the force June 4, 1887.

GEORGE HIATT, patrolman; born in Pand Vermont, Ireland, 1859; came to Chicago July 16, 1880; entered the force June 4, 1887.

MICHAEL KELLY, patrolman; born in Canada 1854; came to Chicago 1872; entered the force December 15, 1884.

ANDREW KALVELAGE, patrolman; born in Chicago 1854; entered the force December 1, 1886.

WILLIAM KAECKE, patrolman; born in Sommerfeld, Germany, 1830; came to Chicago 1857; entered the force April 30, 1867; served as private in Co. "C," 5th Wisconsin Infantry; appointed station keeper at Rawson street station; April, 1874, was pound keeper for the North Division; is lock-up keeper at this station.

ANTON KLINGER, patrolman; born in Prussia, Germany, 1852; came to Chicago 1864; entered the force December 15, 1880.

PETER M. KELLY, patrolman; born in Ireland 1858; came to Chicago 1880; entered the force 1885.

JACOB KLETT, patrolman; born in 1860; entered the force July 12, 1887.

J. LOCHENSTEIN, patrolman; born in Rome, N. Y., April 24, 1855; came to Chicago 1871; entered the force June 14, 1883; detailed for detective duty.

RICHARD McCORMICK, patrolman; born in Chicago 1860; entered the force April 18, 1886.

NICHOLAS MICHELS, patrolman; born in New Strasburg, Ill., 1857; came to Chicago October 10, 1880; entered the force June 3, 1887.

THOMAS J. MORAN, patrolman; born in County Mayo, Ireland, 1849; came to Chicago December 27, 1877; entered the force April 9, 1885.

WILLIAM M. MURPHY, patrolman; born in Chicago 1863; entered the force December 15, 1884.

THOMAS McMAHON, patrolman; born in Chicago 1855; entered the force 1883.

HUGO R. A. MALINOWSKY, patrolman; born in Pomerania, Germany, 1859; came to Chicago September, 1872; entered the force March 25, 1885.

JAMES MOORE, patrolman; born in County Mayo, Ireland, 1854; came to Chicago 1873; entered the force 1883.

BERUT MEYER, patrolman; born in Bergan, Norway, 1828; came to Chicago 1861; entered the force August 15, 1867.

JOHN D. McCARTHY, patrolman; born in Ireland 1857; came to Chicago February 27, 1880; entered the force July 2, 1886.

JOHN O. NORDSTROM, patrolman; born in Sweden 1847; came to Chicago 1867; entered the force December 15, 1884.

LOUIS C. PETERS, patrolman; born in Chicago 1858; entered the force June 4, 1887.

E. W. RUEL, patrolman; born in Green Bay, Wis., 1859; came to Chicago 1880; entered the force December 15, 1884; attended the McCormick riot, also the Haymarket riot under Lieutenant Quinn; received two fragments of the shell in the back and three bullets in the lower limbs, two of which have been extracted.

CHARLES REHM, patrolman; born in DuPage county, Ill., 1842; came to Chicago 1843; entered the force 1868; detailed for detective duty.

BERNARD ROACH, patrolman; born in Oswego, N. Y., 1862; came to Chicago 1867; entered the force June, 1886.

PATRICK RILEY, patrolman; born in Ireland 1854; came to Chicago 1872; entered the force May 7, 1882.

PATRICK SHEARIN, patrolman; born in Ireland 1859; came to Chicago June 4, 1867; entered the force July 7, 1886.

WILLIAM SPAIN, patrolman; born in County Tipperary, Ireland, 1857; came to Chicago 1870; entered the force December 15, 1884.

JOHN STEFFES, patrolman; born in Chicago 1852; entered the force June 1, 1882.

JOHN STIFT, patrolman; born in City of Havre, France, 1847; came to Chicago June, 1850; entered the force April 4, 1872; during the sixteen years of service has made five hundred and twenty arrests, the most important being James Tracy, for the murder of Officer John Huebner, of the Rawson street station, executed September 15, 1882; May 18, 1886, arrested George Engel, one of the anarchists, also August Breitenfeld, Victor Clairmont, Bernard Schrider, John Kraemer, and others, who were in the conspiracy; January 14, 1887, Lorenz Krug, the poisoner of Lucy Heidelmeier, his stepdaughter, sentenced eighteen years in the penitentiary; Eddie Harper for robbery, six years in the penitentiary; assisted in the arrest of Frank Mulkowski for murder; also the poisoner, Meyer.

MICHAEL WHALEN, patrolman; born in Spencer, Mass., 1847; came to Chicago 1866; entered the force 1873.

PETER WELTER, patrolman; born in Tiffin, Ohio, 1860; came to Chicago April 2, 1879; entered the force June 22, 1885.

GUSTAV WILLIAMS, patrolman; born in Sweden 1853; came to Chicago October, 1869; entered the force December 15, 1884.

LARRABEE STREET STATION.—This station was organized August 1, 1865, Sergeant William Macauley, with six men, being in charge. Sergeant John A. Gund succeeded Macauley May 1, 1866, and Sergeant F. E. Gerbing followed, January 31, 1868. Then came Sergeant John Baus, who succeeded Gerbing, Dec. 1, 1868, and has retained the command of the district to the present day. The station was destroyed by the fire of '71, and was rebuilt in 1872. The district patrolled by the force of this station is bounded by Willow and Menomonee streets on the north, Division street on the south, Lake Michigan on the east, and the north branch canal on the west, embracing an area one and three-twentieths square miles, containing a population of about 65,000. The total force at this station, including officers, numbers forty-four men.

JOHN BAUS, lieutenant of police, commanding the Larrabee street district, has been connected with the police force in this part of the city for a long time, that to tell the story of his police career would be to write the history of the rise and progress of the district, while he is so well known, and so universally popular, that nothing short of a volume would satisfy his thousands of friends and admirers. His name recalls the by-gone days of the Chicago police force, the days when the beats were longer, wider and more lonesome, in the present crowded sections of the city, than they are now on the outskirts. When some of the men now on the force were infants, John Baus was chasing grave robbers out of the cemeteries of the North Division, and catching them, too, and he was recognized as a pretty good officer before some of the stalwart young men now swinging batons on the streets, were born. It is a question in the minds of some, whether or not John Baus or Marquette first discovered Chicago, or whether John Baus was not in command of the Larrabee street district before Fort Dearborn was built. To put all these questions at rest, let us take a glance at the facts. He was born at Geraldhausen, in beautiful Bavaria, February 24,

1828. His father was a cabinet maker, and the son became the father's apprentice, and an apt scholar. Attending the Lutheran school, he acquired a good, solid education, and imbibed many of the liberal opinions from close study, which made him a revolutionist, like his father, in 1848. That was the year that tried men's souls in Germany, as in other parts of the world, and like Carl Shurz and scores of compatriots, young Baus found it pleasanter, and perhaps safer, to seek his future in America. He arrived in New York April 23, 1851, and for two years he was located a part of the time at Utica, and a part at Rome, in the Empire state. In 1854 he came West, and settled at Belvidere, Ill., but in 1856 he took a trip East, after an old sweetheart, and married Miss Sabine L. Dapper at Utica. Then he came to Chicago and went into business here. He first became connected with the force in 1857, when John Wentworth was mayor, and like all his brethren in those days he wore a leather badge, carried a heavy hickory stick, and sounded alarms on a "creaker." But he retired after two years, and abandoning his trade (that of a painter), he became a carrier for the *Illinois Staats-Zeitung.* August 6, 1862, he enlisted in Company C, 82nd Illinois Volunteers, infantry, and joined the 11th army corps, engaging in the battle of Chancellorsville, while he was still a new man. He followed the career of his regiment at Chattanooga, through the Cumberland campaign, in the Battle of Mission Ridge, and in many bloody engagements, always behaving himself like a man of iron nerve. He was with Sherman on the march to the sea, and was honorably discharged from the service June 9, 1865. After returning to Chicago, he resumed his trade, but on Sept. 20, 1865, he again entered the police force, being recommended by Capt. Frederick Gund, and he has been connected with the department from that day to this; was made station keeper shortly afterward, at the North Market police station, on Michigan street, and was transferred the following spring to the North avenue sub-station, in the same capacity; again was placed in the North Market station as night station keeper, August, 1866, and on June 1, 1867, was transferred to the North avenue (now Larrabee street) station, as day station keeper; June 13, 1868, was made sergeant; was transferred to the Huron street station later on, but only for a brief period, and transferred back to Larrabee street, from which he has not been changed since, holding the rank of lieutenant during nearly all these years; was in command at this station on the night of the great fire, when he had $75,000 worth of plate and other valuables belonging to W. B. Ogden, and saved them by burying them near his own home, which was destroyed; his wife and son having died before this time, he married again, his second wife being Miss Margaret Dapper of Chicago. There are thousands of Bavarians, and people of Bavarian extraction, in the Larrabee district, and among them Lieut.

Baus is esteemed beyond measure. They have shown their appreciation of his manly character in many ways. "In June, 1871," says one of his biographers, "at the head of a mounted detail, on his historical while horse, he led the escort of the German peace festival procession, said to be the largest and longest column ever in the streets of this city. In 1877, Lieut. Baus took the flag in the competition police drill. During the riot of '77, he drove 2,500 rioters across Madison street bridge with twenty-five policemen, and for this, first received the sobriquet of the "flanker" from the city press. In the Knights Templars and Garfield funeral parades he, mounted, led the procession, as he did the procession on Mayor Harrison's return." He has a family of five children, is a good father, a valuable citizen and an excellent police officer.

JOHN P. NELSON, patrol sergeant; born at Varberg, Sweden, 1843; came to Chicago 1857; entered the force February 22, 1876; assigned to duty at Webster avenue for three months; transferred to Harrison street; there two years; served under Lieut. Ebersold during riot of 1877; transferred to Chicago avenue, where he remained two years; transferred to Central detail and assigned to crossing duty at Washington and State streets, continuing there for seven years and five months; was in Lieut. Hubbard's company in the Haymarket riot; has proved to be an able, efficient and faithful officer in every capacity.

FRANCIS SMITH, desk sergeant; born in Germany 1835; came to Chicago 1867; entered the force 1869; was first assigned to this station; appointed desk sergeant 1875.

EDWARD F. HEDRICK, desk sergeant; born in Germany 1841; came to Chicago 1869; entered the force 1873.

PETER ADAMS, patrolman; born in Chicago 1860; entered the force December 15, 1884; arrested Owen Dolan for burglary; did good service during the street-car strike of 1885 and the riots of 1886.

RICHARD BOLD, patrolman; born in Bavaria 1857; came to Chicago 1876; entered the force June 1, 1882; took active part in the riots of 1886 as acting sergeant.

FRANK BYRNE, patrolman; born in Cavin, Ireland, 1852; came to Chicago 1875; entered the force April 19, 1886.

PATRICK CASEY, patrolman; born in Ireland 1846; came to Chicago May 20, 1864; entered the force February 7, 1881; December 28, 1883, arrested Bernhard Kleen for burglary; sentenced two years in the penitentiary; was at the Haymarket riot.

PATRICK CLIFFORD, patrolman; born in Chicago 1862; entered the force July 1, 1886,

WILLIAM DUNAR, patrolman; born in Germany 1845; came to Chicago October, 1869; entered the force June, 1882; took part in the Haymarket riot.

HENRY DeGAU, patrolman; born in Syracuse, N. Y., 1859; came to Chicago 1862; entered the force December 15, 1884; took part in the Haymarket riot, 1886.

JOHN DELANEY, patrolman; born in Ireland 1847; came to Chicago 1878; entered the force December, 1884; did active service at the Haymarket riot of 1886.

JOHN EIZINGER, patrolman; born in Bavaria, Germany, 1838; came to Chicago 1854; entered the force March 19, 1868; did active service during the fire of 1871; the strikes of 1877; also the West Side car strike of 1885.

FRANK FRIEDEL, patrolman; born in Chicago 1857; entered the force April 19, 1886.

JONH J. GALLAGHER, patrolman; born in Philadelphia, Penn., 1860; came to Chicago 1865; entered the force December 15, 1884; served during the street-car strike of 1885; also the riots of 1886.

WM. T. HIFLICHER, patrolman; born in Chicago 1854; entered the force April 19, 1886; served during the riots of 1886.

DENNIS HAYES, patrolman; born in Canada 1854; came to Chicago 1874; entered the force June, 1888; arrested Kelley, who was sentenced to one year in the penitentiary, and was killed by an officer three weeks after his release while committing a burglary.

OTTO HAERLE, patrolman; born in Chicago 1859; entered the force December 15, 1884; served during the Haymarket riot.

HUGH HERRATY, patrolman; born in Ireland 1849; came to Chicago 1865; entered the force 1878; was at the Haymarket riot of 1886.

MARTIN HUCHS, patrolman; born in Chicago 1862; entered the force December 15, 1884; was at the Haymarket riot.

JOHN F. JORUDT, patrolman; born in Chicago 1859; entered the force April, 1886; was at the Haymarket riot.

MATHIAS JOHANNES, patrolman; born in Germany 1848; came to Chicago 1864; entered the force 1876; served during the riot of 1877; arrested two notorious horse thieves, Reinhold Rudolph and Fritz Laumfeld, who are now serving a three-year term in the penitentiary.

JOHN KEEGAN, patrolman; born in Ireland 1855; came to Chicago 1872; entered the force June, 1882; did active duty during the riots of 1877, 1885 and 1886.

G. J. LORCH, patrolman; born in Chicago 1854; entered the force 1881; arrested two burglars at 167 Larrabee street; served during the street-car strikes.

PATRICK McMAHON, patrolman; born in Ireland 1856; came to Chicago June, 1874; entered the force February 5, 1885; acted during the riot of 1886.

THOMAS H. F. MORAN, patrolman; born in Boston, Mass., 1864; came to Chicago April, 1867; entered the force December 15, 1885; at the Haymarket riot.

FRED MORITZ, patrolman; born in Hanover, Germany, 1852; came to Chicago 1865; entered the force April 20, 1886; did service during the trouble of 1886.

AUGUST H. MUELLER, patrolman; born in Davenport, Iowa, 1859; came to Chicago July, 1859; entered the force June 10, 1885; served at the Haymarket riot.

GEORGE McGOWEN, patrolman; born in Chicago 1859; entered the force December 15, 1884; was at the Haymarket riot of 1886; also street-car strike of 1885.

JAMES O'DONNELL, patrolman; born in Chicago 1860; entered the force 1884; arrested Tony Lawrence, alias Gazzolo, for burglary, the first night he wore a police star; was in the riots of 1886; detailed for detective duty

THOMAS O'SHEA, patrolman; born in Wexford, Ireland, 1849; came to Chicago 1867; entered the force December 15, 1884; did good service at the Haymarket riot.

WILLIAM PARKER, patrolman; born in Rochester, N. Y., 1849; came to Chicago 1871; entered the force December 15, 1884; took part in the car strike of 1885; also the riots of 1886.

THOMAS J. RYAN, patrolman; born in New York city 1849; came to Chicago 1860; entered the force June 14, 1884; arrested William Johnson for attacking a man on Kinzie street; Frank Bush for burglary.

JOHN V. RYAN, patrolman; born in Ireland 1849; came to Chicago July, 1867; entered the force December, 1884; at the Haymarket riot.

JULIUS ROACH, patrolman; born in Germany 1849; came to Chicago in 1872; entered the force December 15, 1884; at the Haymarket riot of 1886.

ROBERT J. SEVLAN, patrolman; born in Chicago 1858; entered the force 1884; took part in the Haymarket riot.

THOMAS H. SEAVY, patrolman; born in Ireland 1850; came to Chicago 1866; entered the force 1884; took part in the Haymarket riot.

MICHAEL WALSH, patrolman; born in Mayo, Ireland, 1854; came to

Chicago 1874; entered the force July 1, 1886; served during the stock yards strike of November, 1886.

LEVI WOOD, patrolman; born in Lake Co., Ill., 1850; came to Chicago 1879; entered the force December 15, 1884; was at the Haymarket riot.

NATHAN J. YOUNG, patrolman; born in Portland, Maine, 1838; came to Chicago 1855; entered the force August, 1870; arrested Thos. McGuire for murder; sent to the penitentiary for life; did active service during the fire of 1871; strikes of 1877, 1885 and 1886.

WEBSTER AVENUE STATION.—This station is located in the heart of a quiet and respectable district, and is the only police station in the city where, up to the present time, it has not been deemed necessary to place a patrol wagon, although arrangements are now being made in that direction. The station is one of the oldest, but events of an exciting nature have never been connected with it to any great extent. The district patrolled by the force of the station is bounded by Fullerton avenue on the north, Wilson and Menominee streets on the south, Lake Michigan on the east and the north branch of the Chicago River on the west. The area is about one and one-tenth square miles and the population 45,000. The force at this station, including officers, numbers 42 men.

ELISHA E. LLOYD, lieutenant of police, commanding Webster avenue district; was born at Long Branch. New York, 1839; came to Chicago in 1854, and entered the force August 14, 1871; served as a Union soldier during the rebellion, and was for fourteen months subjected to the tortures of Andersonville prison; as a patrolman, made several important arrests, sending many notorious criminals to the penitentiary. Has proved himself to be a splendid executive officer, and his district is one of the best managed of any in the city.

WILLIAM HOGAN, patrol sergeant; born in Ireland 1837; came to Chicago 1856; entered the force November 2, 1864.

JOHN QUIRK, desk sergeant; born in Ireland 1829; came to Chicago Sept. 28, 1856; entered the force February 11, 1868, was assigned to duty as patrolman at the Huron street station under Captain Wells Sherman; transferred to Webster avenue February 12, 1871; appointed desk sergeant October 1, 1876.

E. E. LLOYD,
Lieut. Comdg. Webster Ave. District.

AUSTIN J. DOYLE,
Ex-Superintendent of Police.

JOHN P. NYE, desk sergeant; born in Germany 1835; came to Chicago 1857; entered the force September 7, 1869; served eight months under Sergeant Baus in the old North avenue station, nine months on the day squad under Sergeant Mccauley, and as station keeper at Webster avenue since February, 1871.

GEORGE C. BURNETT, patrolman; born in Pennsylvania 1855; came to Chicago in 1870; entered the force January 11, 1887.

WM. W. BURNS, patrolman; born in Watertown, Minn., 1864; came to Chicago in 1881; entered the force July 1st, 1886.

AUGUST BISCHOFF, patrolman; born in Chicago in 1860; entered the force July 1, 1886.

WM. CUSHMAN, patrolman; born in Ludlow, Vermont, 1852; came to Chicago in 1871; entered the force April 22, 1880; assigned to duty at East Chicago avenue station, Captain Hathaway commanding, where he served until December 31, 1880; transferred to Webster avenue station January 1, 1881.

HERMAN B. CROON, patrolman; born in Aurich, Germany, 1854; came to Chicago May 27, 1881; entered the force May 26, 1885; August 25, 1886, arrested John Quinn, a notorious thief; penitentiary one year.

THOMAS J. DONOVAN, patrolman; born in Chicago 1862; entered the force December, 1884.

HENRY DAHME, patrolman; born in Chicago 1855; entered the force December 15, 1884.

JOHN A. ELLIOTT, patrolman; born in Canton, Ill., in 1855; came to Chicago in 1880; entered the force December 15, 1884.

M. J. FRANZEN, patrolman; born in Chicago 1862; entered the force December 15, 1884.

E. I. GARDINER, patrolman; born in Portland, Maine, 1859; came to Chicago in 1865; entered the force December 15, 1884.

PETER GIBBONS, patrolman; born in Chicago 1859; entered the force December 15, 1884.

THOMAS GLAVIN, patrolman; born in Ireland 1859; came to Chicago in 1876; entered the force March, 1885.

MARTIN HOFFMAN, patrolman; born in Germany 1847; came to Chicago 1874; entered the force June 13, 1883.

WILLIAM J. JACKSON, patrolman; born in Gottland, Sweden, in 1848; came to Chicago 1865; entered the force 1873; in 1880, arrested the notorious desperado, Wm. O. Davis, sentenced to fifteen years in the penitentiary; 1879, arrested James Edwards, alias

Graham; burglary; fifteen years at Joliet; was in active service in riots of 1877, 1885 and 1886.

NICHOLAS KRAUS, patrolman; born in Chicago, Ill., 1849; entered the force in 1873.

FREDERICK LUETTICH, patrolman; born in Prussia 1837; came to Chicago 1860; entered the force August 13, 1869; resigned in 1879; re-entered the force December, 1884.

LAURITZ LAURITZEN, patrolman; born in Denmark 1844; came to Chicago 1871; entered the force in 1874; served ten years at East Chicago avenue station.

EDWARD LEE, patrolman; born at Providence, R. I., 1858; came to Chicago in 1860; entered the force 1873; March 12, 1885, arreste Wm. Schroder; burglary; Joliet two years.

JACOB MARUGG, patrolman; born in Switzerland 1849; came to Chicago 1875; entered the force December, 1884.

JOSEPH MERCIER, patrolman; born in Cheshire, Conn., 1858; came to Chicago 1864; entered the force 1883; served at Chicago avenue station four years.

CHARLES MALESA, patrolman; born in France 1842; came to Chicago in 1877; entered the force May, 1882; served four years and seven months at East Chicago avenue station.

WILLIAM B. MACAULEY, patrolman; born in Ireland 1823; came to Chicago 1856; entered the force April 10, 1859; served one year at the old Armory, one year at the old Bridewell, six months at the old North Market, and seven years at the Central station.

TIMOTHY F. MAHONEY, patrolman; born in Oswego, N. Y., 1857; came to Chicago 1879; entered the force December 15, 1884.

GEO. W. MILLER, patrolman; born in Germany 1834; came to Chicago 1849; entered the force 1883; in active service during the Haymarket riot.

ROBT. L. MONAGHAN, patrolman; born in Lake county, Ill., 1848; came to Chicago in 1872; entered the force in 1881.

DUNCAN McCLOUD, patrolman; born in Canada in 1851; came to Chicago 1868; entered the force in December, 1884.

ANDREW NESSER, patrolman; born in Luxemburg 1849; came to Chicago in 1860; entered the force December 15, 1884.

JAS. R. PRENDERGAST, patrolman; born in Ireland 1850; came to Chicago May, 1873; entered the force June 15, 1883; served at the Chicago avenue station till June 1, 1887.

F. P. RYAN, patrolman; born in Chicago 1856; entered the force December 15, 1884.

JOHN SCANLAN, patrolman; born in Ireland 1847; came to Chicago 1866; entered the force August 27, 1873; assigned to Larrabee street station; transferred to Webster avenue station in 1874, to Chicago avenue station in 1878, to Webster avenue station in 1882; served three years in U. S. army; was in active service in the riots of 1877.

JNO. E. SULLIVAN, patrolman; born in Chicago 1860; entered the force July 1, 1886.

WILLIAM SAUER, patrolman; born in Milwaukee county, Wis., 1854; came to Chicago March, 1882; entered the force June 5, 1885; served two years at Chicago avenue station.

FRANK J. THALSTROM, patrolman; born in Chicago 1855; entered the force 1885.

AUGUST L. ZIMMERMANN, patrolman; born in Chicago 1861; entered the force December 15, 1884.

NAME INDEX.

GENERAL INDEX.

This general index, which has been specially prepared for the Patterson Smith edition, provides all references to Chicago policemen who played a significant role in the *History*. The original index to the work, which has been retained on the preceding pages, should be consulted for mentions of policemen not included in the index below.

PATTERSON SMITH SERIES IN
CRIMINOLOGY, LAW ENFORCEMENT, AND SOCIAL PROBLEMS

1. *Lewis: *The Development of American Prisons and Prison Customs, 1776–1845*
2. Carpenter: *Reformatory Prison Discipline*
3. Brace: *The Dangerous Classes of New York*
4. *Dix: *Remarks on Prisons and Prison Discipline in the United States*
5. Bruce et al.: *The Workings of the Indeterminate-Sentence Law and the Parole System in Illinois*
6. *Wickersham Commission: *Complete Reports, Including the Mooney-Billings Report*. 14 vols.
7. Livingston: *Complete Works on Criminal Jurisprudence*. 2 vols.
8. Cleveland Foundation: *Criminal Justice in Cleveland*
9. Illinois Association for Criminal Justice: *The Illinois Crime Survey*
10. Missouri Association for Criminal Justice: *The Missouri Crime Survey*
11. Aschaffenburg: *Crime and Its Repression*
12. Garofalo: *Criminology*
13. Gross: *Criminal Psychology*
14. Lombroso: *Crime, Its Causes and Remedies*
15. Saleilles: *The Individualization of Punishment*
16. Tarde: *Penal Philosophy*
17. McKelvey: *American Prisons*
18. Sanders: *Negro Child Welfare in North Carolina*
19. Pike: *A History of Crime in England*. 2 vols.
20. Herring: *Welfare Work in Mill Villages*
21. Barnes: *The Evolution of Penology in Pennsylvania*
22. Puckett: *Folk Beliefs of the Southern Negro*
23. Fernald et al.: *A Study of Women Delinquents in New York State*
24. Wines: *The State of Prisons and of Child-Saving Institutions*
25. *Raper: *The Tragedy of Lynching*
26. Thomas: *The Unadjusted Girl*
27. Jorns: *The Quakers as Pioneers in Social Work*
28. Owings: *Women Police*
29. Woolston: *Prostitution in the United States*
30. Flexner: *Prostitution in Europe*
31. Kelso: *The History of Public Poor Relief in Massachusetts, 1820–1920*
32. Spivak: *Georgia Nigger*
33. Earle: *Curious Punishments of Bygone Days*
34. Bonger: *Race and Crime*
35. Fishman: *Crucibles of Crime*
36. Brearley: *Homicide in the United States*
37. *Graper: *American Police Administration*
38. Hichborn: *"The System"*
39. Steiner & Brown: *The North Carolina Chain Gang*
40. Cherrington: *The Evolution of Prohibition in the United States of America*
41. Colquhoun: *A Treatise on the Commerce and Police of the River Thames*
42. Colquhoun: *A Treatise on the Police of the Metropolis*
43. Abrahamsen: *Crime and the Human Mind*
44. Schneider: *The History of Public Welfare in New York State, 1609–1866*
45. Schneider & Deutsch: *The History of Public Welfare in New York State, 1867–1940*
46. Crapsey: *The Nether Side of New York*
47. Young: *Social Treatment in Probation and Delinquency*
48. Quinn: *Gambling and Gambling Devices*
49. McCord & McCord: *Origins of Crime*
50. Worthington & Topping: *Specialized Courts Dealing with Sex Delinquency*
51. Asbury: *Sucker's Progress*
52. Kneeland: *Commercialized Prostitution in New York City*

* new material added

* new material added   † new edition, revised or enlarged

PATTERSON SMITH SERIES IN
CRIMINOLOGY, LAW ENFORCEMENT, AND SOCIAL PROBLEMS

* new material added † new edition, revised or enlarged